The Christian Philosophy of

ST. THOMAS AQUINAS

THE RANDOM HOUSE
Lifetime Library

The Christian Philosophy of ST. THOMAS AQUINAS

BY Etienne Gilson *Director of Studies,*
Pontifical Institute of Mediaeval Studies, Toronto

with A Catalogue of St. Thomas's Works
BY I. T. Eschmann, O.P.

TRANSLATED BY L . K. Shook, C.S.B.
President, St. Michael's College, University of Toronto

RANDOM HOUSE · NEW YORK

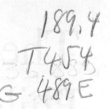

FIRST PRINTING

TO C. G.

WHO IS ONE WITH ME
IN THE LOVE OF
THEOLOGY

FOREWORD

THIS book is the English equivalent of the last French edition of *Le Thomisme. Introduction à la philosophie de saint Thomas d'Aquin*, 5th edition, Paris, 1948. I wish to express my gratitude to my publisher and friend of many years, Mr. Joseph Vrin, for graciously granting permission to put this book at the disposal of the English-speaking public. I also wish to extend my most sincere thanks to Rev. L. K. Shook, C.S.B., Superior of St. Michael's College in the University of Toronto, for englishing a work written in Scholastico-French behind whose language the presence of the technical Latin of Thomas Aquinas is but too easily detected. While reading his translation, it often occurred to me that the writing of a book is sometimes a much easier task than translating it. For his generous and talented cooperation, Father Shook is entitled to my deep gratitude.

To read again in a new language a book written in 1948, but whose origins reach much further back into the past, is an invitation to revise and correct it wherever necessary. This is what I have done.

On the whole, there is no essential difference between this book and the 1948 French edition of *Le Thomisme*. The only important event bearing upon my study of Thomas Aquinas during these eight years, was my discovery (for which I am indebted to Msgr. L. de Raeymaeker, President of the 'Institut Superieur de Philosophie,' Louvain) of Bañes' commentary on the first part of the *Summa Theologiae*. My reading of this commentary confirmed my hope that my fancy had not been deceiving me, for I had merely rediscovered in the twentieth century what had been known at least since the sixteenth.

There has been only one Thomas Aquinas. Even Bañes is not a second one, and anybody mistaking himself for the third leaves himself open to well-deserved ridicule. I find it hard to understand how Bañes, in the field of pure metaphysics, and after subscribing to the correct interpretation of his master Soto, decided that, in a Thomistic substance, accidents could have an *esse* of their own. By and large, however, Bañes appears to me to be by far the most Thomistic of all the Thomists whom it is my privilege to know. This is eminently true concerning the notion of the act of being (*esse*) which is the very core of the Thomistic interpretation of reality. On this precise point, historical research wholly confirms the interpretation of Bañes. It is a sad commentary on the present situation of Thomistic studies that the text of Bañes is almost impossible to find, while another commentary, as misleading as it is painstaking, is still considered the quasi-official interpretation of the doctrine developed by Thomas Aquinas in his *Summa Theologiae*.

This surprising fact perhaps only confirms the time-honored truth that God does not intend to save man through metaphysics. Still, if we must metaphysicize, it is important that we should do so in the proper way. After many years of study, I am more convinced than ever that the basic metaphysical positions of Thomas Aquinas are still far ahead of what is considered most progressive in the philosophical thought of our own times. Personally, I do not say of Thomas that he was right, but that he *is* right. This has not been a preconceived principle guiding my historical study of Thomas Aquinas; it is its conclusion. But only those who have chosen Thomas for their guide know how it is possible to prefer him without despising the rest. All the metaphysical truths contained in other doctrines acquire a still deeper truth in the light of Thomism. But for this proposition to make sense, one must have seen that light.

Pontifical Institute of Mediaeval Studies
Toronto, January 6, 1956.

CONTENTS

ix

The Christian Philosophy of

ST. THOMAS AQUINAS

INTRODUCTION

In THREE of its most important aspects, the personality of St. Thomas lies outside the compass of our work. The saint belongs properly to the field of hagiography. The theologian requires a highly specialized treatment and should by rights be given first place in an exhaustive study of St. Thomas. The mystic and his interior life are to a large extent quite beyond our reach. It is only the philosophical activity which he puts to the service of theology that directly concerns us. Fortunately, there is one phase of his career which affects almost equally every side of this multiple personality, and it seems to correspond with the most central point of view we can take of it. What is most apparent, in the personality of St. Thomas, the aspect under which there is most likelihood of presenting him as he really is, is the teacher or Doctor.[1] The saint was essentially a Doctor of the Church. The man was a Doctor of Theology. The mystic never completely separated his meditations from the teaching which was drawing its inspiration from them. We scarcely run the risk of going astray if we search here for one of the principal sources of the doctrine we are about to study.[2]

i THE CHRISTIAN TEACHER

Man can only choose between two kinds of life, the active and the contemplative. What confers special dignity on the functions of the Doctor is that they imply both of these two kinds of life, properly subordinated the one to the other. The true function of the Doctor is to teach. Teaching (*doctrina*) consists in communicating to others a truth meditated beforehand.[3] It demands of necessity both the reflection of the contemplative in order to discover the truth, and the activity of the professor in order to communicate his findings to others. But the most remarkable thing about this complex activity is that there is an exact correspondence between the higher and the lower, between contemplation and action. According to our definition, then, the function of the Doctor is directed towards a twofold object, interior and exterior, depending upon whether it is a question of the truth which the Doctor meditates and contemplates within himself or of those whom he is teaching. Thus there are two sides to his life, the first of which is the better and which it is his task to regulate.

In the first place, it is clear that the activity of the Doctor is not superimposed artificially upon his contemplative life. Rather, it finds

3

its source in his contemplation and is, so to speak, its outward manifestation. Teaching, as well as preaching to which it is allied, is certainly a work belonging to the active life, but it derives somehow or other from the very fullness of contemplation.[4] This is why it cannot be considered as an interruption of contemplation. When a person turns from his meditation on intelligible realities, the food of contemplation, in order to give himself to works good in themselves but purely exterior, he has to break with meditation. The distribution of alms and the entertaining of guests are excellent things, yet for all this, they exclude meditation properly so-called. Teaching, on the contrary, is the outward expression of inward contemplation. If it is true that a soul truly free from temporal interests preserves something of this liberty, which it has acquired, in each of its exterior acts, certainly there is no place where this liberty can be more integrally preserved than in the act of teaching.[5] To combine thus the active and contemplative life is not, so to speak, a subtraction but an addition. Moreover, it is evident that here is most integrally to be realized that perfect balance between the two kinds of life, a balance which our present human condition demands that we seek.[6] To teach the truth which meditation reveals for us is to expand its contemplation without losing any of it, even increasing its better part.

From this derive several consequences which are important for determining the exact role St. Thomas was assuming as a Christian Doctor. The functions of this role struck him as particularly suited to the religious state of the monks[7] and especially of an order such as the Dominicans, who were at the same time teachers and contemplatives. St. Thomas never grew weary of defending against the attacks of seculars the legitimacy of the ideal to which he had consecrated his life, monastic poverty and the work of teaching. To those who would object to his right to live in absolute poverty, he cited the example of the ancient philosophers who sometimes renounced all riches in order to devote themselves more freely to the contemplation of truth. With how much more right may not he impose upon himself this renunciation, who wishes to follow not only wisdom, but Christ, according to the beautiful words of St. Jerome to the monk Rusticus: *Christum nudum nudus sequere* "naked to follow a naked Christ." [8] To those who question the legitimacy of assuming the honor or accepting the title of Master, St. Thomas replies sensibly that to be a Master is not to assume an honor but to accept a charge,[9] and that the title of Master is not something you give yourself but something you receive, and that it is next door to impossible to prevent people from giving it to you.[10] In reply to those who maintain that the real monk is bound to perform manual labor and that this is hardly compatible with meditation and teaching, St. Thomas makes a large number of distinctions in order to dispense with a manifestly subsidiary obligation like manual labor, and replace it by the *oral labor* of teaching or preaching.[11] Indeed, in his eyes, nothing is more legitimate than a religious order of contemplative and teaching monks.

For a member of such an order, it is highly desirable to aspire to the functions of the Doctor and to spend his life in fulfilling them. True enough, the office of Master is not without its dangers. A man might, for example, teach throughout his entire life out of vainglory, never so much as placing before himself the good of others as an end. Such a life consequently would be unworthy of a true religious.[12] But one who is conscious of doing his teaching as a work of mercy and as true spiritual charity need experience no scruple in desiring to teach.

An objection constantly directed by seculars against the religious coming up for the title of Master was the difficulty of reconciling the monk's humility with this pretension to authority.[13] St. Thomas answers this objection in terms which keep in mind the place of the Master in the University of Paris, and by carefully distinguishing between the candidate for a Master's chair and a candidate for a bishopric. To seek an episcopal see is to look for a dignity not yet actually possessed; but to be named for a Master's chair is not to receive a new dignity but only a chance to communicate one's knowledge to others. To confer a license on someone is not at all to endow him with learning but merely to give permission to teach it. A second difference between the two cases is that the learning required for holding a Master's chair is a perfection of the very individual who possesses it, while the pontifical power of the bishop actually increases his dignity by comparison with other men. A third difference is that it is pre-eminently divine grace which renders a man worthy to receive the episcopal honors, while it is learning which equips a man to teach.

Thus the basic difference between the two cases can escape no one: it is praiseworthy to desire one's own perfection and therefore also to desire learning and the teaching for which learning equips one; but it is wrong to desire power over others without knowing whether one has the grace necessary to wield it. On the contrary, the desire to teach, that is, to communicate to others the learning one possesses, is a desire to perform an act of charity. There is nothing more praiseworthy than to wish to have authorization to teach, provided that one is genuinely capable of doing so. Here again the case is clear-cut and definite. No one can know with certainty whether or not he possesses grace. God alone dispenses this. But anyone can know with certainty whether or not he possesses sufficient knowledge to have the right to teach.[14] It was with complete assurance of possessing the necessary learning, and out of love for the minds he wished to enlighten, that St. Thomas dedicated his whole life to the work of teaching. To contemplate truth by his intellect and to communicate it out of love, such is the life of the Doctor. It is an exalted human imitation of the very life of God.

We must be on our guard lest an equivocation hide from us the exact sense of St. Thomas's words. When he speaks of Doctor or Master, we are inclined to think first of the philosopher while he thinks first of the theologian. The master *par excellence* can only teach wisdom *par excellence*, that is, the kind of knowledge of divine things which is essentially theology. It is only in this sense that the office of Master can legitimately be the object of the ambition of a religious. It is this office that St. Thomas has in mind when he praises the life divided between teaching and the contemplation which inspires it. It is with this office in mind too that he enumerates the various gifts which the Doctor must possess:[15] a full knowledge of the divine things in which he must instruct others—it is faith that confers this; a power to persuade or to demonstrate in order to convince others of the truth—the gift of wisdom serves him here; an ability to develop his thought and to express it in a manner suitable for instructing others—here the gift of knowledge comes to his service.[16] Wisdom and knowledge are here directed primarily towards knowing divine things and employed to teach them, so that if there is a Doctor of philosophical truth in the complex personality of St. Thomas, it is only within the theologian that we can hope to find him.

In fact, his own definition of his role as a philosopher is that he is a philosopher in the service of a theologian. This abstract statement is inadequate because indefinite and many different theologies could use it in order to define their respective positions towards philosophy; yet it is a statement which must be considered at the very outset in its stark simplicity, with all the consequences it implies in the thought of St. Thomas, if we would avoid certain grave errors about the meaning of his doctrine.

St. Thomas considers that a religious may legitimately aspire to the title and to the functions of teacher. But in so far as he can only teach divine things, it is only in relation to the science of divine things that secular sciences can legitimately interest him. This is demanded by the very essence of the contemplative life, of which teaching is but the immediate prolongation into the order of the active life. In order to be the highest form of human life, contemplation must dwell upon the object whose knowledge is the end of this life. Such knowledge and contemplation will be perfect only in the future life and only then will they confer full beatitude upon us, whereas, being in this life but imperfect, they are likewise here accompanied by only a beginning of beatitude. Thus, the study of philosophy is both legitimate in itself and useful in view of this supreme contemplation. Indeed, we shall have occasion to point out that in man's present state, all his knowledge finds its base in the order of sensible things. It is therefore inevitably from a scientific and philosophical knowledge of the universe that the Doctor of Theology must set out to build up the science of its proper object—the word of God.[17] But he need only strive to acquire this knowledge in the measure that it helps him to understand the word of God.[18] One can say, then, that although the study of philosophy and the sciences is useful to the Christian Doctor, it is not his own end.

What, then, do we call the philosophy of St. Thomas? As he had created it only for the sake of the service it renders Christian wisdom, he himself never separated it from this wisdom to give it a name.[19] Probably he did not foresee that the day would come when scholars would go searching through his works to extract the elements of a philosophy from his theology.[20] He never himself attempted such a synthesis. As a theologian, he felt no obligation to do so. But others have since done it, and it is therefore necessary now to find out in what sense it is legitimate to ascribe a philosophy to St. Thomas Aquinas.

ii THEOLOGY AND PHILOSOPHY

In a first sense, "Thomistic Philosophy" may mean a more or less complete exposition of the philosophical notions present in the works of St. Thomas. When such a task is undertaken by a philosopher dominating, as it were, his matter from above, the result is a doctrinal synthesis. Of these there have been not a few. Whatever their value and their compass, such works belong less to history, properly so-called, than to philosophy, but the historian has much to learn from them. Moreover, nothing prevents an historian from constructing such a synthesis by purely historical methods and in view of historical ends. Since the whole of St. Thomas's thought ought to be included in such a work, it would contain necessarily all the philosophical materials St. Thomas amassed for his theological work, including the notions directly borrowed by him from Aristotle, even where he subjected them to no modification.

One can also understand by "Philosophy of St. Thomas," a synthesis of the notions present in his various works, provided these notions be truly his, that is, distinct from the doctrines of his predecessors. The very existence of such an original Thomistic philosophy has often been contested. It is however our intention to prove its existence by showing in what it consists, leaving to those who would like to undertake it, the task of demonstrating where, before St. Thomas, the same doctrinal synthesis is to be found. From this second point of view, however, all the philosophical statements of St. Thomas no longer present themselves on the same plane. What he has borrowed now becomes less important than what he has been able to do with this borrowed material. This explains our choice of Thomistic doctrines for exposition and even their order of examination in this study.

The parts of his philosophy in which St. Thomas shows the most originality, are in general included within his theology. Far from pretending to give an account of his philosophy without drawing freely upon his theological works, it is often in these latter that we shall find the definitive formula of his thought relative to the nature of being, the existence of God and His attributes, creation, the nature of man and the rules of the moral life. The *Commentaries* of St. Thomas on Aristotle are very precious documents and their loss would have been deplorable. Nevertheless, if they had all perished, the two *Summae* would still preserve all that is most personal and most profound in his philosophical thought, whereas, if the theological works of St. Thomas had been lost, we should be deprived of his most important contributions to the common treasure of metaphysical knowledge. It is quite impossible to get a really adequate notion of the philosophy of St. Thomas from his commentaries on Aristotle alone. Christian Doctor that he was, St. Thomas looked everywhere for material to achieve his task. He drew on Aristotle, on Dionysius, on the *Liber de Causis,* on Boethius, on St. Augustine, on Avicenna, on Averroes, for all he could utilize in the elaboration of his work, but he had to transform almost all that he was borrowing in order to organize it into an integral theology. Indeed, we can take it as a general rule that those aspects of Thomistic philosophy have been the more profoundly elaborated which concern more directly Thomistic theology. The theology of St. Thomas is a philosopher's theology; his philosophy is a theologian's.

It can be seen at once why, from this second point of view, it becomes natural to set forth the philosophy of St. Thomas according to the order of his theology. If it is a question of what really interested him in metaphysics, and of the points on which he personally committed himself, then the only synthesis for which we are indebted to him is that of the two *Summae*. It is tempting to extract from the theological works of St. Thomas, the philosophical notions which they contain, and then to reconstruct them into some kind of philosophical order, but this is to imply that St. Thomas perhaps wished to construct a philosophy with purely philosophical ends, not with the ends proper to the Christian Doctor. Above all, it runs the infinitely graver risk of mistaking the true philosophical meaning of his philosophy.

Let us suppose that St. Thomas found in his theological investigations an incentive to carry metaphysics beyond the point where his predecessors had left it. Could we then release Thomistic philosophy from its theological moorings without running the risk of not knowing its origin or its end, of altering its nature, and even of no longer grasping its meaning? This danger has not always been avoided,[21] though it is not unavoidable. If it were impossible to present the philosophy of St. Thomas after the order of his theology without, by the same token, confusing reason with faith, it would be much better to renounce this order. But nothing is less impossible. First, St. Thomas himself has done it,[22] and most of our difficulties on this point arise from the fact that even modern Thomists do not understand theology exactly as their master himself did.

It has become customary to label "theological" any conclusion whose premises presuppose faith in a divinely revealed truth, and to label "philosophical" any conclusion whose premises are purely rational, that is, known by the light of natural reason alone. This is not the point of view stated by St. Thomas himself at the beginning of his Prologue to the Second Book of his commentary on the *Sentences* of Peter Lombard. According to him, the philosopher considers the nature of things as they are in themselves, whereas the theologian considers them in their relation to God conceived as being both their origin and their end. From this point of view, every conclusion concerning God himself, or the relations of being to God, is theological in its own right. Some of these conclusions presuppose an act of faith in the divine revelation, but some of them do not. All of them are theological; those, among them, which are purely rational, belong to theology no less than the others. The only difference is that, since these do not presuppose faith, they can be extracted from their theological context and judged, from the point of view of natural reason, as purely philosophical conclusions. This is an extremely important point in that it enables us to understand how strictly metaphysical knowledge can be included within a theological structure without losing its purely philosophical nature. Everything in the *Summa* is theological, yet, elements of genuinely philosophical nature are part and parcel of Thomistic theology precisely because, according to St. Thomas himself, the distinction between theology and philosophy does not adequately answer the distinction between faith and reason. As will be seen later on, his theology requires the collaboration of purely philosophical elements used in view of an essentially theological end. St. Thomas did this advisedly, clearly realizing the definite position which philosophy occupies in the work of a Christian Doctor. For this position he has found a term which correctly designates the status of the philosophical elements that have been integrated with a theological synthesis. He has called them *revelabilia*. This "revealable" is the proper object of this present work. Our immediate task is to define the nature of the "revealable," that is at least if we are to understand accurately the full meaning of the often-used though rarely-explained expression—the philosophy of St. Thomas Aquinas.

According to some of his modern interpreters, St. Thomas thought of himself as a philosopher who was not anxious to compromise the purity of his philosophy by admitting into it the slightest mixture of theology. But as a matter of fact, the real St. Thomas was afraid of doing just the reverse. In the *Summa Theologiae,* his problem was not how to introduce philosophy into theology without corrupting the essence of philosophy; it was rather how to introduce philosophy into theology without corrupting the essence of theology. Not only the hostility of the "Biblicists" of his time warned him of the problem, but he was himself quite as much aware of it as they were. And the more freely he made use of philosophy, the more was he aware of the problem. As he himself understands it, theology must be conceived as a science of Revelation. Its source is the word of God. Its basis is faith in the truth of this word. Its "formal" unity, to speak like St. Thomas, depends precisely upon the fact that there is a Revelation, which faith receives as Revelation. For theologians who were not in the least worried about philosophy, no problem actually arose. Persuaded that they should add nothing human to the bare deposit of revelation, they could rest assured that they were respecting the integrity and the unity of the Sacred Science. They proceeded from faith to faith, by faith. For St. Thomas Aquinas the problem was rather different. It was a question of how to integrate philosophy into sacred science, not only without allowing either the one or the other to suffer essentially thereby, but to the greater benefit of both. In order to achieve this result, he had to integrate a science of reason with a science of revelation without corrupting at the same time both the purity of reason and the purity of revelation.

This problem did not arise for the first time in the work of St. Thomas. Other theologians before him had discharged into sacred studies a considerable body of philosophical doctrine. Albert the Great, whose encyclopedic theology neglected no science as stranger to his design, was one of these. What characterizes St. Thomas and gives him a special place in this general movement is precisely the intellectual effort he made to introduce this human learning into theology, without disturbing its unity. The moment we put the problem in this manner, we can see in what direction to look for the answer. For theology to remain formally one as a science, all the natural knowledge it contains must be directed and subordinated to the point of view proper to the theologian, which is that of revelation. Thus incorporated into the theological order, human learning becomes a part of the sacred doctrine which is founded on faith. This human learning, assumed by theology for its own ends, is what St. Thomas calls the "revealable," a term for which many different interpretations have been suggested, for failure perhaps to grasp exactly the meaning of the problem to which it brings the solution.[23]

If we adhere to the obvious meaning of the term, the "revealable" is whatever can be revealed. Ingenious exegeses have tried to show that the word "revealable" came from the word "revealed." [24] This is true, but let us add that in Thomistic theology, there is some of the revealable which has been revealed, although it might well not have been, and there is some of the revealable which might well have been revealed but has not been. In order to preserve due respect for the complexity of this problem, we submit that it would be extremely imprudent to draw up *a priori*, without careful consultation of the texts of St. Thomas himself, a list of the revealable truths which God has or has not revealed. Let us ask Thomistic theologians whether the distinction between essence and existence is a truth deriving from natural knowledge or a revealed truth, and most of them will reply that it is from natural knowledge and pertains directly to philosophy. They are right. Nevertheless, St. Thomas is of the opinion that God revealed this philosophic truth.[25] If we but think of the central place of this thesis in Thomistic metaphysics, we begin to wonder what remains in this science which God might not have been able, had He so wished, explicitly or implicitly to reveal. For the moment, then, let us leave the Thomistic notion of the "revealable" an open question, and be content to examine another notion which is of primary importance for determining it.

What makes this enterprise difficult is that we have developed a tendency to approach all problems of Thomistic philosophy from the most formal point of view possible. As the well-known adage puts it: *semper formalissime loquitur Divus Thomas*. It is thus at least that we make him speak. But if he does always speak formally about the abstract, he always speaks concretely about the concrete.[26] Because we have forgotten this, we have lost a whole set of notions essential to the proper balance of Thomism, and have changed into a logic of pure essences a doctrine which its author had conceived as an explanation of facts. Let us, like him, try to speak both languages, and each one at the proper time.

The first notion to be defined is that of "the revealed." To grasp its nature, we ought to consider it *formalissime*. According to St. Thomas, the *revelatum* embraces solely that whose very essence it is to be revealed, because we can only come to know it by way of revelation. In defining the *revelatum*, we do not undertake an empirical examination of anything and everything it has pleased God to reveal to man. What constitutes "the revealed" as such is not the fact that it has been revealed but rather its character of not being accessible save by revelation. Thus conceived, "the revealed" is all knowledge about God beyond the grasp of human reason. God may in addition reveal things accessible to reason, but since they are not inaccessible by the natural light of human understanding, such knowledge is not part of "the revealed." Actually, God has revealed such truths, but it is not of their essence to be knowable only by revelation. Let us say, therefore, that "the revealed" is all that knowledge which, because it is beyond the powers of natural reason, can only be known to man through revelation.[27]

As has just been said, God may have seen fit to reveal some knowledge not essentially part of "the revealed." In order to define the category of knowledge brought within the range of our reason in this manner, a new notion is necessary, but a notion sufficiently concrete and flexible to embrace a large number of heterogeneous facts. Certainly, such a notion will have its own unity. Were it not *one*, it would not exist. Lacking the strict unity of a single essence, it has the best imitation of this, the unity of an order. This is the precise notion of "the revealable" which we must now define.

This time, we can only succeed by proceeding in the contrary manner, that is, empirically, beginning with the facts to be unified. The facts which we must dress up this way are the various things which go to make up the extremely complex event which we know as revelation. It is, indeed, here a question of an event, therefore of a fact in the order of existence, which pertains less to definition properly so-called than to the judging faculty. To encompass *a priori* the limits of this is impossible. But we can progressively construct a concept of it by a series of existential judgments on the factual data which we hope to unify. As has been said, revelation concerns essentially the revealed, but includes many other things. Because it includes them, they pertain in some degree to its order. Taken together, therefore, they will form a class of facts dependent upon a single notion whose unity will derive from their common relation to the divine act of revealing.

Taken in itself, revelation is an act which, like every act, has a certain end in view. This end, for revelation, is to make possible man's salvation. For man, salvation consists in attaining his end. He cannot attain it unless he knows it. Now this end is God, who is infinitely beyond the limits of man's knowledge. If man was to attain his salvation, God had to reveal to him knowledge beyond the limits of reason. The whole body of this knowledge is called sacred teaching, *sacra doctrina, sacra scientia*. Our problem is to know what is the content of this body of sacred teaching.

As St. Thomas conceives it, revelation appears to be a kind of hierarchical operation, using the term "hierarchical" in the sense given to it by Dionysius. Supernatural truth reaches us, so to speak, like the water of a river which passes over a series of waterfalls, from God who is its source to the angels who receive it first according to the order of the angelic hierarchy; then, from angels to men, reaching first the apostles and prophets, then spreading out into the multitude of those who receive it by faith. Sacred science has, then, for its basis faith in a revelation made by God to the apostles and prophets. This revelation confers upon these apostles and prophets a divine, therefore unshakable, authority; and theology rests primarily upon our faith in the authority of those who have spoken in order to teach us this revelation.

Theology therefore depends, first and foremost, upon the body of writings inspired by God and which we call *Sacra Scriptura,* Holy Scripture. Let us say more, it depends solely upon them, because it is the science which they have given us.[28] But here, more than ever, we must be careful to speak concretely of the concrete.

Though theology is of the same nature in all who possess it, it has not in all the same degree of perfection. Its content is not necessarily identical in all. Certainly it contains first of all the *revelatum* properly so called; that is, what it has pleased God to reveal to men for their eternal salvation. But it contains, over and above this, all our rational understanding of this revelation. Clearly, revelation resides in us only to the extent that we can be said to know it. And it is an act which has reached us by a hierarchical order, and this, not only from the Apostle or Prophet to other men, but also from the Christian Doctor to the simple faithful. By the science of the word of God which he constructs, the theologian simply explains, with the aid of natural reason, what has been revealed. This science, therefore, is nothing else than Holy Scripture received into the human understanding, or, to put it in another way, it is only divine revelation spreading itself, thanks to the light of a reason which examines the content of faith, the authority of faith and the ends of faith. We might ask, perhaps, why God did not Himself reveal this knowledge too. It is because such knowledge is not necessary for salvation. In order to attain his end, man must believe in the "articles of faith," all of which God has revealed, and the acceptance of which is sufficient for salvation. But because this other knowledge is not necessary for salvation, it was not revealed. However, it is related to salvation as to an end because it makes more and more explicit the saving word. This is why every legitimate elaboration of Holy Scripture belongs by full right to sacred theology.

The problem would be relatively simple if a new factor did not appear to complicate it. As has been said, there is a certain proportion of philosophy in the composition of the *Summa Theologiae.* The question arises, therefore, how it can be there without compromising either the purity of its own essence or that of theology. Philosophy deals with truths accessible to the human understanding, knowable by natural reason alone, and without the aid of revelation. Since this knowledge does not pass beyond the limits of natural reason, it cannot be considered as belonging to the order of "the revealed." If God has nevertheless revealed it, it is for the very different reason that man needs to know it for his salvation. Such a truth is one which every man needs to know in order to be saved, but which many men cannot discover by natural reason alone, in spite of the fact that it is a truth accessible to reason. For instance, a metaphysician can demonstrate the existence of God, but because all men are not metaphysicians, his demonstration is not easily intelligible to everyone; so God has revealed to man his existence in order that all men might be saved. This natural knowledge, included in the body of revelation, makes up the order of what St. Thomas calls the *revelabilia*. Taken in itself, this "revealable" is philosophical, but it is drawn, so to speak, into the orbit of theology as included in revelation which assumes it in view of its own end. The final cause of theological wisdom blends its various elements into an organic whole and insures its unity.

St. Thomas's commentators have been so eager to multiply formal distinctions that they have gradually altered the primitive Thomistic position on the question. For St. Thomas, the main point was not to safeguard the autonomy of philosophy as a purely rational knowledge; rather, it was to explain how natural philosophy can enter into theology without destroying its unity. This is why he stressed the fact that revelation itself had remained one, although it spoke at the same time of God, an object transcending natural reason, and men, animals and plants, objects of anthropology, or moral, biological and physical sciences: "Since, therefore, as has just been said, Holy Scripture considers certain objects because they have been divinely revealed, all that is, generally speaking, revealable by God shares the formal reason of this science; this is why these things come under Sacred Science as under a single science." [29] Such an organic knowledge of all things as ultimately related to God is no chimera. It actually exists in God's knowledge of Himself and in the knowledge which the blessed have of Him. It is this perfectly unified knowledge which our theology imitates in its fashion by directing all natural knowledge to the supernatural knowledge which we have of God by revelation. St. Thomas's practice would indicate that all philosophy could fall into this category. Moreover, he has said: "The Sacred Science can, without ceasing to be a single science, consider from one point of view the matter dealt with in the various branches of philosophy, to know, in so far as they are revealable, to the end that Sacred Science may thus be like a copy of the Divine Science, which is the only and simple law of all things." [30]

Thus related to the knowledge which God has of Himself,[31] and, as it were, glorified by its theological assumption, philosophy eminently deserves the attention of the Christian Doctor, and it is in this condition that we, in our turn, would like to consider it as the proper object of our study. We are not maintaining that St. Thomas identified the two notions of "revealable" and "philosophy," nor do we claim that the philosophy of St. Thomas cannot be legitimately examined from another point of view.[32] But we beg leave to examine it under the aspect which St. Thomas himself claims to have examined it, that of the Christian Doctor, because it is for having envisaged metaphysics under this definite aspect, that his genius has renovated it.[33]

iii FAITH AND REASON

What, then, are we to understand to be the object of metaphysics, still called "first philosophy" or "wisdom"? According to common usage, the *wise* man is one who puts things in their right place and governs them well. To put a thing into its right place and to govern it well is to make it serve its true end. Thus we see in the hierarchy of the arts that one art governs another and serves in some sort as its principle when its immediate end constitutes the last end of the subordinated art. Medicine, for example, is a principal and directing art so far as concerns pharmacy, because health, which is the immediate end of medicine, is at the same time the last end of all the remedies which the pharmacist prepares. These principal and dominating arts are described as architectonic, and those who practise them are called *wise* men or sages. But they are only called wise with regard to the things they actually know how to employ properly in view of their end. Their wisdom, since it concerns particular ends, is only a particular wisdom. If we imagine, on the contrary, a wise man who does not propose to consider such or such a particular end but the end of the universe, he will not be called wise in any given art, but wise absolutely speaking. He will be the wise man *par excellence*. The object proper to wisdom, first philosophy, is therefore the end of the universe. And, since the end of an object becomes one with its principle or its cause, we find Aristotle giving this definition: first philosophy studies first causes.[34]

Let us now ask what is the first cause or last end of the universe. The last end of anything is clearly what its primary author intended when he made it, or what its first mover intends in moving it. Now we shall see that the first author and first mover of the universe is an Intelligence. The end which He puts before Himself in creating and moving the universe ought therefore to be the end or good of the intelligence, that is, truth. Thus truth is the last end of the whole universe; and since the object of first philosophy is the last end of the whole universe, it follows that its proper object is truth.[35] But we must here avoid a possible confusion. Since the philosopher is to attain the last end and, consequently, the first cause of the universe, the truth we speak of here cannot be any truth whatsoever, but only that truth which is the first source of all truth. Now the disposition of things in the order of truth is the same as in the order of being (*sic enim est dispositio rerum in veritate sicut in esse*), since to be and to be true are equivalent to each other. A truth which is the source of all truth can only be found in a being that is the first source of all being. The truth which is the object of first philosophy, therefore, is this truth which the Word made Flesh came to manifest to the world, as St. John says: "For this was I born, and for this came I into the world, that I should give testimony to the truth." [36] In a word, the real object of metaphysics is God.[37]

This determination, which St. Thomas puts at the beginning of his *Summa Contra Gentiles,* in no way contradicts the one which elsewhere brings him to define metaphysics as the science of being considered simply as being, and of its first causes.[38] If the metaphysician's research deals immediately with being in general, this is not its real end. Philosophical speculation moves beyond being in general towards the first cause of all being: "And moreover first philosophy is wholly directed to the knowledge of God as its last end; and is consequently called the *divine science."* This is why, when he speaks in his own name, Thomas Aquinas lays aside the consideration of being as being and defines metaphysics from the point of view of its supreme object—the primary principle of being, God.

What means have we to attain this object? First, and obviously, we have natural reason. The problem is to know whether our reason is an adequate instrument to attain the objective of metaphysical research; namely, the divine essence. Let us state at once that natural reason, left to its own devices, is adequate to attain certain truths concerning God and his nature. Philosophers can demonstrate that God exists, that He is one, etc. But it is most apparent that there is a knowledge of the divine nature infinitely beyond the grasp of the human understanding. This is a point which it is important to establish in order to silence the unbelievers who consider false all statements about God which our reason is unable to make. Here the Christian sage is about to implement the Greek.

All the demonstrations of this thesis intend to show the disproportion between our finite understanding and the infinite essence of God. The one among them which introduces us most deeply, perhaps, into the thought of St. Thomas derives from the nature of human knowledge. Perfect knowledge, if we accept Aristotle's word for it, consists in deducing the properties of an object, using the essence of this object as the principle of demonstration. It is the mode according to which the substance of each thing is known to us which determines, in fact, the mode of the knowledge we can have of this thing. Now God is a purely spiritual substance. Our knowledge, on the contrary, is the acquired knowledge proper to a being composed of soul and body. It necessarily has its origin in the senses. Our knowledge of God, therefore, begins with such sense data as we can have of a purely intelligible being. Thus our understanding, using the testimony of the senses as its starting-point, can infer that God exists. But it is evident that the simple inspection of sensible things, which are effects of God and, consequently, inferior to him, are unable to bring us to a knowledge of the divine essence.[39] There are, therefore, truths concerning God which are accessible to reason, and others which are beyond it. Let us examine the role of faith in both of these cases.

Abstractly and absolutely speaking, where reason is able to understand, faith has no further role to play. In other words, we cannot both know and believe the same thing at the same time under the same aspect: *impossible est quod de eodem sit fides et scientia.*[40] The proper object of faith, according to St. Augustine, is precisely what reason does not attain. Whence it follows that any rational knowledge that can be resolved into first principles is removed by this very fact from the domain of faith. This is the theoretical truth. But in actual fact, faith must take the place of knowledge in a large number of our affirmations. Not only, indeed, may certain truths be believed by the ignorant and known by scholars,[41] but it often happens that, by reason of the weakness of our understanding and of the wanderings of our imagination, error creeps into our research. Many a person but badly perceives what conclusions ought to follow from a principle; and so he remains quite inadequately informed about truths which can be well enough demonstrated. Disagreement over the same questions, even among reputedly wise men, completely baffles him. It was then most helpful that Providence should propound as truths of faith a number of truths accessible to reason, so that everyone might easily share in the knowledge of God without fear of doubt or error.[42]

If we consider, on the other hand, truths beyond the grasp of our reason, we shall see no less clearly that it was only fitting that they too should have been presented to us as objects of faith. The end of man is God, an end obviously exceeding the limits of reason. Yet man should have some knowledge of his end in order to regulate and order his intentions and actions towards that end. The salvation of man, therefore, demands that divine revelation should make him know a certain number of truths quite beyond the grasp of his reason.[43] In other words, since man requires knowledge of the infinite God, who is his end, and since such knowledge exceeds the limits of his reason, he simply must get it by way of faith. Nor does such faith do violence to our reason. Rather, faith in the incomprehensible confers on rational knowledge its perfection and consummation. We do not truly know God, for example, save when we believe Him to be above anything man can think about Him. Now, certainly, to ask us to accept incomprehensible truths about God is an excellent means of implanting in us a conviction of his incomprehensibility.[44] Moreover, acceptance on faith tends to suppress presumption, the mother of error. Some think they can measure God's nature by the yardstick of their own reason. To propose to them, in God's name, truths above their understanding, brings them back to a just estimate of their limitations. Thus the very discipline of faith turns to the profit of reason.

Is it possible, however, over and above this exterior and simple accord, to admit that an internal accord, one taken from the point of view of truth, can be established between reason and faith? In other words, can we be sure that there is agreement between truths beyond reason and those within the range of reason? The proper response to this question depends on the value we assign to the motives of credibility which faith calls upon. If we admit, as we really should, that the miracles, the prophecies, the marvellous effects of the Christian religion sufficiently prove the truth of revealed religion,[45] then we must also admit that there can be no contradiction between faith and reason. Only the false can contradict what is true. Between true faith and true knowledge there is by definition a natural agreement. But we can give this agreement a purely philosophical demonstration. When a master instructs his disciple, his own knowledge must include whatever he would introduce into the soul of the disciple. Now our natural knowledge of principles comes from God, since He is author of our nature. These principles themselves are also contained in the wisdom of God. Whence it follows that whatever is contrary to these principles is contrary to the divine wisdom and, consequently, cannot come from God. There must necessarily be agreement between a reason coming from God and a revelation coming from God.[46] Let us say, then, that faith teaches truths which seem contrary to reason; let us not say that it teaches propositions contrary to reason. The rustic thinks it contrary to reason that the sun should be larger than the earth. But this proposition seems reasonable to the scientist.[47] Let us rest assured that apparent incompatibility between faith and reason is similarly reconciled in the infinite wisdom of God.

We are not, however, reduced to this act of general confidence in an agreement whose direct perception escapes us. Many observable facts cannot be satisfactorily interpreted unless we accept the existence of a common source for our two orders of knowledge. Faith is above reason, not in what concerns its mode of learning, for indeed its knowledge is of an inferior kind because of its very obscurity, but in that it puts human thought in possession of a truth which it is naturally incapable of grasping. There can result, therefore, from faith a whole series of influences and actions whose consequences within reason itself can be most important. Faith in revelation does not destroy the rationality of our knowledge but rather permits it to develop more fully. Even as, indeed, grace does not destroy nature but heals and perfects it, so faith, through the influence it wields from above over reason as reason, permits the development of a far more true and fruitful rational activity.[48]

This transcendent influence of faith on reason is an essential fact which we must interpret aright if we are not to deprive Thomistic philosophy of its proper character. Much of the criticism directed against it is based on this blending of faith and reason which is said to be found in it. Now it is equally inexact to maintain either that St. Thomas separates faith and reason into water-tight divisions or that he confuses the two continually. Later on, we shall have occasion to ask whether he does confuse them. But for the present, it is enough to see that he does not isolate them from each other and that he was able to keep them in touch with each other in a way which did not force him ultimately to confuse them.[49] The fear experienced by some disciples of St. Thomas, lest the notion become current that his reason has been contaminated by his faith, has nothing Thomistic about it.[50] To deny that he acknowledges or wants the beneficent influence of faith is to force oneself to regard as purely accidental the actual accord between philosophy and theology achieved in his work. It is to manifest an inquietude which St. Thomas himself would not have understood. Aquinas is too sure of his thinking to fear any such thing. His reason advances under the beneficent action of faith. He acknowledges this. But he affirms that, by passing along the road of revelation, reason sees truths which it might otherwise have overlooked. The traveller whom a guide has conducted to the mountain peak sees no less of the view because another has opened it up for him. The panorama is no less real because the helping hand of another has brought him to it. When one has worked a long time at St. Thomas, one becomes convinced that the vast world-system which his doctrine presents took form in his thought in the same measure that the doctrine of faith took form there too. When he tells others that faith is a salutary guide for reason, it is because the memory of the help furnished his own reason by faith is still very much alive in him.

It is therefore no wonder that in what concerns theology primarily, there is room for philosophical speculation, even when it is a question of revealed truths beyond the grasp of our reason. Undoubtedly, reason cannot pretend either to demonstrate or understand these truths. But it is encouraged by the certitude that there is a truth hidden away in them, and it can give us passing if indistinct glimpses into it by means of well-founded comparisons. Sensible objects, the point of departure of all our knowledge, have retained vestiges of the divine nature which created them, because the effect always resembles its cause. Reason therefore can put us on our way to understanding the perfect truth which God will disclose to us in the future life.[51] This statement delimits the role of reason in undertaking to clarify the truths of faith. There is nothing more imprudent than to assume the task of demonstrating them. To attempt to demonstrate what is undemonstrable is to confirm the unbeliever in his unbelief. So evident is the disproportion between the theses to be established and the false proofs brought to the task that, far from serving faith by such arguments, one only holds it up to ridicule.[52] But we can explain, interpret, reconcile what we cannot prove. We can, as it were, lead our adversaries by the hand into the presence of these inaccessible truths. We can point out the probable reasons and the sure authority upon which they are based here below.

But we must go farther. There is place even for demonstrative argumentation where it is a question of truths inaccessible to reason, and, conversely, for the intervention of faith in matters apparently reserved to pure reason. We have seen, indeed, that revelation and reason cannot contradict each other. If, therefore, it is certain that reason cannot demonstrate faith, it is equally certain that all so-called rational demonstration, pretending to establish that faith is in error, itself rests upon a piece of sophistry. However subtle the arguments invoked, it is necessary to adhere firmly to the principle that, since truth cannot be divided against itself, reason cannot be rational if it is opposed to faith.[53] We can safely look for sophistry in any philosophical thesis opposing revelation. Revealed texts are never philosophical demonstrations of the falsity of a doctrine, but they are for the believer the sign that the philosopher who holds it is mistaken, and it is up to philosophy alone to demonstrate where.

With still stronger reason are the resources of philosophical speculation required by faith when it is a question of revealed truths which are also rationally demonstrable. This body of true philosophical doctrine which human thought would rarely possess intact and complete if left to rely only on the resources of reason is rather easily put together even by a purely rational method, once it has been presented by faith. Like a child, understanding when the master teaches what it would not have been able to discover alone, the human intellect takes easy possession of a doctrine whose truth is guaranteed by a more than human authority. Whence the incomparable steadfastness it shows before errors of every kind which bad faith or ignorance can engender among her adversaries. It can always oppose them with conclusive demonstrations capable of imposing silence and restoring truth.

Let us add, finally, that even the purely scientific knowledge of sensible things cannot leave theology completely indifferent. Not that there is no knowledge of creatures valuable in itself and independent of all theology. Science exists as science and, provided it remains within its natural borders, it has a place beyond any intervention by faith. But it is rather faith which cannot afford not to take such science into consideration, first, because the consideration of creatures is useful for instruction in the faith; secondly, because, as we have just seen, natural knowledge can at least destroy certain errors about God.[54]

Although the relationship established between faith and reason is so intimate, they still constitute two formally distinct types of knowledge, and the same can be said of philosophy and theology. In spite of the fact that their territories extend over a certain common expanse, they still do not coincide. Theology is the science of truths necessary for our salvation, and since all truths are not necessary for this, God has not revealed about creatures many things which they are capable of learning by themselves, and the knowledge of which is not necessary for salvation. There is room, then, outside theology for a knowledge of things considered in themselves and for themselves, and which falls into different sciences according to the different genera of natural things, while theology considers them all under the perspective of salvation and in relation to God.[55]

Even where the two disciplines cover the same ground they keep their specific characters and thus are distinguished from each other. Indeed, they differ first and above all in their principles of demonstration, and it is this which definitely prevents the two from becoming confused. Philosophy borrows its arguments from the essences of things and, consequently, from their proper causes. The theologian, on the contrary, argues from the first cause of all things, God, and he appeals to three different classes of arguments, none of which is regarded by the philosopher as satisfactory. Sometimes the theologian affirms a truth on the principle of authority, because it has been passed on to us and revealed by God. Sometimes the glory of an infinite God demands that a certain truth be so. This is called the principle of perfection. Sometimes it is because the power of God is infinite.[56] This does not imply that theology should not be called a science; it only means that it is not science in the philosophical meaning of the word. Just as two natural sciences can establish one and the same fact starting from different principles and arriving by different methods at the same conclusions, so the demonstrations of the philosopher, based on principles of reason, differ specifically from faith, even where both agree on the same truth.

A second difference, closely allied with the first, is to be found, not in the principles of demonstration, but in the order which it follows. In philosophic teaching, whose proper object is the consideration of creatures in themselves, we strive to lift ourselves from creatures to God, so that the consideration of creatures comes first and the consideration of God last. In the doctrine of faith, on the contrary, which only studies creatures in relation to God, it is the consideration of God that comes first and then follows that of creatures. Thus theology follows an order which, taken in itself, is more perfect since it imitates the knowledge of God who, in knowing himself, knows all the rest.[57]

Such is the position of St. Thomas himself; but if we call "philosophy" those parts of his theology which he held as philosophically demonstrated, the problem arises to know what order to follow in presenting the philosophy of St. Thomas. As we have said, in none of his works is the body of his philosophical thought exposed for itself and according to the order of natural reason alone. There is a series of works in which St. Thomas used the philosophical method—the Commentaries on Aristotle and a small number of *Opuscula*. But each *opusculum* gives but a fragment of his thought, and the commentaries on Aristotle, bound to follow the meanderings of an obscure text, only let us suspect imperfectly what might have been the nature of a Summa of Thomistic philosophy organised by St. Thomas himself, with all the sparkling genius that went into the *Summa Theologiae*.[58] Then there is a second group of works, of which the *Summa Theologiae* is the most perfect example, which contain, included in his theology, his main philosophical positions demonstrated according to the *principles* of philosophical demonstration but presented according to the *order* of theological demonstration. It would remain then to reconstruct an ideal Thomistic philosophy by extracting what is best from these two groups of works and by submitting St. Thomas's demonstrations to the exigencies of a new order. But who will vouch that the philosophic order of the demonstration thus adopted will be the same as that which the genius of St. Thomas would have followed? How, above all, could we be sure that in proceeding thus we might not actually dispense with something which St. Thomas esteemed more than all the rest, namely, the tangible satisfaction and benefit which the philosopher receives when, in dealing with the revealable, he integrates it with theology? It would be interesting to know why John of St. Thomas has not written a "metaphysics" of Saint Thomas Aquinas. At any rate, historical prudence is no mean virtue in the practising historian. But more is at stake here. The real question is to know whether one can snatch a philosophy from the milieu in which it was born, plant it elsewhere away from the environment in which alone it has ever actually existed, and not destroy it? If the philosophy of St. Thomas has been constituted as revealable, then to expound it in the order proper to the theologian is simply to respect it.

To do so does not imply that the truth of a philosophy, thus arranged according to the order of faith, is subordinate to that of faith, which rests upon the authority of a divine revelation. What we call Thomistic philosophy is a body of rigorously demonstrable truths and is justifiable precisely as philosophy by reason alone. When we speak of St. Thomas as of a philosopher, it is a question only of his demonstrations. It is of little importance that his thesis comes right where faith would have it. He never calls upon faith, nor asks us to call upon it in those proofs which he regards as rationally demonstrated. Between the claims of these two disciplines, and even when they bear upon the same matter, there remains a strict, formal distinction based on the heterogeneity of the principles of demonstration. Theology places its principles in the articles of faith. Philosophy asks reason alone what it can tell us about

God. Between the two, there is a generic difference: "the theology included in sacred doctrine differs in genus from that theology which is part of philosophy." [59] It can be shown that St. Thomas did not establish this generic distinction as an inefficacious principle, stated but not taken into account. The examination of his teaching, in all its historical significance, compared with the Augustinian tradition most illustriously represented by St. Bonaventure, reveals what profound recasting, what incredibly bold transformations he was willing to carry out on his own responsibility in order to meet the demands of philosophical truth whenever, in his judgment, they were justified by right reason.[60]

Here precisely is to be found the properly philosophical value of the Thomistic system. This is what makes it a decisive moment in the history of human thinking. Fully aware of all the consequences of such an attitude, St. Thomas accepts simultaneously, each with its own exigencies, his faith and his reason. He does not seek to establish, at the cheapest possible price, some superficial reconciliation between Christian faith and commonly received philosophical notions. He prefers that reason should develop its own content in perfect liberty, and that it should display without diminution all the rigors of its demands. The philosophy which he teaches is not philosophy because it is Christian, but he knows that the truer it is, the more Christian it will be, and the more Christian it is, the truer it will be. This is why, equally open to St. Augustine and to Aristotle, he feels free to go beyond both of them every time truth compels him to do so.

Thomas elaborates a new metaphysics of being, renovates the philosophical notion of God and, consequently, the whole philosophy of nature inasmuch as it hangs on the notion of creation, whose implications deeply affect the structure of traditional morality. Rather than follow passively the Aristotelianism of the Averroists, he cracks its framework everywhere, submits the doctrine on which he comments to a profound metamorphosis and charges it with a new meaning. In so far as it affects philosophy, Thomism is an immense effort of intellectual honesty to reconstruct metaphysics in such a way that its actual accord with faith should appear as the necessary consequence of the demands of reason itself, and not the accidental result of a mere desire for conciliation.

Such seem to us to be the contacts and the distinction between faith and reason in the theology of St. Thomas Aquinas. They can neither contradict each other nor ignore each other nor be confused with each other. In vain will reason justify faith. It can never transform it into reason. The moment faith gives up authority for proof, it ceases to believe and begins to know. And in vain would faith move reason from without or beguile it from within. Reason can never cease to be itself. The moment it accepts any substitute for a demonstrative proof of what

it holds forth, it vanishes, giving way to faith. Thus it is the very ex-
clusiveness of their proper essences which allows them to help each
other without contamination. But we are not living in a world of pure
essences, and the complexity of a concrete science like theology can
include both faith and reason, ordering them to the unity of one and
the same end. In *becoming something revealable,* philosophy does not
give up in any way its essential rationality, but it agrees to ordain its
rationality towards a higher end.

We see how, considered in this light and as a discipline which grasps
here below whatever natural reason can conceive about God, the study
of philosophical wisdom appears to St. Thomas as a divine science.
Aristotle had already said this. St. Thomas repeats it, but with a new
meaning. Raised by his efforts to the level of the revealable, it shares
from now on the attributes of theological wisdom which, St. Thomas says,
is at once the most perfect, the most sublime and the most useful
knowledge man can acquire in this life. The most perfect because, to the
extent that he is dedicated to the study of wisdom, man participates even
in this world in true beatitude. The most sublime, because the wise man
takes on in some degree a resemblance to God, God having established
all things in wisdom. The most useful because it brings us to the eternal
kingdom. The most consoling, too, because as Scripture says (*Wisd.* viii,
16), its conversation has no bitterness, its communication no sadness;
one finds there only pleasure and joy.[61]

There are, no doubt, certain minds more vitally touched by scientific
certitude, and they will quickly question the superiority of metaphysical
study. To investigations which do not declare themselves totally powerless even in the presence of the incomprehensible, they prefer the sure
deductions of physics or mathematics. But it is not only its certitude
that ennobles a science, it is its object as well. To minds tormented by
the divine thirst, it is useless to offer the most certain knowledge of
the laws of numbers and the arrangement of the universe. Straining for
an object which eludes their grasp, they endeavor to lift a corner of the
veil, only too happy to perceive, sometimes even under heavy shadows,
glimmerings of the eternal light which must one day shine upon them.
To such, the slightest knowledge touching the highest realities is far
more desirable than the most absolute certitude touching minor objects.[62]
Here we arrive at that point of reconciliation between the utmost scorn
of what concerns human reason, a scorn which St. Thomas himself sometimes shows, and that lively taste for metaphysical discussion and reasoning. It is when it is a question of attaining an object rendered inaccessible
to us by its very essence that our reason reveals itself powerless and
deficient on every side. No one was more aware of this shortcoming than
St. Thomas. If, in spite of all, he unweariedly applied this feeble

instrument to the most exalted objects, it is because the most confused knowledge, knowledge hardly deserving the name, ceases to be despicable when it has for its object the infinite essence of God. Poverty-stricken conjectures, comparisons not totally inadequate, it is from these we draw our purest and most profound joys. The sovereign happiness of man here below is to anticipate, in however confused a fashion, the face-to-face vision of God in the quiet of eternity.

PART ONE

GOD

CHAPTER I

EXISTENCE AND REALITY

IF WE CONSIDER the philosophy of St. Thomas under the aspect of the revealable, its resulting theological order brings it immediately to grips with the problem of the existence of God. This problem itself supposes some preliminary understanding of the meaning of the term "existence," that is, a definition of what is meant by the verbs "to be" or "to exist." St. Thomas himself seems to have been aware of the urgency of this problem since one of his first works is the treatise *On Being and Essence.*

It has often been said that his conception of the real and of being dominates his metaphysics, consequently the whole of his philosophy.[1] Nothing could be more exact. Perhaps we should go farther and say that the question really raised by this notion is the existence of a philosophy proper to St. Thomas. Because historians have not been fully aware of its orginality and depth, even the best of them have felt justified in saying that St. Thomas only repeats Aristotle. Others have held that he actually fails to repeat Aristotle. There are, too, historians who charge that St. Thomas has merely fashioned a mosaic of miscellaneous fragments borrowed from irreconcilable doctrines with no dominating intuition to unify them. Even his most faithful interpreters have themselves sometimes overlooked the Thomistic notion of being, because it is difficult to grasp and because, even after it has been grasped, it is still more difficult to hold on to.

The misconceptions haunting this problem proceed in the first place from the structure of the human reason. This is a point to which we shall have to return. They proceed also, in some measure, from difficulties of terminology, particularly embarrassing in French and English. In Latin, St. Thomas found at his disposal two distinct terms; one, *ens,* designating a being; the other, *esse,* designating the very act-of-being. French has but one word, *être,* which means "what is" and also indicates that what is exists. A similar situation holds in English where both *ens* and *esse* are rendered by "being." Now as we shall have many an occasion to remind ourselves, we are here dealing with two aspects of the real which a metaphysical analysis must carefully distinguish. In order to render their fundamental distinction more clear, it is in general preferable not to translate the *esse* of St. Thomas by "being," but to render *ens* by "being" and *esse* by "act-of-being." [2]

Beginning, as St. Thomas himself does, with the *entia,* or beings which come to us in sense experience, we shall designate them by the term "substances." Each substance forms a complete whole which has a structure that we shall analyze and which constitutes an ontological unit capable of being given a definition. In so far as substance can be conceived and defined, it is called "essence." *Essence*, therefore, is only *substance* as susceptible of definition. To be exact, the essence is what the definition says the substance is. This is why, following the terminology of Aristotle, St. Thomas introduces a third term into his description of the real. To signify what a substance is, is to reply to the question *quid sit* (what is it?), and so, to the extent that it is expressed in the definition, the essence is called the "quiddity." [3] Substance, essence, quiddity; that is, a concrete ontological unit taken in itself, then taken as susceptible of definition, and finally taken as signified by the definition, such is the first group of terms which we shall be constantly using. They are too closely related not to be sometimes employed one for the other, but we should know, whenever it becomes necessary, how to reduce them to their primary meaning.

Since essence is substance in so far as it is knowable, it ought to include the latter in its complete being and not only one or other of the elements of which it is composed. Substance is sometimes defined as "a being by itself." This is not inexact, but is not the whole truth, and it is in completing this formula as it ought to be that we discover the proper sense of the notion of essence. Indeed, substance is not conceivable, and, consequently, is not definable, unless we think of it as a given determined substance. This is why "a being by itself" cannot exist without a complementary determination. The essence alone furnishes this determination. Substance, therefore, must be defined as an essence or quiddity existing by itself in virtue of its own act of being. [4]

We can understand it better if we examine the meaning of the formula "being by itself." Let us take any substance whatsoever, a man, for example. He is said to exist by himself because he constitutes an ontological unit distinct from any other and contains in himself all the determinations necessary for his existence. However, all these determinations do not exist in him by the same title nor in the same manner. There are first of all those without which he could not be called a man and which permit us so to call him. Definitions express these determinations. In the present instance, this substance is a man because it is an animal endowed with reason. Let us assume that such a substance has been concretely realized. Then all complementary determinations will be realized at the same time, and by means of it. Because he is an animal, a man must have a certain color and shape. He will necessarily occupy a certain place in space and a certain relative position. We put the name *substance* on the subject of these complementary determinations which themselves are called accidents. Although, within our experience, there are no substances without accidents any more than there are accidents without substance, still it is the accidents which belong to the substance, not the substance to the accidents.

At this point there is danger of making a fatal mistake, one capable of blocking once and for all the only path to the understanding of Thomism. We often hear it said that this philosophy consists in imagining the structure of the real as analogous to that of human language. Because our phrases are made up of a subject and predicates, St. Thomas would have concluded that the real is made up of substances of which accidents are predicated and of accidents which are attributed to substances. This is completely to misunderstand his thought and to confuse his logic with his metaphysics. To state the problem of being and to define this type of beings known as substances is to become engaged in the mystery of actual existence. The analytic language which we use to describe it is up against an objectively given reality upon which both language and metaphysical knowledge have to model themselves. To speak of things as "substances" is not to conceive of them as groups of accidents bound by some kind of copula to a subject. Quite to the contrary, it is to say that they set themselves up as units of existence, all of whose constitutive elements *are*, by virtue of one and the same act of existing, which is that of the substance. Accidents have no existence of their own to be added to that of the substance in order to complete it. They have no other existence than that of the substance. For them, to exist is simply "to-exist-in-the-substance" or, as it has been put, *"their* being is to-be-in." [5] The full sense of the expression "to be by itself" is here revealed in all its profundity. Substance does not exist by itself in this sense, that there is no cause of its existence. God, who alone exists without cause, is not a substance. Substance exists by itself in this sense that whatever in it is, belongs to it by virtue of a single act of existing, and is accounted for by this act, as by the cause why it exists.

The analysis of what makes up the very core of reality can therefore abstract from accident, denuded of any being of its own besides that of a quality, and focus itself on substance. The only substances of which we may have any direct experience are sensible things whose qualities we perceive. These substances have one remarkable property. They can be distributed into classes, each the object of one concept. This concept can itself be expressed by a definition. However we interpret it, it is a fact that we think by general notions or concepts. For this fact, which is real, to be possible, it is essential that the datum of our sensible experience be at least capable of being conceptualized, that is, that its nature lend itself to knowledge by means of concepts. Let us, then, assign a distinct term to that in the real which makes knowledge of it by concept to be possible. Let us call it the *form* of the substance. We say, then, that every substance implies a form, and that it is by virtue of this form that a substance is classified in a determined species,[6] whose concept the definition expresses. On the other hand, it is also a fact of experience that species do not exist as such. "Man" is not a substance. The only substances we know are individuals. There must be, therefore, in the individual some other element than form, something that distinguishes members of the same species from one another. Let us assign, in its turn, a distinct term to this new element in the real. Let us call it *matter*. Thus we say that every corporeal substance is a unit of existence which, at the same time and indivisibly, is one of form and matter.[7] To ask ourselves what authorizes us to say of this substance that it is a *being,* is to ask ourselves if that by which it *is* ought to be sought in its matter or in its form, or in the composite formed by their union.

We know that it is not the matter by which the substance *is,* because matter cannot have existence apart from some form. It is always the matter of a substance which, because it has a form, is the object of a concept or definition. This, moreover, is why matter can enter into the composition of substance without breaking its existential unity. Taken precisely as matter, quite apart from that of which it is a part, it does not exist. "Indeed, the act-of-existing (*esse*) is the act of something about which one can say: this thing exists. Now we do not say of matter that it exists. We only say this about the whole thing. We cannot therefore say that matter exists. It is the substance itself which exists."[8] Having no existence of its own, matter cannot be the cause of the existence of substance. It is therefore not in virtue of its matter that we say of any substance: it is a *being,* it *is.*

When we turn to form, the same consequences obtain and for the same reasons. Certainly form is a nobler element of substance than is matter, since it is form that specifies substance and confers intelligibility upon it. The form of a human individual, Socrates for example, is that by which the matter is the matter of this given organized body called a human body. Matter is only a potency determinable by the form. But the form itself is the act by which the matter is made to be the matter of such or such a determined substance. The proper role of the form is, therefore, to constitute substance *as substance.* As St. Thomas says, it is what makes it to be substance and enables it to achieve substantiality.[9] Thus conceived, form is *that by which* the substance is *that which is.* We recognize here the distinction, traditional among readers of Boethius, between the *quo est* and the *quod est.*[10] This distinction plays a considerable role in the Thomistic doctrine, where it receives another and deeper meaning than it had in the doctrine of Boethius.

It is, indeed, of the greatest importance to understand clearly on what plane St. Thomas puts these problems when he examines them from the point of view of substance. In the order of the finite which we are at present considering, only substances exist. Composed of matter and form, each of them is a "something which is," an *ens* specifically determined. Every problem concerning the order of substance falls by full right in the plane of being, but it cannot pass beyond it. To explain a being as substance is to say why this being "is what it is." Even this is an important achievement, and we find St. Thomas admiring Plato and Aristotle for having reached such metaphysical heights. However, there remains a still higher one, for once it has been explained why a being is what it is, there remains to explain what makes it exist. Since neither matter nor form can exist apart, it is not difficult to see that the existence of their composite is possible. But it is not so easy to see how their union can engender actual existence. How is existence to arise from what does not exist? It is therefore necessary to have existence come first as the ultimate term to which the analysis of the real can attain.

When it is thus related to existence, form ceases to appear as the ultimate determination of the real. Let us agree to call "essential" every ontology, or doctrine of being, for which the notion of essence and the notion of being are equivalent. We will then say that in an "essential ontology" the form element, which achieves the completion of substance, is the very core of reality. But this can no longer hold for an "existential ontology" where the form is further actuated by existence. From this second point of view, the substantial form appears as a secondary *quo est* subordinated to this primary *quo est* which is the very act of existing. Beyond form which makes a being be such a being belonging to a given determined species, we must therefore place "to be," or the act-of-being, which makes the substance thus constituted a "being." As St. Thomas says: "The act-of-being (*ipsum esse*) is like the act itself with regard to the form itself. For if we say that in composites of matter and form the form is the principle of existence (*principium essendi*), it is because it achieves the substance whose act is the act-of-being (*ipsum esse*)." [11] Thus form is only the principle of existence to the extent that it achieves substance, which is that which exists.

At its own level and in its own order, form too is a cause of existence. In our human experience, existence itself does not exist; it is always the existence of some thing which exists. Supreme constitutive principle of "that which exists by itself," that is, of substance, form therefore deserves to be considered as a principle of actual being. What it is important above all to retain, however, is that substance itself, or the composite, exists only in virtue of a further, and this time, supreme determination, its very act of being. In this sense, the act-of-being is the act of the form, itself the act of the substance. It is, therefore, that which makes the substance to be a "being," as having actual existence: "The form can, however, be called the *quo est* insofar as it is principle of existence (*principium essendi*): but it is the total substance itself that is the *quod est*, and that by which the substance is called being (*ens*) is the act-of-being (*ipsum esse*)." [12] In brief, in concrete substances which are the object of sensible experience, two metaphysical compositions must be ranged according to profundity: the first, that of matter and form, constitutes the very substantiality of the substance; the second, that of the substance with its act of existing, constitutes the substance as "being" because it makes it an existing thing.

This doctrine, whose place in Thomism is central, is worth stopping over long enough, if not fully to grasp its meaning, at least to feel its significance. To assert that the act-of-being has the bearing of an act with regard to form itself—*ad ipsam formam comparatur esse ut actus*—is to affirm the radical primacy of existence over essence. Whiteness is not what it is, it does not even exist, save that there exists a being which exercises the act of being white. Nor is the form of the white substance what makes it to be; it only exists in virtue of the existential act which makes it a real being.[13] Thus understood, the act of existing lies at the very heart, or if one prefers, at the very root of the real. It is therefore the principle of the principles of reality. First absolutely, it even precedes the Good, for a being is only good in so far as it is a being, and it is a being only in virtue of the *ipsum esse* which permits us to say of it: this is "being."[14]

To understand this doctrine in its proper nature, it is necessary to remember that *esse*, like every verb, designates an act[15] and not a state. The state in which the *esse* places that which receives it is the state of *ens*, that is to say, of that which is a "being." Because essences are the proper object of human understanding, we tend ceaselessly to step down from the plane of the act-of-being to that of things (*res*). This is a natural inclination, but the metaphysician must make every effort to remount, that is to emphasize that being has meaning only in relation to actual existence.[16] Beyond what is most perfect and most profound in the real, there is nothing. Now, what is most perfect is the act-of-being (*ipsum esse*) "since it is related to all things as their act. In fact, nothing has any actuality save in that it exists. The act-of-being (*ipsum esse*) is the actuality of everything else, even including forms. Its relation to other things therefore is not that of receiver to received but of received to receiver. Indeed, when I say of a man, or of a horse, or of anything else: that exists, the act-of-being (*ipsum esse*) is taken as formal and received, and not as that to which the act-of-being belongs."[17] St. Thomas is here noticeably making, as it were, a supreme effort, so much so that the meaning fairly rings through the formulae, to express the unique character of *ipsum esse* and its transcendence. But precisely because it is the summit of the real, it is also its heart. "The act-of-existing is more intimate to anything whatsoever than is what determines it."[18]

It is hard to conceive a metaphysics more fully and more consciously existential than that of St. Thomas Aquinas. It is actually this that makes his doctrine so difficult to teach without betraying it. We betray it first, and only too often, by presenting it as a philosophy occupied principally with forms, whereas it never speaks of them save as of constituent elements of actual beings. But something more serious is involved, for we betray it still more commonly by substituting form for the act-of-being as the supreme constituent of "being." Nowhere does this mistake do more harm than on the question which is now at stake. Centuries have passed judgment on the Thomistic distinction between essence and existence, and never has a doctrine been so bitterly discussed and so little understood. The very title under which this controversy has become notorious explains why. To speak of the distinction between essence and existence is to express oneself as if existence were itself an essence—the essence of the act-of-being. This is to treat an act as though it were a thing. Thus one is almost infallibly condemned to envisage the composition of essence and existence as a sort of chemical mixture in which some very powerful technician, God for example, takes an essence from one side, an existence from another, and makes a synthesis of them under the action of the creative ray.

What Thomas Aquinas has in mind is something else and, unfortunately, something far more difficult to understand. In fact, the only real explanation is the most difficult one. It goes directly to the very heart of the act-of-being. To posit such an act, without other determination is to posit it as absolute, since it is wholly act-of-being, and it is also to posit it as unique, since nothing can be conceived as being, which the pure act-of-being is not. If we are speaking of this act-of-being, no problem of essence and existence can arise. It is what we shall later call God. But the existing beings here under consideration are of a different sort. They are, as we have said, concrete substances, objects of our sense experience. None of them is known to us as a pure act-of-being. We find each distinguished from the others as being "an existing animal," or "an existing man." This specific determination of the acts of existing, by their forms which place each of them in a definite species, is precisely what we call their essence. Now, in the case of such beings, the only ones we know empirically, the problem of their existence challenges our thinking. Whether the pure act of existing exists or not, we do not know at this stage of our investigation. But it is at least clear that if such a being exists, it exists somehow or other in its own right, as one whose very essence is to exist. But it is quite otherwise with a tree, an animal or a man. Their essence is to be either a tree or an animal or a man. In no case is it their essence to exist. The problem, then, of the relation of the essence to its act-of-being (*esse*) arises inexorably about every being whose essence is not to exist.

Such also is the so-called distinction between essence and existence, which it would be better to call the distinction between essence (*essentia*) and the act-of-being (*esse*). It cannot be doubted that this distinction is real, but it arises in the metaphysical order of act and potency, not in the physical order of the relation of parts within a material whole. This distinction is real in the highest degree, since it expresses the fact that a being whose essence is not its act of being has not of itself the wherewithal to exist. We know from experience that such beings exist, since they are all we know directly. They exist therefore, but we know too that they do not exist in their own right. Since their lack of existential necessity is congenital, it is with them as long as they endure. So long as they exist, they remain beings whose existence finds no justification in their own essence. It is this that is the distinction between essence and the act-of-existing. And because it is profoundly real, it poses the problem of the cause of finite existences, which is the problem of the existence of God.

When it is put thus on the plane of the act-of-being, this distinction ceases to exclude the unity of substance. On the contrary, it demands it, and for the following reason. The conceptual nature of our knowledge invites us naturally to conceive of existence as an undetermined value to which the essence is added from without in order to determine it. We can see that reason is here reaching its limit from the difficulty St. Thomas experiences in trying to give verbal expression to such a relationship. It is a general rule that in any relation between determinant and determined, the determined is in the realm of potency, the determinant in that of act. But his rule cannot apply in the present case. Whatever we imagine determines the act-of-being, the form or the matter, for example, it cannot be pure nothingness. Therefore, it is something pertaining to being in virtue of an act-of-being. It is, therefore, impossible that the determination of an act-of-being should come to it from without, that is, from something not itself. Indeed, the essence of a finite act-of-being consists in *only being* such or such an act-of-being (*esse*),[19] not the pure, absolute and unique *Esse* we have spoken about. The finite act-of-being, then, is specified by what it lacks so that here it is the potency which determines the act, at least in the sense that its proper degree of potentiality is inscribed in each finite act-of-being. The vigor of the formulas St. Thomas uses, relating these thoughts in rather trenchant terms, shows adequately that the limits of language are here being reached together with the limit of being. Each essence is set up by an act-of-being which it is not and which includes it as its own determination. Outside the pure act of existing, if it exists, nothing can exist save as a limited act-of-being. It is therefore the hierarchy of the essences which establishes and governs that of beings, each of which expresses only the proper area of a certain act-of-being.

Other philosophers had preceded St. Thomas along this road, and they all helped him to follow it to its end, particularly, however, those among them for whom the problem of existence had distinctly arisen. Alfarabi, Algazel, Avicenna among the Arabs, Moses Maimonides among the Jews, had already noticed the remarkable place which existence occupies in relation to essence. It is probable that their attention was drawn to this point by the religious notion of creation. What seems most to have struck these philosophers, however, is that no matter how far they went with the analysis of essence, it never included existence. Thus wherever essence is to be found, existence is added to it so to speak from without, as an extrinsic determination. Given their starting point these philosophers could reach no other conclusion. They all began with essence. They then sought to analyze it and to discover in it existence. Not finding it there, they concluded that it was foreign to essence, as, in a way, it is. The essence of man and of horse remain for thought exactly what they are whether we attribute existence to them or not. Like the hundred dollars to be made famous by critical idealism, these essences in no way change content whether they are thought of as existing or not existing. It would be quite another matter, observes Alfarabi, if existence fell within the comprehension of essence: "If the essence of man implied his existence, the concept of his essence would also be the concept of his existence and it would be enough to know what a man is in order to know that he exists. Hence every representation of a thing would be accompanied by an affirmation. . . . But this is not so at all. We doubt the existence of things until we receive a direct perception of them through the senses directly, or mediately by a proof." Then comes the formula defining the exteriority of existence to essence: what does not belong to essence as such, and yet is added to it, is an accident belonging to it. Therefore, Alfarabi concludes, "existence is not a constituent character, it is but an accessory accident." [20]

This doctrine of the accidental nature of existence is the one which St. Thomas, following Averroes, often attributes to Avicenna. Actually Avicenna only accepted it with limitations. The expression "accident" was for him not much more than a makeshift. It did not adequately express the intimate relationship of existence to essence. Nevertheless, Avicenna did accept it,[21] and well had to. For where existence is conceived of as a property of essence, and yet is not essence, then it can only be an accident. Algazel, with his habitual lucidity, has synopsized the doctrine in his chapter on accidents. What struck him most of all was that substances had not the same status as accidents, and that among the nine categories of accidents, no two existed in the same way. Existence, therefore, cannot be a genus common to the various categories of accidents, and still less a genus common to accidents and substance. This is what Algazel calls the *ambiguity* of the notion of being, and that St. Thomas calls its *analogy*. No matter what one calls it, it is impossible to identify being with essence, without having to conceive of existence as an accident. Thus Algazel concludes: "It is therefore clear that being belongs to the order of accidents." [22]

There was something very attractive about this doctrine for St. Thomas Aquinas, particularly the sharp feeling for the specificity of the existential order which it revealed. At least these philosophers deserved credit for having understood that, since the act of existing cannot be thought of as included in the essence, it must be added to it. St. Thomas has often followed the method of demonstration used by Alfarabi and Avicenna, and nowhere more closely than in his own treatise *On Being and Essence:* "All that is not in the concept of essence comes to it from outside and makes a composition with it. Indeed, no essence can be conceived of apart from whatever forms part of the essence. Now there can be a concept of any essence or quiddity without a concept of its existence. For example, I can have a concept of *man*, or *phoenix*, without knowing whether they exist in nature. It is therefore clear that the existence (*esse*) is something other than the essence or quiddity." [23]

However much has passed from Avicenna and his group into St. Thomas Aquinas, he rarely cites them except to criticize them. Indeed, what radical opposition between them on this common ground! The doctrine of Avicenna had made the act-of-being an accident of essence; St. Thomas makes it the very root and core of being.

Such is the difference between an essential notion of being like that of Avicenna and an existential one like that of St. Thomas Aquinas. For a philosopher who begins with essence and proceeds by way of concepts, existence will inevitably turn out to be an extrinsic appendix to essence. But if he begins with the concrete existing thing received from sense experience, the relationship must necessarily be reversed. Even then, of course, existence does not appear to be included in essence, and it still remains true to say that it is not in virtue of itself that essence exists. But it also appears that it is the existence which includes the essence, and that yet it is distinct from it because the act-of-being and its essential determinations refer to two irreducibly ultimate kinds of acts, the one in the order of existence, the other in the order of essence, whose composition makes up a "being."

The misconception lying in wait for the interpreter of this doctrine is the illusion that the relation of essence to existence is that of an incomplete being to another incomplete being. All that is most profound in the thought of St. Thomas flatly contradicts this attitude. The act-of-being (*esse*) is there distinct from all the rest because it belongs to a different order from the rest, being that without which the rest would not be. That is why his distinction between essence and existence ought never to be thought of apart from that other thesis which provides it with a basis, rather than completes it, the intimate union of essence and existence in the concrete existing thing. Such is the meaning of his criticism of Avicenna on this point. *Esse* (to be) does not come from *essentia*, but *essentia* comes from *esse*. We do not say of any object that it *is* because it is a *being,* but we say, or should so conceive it, that it is a *being* because it *is.*[24] It is for this very reason that the act-of-being is not an accident of essence: "The act-of-being is the most intimate element in anything, and the most profound element in all things, because it is like a form in regard to all that is in the thing." [25] Between the Avicennian extrinsicism and the Thomistic intrinsicism of existence, no conciliation is possible. To pass from one to the other is not to achieve an evolution but a revolution.

This is what has led many to think that St. Thomas simply took Averroes' part against Avicenna on this important point. This illusion is excusable in that St. Thomas, always inclined to formulate his own thought in the words of others, has often cited texts of Averroes to attack the position of Avicenna. And, indeed, Averroes had criticized this doctrine in which he saw only naïveté and the expression of common opinion. According to him, the Arabian word meaning "to exist" came from a root originally meaning "found," because it seems to have been a common notion that, for any given thing, to exist meant approximately "to be found there." *Sein,* we should say today, is a *Dasein.* Not at all surprising from the moment existence had become an accident. But how are we to conceive of this accident in relation to the rest? If we try to formulate such a relation philosophically, the difficulties become insurmountable. It can be said of everything, substance or accident, that it exists. Shall we have to imagine, therefore, that the existence of an accident is an accident added to another accident? Or that substance, which is being by itself, is a being only by accident?[26] Besides, what exists by itself is necessary, and, in its turn, the necessary is only necessary because it is simple. Now, if existence were added to substance as an accident, substance would be a composite, therefore a pure possible. Being no longer necessary, it would no longer be substance.[27] However considered, Avicenna's doctrine leads to impossibilities.

It is easy to see what use St. Thomas could make of Averroes against Avicenna. He could use Averroes to show that the unity of substance is jeopardized if existence is only an accident. Existence is consubstantial with substance, and here Averroes is right, but too easily right, for, indeed, according to him, substance and existence are one. This we see from the manner in which the two notions of substance and the necessary become identified in his criticism of Avicenna. Not so in the doctrine of St. Thomas for whom even the existence of the necessary is not necessary by full right. It only becomes necessary from the moment that the necessary exists. If Averroes is right against Avicenna, St. Thomas does not admit that it is because of the reasons he gives. Rather, Avicenna is right at least in not confusing existence with the "being by itself" of substance. It is distinct from it because it is its act.[28]

In order to piece together the authentic thought of St. Thomas, we

need not search in Avicenna nor Averroes, nor in some eclectic compromise straightening out their dispute. High above both of them, it
shines forth from the brilliance of the act of existing. By transcending
the plane of the ontology of essence common to both of them, St. Thomas
nullifies their dispute. By lifting himself to this level he sees at one
glance what distinguishes essence and existence and what unites them
in the real. They are different because it is not in essence that the root
of the act-of-being lies. Rather this act dominates essence and is its act.
But they are closely united too, because if essence does not contain the
act-of-being, it is itself so thoroughly actuated by it that existence is that
which is most intimate and profound in it. Avicenna and Averroes
quarrel because they remain on the same plane. St. Thomas contradicts
neither of them but by-passes them, going to the very root of being, the
actus essendi, the *ipsum esse.*

In noting the difficulty of the approach to this existential order, we
pointed out that it was contrary to the natural tendency of reason. The
time has come to explain ourself. To the question, how do we know
being? the reply is simple, and supported by many texts in St. Thomas.
Being is a first principle, and even the first of first principles, because
it is the first object presented to the understanding.[29] Whatever we
conceive, we apprehend as something that is or can be. We might almost
say that because this notion is absolutely first, it accompanies all our
representations. This is true and the reply is a good one provided we
properly understand it as referring to *ens,* carefully guarding the rights
of *esse.* It cannot be said too often that *ens* is and can only be ultimate
in so far as it refers to the act-of-being: *ens* signifies *habens esse.*[30]

Why does our understanding naturally desert the plane of the act of
existing to go down again to that of essence? It is because the human
understanding moves about easily in the realm of abstract concepts,
and because we have an abstract concept for essence but not for the act
of existing. In a text frequently quoted because so succinct, St. Thomas
distinguishes between two operations of the understanding. The first is
that which Aristotle calls the intellection of simple objects (*intelligentia
indivisibilium*), which consists in apprehending essence as something
indivisible. The second is that which combines essences among themselves
or separates them, forming propositions. This second operation, which
St. Thomas calls *compositio,* is called today "judgment." These two
distinct operations both concern the real, but they do not penetrate it
equally far. Intellection reaches the essence which the definition formulates. The judgment reaches the very act-of-being: *Prima operatio
respicit quidditatem rei, secunda respicit esse ipsius.*[31] When we speak of
the being of any being (*ens*), we are speaking of something having an
act-of-being (*habens esse*). What comes first in the understanding is
therefore the essential being; it is not yet the act whereby it is, or exists.

After all, nothing is more natural. To be is to exercise an act. It requires therefore an act to express it. To the static character of the essence corresponds that of the definition simply presented to the intuition of the intellect. To the dynamic character of the act of existing corresponds that of the judgment, which, because it is an active operation, can express the energy whose act generates a being and assures its unity. This is why, moreover, the active spring of the judgment, its copula, is always a verb, the verb "is." The judgment puts all its relations in terms of existence because its proper function is to signify the act of existing.

All this becomes evident in the case of a judgment of existence, for example: *Socrates is.* Such a proposition clearly expresses by its very composition the composition of the substance Socrates and its existence in reality. In propositions such as *Socrates is man* or *Socrates is white,* the verb *is* plays no more than the role of copula. It signifies simply that it is of the essence of Socrates to be a man, or that the accident *white* is in the substance Socrates. Its existential value is then less direct and consequently less apparent. We shall see that it is there none the less.

Let us first note that, as St. Thomas points out, the copula *is* refers always to the predicate: *semper ponitur ex parte praedicati,*[32] and no longer to the subject as in the case of existential judgments. In *Socrates is* the verb signifies Socrates himself as existing. In *Socrates is white* it is no longer the existence of Socrates but that of the *white* in Socrates that is signified. Employed thus as copula, the verb *is* is no longer taken in its principal and full signification, that of the actual existence, but in a secondary signification, deriving nevertheless from the principal. What is first presented to the thought when we say *is,* is the very act of existing, that is, that absolute actuality which actual existence is. But beyond the actuality of the act of existing, which is its principal signification, this verb designates secondarily all actuality whatsoever in general, notably that of the form, whether substantial or accidental. Now, to form a judgment is to signify that a certain form, therefore a certain act, exists *actually* in a subject. *Socrates is man* signifies that the form *man* inheres in Socrates as constitutive act of his substance. *Socrates is white* signifies the actual determination of the subject Socrates by this accidental form *white.* What the copula designates exactly, is, therefore, still a composition, no longer now that of essence and existence, but that of the form with the subject which it determines. And as this composition is due to the actuality of the form, the verb *is,* which signifies principally the actuality, is naturally employed to designate it.[33] That is why this verb is the only one to play the role of copula. It is because the verb *is* first signifies actuality that it can signify secondarily, or, as St. Thomas says, "consignify," the composition of every form with the subject of which it is the act. The formula in which this composition is expressed is precisely the proposition or judgment.

We understand now why judgment alone can penetrate to existence. To formulate an experience such as ours in which all its objects are composite substances, we need a thought itself composite. To express the activity of the principles which determine these substances, our thought must duplicate the exterior act of the form by the interior act of the verb. Because the very root of the real is an act, the act of judging alone can attain the real in its root. This is what it does, first of all, in using the verb *is* as a copula, in order to state that such or such a substance "exists-with-such-a-determination." It may so exist only in my thought, or also as real, but as yet we know nothing of this. In so far as the proposition uses this verb as a copula, it expresses nothing more than the community of act of the subject and of its determination. In order that the unity thus formed may be affirmed as existing in reality and outside of our mind, it must be actuated by an act of existing. It is only then that our intellect uses the verb *is* with the existential signification, which is its proper signification, for just as the act of existing is the act of all acts (*actualitas omnium actuum*), the first signification of the verb *is*, is actual existence: *"Est" simpliciter dictum, significat "in actu esse."*

This radical ordination of the judgment to the existing real had already been stressed by Aristotle on the plane of substantial being as he himself understood it. For Aristotle, it is quite true that substances alone exist, but it is equally true that, for him, to exist is simply to be a substance, or, in other words, that to be is before all to be something. More particularly, and in the fullest sense, it is to be one of those things which, owing to their form possess in themselves the cause of what they are. Thus, the being at which Aristotle stops is "that-which-has-the-act-of-being," minus the act-of-being itself. And indeed, as St. Thomas puts it, *ens* does not signify principally the *esse*, but the *quod est*, not so much the act-of-being as the thing possessing it: *rem habentem esse*.[34] Aristotle, therefore, was right in throwing into relief the role of an act played by the form in the constitution of the substance and, as well, the actuality of the substantial being, but his metaphysics has not gone beyond the plane of "entitative" being, which is that of the *ens*, towards attaining the very existential act of the *esse*.

Here, then, is the reason for a fact noted by one of the best Aristotelian scholars, "in the verb *esti*, the meaning *to exist* and that belonging to the copula are strangely confused," for "Aristotle mixes very confusedly the two senses of the verb *to be*,"[35] that is, the being of existence and that of predication. Perhaps it would be better to say that, rather than mix them, Aristotle did not distinguish them. We, who distinguish them carefully, find these two senses confused in his text. For him, to say that a just man exists, or that a man is just, was always to say that a man exists with the determination: to be just. It all came to the same thing.

In turning the ontology and logic of Aristotle to his own account, St. Thomas transposed them from their original tone, that of essence, to his own tone, that of existence. Whence this first conclusion which is to affect our whole interpretation of Thomism: in entering the doctrine of St. Thomas, the metaphysics of Aristotle has received an entirely new existential meaning.

This first remark calls for a second. It is a rather curious fact that the doctrine of St. Thomas, depending upon the way one looks at it, appears the most complete or the most empty of all. The fervent enthusiasm of its partisans is only equalled by the scorn of its adversaries. This is because if one interprets Thomistic philosophy as a metaphysic of substance, one reduces it to the Aristotelian level of the *quod est*. In this expression, as St. Thomas himself notes, the *quod* designates the thing, and the *est* its act of existing. Now, as we have seen, the principal and direct signification of *ens* is not the act of existence, but the existing thing.[36] Thomism thus becomes a "thingism," which can be freely charged with turning into things all the concepts it touches, thereby transforming the living tissues of the real into a mosaic of entities enclosed in their respective essences.

The best interpreters of St. Thomas know very well that he had himself, on the contrary, a very lively awareness of the plenitude and continuity of the concrete. But those of them who reduce the act-of-being to *that which is,* run into serious difficulties when they try to express this awareness by the concept of being. As a concept, being is both the most universal and the most abstract of all. Its extension is the richest, its comprehension the most poor. A philosopher who would begin with the concept of being alone undertakes to deduce the concrete from the abstract. Since the time of Descartes, this has been a common charge against St. Thomas and against Scholasticism in general. To obviate this reproach, one has sometimes attempted to enrich the ontological void of the concept of being, to nourish it and fill it up by conferring upon it the fullness of an intuition of existentiality. This is to come closer to the truth, but it is not yet to attain it. Conceived as an intellectual intuition of "being as being," the proper object of metaphysics, this knowledge would permit us to attain by simple sight the inexhaustible and incomprehensible reality of "real being in all the purity and amplitude of its own intelligibility or its own mystery." Understood thus, the intellectual view of being would require, not, to be sure, a special faculty, but that special light of the intellect which makes the metaphysician[37] and which permits *metaphysical experience*.[38]

We should be very careful not to deny that such an experience is possible. Perhaps a special gift is necessary here, one approaching religious grace rather than the natural light of the metaphysician. For indeed all men have the same natural light, but some make better use of it than others. To confine ourselves to the properly metaphysical order of human knowledge, however, let us observe first that the concept of being occupies in it indeed a privileged and unique place. We cannot think of actual existence without enclosing it in an abstract concept; and whatever act-of-being we experience, the concept is always the same. All *esse* (to be) is, for us, the act of an *ens* (being). It is therefore perfectly true to say that one cannot think of *ens* without *esse* (at least if one thinks here as one ought) and much less of *esse* without *ens*. The act-of-being is always that of something having existence.[39] Being, therefore, is certainly first in the order of the concept, and since our judgments are made up of concepts, it is also first in the order of judgment.[40] Nevertheless, the concept of being always registers in the same manner an infinity of acts of existing, all different. It represents what St. Thomas has called many a time, *ens commune:*[41] the abstract notion of being, understood in its universal and pure indetermination. That it requires an effort to attain it and that this effort is difficult, we readily concede. But it is an effort which is developed entirely in the order of the abstract concept. The very judgments it demands tend towards definitions of quiddities. Everything looks, indeed, as if the being as being of Thomistic metaphysics was only the most abstract of abstractions.

No one doubts, of course, that it is this. But the metaphysics of St. Thomas has much more to it than this. When it is reduced to the quidditative order, it becomes a science of the notion of being and of the thing, that is to say, the abstract expression of what, in the real, is capable of definition. Thomism thus conceived has been the object of a good many syntheses, at least one of them being a masterpiece,[42] but it is not the Thomism of St. Thomas. What characterizes his is that in it every concept of thing connotes an act of existing. His metaphysic of being as being "consignifies" existence. It does not "signify" it unless precisely it uses the second operation of the understanding and employs all the resources of the judgment. The feeling, so just in itself, that the universal concept of being is the contrary of an empty notion, finds justification here. Its wealth consists, first, of all the judgments of existence it virtually comprises and connotes, but much more of its permanent reference to the infinitely rich reality of the pure act of existing. This is why St. Thomas's metaphysics pursues through the essence of beings that supreme existant, God.

In a philosophy where the the act-of-being can only be conceived in and by an essence, but where every essence points to an act-of-being, the concrete wealth is inexhaustible. Reason dislikes the undefinable, and because pure existence is undefinable, philosophy does all it can to avoid it.[43] It is inevitable that this natural tendency of the reason should affect our interpretation of Thomism. Even one who denounces this tendency with all his might knows well that he is going to yield to it. We must at least know it as a temptation inviting us into error. Kept on the plane of the quiddity, Thomism will spend its strength making one inventory after another of its inheritance. Raised to the plane of the judgment, Thomism will again make contact with the very heart of the reality it is interpreting. It will become fecund once more, and again will be able to create. If history has any lesson for us on this point it is because it enables us to watch that flowering of new truths which marked the appearance of Thomism. The first of these fruits was the complete renovation of the problem of the existence of God.

CHAPTER II

IT IS WISELY SAID, writes St. Thomas, that he who would become educated should begin by trusting his teacher. He will never master his science unless he presumes in the beginning that the doctrine being presented is true even if, for the moment, he cannot tell why.[1] This remark is particularly applicable to the Thomistic doctrine of knowledge. We have already met this doctrine of knowledge in the preceding chapter. Now again we shall find that it has been presupposed in all the proofs of the existence of God. When we come later to study God's essence, the theory of knowledge will still dominate every affirmation. As he is following the theological order, St. Thomas does not hesitate to make this theory yield some of its most important consequences long before undertaking to justify it.

Certain philosophers regard the existence of God as a self-evident truth. We must begin therefore by examining their reasons, because if they are valid, they render all demonstration of God's existence superfluous and even impossible.

I. THE ALLEGED EVIDENCE FOR THE EXISTENCE OF GOD

Among those who consider that the existence of God is not an object of demonstration are the simple faithful who have been familiar with His name from their childhood and for whom prayer is a habit. They mistake their very habit of believing in Him for a proof of His existence.[2] St. Thomas sets this group aside as not, in general, coming into our discussion. He is addressing rather the philosophers and theologians who, for different reasons, find the existence of God immediately evident.[3] Although he mentions a large number of these in the *Summa Contra Gentiles*, they can all be satisfactorily dealt with in the three main positions treated in the *Summa Theologiae*.[4] The arguments which St. Thomas retained for discussion in this work are not presented in any systematic order. His treatment does not even necessarily imply that those responsible for the arguments he is using themselves expressly subscribed to the thesis which he is attacking. In fact, all the theologians from whom these arguments are more or less directly borrowed did actually try to demonstrate the existence of God. Such is clearly the case of St. John Damascene, for example, whose demonstrations have played a role in the history of the problem; and yet St. Thomas places him among those who think that the existence of God is not an object of demonstration. Here, as in many other places, St. Thomas is but borrowing themes which allow him to emphasize important points. These themes can be only pretexts for philosophical variations. The very fact that he chooses them may, of course, express some profound historical intuition. But St. Thomas has selected them primarily for the sake of discussion.

The first of the three arguments presented in the *Summa Theologiae* is a simple one. John Damascene says, at the beginning of his *De Fide Orthodoxa* that "the knowledge that God exists is naturally implanted in everyone." [5] That John Damascene has in the same work demonstrated God's existence by change and by finality is of no importance here, for if it were true that every man knows from birth that God exists, it would assuredly be impossible to demonstrate it.

The second argument arises from the principle that every proposition for which it is enough to understand the terms in order to know that it is true, is immediately evident. This is what is called a self-evident proposition, one "known by itself," that is, the truth of which is clear as soon as the statement of it is understood. An example of such a principle is: "The whole is greater than the part." Now the proposition "God exists" is like this. The word "God" is defined as "that than which nothing greater can be conceived." Let someone hear this word spoken, and he will form this proposition in his thought. At this moment, God exists in his thought, at least in the sense that He is placed in existence as an object of thought. Now it cannot be that God only exists by such a title. Indeed, what exists in thought and in reality at the same time is greater than what exists in thought alone. If therefore, the word "God" signifies: "That than which nothing greater can be conceived," then God exists both in thought and reality at the same time. The existence of God is therefore self-evident, in virtue of the very definition of His name.[6]

The third argument which St. Thomas retains in the *Summa Theologiae* is more simple and more direct. "It is self-evident that truth exists, for he who denies that truth exists concedes that truth exists. Indeed, if truth is not, it is true that truth is not. But if anything is true, then truth must exist. Now God is truth itself, as St. John says (XIV, 6): 'I am the way, the truth and the life.' It is therefore self-evident that God exists." [7]

Of these three arguments for the existence of God, the first is borrowed from an author who has elsewhere actually demonstrated God's existence; the second is a résumé of what St. Anselm considered to be the demonstration *par excellence;* the third comes from texts of St. Augustine, who certainly never thought the existence of God too evident for demonstration. St. John Damascene, St. Anselm and St. Augustine are certainly not responsible for the conclusion St. Thomas drew from the arguments he borrowed from them. But it does not follow that St. Thomas's conclusion was therefore arbitrary. The notion that God's existence is self-evident represents accurately the average opinion of a whole group of theologians with whose work he was familiar. And the arguments recorded by St. Thomas are the ones used by these theologians to justify this opinion. The ground upon which St. Thomas conducts this discussion is, therefore, that of the theological synthesis so widespread in the thirteenth century, and which was less a systematic elaboration of the principles of St. Augustine himself than a blending of theses borrowed from Augustine, Gabirol and other representative of the neoplatonist tradition.

The thirteenth-century work which best represents it is almost certainly that vast compilation known to the Middle Ages under the title of the *Summa Theologica* of Alexander of Hales. The three arguments discussed by St. Thomas are there;[8] and they are also to be met in St. Bonaventure's Commentary on Peter Lombard.[9] It is to works of this kind that we must look rather than to the original sources of the theses, if we are to understand St. Thomas's attitude towards them. They represent the state of the question in his day. But this state had its own causes in the philosophy of the past, and it is not useless to recall it, especially if we wish the thought of Thomas Aquinas to be accurately understood.

2. THE THEOLOGIES OF ESSENCE

It is remarkable that to the question, "What is being?" Plato replies by describing a certain manner of existing. For him there is only being where intelligibility is possible. How could we say that a thing is, without being able to say what it is? Moreover, for it to be something, it must remain that thing. To admit that a thing changes is to state that it is no longer what it was; and that it is about to become something which as yet it is not. How are we to know as being, what is never ceasing to become something else? In the doctrine of Plato, then, the three notions—being, intelligibility and immutability—are intimately linked together. That alone deserves to be called being which, because it always remains the same, is a possible object of intellection. "What is it that is and is never born, and what is ever being born but never is?" asks Plato in the *Timaeus* (27 d). This same principle enables us to understand Plato's reply to the question posed by the *Sophist*—what is being?[10] What remains constant throughout all the vagaries of his dialectic is that the expressions εἶναι, "being," εἶναι τι, εἶναι τι τῶν ὄντων, "to be something," "to be one of the beings" are equivalent in Plato's mind. This is why the term οὐσία [entity] is so difficult to translate in his texts. One rightly hesitates to render it by "essence" or by "substance"; neither of these two terms suggests its power and true import. The οὐσία is what truly possesses being because it always remains what it is.[11] Here, as elsewhere, the Platonic τὸ ὄν is defined by contrast with τὸ γιγνόμενον, being is the contrary of becoming.[12]

In a philosophy where being is thus reduced to the stability of essence, how are we to determine what is, in order to distinguish it from what is not? This, replies the *Sophist*, finally, is the business of the dialectitian.[13] Armed with his method, his eye on the intelligible, he can say of each essence "what it is," and consequently "that it is," but also "what it is not," and consequently "that it is not." In a doctrine of this kind, the empirical opposition between *existence* and nothingness tends therefore to be reduced to the dialectical distinction between *same* and *other*. Every time the dialectician defines an essence he affirms simultaneously that it is what it is, and that it is not other than what it is. From this point of view, which is that of essence, the notions of *being* and *non-being* remove any existential connotation. As Plato says in the *Sophist:* "When we affirm non-being, it is not at all, it seems, to specify the contrary of being, but only something other." [14] While in an existential ontology there is a strict opposition between existence and nothingness, in an ontology of essence, on the contrary, being and non-being mutually imply each other. An essence can only be affirmed once with reference to being, since it is only itself. But for the once that it is, there is an indefinite number of times that it is not, since it is other than all the other essences. If an essence shares only once in the same and in being, against the innumerable times that it shares in the other and in non-being, being is so far from excluding non-being that it cannot be affirmed once without affirming non-being an infinite number of times. We can be sure that we are in the authentic Platonic tradition whenever the notions of existence and nothingness are reduced to the purely essential notions of "the same and the other," *de eodem et diverso*.

This is precisely the notion of being that St. Augustine inherited from Plato. For him as for Plato the radical existential opposition between being and nothingness disappears before the distinction between what "truly is" and what "truly is not." Being thus acquires that variable value which it always has in an ontology of essences. In the fullest sense, it is defined as the absolutely immutable, self-identical and at rest, as opposed to non-being conceived as changing, other and pure motion. Between the purely immutable and pure duration are ranged all the beings of which it cannot be said that they absolutely are not, since they participate in some stable essence, but of which it cannot any the more be said that they "truly are," because they are born and perish. Now to be born is to pass from non-being to being, as to perish is to pass from being to non-being, and wherever there is non-being, being is deficient to that extent.[15] We are, therefore, clearly established on the plane of the *vere esse*, to be truly where being is a variable value measured by the stability of the essence. If God is to be placed there as principle of all, it is because He is truly, that is in the supreme degree, since He is supremely immutable.[16] Inversely, whatever is supremely immutable is in the supreme degree, and is God. Such is truth, which cannot change, since it is necessary and eternal. We progress in being at the same time as in the immutable, and we attain simultaneously in God the supreme degree of both. God alone is supreme being, because as He is the stable totality of being, He cannot change either by losing anything or acquiring anything.[17]

Thus conceived, God clearly occupies the summit of being. But He is there as supreme in the order of οὐσία [entity]. Before St. Augustine, both Cicero and Seneca had rendered this Greek term by its Latin equivalent, *essentia*.[18] The debates which were to culminate in the definition of the dogma of the Trinity had also conferred a dignity upon it, by designating the divine reality as an essence common to the three distinct persons. We can see, then, why Augustine had preferred this term to any other to designate the divine being in its most profound reality. In a remarkable passage, St. Augustine records his views on the subject in a few lines: "God, however, is unquestionably substance, or, if this name suits Him better, essence. This is what the Greeks call οὐσία. Indeed, *essentia* draws its name from *esse*, as *sapientia* from *sapere* and *scientia* from *scire*. And who 'is,' more than He who said to his servant Moses: *I am who am*, and, later, *Say you to the people of Israel: He who is sent me to you* (Exod. III, 14). Other things called essences, or substances, call for accidents which cause change in them, little or great. But in God no such accident is possible. This is why there is only one immutable substance or essence, which is God, to which being itself (*ipsum esse*), from which essence draws its name, belongs supremely and in all truth. For that which changes does not keep its very being, and that which is capable of changing, even if it does not change, is capable of not being what it was. There only remains, therefore, that which not only does not change but is even absolutely incapable of changing which we can truthfully and honestly speak of as a being." [19]

This God *essentia* of St. Augustine remained St. Anselm's. Towards the end of the *Proslogion*, St. Anselm uses grammatical forms which show that the God he has in mind is the God of *Exodus*. But in the same text, we can see too how faithful he remains to the ontology of essence handed on by Plato to his successors: "Thus, O Lord, Thou alone art what Thou art, and Thou art Who is." Obviously we have here to deal with the *Qui sum* of Holy Scripture. Now St. Anselm says that it is proper to God to be "What He is." And he gives exactly the same reason as St. Augustine before him: "That in which there is something mutable is not entirely what it is." God's proper attribute is to be always the same, without any mixture of "other." Consequently He is Being, purely and simply. "But Thou, Thou art what Thou art, because all Thou hast ever been or that Thou art in any manner whatsoever, Thou art it always in all its entirety. And Thou art *Who is* purely and simply, because there is in Thee neither *have been* nor *ought to be*, but only *present being*, and because it is inconceivable that at any time Thou wert able not to exist." [20] This is why, although he uses upon occasion terms such as "substance" or "nature," [21] St. Anselm prefers "essence" to designate God, taken as Being itself, which is outside of and above all substance.[22] For *essentia* is to *esse* and to *ens* as *lux* is to *lucere* and *lucens*. Essence therefore is for him *what is* or *what exists*, or *what subsists*, and it is as supreme essence that God is the supreme existant.[23]

By this text from the *Monologium* we see how much closer St. Anselm was to the *Proslogion* than he thought. All St. Anselm's arguments for the existence of God are related by the fundamental notion of being-essence which produces them. For the Good is proportional to Being, or, to put it better, since it is the perfection of the essence which measures it, Being is proportional to the Good. Hence the so-called physical proofs of the *Monologium*. However, they are only so qualified by analogy with the proofs of St. Thomas. Foreign to the plane of existence, they are limited to showing that the essence of things more or less good and more or less great presupposes the essence of a supremely good, supremely great and supremely being.[24] This same notion provides the key to the treatise of Anselm *On Truth,* which proves that whatever is true, in whatsoever sense, is true only in virtue of an unique and supreme Truth.[25] Finally, it is this same notion that inspires the celebrated argument of the *Proslogion*. God is entity (*essentia*); the entire problem is, therefore, to know whether entity, whose very definition is to be "what exists," can be conceived as not existing. The solution forces itself upon us. He who is being by definition is "that than which nothing greater can be conceived. Now to understand this *that* properly is to conceive it in such a way that, even in thought, it cannot not be. One who understands that God is in this way cannot, therefore, think that He is not." [26] It is indeed the modality of the divine being which establishes the necessity of His existence in a doctrine where existence is a modality of essence. Not for a moment do we escape from the order of essentiality.

The same tradition carries on between St. Anselm and St. Thomas, thanks to several works the most significant of which is the *De Trinitate* of Richard of St. Victor. This theologian asked himself what was the meaning of the two notions "essence" and "existence" in relation to each other. In his discussion of the mystery of the Trinity, Richard remarked that when we wish to distinguish between the Persons of the Trinity, we must consider each of them from two points of view: what being each is, and where its being comes from. To say what each Person is (*quale quid sit*) is to examine its essence. To say where it gets the being that it is, is to examine it from the point of view of existence. Thus, in Richard's thought, existence is only essence in relation to its origin. Indeed, he actually remarks that the term *existence* connotes the two notions simultaneously. *Existere* is *sistere ex,* where *sistere* designates essence and *ex* designates origin. As Alexander of Hales later observed, *existere* is *ex alio sistere,* which amounts to saying that "The word 'existence' signifies essence with reference to its source." [27]

The so-called *Summa* of Alexander of Hales followed Richard of St. Victor on this point and so inevitably reduced all problems of existence, including that of the existence of God, to problems of essence.[28] We find there first of all the identification of *essentia* with the οὐσία of the Greeks, justified by the text of the *De Trinitate* of Augustine, Book IV, ch. ii, already cited. Next comes the identification of *ens* (God) with *essentia,* for if we take it by itself, abstracting from any notion of dependence, of composition or of mutability, *essentia* (entity) is no more than the property of being, purely and simply. This term becomes, then, the proper name of the divine "essentiality" since "essence" thus understood designates "essentiality" without the addition of anything.[29]

This explains why what we call the proofs for the existence of God appears here under the general heading: "On the essentiality of the divine substance." What is really at stake is to show that the property of being rightly belongs to the divine substance, that is, to prove that the divine substance, being what it is, must necessarily be. The real difficulty for the author of the *Summa* is not to prove that God exists, but rather to find such a formulation of the problem that one can at least believe that there is room for proving it. This is unquestionably why we find him using the term "substance" although he has said, following St. Augustine, that "essence" would be the more correct term. But how is it to be shown that the existence of that whose essence it is to be needs to be proved? The whole question is reduced to finding out whether there exists a substance whose being is inseparable. If he can establish that there is an essence which implies being, he will have a proof for the existence of God.

In such a doctrine, the proofs amount naturally to an examination of essences. It is a question of determining whether or not an essence implies the necessity of existing. The so-called "physical" proofs retain therefore the purely essential character they had in St. Anselm. Change is not presented as an existential fact but as the purely essential index of ontological deficiency. Anything which changes appears at once as not-necessary and consequently non-being. Thus the two notions of mutable and creature are equivalent in Alexander's *Summa.* We thus run into arguments like the following which, in a metaphysics of existence, are fallacious: It is obvious that the created universe, whether considered as finite or infinite, is entirely caused; now nothing is the proper cause of itself; therefore, the universe has necessarily a cause which is not itself caused.[30] And indeed, *if* being is immutable, mutability is evidence of a certain degree of non-being, characteristic of the state of creature wherever observed, and postulates the existence of the purely immutable being which we call God.

It is natural that, in the same chapter, Alexander should borrow from St. Anselm, who was himself inspired by St. Augustine, a proof for God by the existence of truth.[31] It is another proof of the same kind. We cannot conceive of a time when it was not true that something was going to be, nor of a time when it will cease to be true that something is going to be; it is therefore always true that there has been and that there will be something; therefore truth has neither beginning nor end. Thus, adds Alexander, Truth is eternal. We call it the divine essence: *et hanc dicimus divinam essentiam*. This time there is no mistaking it: whoever succeeds in reaching the essence "God" reaches God.

In these conditions, the simplest procedure was to follow St. Anselm's royal road towards God, a road on which one had no sooner to set out than he arrived. Alexander sets out along it with evident satisfaction. Since essence here precedes existence, existential being is always confused with the being of predication: "The best is the best, therefore the best is, because in the notion *is the best*, the intellect includes being." [32] To show the divine *essentiality* is identical with showing that God exists; and, to establish it, it is enough to show that the non-existence of God is unthinkable: *ad divinam essentialitatem declarandam, ostendendum est eam sic notam esse ut non possit cogitari non esse*.[33] We can certainly agree that St. Thomas was not misrepresenting those whom he charged with making a self-evident truth of the existence of God.

A rapid examination of the texts of St. Bonaventure leads to the same conclusions. We have observed elsewhere that he tended to make the existence of God appear evident rather than to demonstrate it.[34] Now we can see the real reason why. Since the divine "essentiality" dominates the whole problem, he is less concerned with establishing the existence of God than of showing his eminent "knowableness." Since God is being by definition, to speak of God is to speak of being. Hence the typical statement: "If God is God, God is; Now the antecedent (sc. God is God) is so true that the non-existence of God is inconceivable; it is, therefore, an inevitable truth that God is." [35] This would be surprising to us, did we not know what notion of being dictated these formulas. For the existence of God to be similar to the being of the copula which predicates God of Himself, St. Bonaventure must think of it as being the same as the relation of the divine essence to itself, that is, he must reduce existential being to essential being. We thus come directly to some statements as close as possible to those that St. Thomas will criticize: "The truth of the divine being is evident both in itself and when demonstrated. In itself, for the principles are evident in themselves, because we know them from the moment we know the terms, and because the cause of the predicate is included in the subject. Such is the case here, because God, or supreme truth, is that being, than which none better can be conceived. Therefore it cannot not be nor be conceived as not being. Indeed, the predicate is included in the subject: *praedicatum enim clauditur in subjecto*. And this truth is not only evident in itself but also by demonstration, for all truth and nature prove conclusively that divine truth is, since, if there is being by participation and by another, it is because there is being by essence and by itself." [36] In short, the existence of any truth whatsoever testifies that God exists, but this is because the only being which is here at stake is that of an essence, which is the essence of truth.

3. THE EXISTENCE OF GOD AS A PROBLEM

When St. Thomas substituted the point of view of existence for that of essence he found that he had not only to look for new proof for the existence of God, but that he had, above all, to emphasize the fact that the existence of God requires demonstration properly so-called. It is therefore the specificity of the existence of God as a problem which is immediately affirmed in his doctrine, as against the reduction of the problem to that of the divine essentiality in the theologies of essence. Most significant in this regard is the attitude St. Thomas adopts in his *Commentary on the Sentences*. No more than the others does he here undertake to demonstrate the existence of God because this task is not forced upon Commentators of Peter Lombard. But, at the very place where the *Summa* of Alexander and the *Commentary* of St. Bonaventure undertake to show that the existence of God is evident, St. Thomas devotes an article to proving that it is not.

We have identified the theses to which St. Thomas objects, but we must now be more precise about the real sense and significance of his refutation of them. His basic objection amounts to this: that all the arguments that God's existence is self-evident depend upon a common error— they mistake for God Himself what is only an effect caused by God. For example, if we admit with John Damascene that we have natural knowledge of the existence of God, this knowledge will be at most an effect of God or His image stamped in our thought. But to infer from this that God exists, demands a demonstration. If we say with the Augustinians that God can be immediately known by the intellect as light is immediately visible to the sight, or that God is more interior to the soul than the soul itself, it must be replied that the only beings directly accessible to our knowledge are sensible things. A demonstration is therefore necessary if the reason is to ascend from the realities thus given to it in experience to the reality of God who is not so given. St. Anselm's argument contains the same error. If we begin with the principle that there is a being than which none greater can be conceived, it goes without saying that such a being exists, but his existence is only evident by virtue of this supposition. In other words the argument amounts to saying that we cannot understand that God exists and conceive at the same time that He does not exist. But we can very well think that there does not exist a being than which none greater can be conceived. In brief, the idea of existence is never the equivalent of existence. Existence is established or demonstrated, it is not deduced.[37]

So far as we can judge from the text of St. Thomas, his attitude may be best explained by his familiarity with a world inadequately understood by many theologians, the world of the philosophers. Useful as the philosophy of Aristotle was to Christians, the universe it described was hardly a Christian universe. Even in the first book of the *Metaphysics* we meet Democritus and others who seem to have dispensed with a first efficient cause and hence with God.[38] That such men exist may surprise holy men, and often even certain theologians, but they exist all the same and must be reckoned with. There would be no atheists if the existence of God were so evident that it required no demonstration. Besides, Aristotle himself has demonstrated the existence of God in both the *Physics* and the *Metaphysics*. It cannot have been so self-evident or he would hardly have demonstrated it. And it required demonstrations, because where intuitive experience of God is wanting, His existence can only be affirmed after an induction based on His effects.

In sketching, in his *Commentary on the Sentences,* the course of such a proof, St. Thomas makes this interesting remark: "And such is Avicenna's proof in his *De Intelligentiis*, ch. I." [39] Perhaps there is more here than a coincidence. It is not surprising that one of the most clearly existentialist of his predecessors should have called St. Thomas's attention to the existential aspect of the problem. But no one teaches us something we do not already vaguely know ourselves, and it might easily be shown that Avicenna was actually anticipating the essentialism of Duns Scotus rather than the existentialism of St. Thomas. Whatever the case, St. Thomas was never to modify the position he adoped here in the *Commentary on the Sentences.* In his two *Summae,* he but returns, in all essentials, to his earlier rejection of the alleged evidence for the existence of God.

To the thesis, based on a text of John Damascene, that we have innate knowledge that God exists, St. Thomas is careful not to deny that there may be something innate about our knowledge of the existence of God. As usual, St. Thomas does not completely reject a thesis which he thinks susceptible of a sane interpretation. This principle governs the whole of his textual exegesis. In the present case, he notes that what is innate in us is not the actual knowledge that God exists, but the natural light of reason and its principles, through which we can return to God, the first cause, by way of His effects. How justified was this reservation, we shall see when the time comes to study the origin of knowledge. When it is said furthermore that we know God naturally since we tend towards Him as to our end, we shall have to admit this too up to a certain point and in a certain sense. For it is true that man tends naturally towards God, since he tends towards his beatitude, which is God. But a distinction must be made. Man tends towards happiness, and his happiness is God, but he can tend toward happiness without knowing that his happiness is God. Some actually place their sovereign good in riches, others in pleasure. It is therefore in a very confused fashion that we tend naturally toward God and that we know him. To know that a man is approaching is not to know Peter, even though it is Peter who is approaching. Similarly, to know that there is a sovereign good is not to know God, even though God is the sovereign Good.[40]

This argument, which first appears as a discussion of a purely epistemological order, rests ultimately on an observation of metaphysical significance. What dominates the problem is the fact that the being we know is not that of God. Because every object of experience needs God as its cause, we can proceed from this to show that God exists. But because the existence given us is not that of God, we must demonstrate it. This is why the argument from truth, whatever its form, cannot be taken as conclusive. We are told that truth exists, that God is truth, and that consequently He exists. Now it is quite true that there is truth, as there is being; but the fact that truths exist only implies the existence of the truths in question, just as the fact that certain beings exist only implies of itself their existence. If what we wish to attain is the existence which we think about, then to pass from truths empirically given to their first cause is to pass from one existence to another. This can only be done by an act of faith or through a demonstration.[41]

There still remains the argument of the *Proslogion*, given so many forms by Alexander of Hales and St. Bonaventure: it is unthinkable that God does not exist. For St. Thomas, this argument has two chief weaknesses. The first is to suppose that by the term *God*, everyone necessarily intends to designate a being such that one cannot conceive a greater. Many of the ancients, for example, considered that the universe was God, and a being superior to the universe can easily be conceived. Moreover, among all John Damascene's interpretations of this name, none is reducible to this definition. For many minds, the existence of God is not evident *a priori*. The second weakness in this argument is that, even if the definition that God is that than which none greater can be conceived is conceded, the real existence of such a being does not necessarily follow. In no way does it follow. From the fact that we understand this definition, it follows only that God exists for our understanding, not that He exists in reality.[42] There is, therefore, no contradiction in holding at the same time that God cannot not be conceived as existing, and that nevertheless He does not exist. The case would be different if it was conceded that there exists a being than which none greater can be conceived. Evidently if such a being exists He is God. But since, by hypothesis, the adversary denies the existence, we cannot possibly make him agree with us, following this course.

It is not the conclusion which separates St. Thomas from his adversaries, for all agree about it, it is the means of justifying it. They both accept the existence of God and that existence is His by full right. But they do not agree on the problem of method, which is basically a problem of metaphysics. Proceeding from essence to existence, we have to look for the proof of God's existence in the notion of God. Proceeding from existence to essence, we have to use proofs for the existence of God to form a notion of His essence. St. Thomas holds this second point of view. After establishing the existence of a first cause, he will establish, through the very proofs of its existence, that this first cause is the being than which none greater can be conceived and which cannot be conceived as not existing. The existence of God will, then, be a demonstrated certitude, and at no time the result of an intuition.

For this knowledge to be as evident for us as it is in itself, we should have to see the divine essence, and this is not granted to man naturally. It will be evident for us, of course, in heaven, where we shall behold God's essence. Then God's existence will be known to us of itself, and we shall know then much better than now that a thing cannot be and not be at the same time and under the same aspect. For in nothing which we know does the essence include its existence. It cannot, accordingly, not exist, if it exists, but it might be able not to exist. The impossibility of affirming the non-existence of an actually existing thing therefore is a conditional as the very existence of the thing. Those who, on the contrary, see the divine essence, see there the existence of what cannot not exist.[33]

We can see from all this how far from verifying their position are those who maintain that here below our knowledge of the existence of God is evident. They are perfect believers who take their faith for evidence. Their mistake does them personally no harm. But it is dangerous to lead unbelievers to think that such reasons for the existence of God are the only ones a philosopher can have. Before inadequate arguments, those who have neither faith, nor God, nor demonstrations of His existence, conclude that God does not exist. As for those who perceive the weakness of such arguments, but believe in the existence of God, they simply come to the conclusion that this truth is neither evident nor demonstrable, and can only be accepted by an act of faith.

Moses Maimonides knew theologians of this kind.[44] The only reason capable of giving philosophical justification to their attitude would be that demonstration had to find its starting point in some knowledge of the essence of God. As we have just seen, such knowledge is neither necessary nor possible. To see the essence of God is to have an intuition of His existence, and this intuition removes all possibility of demonstration. Not to see the essence of God is not to have the proper concept necessary for certitude about His existence. Man has, then, no other recourse here below than to return to God by way of thought, beginning with the sensible knowledge coming from His effects. In doing this, we do no more than give philosophical meaning to the words of the Apostle: *"The invisible things of Him, from the creation of the world are clearly seen (Rom.* I, 20). Certainly all theologians and Christian philosophers who have spoken about the existence of God have quoted these words, but St. Thomas took them in all their living force. For him they signify that man can start from God's effects and come to know His existence; and that man can only know God's existence by starting from His effects. From this point on, it becomes a matter of proceeding from the existences given in experience to the inferred existence of their cause. In this revealing in its purity the profound meaning of the rather simple question: *Is there a God?* St. Thomas gave its full meaning to the very problem he was about to resolve. It was he who made it what we shall henceforth rightly call it, the problem of the *existence* of God.

CHAPTER III

THE Thomistic proofs for the existence of God appear in the *Summa Theologiae* and the *Summa Contra Gentiles*.[1] The five ways of the *Summa Theologiae* are presented in a succinct and simplified fashion, for after all, it is addressed rather to beginners, as the *Prologue* states. They tend also to treat the more metaphysical aspects of the problem. In the *Summa Contra Gentiles,* on the contrary, the philosophical demonstrations are minutely developed. They approach the problem from a more physical aspect and they appeal more forcefully to sensible experience. We shall treat of the proofs successively from these two accounts.

I. PROOFS FROM MOTION

Although St. Thomas rightly regarded his five demonstrations as equally conclusive, their various bases are not all equally easy to grasp. The proof based on the consideration of motion is the simplest of the four.[2] This is why St. Thomas strives to elucidate it completely, demonstrating even its minutest propositions.

The demonstration appears originally in Aristotle.[3] Naturally it remained unknown as long as Aristotelian physics was itself unknown, that is, until about the end of the twelfth century. If we consider as characteristic of this proof the fact that its point of departure is in the consideration of cosmic motion, and that it bases the principle that "nothing moves of itself" upon the concepts of potency and act,[4] then we can say that it reappears for the first time in Adelhard of Bath. It is to be found in its complete form in Albert the Great who gives it as an addition to the proof of Peter Lombard, and who borrowed it undoubtedly from Maimonides.[5]

The *Summa Theologiae* presents the demonstration as follows. It is certain that there is motion in the world because our senses tell us so. Now anything which moves is moved by some thing. Nothing indeed is moved save according as it is in potency with regard to that towards which it is moved. Nothing moves, on the contrary, save according as it is in act. For to move a thing is to make it pass from potency into act. Now a thing cannot be brought from potency into act except by a being in act. Hence, it is heat in act, for example, fire, which makes wood, which was hot only in potency, hot in act, and in making it burn, moves it and alters it. But it is impossible for a thing to be in act and in potency at the same time under the same relationship. Thus, what is hot in act cannot be at the same time cold in act, but cold only in potency. It is therefore impossible that a thing be in the same manner and under the same relationship, mover and moved, that is, that it move itself. From this we see that whatever is moved is moved by something else. If, however, that by which a thing is moved is itself moved, it is moved in its turn by some other mover, which mover is moved by another, and so on. But this cannot proceed to infinity, for there would then be no first mover and, consequently, no mover at all, because the second mover only moves because the first moves it, even as the baton only moves because the hand moves it. To explain motion, therefore, it is necessary to go back to a first mover whom nothing moves, that is, to God.[6]

The very general character of the idea of motion here will have been noticed.[7] It has been reduced to the notions of potency and act, transcendentals which divide all being. What provides the basis for the entire proof in the *Summa Theologiae* is given as but one of the possible grounds of the proof in the *Summa Contra Gentiles;*[8] and this proof itself is given under two forms, direct and indirect.

The direct proof proposed by Aristotle can be summarized thus:[9] Whatever is moved is moved by something else. Now our senses tell us that there is motion, the solar movement, for example. The Sun, therefore, is moved because something moves it. Now whatever it is that moves the sun is either moved or not moved. If it is not moved, then our conclusion is right, namely, that we have to affirm that there is an unmoved mover whom we call God. If it is moved, it is because another mover moves it. We must then either go back to infinity or else we must affirm that there is an unmoved mover. Now we cannot go back to infinity; therefore we must affirm that there is a first unmoved mover.

In this proof, two propositions must be established; first, that everything is moved by something else, and secondly, that we cannot go back to infinity in the series of movers and things moved.

Aristotle proves the first proposition by three arguments. Here is the first, which itself supposes three hypotheses. First, for a thing to move itself, it must have in itself the principle of its movement, otherwise it would obviously be moved by something else. The second is that this thing should move immediately, that is, move itself by reason of its whole self, and not by reason of one of its parts, as the animal is moved by the movement of its foot, in which case it cannot be said that the whole moves itself, but only that one part of the whole moves another part. The third is that this thing be divisible and possess parts, since, according to Aristotle, whatever moves is divisible. This granted, we can show thus that nothing moves itself. If we suppose that a thing moves itself, it is moved immediately; and therefore, when one of its parts is at rest, the whole is at rest.[10] If, indeed, one part were at rest and another part in motion, it would no longer be the whole thing itself which would be moved immediately but only the part in movement while the other part was at rest. Now nothing whose rest depends upon the rest of another moves itself. Indeed, if the rest of one thing depends upon the rest of another, its movement too must depend upon the movement of another, and consequently, it does not move itself. And since what one considers to be moving itself is not moving itself, it necessarily follows that whatever moves is moved by another.[11]

Aristotle's second demonstration of this principle is an induction.[12] Whatever is moved by accident is not moved by itself; its motion depends upon the motion of another. This is also evident in anything which is subjected to violent motion: if it is moved by violence it is not moved by itself. But this is also evident in anything which is moved by nature and contains within itself the principle of its movement, like the animals who are moved by their soul; and finally it remains true in anything which is moved by nature, without having in itself the principle of its motion, as heavy or light bodies which are moved by their place of origin. Now whatever is moved is moved by itself or by accident. If it is moved by accident, it is not moved by itself. If it is moved by itself, it is moved either violently or by nature. If it is moved by nature, it is either by its own nature as in the case of an animal, or not by itself, as the heavy or light bodies. Thus whatever is moved is moved by another.

Aristotle's third proof is as follows:[13] Nothing is in potency and act at the same time under the same relation. But everything is in potency in so far as it is moved, for movement is the act of what is in potency inasmuch as it is in potency. Now, whatever moves is, in so far as it moves, in act, for nothing acts save according as it is in act. Therefore nothing is at the same time and under the same relation mover and moved; and consequently nothing moves itself.

It remains to prove our second proposition, namely, that it is impossible to go back to infinity in the series of movers and things moved. Here again we find Aristotle giving three reasons.

The first is as follows:[14] If we go back to infinity in the series of movers and things moved, we must affirm that there is an infinite number of bodies, for whatever is moved is divisible, and consequently is a body. Now every body which moves something moved, is moved at the same time that it moves. Therefore this entire infinity of bodies which move because moved must move simultaneously when one of them moves. But since each one of them, taken by itself, is finite, it must move in finite time, therefore the infinity of bodies which must move at the same time it moves, must move in finite time. Now this is impossible. It is therefore impossible to go back to infinity in the series of movers and things moved.

Here Aristotle proves that it is impossible for an infinite number of bodies to move in finite time. What moves and what is moved must exist together, as can be demonstrated inductively by running through all the species of movement. But bodies can only exist together by continuity or by contiguity. Since, therefore, all these movers and things moved are necessarily bodies, they must form a single mobile whose parts are continuous or contiguous.[15] Thus, something infinite is moved in a finite time. Now in his *Physics*, VI, 7 and VII, 1, Aristotle has proved that it is impossible that one infinity should move in finite time.[16]

The second reason proving the impossibility of infinite regression is this.[17] When a series of movers and things moved are ordered, that is, when they form a series where each one moves the next, it is inevitable that, if the first mover disappeared or ceased to move, none of the rest would any longer be either a mover or moved. It is the first mover, indeed, which confers the power of moving on all the others. Now if we have an infinite series of movers and things moved, there will no longer be a first mover and all are intermediate movers. Therefore, if the action of the first mover is wanting, nothing will be moved and there will be no movement in the world.

The third reason is the same as the preceding one, save that the order of the terms is reversed. We begin with the higher term and reason thus. The instrumental moving cause can only move if there exists some principal moving cause. But if we go back to infinity in the series of movers and things moved, all will be at the same time mover and moved. There will therefore only be instrumental moving causes, and, since there will be no principal moving cause, there will be no movement in the world.

Thus are the two propositions proved which we found at the basis of the first demonstration by which Aristotle established the existence of a first immobile mover.

The same conclusion can be established indirectly, that is by establishing that the proposition "whatever moves is moved" is true neither by accident nor by itself.[18] If indeed whatever moves is moved, and if this proposition is true by accident, then it is not necessary. It is therefore possible that none of all the things that move is moved. But the adversary himself has admitted that what is not moved does not move: if therefore it is possible that nothing is moved, it is possible that nothing moves and that, consequently, there may be no motion. Now Aristotle holds that it is impossible that at any moment whatsoever there be no motion. Our point of departure is, accordingly, unacceptable. Consequently, the proposition "whatever moves is moved by another" is not true by accident.

The same conclusion can again be demonstrated by an appeal to experience. If two properties are accidentally joined in a subject, and if we can find one of them without the other, it is probable that we can also find the second without the first. For example, if we find *white* and *musician* in Socrates and Plato, and if we can find *musician* without *white,* it is probable that we could also find *white* without *musician.* If, then, the properties mover and moved are accidentally joined in some subject, and if we find somewhere the property of being moved without the property of mover, it is probable that we could find a mover which is not moved.[19]

The proposition "whatever moves is moved" is not therefore true by accident. Is it true by itself? [30] If it is true by itself, there arises still an impossibility. Whatever moves can either receive a movement of the same kind as it gives or of a different kind. If it is a movement of the same sort, then it follows that whatever causes alteration will be altered, whatever heals will be healed, whatever instructs will be instructed and this under the same relation and according to the same science. But this is impossible, for if he who instructs must be in possession of the science, it it equally necessary that he who learns this science be not in possession of it. If, on the other hand, it is a question of a motion that is not of the same species, so that what imparts a motion of alteration receives a local motion, and what moves according to place receives a motion of increase, and so on, the result will be, since the genera and species of movement are in finite number, that it will be impossible to proceed to infinity. Thus there will be a first mover that is not moved by another.

We may say, perhaps, that after having run through all the genera and all the species of movement, we must return to the first genus and close the circle. Thus, if what imparts local motion is altered, and if what causes alteration is increased, then what gives increase will in its turn be moved locally. But we would always come to the same conclusion. What moves according to a given species of movement would be moved according to the same species. The only difference is that it would be moved mediately rather than immediately. In both cases, the same impossibility forces us to affirm a first mover whom nothing exterior causes to move.

But our second demonstration is not finished. From the fact that there exists a first mover who is not moved from outside, it does not follow that an absolutely immovable first mover exists. This is why Aristotle says that the formula "an unmoved first mover" can be taken in two senses. First, it can signify an absolutely immovable first mover; if we take it to mean this, our conclusion stands. Secondly, it can signify that this first mover is not moved from outside but that it can move itself, and consequently is not absolutely immovable. But is this first mover which moves itself moved in its entirety by its entire self? Then we fall again into the preceding difficulties, namely, that the same being is instructing and instructed, in potency and act at the same time and under the same relation. But if we say, on the contrary, that only one part of this being is moving, while the other part alone is moved, then we reach our conclusion: there exists a mover which is only mover, that is, which moves without being moved.[21]

Here we reach the last stage of this long inquiry. In the case of animals, the moving part of the being which moves itself is itself moved, if not from outside, at least from within, by the desire which it has for the desirable. On the contrary, to be desired, the desirable has itself nothing other to do than to be what it is. If it moves in so far as desired, itself remains totally immovable, as a beautiful object towards which he who sees it moves itself. Thus, above the mover that moves itself by desire, there is the very object causing its desire. This object then occupies the summit in the order of moving causes, "for whatever desires is, so to speak, a mover moved, whereas the desirable is a mover which is not at all moved." Since this supreme desirable is thus the first cause of all movement, we must place it at the origin of becoming: "There must be a first, separated mover, absolutely unmoved, which is God." [22]

Such are the essential elements of the demonstrations of the existence of a first mover given in the *Contra Gentiles*. We can see without effort that in the thought of St. Thomas the notion of immovable mover and the notion of God are not distinct. In the *Summa Theologiae* he considers it enough to name the first mover which nothing moves for everyone to be quite sure that he is speaking about God.[23] However, St. Thomas does not insist that we receive this conclusion as purely and simply evident. We shall have the complete demonstration when we see all the divine attributes within the reach of human reason evolving from the notion of a first immovable mover. The *Compendium Theologiae*, beginning from this principle, clearly demonstrates the simplicity, the aseity, the unity, and, in a word, all those attributes describing from our point of view the essence of God.[24]

One can also note in the preceding demonstrations the absence of any allusion to any beginning of motion in time. The proof does not consist in showing that present motion requires a prime cause in the past, which would be God. It aims simply at establishing that, in the actually given universe, the actually given motion is unintelligible without a first mover who, in the present, is the source of movement for all things. In other words, the impossibility of going back to infinity does not refer to an infinite regression in time, but in the present instant in which we are considering the world.[25] We can put this in another way by saying that the structure of the proof would be the same if we admitted the hypothesis of the eternity of the world. St. Thomas knows this and explicitly says so.[26]

If, however, we accept the Catholic dogma that the world and motion took their beginning in time, we are in a much more favorable position to demonstrate the existence of God. For if the world and motion had a beginning, the need for affirming a cause producing motion and the world becomes self-evident. Whenever something new occurs, there must be a cause for what is new, for nothing can of itself pass from potency into act or from non-being to being. Such a demonstration is relatively easy. The demonstration is not at all easy if we hypothetically concede the eternity of the world and of motion. Yet it is this kind of demonstration, difficult and obscure as it is, which St. Thomas has preferred to give. He held that to demonstrate the existence of God by the need of a creator to make motion and all things appear in time is not, from the strictly philosophical point of view, a convincing demonstration,[27] because it cannot be proved by simple reason, as we shall see later on, that the world had a beginning.

Here St. Thomas is definitely and irreducibly at odds with most of the other theologians, but he carries his fidelity to the Peripatetics even to this point. To demonstrate the existence of God on the supposition that the world is eternal would be, in the last analysis, to make the question one of faith, dependent upon our belief in the account in *Genesis*. It would cease to be a philosophical truth proven by demonstrative reason. But by demonstrating the existence of God on the hypothesis of eternal motion, St. Thomas demonstrates it *a fortiori* for the hypothesis of a universe begun in time. His proof is philosophically sound; it borrows nothing from revelation.

It is important to understand why a regression to infinity in the present instant in which we are considering the world is an absurdity. It is because the causes whose series we are here considering are hierarchically ordered. For, in the physical universe in which the proof by the first mover is located, whatever is moved is moved by a moving cause which is superior to it, and, consequently, is the cause of its motion and its moving force at the same time. The higher cause has not only to account for the motion of some individual or other—a stone moves a stone—but of the motion of the species. If we consider what happens within the species, we easily discover there the sufficient reason of the coming to be of individuals or of their motions. But each particular moving cause, taken within the species, cannot be considered the first source of its movement. And the problem arises similarly for all individuals of the species under consideration, since, for each of them, the nature defining it is that of the species. It is therefore outside the species and above it that we must necessarily look for the sufficient reason for the efficacy of individuals.[28] Either we shall have to suppose that what receives its nature is at the same time cause of it and that consequently it is cause of itself, which is absurd, or we must consider that whatever acts in virtue of a nature which has been received is only an instrumental cause which is related, through higher causes, to a first cause.[29] The hierarchical series of the moving causes is not only not infinite, but its terms are not very numerous. There are the elements, the ascending series of the heavenly bodies, the separate Intelligences, and God.[30]

This is the most celebrated and the most frequently cited of St. Thomas's five demonstrations of the existence of God. Undoubtedly St. Thomas himself had a particular preference for it. But its interpretation is far from easy. At first glance it seems to be only the repetition of a text of Aristotle. In reality it is not one text of Aristotle but is a synthesis of texts from Books VII and VIII of the *Physics* and Book XI of the *Metaphysics*. Upon close examination it proves to be composed of two parts of unequal length. One, developed fully, is based on the *Physics*, the other, quite brief, on the *Metaphysics*. A comparison of the two texts reveals that they are very different. The text in which he uses the *Physics* leads the reader towards a conclusion that is really in the realm of physics, or, to be more exact, of cosmography: the existence of a first mover which moves itself, and, in moving itself, causes motion in the entire universe. Since this first mover is not completely immovable and separated, it is not the God whose existence Thomas intends to demonstrate. The problem of the existence of a God truly super-natural is directly treated only in the second part of the proof, as a metaphysical problem the solution of which is provided by Aristotle's *Metaphysics*. St. Thomas accepts this solution and reproduces it with remarkable fidelity. The first physical mover moves itself in that it desires God. God himself is completely immovable and separated, since He moves simply as desired. How are we, in our turn, to interpret St. Thomas's proof from motion? Does he conclude that there is a first cause which only moves in so far as it is the object of desire? Or does he go beyond Aristotle to a first efficient cause of motion? Since the same problem arises in regard to St. Thomas's other demonstrations of the existence of God, we shall defer discussion until they too have been examined.

2. PROOF BY EFFICIENT CAUSE

The first proof of the existence of God is drawn from the Aristotelian notion of moving cause. The second proof of the existence of God is drawn from the Avicennian notion of efficient cause, *ex ratione causae efficientis*.[31] According to Thomas himself, it has its first origin in Aristotle[32] who says that a regression to infinity is impossible in any of the four kinds of causes: material, moving, final, and formal, concluding that we must always go back to a first principle. We shall say later on why this historical indication fails to convince us. But Avicenna,[33] Alan of Lille,[34] and Albert the Great[35] have resorted to similar demonstrations. Of all the forms which these thinkers give the argument, Avicenna's is the most interesting because so much closer to the proof of St. Thomas. They are not so similar that we may not legitimately suppose[36] that St. Thomas reached his conclusions independently by direct and personal examination of the text of Aristotle, but he has certainly not found in Aristotle the distinction, which the second way presupposes, between the causality by way of motion and efficient causality, whose proper effect is Being.

Let us consider sensible things, the only possible point of departure for a demonstration of the existence of God. We note in them an order of efficient causes. But we never meet, nor can we meet a being which is its own efficient cause. Since the cause is necessarily anterior to its effect, a being would have to be anterior to itself in order to be its own efficient cause, which is quite impossible. On the other hand, it is impossible to go back to infinity in the series of efficient causes. Now we have observed that there is an order of moving causes, that is, that they are so arranged that the first is the cause of the second and the second of the last. This affirmation is true of efficient causes, whether it is a question of a sole intermediate cause binding the first to the last or of several intermediate causes. In both cases, and whatever the number of intermediate causes, it is the first cause that is the cause of the last effect, so that if the first cause is suppressed, the effect is suppressed. Thus if there is no first term in the series of efficient causes, there will be neither intermediate terms nor a last one. If, then, there were an infinite series of causes arranged in this way, there would be neither intermediate efficient causes nor last effect. But in the world around us, we observe that there are such causes and such effects. It is therefore necessary to affirm a first efficient cause, which everyone calls God.[37] The text of the proof in the *Contra Gentiles* is almost identical with that of the *Summa Theologiae*. Since the only differences are in the manner of expression, it is useless to repeat it.

We should note the close relationship between St. Thomas's second proof for the existence of God and the first. In both cases the necessity for a first cause is based on the impossibility of going back to infinity in an ordered series of causes and effects. Nowhere more than here is one more likely to accept the recently suggested thesis that there are not five proofs of God's existence, but only one divided into five parts.[38] If we mean by this that the five proofs of St. Thomas are conditioned upon one another—and some have gone so far as to regard the proof by a first mover as a mere preparation for the proof—the conclusion is unacceptable.[39] Each proof is sufficient in itself. This is eminently true of the proof by the first mover: *prima et manifestior via*. But it is correct to say that the structure of the five proofs of St. Thomas is identical, even that they form one whole and reciprocally complete one another. Any one of them is enough to establish the existence of God but each begins from a different series of effects and brings out a different aspect of the divine causality. While the first brings us to God as the cause of cosmic motion and of all motion dependent upon it, the second leads us to Him as the cause of the very existence of things. We knew that God was moving cause. We know now that He is cause of being. In a doctrine which obliges the quest for God to start from the consideration of the physical universe, the multiplication of converging proofs cannot be considered a matter of indifference. Each different approach discloses to us a different aspect of the divine causality.

Finally, it should be pointed out that if the proof from the efficient cause, like that from the first mover, rests on the impossibility of carrying the series of causes to infinity, it is because in this case too causes arranged according to the order of essences are causes arranged hierarchically. An infinite series of efficient causes within the same species is not only possible, but even, in the Aristotelian hypothesis of the eternity of the world, necessary. A man can beget a man who, in his turn, begets another, and so on to infinity. A series like this has no internal order, because it is as man and not as son of his father that a man begets another. But do we want to find out the cause of his own specific form as such, the cause in virtue of which he is man and able to beget another? It is clearly no longer in his own kind but in a being of a higher degree that we shall discover it. And just as this superior being explains at once the existence and the causality of the beings whose species is subordinated to its own, so it holds in its turn its own being and causality from a still higher being. Hence the necessity of a first term: the first term contains virtually the causality of the entire series and of each of the terms belonging to it.[40] In the doctrine of St. Thomas one cannot say that there is just one efficacy, but there is only one solitary source of efficacious causality for the entire world. No thing gives existence, save inasmuch as there is in it a participation of the divine power. This is also why, in the order of efficient causes as in that of moving causes, we must proceed to and stop at a supreme degree.

St. Thomas indicates the historical source of this second proof in the *Contra Gentiles* where there is an explicit reference to Book II of the *Metaphysics* of Aristotle. He even presents it as a proof by Aristotle himself in order to show "that it is impossible to proceed to infinity in efficient causes, but that we must come to one, first cause, whom we call God." But if we examine the passage which St. Thomas seems to have had in mind (Met., II, 2, 994, a 1-19), we are struck by the fact that here there is no direct question of an efficient cause. Aristotle is showing that it is impossible to go back to infinity in any of the four kinds of causes, material, moving, final and formal, but there is no question of the efficient cause properly so called. The problem, then, that came up before in the matter of the moving cause reappears here with an even greater urgency. Is St. Thomas just following Aristotle, or is he putting to his own use the letter of arguments to which he is giving quite a new sense?

3. THE PROOF FROM NECESSARY BEING

The point of departure for the third proof is in the distinction between the possible and the necessary.[41] Two premises can be regarded as the basis of the proof. The first is that the possible is contingent, that is, can either be or not be, and so is opposed to the necessary. The second is that the possible has not its existence from itself, that is, from its essence, but from an efficient cause which communicates it to it. With these propositions and the principle already demonstrated that it is impossible to go back to infinity in the series of efficient causes we have at our disposal everything necessary to establish our demonstration. But it is well to begin by indicating the historical conditions of its appearance.

To the extent that this third proof considers that the possible has no existence of its own, it takes for granted the distinction between essence and existence in created things. It was the Arabian philosophers, and chiefly Alfarabi, as we have seen, who first clarified this distinction. But it had provided Avicenna with the basis of a distinct demonstration in which we see the two premises which we have just affirmed at work.[42] A modified form of this demonstration is to be found in Maimonides who got it no doubt from Avicenna.[43] Finally we find it in the *Summa Theologiae* where it follows the demonstration of the Jewish theologian.[44]

Maimonides sets out from the fact that there are beings[45] and that they can be in one of three possible conditions only: 1) no being is born or perishes; 2) all beings are born and perish; 3) there are beings which are born and perish, and there are beings which are not born and do not perish. There is no question about the first case. Experience is continually showing us that there are beings which are born and perish. The second case cannot stand long under examination. If all beings can be born and perish, it would follow that at a given moment all beings would necessarily have perished. For indeed, as far as individuals are concerned, a possible may or may not be realized, but what is possible for a species, whose duration is eternal, must inevitably come to pass,[46] otherwise the word possibility is vain. Therefore, if disappearance were a true possible for all beings, considered as forming one sole species, they would have already disappeared. But if they had fallen into nothingness, they would never have been able of themselves to come back into existence, and consequently today there would still be nothing existing. But we see that something does exist. We must then admit that only the third hypothesis is true. Certain beings are born and perish, but there is one withdrawn from all possibility of destruction and who possesses necessary existence, namely, the first being, God.

This demonstration does not appear in the *Summa Contra Gentiles*, but it appears almost word for word as the third way to the existence of God in the *Summa Theologiae*. There are, says St. Thomas, things which are born and corrupt, and which, consequently, can either be or not be. But it is impossible that everything of this kind should always exist, because when the non-being of a thing is possible, there finally comes a moment when it does not exist. If therefore the non-being of everything were possible, there would have come a moment when nothing would have existed. But if it were true that such a moment had come, then even now nothing would exist, because what does not exist cannot begin to be without the intervention of something which does exist. If, therefore, at this moment no being existed, it was absolutely impossible for anything to begin to be, and nothing would any longer exist, which is clearly false. We cannot say, then, that all beings are possible beings, and we must acknowledge the existence of something that is a necessary being. This necessary being can have its necessity from itself or from another. But we cannot go back to infinity in the series of beings which hold their necessity from another, no more than in the series of efficient causes, as already shown. We must then inevitably affirm a being which, necessary of itself, does not hold the cause of its necessity from others, but which is the cause of the necessity of others. This is the being that is called God.[47]

St. Thomas's third proof for the existence of God is related to the first in that it assumes, in an even more obvious way, the thesis of the eternity of the world. If the Jewish philosopher and the Christian philosopher both admit that in the event that the non-being of all things had been possible, the moment would necessarily have come when nothing would have existed, it is because they are reasoning within the hypothesis that time is of infinite duration. Where there is infinite duration, it is unthinkable that a possible worthy of the name be not realized. No doubt, and we have already noted this in so far as St. Thomas is concerned, they do not really accept the eternity of the world. But as Maimonides says, they wish "to confirm the existence of God, in which we believe, by a method of demonstration that is incontestable so as not to found this true and important doctrine upon a basis that anyone can shake and which many can even consider as null and void." [48] Maimonides and St. Thomas are in complete agreement on this point.

It is easy to ascertain the new gains assured by this third demonstration: God, already known as moving cause and efficient cause of all things, is henceforth known as a necessary being. This is a conclusion which we shall have to recall more than once. Here again the problem arises of the extent to which St. Thomas is merely following the men whose arguments he borrows. Certainly in so far as concerns Avicenna, whose principles underlie the proof, the question cannot be avoided. The notion of "necessary being" implies the notion of being, and since, as we have seen, this demonstration is based on the distinction between essence and existence, it is probable that what was new in St. Thomas's notion of existence has given an equally new sense even to those elements of his proof which are the most obviously borrowed from Avicenna.

4. PROOF FROM THE DEGREES OF BEING

The fourth proof of the existence of God is based on an examination of the degrees of being. Of all the Thomistic proofs none has been subjected to so many different interpretations.[49] A look at the two accounts given by St. Thomas will enable us to determine the difficulties that arise and to suggest a solution.

In the *Contra Gentiles* St. Thomas says that a further proof can be found in Book II of Aristotle's *Metaphysics*.

Aristotle teaches[50] that things possessing the supreme degree of truth possess also the supreme degree of being. In another place, he shows[51] that there is a supreme degree of truth. Wherever we have two falsehoods, one is always more false than the other, hence one of these is always truer than the other. But more or less true only indicates approximation to what is absolutely and sovereignly true. Hence the final conclusion that there exists something that is sovereignly, and in its supreme degree, being. And it is this to which we give the name God.[52]

In the *Summa Theologiae,* St. Thomas announces that he is going to take his proof from the grades or degrees that can be found in things. We observe that among things there are those that are more or less good, more or less noble, more or less true, and so on for all perfections. But more or less are only applicable to different things according as they approach in varying degree whatever is this perfection in its highest degree. For example, what more closely approaches supreme heat is hotter. Thus there exists something that is true, good, and noble in their highest degree, and which consequently is the highest degree of being. For, according to Aristotle,[53] what possesses the highest degree of truth, possesses also the highest degree of being. On the other hand, what is said to constitute the highest degree in a genus is cause and measure of whatever belongs to that genus. Fire, for example, which is the highest degree of heat is the cause and measure of all heat. There should therefore exist something else that is the cause of being, and of goodness and of the perfections of every rank which are in all things, and it is this that we call God.[54]

We have indicated already that the interpretation of this truth has given rise to many controversies. This is because, rather different from the others, it presents clearly enough a purely conceptual aspect. Certain philosophers distrust it. Staab,[55] for example, only concedes that it is a demonstration of probability. Grunwald[56] observes that the proof proceeds from the abstract concept to the affirmation of being. No doubt, he says, it was St. Thomas's realization of this inconsistency that led him to modify his proof in the *Summa Theologiae.* By constantly appealing, in this second version, to sense experience, using fire and heat as an example, he was trying, we are told, to place demonstration on a more empirical basis. And this *modulation,* intended to bring the proof down from the heights of idealism to the depths of Thomistic realism, was perceptible in the simple comparison of the two texts. On the other hand there are many historians who admire this proof unreservedly. More

Thomistic in this than St. Thomas himself, they give it a preferred position among the proofs.[57] These varying appreciations are interesting because they betray differences of interpretation.

No problem arises over the statement of fact that there are degrees of
being and of truth in things. Nor is there any difficulty about the conclusion St. Thomas draws from it: that there is a supreme degree of truth.
Some have wondered whether this conclusion should be understood in a
relative or an absolute sense. Kirfel[58] understands it in the relative sense,
that is, as the highest degree actually found in each genus. Rolfes[59]
understands it as the highest possible degree, in the absolute sense. And
Pègues writes to the same effect: "It is a question first and immediately
of the being that surpasses all others in perfection, but by this we come
to the most perfect that can be conceived." [60]

The interpretation which takes "the supreme degree of being" (*maxime
ens*) in the relative sense is easily explained. Its purpose is to eliminate
any trace of what might be taken for ontologism from the Thomistic
proof. St. Thomas says: there are degrees in error and truth, therefore
there is a supreme truth and consequently a supreme being who is God.
But is not this to pass, like St. Anselm, from thought to being, from
the order of knowledge to the order of the real? Nothing is less Thomistic
than such an attitude. And it is to avoid this difficulty that St. Thomas
has added an induction that raises us from the relatively highest degree
that we observe in all order of reality to the absolutely highest degree
of being, that is, to the highest being which can be conceived.

We can understand how important, in a hypothesis like this, is the
addition found in the proof in the *Summa Theologiae*. The *Contra Gentiles* concludes the proof with an affirmation of the existence of a *maxime
ens*, which is at once identified with God. The *Summa Theologiae* demonstrates further that what is *maxime ens* is also the universal cause of
being and, consequently, can be nothing but God. Why this addition to
the demonstration?

If we take the expression *maxime ens* in the relative sense, it is easy
to understand it. In this case it is not immediately evident that this
supreme degree of being is God. It can be a very high degree which is
still finite and within our grasp. But by assimilating it to the universal
and supreme cause, we establish that this *maxime ens* is God. Taken
absolutely, it is clear that this supreme being is God, and it is hard to
see why St. Thomas should have drawn out his proof to such length,
above all in a work like the *Summa Theologiae* where he wishes to be
clear and brief.[61]

These are ingenious arguments but they only serve to create difficulties
where there ought not to be any. The first of such difficulties is this:
that if *maxime ens* must be taken in a purely relative sense, the whole

argument of the *Contra Gentiles* is but a crude paralogism. St. Thomas is reasoning in this way: that which is the supreme truth is also the supreme Being; now there is a supreme Truth; therefore there is a supreme Being, who is God. If *maxime verum* and *maxime ens* have but a relative sense in the premises, how can it be given an absolute sense in the conclusion? Yet the proof demands this because the conclusion comes immediately to God.

If we are to be referred on this point to the supposedly more complete proof of the *Summa Theologiae*, we only find that the literal text gives scant support to such an interpretation. St. Thomas's example of the more and less hot should cause no illusions. It is simply a comparison, a *manuductio* to help us understand the principal thesis. Certainly the "supremely hot" is but a relative supreme degree. Strictly speaking the "supremely true" and the "supremely noble" could have been used as other examples of relative supreme degrees. But the discussion seems difficult in what concerns the "supreme Being." It is possible to conceive of a relatively supreme degree in any order of perfection whatsoever, except in that of being. From the moment St. Thomas affirms a truth *par excellence* which is also being *par excellence,* then either his terminology has no conceivable meaning or he is affirming, purely and simply, the supreme degree of being, which is God. As to the appeal to the relation of causality which terminates the demonstration of the *Summa Theologiae,* it is not at all intended to establish the existence of the supreme Being. This conclusion is now already reached. It is intended simply to show that in this First Being, whom we place above all beings, there is the cause of all perfections to be found in second things. This conclusion shows in what sense, like the preceding ones, the fourth way manifests the existence of God as the cause of observable facts.

St. Thomas, therefore, has drawn his conclusion of the existence of God directly from the degrees of being. Can such a form of argument be interpreted as inferring actual existence from reality? The very sources of the proof would lead one to believe so. Among the primary sources of this proof, we recognize, besides Aristotle,[63] the celebrated passage of *The City of God* where St. Augustine praises the Platonic philosophers for having seen that in all more or less beautiful things the form by which any being whatsoever is beautiful can only come from a prime, absolute and immovable form, by which all that is, and is beautiful, was made.[64] But to argue from the Platonic inspiration of the proof to its purely conceptual character, or to say, with Grunwald, that it is a waste of time and labor to reduce this idealist argument to the properly Thomistic point of view of moderate realism,[65] is perhaps to proceed too hastily.

St. Thomas's criticism of the *a priori* proof of the existence of God has led us indeed to this conclusion: that it is impossible to place the point of departure of the proof in the consideration of the divine essence, and that consequently we must start from the consideration of sensible things. But sensible things are much more than material things. St. Thomas is quite right in taking the sensible in its most complete form and with all the conditions which, according to his teaching, it requires. Now, we shall see later on that the sensible is constituted by the union of the intelligible and the material. And if the purely intelligible form does not fall directly within the grasp of our understanding, it is none the less true that our understanding can abstract from sensible things the intelligible to be found there. Thus envisaged, the beautiful, the noble, the good, the true (for there is a certain element of truth in things) constitute realities which we grasp. The fact that their divine exemplars escape us does not mean that their finite participations need escape us as well. But, if it is this way, nothing prevents our taking them as points of departure for a new proof. Motion, efficient causality, and the being of things are not the only realities that demand explanation. What is good, noble, true in the universe also requires a first cause. In seeking out the origin of the degrees of perfection observable in sensible things we exceed in no way the limits which we had previously set for ourselves.

Obviously, the fourth way openly relies upon the validity of the Platonic and Augustinian notion of participation. But we shall see that, taken in a new sense, exemplarism is one of the essential elements of St. Thomas's thought. He maintains that the lower degrees of perfection and being suppose a being in which perfections and being meet in their highest degree. He also maintains that to possess a perfection incompletely and to possess it from a cause are synonymous. A cause can only give what it has. Anything that does not possess a perfection of itself and only possesses it incompletely must hold it from something possessing it of itself and in the highest degree.[66] But it does not therefore follow that this proof of St. Thomas is reduced, as has been charged, to a purely abstract and conceptual deduction. All the proofs equally suppose the intervention of intellectual conceptions transcending sensible knowledge and suppose that the sensible itself should furnish them with an empirical basis on which to rest in order to raise us to God. Now this is precisely the case, since the very intelligibility of things comes from their resemblance to God.[67] This is why the conception of a universe, hierarchized according to the degrees of being and perfection, is involved right from the beginning of the proof of the existence of God by the prime mover or by the efficient cause. If therefore this new demonstration were to be considered as essentially Platonic, it would be necessary, in sound logic, to concede that the earlier demonstrations are so too.

5. THE PROOF FROM THE FINAL CAUSE

The fifth and last proof is based on the consideration of the government of things. There is no point in going into its philosophical origins since the idea of a God giving order to the universe is the common property of Christian theology. There are many texts of Holy Scripture upon which to establish it. St. Thomas himself appeals to St. John Damascene,[68] who appears to have furnished him with the framework of his argument. It runs as follows in the *Contra Gentiles*: It is impossible that contrary and disparate things should be in accord and reconciled within the same order, either always or very often, unless there exists a being governing them and causing them, collectively and individually, to tend towards one determined end. Now we observe that in the world things of different natures are reconciled within one and the same order, not merely from time to time and by chance, but always or practically always. There must then exist a being by whose providence the world is governed, and it is this being that we call God.[69] The *Summa Theologiae* argues in precisely the same manner but specifying that this providence which orders the world, by which all things are disposed towards their end, is an intelligence; and one might in the end come to the same conclusion by following different ways, notably by reasoning and logically from human acts.[70]

Although more familiar to theologians and more popular than the preceding, this last proof and the conclusion it establishes is, in St. Thomas's opinion, no less valuable than the others. It may be distinguished from the others in that the final cause is very different from the other causes, and holds a more eminent place in the order of causality. Assuredly this proof has varying degrees of profundity.[71] In its most obvious aspect, it argues to some supreme artisan or demiurge, more or less resembling the Author of Nature so dear to the eighteenth-century Frenchman. In its profounder aspect it sees in the final cause the reason for which the efficient cause moves, that is, it sees in it the cause of the cause. It arrives, therefore, not only nor first of all at the reason for what order there is in nature, but also and pre-eminently at the reason for nature itself. In brief, beyond the intelligible manner of existing, the final cause attains the supreme reason for which things exist. It is this reason exactly which the proof by the final cause seeks, and this it attains when it reaches the conclusion that God exists.

The proof by finality, like the preceding proof, is existential and has the same structure. To admit that sensible things are ordered by chance is to admit that there is room in the universe for an effect without a cause, namely, their very order. For if the proper form of each body is enough to explain the particular operation of this body, it does not at all

75

explain why different bodies and their different operations are ordered in a harmonious whole.[72] We have, therefore, in the proof by finality, as in all the preceding proofs, a sensible datum which looks for its sufficient reason in God and finds it in Him alone. The thought interior to things is explained, as are the things themselves, by their distant imitation of the thought of the provident God who rules them.

The various "ways" St. Thomas follows to arrive at the existence of God are manifestly distinct from one another if we consider their sensible starting points, and they are quite as manifestly connected if we consider their structure and relations.[73] In the first place, each proof is based on the empirical observation of a fact, because no existence can be inferred save by starting from some other existence. Thus all the Thomistic proofs differ from the Augustinian proofs by truth, or the Anselmian proof by the idea of God. There is motion, there are reciprocal actions, beings that are born and die, things more or less perfect, and there is order in things. And it is because all this *is* that we can affirm that its cause exists. The presence, then, of an existential base is a first characteristic common to the five proofs for the existence of God.

A second characteristic trait is that they all make use of the causal inference. Properly considered, there is not one of them that does not show that God is the only conceivable cause of the sensible experience from which it starts. This is because the notion of cause is for St. Thomas a first principle, that is, immediately known by the natural light of reason from the moment it awakens at the contact of experience. To existence empirically given, each proof adds a rational and necessary element, which makes all existence intelligible by binding it to the existence of its cause. All movement supposes a mover; every effect, a cause; every contingent being, a being *per se;* every hierarchy, a highest term; every order an orderer.

But it is fitting to add a third characteristic to the preceding. If, indeed, we except the proof by finality, all the proofs suppose that the effects with which the arguments deal are arranged in a series of more and more perfect causes. This aspect of Thomistic thought is very apparent in the fourth way, but is no less perceptible even in the first. It is this hierarchical subordination of essentially ordered effects and causes which makes impossible a regression to infinity in the series of causes and permits the reason to affirm the existence of God. Let us note, nevertheless, to avoid all equivocation, that the hierarchy of causes to which St. Thomas assigns a first term is much less necessary as a ladder ascending towards God than as something enabling us to consider the whole series of intermediate causes as one sole second cause, of which God is the first cause. To be sure, St. Thomas takes a certain imaginative pleasure out of ascending these degrees, but as far as concerns his metaphysical reason, they form but one degree, since the efficacy of each intermediate cause presupposes that the complete series of its conditions is actually realized. And thus we come back to our first general characteristic of the proofs: we have to start from an existence. When we can assign the complete, sufficient reason of any single *existence*, empirically given, we can prove the *existence* of God. In appearance nothing could be simpler than such a formula, but it is not as easy to understand as many imagine. The quickest way of grasping it satisfactorily is the one which at first blush appears to the most involved. Unless we go into them historically, we are not likely to discern the true meaning of the Thomistic proofs for the existence of God.

6. SIGNIFICANCE OF THE PROOFS FOR THE EXISTENCE OF GOD

Nowhere is the absence of an exposition of his own philosophy by Thomas Aquinas himself more seriously felt than on the question of the existence of God. Here especially do we have to show that St. Thomas is transforming all he borrows. This would be a great deal easier were it not that he constantly gives expression to his own meaning in a form already used by others before him. He nowhere offers an explanation of why he does this, and the historian is left to his own surmises. There may be several concurring reasons. The modesty of the man and the saint must have contributed something and also his sincere desire to make others as sure as he himself was of the very real agreement there is between faith and reason. Thus it was more important to show that the ways pursued in different philosophies lead to the same truth than to propose further demonstrations of a totally new kind. St. Thomas did not consider himself to be the first to prove effectively the existence of God. He did not think this as philosopher, and as theologian he would have shuddered at the very suggestion. Whatever his reasons, he borrowed the language of others. Thus the need here to scrutinize his texts in order to extract his personal thought from words and expressions which were not his own.

We can speak about his terminology and formulae this way when we become aware of the extreme diversity of their sources. St. Thomas borrows now from Aristotle, now from Avicenna, and now from St. John Damascene or St. Augustine. No matter how eclectic we suppose him to be, he cannot have collected thoughts so infinitely varied without modifying them considerably. We shall see that he did modify them, and his personal contribution to the problem was precisely the modification he imposed upon them. It mattered little to him that his proofs were of different origin; his hope was above all to show that they were all good, provided they could be made to come to the right conclusion.

Thus envisaged, the number of the Thomistic proofs for the existence of God loses considerable of its importance. Our attention has rightly been called to "the empirical character of the five ways . . . a sort of stock-taking which makes no claim to be exhaustive, much less to present the constituent parts of a necessary division." [74] Not only their number, but their original meaning in the doctrine from which they are borrowed loses much of its interest. The point in trying to get back to their original sense is less to determine what St. Thomas is preserving than to see what he is adding. Indeed it is perhaps rather to see, where he appears to be adding nothing, how he is transforming it into something else entirely by merely transposing it to another plane.

The proof by the first mover is characteristic in this regard and is more or less typical of the others. As we observed when analyzing it,[75] it argues to the existence of a first desirable and immovable source of all the movement of the universe. We have also observed that such was Aristotle's position.[76] It appears, however, at first glance, that St. Thomas could not hold this. The God of whom he is thinking, both as Christian doctor and philosopher, does not cause motion simply as a final cause but as an efficient cause, without, however, being moved himself, and remaining always separate. We have only two choices here. Either St. Thomas did not understand that Aristotle's proof could not be taken over as it stood, in which case he was guilty of misinterpretation; or he did understand this, and therefore could only press the proof by the first mover into service by giving it a new meaning.

Now there are many signs that St. Thomas's first mover is not a simple final cause. In the first place, it is remarkable that in the *Summa Theologiae* the immovable First Mover is not at all presented as being only a supreme desirable. Reading this text just as it is, everyone will understand it. Everyone understands it in fact to prove the existence of a first efficient cause of motion. One has only to read it again to be assured of this.[77] But this is not all. The distinction between the Aristotelian level of substance and the Thomistic level of existence ought to intervene here, at least if we are to attribute to the texts of St. Thomas their Thomistic meaning. We all know that in Aristotle the motion of the heavenly bodies is the cause of all motion, the term "motion" being understood here as everywhere in the sense of "passing from potency to act." The generation of beings which we are constantly witnessing in experience are motions of this kind. They are, therefore, caused by the motion of the heavenly bodies. As the first cause of this motion is the immovable First Mover, then, even under the simple title of First Mover, it can be called the cause of all the beings succeeding one another in the world. Moreover, St. Thomas has strongly emphasized this in order to defend Aristotle against the charge of having made of God a mere moving cause. These common causes of beings, eternal and separated substances, are also supreme beings, and, consequently, causes of other beings. "Whence it is evident," concludes St. Thomas, "how false is the opinion of those who maintain that Aristotle did not think that God was the cause of the substance of the heavens but only of its motion." [78] Indeed, "On this first principle, which is the first mover as end, depends the heavens, both as to the perpetuity of its substance and as to the perpetuity of its motion. Consequently, all nature depends on such a principle, since all natural beings depend upon the heavens and their motions." [79] Let us go farther. Aristotle shows that the immovable first mover is not only intelligible and desirable, but intelligent and living. In short, the first mover is truly God.[80] It is, therefore, God as immovable first mover that Aristotle affirms to be the cause of motion and of substances.

Can we go beyond this point, without going beyond Aristotle? St. Thomas, who always brings Aristotle as close to the truth as he can, has at least tried to do so. He strives to make him say that all motion and all nature depend upon the First Mover, not only as upon a final cause, but upon a will. He makes the attempt in this additional remark: "We must pay attention to this, that Aristotle is here saying that the necessity of the first movement is not an absolute necessity, but a necessity depending upon an end. Now the end is that principle which he afterwards names God, to whom the end of motion is to assimilate beings (*inquantum attenditur per motum assimilatio ad ipsum*). On the other hand, the assimilation to a willing and intelligent being, as he shows God to be, is understood in terms of will and intelligence. Thus the products of art are assimilated to the artisan in so far as in them the will of the artist is fulfilled. It follows from this, therefore, that all the necessity of the first movement is subject to the will of God." [81]

Strictly speaking, St. Thomas is not here going beyond the letter of Aristotle, save perhaps in speaking of Aristotle's God as having a will, when, in the passage from the *Metaphysics* upon which he is commenting, Aristotle does not say this. However, as Aristotle is there showing the immovable First Mover as supreme delectable and as living, he could strictly speaking be said to have a will. We say, strictly speaking, because Aristotle is only speaking in this Book XII, chap. VII of the *Metaphysics* of the life and pleasure of a Supreme Intelligence, which is also the supreme Intelligible.[82] But if we admit that this is so, all that St. Thomas can rightly draw from this text of Aristotle is that the first motion, cause of all others, is that of a will being assimilated to what the First mover wills in willing itself, not a motion willed by a supreme will. In fact, St. Thomas says no more about it; so that even in his commentary upon it, the hiatus separating the "final cause" God of Aristotle from the "efficient moving cause" God of Thomism is still not removed.

But even if it were removed, we should have a second gap to cross, and this time a veritable abyss, because it separates the entitative being of nature or substance from existential being properly so called. St. Thomas always maintains, as we shall see better when we deal with creation, that Aristotle affirmed his immovable First Mover as the cause of the whole substance, and, consequently, of all substances. This is clearly what we have just found St. Thomas saying *a propos* of the text of the *Metaphysics*. There is nothing more interesting than to compare with his commentary the terms he uses when speaking freely and for himself about the moving causality of the Christian God. Since he has begun with Aristotle's proofs, it is still the God of these proofs with whom he sets out. But now it becomes evident that the entire substantialist metaphysic of Aristotle is transferred to a much more profound plane. "It has been shown above, by a demonstration from Aristotle, that a first efficient cause exists, which we call God. Now the efficient cause brings its effects to actual existence (*suos effectos ad esse conducit*). God is, therefore, the cause by which other things exist. It has also been shown by an argument of the same Aristotle that there exists an immovable first mover whom we call God. Now in any order of motions whatsoever, the first mover is the cause of all the motions in the series. Since therefore the motions of the heavens bring many things to exist, motions of which God has been shown to be the first mover, it must be that God is the cause of the existence of many things." [83]

The interpreter of St. Thomas has to make his choice. The first efficient cause cannot cause the existence of the effects which other causes produce if it does not first cause the existence of these causes.[84] The immovable First Mover cannot cause the existence of the effects of the motions of the heavens if it does not first cause the existence of this motion. It would not cause it, if its action simply consisted in motivating by its presence the motion of a first movable. This would be to give to this first movable a motive for moving itself; it would not be to confer existence to its motion. It seems true to say that the Thomistic proofs for the existence of God are developed immediately upon the existential level as demonstrations that there exists a first moving cause of the heavenly motions and, through them, of the very beings that come to be owing to their influence; a first efficient cause of all the causes and of their efficacy; a necessary existant, cause of the actualization of all possibles; a first term in the orders of Being, Good, True, cause of everything contained in these orders; a Last End, whose existence is the why of every "why—something—exists."

Thus interpreted in the fullness of their meaning, the Thomistic proofs of the existence of God rejoin another order of considerations which we have already met several times. To say that an existing thing requires an extrinsic cause of its existence is to say that it does not contain it in itself. From this point of view, the proofs of the existence of God consist in constructing a chain of causes which binds all beings which are by another to the one being who is by itself. Beings by another, which have not in themselves the wherewithal to exist, are those same beings whose essence, we were saying, is distinct from their existence,[85] as opposed to being by itself whose very essence is to exist. We can say, therefore, that all the Thomistic proofs for the existence of God amount, in the last analysis, to a search, beyond existences which are not self-sufficient, for an existence which is self-sufficient and which, because it is so, can be the first cause of all others.

The reason why St. Thomas did not directly approach the problem from this angle in the *Summa Theologiae* and in the *Summa Contra Gentiles* is no doubt the same as that for placing the proof by motion before the others. "The first and most manifest way," he says of this proof. It is the most manifest because there is no sensible experience more common and more striking than that of motion. If it is motion that is most apparent in the sensible world, it is the distinction between essence and act-of-being that is most secret. What indeed is this distinction if not the translation, in abstract terms, of the ontological deficiency revealed in a being by the fact that it changes, that it is only a cause in so far as caused, only a being in so far as it is a possible realized, and that it is neither first in its own order nor last in the order of ends? On the other hand, precisely because the distinction between essence and existence translates the state of second cause, whatever its order of causality, into one and the same formula, it qualifies all the proofs. It is not a sixth way. It is rather the ultimate metaphysical implication of the other five, in the light of the Thomistic interpretation of the notion of being.

It is therefore natural to find this interpretation in one of Thomas's more deeply metaphysical writings, his short treatise *On Being and Essence*. In this work dating from the beginning of his career, he inaugurated his method of entrusting his most personal contributions to the patronage of others. When, in this treatise, he has made his distinction between essence and existence, which we have dealt with above,[86] St. Thomas continues as follows: "Whatever is proper to anything is either caused by the principles of its nature, as, for example, the aptitude for laughing in man, or comes to it by some extrinsic principle, as the light that is in the air under the influence of the sun. Now it cannot be that the act-of-being (*ipsum esse*) is caused by the very form or quiddity of the thing, caused, I say, as by an efficient cause, for then a thing would itself be the cause of itself, a thing would itself bring itself into existence, which is impossible. It is necessary, therefore, that everything whose act-of-being is other than its nature should have its act-of-being from another. And as whatever exists by another can be reduced to what is by itself as to its first cause, there must be one thing that is the cause by which all things exist, because it alone is the act-of-being. Otherwise we should have to go to infinity in causes, for anything that is not act-of-being only has a cause which makes it exist, as has been said."[87]

Contrary to what we ourselves have once believed, this development is not intended by Thomas Aquinas to be a proof of the existence of God. It is not presented as such in *On Being and Essence*. Nor is it mentioned, in either one of the two *Summae,* as a supplementary way to the conclusion that there is a God. If one considers the problem closely enough, the reason why it should be so becomes apparent. An essential feature of a Thomistic way to the knowledge of the existence of God is that it should start from sense experience. Now, to the best of our knowledge, Thomas Aquinas has never attempted such a demonstration. Nor does one see how the thing could be done. The distinction of essence and existence presupposes the very notion of the pure act of being which its alleged demonstrations are supposed to justify. What here is at stake is the metaphysical intuition of the first principle, which is the notion of being. At this highest metaphysical level, it is not a question of proof, but of sight.

The large number of Christian philosophers and theologians, even among the so-called Thomists, who have rejected the distinction of essence and existence understood in its Thomistic meaning, clearly shows that no demonstration is here at stake. Above all, the careful procedure of Thomas Aquinas himself in handling the notion invites us to consider it less as the conclusion of some dialectical argument than as a prime source of intelligibility whose existence is known by the very light it sheds upon all the problems of metaphysics. So Thomas Aquinas will not attempt to prove it, but we shall see him progressively leading us to it, starting from the very demonstrations of the existence of God, as if it were for him a question of purifying our sight until it becomes able to stand the light of the first principle.

In the present problem, the distinction of essence and existence throws into relief the existential nature both of the effect whose cause is being sought and of the very cause which explains it. This cause is a God whose essence is the very act-of-being *Deus cujus essentia est ipsummet esse suum.* A God of whom some go so far as to say that He has no essence or quiddity since He is all act-of-being: *non habet quidditatem vel essentiam, quia essentia sua non est aliud quam esse suum.*[88] Otherwise put, God is actual being pure and simple, without any addition, distinct from any other existing thing because of His very purity, as a color existing in its pure state would differ from broken colors because of its purity and separation.[89] Such is the God whom the proofs of St. Thomas strive for, but whom we only approach by meditation on that same Being whose existence they conclusively demonstrate.

This last aspect of the God of St. Thomas remains perhaps the least known by his interpreters. One hesitates between saying that it escapes them so often although it marks the point at which St. Thomas and Aristotle are farthest apart or that it escapes them for this very reason.

In positing his immovable First Mover as a thinking thought, Aristotle had guaranteed the purity of the highest act by enclosing it in the splendor of divine isolation. Aristotle's God is not merely "separated" as ontologically distinct from everything else, but as ontologically absent from anything else. The only kind of presence He can fittingly have for things is the desire which they experience for Him and which moves them towards Him. Now this desire for God is their desire. It is of the being experiencing it, not of the being who is its term. It is quite otherwise in St. Thomas's world. The relation of things to God is defined there in the order of existence. This is why the dependence of things upon their principle attains there a depth that cannot be expressed either in Aristotle's language or Plato's. It is in its very existence that the universe of St. Thomas is a religious universe.

To formulate the relation of the world to God in the language of Plato, we must have recourse to the relations between image and model. St. Augustine normally used the same terminology and so too did St. Bonaventure and the thirteenth-century Augustinians. For all of these, the sensible world is a mirror in which reflections of God are to be found— a collection of images for an illustrated theology. The universe itself is indeed that. Christian spirituality could not consent to part with its divine "speculations" in the mirror of nature, so splendidly rationalized by St. Bonaventure, so divinely lived by St. Francis of Assisi. The question, then, is to know whether this kind of meditation gives an insight into the deepest metaphysical resemblance of things to God. The reply to this has to be affirmative, at least if the contemplation of God in the *being* of things penetrates to their *act-of-being*. It is true that things are good in so far as they are. It is true that they are beautiful. It is true that they are causes and that they have marvellous energy and fecundity in whatever they do. In all this they imitate God and represent Him. But the most marvellous of all the things a being can do is *to be*. Things exist, and this is what is most profound in them because in this they best imitate their cause. Herein lies the true meaning of the proofs for the existence of God—we come to *Him Who Is* by starting with those objects of which it can be said that they *are*. "Things which exist by God resemble Him, in so far as they are beings, as the first and universal principle of all that *is*." [90]

CHAPTER IV

It is hardly credible that the existential nature of the problem of the existence of God ever had to be discovered. It is even less credible that Christian theologians had to discover the existential nature of the Christian God. Was it not enough to open the Scriptures in order to discover it there? When Moses wished to know the name of God in order to reveal it to the Jewish people, he directly addressed God Himself and said to Him: "Lo! I go to the children of Israel, and I shall say to them: the God of your fathers sends me to you. If they ask me His name, what shall I say to them?" And God said to Moses: "I Am Who Am." And He added: "Thus will you reply to the children of Israel: *He Who Is* sends me to you." (Exod., III, 13-14) Since God Himself called Himself *I am*, or *Who is*, as the name properly belonging to Him,[1] how could Christians have ever been ignorant that their God was the supremely existing being?

We do not say that they did not know this. Indeed, everyone believed it, many struggled to understand it, and a certain number before St. Thomas carried the interpretation even to the level of metaphysics. Certainly the identification of God and Being is the common possession of Christian philosophers as Christian.[2] But the agreement of Christians upon this point did not prevent philosophers from being divided on the interpretation of the notion of being. Holy Scripture provides no treatise on metaphysics. The first Christians who wanted to think philosophically about the content of their faith had at their disposal only the philosophical techniques elaborated by the Greeks for altogether different ends. The history of Christian philosophy is in large measure that of a religion becoming progressively conscious of philosophical notions which as a religion it could, strictly speaking, do without. But she recognized more and more clearly that these notions were capable of defining the philosophy of those faithful who wished to have one. It is easy to understand how Christian thinkers had to struggle a long time in order to clarify the meaning of this basic text of *Exodus*. It was only gradually that a metaphysical interpretation was found. The mere inspection of the two distinct notions of being which turn up in the study of the problem of the existence of God is enough to show us this. History permits us to make a living analysis by comparing the essentialist interpretation of the text of *Exodus*, at which St. Augustine finally stopped, with the existential interpretation of the same text developed by St. Thomas Aquinas.

St. Augustine was so sure that the God of *Exodus* was Plato's being that he wondered how to explain the coincidence without admitting that

Plato had somehow or other known *Exodus:* "But what makes me almost subscribe to the idea that Plato was not completely ignorant of the Old Testament is that when an Angel conveys the words of God to the holy man Moses, who asks the name of the one who is ordering him to proceed to the deliverance of the Hebrew people, the reply is this: *'I am Who am; and you are to say to the children of Israel: it is He Who is who has sent me to you.'* As if, in comparison with him who truly is because he is immovable, he who has been made movable did not exist. Now Plato was intensely convinced of this and he took great care to say so." [3] Clearly, the Being of *Exodus* is here conceived as the immovable entity of Plato. Reading these lines, we are bound to suspect that the accord at which Augustine marvels conceals a little confusion.

Such, indeed, was St. Augustine's notion of God and being. "The first and highest being is that which is entirely immovable, and which can say by full right: *'I am Who Am; and you will tell them, He Who is has sent me to you.'* " [4] But Augustine had a very deep sense of the difficulty of the problem, and he never, perhaps, expressed his final thought on this question better than in a homily on the Gospel of St. John. It is better to cite the entire text because we can sense in it both the depth of Augustine's Christian feeling and the Platonic limits of his notion of being.

"Nevertheless, pay good attention to the words spoken here by Our Lord, Jesus Christ: *if you do not believe that I am, you will die in your sins* (John, VIII, 24). What is this: *si non credideritis quia ego sum? I am,* what? There is nothing added; and because there is nothing added, his word embarrasses us. We were waiting for him to say what he was, yet he did not say it. What did we think he was going to say? Perhaps, *if you do not believe that I am the* Christ; *if you do not believe that I am,* the Son of God; *if you do not believe that I am* the Word of the Father; *if you do not believe that I am* the author of the world; *if you do not believe that I am* the former and reformer of man, his creator and recreator, he who made him and remade him; *if you do not believe that I am* that, *you will die in your sins.* This *I am,* he says he is, is embarrassing. For God also had said to Moses: *I am Who Am.* Who can say rightly what is this *I am?* By his angel, God sent his servant Moses to deliver his people from Egypt (you have read what I am saying here, and you knew it, but I am recalling it to you); God was sending him trembling, reluctant but obedient. In order to find some excuse Moses said to God who, he knew, was speaking to him through the angel: if the people ask me, who then is the God who sent thee? What shall I reply? And the Lord said to him: *I am who am;* then he repeated: *it is He Who Is who has sent me to you.* Here, again, he did not say: *I am* God; or *I am* the maker of the world; or *I am* the creator of all things; or again, *I am* the propagator of this very people who must be liberated; but he only said this: *I am Who Am;* then, *you will say to the children of Israel, He Who Is.* He did not add: *He Who Is* your God; *He Who Is* the God of your fathers; but he only said this: *He Who Is sent me to you.* Perhaps it was difficult for Moses, even as it is difficult for us too—and even more difficult for us—to understand these words: *I am Who Am;* and, *He Who Is, has sent me to you.* Moreover, even if Moses understood them, how could they to whom God was sending him have understood them? God has then postponed what man could not understand and added what he could understand. This he added, indeed, when he said: *I am the God of Abraham, and the God of Isaac, and the God of Jacob* (Exod., III, 13-15). This, you can understand; but what thought can comprehend *I am?"*

Let us pause here briefly to greet in passing this first meeting, in God's own words, between the God of Abraham, of Isaac and of Jacob and the God of the philosophers and scholars. Augustine knows very well that it is the same God. No more than the people of Israel can he hesitate over the identity of the living God of Scripture. But it is the *Qui est* that intrigues him, for God no more explained it to Moses than to Augustine or to us, as if, having revealed to men the truth that saves, He had reserved the understanding of it to the patient efforts of the metaphysicians. However, faithful to the teaching of the "interior master," [5] Augustine is going to pray here to God Himself to enlighten him on the meaning of His words.

"I am going to speak, now, to Our Lord Jesus Christ. I am going to speak to him and he will hear me. For I believe that he is present; I do not doubt it in the least, since He said: *Behold I am with you even to the consummation of the world* (Matt., XXVIII, 20). O Lord, our God, what have you said: *If you do not believe that I am?* Indeed, of all you have made, what is there that is not? The heavens, are they not? The earth, is it not? And the things that are on the earth and in the heavens, are they not? And the very man to whom you are speaking, is he not? If they are, if all these things you have made are, what then is being itself—*ipsum esse*—which you reserved for yourself as something proper to you, and which you have not given to others, in order to be the only one to exist? Must we then understand: *I am Who Am,* as if the rest were not? And how are we to understand the *If you do not believe that I am?* Those who understood it, then, were they not? Even if they were sinners they were men. What are we to do? Let being itself —*ipsum esse*—say what it is; let it speak it to the heart; let it say it within; let it speak it within; let the interior man understand it; let thought understand that to be truly is, to be always in the same way."

Nothing could be clearer than this statement: *vere esse est enim semper eodem modo esse . . .* To identify thus the true being (*vere esse*) which

God is with "immovable being" is to assimilate the *Sum* of *Exodus* to the οὐσία of Platonism. Here we are again face to face with the same difficulty we had when it was a question of translating this term in the dialogues of Plato. The Latin equivalent of οὐσία is *essentia* and it seems, certainly, that Augustine identified in his mind the God of Abraham, of Isaac and of Jacob with that alone which, being immovable, can be called *essentia* in all the fullness of the term. How would it be otherwise since to be is "to be immovable"? Hence this formal statement of the *De Trinitate:* "Perhaps it ought to be said that God alone is *essentia*. For he alone truly is, because he is immovable, and it is this he declared for Moses his servant when he said *I am Who Am* and *you will tell them that it is He Who Is who has sent me to you* (*Exod.*, III, 14)."[7] Hence the divine name of names, *Sum,* is best translated into philosophical language by the abstract term *essence* which itself denotes the immutability of *"that which is."*

We see here the source of that doctrine of divine *essentialitas* which was later through St. Anselm to influence so profoundly the theology of Richard of Saint-Victor, Alexander of Hales and St. Bonaventure. To pass from this philosophical interpretation of the Text of *Exodus* to the one St. Thomas was going to propose, it was necessary to bridge the gap between being of essence and being of existence. We have seen how St. Thomas's proofs for the existence of God have prepared that bridge. It only remains to recognize the proper nature of the God whose existence they have demonstrated, that is, to recognize Him as the supreme act of being.

There is nothing more convincing in this regard than the order followed by the *Summa Theologiae*. Knowing that a thing is, one has only to ask in what way it is, in order to know what it is. Indeed, and we shall have to say why, we do not know what God is, but only what He is not. The only conceivable manner of circumscribing His nature is therefore to remove successively from our notion of Him all the modes of existing which cannot be His. Now it is remarkable that the first of the ways of being which St. Thomas eliminates as incompatible with the notion of God is composition. He does this by establishing at the outset that God is simple, not in the hope of giving us a positive concept of a simplicity like God's but to make us conceive of Him, at least negatively, as the being free from all composition whatsoever. What can we hope to find at the end of the analysis announced if not *being,* free from all that is not being? To progress towards this conclusion will be to do no more than to make evident a notion virtually included in the proofs for the existence of God.

In following St. Thomas's analysis it is well to fix the attention at least as much on the reasons for which all compositions are eliminated one after the other as on the nature itself of the compositions thus eliminated. Let us begin with the grossest among them, that of conceiving of God as a body. To eliminate body from the notion of God, it is enough to look again at the principal proofs of His existence. God is the first immovable mover; now no body moves unless it is moved; God is therefore not a body. God is the first being, and is therefore being in act, *par excellence;* now all body is continuous and, as such, divisible to infinity; all body is therefore divisible in potency; it is not being, in pure act; hence, it is not God. The existence of God has already been shown to be the most noble of *beings;* now the soul is more noble than the body; it is impossible therefore that God is a body.[8] Clearly, the principle dominating these various arguments is one and the same. In each case, it is a question of establishing that whatever is incompatible with the pure actuality of being is incompatible with the notion of God.[9]

According to this principle, we must deny that God is composed of matter and form, for matter is what is in potency, and since God is pure act, without any mixture of potency, it is impossible that He is composed of matter and form.[10] This second conclusion immediately entails a third. According to our definition,[11] essence is only substance as intelligible through the concept of its quiddity and susceptible of definition. Thus understood, essence expresses, before anything else, the form or nature of substance. It includes whatever falls under the definition of species, and only this. For example, the essence of man is *humanitas*, which notion covers everything by which man is man—a reasoning animal composed of soul and body. It is to be noted, however, that essence embraces only that part of the substance which all substances of the same species have in common and not what each substance possesses as an individual. It is of the essence of humanity that every man should have a body. But the notion of humanity does not include the very body, the members, the flesh, the particular bones belonging to the substance of a given man. All these individual determinations belong to the notion of man since no man can exist without them. Thus, man (*homo*) is said to designate the complete substance taken with all the specific and individual determinations which render it capable of existing, whereas humanity designates the essence or formal part of the substance, man. It is the element which defines man in general. From this analysis, it follows that in all substances composed of matter and form, substance and essence do not exactly coincide. Since there is more in the substance man than in the essence humanity, man and humanity are not wholly identical. Now we have said that God is not composed of matter and form. There cannot, then, be in Him any distinction between essence on the one hand and substance or nature on the other. We can say that man is man in virtue of his humanity but not that God is God in virtue of His deity. God (*Deus*) and deity (*deitas*) and anything else that can be attributed to God by way of predication are all one and the same thing.[12]

This last formula enables us to recognize at once the opponents whom St. Thomas had in mind in this discussion and at the same time to understand the exact meaning of his position. At the point of his analysis just reached, St. Thomas has not yet arrived at the order of existence, the ultimate term towards which he is tending. Thus far it is only a question of a notion of God which does not go beyond substantial being. What he is asking himself is simply whether on this level which is not yet that of the act of being, it is possible to distinguish God's substance (what God is) from His essence (that by which He is). In this case, that by which God is God, is called His deity and the problem is reduced to asking whether God (*Deus*) is distinct from His *deitas* or identical with it.[13]

This thesis came from a Platonism different from St. Augustine's, that of Boethius. It is a rather curious fact that Plato's thought should have exercised so profound an influence on the thought of the Middle Ages which knew almost nothing of his works. But his thought reached the Middle Ages through several schools which he had directly or indirectly influenced. We have already met the Platonism of St. Augustine and its derivatives, and we shall be meeting the Platonism of Dionysius the Areopagite and its derivatives. But we must also take into account that of Alfarabi, Avicenna and their disciples, as well as that which falls under examination here, the Platonism of Boethius, by no means the least important.

There have then been several forms of Platonism, not just one, behind medieval philosophies, and it is important to know how to distinguish them. But it is important also to remember that by their relationship to a common origin, these various Platonisms have constantly tended to reinforce one another, to unite, and sometimes even to become confused. The Platonic current is like a river issuing from St. Augustine, being enlarged by the tributary from Boethius in the sixth century, from Dionysius, Scotus Erigena in the ninth century, from Avicenna and the *Book of Causes* in the twelfth century. Other less important tributaries like Hermes Tresmegistus, Macrobius and Apuleius, for example, can be cited, as well as the translation of the *Timaeus* by Chalcidius, with its commentary, the only fragment of Plato himself which was, if not known, at least used during the high Middle Ages. Thus St. Thomas found himself face to face with many allied forms of Platonism to which he had sometimes to adjust himself, which he had sometimes openly to combat, and against which he had always to be on guard.

In the case in question, the root common to the Platonism of Boethius and Augustine is the ontology which reduces existence to being and conceives of being as *essentia*. But this principle is developed differently by Boethius than by St. Augustine. Boethius seems to have begun with the celebrated remark made by Aristotle, as it were in passing, which was to give rise to such numerous commentaries: "what man is is different from that fact that he is" (II *Anal.*, II, 7, 92 b 10-11). This remark could have introduced, *a propos* of a question of logic, the frequently discussed problem of the relation between essence and existence. Aristotle himself never raised the problem, for the simple reason that, as his faithful commentator Averroes very well saw, he never made the distinction between what substances are and the fact that they are. Aristotle is not saying in this passage that the essence of a substance is distinct from its existence, but simply that one cannot conclude from the mere definition of substance that it exists.

When in his turn Boethius took up the problem, he raised it to the plane of metaphysics. The very obscurity of his terse definitions tended to focus the attention of his commentators upon them.[19] Boethius distinguished between being and what is: *diversum est esse et id quod est.*[15] But his distinction between *esse* and *id quod est* does not mark a distinction between essence and actual existence.[16] It designates, rather, the distinction between the thing itself that is (*id quod est*) and the form (*esse*) whereby it is that which it is. For this reason, the form (*esse*) of a substance is also called its *quo est:* that by which the substance is. Such a form is simple by definition; *ipsum esse nihil aliud praeter se habet admixtum;*[17] on the contrary, the *quod est* only exists in so far as it is informed by the form that gives it being: *quod est, accepta essendi forma est atque consistit.*[18]

To comment on Boethius through Gilbert de la Porrée is certainly to explain *obscurum per obscurius.* However his modern commentators interpret Gilbert himself, they agree that, in his texts, "one must not translate *essentia* by essence. This term evokes, in its true meaning, a distinction, within being itself (essence and existence), which did not as yet exist in Latin thought. *Esse,* too, is taken as a form. *Esse* and *essentia* are in this sense equivalents. God's *essentia* is the *esse* of all being and, at the same time, form *par excellence.*" [19] Since it is here a question of a basic metaphysical position[20] it was to dominate even the problem raised by the notion of God. Indeed, Gilbert conceived God, the form of all being, as Himself defined by a form determining our notion of Him as God. Thought, therefore, would conceive of this *quod est,* which God is, as determined to being by the form *divinitas.* It is impossible to think that Gilbert conceived of God as composed of two really distinct elements, God (*Deus*) and divinity (*divinitas*), but he seems at least to have admitted that as far as we are concerned, God can only be conceived as a *quod est* informed by a *quo est,* which is His divinity.[21] The influence of this doctrine has been considerable. Accepted or amended by some, condemned by others, it has left its traces even upon those who rejected it most energetically. This is hardly surprising, because philosophers frequently reject consequences whose principles they still accept. In order to set aside Gilbert's doctrine, it was necessary to pass beyond the realism of *essentia* to that of existence. In brief, it was necessary to bring about that philosophical reform which we associate with the name of St. Thomas Aquinas.

Put in terms of Thomistic philosophy, the distinction between *Deus* and *divinitas* was equivalent to conceiving of the divine being as a kind of substance determined to be such by an essence which would be the essence of divinity. It may be that this conclusion is practically inevitable so long as one seeks to circumscribe the divine being by the conceptual definition of an essence. Even if he affirms, as does Gilbert, that God is His divinity, whoever seeks to define such an essence can only do so by conceiving of God as being God by the very *divinitas* that He is. This is to reintroduce into Him, at least in what concerns thought, a distinction between potency and act, incompatible with the pure actuality of the divine being.[22] In order to overcome this difficulty we must, with St. Thomas, pass beyond the identification of God's substance with his essence and posit the identity of his essence with His very act-of-being. What distinguishes his position from that of the followers of Gilbert is not that it gives testimony of a more lively sense of the divine simplicity. All Christian theologians know that God is absolutely simple; and they say so, but not in the same way. The lesson St. Thomas gives us here is that we cannot say this properly if we remain on the plane of substance and essence, which are objects of quidditative concepts. The divine simplicity is perfect because it is the simplicity of pure act. We cannot define it; we can only affirm it by an act of the judging faculty.

In order to understand the position of St. Thomas on this decisive point, we must first remember the privileged role he attributes to *esse* in the structure of the real. For him each thing has its own act-of-being. Let us say, rather, there is no real apart from distinct acts of existing, by virtue of each of which a distinct thing exists. We must, then, posit as a fundamental principle that everything is, in virtue of the act of existing proper to it: *unumquodque est per suum esse*. Since it is here a question of a principle, we can be certain that its scope extends even to God. It would perhaps be better to say that it is the very being of God which is at the basis of the principle. For God is, as the third proof for His existence shows, the necessary being. He is therefore an act of existing of such a kind that His existence is necessary. This is what is meant by being necessary *per se*. To posit God in this way is to affirm an act of existing which needs no cause of its own existence. Such would not be the case were His essence distinguished, in so far as it is, from His existence. If, indeed, the essence of God determined in any degree this act of existing, the latter would no longer be necessary. God is, therefore, the act-of-being that He is. Such is the meaning of the expression: *Deus est suum esse*.[23] Like whatever exists, God is by His own act-of-being; but, in His case alone, we have to say that *what* His being is is nothing else than that by which He exists, namely, the pure act of existing.

Any one of the proofs for the existence of God would lead to the same conclusion precisely because they all set out from contingent existences in order to reach the first *esse* which causes them. As St. Thomas himself says of this thesis: it can be shown in many ways. God is the first cause; He has therefore no cause; now God would have a cause if His essence were distinct from His existence, because then it would not be enough, in order to exist, to be what He is. It is therefore impossible that God's essence be anything other than His act-of-being.

We can begin too, if it seems preferable, from the fact that God is act, free from any potency. Then the question is: What is most actual in all given reality? According to our analysis of the metaphysical structure of the concrete the answer must be: The act-of-being, because to be is the actuality of all form, or nature. Actually to be good is to be a good being which exists. Humanity only has actual reality in an actually existing man. Let us suppose, therefore, that the essence of God were distinct from His existence. The divine act of existing would then be the act of the divine essence. This latter would therefore be, with regard to God's *esse,* as potency to act. Now God is pure act; therefore, His essence must be his very act-of-being.

It is possible also to proceed even more directly, starting from God posited as being. To say that God's essence is not His *esse* would be to say that *what* God is has *esse* but is not itself *esse.* Now what has the act-of-being but is not the act-of-being is only by participation. Since, as we have just seen, God is His essence or His very nature,[24] He is not by participation. This is, moreover, what we mean when we call Him the first being. Thus God is His essence, and His essence is the act itself of being; He is, therefore, not only His essence but His act-of-being.[25]

Such is the God whom the five proofs of St. Thomas seek and finally attain by five different ways. The question here was incontestably a philosophical one. Historically located, this conclusion appears to be the result of an effort extending over several centuries to attain the very root of being, which was then to become identified with the act-of-being. Going beyond the Platonic ontology of essence and the Aristotelian ontology of substance, St. Thomas in one long stride also went beyond both the first substance of Aristotle and the God *essentia* of St. Augustine and his disciples. St. Thomas never says that God has no essence.[26] If we think of his many opportunities to say this, we must presume that he had good reasons for avoiding the expression. The simplest reason is probably that, since we only know beings whose essence is not their act-of-being, it is impossible for us to conceive of a being without essence. Also, in the case of God, we conceive less of an act-of-being without essence than of an essence which, by passing as it were to its limit, comes at length to be one with its own act-of-being.[27] Moreover, the case is similar with all the attributes of God in the doctrine of St. Thomas. Just as we do not say that

God has no wisdom, but that His wisdom is His own being, so we do not say that He has no essence but that His essence is His act-of-being.[28] To grasp in one glance the extent of St. Thomas's reform on the plane of natural theology, we have only to measure the distance separating the God *Essentia* of St. Augustine from the God of St. Thomas whose *essentia* is, as it were, absorbed by its *Esse*.

However, this pure act-of-being which St. Thomas the philosopher met at the end of metaphysics, St. Thomas the theologian had met too in Holy Scripture. It was no longer the conclusion of rational dialectic but a revelation from God Himself to all men that they might accept it by faith. There is no doubt that St. Thomas thought that God had revealed to men that His essence was to exist. St. Thomas is not lavish with epithets. Never did a philosopher yield less frequently to the temptation to wax eloquent. Here, however, seeing these two beams of light so converging that they fused into each other, he was unable to withhold a word of admiration for the overwhelming truth blazing forth from their point of fusion. He saluted this truth with a title exalting it above all others: "God's essence is therefore His act-of-being. Now this sublime truth (*hanc autem sublimem veritatem*), God taught to Moses when Moses asked what to reply if the children of Israel should ask His name. (*Exod*. III, 13). And the Lord replied: I am Who Am. You may say this to the children of Israel: *He Who Is* has sent me to you. Thus He showed that His proper name is *Who Is*. Now every name is intended to signify the nature or essence of something. It remains then that the divine act-of-being itself (*ipsum divinum esse*) is the essence or nature of God." [29]

Let us note well that for St. Thomas this revelation of the identity of essence and existence in God was the equivalent of a revelation of the distinction between essence and existence in creatures. *Who Is* signifies: He Whose essence is to exist; *Who Is* is the proper name of God; consequently, the essence of anything that is not God is not to exist. We could, if we had to, make this simple inference by our reason. But we do not have to, the text is explicit: "It is impossible that the substance of any being other than the First Agent be its very act-of-being. Hence the name which *Exodus* (3:14) gives as the proper name of God, *Who Is*. It belongs properly to Him alone that His substance be nothing other than His act-of-being." [30]

These positions have two principal consequences. First, Thomistic existentialism concerned not merely natural theology, but theology in the strict sense. It is here indeed a question of a literal interpretation of the word of God. To appreciate the importance of what is at stake we have only to compare St. Thomas's interpretation of the text with St. Augustine's. When St. Augustine read the name of God, he understood "I am he who never changes." St. Thomas reading the same words understood them to mean "I am the pure act-of-being."

Whence, this second consequence, that no historian can consider St. Thomas's thinking to be a combination of distinct schools of thought. Neither the identity of essence and existence in God nor the distinction between essence and existence in creatures belongs to the *revelatum,* properly so-called, since neither of these truths is beyond the range of natural reason considered as a judging faculty. Both are, nevertheless, for St. Thomas part of the revealable, and even of the revealable which has been revealed. Nowhere, perhaps, can we see more clearly how complex is the economy of revelation, the act by which God makes Himself known to man, in the teaching of St. Thomas. St. Thomas was far from believing or having others believe that God had at one time revealed to Moses the twenty-second chapter of Book II of the *Summa Contra Gentiles.* If anyone should think this, it is not St. Thomas who is naïve. God has given us His name; it suffices that man believe it lest any false god afterwards seduce him. But the theology of the Christian Doctors is only revelation investigated by reason working in the light of faith. Time was necessary for reason to do its work. St. Augustine was on the right path; St. Thomas but followed the same road to its end. Everyone is free to imagine St. Thomas's genius as a living classification of the sciences. But those of us who do this will soon be at grips with this thorny problem: Is it St. Thomas the theologian who, reading in *Exodus* the identity of essence and existence in God, taught St. Thomas the philosopher the distinction between essence and existence in creatures? Or is it St. Thomas the philosopher who, pushing his analysis of the metaphysical structure of the concrete even as far as the distinction between essence and existence, taught St. Thomas the theologian that *He Who Is* in *Exodus* means the *Act-of-Being?* St. Thomas himself as a philosopher thought of these two propositions as the two sides of one and the same metaphysical thesis. And from the day he understood them, he always thought of them as being in Holy Scripture. The word of God is too profound for human reason to exhaust its meaning. But it is always the same meaning of the same word which the reason of the Doctors of the Church ever pursues to depths more and more profound. The genius of St. Thomas is one and his work is one. One cannot separate, without destroying its perfect balance what God has revealed to men from the meaning of what He has revealed.

This sublime truth is, for the historian at least, the key to the understanding of Thomism. His best interpreters have all seen this, and we need only repeat it after them. But each age repeats it in its own way, because new obstacles arise to obscure the meaning of the fundamental notion of existing. Today two distinct causes are moving concurrently in this direction. On the other hand, the permanent tendency of the human understanding to feed on quiddities inclines us to break up the unity of Thomism into a mosaic of essences. These, like the pieces in a jig-saw puzzle, are arranged side by side, powerless to communicate with one another.

On the other hand, the progress of historical studies reveals for us in ever-increasing number the doctrinal sources on which St. Thomas drew in order to construct his work. So much is this so, that his work is apt to appear more and more as a mosaic of borrowed fragments of whose heteroclite nature he seems to have been unaware.

Thomism, indeed, can appear as the emptiest or fullest of philosophies, as the most inconsistent of eclecticisms or the luckiest stroke of drilling ever attempted through the thickness of concrete reality, according as it is interpreted as a logic of abstract being or a metaphysic of the act-of-being. We must, then, be neither scandalized nor disturbed when some find fulness and light where others find but obscurity and emptiness. St. Thomas's philosophical work is above all else the first discovery, through human reason, of the *Ultima Thule* of metaphysics. It is difficult to reach it and almost as difficult to stay there. This, however, is what we must try to do in following, even to its final consequences, this sublime truth— *hanc sublimem veritatem*—whose light illumines the whole of Thomism.

At the beginning of this quest, let us provide ourselves with this formula, the fullest and clearest of all those which Thomas himself has provided: "Being (*esse*) is used in two senses. In the first it denotes the act-of-being (*actum essendi*). In the second it denotes the composition of the proposition made by the mind in joining a predicate to a subject. If we take being in the first sense, we cannot know what God's being is (*non possumus scire esse Dei*), any more than we can know His essence. But we can know that the proposition we form about God in saying 'God is' is true; and we know this from His effects." [31]

CHAPTER V

THE ATTRIBUTES OF GOD

A COMPLETE STUDY of the problems relative to God, once His existence has been demonstrated, should fall under three principle headings: first, the unity of the divine essence; secondly, the trinity of divine persons; thirdly, the effects produced by the divinity.[1] The second of these depends in no way upon philosophical knowledge; although man is not forbidden to apply his mind to this mystery, he cannot pretend, without destroying it as a mystery, to demonstrate it by means of reason. The Trinity is known to us by revelation alone. It eludes the grasp of human understanding.[2] Natural theology, then, could only examine two of these subjects, the being of God and the relationship between God and His effects.

It should be added that even in these two cases, the human reason cannot clarify everything. As we have said, it is not at home save in the order of the quiddity and of definition. To define an object is first of all to assign its genus (e.g., "animal"); to genus is added its specific difference (e.g., "rational animal"); finally, this specific difference can be further determined by individual differences (e.g., "Socrates.") Now in the case of God all definition is impossible. He can be named; but to give Him a name is not to define Him. In order to define Him we should have to assign Him a genus. Since God is called *Qui est*, He has no genus, because, if He had a genus, He would have an essence distinct from His act of being. Moreover, as has already been observed, if God had a genus, this genus would have to be determined by a difference not included in it. Now it is impossible to conceive of anything that is not something, and which, consequently, is not contained in being. Outside being there is only non-being, which is not a difference because it is nothing. Thus we cannot say that the essence of God belongs to the genus being; and, as we cannot assign Him any other essence, all definition of God is impossible.[3]

All this does not mean that we are reduced to complete silence. Failing to arrive at the essence of God, which has no quiddity distinct from the pure act of being, we can seek to determine what it is not. Rather than begin with an inaccessible essence and add to it positive differences which would make as know more and more about it, we can gather a more or less considerable number of negative differences which give us a more and more precise knowledge of what God is not.

It might be asked, perhaps, whether by this procedure we will arrive at true knowledge. The answer to this is: Yes. Certainly such knowledge is imperfect, but it is better than ignorance pure and simple. What is more, it eliminates a kind of positive pseudo-knowledge which pretends to say what the essence of God is but presents it as it cannot possibly be. But when we posit an unknown essence and distinguish it from an ever larger number of other essences, each negative difference determines with increasing precision the preceding difference and thus encircles ever more closely the outline of the central object. For example, to say that God is not an accident but a substance is to distinguish Him from all possible accidents. If we add then that God is not a body, we determine with more precision the place He occupies in the genus of substances. Thus, proceeding in orderly fashion and distinguishing God from all that is not God by negations of this kind, we come to a knowledge of His substance, not positive but true because we know Him as distinct from everything else.[4] Let us follow this path as far as it can lead us. It will be time enough to follow a new one when we have gone as far as this will take us.

I. THE KNOWLEDGE OF GOD BY WAY OF NEGATION

To make God known by way of negation is to show not how He is, but how He is not. Moreover, this is what we have already begun to do in establishing His perfect simplicity.[5] To say that God is absolutely simple, since He is the pure act of existing, is not to have a concept of such an act, but to deny Him, as we have seen, any composition whatsoever: composition of whole and parts as is found in bodies, that of form and matter, that of essence and substance, and finally that of essence and existence, which led us to affirm God as a being whose essence is to exist. Beginning from here, we can add to the divine simplicity a second attribute which follows necessarily from the first, His perfection.

Here again, it is impossible for us to conceive of a perfect being, but we must affirm God to be such, denying Him all imperfection. Moreover, this is what we do in affirming that God is perfect. Just as the judgment concludes that God exists, although for us the nature of His act of existing is inconceivable, so it concludes that God is perfect, although the nature of His perfection is beyond the reach of our reason. For us to eliminate all conceivable imperfections from the notion of God is to attribute to Him all conceivable perfection. Human reason can go no farther in its knowledge of the divine, but it should at least go thus far.

This being, from whom we remove all the imperfections of creatures, is not reduced to an abstract concept by our understanding of what is common to all things, as the universal concept of being would be. It is in some degree the meeting point and, as it were, the *locus metaphysicus* of all judgments of perfection. This need not be understood in the sense that being must be reduced to a certain degree of perfection, but rather, inversely, in the sense that all perfection consists in the possession of a certain degree of being.

Let us consider, for example, the perfection known as wisdom. To possess wisdom is *to be wise*. It is because man gains a degree of being in becoming wise that he gains also a degree of perfection. For a thing is said to be more noble or less noble, more perfect or less perfect in the measure in which it *is* a determined mode in the scale of perfection. Accordingly, if we suppose a pure act-of-being, this absolute act-of-being will also be absolute perfection, because perfection is only a certain way of being. Now we know a thing that is the absolute act-of-being; it is the same thing of which we have said that it is the act-of-being. What is its act-of-being, that is, that whose essence is only to exist, is necessarily absolute being as well. In other words, it has the power to be in its supreme degree. A white thing, indeed, cannot be perfectly white because it is not whiteness; it is white only in that it participates in whiteness, and its nature is perhaps such that it cannot participate in integral whiteness. But if there existed a whiteness in itself and whose being consisted precisely in being white, it would not be deficient in whiteness in any degree. Similarly for what concerns being. We have already proven that God is his act-of-being. He does not, accordingly, receive it. But we know that to be a thing imperfectly amounts to receiving it imperfectly. God, who is His act-of-being, is the pure being to whom no perfection is wanting. And since God possesses all perfections, He presents no defect. Just as everything is perfect in the measure in which it is, so also everything is imperfect in the measure in which, under a certain aspect, it is not. But since God is pure being, He is entirely free from non-being. Thus God has no defects and possesses all perfection; that is, He is universally perfect.[6]

How then does the illusion arise that in denying God a certain number of modes of being we lessen His degree of perfection? It arises from an equivocal understanding of the meaning of the words *only to be*. Unquestionably, what only exists is less perfect than what is living. But this is the way we reason about the being of essences which are not their very act-of-being. With them it is a question of imperfect and participated beings which increase in perfection as they increase in being (*secundum modum quo res habet esse est suus modus in nobilitate*), and we easily conceive consequently that what *is* the perfection of the body only is inferior to what *is*, in addition, the perfection of life. The expression *only to be* denotes, then, nothing else than an inferior mode of participation in being. But when we say of God that He is his act-of-being only, so that He is neither matter, nor body, nor substance, nor accident, we mean that He possesses absolute being, and we put aside whatever would be incompatible with the plenitude of His perfection.[7]

To be perfect is to lack no good. To say that God is perfect is equivalent to saying that He is the good. And since His perfection is only the purity of His act-of-being, it is as pure actuality of being that God is the good. To affirm in this way that God is good is not to imagine that He has some supplementary quality added to His being. To be is to be good. As Augustine said in the *De Doctrina Christiana* (Bk 1, ch. 32) and as St. Thomas repeats to strengthen his own thesis—*inquantum sumus, boni sumus.* However, let us carefully mark the transposition necessary before St. Augustine's thought can be integrated with Thomism. True, it makes the adjustment gracefully even as does the thought of Aristotle which St. Thomas places in the same crucible. Why, St. Thomas would ask, can we say with St. Augustine that we are good insofar as we are? Because the good and being are really identical. To be good is to be desirable. As Aristotle says in Book I of the *Nicomachaean Ethics,* Chapter I, the good is "what all desire." Now everything is desirable in so far as it is perfect, and everything is perfect in so far as it is in act. To be, is, therefore, to be perfect, and, consequently, to be good. We could hardly wish for more complete agreement among Aristotle, Augustine and Thomas Aquinas. However, St. Thomas does not bring his predecessors into accord by an arbitrary and eclectic conciliation. He transforms the thought of the two authorities he invokes. To make a total metamorphosis of their common ontology of essence, St. Thomas has only to transpose their theses from the tone of being to that of the act-of-being. He actually does this in so simple a phrase that there is danger of its profound meaning escaping us: "It is therefore clear that a thing is good in so far as it is being; indeed, *esse* (to be) is the actuality of everything, as can be seen from what has been said." [8] Thus the identity of the good and of being as taught by his predecessors, becomes for St. Thomas the identity of the good and the act-of-being.

Therefore, we must also transform the doctrine of the primacy of being over the good to that of the primacy of the act-of-being. Once again, and even more strikingly than in the preceding case, St. Thomas relies upon a Platonic text to effect this transformation, this time from the *De Causis,* Section IV: the first created thing is being (*primum rerum creatarum est esse*).[9] The primacy of the act-of-being is presented, indeed, as a primacy of being when placed in the order of knowledge. Being is the first intelligible object; we can, then, only conceive as good what we have first conceived as being.[10] But we must go farther. Since being (*ens*) is what has actual existence (*habens esse*), the noetic primacy of being over the good is only the conceptual expression of the ontological primacy of the act-of-being over the good. In order to be good, a thing first has to be. At the root of all good, there is a being which is the definite perfection of a certain act-of-being. If God is perfect, it is because for a being "which is its act-of-being, it is proper to be in the fullest sense of the term." [11] Similarly, if any given thing is good, it is because for a being which is a certain essence, it is proper to be good according to the degree of this essence. The case of God remains, however, unique, because we must here *identify* what is called good with what is called "to be." The same conclusion is also valid for all the particular perfections we should like to attribute to God. "Since indeed a thing is good in so far as it is perfect, and since the perfect goodness of God is His divine act-of-being itself (*ipsum divinum esse est ejus perfecta bonitas*), it is the same thing for God to be and to live, and to be wise, and to be happy, and, generally speaking, to be anything at all which seems to imply perfection and goodness. This amounts to saying that the total divine goodness is the divine act-of-being itself (*quasi tota divina bonitas sit ipsum divinum esse*).[12] In brief, for God to be good and for God to exist is one and the same thing.[13]

To affirm that God is perfection and the absolute good is at the same time to affirm that He is infinite. According to Aristotle, *Physics*, III, 6, all the ancient philosophers admitted that God was infinite. St. Thomas saw very well the sense in which they admitted it. Since they considered the world eternal, they could hardly regard the principle of a universe of infinite duration anything other than infinite. Their error concerned the kind of infinity belonging to a principle like this. Considering it to be material, they attributed to it a material infinity. Some of them posited an infinite body as the first principle of nature. And indeed matter is infinite in a sense, in that it is not of itself finite or determined. It is the form that determines it. On the other hand, the form is, of itself, not finite, or incompletely determined, since, common to the species, it is only determined by matter to be the form of a given singular thing. It is to be remarked, however, that the two cases are very different. Matter gains in perfection by being determined by form. Thus, non-finiteness is in it the mark of a real imperfection. On the contrary, form loses something of its natural amplitude when it is, so to speak, contacted within the dimensions of a given matter. The non-finiteness of form which is measured by the amplitude of its essence, is therefore rather a mark of perfection. Now in the case of God, what is at stake is the apex of actuality, since, as we have said, the act-of-being is the most formal of all that there is: *illud quod est maxime formale omnium, est ipsum esse*. God is absolute and substantial *esse*, who is neither received nor contracted by any essence, since He is *suum esse*. Clearly, pure and absolute Act-of-Being is infinite in the most positive sense of the term and by full right.[14]

If He is infinite it is impossible to conceive of the real where this God is not present. Otherwise there would be being exterior and foreign to his, constituting limits for him. This consequence, of the greatest importance in Thomistic metaphysics, affects both our notion of God and our notion of created nature. To deny that there is anything in which God is not present is to affirm that He is in all things. But we cannot affirm this without denying in turn that He is in beings as a part of their essence or as an accident of their substance. The principle by which we

affirm His omnipresence is that which we have from the proof for His existence: *Deus est ipsum esse per suam essentiam.* If we suppose that Being
(*ipsum esse*) acts as a cause, and we shall see later on that He does so in
the role of creator, His proper effect will be the being of creatures. This
effect God will not only cause at the time of their creation, but as long as
they last. These things exist in virtue of the divine act-of-being as the light
of the sun exists in virtue of the sun. While the sun shines, it is day; when
its light ceases to reach us, it is night. So, let the divine act-of-being cease
for a moment to keep things existing, and there is nothingness.

Hence the Thomistic universe even on the plane of metaphysics takes
on the appearance of a sacred universe. Other natural theologies, St.
Augustine's for example, are pleased to contemplate the footprints of
God in the order, in the rhythms and forms of creatures. St. Thomas
finds pleasure in all this too. These natural theologies go farther, and
they see this order, these rhythms and these forms conferring upon creatures the stability of being, and so the whole world is a mirror reflecting
to the eyes of reason the immutability of the divine being. St. Thomas
follows them here too, and then takes the lead and moves far beyond
them. The Thomistic universe is a world of beings, each one of which
gives testimony of God by the very fact that it is. All things therein
are not of the same rank. There are glorious beings like the angels, noble
ones like men, and more modest beings like beasts, plants and minerals.
Of all these beings there is not one which does not bear witness that God
is the supreme act-of-being. Like the highest of the angels, the humble
blade of grass bears this resemblance to God. The world of St. Thomas
is one where it is a marvellous thing to be born. It is a sacred world, one
impregnated to its every fibre with the intimate presence of a God whose
supreme actuality preserves it in its own actual existence.

To have once crossed the threshold of this enchanted universe is to
be no longer able to live in any other. The plain technical language in
which Thomas speaks of it has misled many of his readers about its
nature. Yet it is there that his simple formulas are beckoning us, formulas
besides which all others used before him seem suddenly so feeble. The
thought that all things were full of gods was beautiful indeed. Thales
of Miletus once thought this way, and Plato after him. But in this new
world of St. Thomas all things are filled with God. Or better, perhaps,
God is the act-of-being of all that exists, not in this sense that He is
their essence, but in that He is their cause, since all acts-of-being only
exist by His: *Deus est esse omnium, non essentiale, sed causale.*[15] Or to
put it in another way with St. Thomas, returning simply to the conclusion of our analysis of being:[16] "As long as one thing is, God must be
present in it in that it is. Now to be is that which is most intimate in
each thing, and it is that which is most profound in it, because the act-

of-being is formal with respect to all that there is in it. God must, therefore, be in all things, and that intimately: *unde oportet quod Deus sit
in omnibus rebus et intime.*" [17]

God is, therefore, everywhere, that is, in all places. This is a time-
worn phrase, which is often little more than a pious statement. There,
however, in its Thomistic context, it takes on a significance which gives
substance to piety. To be in all places means to be the act-of-existing of
whatever exists in place.[18] It is perhaps even better to say that God is
present in all conceivable ways of being present. Because His presence
impregnates each being in its very act of existing, root of all other acts,
God is in all things by His essence, as the *Esse* causing their *esse.* For
the same reason He is in them by His presence, for what has no existence
except from Him is naked and open to His eyes. And for the same
reason again, He is in them by His power, for nothing acts save in so
far as it is, and since God is the cause of the being of each thing, He
is the cause too of its actions or operations.[19] It pertains to God, then,
to be in all things by His essence, by His presence and by His power,
because He is there by Himself (*per se*) in virtue of the fact that He
is the pure act-of-being.

We come now to that divine attribute which St. Augustine so rightly
emphasized but which no one before St. Thomas really grasped—the
divine immutability. To say that God is immovable was, for St. Augustine,
to have reached the ultimate hidden depths of the divine nature. For St.
Thomas there is something still more ultimate, the very reason for this
immutability. To change is to pass from potency to act; now God is
pure act; He can, accordingly, in no way change.[20] We have met this
already in proving God's existence as first immovable mover. To deny
that He is subject to movement is to affirm His complete immutability.[21]
Completely immovable, God is, by the same token, eternal. Once more,
let us avoid trying to conceive as an essence what an eternal act-of-being
must be. The only mode of existing which we know is that proper to
beings living in time. Theirs is a mode of existing in which an after
continually replaces a before. All we can do is deny that God's act-of-being admits of a before or after. This has to be the case because God is
immovable and because His being undergoes no succession. To say that
a duration admits of no succession is to affirm that it has no terminus,
whether beginning or end. It is to posit it as doubly *interminable.* But it
is at the same time to affirm that it is not truly what we call a duration,
since it is without succession. Eternity is all at once (*tota simul
existens*).[22] This eternity is the stability of the very act-of-being which
is God. And since God is His essence, He is His eternity.[23]

The simplest way of summarizing what precedes is to say that God
is one, for what we have done thus far amounts to denying any multiplicity in His essence. Like the good, the one is only *being* itself under

one of its aspects. This time it is no longer being in so far as desirable, it is being as undivided. Indeed, a being divided is no longer the being it was; the result is two beings, each of which is one. We cannot speak of *one being* save where there is a *being one*. As St. Thomas puts it so energetically, *unumquodque, sicut custodit suum esse, ita custodit suam unitatem,* just as each thing preserves its being, so does it preserve its unity.[24]

Does this mean that the two terms, *one* and *being* can be indiscriminately used, one for the other? Not at all! It is the same in the case of the one as in that of the good. It is not the one that exists; it is being that is one, even as it is being that is true and beautiful. These properties, often called the *transcendentals* have no meaning or reality outside being, which affirms them in affirming itself. Thus it is not meaningless to say that "being is one." Our reason adds something to its notion of being in conceiving of it as undivided, that is, as one.[25] It is the same with our notion of God. To say that God is one is to say that He is the being that He is. Not only is He this, but He is this pre-eminently, since He is His own nature, His own essence, or rather His own act-of-being. If *the one* is only undivided being, what is supremely being is also supremely one and supremely undivided. Now God is supremely being, for He is *esse* itself, pure and simple, without any other qualification of nature or essence added in order to determine it. And God is also supremely undivided, since the purity of His act-of-being makes Him perfectly simple. It is therefore quite clear that God is one.[26]

2. THE KNOWLEDGE OF GOD BY WAY OF ANALOGY

The preceding conclusions really amount to a series of negative judgments. An absolutely simple being, one without any conceivable essence apart from its act-of-being is not an object falling within the range of human understanding. Further, there is not even hope of ever coming to this simple being through the imagination. There is here an essential disproportion between the understanding and its object with nothing, save God Himself in another life and for man in another state, can make proportionate. In his present state man draws his concepts from sensible knowledge. Beginning from sensible knowledge it is impossible to come to the pure being of God; and it would be necessary to do just this in order to achieve positive knowledge of God. But sensible things are effects of God. We can use them to seek Him indirectly as their cause. We have done this in proving His existence by starting from the sensible world. We ought also to be able to use it in order to prove, not that He is, but what He is.[27] The problem here presented is to know whether, in launching into this second way, we can hope to know anything more about Him than what He is not.

To describe the nature of God is to attribute perfections to Him and, consequently, to give Him various names. It is to call Him good and wise and powerful, and so on. The general principle governing these attributions is that God, the first cause, ought to possess in an eminent degree all the perfections to be found in His creatures. The names denoting these perfections must be fitting. But they are only fitting in a certain sense, because it is a matter of transferring them from the creature to the creator. This transference makes of them metaphors in the proper sense of the term, and these metaphors are doubly deficient. For one thing, they designate the being of God by means of names intended to designate an infinitely different way of being, that of created things. Again, names which we use to designate an object are woven into our very manner of conceiving that object. The natural objects of our understanding are corporal substances, composed of matter and form, each of which is a complex *quod est* determined by a simple *quo est* which is its form. The substance exists, but it is complex, whereas God is simple. The form is simple, but it does not exist, whereas God exists. In our human experience we have no example of a simple act-of-being; so much so, that all the names transferred from creatures to God only apply to Him in a sense which eludes us. Let us take, for example, goodness and the good. A good is a substance which exists, and God also exists; but a good is a concrete substance which can be broken up for analysis into matter and form, essence and existence, which is not at all the case with God. As for goodness, it is a *quo est,* that by which a good is good; but it is not a substance, whereas God is supremely subsistent. In brief, the names of such perfections denote something belonging to God, the supremely perfect being, but the manner in which these perfections belong to him escapes us, even as does the divine act-of-being which they are.[28]

How are we to characterize the nature and range of so deficient a knowledge of God? Since we wish to speak of Him as cause of creatures, the whole problem bears on the degree of resemblance to God we can attribute to His effects. But it is a question of effects much inferior to their cause. God does not bring forth creatures as a man engenders a man. A man, who has been engendered, possesses the same nature and bears with due right the same name as the one who engendered him (a child is called a man in the same way as the father). But the effects created by God are not one with Him either in name or in nature. Although here the effect is most deficient in relation to its cause, the case is not unique. Even in nature, certain efficient causes produce effects of an order specifically inferior to themselves. Since they produce them, these causes must in some way contain these effects, but they contain them in another manner and under another form. Thus, for example, solar energy causes at the same time terrestrial heat, drought and many other effects. We do not, however, call this energy heat or drought, but it is their cause. Because it is their cause, and proceeding from its effects, we say that the sun is a hot body. Causes of this kind are called *equivocal* causes, and their order of perfections transcends that of their effects.[29]

It is precisely as equivocal cause that God contains the effects He creates and that, consequently, their perfections can be attributed to Him.[30] We know that they are in Him but we do not know how. All we know is that in Him they are what He is and as He is. Thus nothing can be said univocally of God and His creatures. Their perfections and various efficacies are first contained in the one and simple perfection of God. What is more, what they possess in virtue of essences distinct from their existences is first of all in God by virtue of His pure act-of-being. As St. Thomas says, *nihil est in Deo quod non sit ipsum esse divinum:* whatever is in God is the very divine being itself.[31] Now there seems to be no conceivable mean between the univocal and the equivocal. The conclusion is therefore inevitable that all we say about God by starting from his creatures is equivocal; and this, from the point of view of natural theology, is somewhat discouraging.

St. Thomas has altered this conclusion, as we shall see, although perhaps not so radically as is commonly thought. He seems never to have said that the names we give are not equivocal, but only that they are not altogether equivocal. When different things bear by chance the same name, they are purely equivocal. Their common name implies no real relation nor any resemblance between them. The word "dog" for the constellation and the animal is purely equivocal, for their name is all they hold in common. It is not thus with the names we give to God, since they are related as cause and effect.[32] There is always then a positive element in what we say about God, that there must be a kind of resemblance, not between God and the things, but rather between them and God. It is the resemblance which an effect always preserves in relation to its cause, however inferior to it it may be.

This is why St. Thomas repeats so often the assertion that we do not speak about God *secundum puram aequivocationem* and that man is not condemned to say nothing of God *nisi pure aequivoce* or *omnino aequivoce*.[33] This manner of speaking "not altogether equivocally" about God is what St. Thomas calls *analogy*.

Judging from the numerous articles, papers and volumes devoted to this subject,[34] we might easily think that St. Thomas had explained himself at length. But this is not so. His texts on the notion of analogy are relatively few, and in each case they are so restrained that we cannot but wonder why the notion has taken on such an importance in the eyes of his commentators. Perhaps it is due to a secret longing to redeem from an all too-apparent misery the knowledge of God which St. Thomas will concede us. Commentators have gradually come to the stage where they speak of analogy as an almost positive source of knowledge giving us a more or less confused insight into a quasi-quidditative being of God. Perhaps it is not necessary to force the Thomistic texts in order to find in this notion all that we might hope for. Rather, it is quite enough to interpret them as St. Thomas himself did, not in the order of the quidditative concept, but in that of the judgment.

What St. Thomas asks of the notion of analogy is that it permit the metaphysician or the theologian using metaphysics to speak of God without constantly falling into pure equivocation and even sophistry. That the danger is avoidable, he saw in the fact that Aristotle had, by demonstrative reason, proven a great deal about God. But Aristotle's God inaccessible as he was, was far less so than the WHO IS of Thomas Aquinas.[35] To avoid complete equivocation, then, it becomes necessary to rely upon the relation binding each effect to its cause, the only link enabling us to make an accurate ascent from creature to creator. This relationship St. Thomas calls analogy, that is to say, proportion.

Analogy or proportion, as conceived by St. Thomas, is to be found in two principal cases. First, several things are in relation to one other thing, although their relations to this other are different. There is said to be analogy among the names of these things because they are all in relation to the same thing. So we can speak of a healthy medicine and a healthy urine. The urine is healthy because it is a sign of health; a medicine is healthy because it is the cause of health. There is, then, analogy between all things that are healthy, in no matter what sense they are so, because whatever is healthy is so in relation to the state of healthiness in a living being. In the second case it is no longer a question of analogy or proportion binding together several things because they are all in relation to another thing, but of the analogy binding one thing to another because of the relationship uniting them. For example, we speak of a healthy medicine and a healthy person because this medicine causes the health of this person. It is no longer here the analogy of the sign and of the cause of one and the same thing (urine and medicament), but rather the analogy of the cause and its effect. Certainly, when we say that a medicine is healthy, we are not pretending that it is in good health; the term "healthy" is not therefore *purely univocal* in the remedy and in the sick person. But the remedy is nevertheless healthy, since it causes health. Thus the term "healthy" is not *purely equivocal* in the remedy and the sick person.

It is precisely in this sense that we can name God from His creatures. God is not more good, just, wise, powerful than the healing remedy is healthy. Nevertheless, what we call goodness, justice, wisdom, power is certainly in God since God is its cause. We therefore know with certitude that when a thing has a positive perfection, God is that positive perfection. But we also know that this positive perfection is God only as the effect is its cause, that is, according to a necessarily deficient mode of

being. To affirm thus of God the perfections of creatures, but according
to a mode that eludes us, is to be between the purely univocal and purely
equivocal.[36] Signs and effects of God, the perfections of things are not
what God Himself is; but God Himself is, in an infinitely higher mode,
what things are. To speak of God by analogy is to say in each case that
God is pre-eminently a certain perfection.

The meaning of this doctrine has been much discussed, some emphasizing as strongly as possible the agnostic element which it admits, others
energetically insisting on the positive value of the knowledge of God which
it preserves. The discussion can last as long as each side can discuss new
texts, all authentically Thomistic, to justify its thesis. On the plane of
the quiddity, there is no mean between the univocal and the equivocal.
Here the two interpretations in question are irreconcilable, and this is
why, anxious to avoid pure agnosticism with respect to God, Duns Scotus
will uphold the doctrine of the univocity of being, as well as of all the
terms signifying divine attributes.[37] But this is not the case if we transfer
the question to the plane of the judgment. In the case of God, every judgment, even if it takes the form of a judgment of attribution, is really a
judgment of existence. Whether one speaks of His essence or His substance
or His goodness or His wisdom, one only repeats— He is *esse*. This is why
His name of names is HE IS. If we take the divine attributes one by one
and ask if each is in God, we shall have to reply that it is not, at least as
such and as a distinct reality. And since we can in no way conceive of an
essence which is only an act-of-being, we can in no way conceive of what
God is, even with the help of such attributes. To make St. Thomas say
that we have at least an imperfect knowledge of what God is is to betray
his expressly stated thought. Indeed he not only says that the vision of
the divine essence is not given to us here below, but he states clearly that
"there is something pertaining to God which is entirely unknown to man
in this life, namely, what God is." To say that *quid est Deus* is something
omnino ignotum for man in this life,[39] is to affirm that all knowledge, perfect or imperfect, of the essence of God is radically inaccessible here below. To every interpretation of St. Thomas to the contrary, the deserv-
edly famous text of the *Contra Gentiles* presents an insuperable obstacle:
"We cannot grasp what God is, but what He is not, and the relation other
things have with Him." [40]

On the other hand, St. Thomas certainly concedes us a certain knowledge of God, a knowledge of what St. Paul calls in his *Epistle to the Romans* the *invisibilia Dei*. But we must see where this stops. First of all, if
in this text it were a question of a knowledge of God Himself, St. Paul
would not say *invisibilia* but *invisible*, for God is one, His essence is one,
as the blessed see Him, but as we do not see Him. St. Paul's words in no
way lead us to qualify the statement that we cannot know the divine essence. All St. Paul concedes us is a knowledge of the *invisibilia*, that is,

of several aspects of God, several ways of looking at Him (*rationes*) which we designate by names borrowed from his effects, and which we attribute to God. "In this way, the understanding envisages the unity of the divine essence under the reasons of goodness, of wisdom, of virtue, and of other things of the same sort, which are not in God (*et hujusmodi, quae in Deo non sunt*). He has therefore called them the *invisibilia* of God because what in God corresponds with these names or reasons, is one, and we do not see it." [41]

Unless we admit that St. Thomas has glaringly contradicted himself, we must suppose that the knowledge of God which he concedes us is not that of His essence, that is, with His *esse*. Such, in fact, is the case, and he repeats it unceasingly. Every effect of God is analogous to its cause. The concept which we form of this effect cannot at all be transformed for us into the concept of God which we lack. But we can attribute to God, by an affirmative judgment, the name which designates the perfection corresponding to this effect. This procedure does not affirm that God is like the creature. It is based on the certitude that, since every effect resembles its cause, the creature with which we start certainly resembles God. [42] So we attribute to God several names, such as good, intelligent or wise; and these names are not synonyms, since each of them designates our distinct concept of a distinct, created being. [43] Nevertheless, this multiplicity of names designates a simple object, because we attribute all of them to the same object by way of judgment.

If we think about it, we can see how much the nature of the judgment predestines it to play such a role. To judge is always to affirm unity by a complex act. Where our judgments concern God, each of them affirms the identity of a certain perfection with the divine *esse* itself. This is why our understanding "expresses the unity of the thing by a composition of words, and this composition is a mark of identity when it says *God is good* or *God is goodness*, in such a way that the diversity in the composition of the terms can be attributed to the knowledge of the understanding, whereas the unity is attributable to the thing known." [44] What St. Thomas calls our knowledge of God consists then in the last analysis in our ability to form valid affirmative propositions about Him. Unquestionably, each of these propositions amounts to predicating the same thing about Him. But the understanding can do this by reasoning as if the subject of its proposition were a sort of substratum, to which the predicate would have come to be added as a form. Thus in the proposition "God is good," we speak as though God were a real subject informed by goodness. This is necessary, because a judgment is made up of several terms. But let us not forget, on the other hand, that a judgment is not a simple juxtaposition of these terms, it is a *composition* of them, a term which St. Thomas almost always uses, not in the passive sense of having been composed, but in the active sense of the act of composing. Now in making the *compo-*

sitio of the terms in the judgment, it is precisely their real identity which the understanding signifies, since it is the proper function of the judgment to signify this identity—*identitatem rei significat intellectus per compositionem*. And what is true of each of our judgments of God taken separately is equally true of them taken together. As we have said, no two names given to God are synonymous. Our understanding grasps Him in many ways even as creatures represent Him in many ways. But since the subject of all our judgments about God remains one and the same, we can say here that although our understanding knows God through many concepts, it nevertheless knows that it is the same reality which corresponds to all its concepts.[45]

Thus we see how the two interpretations, the affirmative and negative, of St. Thomas's natural theology meet upon a higher plane, for both are true in their own way. It is exact that, according to St. Thomas, none of the definite forms signified by the divine names exists in God: *Quodlibet enim istorum nominum significat aliquam formam definitam, et sic non attribuuntur.*[46] It cannot then be said that goodness as such, intelligence as such, nor power as such exist as definite forms in the divine being. But it is equally inexact to say that we affirm nothing positive about God when we say that He is good, just or intelligent. What we affirm in each case is the divine substance itself.[47] To say *God is good* is not simply to say *God is not bad*. It is not even simply to say *God is the cause of goodness*. The true sense of the expression is that "what we call goodness in creatures pre-exists in God, and in a much higher degree. But it does not result from this that it pertains to God to be good in so far as He is the cause of goodness, but rather, on the contrary, that it is because He is good that He diffuses goodness into things."[48] There is no contradiction in these two theses for the simple reason that they are but the two sides of one doctrine, the one which St. Thomas so strongly emphasizes concerning the divine act-of-being.

What do we know about God? Unquestionably this, that the proposition "God exists," is a true proposition; but what God's act-of-being is we do not know, for, "God's existence is the same as His substance, and as His substance is unknown so also is His existence."[49] And the situation is exactly the same with the divine attributes. After we have shown what they are we still do not know what God is. "We do not know what God is."[50] St. Thomas goes on repeating. The illusion that the case can be otherwise comes from the fact that we think we know of what *esse* it is a question when we prove that God exists. And with more reason we think we know of what goodness, of what intelligence, of what will it is a question when we prove that God is good, intelligent and willing. But actually, we know no more about them, because they all signify the divine substance, identical with the *esse* of God, and, like it, unknown to us.[51] But in spite of all this, we are quite sure that even as the proposition

"God exists" is true, so the propositions "God is good," "God is life," "God is intelligent," and others of the same kind, are also true. That God is what we call goodness, life and will we know as surely as we know that He is what we call being. But the meaning of these terms does not change when we apply them to God. All these judgments direct our understanding toward the same goal, the direction of which is known to us but which, because it is at infinity, is beyond the reach of our natural forces. For we do not attain it by multiplying the affirmative propositions which denote it. But yet to make these propositions is neither to waste our words nor our efforts because it is at least to turn ourselves toward Him.

3. THE PERFECTIONS OF GOD

Among the perfections we can attribute to God by analogy with His creatures, three deserve particular attention because they constitute the highest perfections of man, himself the most perfect of terrestrial creatures. These are intelligence, will and life. Some, no doubt, will call this anthropomorphism. But since we are obliged to start from God's effects, it seems wiser to start with man than with a stone. What risk, indeed, do we run of conceiving God in the image of man in a doctrine in which we know beforehand that our concept will always be infinitely lower than its object, no matter which effect we take for our starting point?

God's intelligence can be immediately deduced from His infinite perfection. When we attribute to the creator all the perfections of creatures, we can hardly deny Him the noblest of all intelligence, or that by which one being can in a certain way become all beings.[52] But there is a deeper reason than this, one based on the very nature of the divine being. We can first of all state that any being is intelligent in the measure in which it is divested of matter.[53] We can next admit that knowing beings are distinguished from beings deprived of knowledge in that the latter possess only their own form, while knowing beings can apprehend too the form of other beings. In other words, there is a correspondence between the knowing faculty and an increased breadth and extension of being in the knowing subject. Privation of knowledge corresponds with limiting and restricting of the being of the subject deprived of it. Aristotle expresses this as follows: "the soul is in a sense all things."

A form, then, will be more intelligent as it is more capable of becoming, by way of knowledge, a larger number of other forms. Now it is only matter that can restrict and limit this extension of form; this is why it can be said that the more immaterial the forms, the more they approach a sort of infinity. It is therefore evident that it is the immateriality of a being which confers knowledge upon it, and that the degree of knowledge depends upon the degree of immateriality. A short inductive survey will serve to convince us of this. Plants are deprived of knowledge by reason of their materiality. The senses, on the contrary, are already endowed with knowledge because they receive sensible species deprived of matter. The intellect is capable of a still higher degree of knowledge, being more thoroughly separated from matter. So its proper object is the universal and not the singular, since it is matter that is the principle of individuation. Finally we come to God who is, as has already been demonstrated, completely immaterial. He is also, therefore, intelligent in the highest degree: "since God is in the highest degree of immateriality, it follows that He occupies the highest place in knowledge." [54]

By putting this conclusion beside our other one, that God is His being, we find that God's intelligence becomes one with His existence. Knowledge is the act of being intelligent. Now the act of a being can pass into another being exterior to it. The act of heating, for example, passes from what heats into what is heated. But certain acts are immanent in their subject, and the act of knowledge is one of these. The intelligible experiences nothing from the fact that the intelligence apprehends it. But it remains what it is while the intelligence acquires its act and its perfection. Therefore, when God knows, His act of intelligence remains immanent to Him. But we know that whatever is in God is the divine essence. The intelligence of God, therefore, is one with the divine essence, and consequently, with the divine act-of-being which is God Himself; for God is the identity of His essence and His act-of-being, as has been demonstrated. [55]

Thus we see again that God understands Himself perfectly, for, if He is the supreme Intelligent, as we have seen above, He is also the supreme Intelligible. A material thing only becomes intelligible when it is separated from matter and from material conditions by the light of the agent-intellect. Consequently, we can say of the intelligibility of things what we said of their degree of knowledge: it increases with their immateriality. In still other terms, the immaterial as such, and by its nature, is intelligible. On the other hand, every intelligible is apprehended according as it is one in act with the being that apprehends it; now the intelligence of God is one with His essence, and His intelligibility is also one with His essence; the intelligence therefore is here one in act with the intelligible, and consequently God, in whom the supreme degree of knowledge and the supreme degree of knowability are joined, understands Himself perfectly. [56] Let us go further. The only object which God knows by Himself and in an immediate manner is Himself. Indeed it is evident that in order to know immediately by Himself an object other than Himself, God would have to turn from His immediate object, which is Himself, in order to turn toward another object. But this other object could only be inferior to the first; and the divine knowledge would then lose some of its perfection, and this is impossible. [57]

God knows Himself perfectly and He knows only Himself immediately.

This does not mean that He does not know anything other than Himself. Such a conclusion would contradict absolutely what we know about the divine intelligence. Let us start from this principle that God knows Himself perfectly—a principle, moreover, evident outside of all demonstration, since the intelligence of God is His being, and since His being is perfect; it is evident that to know a thing perfectly it is necessary to know its power perfectly, and to know its power perfectly it is necessary to know the effects to which this power extends. But the divine power extends to other things than God Himself, since He is the first efficient cause of all beings. It is therefore necessary that in knowing Himself God know all the rest. This consequence becomes more evident still if we add to what precedes that the intelligence of God, the first cause, is one with His being. Thus it follows that all the effects which pre-exist in God as in their first cause are first in His intelligence, and that they all exist in Him under their intelligible form.[58] This truth of capital importance requires some precision.

When we extend God's knowledge to all things, we do not make it dependent upon anything. God sees Himself in Himself, for He sees Himself by His essence. In what concerns other things, on the contrary, He does not see them in themselves but in Himself, in so far as his essence contains in itself the archetype of all that is not Himself. Knowledge, in God, is not specified by anything else than the very essence of God.[59] But the real difficulty is not here. It consists rather in determining under what aspect God sees things. Is His knowledge of them general or particular? Is it limited to the real or does it extend to the possible? Must we, finally, subject even future contingents to it? Such are the debatable points which it is important to discuss, and the more rigidly in that they have furnished material to the gravest of Averroist errors.

It has been held, indeed, that God knows things with a general knowledge, that is, as beings, but not with a distinct knowledge, that is, as they constitute a number of distinct objects, each endowed with its own reality. There is no need to be too insistent here, for such a doctrine is obviously incompatible with the absolute perfection of the divine essence. God would not know Himself if He did not know distinctly all the modes in which His own perfection is participable. Nor would He know perfectly the nature of being if He did not know distinctly all the possible modes of being.[60] God's knowledge of things is therefore a proper and determined knowledge.[61]

Is it fitting to say that this knowledge extends even to the singular? Some have contested this, not without some appearance of reason. To know a thing, indeed, comes down to knowing the constituent principles of that thing. Now every singular essence is constituted by a determined matter and a form individuated in this matter. The knowledge of the singular as such supposes then the knowledge of the matter as such. But we see that in man the only faculties that can apprehend the material and the singular are the imagination and the senses, or other faculties resembling these in that they also use material organs. The human intellect, on the contrary, is an immaterial faculty. Moreover, as we can see, its proper object is the general. But the divine intellect is clearly much more immaterial than the human intellect. Its knowledge must then be even farther removed than human intellectual knowledge from every particular object.[62]

The principles of this argument do not support its conclusion. They permit us, in fact, to affirm that one who knows a determined matter and the form individuated in this matter knows the singular object constituted by this form and this matter. But the divine knowledge extends to the forms, to the individual accidents and to the matter of each being. Since His intelligence is one with His essence, God knows inevitably whatever is in His essence in any manner whatsoever. Now what possesses being in any way and no matter to what degree is in the divine essence as in its first cause, since His essence is pure being. But matter is a certain mode of being, since it is being in potency. Accident is also a certain mode of being, since it is that which is in another (*ens in alio*). Matter and accidents, like form, come under the essence and, consequently, under the knowledge of God. Thus one cannot deny Him knowledge of singulars.[63] In all this, St. Thomas openly resists the Averroism of his time. A Siger of Brabant, for example,[64] interpreting the doctrine of Aristotle on the relations of God and of the world in its strictest sense, saw in God only the final cause of the universe. According to him God was not the creative cause of physical beings in either their matter or their form; and not being their cause, He had neither to administer to them as their providence, nor even to know them. It is the denial of God's creative causality which led the Averroists to deny God knowledge of singulars. And it is the affirmation of the universal divine causality which led St. Thomas to attribute it to Him. *Esse* itself, the God of St. Thomas, causes and knows the totality of *esse*.

God therefore knows all real beings, not only as distinct from one another, but also in their very individuality, with the accidents and the matter which make them singulars. Does He likewise know possibles? There can be no reasonable doubt about this. What does not actually exist, but can exist, is at least a virtual existence and is in this to be distinguished from pure nothingness. Now it has been shown that because He is the act-of-being, God knows everything that exists, of whatever sort its existence may be. God therefore knows possibles. When it is a question of possibles not actually existing but which have existed or will exist, God is said to know them by His science of vision. When it is a question of possibles which might have been realized, but which do not exist, have never existed, nor will ever exist, God is said to know them by His science of simple intelligence. But possibles never escape God's perfect intellection.[65]

This conclusion extends to that class of possibles of which we cannot say that they have or have not to be realized, that is, to future contingents. A future contingent can be considered in two ways: in itself and actually realized, or in its cause and capable of realization. For example, Socrates can be sitting or standing. If I see Socrates sitting, I see this contingent actually present and realized. But if I simply see in the concept of Socrates that he can be sitting or not sitting as he wills, I see the contingent in the form of a future not yet determined. In the first case there can be certain knowledge; in the second, certain knowledge is impossible. Therefore, to know a contingent effect only in its cause is to have but a conjectural knowledge of it. But God knows all future contingents both in their causes and in themselves as actually realized, and this at the same time. Although future contingents are realized successively, God does not know them successively. We have established already that God is placed outside of time; His knowledge, like His being, is measured by eternity. Now eternity, which exists all at once, embraces the whole of time in an immovable present. God, then, knows future contingents as actually present and realized;[66] and nevertheless, His necessary knowledge of them in no way deprives them of their character of contingency.[67] In this way St. Thomas puts himself at some distance from Averroism, and even from the most authentic Aristotelianism.[68] According to Averroes and Aristotle, the essential characteristic of a future contingent is that it can come to pass or not. It is inconceivable therefore that it can become the object of a science for anyone at all; and, from the moment that a contingent becomes known as true, it ceases to be a contingent and becomes immediately necessary. But Aristotle did not conceive of God as the pure act-of-being, efficient cause of all existence. Supremely necessary in itself, the divine thought dominating Aristotle's world thought nothing save what was necessary. It was neither creative nor universally provident because it was not the cause which made the universe exist.

We have now determined in what sense intelligence is to be attributed to God. It remains to determine in what sense will is to be attributed to Him. We can conclude that God wills from the fact that He knows. Since it is the good as known that constitutes the proper object of the will, it follows necessarily that the good be also willed from the moment that it is known. From this it follows that a being which knows the good is by the same fact endowed with will. Now God knows the good. Since, indeed, He is perfectly intelligent, as has already been demonstrated, He knows being as being and as good at the same time. Thus God wills only because He knows.[69]

This conclusion is valid not only for God but for every intelligent being.

For the relation of a thing to its natural form is such that when it does not possess it, it tends toward it, and, when it does possess it, it rests in it. Now the natural form of the intelligence is the intelligible. Thus every intelligent being tends toward its intelligible form when it does not possess it, and rests in it when it does possess it. But this inclination and this complacent rest pertains to the will. We can therefore conclude that in every intelligent being there must also be a will. God possesses intelligence and therefore will as well.[70] But we know from elsewhere that God's intelligence is identical with His act-of-being. Since He wills in so far as He is intelligent, His will too must be identical with His act-of-being. Consequently just as God's knowing is His act-of-being, so His willing is His act-of-being.[71] Thus will does not, any more than intelligence, introduce composition into God.

We shall see issuing from this principle consequences parallel to those we have previously deduced concerning God's intelligence. The first is that the divine essence constitutes the first and principal object of the will of God. The object of the will, we have said, is the good apprehended by the intellect. Now what the divine intellect apprehends immediately and by itself is nothing else than the divine essence, as has been demonstrated. The divine essence is, therefore, the first and principal object of the divine will.[72] This only confirms our former certitude that God is dependent upon nothing exterior to Himself. But it does not follow that God wills nothing exterior to Himself.

Will, indeed, proceeds from intelligence. Now the immediate object of the divine intelligence is God. But we know that in knowing Himself God knows all other things. Similarly God wills Himself as immediate object, and wills all other things in willing Himself.[73] This same conclusion can be established by a more profound principle which even reveals the source of creative activity in God. Every natural being has, indeed, with reference to its own good, not only that inclination making it tend toward it when it does not possess it, or making it rest in it when it does possess it, but it tends, too, to expand, as much as this is possible, to diffuse its own good into other beings. This is why every being endowed with will tends naturally to communicate to others the good it possesses. This tendency is eminently characteristic of the divine will from which we know every perfection derives by way of resemblance. Consequently, if natural beings communicate their proper good to others in the measure in which they possess a perfection, much more does it pertain to the divine will to communicate its perfection to others by way of resemblance and in the measure that it is communicable. Hence God wishes Himself to exist and wishes others to exist, but he wills Himself as an end, others as related to their end, that is, to the extent that it is fitting for other beings to participate in the divine goodness.[74]

From the point of view just defined, we see immediately that the divine will extends to all particular goods just as the divine intelligence extends to all particular beings. It is not necessary, in order to preserve the divine simplicity intact, to concede only that He wills other beings in general, that is insofar as He wishes to be the principle of all the goods issuing from Himself. There is nothing to prevent the divine simplicity from being the principle of a host of participated goods, nor God from remaining simple while willing such and such a particular good. From the moment that the good is known by the intelligence it is, by the same fact, willed. Now God knows particular goods, as has already been demonstrated. His will, therefore, also extends to particular goods.[75]

It extends even to simple possibles. Since, indeed, God knows possibles, including future contingents, in their proper nature, He wills them also with their proper nature. Now it pertains to their proper nature that they must be or not be realized at a determined moment in time. It is thus that God wills them, and not only as existing eternally in the divine intelligence. This does not signify that God, in willing them in their proper nature, creates them. For will is an action which is completed interiorly in the one willing. God, in willing temporal creatures, does not thereby confer existence upon them. This existence only belongs to them through one of the divine actions whose terminus is an effect exterior to God, namely, the actions of producing, creating and governing.[76]

Now that we have determined the objects of God's will, let us see in what ways it is exercised. First of all, are there things which God cannot will? To this question the answer has to be: Yes. But such an affirmation must at once be qualified. The only things which God cannot will are those which, in the last analysis, are not things at all; namely, those which include in themselves a contradiction. For example, God cannot will that a man be a donkey, because He cannot will that a being be reasonable and deprived of reason at one and the same time. To will that the same thing be, at the same time and under the same relation, itself and its contrary is to will that it be and that it not be at the same time. It is to will what is, of itself, contradictory and impossible. Let us recall, moreover, the reason why God wills things. He only wills them, we have said, insofar as they participate in His resemblance. The first condition they must fulfil to resemble God is to be, because God is the First Being, and source of all being. God would not be right in willing what is incompatible with the nature of being. To affirm the contradictory is to affirm a being which destroys itself. It is to affirm being and non-being at the same time. God cannot, therefore, will what is contradictory.[77] This is the only limitation that can rightly be placed on His all powerful will.

Let us try to envisage what God is able to will, that is, all that can, in any way whatsoever, be properly called being. If it is a question of the divine being itself, considered in its infinite perfection and its supreme goodness, we must affirm that God necessarily wills this being and this goodness, and that he cannot will what is contrary to them. It has been proven already, indeed, that God wills His being and goodness as His principal object, and as His reason for willing other things. Consequently, God wills His own being and goodness in everything He wills. It is impossible, on the other hand, that God should not will a thing with an actual will, for then He would be willing in potency only. This is impossible because His will is His act-of-being. God, therefore, wills necessarily, and He wills necessarily His own act-of-existing and His own goodness.[78]

But the situation is not the same where other things are concerned. God only wills them insofar as they are related to His goodness as to their end. Now when we will a certain end we do not necessarily will the things related to it, save when they are of such a nature that it is impossible to attain this end without them. If, for example, we will to live, we necessarily will food; and if we wish to cross the sea, we are constrained to wish a means of transportation. But we do not have to will something without which we can attain our end. If, for example, we wish to take an outing, we are not obliged to wish a horse, for we can take an outing without one. And so it is for all the rest. Now God's goodness is perfect. Nothing capable of existing outside of it increases His perfection in any way. Thus God, who wills Himself necessarily, is in no way constrained to will anything else.[79] What remains true is that if God wills other things, He cannot not will them, for His will is immutable. But this purely hypothetical necessity introduces into Him no true and absolute necessity, that is, no constraint.[80]

It might be objected that if God wills other things with a will free from all constraint, He does not will them without a reason, since He wills them in view of their end which is His own goodness. Are we to say, then, that the divine will remains free to will things, but that if God wills them, a cause can be assigned to His will? This would be to express it badly because it is not true that the divine will is caused in any way. We will grasp this more easily if we remember that will proceeds from understanding, and that the causes by which a being endowed with will wills belong to the same order as those by which an intelligent being knows.

In the case of knowledge, things take place in such a way that if the intellect understands the principle and the conclusion separately, its knowledge of the principle is the cause of the knowledge it acquires of the conclusion. But if this intellect perceived the conclusion in the very bosom of the principle, thus grasping both in one single intuition, its knowledge of the conclusion would not be caused by its understanding of the principle, because nothing is its own proper cause; and yet the intellect would understand that the principles are the causes of the conclusion. It is the same in the case of the will, where the end is in the same relation to the means as the principles are to the conclusions in the case of the intellect. If one were to will the end by one given act, and the means to this end by another act, the act by which it would will the end would be the cause of that by which it would will the means. But if it will both means and end by one single act, this could no longer be said, because it would be to assert that one and the same act is its own cause. Nevertheless, it would remain true to say that this will wills to order the means in view of their end. Now just as God, by one single act, knows all things in His essence, He wills, by one single act, all things in His goodness. Just as in God, His knowledge of the cause is not the cause of His knowledge of the effect, and yet He knows the effect in its cause, so His willing of the end is not the cause of His willing of the means, and yet He wills the means as ordered to their end. He wills, therefore, that *this* be because of *that;* but it is not because of *that* that He wills *this*.[81]

To say that God wills the good is to say that He loves it, for love is nothing else than the first movement of the will in its tending toward the good. In attributing love to God, we must not imagine Him as moved by a passion or inclination distinct from His will and moving Him. Divine love is only the divine willing of the good. Just as this willing is only the *esse* of God, divine love in its turn is this same *esse*. Such, too, is the teaching of Holy Scripture: God is Love (*Deus caritas est,* John, *Epist.,* IV, 8). Once again natural theology and revealed theology find common ground on the level of existence,[82] as could be shown point by point in an analysis of the object of divine love. It is God's will that is the cause of all things. Cause of the fact that *they are,* the divine will is therefore cause of *what they are.* Now God has only willed that they be, and that they be what they are, because they are good in the very measure in which they are. To say that the will of God is the cause of all things, is therefore to say that God loves all things, as reason points out and as Scripture teaches: "For thou lovest all things that are, and hatest none of the things thou hast made" (Wisd., XI, 24).

Let us note, too, that the divine simplicity is in no way divided by the multiplicity of the objects of the Divine Love. We must not imagine that the goodness of things moves God to love them. It is He who creates their goodness and infuses it into them. To love His creatures is for God but to love Himself in the simple act by which He wills Himself and which is identical with His act-of-being.[83] Thus God loves all in loving Himself; and as every being has as much good as it has being, God loves each being in proportion to its proper degree of perfection. To love one thing more than another is, for Him, to will it better than another.[84] To prefer one thing to another is to will like Him that some things be in fact better than other things.[85] In brief, it is to will that they be exactly what they are.

Intelligent and free, God is also a living God. He is such, first of all, by the very fact that He possesses intelligence and will, for it is impossible to know or to will without living. But He lives, too, for a more direct and more profound reason, a reason drawn from the very notion of life.

Among the various kinds of beings, life is attributed to those containing an interior principle of motion. This is so true that we extend it spontaneously to inanimate beings themselves when they appear to have spontaneous motion. Water surging from a spring we think of as living water in contrast to the dead waters of a cistern or a pond. Knowing and desiring are among those actions whose principle is interior to the being performing them. In the case of God it is much more evident that such acts lie in His most hidden depths since, as first cause, He is pre-eminently the cause of His own operations.[86]

Thus God appears to us as a living source of efficacy whose acts spring eternally from His being, or, more precisely, whose operation is one with His act-of-being. What we mean by the term "life" is, in the case of a being, the very fact of living, considered in the abstract, just as the term "race" is a simple word to express the concrete act of racing, but with much greater reason since the life of a being is what actually makes it exist. In the case of God the conclusion comes home more forcibly since He is not only His own life as other particular beings are the life which they have received, but because He is His life as one who lives by reason of Himself and as the cause of the life of all other things.[87] It is from this eternally fecund life of an intelligence ever in act that the divine beatitude flows, the beatitude in which ours can only be a participation.

Beatitude is, indeed, inseparable from the notion of intelligence, since to be happy is to know that one possesses one's own good.[88] A being's proper good rests in the accomplishing as perfectly as possible its most perfect operation; and the perfection of an operation depends upon four principal conditions each of which is eminently realized in the life of God.

First, this operation must be sufficient in itself and be integrally completed within the being performing it. This is necessary because an operation which is completely developed within a being is performed in the last analysis for that being's own profit. What is achieved is its own acquisition and constitutes a positive gain which serves its own advantage.[89] On the contrary, operations which are terminated outside their author are of less benefit to their author than to the work they produce. The good they constitute cannot be of the same order as the preceding. It is therefore an operation immanent in God which will form his beatitude.

The second condition of this operation is that it be accomplished by the highest power of the being under consideration. In the case of man, for example, beatitude cannot consist in the act of a purely sensible knowledge, but only of a perfect intellectual knowledge.

But we have to take into account, moreover, the object of this operation. Thus in our case, beatitude supposes an intellectual knowledge of the supreme intelligible. This is the third characteristic.

The fourth is to be found in the very manner in which the operation is accomplished. It must be perfect, easy and delectable. Such, precisely and in the most perfect degree, is God's operation. He is pure intelligence, totally in act. He is His own proper object, that is, He knows perfectly the supreme intelligible. Finally, since He is the act by which He knows Himself, He does it easily and in joy. God is therefore blessed.[90] Once again let us say rather: God is His own beatitude since He is happy by an act of intelligence and since this act of intelligence is His very substance. His is a beatitude, consequently, which is not only very perfect, but without any measure in common with other beatitude. To enjoy the Sovereign Good is assuredly happiness. But to possess one's self as being oneself the Sovereign Good, is no longer only to participate in happiness, it is to be it.[91] With this attribute, then, as with all the others, we can say that it belongs to God in a unique sense: *Deus qui singulariter beatus est.* It is because He *is* beatitude that the creature *has* it.

These last considerations bring us to the point where we should pass from the divine essence itself to an examination of its effects. Such a research would be completely closed to us if we had not previously determined, in so far as it is possible to do so, the principal attributes of God, the efficient and final cause of all things. Whatever the importance of the results obtained, if we regard them from the point of view of our own human knowledge, it is well not to forget their extreme poverty in comparison with the infinite object which they would seem to make us know. Certainly it is a precious blessing to know that God is eternal, infinite, perfect, intelligent and good. But let us not forget that the "how" of these attributes escapes us. If some scraps of certitude were to make us forget that the divine essence remains unknown to us here below, it would be far better not to possess them. Our intellect cannot be said to know what a thing is save when it can define it, that is, when it represents it under a form corresponding at every point to what it is. We should not forget that all our intellect has been able to conceive about God has been conceived in a deficient manner, because God's act-of-being eludes our every grasp. We can conclude, therefore, with Dionysius the Areopagite,[92] by placing the highest knowledge which we are permitted to acquire concerning the Divine nature in this life, in the certitude that God remains above everything that we think about Him.[93]

4. THE CREATOR

We have seen that, according to St. Thomas, the sole object of philosophy as revealable is God whose nature we must consider first, then His effects. It is time now to turn to this second aspect. But before examining the effects of God, that is, creatures taken in their hierarchical order, we should once again consider God Himself in the free act by which He gives existence to all the rest.[94]

The way by which all beings emanate from their universal cause is called creation. Creation signifies either the act by which God creates, or those things which result from His act of creating. In the first sense, there is creation when there is absolute production of an act-of-being. Applying this notion to the ensemble of existing things, we say that creation, which is the production of a being, consists in the act by which *He Who is,* that is, the pure act-of-being, causes finite acts-of-being. In the second sense, creation is neither an approaching into being (since nothingness cannot approach anything), nor a transmutation by the Creator (since there is nothing to transmute), it is only an "entering into being, and a relation to the creator from whom it has being." [95] It is this we wish to express as best we can by saying that God has created the universe out of nothing, or again, that creation is the passage from non-being, or nothingness, to being. It is important to note that in statements of this sort the prepositions "out of" and "from" in no way imply a material cause. They simply denote an order. God has not created the world from nothing in the sense that He made it spring from nothingness as from a kind of pre-existing matter, but in the sense that where there was nothing, being appeared. To create from nothing does not mean to create from something. Far from asserting that there is matter at the base of creation, this expression radically excludes anything of the sort which we might possibly imagine.[96] It is perhaps in this sense that we say that a man is sad over nothing when his sadness has no cause.[97]

This conception of the creative act almost invites objections from philosophers, because it is so contrary to their ordinary habits of thought.[98] For the physicist, for example, any act whatsoever is, by definition, a changing, that is, a sort of movement. Now whatever passes from one place to another, or from one state into another, presupposes an initial place or state, the point of departure of the change or movement. So true is this that where there is no point of departure, the very notion of change becomes impossible. For example, I move a body. It was therefore in a certain place, from which I was able to cause it to pass to another. I change the color of an object. It had to be an object of some color or other in order that I could change it to another. Now in the case of the creative act as just defined, it is precisely this point of departure that is lacking. Without creation there is nothing; with creation there is something. But does not this notion of a passage from nothingness to being involved a contradiction? Does it not presume that what does not exist can nevertheless change its state? Does it not suggest that what is nothing can somehow or other become something? From nothing, nothing comes, is the philosopher's preliminary objection to the very possibility of creation.

This objection, however, only has force in the measure to which its point of departure is conceded. The physicist argues from the notion of movement. He claims that the conditions required for movement are not satisfied in the case of creation and concludes that creation is therefore impossible. Actually the only legitimate conclusion to be derived from his argument is that creation is not a movement. Such a conclusion is completely legitimate. It is absolutely true that all movement is a changing of the state of a being. But when we hear of an act which is not a movement we are at a loss how to think about it. No matter how we try, we always *imagine* that creation is a kind of change, which renders its notion both contradictory and impossible. But in actual fact, it is something quite different, something we are at a loss to put into words, so unfamiliar is it to the conditions of human experience. To call creation "the giving of being" is misleading, for how can something be given to what does not exist? To call it "a receiving of being" is scarcely any better, for how is something to be received by what is nothing? Let us call it then, "a reception of the act-of-being" without pretending to be able to represent it to ourselves.[99]

The act-of-being itself can only be conceived in the notion of being. It is hardly surprising that the relation between two acts-of-being, one of which is that act-of-being itself and the other but the proper effect of the first, remains inconceivable. This is a point on which St. Thomas has explained himself many a time and as precisely as we could wish. It is also at a point where we are naturally very much tempted to relax a little the rigor of his principles. Each time he speaks directly of creation as such, St. Thomas uses the language of the existential act, not that of being. "God brings things into being from nothing." [100]

It is a question here, therefore, of an act which, beginning from *Esse* terminates directly and immediately with *esse*. In virtue of this, "to create is the proper action of God and of Him alone." And the proper effect of this properly divine activity is also the most universal effect of all, the one presupposed by every other effect, the act-of-being: "among all effects the most universal is being itself . . . now to produce being absolutely, and not merely as this or that being, belongs to the nature of creation. Hence it is manifest that creation is the proper act of God alone." [101] This is why, when St. Thomas asks what is in God the root of the creative act, he refuses to place it in any one of the divine persons: "To create, indeed, is properly to cause or to produce the being of things. Since anything which produces, produces an effect resembling itself, we can see by the nature of an effect that of the action producing it. What produces fire is fire. This is why to create belongs to God according to His act-of-being, which is His essence, which is common to the three persons." [102] An instructive theological application since it brings to light the ultimate, existential significance of the Thomistic notion of creation: "Since God is being itself by His own essence, created things must be His proper effect." [103]

If this is the kind of production designated by the word "creation," we see at once why God alone can create. The Arabian philosophers, and

notably Avicenna, deny this. The latter, while admitting that creation is
the proper action of the universal cause, regards certain inferior causes,
acting as instruments of the first cause, as capable of creating. Avicenna
teaches particularly that the first separated substance created by God
creates after itself the substance of the first sphere and its soul, and that
afterwards the substance of this sphere creates the matter of inferior bodies.[104] Similarly the Master of the Sentences[105] says that God can communicate the power of creating to the creature, but only as His minister
and not by its own authority. Now this notion of the creature—creator
is contradictory. Any creation through the mediation of a creature would
evidently presuppose the existence of this creature. But we know that the
creative act presupposes nothing anterior, and this applies both to efficient
cause and to matter. It causes being to succeed non-being, purely and simply. Creative power is, therefore, incompatible with the condition of creature, for a creature does not possess being of itself and cannot confer an
existence which does not belong to it by its essence. It can only act in virtue of the act-of-being which it has previously received.[106] God, on the
other hand, is being *per se* and can also cause being. He alone is being
per se, and He alone can produce the very existence of other beings. To
His unique mode of being there corresponds a unique method of causality.
Creation is the action of God alone.

It is interesting to look into the reasons given by the Arabian philosophers for assigning to creatures the power to create. According to them,
a cause that is one and simple can produce but one effect. Only one
can proceed from the one. If then we are going to explain how a number
of things can proceed from a first and simple cause [God], we have to
grant a succession of unique causes producing but one effect each. Now
it is quite true to say that from a principle that is one and simple but
one can proceed; but this only holds for what acts by the necessity of
nature. Thus it is basically because they consider creation to be a
necessary production that the Arabian philosophers posit creatures which
are at the same time creators. If we are to provide a complete refutation
of their doctrine, we must examine whether God produces things by the
necessity of nature and whether the multitude of created beings comes
from His one and simple essence.

St. Thomas's reply to these two questions is contained in a single statement. We affirm, he says, that things proceed from God by way of knowledge and intelligence. By this mode, a multitude of things can proceed
immediately from a God who is one and simple and whose wisdom embraces all beings.[107] Let us examine the implications of this statement
and see what new depths it opens in the notion of creation.

There are three reasons for saying that God has given being to creatures
by a free act of His will and without any natural necessity. First, we are
obliged to recognize that the universe is ordered in view of a certain end,

otherwise everything in the universe must be produced by chance. Thus God had an end before Him in making it. It is quite true that nature, like the will, can act for an end; but nature and will tend toward their end in different ways.[108] Nature does not know the end nor the reason of the end, nor the relation of the means to their end. It cannot, accordingly, propose an end to itself, nor move toward it, nor order and direct its actions in view of this end. The being acting through will possesses all the kinds of knowledge which nature lacks. It acts for an end as knowing it, as proposing it to itself, and, so to speak, as moving toward it, and as ordering its actions in relation to it. In a word, nature only tends toward an end because it is moved and directed toward this end by a being endowed with intelligence and will, as an arrow moves toward a determined target because of the guiding hand of the archer. Now what is through another is always posterior to what is by itself. If therefore nature tends toward an end assigned to it by an intelligence, then that first being, from which it has both its end and its disposition to that end, must have created it, not by the necessity of nature, but by intelligence and will.

Secondly, nature, unless hindered, always works in one and the same manner. The reason for this is that everything acts according to its nature, so that it acts in the same way in the degree to which it remains itself. But whatever acts according to nature is determined by a single mode of being. Thus nature always achieves one and the same action. The divine being is not at all determined to a single mode of being. On the contrary, we have seen that it contains within itself the total perfection of being. If therefore it acted by the necessity of nature it would produce an infinite and undetermined kind of being. But two simultaneous, infinite beings are impossible.[109] Consequently, it is contradictory that God should act by the necessity of nature. Now there is only one possible kind of action outside of natural action, that is, voluntary action. Let us conclude, therefore, that things proceed, as so many determined effects, from the infinite perfection of God, according to the determination of His intelligence and will.

Thirdly, the last reason is derived from the relation binding effects to their cause. Effects only pre-exist in their cause according to the mode of being of this cause. Now the divine being is its intelligence. Its effects pre-exist in it, therefore, according to a mode of intelligible being. It is also according to a mode of intelligible being that they proceed from it, that is, in the last analysis, by a will. God's inclination to accomplish what His intelligence has conceived belongs, indeed, to the domain of the will. It is therefore the will of God which is the first cause of all things.[110] There still remains to be explained how a multitude of particular beings can derive from this one, simple being. God is the infinite being from which everything that exists holds its being. On the other hand, God is absolutely simple and whatever is in Him is His own *esse*. How can a diversity of finite things pre-exist in the simplicity of the divine intelligence? The theory of ideas will enable us to resolve this difficulty.

By ideas we mean forms considered as existing outside things themselves. Now the form of a thing can exist outside the thing for two different reasons: either because it is the exemplar of that of which it is called the form, or because it is the principle by which that thing can be known. In both senses we must posit the existence of ideas in God.

First of all, ideas are found in God under the form of exemplars or of models. In every generation which does not result from mere chance, the form of what is generated is the end of the generation. Now, what acts could not act in view of this form unless it had its similitude or model within itself. But it can have this in two ways. In the case of certain beings the form of what they have to realize pre-exists according to its natural being. Thus man generates man, and fire generates fire. Such actions are by way of nature. In the case of other beings, on the contrary, the form pre-exists as a purely intelligible being. Such action is by way of intelligence. It is thus that the similitude or model of the house pre-exists in the architect's mind. Now we know that the world does not result from chance. We know too that God does not act from necessity of nature. We must then admit, in the divine intelligence, the existence of a form in whose likeness the world has been created. This we call an idea.[111]

Let us go further. There exists in God not only an idea of the created universe but also a host of ideas corresponding to the various beings which make up this universe. This proposition becomes evident when we consider that when any effect whatsoever is produced, its last end is just what the producer principally intended to realize. Now the final end in view of which all things are disposed is the order of the universe. God's proper intention, then, in creating all things was the order of the universe. But if God's intention was to create the order of the universe, then He must necessarily have had within Himself the idea of universal order. Now there is no true idea of a whole without the ideas of the parts of which it is composed. Thus the architect has no true idea of a house unless he has within him the ideas of each of its parts. It is absolutely necessary, therefore, that the proper ideas of all things be contained in God's thought.[112]

At the same time, however, we see that this plurality of ideas is not inconsistent with the divine simplicity. Any difficulty one finds here arises from sheer equivocation. There exist, actually, two kinds of ideas: those from copies and those from models. Ideas formed from the likeness of objects fall into the first category. These are ideas by *means of which* we understand forms making our intellect pass from potency to act. It is only too evident that if the divine intellect were composed of a number

of ideas of this sort its simplicity would be destroyed. But this does not
at all follow when we place ideas in God in a form similar to that of the
idea in the mind of the workman. The idea is no longer that *by which* the
intellect knows but *that which* the intellect knows and that by which the
intelligent being can accomplish its work. A plurality of ideas of this kind
introduces no composition into the intellect in which they are found. The
implication is, rather, that they are known in God's knowledge of Himself.
We have already said that God has perfect knowledge of His own essence.
He knows it under all the modes by which it is knowable. Now the
divine essence can be known not only as it is in itself but also as it is
in some way participable by His creatures. Every creature possesses its
own being which is nothing other than a kind of participation in the likeness of the divine essence. The idea proper to this creature only represents
this particular manner of participation. Accordingly, insofar as God
knows His essence as imitable by a given creature, He possesses the idea of
that creature. And so it is with all the other ideas in God.[113]

We now know that creatures pre-exist in God under the mode of
intelligible being, that is, in the form of ideas, and that these ideas introduce no complexity into the divine thought. There is nothing, then, to
prevent us from considering Him as the unique and immediate author
of the host of beings constituting this universe. But the most important
result of all these considerations is to show us how vague and inadequate
was our first attempt to determine the creative act. When we said that
God created the world *ex nihilo,* we were removing from the creative act
any notion likening it to the activity of the workman who adapts pre-
existing matter to the work he has in mind. But if we take this expression
in a negative sense, as we have seen we must, it leaves totally unexplained
the first origin of things. It is only too certain that nothingness is not
the original womb from which all creatures can come forth. Being can
only issue from being. We now know from what first being all others
have issued. They only exist because all being is derived from the divine
being: *omnis essentia derivatur ab essentia divina.*[114] This formula
does not do violence to the true thought of St. Thomas, for no being exists
save because God *is* virtually all beings: *est virtualiter omnia;* and it
adds nothing to the often repeated assertion of the philosopher that each
creature is perfect in the very measure in which it participates in the
divine being.[115]

It may be asked how creatures can be derived from God without either
being confused with Him or added to Him. The solution of this problem
brings us again to the problem of analogy. Creatures have no goodness,
no perfection, no modicum of being which they do not hold from God.
But we know already that these things are not in creatures in the same
way that they are in God. The creature is not what he possesses. God is
what He possesses. He is His act-of-being, His goodness, His perfection.

This is why creatures, even though they derive their act-of-being from that of God Himself, since He is *Esse* in its absolute sense, possess it nevertheless in a participated and deficient manner which keeps them infinitely distant from the Creator. A mere *analogue* of the divine being, created being can neither constitute an integral part of the divine being, nor be added to it, nor subtracted from it. Between two magnitudes not of the same order, there is no common measure. The problem, then, is a false one. It vanishes from the moment the question is properly stated.

There remains to be discovered why God wished to realize outside of Himself the many particular beings which He knew as possibles. In Him, and considered in His intelligible being, the creature is indistinguishable from the divine essence. Still more precisely, the creature as idea is nothing else than the creative essence.[116] How is it that God has projected outside of Himself, if not His ideas, at least a reality whose whole being consists in imitating certain of the ideas which He thinks in thinking Himself?

We have already met the only explanation within the reach of the human reason: the good naturally tends to diffuse itself outside itself. Its characteristic is that it seeks to communicate itself to other beings in the measure in which they are capable of receiving it.[117] What is true of every good being in the measure that it is such is eminently true of the Sovereign Good we call God. The tendency to expand outside itself and to communicate itself expresses no more than the superabundance of an infinite being whose perfection overflows into a hierarchy of participated beings. Even so the sun, without having either to reason or to choose, by the mere fact that it is at hand, shines upon all that share its light.

This comparison, which was used by Dionysius, requires further clarification. The internal law ruling the essence of the Good and bringing it to communicate itself must not be thought of as a natural necessity constraining God. If the creative action is like solar illumination in that God, like the sun, lets no being escape His influence, it differs from it, too, regarding privation of will.[118] The good is the proper object of the will. It is therefore the goodness of God, as willed and loved by Him, that is the cause of the creature. But it is only the cause of the creature through the intermediary of the will.[119] Thus we affirm at the same time that there is in God an infinitely powerful tendency to diffuse Himself externally or to communicate Himself, and that nevertheless He only communicates or diffuses Himself by an act of the will. These two affirmations, far from contradicting each other, corroborate each other.

The voluntary, indeed, is nothing else than the inclination toward the good which the understanding grasps. God, who knows His own goodness both in itself and as imitable by creatures, wills it therefore in itself and in creatures who can participate in it. But the fact that the divine will is like this does not mean that God is subject to any kind of necessity.

The divine Goodness is infinite and total. All creation cannot increase this goodness by any amount, however little. Inversely, were God never to communicate His goodness to any creature, it would still remain undiminished.[120] No creature can introduce necessity into God's will.

Ought we to say that if God willed to realize creation, it had to be the one He actually realized? By no means, and for the same reason! God wills necessarily his own goodness, but this goodness is not increased because of the existence of creatures, and it would not diminish were they to disappear. What is true is that the present world is perfect in itself. It is the best possible world which it was possible to make with the kind of beings God chose to create. But He could have created another one, made up of better beings and which was a better universe. Consequently, just as God manifests His goodness by means of the things actually existing and by the order which He introduces here and now into the very depths of these things, so He could manifest it by means of other creatures disposed according to some different order.[121] For an infinite Creator, there is no such thing as a best possible finite universe. The same question could have been asked about any created world.[122] Just as God was free to create or not create a universe, He might have created it better or worse without His will being subject to any kind of necessity.[123]

In every case, since all that is is good insofar as it is, any universe created by God would have been good. Every difficulty that could arise on this point springs from the same confusion. It supposes that creation establishes a relation between God and creature as with an object. Hence one is led naturally to search out the cause determining the divine will in the creature. But in reality, creation does not introduce into God a relation with the creature. Any relation here is unilateral and is established only between the creature and the Creator as between a being and its cause.[124] We must adhere firmly, then, to this conclusion, that God wills Himself, and only Himself, necessarily; and that even though the superabundance of His being and His love carries Him to willing and loving Himself even in the finite participations of His being, we must see here only a gratuitous gift and nothing remotely resembling necessity.

To attempt to push this inquiry further would be to exceed the limits of the knowable or, more exactly, to seek to know what does not exist. The only further questions one can ask are the following: Why did God create the world when He did not have to do so? Why did He create this particular world when there were so many others He might have created? But such questions do not demand a reply unless one finds inadequate the simple statement that these things are so because God willed them. We know that the divine will has no cause. Certainly effects presupposing some other effect are not dependent upon the will of God alone. But first effects do depend upon the will of God alone. We say, for example, that God willed to give man his hands that they might obey the intellect and carry out its orders. He willed to give man his intellect because without it he would not be a man. Finally He willed that there be men for the greater perfection of the universe and because He willed that such creatures should exist in order to enjoy Him. But it remains absolutely impossible to assign an ulterior cause to this last will. The existence of the universe and of creatures capable of enjoying their creator has no other cause than the pure and simple will of God.[125]

Such is the true nature of the creative act insofar as it is given to us to understand it. It now remains to consider its effects. Before examining these, both in themselves and according to the hierarchy in which God has placed them, we must examine in general the view of the world proper to St. Thomas in order to distinguish the original features setting it apart from all those preceding it and the greater part of those which follow it.

CHAPTER VI

THE UNIVERSE OF ST. THOMAS

IT IS IMPOSSIBLE to appreciate St. Thomas's view of the world at its true value or to understand it fully without first placing it in its proper historical perspective. It is not difficult to do this to the extent that St. Thomas himself has done it. But beyond this point one runs into ever-increasing difficulties which become finally insurmountable. However, we can at least try to define its nature, leaving to each investigator the task of proposing a definitive interpretation.

St. Thomas clearly saw the general stages in the development of the problem of the basic origin of things, and he pointed it out with considerable accuracy so that there should be no danger of seriously misrepresenting his thought. On two distinct occasions he described them in the same manner, like a philosopher anxious to discover in the very structure of human knowledge the reason for the various phases through which the study of the problem has passed.

Our first knowledge has to do with the sensible, that is, with the qualities of bodies. The first philosophers, therefore, thought that there were no beings other than material beings, that is, sensible bodies. For them, these bodies were uncreated. The production of a new body was simply the appearance of a new grouping of sensible qualities. Such philosophers did not push the study of the origin of things beyond the problem of their accidental transmutations. They explained these transmutations as various types of motion, as, for example, rarefaction and condensation, and they explained these motions from principles which varied according to their particular doctrine, by Affinity, Discord, Intellect and so on. Such was the contribution of the Pre-Socratics to the problem. It is not surprising that they got no further than this, since it is by slow steps that men progress to the knowledge of truth.

At the second stage of this evolution we meet the work of Plato and Aristotle. These philosophers observed that every corporeal being is formed from two elements, matter and form. Like their predecessors, neither Plato nor Aristotle questioned the origin of matter. So far as they were concerned, it was without cause. As for the forms of things, however, they assigned them an origin. According to Plato, substantial forms came from the Ideas. According to Aristotle, Ideas were not enough to explain the generation of new substances continually observed in experience. Even if they exist, which Aristotle did not concede, Ideas are not causes. It would be necessary, therefore, to admit in every hypothesis, a cause for these participations of matter in the Ideas which we call "substantial forms." It is not health-in-itself which heals the sick, it is the physician.[1] In the case of the generation of substances, the efficient cause is the movement of the sun across its ecliptic course. Indeed, this motion permits at the same time both the continuity required to explain how generations and corruptions are continuous, and the duality without which it would be impossible to understand how it can cause generations and corruptions.[2]

Whatever may be the full detail of these doctrines, it is enough for us to remember this one point: whenever a cause is given for the uniting of forms to matter, the origin of substances is thereby assigned. The foregoing philosophers set out from substances already constituted. As if there was no call to justify their existence, they merely explained why, when specifically distinct substances are given, the individuals are distinguished from one another within the bosom of each species. To pass in this way from what makes a being to be *this* being to what makes it such and such a being is to progress from the plane of the accident to that of substance. An indisputable progress, though not yet a definitive one.

To explain the existence of a being is to explain the existence of the whole being. Now the pre-Socratics had, indeed, justified the existence of individuals as such. Plato and Aristotle had justified the existence of substances as such. But not one of these seemed even to have dreamed that there was any occasion to explain the existence of matter. Nevertheless matter, like form, is a constituent element of bodies. After Plato and Aristotle, then, there remained a last possible advance: to assign the ultimate cause of the total being, of its matter, its form, its accidents. In other words, it is not enough to show why it is *this* being and why it is such and such a being, but it must also be shown why it is "being." When we ask why beings exist as such, matter and form and accidents included, there is but one possible answer—God's creative act.[3] When it has arrived at this point, the human reason has exhausted the question to its limit and the problem of the basic root of being is resolved.

This text alone would justify our concluding that in St. Thomas's eyes, Aristotle's doctrine did not completely solve the problem of being. If we only think what an infinite distance lies between a God who is a creator and one who is not a creator, we can conclude that St. Thomas saw his God as very different from Aristotle's. St. Thomas pointed out this weakness of Aristotelianism as one of the capital errors opposed to the articles of the Christian faith.[4] To whom must we give the credit for going beyond Plato and Aristotle to the heart of the problem of the origin of being as being? To our knowledge at least, St. Thomas has never said. The text of the *Summa Theologiae* which we have just been examining refers to the authors of this metaphysical reform anonymously: "*Then others* (after the time of Plato and Aristotle) advanced further and raised themselves to the consideration of being as being."

It might be here a question of those Platonists whom Augustine praises for carrying Plato's conclusions so far. But St. Thomas never read Plotinus. Following St. Augustine,[5] he is speaking of these philosophers by hearsay. Forced to say whether the pagan philosophers had ever reached by reason alone the notion of creation, St. Thomas would probably have replied: it seems so, if what Augustine tells us about some of the Platonists is true. But he knew the position of Plato and Aristotle too well to admit that they had ever gone so far.[6] Thomas Aquinas must have had someone else in mind.

The difficulties become considerable when we seek to discover what place St. Thomas assigned himself among those philosophers who put the problem of the origin of being in its complete form. Always well-disposed toward philosophers, St. Thomas was doubly so here. And he was careful not to differ externally from the authoritative theologians whose faith he shared. Thus it is that we are forced to introduce between St. Thomas and his predecessors some distinctions which might not have met his approval. To be sure of ourselves, we should have to know to what extent St. Thomas was aware that he was an innovator in disengaging the existential character of being far better than his predecessors had done. We should have to know how conscious he was that he was an innovator in relation to men like St. Augustine and Dionysius the Areopagite whose authority in the Church was so enormous. But we do not know all this. Let us be content, then, at our own risk, to point out a number of differences in doctrine in which St. Thomas himself undoubtedly saw but different formulations of one and the same truth.

On the metaphysical foundation of the Augustinian group we have already explained ourselves at considerable length.[7] Since Moses said so, St. Augustine never wearied of repeating that God is *I Am*. But he always regretted that Moses, having said this, never explained the meaning of his words. Augustine was obliged to provide his own commentary. For him the words of *Exodus* meant: I am the immutable being, I am "He who never changes."

Setting out from this principle, Augustine seems to have met no grave difficulty in resolving the problem of the divine names. Whatever unity, order, intelligibility and beauty is to be found in nature provided him with a basis for as many attributes of God. To do this, he had only to carry each positive good to its highest perfection and to attribute it to God under this form, adding that what we learn as a host of distinct attributes are, in God, identical with His being. "God is what He possesses" is St. Augustine's oft-repeated formula, whose implications he worked out on the level of *essentia* as St. Thomas was to do on the level of the act-of-being. The serious difficulties ahead of him lay somewhere else, namely, at the point where, in seeking to define the relation between beings and Being, he was to come to grips with the problem of creation.

Like all Christians, St. Augustine knew that to create meant to produce beings out of nothing. No one can reasonably charge that he made any mistake about the meaning of the term. But the question arises as to what creation meant for him when placed under the light of natural reason for purposes of definition. St. Augustine always presents the creative act as the production of being by Being, a creation *veri nominis*, bearing upon being itself. "How, O my God, have you made the heavens and the earth? It is not in the universe that you have created the universe, because there was no place where it could be born before it was made to be. You had nothing at hand that could be of service in forming the heavens and the earth. Whence would you have received this matter not made by you and out of which you would have made things? What is there, indeed, that *is,* if not because you *are?*" And again: "It is you, O Lord, who have made the heavens and the earth; . . . you who *are,* because they are." [9] A truth could not be stated better, nor could its limitations be better revealed. St. Augustine knows very well that God exists and that the creative act has made the world exist. But just as he can only understand the existence of God conceived as the divine being, so also does he confuse the existence of things with their being. Creation, then, becomes the act in virtue of which "He who is what He is" makes things be what they are.

Hence the embarrassment of those interpreters who push the analysis of certain texts of St. Augustine to this point. One can speak only about one thing at a time. To be perfectly fair here one would have to say both that St. Augustine knows very well the meaning of creation, that is, of the production of being; and that his Platonism of being leaves him helpless to affirm clearly the act-of-being. So it is, as one of his best interpreters has observed, that all his explanations of creation tend naturally toward the level of participation.[10] For St. Augustine, the terms *creata* and *facta* are simple words borrowed from common speech. Whenever he looks for their technical equivalent in order to designate created beings as such, his choice falls upon the expression: things formed from the unformed, *ex informitate formata.*[11] Here it is as though the proper and direct effect of the creative act was, not the act-of-being, but that condition of the real which justifies the use of the term *being* in speaking of it. The unformed, in the present instance, is matter. The informing of matter is its intelligible determination by the divine idea. St. Augustine certainly knows that matter is itself created, or, as he puts it, concreated with form. But it is precisely this stabilization of matter by the rule of form which is evoked by the word creation in his thought. And necessarily so! In a doctrine in which being and immutable being are one and the same thing, creation consists in producing essences, which can only be called beings because their relative stability imitates the perfect immobility of Him Who Is.

Thus, however envisaged, the natural theology of St. Augustine seems to be dominated by the Platonic ontology of essence. Puzzled by the mystery of the divine name, he found himself similarly embarrassed when it came to explaining the being of things. Corresponding to the texts in which he complained because Moses had not explained the *Qui Est* of *Exodus,* we find now the passage from the *Confessions* where he deplores the fact that Moses failed to dwell on the first verse of *Genesis:* "In the beginning God created heaven and earth." Moses wrote this and moved on: *scripsit et abiit.* Were he still here, says Augustine, I should cling to him, I should pray him, beg him in God's name to explain its meaning; but Moses is no longer here, and even if he were, how should we understand the meaning of his words? [12]

Whenever St. Augustine finds himself face to face with being, he speaks like one haunted by the restlessness that springs from believing more about it than he knows about it. He is ever turning toward the divine being for further knowledge. What he holds from Plato shackles his native impulse: "The angel—and in the angel the Lord—said to Moses who was asking his name: 'I am who am. Thou shalt say to the children of Israel: *He Who Is* hath sent me to you.' The word 'being' means 'to be immutable' (*Esse, nomen est incommutabilitatis*). All changing things cease being what they were and begin being what they were not. Nothing has true being, pure being, authentic being save what does not change. He has being, to Whom it has been said: Thou wilt change things, and they will be changed, but Thou, thou remainest the same (Psalm CI, 27-8). What is meant by 'I am who am,' if not 'I am eternal'? What is meant by 'I am who am' unless 'I cannot change'?" [13]

By a strange paradox, the philosopher who most completely identified God with the transcendent immutability of Essence was the Christian most aware of the immanence of divine efficacy in nature, in the universal history of humanity, in the personal history of the individual conscience. When he speaks of these things as a theologian, St. Augustine seems infallible. Here he is without rival in the history of Christian thought. He has only disciples. His greatness is not the philosopher's but the theologian's whose philosophy lags behind his theology without retarding its progress.

The point at which Augustine felt the presence of God in nature could easily be shown from his doctrine of providence. But it is better to insist upon the Augustinian immanence of God in the history of the world and of souls because nowhere is the philosophical inadequacy of Christian Platonism more evident. Augustine's entire religion, as it appears in *The City of God,* is based on a history dominated by the memory of two major events, Creation and Redemption, and upon the expectation of a third, the Last Judgment. In order to make a philosophy of history out of this theology of history Augustine drew but lightly upon his ontology of the Immutable. Instead of having to explain the detail of existences by a supreme Existing Being, he had to explain what is always other through what remains immutably the same. In brief, he could not explain philosophically the relation between history and God save in terms of the opposition between time and Eternity. It is conceivable that time is in eternity,[14] but how is it conceivable, inversely, that Eternity may be in time? Yet it must be, at least if God's presence in history is to be assured. We willingly accord St. Augustine the full measure of success possible here, but we have also to recognize that to justify Christianity as history by means of an ontology in which becoming hardly deserves to be called being was a very difficult undertaking.

Perhaps as much ought to be said about the relation between St. Augustine's spirituality and his metaphysics. No one has felt more intensely than he God's immanence in the soul which He transcends: "You were more interior than my own interior and higher than my highest self." [15] Yet it is none the less true that Augustine was far better equipped to establish God's transcendence than to justify His immanence in the soul. The pathos of the *Confessions* depends in part upon its picture of a soul saturated with God's presence but failing to grasp it. Each time Augustine dares to say that God is within him, he hastens to add an *An potius* . . . "I should not be, O my God! I should absolutely not be, wert Thou not within me. Or rather, I should not be, were I not in Thee, from Whom, by Whom and in Whom all things are." [16] So it is that all his proofs for the existence of God, which are but so many impassioned searches for the divine presence, always bring Augustine to place God less within the soul than beyond it.[17] Each proof tends to terminate in mystical experience, where the soul finds God only by escaping from its own becoming and rooting itself for the moment in the stability of the Immutable. These short experiences only serve to anticipate in time, by suspending its limitations, the final vicissitude of universal history in which the entire order of becoming will be transformed into the stable peace of eternity.

Augustine knows better than anyone that everything, even becoming, is the work of the Immutable. But it is precisely at this point that he finds the mystery most obscure. No doubt no one could have cleared it up. But, at least, it was possible to show what latent intelligibility lay locked in the mystery. This was only possible by reducing the antinomy of time and Eternity to the analogy of being to Being, that is, by moving from God as Eternity to God as Act-of-Being. "Eternity, it is the very substance of God":[18] these words of Augustine clearly mark the ultimate limits of his ontology. They explain how his thought had conceived as an antinomy of Eternity and Mutability the relation of man to God which, his experience assured him, resembled the intimacy of a mutual presence. "God is his own act-of-being": these words of St. Thomas mark clearly the decisive progress attained by his ontology; they explain also the ease with which his thought could bind time to eternity, creature to Creator. For "He Who Is" signifies God's eternal present,[19] and the immanence of the divine efficacy in His creatures is, at the same time, cause of their being and of their duration: "Being is innermost in each thing, and most fundamentally present within all things. . . . Hence it must be that God is in all things, and innermostly." (ST. I, 8, 1)

We who are so far removed from the scene of battle might regard the Augustinian obstacle as far more formidable than the Dionysian. Not so, however, for the thirteenth century. For later generations the imposing figure of Denis the Areopagite has been reduced to the much more modest stature of the Pseudo-Dionysius, whose doctrinal authority has steadily diminished while Augustine's, if it has not increased, has at least held its own. Moreover, by its very nature, Dionysius' work presented St. Thomas with a problem that was serious in a way quite different from Augustine's. As we have said, Augustine's philosophy lagged behind his theology, but his theology itself was perfectly sound. Hence St. Thomas could take it as it stood, find therein exactly the same truth, but penetrate it more deeply than Augustine had done. We are far from being able to say as much of Dionysius' theology. Resplendent with the authority which the thirteenth century gave him, Denis must have seemed to St. Thomas to say many things which he could scarcely have thought. St. Thomas's clever sleight of hand in appropriating the riskiest Dionysian formulas must not blind us to the fact that he never took over a formula without altering its content.[20] The sleight-of-hand artist is indeed a magician. Sometimes St. Thomas is hard put to it to extract from these Sybilline formulas the correct meaning with which he actually charges them. At such moments he pauses to grumble a little. "In all his books Denis employs an obscure style," and that he should do so deliberately, *ex industria,* does not alter the case. Again, he was so like the Platonists! *Platonicos multum imitabatur.* But St. Thomas does not give up; and from his furious labor there issues a Thomistic Denis in whom the historical Denis is scarcely discernible.

In its more obvious aspects, the work of Denis is presented as a commentary on Sacred Scripture, that is, as the work of a Christian theologian.[21] This is pre-eminently the case with his treatise *On the Divine Names.* Here he deals directly with the problem of our knowledge of God and resolves it in a manner that must have caused St. Thomas much perplexity in the reading of it. Like Augustine, Denis borrows the essentials of his philosophical technique from the Platonism of Plotinus. Also like Augustine, he has to use this technique in order to elucidate Christian dogma. But the Greek concedes far more to Plotinus than Augustine ever did.

The chief characteristic of the philosophy of Plotinus is that it is built upon a metaphysics of the One rather than of Being. To affirm that the One is the first principle of everything that is, is to admit at the outset that the One is not a being. Since it is the principle of whatever deserves the name of being, it is not itself a being. Being, properly so-called, makes its first appearance in the universal hierarchy with the νοῦς, or Intelligence. At the same time that it is the first being, this second hypostasis is the first god. In such a sense, this theology was manifestly unusable for a Christian. To identify the God of *Exodus* with the One is either to reduce the latter to the level of being, which Plotinus regards as inferior to the One; or else it is to raise God above being which, for Christianity, is the least inappropriate of all the divine names. The first of these alternatives betrays Plotinus, the second the Scriptures. St. Augustine did not hesitate to betray Plotinus. Let us observe how Denis tries to betray neither more than is necessary, and avoids complete acquiescence with either.

The expression *superessentialis divinitas* often turns up in Erigena's translation of Denis. This pays homage to Plotinus and at the same time betrays his thought. But it is the only course for a Christian. If, like Plotinus, we identify Intelligence, Being and God, we can no longer say that God is above intelligence and being. But if we make the transposition demanded by Christianity and identify God with the One of Plotinus, we have to think of God as above intelligence and being. We arrive thus at Plato's Good, or at Plotinus's for that matter, but here conceived as a God who is beyond being (ἐπέκεινα τῆς οὐσίας). Thus, for Denis, God is *superessentialis,* and is so by full right. Now being and essence are One. A superessential God is not, therefore, a being. Indeed he is much more than a being, and precisely because he is more than a being, he is not a being. This amounts to saying that God is a non-being, and that the *non ὄν* or "what is not" is the supreme cause of all that is.[22]

Starting with this notion, the Platonic hierarchy of principles will necessarily tend to be re-established within the Christian order. Taken by Himself, God will be identified with the One, that is, with perfect simplicity transcending the order of number. The One does not generate number by way of division, because it is indivisible. If we must find a simile for this we can compare it to the center of a circumference at which all the radii coincide. Or again, it is like a Monad, anterior to all number, which contains all beings without being one of them. Similarly, the One, which precedes being, contains within itself all the being which itself is not. But as this being is not the One, it will be called "the being of existing things": *ipsum esse existentium.*[23] This is a formula whose influence was to be deep and lasting, as we shall see. However, if we wish to designate the first principle in all its creative fecundity, we give it its honorary title which Plato had conferred upon it: the Good, or the *Optimum.*[24] From this it becomes clear that if it must be taken as the supreme "non-being," this is by way of excess and not of defect. Taken in the full sense, as it ought to be, this apparent negation affirms a first principle which, placed beyond life, knowledge and being, is the cause of whatever possesses them. Whatever is, is only by participation in the Good, which itself transcends being.[25]

In a doctrine in which the primacy of the Good is so forcefully affirmed, the I Am Who Am of *Exodus* is necessarily subjected to a restricted interpretation greatly diminishing its significance. In writing a treatise on the divine names, that is, on the names given to God in Sacred Scripture, Denis could not ignore this text. But he simply cites it, along with several others, as providing one of the names of the unnameable.[26] To speak of being *à propos* of God, is not to speak of Him but of His effect. Being, of course, always bears the mark of the One, which is its cause. It is even because it is the effect of the One that being only is insofar as it is one. The imperfect, unstable and always divisible unity of beings is nevertheless in them like the causal energy by which they are. Let the transcendent One cease to penetrate a being with its light and it ceases at once to exist. It is in this profound sense that God can be called the being of everything that is: ὤν *totius esse*. Yet God only appears under the aspect of being as the cause which makes things to be. To be exact, being is but the revealing or manifestation of the One; in a word, its "theophany." [27] As to the One, it remains *ante* ὤν: it is not entangled in the order of its participations.[28]

From the point of view of the history of Christian theology, this doctrine, compared with St. Augustine's, seems to be a step backward. In Augustine, the influence of Plotinus had only been generalized under certain extremely rigid conditions. Although, in his doctrine, being is considered as a Platonic kind of intelligible and immutable essence, God is not only identified with the Good and the One, as in Denis, He is also identified with Being. A decision of capital importance which Denis seems not to have adopted, and an oversight involving Christian commentators and historians in countless difficulties. Either they perceive the danger and re-integrate being into Denis's One and so conform his teaching to the norm of orthodoxy, or they accept it literally, and give it a more and more pantheistic flavor as they explain it more fully. What most interests us for the moment is how a theologian, as manifestly Christian as Denis, could have developed such a doctrine without embarrassment.

To maintain that his feeling for God was pantheistic is to go counter to the obvious sense of all his texts. In these God always appears to be before (*ante*) or above (*super*) whatever topic is under discussion. Denis had an acute, almost exasperated feeling for the divine transcendency. If, while experiencing this feeling, he was able to maintain that God is the being of all that is, it is precisely because, for him, God is not being. He has being only in the sense that He is, in the capacity of its cause, "the being of that which is." If, on the contrary, we read his doctrine so as to translate it into the language of a theology in which God is essentially being, we make it pantheistic. If Denis never has any fears on this score, it is because in his thought there can be no confusion of being between things and God for the very simple reason that things are, while God, since He is the One, is not.

This inferiority of being to God is clearly marked in the special metaphysical regulation which Denis imposes on the Ideas. The Ideas, like everything intelligible and immutable, are. It can even be said that they pre-emimently are. Because they are, they are principles and causes: *et sunt, et principia sunt, et primo sunt, deinde principia sunt.*[29] Only, by an inevitable consequence, since they are, they are not God. The very title of the fifth chapter of *The Divine Names* is enough to prove that this is the way this doctrine goes: "On Being, and also on the Ideas" (*De ente, in quo et de paradigmatibus*). Where we begin to speak of being, we begin naturally by speaking of the first beings, the Ideas. The opening of this chapter is likewise remarkable: "Let us pass now to the true theological name of the *essentia* of what truly is. We only remark that it is not our intention here to show the superessential essence. Since it is superessential, it is ineffable, unknowable and absolutely inexplicable. It is transcendent Unity itself (*superexaltatem unitatem*). But we wish to praise the procession, maker of substance, of the principal divine essence, in all existing things."[30] It would be impossible to mark more strongly the breach between the order of being and its principle, and the "superexistentiality" of the latter. By the same stroke, the divine ideas are excluded from this same "superexistentiality." For they only are because they participate in it. In a system in which being proceeds, not from Being, but from the One and the Good, one enters simultaneously into the order of being and into that of participation. Hence, in Denis, that characteristic doctrine which makes of ideas "participations *per se*," anterior to all others, causes of all others, and which, because they are the first participations (*primum participantia*), are also the first beings (*primum existentia*).[31]

One of the first consequences of this doctrine is to de-existentialize completely the notion of creation. For St. Thomas, God gives existence because He is the Act-of-Being. For Denis, the One gives being because it itself does not exist. Hence, a second consequence, that the invisible things of God (*invisibilia Dei*) cannot be known if one begins from the created world. In such a doctrine, reason can mount from being to being right up to the divine Ideas, which are the first beings. Here it is stopped by an impassable abyss, for it can go no higher without mounting to God, who transcends being itself. How could reason possibly do this, since everything which it knows *is?*

The negative theological method had, perforce, to become the Dionysian method *par excellence*. To begin with, whatever Denis says on the subject is in such agreement with what St. Thomas is to say that it is not surprising that the latter often cites it approvingly. Yet let us observe just how he cites it: "Denis says (in his *Divine Names*) that we reach God from creatures, namely, by causality, by elimination, by eminence."[32] Here is the Thomistic method as we have already described it. But how far we are from the text to which St. Thomas appeals! He has in mind John Sarrozin's version of Denis's text: *"Ascendemus in omnium ablatione et excessu et in omnium causa."* St. Thomas has been praised for improving upon the logical order of these operations by reversing the order of the words: *per causalitatem, per remotionem, per eminentiam.*[33] Really, it is the entire doctrine of Denis which is here inverted. The text of the *Divine Names,* ch. VII, says that we arrive at the cause of all by eliminating the given and transcending it.[34] To follow such a method is to begin with the sensible datum in order to ascend to its cause. It is also to rely upon a certain relationship, a kind of analogy, between the effect and its cause. But in this case we do not rely upon such a relationship save to deny that it teaches anything about the nature of the cause. Could it be otherwise in a universe in which things are because God is not?

The two consequences of this principle which we here emphasize are but the two sides of a single thesis: creation does not consist in a relationship between beings and Being; the creative cause cannot be known from created beings. All that Denis will grant is that, beginning from things, we can arrive at a kind of knowledge of the Ideas of God, which, as we have just seen, are not God. To the question "How do we know a God who is neither intelligible, nor sensible, nor in a general way any of the things which exist?" Denis replies by asking another question: "But may we not say that we know God in some other way than by His nature?" And here is his explanation: "For this nature is something unknown which surpasses all understanding, all reason, all thought. When we begin with the disposing of all things which it proposes to us, including, as it were images and assimilations to its divine exemplars, rooting them out and transcending them, we raise ourselves, in the measure of our strength, thanks to the life and to the order of the whole, right up to the cause of all things."[35] To know God, therefore, in this life is only to know some image of Ideas beyond which He dwells as in an eternal inaccessibility.

In order to remove the Dionysian obstacle, a transformation had to be effected in the very notion of God. Though admirably conceived as the principle of rational intelligibility, Denis's One could only with difficulty fulfil the functions which all religion expects of God. At the very most it permitted the return to some doctrine of salvation by knowledge like that elaborated by Plotinus. It could in no way guarantee that intimate and personal union with God which man seeks in religion. Thus we find St. Thomas constantly re-establishing, on the plane of existence and existential causality, all the relationships between the creature and God, which Denis conceived as participations of being in the One.

For Denis, God was a *superesse,* because He was "not yet" the *esse* which He only becomes in His highest processions. For St. Thomas, God is the *superesse* because He is superlatively being: the *Esse* pure and simple, taken in its infinity and perfection. Touched by a magic wand, the doctrine of Denis issues forth transformed. St. Thomas has preserved it in its entirety, but nothing retains its former meaning.[36] God's *esse,* it is true, still remains unknowable, so far as concerns us. But what no longer is the case is that our knowledge of things is a knowledge of something which God is not. We can now say of everything that is that God is it too. Indeed, we can say that He is it pre-eminently; that its being belongs to Him before it belongs to His creature. It is God's manner of being which completely escapes us.[37] When all the necessary eliminations have been made, this at least remains, that each human concept of each being and of each mode of being authorizes us to conclude: Since that of which I have a concept, is, God is it. In such a doctrine, the *invisibilia Dei* continue to transcend our knowledge; but they transcend it in being's own line, since all God's attributes, known from created being, only become invisible to us when identified with the perfect simplicity of *Esse.*

In achieving this decisive progress, St. Thomas finally resolved the fundamental problem of the origin of finite being. From the very beginning, Greek thought had found itself at grips with this difficulty: how to place in the same explanation of the real the gods of religion and the principles of philosophy. In order to understand what things are, there must be principles, but to understand that things are, there must be causes. The Greek gods precisely were such causes. Entrusted to resolve all problems about the origin of things, they intervened each time it was a question of supplying a reason for some existence, whether it was that of the world itself, as we see in the case of Hesiod's *Theogony,* or in the *Iliad,* or whether it was simply that of the events which take place in this world. It could easily be shown that this dualism of essence and existence explains that of philosophy and myth in the work of Plato. All Plato's myths are existential as all his dialectic is essential. Hence none of Plato's Ideas, not even the Good, is a God; nor none of Plato's gods, even the Demiurge, an Idea. In order to resolve this antinomy, it was possible to decide to identify Plato's Good and the supreme God. But this was not to resolve the antinomy; it was only to move it into the First Principle itself. We have shown this to be the case with St. Augustine and of Denis the Areopagite. How can we make a God out of an

essence without at the same time making an essence of a God? Once
God has been essentialized, one quickly has to face, as did St. Augustine,
the difficulty of justifying existences, beginning from the *Essentia* assigned
to them as their principle. The only other course, to avoid the difficulty,
is to remove with Denis the first principle beyond both essence and existence, thereby denying creatures any positive knowledge of the creator.

It is quite different in a natural theology like that of St. Thomas. His
God is *Esse*. Now the act of being is like the very stuff from which things
are made. The real, therefore, is only intelligible by the light of the
supreme Act-of-Being, which is God.

In St. Thomas's work God plays the role of a supreme principle of
intelligibility, as we established when treating the proofs for His existence,
and verified again with each of His attributes. By Him and by Him
alone, all that participates in any way in unity, goodness, truth and
beauty is one, good, true and beautiful. Thus the God of religion has
here truly become the supreme principle of philosophical intelligibility.
But, it may be added, this principle of intelligibility itself coincides with
the God of religion. This coincidence does not come about without danger
both for God's divinity and for the intelligibility of the principle save
in a doctrine in which, as in that of Thomas Aquinas, all these problems
are ultimately settled on the plane of existence, there the radical cause
of all existences is, at the same time, their supreme principle of intelligibility.

Such, indeed, is St. Thomas's God—not only the principle but the
creator, not only the Good, but the Father. His providence extends to
the least detail of being because His providence is only His causality. To
cause an effect is but to propose to Himself its achievement. Moreover,
it must be said of everything that is and acts that it depends immediately
upon God in both its being and operations.[38]

What God is in His eternal self, He remains as cause of events. Creatures passing through time have given Him various names. But each
name marks a relationship between creatures and Him, not between Him
and creatures. Man emerges from nothingness—and calls God his creator.
Man recognises this creator as his supreme master—and calls him Lord.
Man sins, is lost, is saved by the Word made Flesh—and he calls God
his Redeemer. This long history is developed in time and in a changing
world, but God is no more changed by it than a column which moves
from right to left as we pass to and fro before it. God is Creator for
those whom He creates and whom His eternal efficacy redeems each
moment from nothingness. He is Savior for those whom He saves and
Lord for those who profess to serve Him. But in Him creation and redemption are but His action which, like His power, is one with His act-
of-being.[39] In order that the first principle of philosophy rejoin in this

way the God of religion, and in order that the same God of religion be Author of Nature and God of history at the same time, it has been necessary to follow the meaning of the name of God in its profoundest existential implication. *I Am* is the only God of whom it can be said that He is God of philosophers and scholars, and God, too, of Abraham and of Isaac and of Jacob.

PART TWO

NATURE

CHAPTER I

CREATION

THE PROBLEM of the beginning of the universe is one of the most obscure that philosophers can approach. Some would show that the universe has always existed. Others would establish, on the contrary, that the universe necessarily began in time.[1] Supporters of the first thesis claim Aristotle's authority, though the philosopher's texts are far from explicit on the point. In Book VIII of the *Physics* and Book I of the *De Coelo*, Aristotle seems only to have established the eternity of the world in order to refute the teachings of certain ancients who assigned a most unacceptable sort of beginning to the world. He tells us, furthermore, that there are dialectical problems for which there is no demonstrable solution, for example, that of knowing whether the world is eternal.[2] The authority of Aristotle not only is insufficient to settle the question, but it cannot even be invoked on the point.[3] In reality we are here in the presence of a clearly characterized Averroistic teaching,[4] condemned by Stephen Tempier, Bishop of Paris, in 1270: "that the world is eternal and that there never was a first man." Among the numerous arguments upon which this teaching claims to be based, it is important to keep in mind especially the one appealing to the all-powerful causality of the creator because it makes us penetrate to the very heart of the matter.

To posit the sufficient cause is to posit at the same time its effect. A cause whose effect does not result immediately is a non-sufficient cause because imperfect, that is, because something it needs to produce its effects is wanting. Now, God is the sufficient cause of the world, either as final cause since He is the Sovereign Good, or as exemplary cause since He is supreme Wisdom, or as efficient cause since He is Omnipotence. But we know from elsewhere that God exists from all eternity. The world, therefore, like its sufficient cause, also exists from all eternity.[5] Moreover, it is evident that the effect proceeds from its cause by reason of the action which the cause exercises. But God's action is eternal. Otherwise we should have to admit that God was first in potency with regard to His action and that then He was brought from potency to act by some anterior agent, which is impossible.[6] Or, indeed, we should lose sight of the fact that God's action is His own substance, which is eternal.[7] It is therefore necessarily true that the world has always existed.

Next, if we consider the problem from the point of view of creatures, we can observe that we are forced to the same conclusion. We know that in the universe there exist incorruptible creatures, like celestial bodies or intellectual substances. What is incorruptible, that is, what is capable of existing always, cannot be considered as now existing and now not existing, for it exists just as long as it has the power to be. Now, anything which begins to exist belongs in the category of things which now exist and now do not. Therefore, nothing incorruptible can have a beginning. We can conclude, then, that the universe, outside which incorruptible substances would have neither place nor reason to be, exists from all eternity.[8]

Finally, we can deduce the eternity of the world from the eternity of motion. Nothing begins to move unless either the mover or the thing moved is in a different state from that in which it was a moment ago. In still other words, a new motion is never produced without a previous change either in the mover or in the thing moved. But to change is nothing else than to be moved. There is, accordingly, always a motion previous to the one that is beginning. Consequently, as far as we might wish to go back in this series, we always encounter motion. But if motion has always existed, there must also have always existed a thing moved, for motion only exists in a thing moved. The universe has, therefore, always existed.[9]

These arguments are all the more convincing as they seem to be based on the most authentic Aristotelian principles. But they cannot be taken as genuinely conclusive. First of all, we can eliminate the last two arguments by means of a simple distinction. From the fact that there has always been motion, in the sense just demonstrated, it does not at all follow that there has always been something moved. The only conclusion justified by such an argument is that there has always been motion from the moment of the existence of a thing moved. But this thing moved could only have come into existence by creation. Aristotle established this proof in Book VIII of the *Physics*[10] against those who admit eternal moveable objects and yet deny the eternity of motion. It has no force against us, who maintain that there has been motion ever since movable things have existed.

The same holds for the proof based on the incorruptibility of heavenly bodies. We must grant that what is naturally capable of existing forever cannot be considered now to exist and now not to exist. However, it must be remembered that for a thing to be capable of always existing, it must first exist, and that nothing can be incorruptible before it exists. This argument of Aristotle, found in Book I of the *De Coelo,* does not conclude simply that incorruptible bodies never began to exist, but that they did not begin to exist by way of natural generation like other beings subject to generation or corruption.[11] Thus the possibility of their having been created is fully safeguarded.

Need we, on the other hand, grant the eternity of a universe we know to be the effect of an eternal, sufficient cause and an eternal action, the omnipotent efficacy and eternal action of God? There is nothing to force us to do this if it is true, as we have previously demonstrated, that God does not act by the necessity of nature but by free will. No doubt, it might at first glance appear contradictory that an omnipotent, immovable, immutable God should have willed to confer existence, in a determined point in time, on a universe which did not exist before. But this difficulty becomes a mere illusion, easily dissipated, as soon as we re-establish the true relationship between the duration of created things and the creative will of God. We already know that if it is a question of finding a reason for the production of creatures, there is room for a distinction between the production of one particular creature and the exodus (*exitus*) by which the entire universe has issued from God.

In accounting for the production of any given creature, it is possible to explain it either by reference to some other creature or by reference to the order of the universe, in which every creature is ordered as a part of the whole. But when we consider the coming to be of the entire universe, it is no longer possible to look to other created reality for the reason why the universe is what it is. As has been seen, the reason for the definite setting up of the universe cannot be drawn from the divine power, which is infinite and inexhaustible, nor from the divine Goodness which is self-sufficient and in need of no creature. The only reason for the choice of this particular universe is the pure and simple will of God. Let us apply this conclusion to God's choice of the moment fixed by Himself for the appearance of the world. We must say, in this case, that just as it depends on the simple will of God that the universe has a definite quantity so far as the relation of dimension is concerned, so also it depends upon this same will of God that the universe has a definite quantity of duration. This is particularly so inasmuch as time is a quantity truly extrinsic to the nature of the thing existing in time and altogether a matter of indifference so far as the will of God is concerned.

It may be objected that a will only delays something it proposes to do because it suffers some modification causing it to decide to do at a certain moment in time what it had been proposing to do at another. If, then, the immovable will of God wills the world, it must always have willed it, and, therefore, the world has always existed. But such a process of reasoning subjects the action of the first cause to the conditions governing the action of particular causes which act in time. The particular cause is not the cause of the time in which its action takes place. God, on the contrary, is the cause of time itself, for time is included in the universality of things created by Him. Hence, when we are speaking of the way in which the being of the universe has issued from God, we need not wonder why God willed to create this being at one moment rather than another. Such a question supposes that time pre-exists creation, while in reality it is subject to it. The only question we might ask ourselves about universal creation is, not why God created the universe at a given moment of time, but why He has assigned this kind of measure to the duration of this time. Now, the measure of this time depends solely upon the divine will. And since the Catholic faith teaches us that the world has not always existed, we can admit that God willed to set a beginning to the world and to assign it a limit in duration as He assigned it one in space. The words of Genesis:[12] "In the beginning God created heaven and earth" remain, therefore, quite acceptable to reason.[13]

We know that the eternity of the world cannot be demonstrated. Let us see if it is not possible to go farther and demonstrate that it is not eternal. Many theologians adopted the position that they could demonstrate that the world is not eternal. St. Thomas considered their arguments unacceptable. The first argument, which we already know from the pen of St. Bonaventure, maintains, against Averroes, that if the universe has existed from eternity, there ought now to be an infinite number of human souls. Since the human soul is immortal, all those which have existed during infinite time should still be in existence today. There is, then, an infinite number of them. Now this is impossible. Therefore the universe had a beginning.[14] It is only too easy to object to this argument by pointing out that God could have created the world without men or souls, and besides, that it has not yet been demonstrated that God could not have created an actual infinity of simultaneously existing beings.[15]

Again, the doctrine of the creation of the world in time is based on the principle that it is impossible to go beyond the infinite. If the world has not had a beginning, an infinite number of celestial revolutions must have taken place, so that to reach the present day the universe must have passed through an infinite number of days; which is impossible. Therefore, the universe has not always existed.[16] But this reason is not conclusive, for even if we grant that an infinite number of simultaneous beings is impossible, it still remains that an infinite number of successive beings is possible, because every infinity considered as successive is really finished by its present term. The number of celestial revolutions which would have taken place in a universe of infinite past duration would be, properly speaking, a finite number. And it would not be impossible for the universe to have passed through this number in order to reach the present moment.

Finally, if we wish to consider all the revolutions taken together, it must be admitted that, in a world which had always existed, none of them could have been the first. Now every passage supposes two terms, a term from which and a term to which. Since the first of these is wanting in an eternal universe, the question of whether the passage from the first day to the present is possible does not even arise.[17]

We might establish an argument to deny the eternity of the world on the ground that it is impossible to add to the infinite, because what receives an addition becomes larger, and nothing is larger than the infinite. But if the world has no beginning, it has had, perforce, an infinite duration, and nothing more can be added to it. Now such a statement is false since each day adds one more celestial revolution to the preceding revolutions. The world cannot, then, have always existed.[18] But the distinction already made removes this new difficulty; for there is no reason why the infinite cannot receive an addition on the side on which it is really finite. From the fact that eternal time can be affirmed of the origin of the world, it follows that this time is infinite so far as the past is concerned, but finite at its present extremity, for the present is the terminus of the past. Thus considered, the eternity of the world is not an impossibility.[19]

Hence, it cannot be demonstrated by reason that the world is not eternal. This truth, like the mystery of the Trinity, must be accepted on faith. The arguments, probable as they are, on which some pretend to establish it, must be demolished lest the Catholic faith seem to rest on empty reasons rather than on the unshakeable teaching of God.[20] The creation of the world in time cannot be necessarily deduced from a consideration either of the world itself or of God's will. The principle of any demonstration is to be found in the definition of the essence, from which the properties can be deduced. Now essence, in itself, is indifferent to time or place. That is the reason why universals are said to exist always and everywhere. Because they are indifferent to existence, the definitions of man, of heaven or of the earth do not imply in any way that such beings have always existed. Nor do they imply that such beings have not always existed.[21] Much less can this demonstration be established from God's will, for this will is free and has no cause. We can prove nothing about it, save in regard to those things which must necessarily be willed. But the divine will can be made known to man by revelation, on which faith is founded. On the strength of the divine word, we can believe that the universe had a beginning even if we cannot know it.[22]

The soundest position on this difficult question lies somewhere between the Averroists and the Augustinians. Against the Averroists, St. Thomas maintains the possibility of the world's beginning in time. But he maintains also, even against those who do not like the idea (*contra murmurantes*), the possibility of its eternity. Certainly, in order to resolve the problem of creation, St. Thomas has made use of the work of his predecessors, notably of Albert the Great and Moses Maimonides. But his position is not to be identified with that of any predecessor. Maimonides will only admit creation on the ground of faith.[23] But St. Thomas bases it on demonstrative reason. The two agree on two points: that it is impossible to demonstrate the world's beginning in time, and that it is always possible to deny the eternal existence of the universe.[24] Albert the Great, on the other hand, admits with Maimonides that creation *ex nihilo* can only be known by faith. St. Thomas, closer here than his master to the Augustinian tradition, thinks such a demonstration to be possible. On the other hand, he regards creation of the world in time to be indemonstrable.

Albert, however, closer here than his disciple to the Augustinian tradition, thinks that the beginning of the world in time can be demonstrated, once creation itself has been admitted. Against both of these philosophers, St. Thomas maintains the possibility of demonstrating the creation of the universe *ex nihilo*. In this we see him resolutely opposed to Averroes and his disciples. But, in conceding, with Maimonides, the logical possibility of a universe created from all eternity, he refuses to confuse truths of faith with those which are objects of proof. Thus there is realized in his thought that accord which he endeavors to establish between the infallible teaching of Christianity and whatever unquestionable truth the doctrine of Aristotle contains.

Let us suppose that the moment has come when all the possibles, which are to constitute the universe when they are realized, issue from God in order to pass into being. The problem which then arises is to know why and how a host of distinct beings, not just one being, is produced by the creator. The Arabian philosophers and particularly Avicenna, whose opinion we have already met, want to explain the plurality and diversity of things by means of the necessary action of the first efficient cause, God. Avicenna supposes that the First Being understands himself and that, insofar as he knows and understands himself, produces one sole effect—the first intelligence. It is inevitable, and on this point St. Thomas will follow Avicenna, that the first intelligence will lack the simplicity of the First Being. This intelligence, indeed, is not its own being. It possesses it because it receives it from another. It is therefore in potency in regard to its own being. In this intelligence, potency begins to mix with act. Let us consider, in turn, this first intelligence insofar as it is endowed with knowledge. First, it knows the First Being, and from this very act there proceeds an intelligence inferior to the first. Secondly, it knows what potency is within itself. From this knowledge proceeds the body of the first heaven which this intelligence moves. Finally, it knows its own proper act. From this knowledge proceeds the soul of the first heaven. By continuing in this fashion we may see why different beings are multiplied by a multitude of intermediary causes, beginning from the First Being, God.[25]

But this position is untenable. One decisive reason for this is that Avicenna and his disciples here attribute to creatures a creative power which belongs to God alone. We have already dealt with this point above, and it is superfluous to return to it here. A second reason is that this teaching of Avicenna and his disciples attributes the origin of the world to chance. In their hypothesis, the universe does not wholly arise from the intention of the first cause but largely from the conjunction of many causes whose effects are piled one upon another. This is the very meaning of chance. Avicenna's teaching, therefore, reasserts that the multiplicity and diversity of things contributing to the completion and perfection of the universe comes from chance. This is clearly impossible.[26]

The primary origin of the multiplicity and distinction of things is not in chance, but in the intention of the first cause, God. Moreover, it is not impossible to show a certain expediency in having the creator produce a multiplicity of creatures. Every being which acts tends to induce its likeness into the effect which it is producing. It is the more successful in accomplishing this as it is itself more perfect. Thus, the more heat a being possesses, the more heat it gives off. And the more excellent an artist a man shows himself to be, the more perfect is the artistic form he introduces into matter. Now God is the sovereignly perfect agent. It is therefore in conformity with His nature to introduce His likeness perfectly into things; that is, as perfectly as is consonant with the finite nature of created things. Now it is evident that no one species of creatures can successively express the creator's likeness. Since here the effect—of finite nature—is not of the same order as its cause—of infinite nature—one single species can only obscurely and inadequately express the cause from which it springs. For a creature to represent its creator as perfectly as possible, it would have to be its equal, which is a contradiction.

We know of only one single case in which there proceeds from God a person expressing Him totally and perfectly. This is the procession of the Word. There, however, it is not a question of a creature nor of a relationship of cause and effect, but of something remaining within God Himself. On the contrary, where it is a question of finite and created beings, it will take many such to express under the greatest possible number of aspects the simple perfection from which they proceed. The reason, therefore, for the multiplicity and variety of created things is that such multiplicity and variety are necessary to express as perfectly as creatures can the likeness of God, the creator.[27]

But to posit creatures of different species is necessarily to posit creatures of unequal perfection. In what way are we to distinguish the many distinct things which express the divine likeness? It can only be by either their matter or their form. Any distinction that is theirs from difference of form divides them into separate species. Any distinction of matter makes of them numerically different individuals. But matter only exists in view of form; and beings numerically distinct by their matters are so only to make possible formal distinction differentiating their species from other species. In incorruptible beings, there is only one individual to each species; that is, there is neither numerical distinction nor matter. This is because the individual is incorruptible and itself sufficient to assure the conservation and differentiation of the species. In beings capable of generation and corruption, many individuals are necessary in order to conserve the species. Within the species itself, beings as numerically distinct individuals only exist that the species may subsist formally distinct from other species. The true and principal distinction which we can observe in things is in their formal distinction. Now no formal distinction is possible without inequality.[28] The forms which determine the different natures of beings, and by reason of which things are what they are, in the last analysis are only different quantities of perfection. This is why we can say with Aristotle that the forms of things are like numbers whose species are changed by the addition or subtraction of a unit. Since God cannot adequately express His likeness in any single species, and since He wishes to produce in being a plurality of formally distinct species, He has necessarily to produce unequal species. Hence we see that in natural things species are ordered hierarchically and arranged according to grades. Just as the compounds are more perfect than the elements, just as plants are more perfect than minerals, so animals are more perfect than plants, and men than other animals. In this progression each species surpasses the preceding in perfection. The reason why the divine wisdom causes the inequality of creatures is the same as that which makes it will their distinction; that is, the highest perfection of the universe.[29]

It is not impossible to raise a difficulty at this point. If creatures can be placed in hierarchical order according to their unequal degrees of perfection, it is not at once clear how they can proceed from God. Indeed, an excellent being can only will excellent things; and among truly excellent things, grades of perfection are not discernible. Therefore God, who is excellent, must have willed that all things be equal.[30] But such an objection is based upon an equivocation. When an excellent being acts, the effect produced must be excellent in its totality. But it is not necessary that each part of this total effect be itself excellent. It is sufficient that it be excellently proportioned to the whole. Now this proportion can demand that the proper excellence of certain parts be itself mediocre. The eye is the noblest part of the body; but the body would be badly formed if all its parts possessed the dignity of the eye, or if each part were an eye. Each of the other parts has its function, which the eye, in spite of its perfection, cannot fulfill. It would be similarly unfitting for each part of a house to be a roof. Such a dwelling could not achieve its perfection, nor fulfill its end, which is to protect its inhabitants against rain and heat. Far from being contradictory to the excellence of the divine nature, the inequality we can see in things is actually a patent mark of God's sovereign wisdom. We do not mean that God has necessarily willed the finite and limited beauty of creatures. We know that His infinite goodness can receive no increase from His creatures. But we are simply saying that it is consonant with the order of His wisdom that the unequal multiplicity of creatures should assure the perfection of the universe.[31]

The reason for a difference between the degrees of perfection of the various orders of creatures is thus clearly apparent. But we can still legitimately wonder whether this explanation exonerates the creator for having willed a universe in which it was not impossible to encounter evil.

We say, indeed, that the perfection of the universe demands inequality among beings. Since God's infinite perfection can only fittingly be imitated by a host of finite beings, it is fitting that all the degrees of goodness be represented in things so that the universe may constitute a sufficiently perfect image of the creator. Now to possess so excellent a perfection that one can never lose it is one grade of goodness. It is quite another to possess a perfection which one can at a given moment lose. We also find these two grades of perfection represented in things. Some things are of such a nature that they can never lose their being; these are incorporeal and incorruptible creatures. Others can lose their being; for example, corporeal and corruptible creatures. Hence, by the very fact that the perfection of the universe demands the existence of corruptible beings, it demands that certain beings be capable of losing their degree of perfection. Now the loss of a grade of perfection, and consequently deficiency in some good, is the basis of the definition of evil. The presence of corruptible beings in the world inevitably implies the presence of evil.[32] To say, then, that it is consonant with divine wisdom to will the inequality of creatures is to say that it is fitting for it to will evil. Does not an affirmation of this sort endanger the infinite perfection of the creator?

In one sense this objection presents the human mind with an insoluble problem. The production of creatures amounts inevitably to furnishing a subject for, and a support for, imperfection. This is not mere convenience; it is a real necessity. It is characteristic of creatures to be deficient in degree and mode of being: *Esse autem rerum creatarum deductum est ab esse divino secundum quandam deficientem assimilationem.*[33] Creation is not only an exodus; it is also a descent: "No creature receives the whole fulness of divine goodness because perfections come from God to creatures by a kind of descent." [34] We must observe a continuous series of reductions of the grade of being as we pass from superior to inferior. This deficiency appears even with the first degree of created beings. Even in the highest of creatures, the deficiency in being is, strictly speaking, infinite, because it measures the gap between what is being *per se,* and what only possesses being as received from another.

Undoubtedly, and we shall see why later on, a finite and limited being is not a bad being, if there is no defect in its proper essence. But we also know that a universe of finite beings demands a multiplicity of distinct essences; that is, a hierarchy of unequal essences some of which are incorruptible and removed from evil, others corruptible and subject to evil. Now, we have said that it is impossible to determine why God willed these imperfect and deficient creatures. A *reason* can be assigned: the divine goodness willing to diffuse itself outside of itself into finite participations of its sovereign perfection. But no *cause* can be assigned because God's will is the first cause of all beings, and, consequently, no being can play the role of cause where He is concerned. Now, how is it metaphysically possible for a limited and partially evil world to issue from a perfect God without the corruptions of the creatures reflecting upon the creator? This question the human mind simply cannot leave unanswered. This apparently frightening problem rests ultimately on a confusion.

Is it best to appeal, as the Manichaeans do, to an evil principle, creator of all that is corruptible and deficient in the universe? Or ought we to consider that the first principle of all things has established the grades of being in a hierarchy by introducing into the universe, within each essence, the proportion of evil necessary to limit its perfection? To do this is to misunderstand that basic truth proposed by Dionysius:[35] Evil does not exist: *Malum non est existens neque bonum.* We have already met the thesis that whatever is desirable is a good. Now every nature desires its own existence and its own perfection. The perfection and being, therefore, of every nature are truly goods. But if the being and perfection of all things are goods, then it follows that evil, which is the opposite of good, has neither perfection nor being. The term *evil,* therefore, can only signify a kind of absence of good and of being, for, since being, as such, is a good, the absence of the one necessarily involves the absence of the other.[36] Hence, evil is, if we may use the expression, a purely negative reality. More exactly, it is in no degree an essence or a reality.

Let us state this conclusion precisely. What is called an *evil* in the substance of a thing is only a lack of some quality which ought naturally to be there. For a man to have no wings, is not an evil, because it is not the nature of the human body to possess wings. Similarly, there is no evil in not having fair hair. The possession of fair hair is compatible with human nature but is not necessary to it. On the other hand it is an evil for a man to have no hands, while it is not so for a bird. Now the term *privation,* considered strictly and in its proper sense, designates the absence or want of what a being ought naturally to possess. It is to privation of this kind that evil is limited.[37] Evil is a pure negation within a substance. It is not an essence, not a reality.[38]

Since there is nothing positive about evil, its presence in the universe is unintelligible apart from the existence of real and positive subjects to support it. This conclusion is somewhat paradoxical. Evil is not a being; all good, however, is being. Is it not strange to maintain that non-being demands being in which to subsist as in a subject? Such an objection only holds against non-being taken as a negation, in which case it is irrefutable. The mere absence of being cannot demand a subject to support it. But we have just said that evil is a *negation in a subject,* that is, a lack of what is normally a part of that subject; in a word, a *privation.* There can be no privation, and therefore no evil, without the existence of substances or subjects in which privation can be established. Thus it is not true that all negation demands a real and positive subject, but only those particular negations called privations, because "privation is a negation in a subject." The only true support of evil is the good.[39]

The relation between evil and the good which supports it is never such that evil can consume or, as it were, totally exhaust the good. Could it do so, evil would consume and totally exhaust even itself. So long, indeed, as evil subsists, it must have a subject in which to subsist. Now the subject of evil is the good. Hence there always remains some good.[40] Better still, we can assert that evil has, in a sense, a cause, and that this cause is nothing else than the good. Indeed it is absolutely necessary that whatever subsists in some other thing as in its subject have a cause. This cause must be attributable either to the principles of the subject itself or to some extrinsic cause. Now evil subsists in the good as in its natural subject. Therefore it has to have a cause.[41] But only a being can serve as a cause, because in order to act, it is necessary to be. Now all being, as such, is good. Good, as such, therefore, remains the only possible cause of evil. This may easily be verified by an examination of each of the four kinds of causes.

First: it is quite evident that the material cause of evil is the good. Such a conclusion follows from the principles we have already set forth. It has been proven that the good is the subject within which evil subsists; that is, that it is its true matter, although it is only its matter *per accidens*. Secondly: evil really has no formal cause. Rather it is reduced to a simple privation of form. Thirdly: the same holds for the final cause, because evil is simply the privation of order in the disposition of means to an end. Evil sometimes admits of a final cause *per accidens*, as when a distinction is made between the evil which is found in the actions of various beings and that which is found in their effects. Evil can be caused in an action by the lack of some one of the principles which lie behind this action. Thus the faulty movement of an animal can be accounted for by weakness in its motive faculty, as is the case in infants, or by the malformation of a member, as is the case in cripples. Fourthly: evil is also found in the effects of efficient causes, and this for a variety of reasons.

It can, first of all, appear in an effect which is not the proper effect of these causes. In this case, the lack comes either from the active power or from the matter on which it is acting. It comes from the active power itself, considered in all its perfection, when the efficient cause is unable to achieve the proposed form without causing the corruption of another form. Thus the presence of the form of fire demands the privation of the form of air or water; and the more perfect the active power of the fire, the more successful it is in impressing its form in the matter upon which it is acting, and the more, too, does it totally corrupt the contrary forms which it encounters. The evil and the corruption of air and water are caused by the perfection of the fire; but they only result *per accidens*. The end toward which the fire tends is not to deprive the water of its form, but to introduce its own form into the matter. It is only because it tends toward this end that it finds itself causing evil and privation. If we consider, finally, those deficiencies which can appear in the proper effects of fire, for example, the inability to heat, we must find their source either in a failure of the active power itself, and we have already spoken of this, or in a bad disposition of the matter, badly prepared perhaps to receive the action of the fire. However, all these deficiencies can only reside in a good. Only good or being can act or be causes. Therefore we can legitimately conclude that evil has no other causes than causes *per accidens*. With this reservation, the only possible cause of evil is its contrary, the good.[42]

Hence, finally, we can move on to a last conclusion, one which we must hold firmly, strange as it may seem: the cause of evil always resides in a good; and yet God, the cause of all good is not the cause of evil. From the foregoing considerations one thing remains clear: that whatever evil is reduced to a defect in some action, its cause is invariably a defect in the being which acts. Now there is no defect in God, but on the contrary a sovereign perfection. Evil, caused by a defect in the acting being, cannot be caused by God. But if we consider the evil which exists in the corruption of certain beings, we must, on the contrary, reduce it to God as to its cause. This is equally evident among beings which act by nature and those which act by will. We have posited that when a being acts so as to cause a form, the production of which entails the corruption of some other form, its action must be regarded as the cause of this privation and defect. Now the principal form which God clearly intends in created things is the good of the universal order. But the order of the universe demands, as we already know, that certain things be deficient. God, therefore, is the cause of corruptions and defects in all things, but only because He wills to cause the good of the universal order, and, as it were, *per accidens*.[43] In sum, the effect of the deficient secondary cause can be attributed to the first cause, free from all defect, in what concerns the being and perfection of such an effect, but not in what concerns evil and defectiveness. Just as the movement in a lame man's gait can be attributed to his motive faculty while the limp is imputable to his deformed limb, so being and bad action may be attributed to God, while the defect in such action is to be imputed to the deficient secondary cause, not to the omnipotent perfection of God.[44]

Thus no matter from what side we approach the problem, the conclusion is always the same. Evil taken by itself is nothing. It is inconceivable that God can be its cause. If we ask what is its cause, our answer is that it is the tendency of certain beings to return toward non-being. Undoubtedly we can conceive of finite and limited beings in which there would be no evil. In fact, there are in the universe incorruptible creatures never lacking anything which belongs to their nature. But there is some good even in these beings of less perfection, corruptible creatures. If God has created them, it is because it was consonant with the divine perfection to form a more perfect image of Himself by expressing Himself in unequal creatures, some of which were corruptible, some incorruptible. Whether we regard the one or the other, we see in either only goodness, being and perfection. In this descent of all things from God we find only effusion and transmission of being. The vilest of all creatures whose infinitesimal perfection is almost entirely consumed by evil still enriches with its tiny share the total perfection of the universe. With its wretched degree of being, it still expresses something of God. Let us examine, then, the hierarchy of created goods which God, freely and without cause, formed to His own image. Let us begin with the highest grade in this hierarchy with the creatures entirely free from all matter, and commonly called angels.

CHAPTER II

THE ANGELS

THE ORDER of creatures in which the highest degree of created perfection is realized is that of pure spirits, commonly called angels.[1] Some historians pass over in complete silence this part of St. Thomas's work or at best dismiss it with a few allusions. Such an omission is particularly regrettable in that St. Thomas's study of the angels is not entirely or specifically a theological inquiry. Angels are creatures whose existence can be demonstrated. In certain exceptional cases they have even been seen. To disregard them destroys the balance of the universe considered as a whole. Finally, the nature and operation of inferior creatures, men for example, can only be well understood by comparison and contrast with angels. In short, in a doctrine in which the ultimate reason of beings is often drawn from the place they occupy in the universe, it is difficult to omit the consideration of one whole order of creatures without upsetting the equilibrium of the system. St. Thomas's treatise on the angels is the culminating point of a long development in which there converge heterogeneous elements of both religious and philosophical origin.

We know today[2] that three springs fed this part of the Thomistic system. First, astronomical theories about certain spiritual substances considered as the causes of movement of the spheres and heavenly bodies. Secondly, metaphysical speculation about pure spirits considered as degrees of being and, so to speak, as marking stages in the progressions by which the many issue from the One. Finally, the Biblical accounts of angels and demons.

The astronomical data which we spoke of comes directly from Aristotle who was in this influenced by Plato. According to Aristotle, the first immovable mover moves insofar as desired and loved. But desire and love presuppose knowledge. Hence, the heavenly spheres can only be moved by intelligent substances acting as motive forces. Plato had already placed the principle of universal order in the world-soul and had considered the heavenly bodies to be moved by divine souls. The successors of Plato and Aristotle waver between these two points of view. While the Platonists, properly so-called, attribute real souls to the heavenly bodies, the Fathers and Doctors of the Church adopt a more reserved attitude. None holds this doctrine unreservedly; some consider it possible; many reject it. As for Aristotle's doctrine, which seems to have held for motive intelligences without attributing souls in this strict sense to the heavenly bodies,[3] it will be interpreted in various ways during the Middle Ages. Some Arabian commentators like Alfarabi, Avicenna and Algazel place the first principle of astronomical motion in real souls, while others put this principle of motion either in a soul stripped of every sensible function and reduced to its intellectual role (Maimonides), or in an intelligence pure and simple (Averroes). Many Scholastics held this last view, against Avicenna. They did not consider the heavenly bodies to be the cause of their own motion, as is the case with the elements. Nor did they consider that the spheres were directly moved by God. But they said that pure Intelligences, created by God, were the cause of astronomical motion.

Metaphysical speculation on the hierarchical grades of being, very important here, originates in the neo-Platonic doctrine of emanation. There is, even in Plotinus, besides the four degrees characterizing the exodus of things from the One, a kind of rough differentiation within the first degree itself; that is, within the Intelligence. Plato's Ideas preserve in them a subsistence of their own, a sort of individuality. They are even arranged in a kind of hierarchical subordination analogous to that of species under their genus and of particular disciplines under science in general. We find this organization completed by the successors and disciples of Plotinus: Porphyry, Jamblicus and above all Proclus. It is to this last-named philosopher that we owe the precise formulation of the doctrine of the intelligences: their absolute incorporeity and simplicity, their subsistence beyond time, the nature of their knowledge, etc.

From the earliest times there has been a pronounced tendency to bring together these pure intelligences, which lie between the One and the rest of creation, and certain other beings of a very different origin. Eventually, the two were completely identified. We are speaking, of course, of the angels, who in Holy Scripture are messengers between God and man. Philo at an early date speaks of pure spirits which people the air, called demons by the philosophers, angels by Moses.[4] Porphyry and Jamblicus reckon angels and archangels among the demons. Proclus has them entering into composition with demons, properly so-called, and with heroes to form a triad whose duty it is to fill up the gap between the gods and men.[5] Proclus also gives precise expression to the doctrine of angelic knowledge which was to prevail in the Schools. He speaks of it as a simple, non-discursive, illuminative knowledge. Denis the Areopagite gathers all this data together and makes a definitive synthesis of the biblical concept of angelic messengers and the speculation of the neo-Platonists. Patristic and medieval philosophy only accepts this synthesis and specifies its details.[6] From this time on, angels are more and more considered to be pure spirits. Gradually, the neo-Platonic notion of the total incorporeity of the angels triumphs over the early doubts and hesitations of the Patristic period [7] and, while certain Scholastics maintain the distinction between matter and form in angelic substances, they do not do so in any corporal, luminous or ethereal sense but as simple potency and a principle of change. The pseudo-Areopagite not only defines the angels of the Scriptures as pure spirits but he arranges them in scholarly fashion[8] into three hierarchies each of which itself falls into three classes. It is this arrangement which appears unchanged in St. Thomas's doctrine.

There only remains to unite angels thus conceived with the intelligences to whom the philosophers assigned the motion of spheres. Such an identification was not *a priori* necessary. Indeed, apart from a few isolated indications in a number of neo-Platonists, we have to wait for the Arabian philosophers to find it definitively stated.[9] The Arabians and Jews liken the orders of angels distinguished in the Koran and Bible either to the intelligences which move the heavenly bodies or to the souls of heavenly bodies which are dependent upon these intelligences. The influence of Avicenna and Maimonides is pronounced here. The Scholastics in the West, however, are far from accepting their conclusions without modification. Albert the Great flatly refuses to identify angels and intelligences. Nor do St. Bonaventure and St. Thomas Aquinas accept any such assimilation. Only the Averroists could be fully satisfied with it, and only they accepted it without restriction.

These are the historical elements, varied in nature and from many sources, which St. Thomas was able to fashion into a coherent and, in many respects, original synthesis. Holy Scripture attests the actual existence of angels: "Who makest thy angels spirits." [10] Nothing gives greater satisfaction to the reason than does this attestation of Scripture because on its own side, philosophical reflection necessarily leads us to affirm the existence of incorporeal creatures. God's principal end in creation is the supreme good constituted by assimilation to God. We have already seen that herein lies the only reason for the being of the universe. Now an effect is not perfectly assimilated to its cause if it does not imitate that by which its cause is capable of producing it. Thus the heat of a body resembles the heat which produces it in that body. But we know that God produces creatures by intelligence and by will. Thus the perfection of the universe demands the existence of intellectual creatures. Now the object of the intellect is the universal. Bodies insofar as they are material, and all corporeal powers are on the contrary determined by nature to a particular mode of being. There should be some genuinely intellectual creatures, then, which are simply incorporeal, and this amounts to saying that the perfection of the universe demands the existence of beings totally stripped of matter or of body.[11] Moreover, the general plan of creation would show an obvious gap if there were no angels in it. The hierarchy of beings is continuous. All nature of a superior order touches, in its least noble element, what is most noble in creatures of the order immediately below it. Thus intellectual nature is superior to corporeal nature, and yet the order of intellectual natures touches the order of corporeal natures by the least noble intellectual nature, and this is the rational soul of man. On the other hand, the body to which the rational soul is united is, by the very fact of this union, in touch with the highest grade in the genus of bodies. It is fitting, therefore, in order to preserve proper proportion, that the order of nature keep a place for intellectual creatures which are superior to the human soul; that is, for angels, who are in no way united to bodies.[12]

At first sight it may seem that such an argument is reduced to a mere reason of convenience and harmony. We should be wrong, however, in seeing in it a satisfaction provided for our logical and abstract need of symmetry. If it is satisfying for reason to admit the existence of intelligences free from bodies which are to souls joined to bodies what bodies ennobled by souls are to bodies deprived of souls, it is because there is no discontinuity in the hierarchy of created perfections. And this very absence of discontinuity constitutes the profound law which governs the procession of beings from God. Thomas Aquinas refuses to divide the creative activity into fragments as do the Arabian philosophers and their Western disciples. But although he does not admit that each higher grade of creatures gives being to the grade immediately below it, he firmly maintains this hierarchical multiplicity of grades. One sole and unique creative power produces and sustains creation in its entirety. If it no longer spurts forth like a new spring at each step of creation, it still extends to every one of them.

This is why the effects of the divine power are naturally ordered in a continuous series of decreasing perfection. It is why the order of created things is such that, in order to cover it from one end to the other, it is necessary to pass through all its intermediary grades. Immediately below celestial matter, for example, comes fire. Below fire comes air. Next comes water; and finally, below water, comes earth. All these bodies are arranged in this way according to the order of nobility and decreasing rarity. Now we discover at the highest degree of being an absolutely simple being, God. It is impossible to put immediately beneath God corporeal substance which is eminently composite and divisible. A great number of middle terms must be posited by which we can descend from the sovereign simplicity of God to the complex multiplicity of material bodies. Some of these grades will be made up by intellectual substances united to bodies. Others will be made up by separate intellectual substances free from all union with matter. It is to the latter that we give the name of angels.[13]

Thus angels are completely incorporeal. Can we go further and consider them as totally immaterial? Many philosophers say not. Even granting that the excellence of the angelic nature implies their incorporeity, one may hesitate to consider them as not even composed of matter and form.

By matter we do not necessarily here mean a body but, in the large sense, all potency which enters into composition with act in constituting a given being. Now, the only principle of motion and change which there is, is to be found in matter. Hence there is necessarily matter in anything which is moved. But created spiritual substance is moveable and changeable, because only God is unchangeable by nature. Therefore there is matter in every created spiritual substance.[14] Secondly, we must consider that nothing is agent and patient at the same time under the same relationship, and, moreover, that nothing acts except by its form nor is acted upon except by its matter. Now the created spiritual substance known as an angel acts insofar as it enlightens the angel immediately inferior to it, and is acted upon in that it is enlightened by the angel immediately superior to it. Therefore the angel is necessarily composed of matter and form.[15] Finally, we know that whatever exists is either pure act, or pure potency, or composed of potency and act. But the created spiritual substance is not pure act, because God alone is pure act. Nor is it pure potency, as is evident. It is therefore composed of potency and act, and this amounts to saying that it is composed of matter and form.[16]

These arguments, inviting as they are, are incompatible with the Thomistic notion of the first cause of the universe. We know that the need for positing incorporeal creatures like the angels is based, in the Thomistic system, on the necessity for an order of pure intelligences placed immediately under God. Now the nature of pure intellectual substances must be in harmony with their operation. And the proper operation of intellectual substances is the act of knowing. It is easy, on the other hand, to determine the nature of this act from its object. Things are ready to fall into the grasp of the intelligence in the measure in which they are free from matter. Forms which are inserted in matter, for example, are individual forms. They cannot, as we shall see, be apprehended as such by the intellect. Pure intelligence, whose object is the immaterial as such, must therefore also be free from all matter. The total immateriality of angels is therefore demanded by the very place they occupy in the order of creation.[17]

This means that the objection drawn from the mobility and mutability of the angels cannot be regarded as decisive. The modifications to which they are subject in no way effect their very being, but only their intelligence and their will. To account for this, therefore, it is enough to admit that their intellect and their will can pass from potency to act; but nothing forces us to posit a distinction of matter and form within their unchanging essence.[18] The same holds for what concerns the impossibility of their simultaneous activity and passivity. The illumination which an angel receives and that which it transmits suppose an intellect that is at one time in act and at another in potency. It does not at all suppose a being composed of form and matter.[19]

There is one last objection—that a spiritual substance which is pure act would be identical with God. Hence, it is said that we must admit into the nature of angels a mixture of potency and act; that is, in the last analysis, a mixture of form and matter. In one sense, we can accept this argument completely. It is incontestable that the angel, placed immediately below God, must be distinguishable from Him as the finite from the infinite. Its being is necessarily comprised of a certain amount of potentiality limiting its actuality. And if we take *potency* as a synonym for *matter,* we cannot deny that the angels are to some extent material. But it is not necessary to identify potency with matter in this way, as will be revealed by a consideration of material things.

In material substances we can discern a double composition. First, we see that they are composed of matter and form. By this each of them constitutes a nature. But if we consider this nature itself, composed as it is of matter and form, we observe that it is not its own act-of-being. Taken in relation to the *esse* it possesses, this nature is in the relationship of all potency to its act. In other words, if we abstract from the hylomorphic (matter and form) composition of a created being, we can still find in it the composition of its nature or essence with the existence which the creator has conferred upon it and in which He preserves it. This, which is true of any material nature whatsoever, is equally true of a separated intellectual substance like an angel. If we imagine a form endowed with a determined nature and subsisting by itself apart from all matter, such a form is still related to its act-of-being as potency to act. Hence it is infinitely removed from the First Being, or God, pure act and comprising in itself the whole plenitude of being. This means that it is not necessary to introduce any matter into the angelic nature in order to distinguish it from the creative essence. It is pure form, simple intelligence, free from all matter. Yet it has only a limited amount of being.[20]

The Masters who held for matter in angelic substances were attracted to such a position because it helped them to distinguish between individual angels. It is matter alone which provides the basis for numerical distinction among the beings within each species. If angels are pure forms which no matter can limit, or individuate, it appears to be impossible to distinguish them.[21] To this we have to reply simply that there do not exist two angels of the same species.[22] The reason for this is obvious. Beings of the same species but which differ numerically according to the distinct individuals within the same species possess a similar form united with different matters. But if angels have no matter, then each is specifically distinct from all the others. The individual as such here forms a species apart.[23] We cannot object to this conclusion without making the multiplication of individual angelic natures within each species impossible and reducing the total perfection of the universe. That which distinguishes beings specifically from each other, namely form, clearly surpasses in dignity the material principle of individuation by which beings are only put in a species and particularized. The multiplication of species adds more nobility and perfection to the entire universe than does the mere multiplication of individuals within the limits of the same species. Now the universe owes its perfection mainly to the separated substances which it contains. To substitute a multitude of different species for a multitude of individuals of the same species is not to reduce the total perfection of the universe. Rather, it is to increase and multiply it.[24]

No doubt many of our contemporaries will consider this kind of discussion foreign to philosophy. But there is no better vantage point for revealing the meaning and significance of the existential reform imposed by St. Thomas upon Greek metaphysics. We simply must insist upon this, particularly in that this reform is one of the major events in the whole history of philosophy. If we do not grasp its meaning, we allow its fruits to perish.

Reduced to its essentials, this medieval controversy on the hylomorphic composition of angels tends to resolve the problem of how to conceive of simple spiritual substances which are not gods.

The whole of natural theology was occupied with this problem which became thus a veritable watershed dividing Christian philosophy from Greek. For Aristotle, all beings fall into two classes—those having a nature and those not having one.[25] All beings composed of matter and form have a nature. They are recognizable in that they have within themselves the principle of their own motion and their own repose. This principle is nature itself, "for nature is a principle and a cause of movement and repose for the thing in which it resides immediately, by essence and not by accident." [26] Since it is an active thing, the nature of a being cannot be its matter. Therefore it is its form. But since this being is the seat of movement, there must be matter in it, matter being the principle of that potentiality which by means of movement its nature brings into act. Thus we call every being composed of matter and form,[27] a "natural being." In it, nature is only its form considered as the internal cause of its becoming.

The science of natural or "physical" beings, we call Physics.[28] Beyond this science there is another—the science of beings which are beyond physical beings. Hence it is called the science of "meta-physics," or, as we say, Metaphysics. What distinguishes this second group of beings from the first is that they are forms subsisting in themselves and free from all matter. Without matter, such beings are entirely in act; they are said to be pure acts. For the same reason, they are not the seat of any movement; they are said to be immovable pure acts. Withdrawn from movement, such beings have no nature and are not natural beings. Thus they can be called "metanatural" quite as well as "metaphysical." Both amount to the same thing. Inversely, since they are above natural beings, these pure acts of Aristotle can be "superphysical" beings or "supernatural" beings. It makes no difference. So, for Aristotle, the boundary between the natural and the supernatural is that which separates material forms from pure forms. Owing to the force of circumstances, it is this same boundary which separates the natural world from the divine world. In this sense, since it is the science of the divine, Aristotle's metaphysics has full right to the title of the divine science, or theology. It is even theology according to the basic meaning of the term. As there are no beings more divine than those with which *Metaphysics* is concerned, there is no place for any theology, indeed, for any science, beyond it.

The result of these distinctions is that these pure forms, which the Christian theologians were calling angels, rightfully belonged in that class of beings which Aristotle called gods. Hence the perplexity of these theologians. The Bible forbade them to deny the existence of angels. They could make corporeal beings of them, and this they tried sometimes, but too many sacred texts called for regarding them as pure spirits for this thesis to prevail. To make gods of them would have been to fall back into polytheism. St. Thomas's treatise *De Substantiis Separatis,* an incomparably rich historical work, enables us to some extent to follow step by step the evolution of this problem and to disentangle the various doctrines which its history implies. By all evidence, the problem, for Christian thinkers, boiled down to finding another criterion for the divine than that of immateriality. But time was needed to find it out. They had to wait for the existential metaphysics of St. Thomas Aquinas.

Here as elsewhere the hardest obstacle to remove was the Platonism of essence. Aristotle himself had failed to brush it aside, or, rather, had not even tried. For him, as for Plato, being was ultimately identified with the immovable. What he called "being as being" was accordingly "being as not becoming." It is true, and the point is important, that the stability of all "being as being" expressed for Aristotle the purity of an act. Moreover, this is why, unlike Plato's Ideas, pure acts exercise a causality other than that of principles in the intelligible order; because they are Acts, Aristotle's highest principles are truly gods. They are eternal immovables, causes of an eternal becoming. However, when all is said, their very actuality is reduced to that of a perfect essence whose pure immateriality excludes all possibility of change. For those who were positing angels as so many immaterial substances, Aristotle was providing no excuse for not making so many gods of them.

This explains why the thesis of the hylomorphic composition of angels received such a fine reception among Platonists of every sort, and how it came to offer so vigorous a struggle against its rival. Just as they could not conceive of being, other than as a mode of being, so they could not conceive of an absolutely immaterial being which was not a god.[29] In pushing his analysis of being as far as the very act-of-being, St. Thomas was eliminating one of the principal reasons used to support such a hylomorphism. If the divine is identified with the purely immaterial, and being with essence, then all being whose essence is purely immaterial has a right to be called a god. But if the reality of essence is rooted in its act-of-being, it is at once evident that further distinctions are to be introduced among immaterial beings.

An immaterial substance is completely in act in the order of form but not necessarily in that of the act-of-being. Free from all potentiality as regards matter, this substance nevertheless remains in potency in what concerns its own proper *esse*. Of all substances, only one escapes this particular servitude, that one substance whose *essentia* is one with its *esse;* namely, God. "Form is act" objected the defenders of the hylomorphism of the angels; "and what is form only is pure act; now the angel is not pure act, for this pertains to God alone; the angel, therefore, is not only form, but has a form that is in matter." But St. Thomas could now reply to this that "although there is no composition of form and matter in the angel, there is nevertheless in him act and potency."

We can verify this by considering material things, for in these we encounter two compositions. The first is that of form and matter, a composition to be found in all natures. But a nature is not its act-of-being; rather, the act-of-being is the act of nature. Hence nature itself stands in relation to its act-of-being as potency to act. If the matter is removed, and if we suppose that the form itself subsists without matter, this form still remains with regard to its act-of-being, in the relationship of potency to act. It is in this sense that we must understand the composition of angels. . . . But in God, there is no difference between the act-of-being and what He is . . . and hence God alone is pure act.[30] Whether he was aware of it or not, St. Thomas was here destroying the entire Aristotelian theology of Immovable Movers; he was erecting, above the essentiality of Plato's Ideas, above, even, the substantiality of Aristotle's pure acts, sublime in its solitude, the unique Pure Act-of-Being.

Here we are, then, with a number of angelic creatures both specifically and numerically distinct from one another. Their number is certainly enormous, much greater, indeed, than the number of material things; that is, if we admit that God ought to have produced a greater abundance of more perfect creatures in order to safeguard the high excellence of the universe as a whole.[31] We know, besides, that species differ from one another just as numbers do; that is, that they represent greater or lesser amounts of being and perfection. There is reason, then, for trying to find out in what way this host of angels is ordered and distributed.[32]

If each angel, considered by itself, constitutes a single species, it must be possible to descend by continuous transition from the highest angel—"the nature closest to God"[33]—to the lowest—whose perfection is nearest that of the human species. But it is only too evident that we should become lost in trying to follow so vast a number of grades of being, particularly since individual knowledge of angels is not given to us in this world.[34] The only possibility left us is to attempt a general classification in orders and hierarchies based on their diverse activities. The proper activity of pure intelligences is clearly intelligence itself or, if we may speak in such a way, the act of "intellecting." It is, then,

by the differences in their proper mode of intellection that the angelic
orders are distinguished.

Taken this way, the whole angelic hierarchy, collectively considered,
is radically different from the human order. Of course, for both angels
and men, the first origin of knowledge is the same. In both cases, this is
the divine illumination that is given for the enlightenment of creatures.
But angels and men perceive these illuminations in different ways. Men,
as we shall see later, extract from sensible things the intelligible which
is hidden in them. Angels perceive the intelligible immediately and in
its intelligible purity. Thus they have been given a mode of knowledge
exactly proportionate to their place in general creation; that is, between
that pertaining to man and that which pertains only to God. The angelic
being is immediately below God, but with this difference, that its essence
is not identical with its existence. This multiplicity, characteristic of
creatures, is to be found in its way of knowing. God's intelligence is one
with His essence and His being because His being, which is purely and
simply infinite, embraces being in its entirety. But the angel is a finite
essence endowed by God with a certain act-of-being and its knowledge
does not extend by its own right to all being.[35] Moreover, the angel is
a pure intelligence; that is, is not naturally joined to a body. It cannot,
therefore, apprehend the sensible, as such. Sensible things, indeed, fall
within the grasp of the common sense; intelligible things fall within the
grasp of the intellect. But every substance which extracts its knowledge
from the sensible is united by nature with a body, since sensitive knowledge requires senses and, consequently, corporeal organs. Angelic substances, separated from all body, cannot, therefore, find their medium of
knowledge in the sensible.[36]

Thus the very nature of the being conferred by God on the angels
brings with it an original mode of knowing. It cannot in any way resemble
abstraction, by which man discovers the intelligible buried in the sensible.
Nor can it in any way resemble that act by which God *is* the intelligible
and at the same time apprehends it. It can only be a knowledge acquired
through species which are received by the intelligence and which enlighten
it. But such species are purely intelligible; that is, proportionate to a
completely incorporeal being. To satisfy all these conditions, we say
that angels know things through species which are connatural to them;
that is, by innate species.[37] All the intelligible essences which pre-existed
from eternity in God in the form of ideas proceeded from Him at the
moment of creation in two distinct and parallel lines. On the one hand,
they were individuated in material beings and constituted their forms.
On the other, they flowed into angelic substances, thus conferring upon
them knowledge of things. We can say then that the intellect of angels
is superior to our human intellect, just as a being endowed with form is
superior to formless matter. And if our intellect is like a blank tablet on

which nothing is written, the intellect of the angel is rather like a canvas covered with its painting or, better, like a mirror reflecting the luminous essences of things.[38]

This innate possession of intelligible species is common to all angels and is characteristic of their nature. But all angels do not possess the same species; and here we are coming to the basis of their distinction. What constitutes relative superiority among created beings is their greater or lesser proximity and resemblance to the first being, God. Now God's total fullness of knowledge is all together at one single point—His essence, in which He knows all things. This intelligible fullness is in created intelligences, but in an inferior way and less simply. The intelligences inferior to God know by a multiplicity of means what God knows in a single object. The lower the nature of the intelligence, the more numerous its means of knowing. In brief, the superiority among angels is greater the fewer the species necessary for them to apprehend all intelligibles.[39]

We now know that, in the case of angels, each individual angel is a new and distinct grade of being. The simplicity of their knowledge is graded and subdivided unceasingly from the first angel to the last. Yet, in general, three principal grades can be distinguished. First come those angels who know intelligible essences as proceeding from the first universal principle, which is God. This mode of knowing belongs properly to the first hierarchy which is in immediate attendance upon God and of which we can say with Dionysius[40] that it sojourns in the vestibule of the divinity. Secondly come those angels who know intelligibles as subjected to the most universal created causes. This mode of being is proper to the second hierarchy. Thirdly, come those angels who know intelligibles as applied to singular beings and dependent upon particular causes. These last form the third hierarchy.[41] There is, then, decreasing generality and decreasing simplicity in the distribution of the knowledge of the angels: some are turned toward God only and consider intelligible essences in Him alone; others consider them in the universal causes of creation, that is, in a plurality of objects; others, finally, consider them in their determination to particular effects, that is, in a multiplicity of objects equal to the number of created beings.[42]

When we try to be more specific as to how separated substances apprehend their object, we observe further that there are three different orders within each of these hierarchies. We have said that the first hierarchy considers intelligible essences in God Himself. Now God is the end of every creature. Angels of this hierarchy consider, therefore, under their proper object, the highest end of the universe which is the goodness of God. Those of them who behold it most clearly are called Seraphim because they are aglow or, as it were, on fire with love for this object which they know with an exceedingly perfect love. The other angels of the first hierarchy contemplate the divine goodness not directly and in itself but insofar as it is Providence. They are called Cherubim; that is, fulness of science, because they see clearly the first operative virtue of the divine model of things. Immediately below the preceding come the angels who consider the actual disposition of the divine judgments. Since the throne is the sign of judicial power, they are called Thrones. All this does not imply that God's goodness, His essence, and the science by which He knows the arrangement of beings, are in Him three distinct things. Rather it means that these three things form three aspects under which finite intelligences, such as the angels, can behold His perfect simplicity.

The second hierarchy does not know the reasons of things in God Himself, as in a sole object, but in the plurality of universal causes. Thus its proper object is the general disposition of means in view of their end. Now this universal disposition of things supposes the existence of many directors; these are the Dominations, whose name indicates authority because they prescribe what others must carry out. The general directives issued by these first angels are received by others who multiply them and channel them according to the various effects to be produced. These angels are called Virtues, because they confer on the general causes the energy required that their numerous operations be carried out without fail. This order, then, presides over the operation of the universe as a whole; and to it is attributed not unreasonably the movement of the heavenly bodies, universal causes from which proceed all the particular effects which take place in nature.[43] To these spirits too belongs, apparently, the carrying out of those divine effects which are outside the ordinary course of nature and which are often immediately dependent upon the influence of the stars. Finally, the universal order of Providence, already instituted in its effects, is preserved from all confusion by the Powers, whose task is to remove all those baneful influences which might possibly trouble it.

With this last class of angels we come to the third hierarchy which knows the order of Providence, not in itself, nor in its general causes, but as it can be known in the multiplicity of particular causes. These angels are placed in immediate charge of the administration of things human. Some of these are particularly charged with the common good and general welfare of nations and cities. They are called, by reason of this dignity, Principalities. The distinction of kingdoms, the transference of temporary supremacy to one nation rather than to another, the leadership of princes and great men belong directly to their ministry. Beneath this very general order of goods comes one which effects both the individual taken by himself and, under the same title, a great number of individuals. Such are the truths of faith, which must be believed, and divine worship, which must be respected. The angels for whom these goods, which are both particular and general at the same time, are the proper object, are called Archangels. They also bring to men the most solemn messages from God. It was the archangel Gabriel who came to announce the incarnation of the Word, the only Son of God, a truth all men are obliged to accept. Finally, there is a still more particular good. It is one that concerns every individual man, considered in himself. In charge of this order of goods are the Angels, properly so-called. They are the guardians of men and God's messengers for less important announcements.[44] With them, we reach the end of the lowest hierarchy of separated intelligences.

It is easy to see that the foregoing arrangement concerns the continuity of a universe in which the lowest members of a higher grade approach very closely the highest members of the lower grade. Thus the least perfect members of the animal kingdom are not very far removed from plants. The first and highest order of being is that of the Divine Persons which terminates in the Spirit, that is, in Love proceeding from the Father and the Son. The Seraphim are closely united with God in a burning love. They stand, therefore, in close affinity with the third person of the Trinity. The third degree of this hierarchy, the Thrones, has an equally close affinity with the highest degree of the second, the Dominations. It is they, indeed, who transmit to the second hierarchy the illuminations necessary for the knowledge and execution of the divine decrees. Similarly, the Powers are in close affinity with the Principalities, because there is very little distance between those who make particular effects possible and those who produce them.[45] The grouping of the angels in a hierarchy thus places us in the presence of a continued series of pure intelligences through which the divine illumination shines from one end to the other. Each angel transmits to the one immediately below it the knowledge which it receives itself from above. But it transmits it particularized and broken up to match the capacity of the angel which follows it. The angel proceeds much as our teachers do. They perceive directly the consequences which lie hidden in principles. But when they expound them, they make many distinctions in order to bring them within the reach of their listeners.[46]

In this way the elements which St. Thomas owes to philosophic tradition are brought into a harmonious synthesis. He confirms the existence of angels in the strict sense in their biblical role of announcers and messengers. He refuses to reduce them, as do the oriental philosophers, to the very small number of separated intelligences which move and guide the celestial spheres. Yet he continues to assign these functions to the angels. Finally, the neo-Platonic hierarchy as adopted by the pseudo-Dionysius reappears in St. Thomas's hierarchy of pure intelligences. But St. Thomas binds these notions of such varied origin to his own principles. He places his imprint firmly upon them. In distributing the angelic hierarchies according to the progressive darkening of their intellectual illumination, he is conferring a totally new organic structure upon the world of separated substances. The internal principle governing it all is the same as that he puts at the very source of universal order. In one stroke the angelic world finds that it occupies a place in creation of such importance that it simply must be considered if the universe is to remain intelligible. Between God's pure actuality and man's rational knowledge based upon sensible things, the angels introduce an infinite number of intermediary degrees. As we come down this long chain, we find two parallel and diminishing graduations: a knowledge becoming less and less simple, and an *esse* whose actuality grows less and less pure. No doubt, the vast host of angels, finite creatures, does not fill completely the gap between God and creation. But if there is always discontinuity in the way the act-of-being is possessed, there is henceforth continuity of order. *Ordo rerum tales esse invenitur ut ab uno extremo ad alterum non perveniatur nisi per media.* Knowledge comes down in stages from God, the source of all light. It comes first to the angels, natural intelligences full of intelligible essences. Then it comes to men whom we see seeking and gathering the intelligible so generously expanded in sensible things. Finally its ray comes to be imprisoned in matter under the form of finality.

CHAPTER III

THE CORPOREAL WORLD AND THE EFFICACY OF SECOND CAUSES

AN EXAMINATION of the universe as a whole certainly must begin with the study of pure intelligences. But the next step in the process is not so obvious. Indeed two different procedures are possible. They correspond to the two principles by which the arrangement of this universe is directed. One procedure is to follow the hierarchy of created beings, taken in their diminishing order of perfection, and so pass from the study of the angels to the study of man. The other procedure is to abandon the above point of view and to regard the order of ends. This attitude is suggested by the account of creation in Genesis. Man, who so far as the order of perfection is concerned, ranks immediately after the angels, does not appear in the Scriptural account until the completion of creation of which he is the true end. It is for man that the incorruptible heavenly bodies have been created. It is for him too that God divides the waters with the firmament, and calls the dry land to appear from under the waters and peoples it with animals and the green herb. Consequently, it is quite legitimate to place the study of corporeal things right after that of the purely spiritual. In this way it is possible to conclude with the examination of man who is the bond of union between the world of intelligences and the world of bodies.[1]

The field of natural philosophy is the one where St. Thomas has made fewest innovations; that is, at least, if we restrict it to physics and biology, properly so-called. Here the Christian doctor adds nothing to Aristotle, or so little that it is hardly worth mentioning. We will not find in him the curiosity of a Robert Grosseteste for the fertile speculations of mathematical physics. No doubt the very spirit of his Aristotelian philosophy was opposed to this; although it was not opposed to his following the studies of his master, Albert the Great, in the field of zoology and in the natural sciences. Yet, here again we see him escape. The questions of the *Summa Theologiae* given to the commentary on the work of the six days provide him with many an occasion to exercise his natural ingenuity in one or other of these two directions. But St. Thomas has no heart for the task and saves his ingenuity for other subjects. The essential thing in his eyes is to preserve the very letter of Scripture intact. He is well aware, however, that the Book of Genesis was not a treatise on cosmography for the use of scholars. It was a statement of the truth intended for the simple people whom Moses was addressing. Thus it is sometimes possible to interpret it in a variety of ways.[2] So it is that when we speak of the six days of creation, we can understand by it either six successive days, as do Ambrose, Basil, Chrysostom and Gregory, and as is suggested by the letter of the text, which, however, is not addressed to scholars. Or we can, with Augustine, take it to refer to the simultaneous creation of all beings, with days symbolizing the various orders of beings. This second interpretation is at first sight less literal, but is, rationally speaking, more satisfying. It is the one that St. Thomas adopts, althought he does not exclude the other which, as he says, can also be held.[3]

In whatever way or ways he judges it possible to reconcile the visible universe as he sees it with the account of Genesis, St. Thomas accepts essentially the universe of Aristotle. It consists of a series of seven concentric, planetary spheres. These spheres are contained within an eighth sphere, that of the fixed stars; and they themselves contain the Earth which is their center.[4] The matter of each of the celestial spheres is strictly incorruptible, because for a thing to corrupt it must change. But for it to change it has to be capable of becoming something other than it is. It must, as we say, be capable of being *in potency*. Now the matter of the heavenly spheres is in some way saturated by its form, and is no longer in potency to any kind of being whatsoever. It is all it can be; and can no longer change except in place. To each sphere is assigned a motive Intelligence which maintains and directs its circular movement. But it is not, properly speaking, either its form or its soul. Beneath the lowest sphere, that of the Moon, the four elements, fire, air, water, earth, are ranged. By rights each of these ought to be completely gathered together in its natural place. When it is in its natural place it is in a state of rest and equilibrium. Actually, however, the elements are more or less mixed up. It is their tendency to return to their natural place which produces the various movements by which they are agitated. Fire moves upwards; earth downwards; air and water settle between the two in the intermediary places where they belong. This whole cosmology falls within frameworks drawn from other sources. Where St. Thomas is at home and able to perform with ease the task that comes more naturally to him is in the metaphysical investigation of the principles of natural philosophy. Here once again the Christian philosopher proves his originality. Here it is a question of the relation that binds being and the efficacy of second causes to God. Here he feels himself directly interested in its exact determination.

In studying the notion of creation, we came to the conclusion that only God is a Creator, since creation is an act proper to Him[5] and since nothing exists which was not created by Him. Perhaps it is not out of place to recall this general conclusion when we are about to launch into the study of bodies. The more so since the error that the nature of bodies was itself something bad and that they were consequently the works of some evil principle other than God had become very widespread.[6] This was a doubly pernicious error. First, because all existing things have at least one constitutive element in common—their *esse*. There must be some principle from which they have this element and which causes them to be, whatever may be their manner of being, whether invisible and spiritual or visible and corporeal. Since God is the cause of being, his causality extends necessarily to bodies as well as to spirits. Secondly, there is a reason based on the end of things, which is capable of convincing us that God has no other end than Himself. But things have an end other than themselves— God. This is an absolute truth, which holds for every order of reality whatsoever, and for bodies no less than spirits. But there is something that must be added to it. A being cannot exist for God unless it also exists for itself and for its own good. Thus in this huge organism called the universe each part has first its own act and its own end, as the eye is for seeing. In addition, each of the less noble parts exists with a view to the more noble, as creatures lower than man are in the universe with a view to man. Further, all these creatures, taken one by one, are only in the universe with a view to the collective perfection of the universe. Finally, the collective perfection of creatures, taken all together, is only here in the universe as an imitation and representation of the glory of God Himself.[7] This radical metaphysical optimism does not exclude anything deserving, in any sense whatsoever, the name of being. It does not exclude the world of bodies any more than anything else. Matter exists with a view to form; lower forms with a view to higher, and higher forms with a view to God. Whatever is, therefore, is good.[8] Consequently, whatever is, has God for its cause in spite of the objection raised.

In analyzing this conclusion, we see a first consequence issue out of it: God is the first and immediate cause of bodies, that is to say, not of their form taken by itself, nor their matter by itself, but the substantial unity of their matter and form. Here is how we are to understand this.

What experience gives us to grasp immediately are bodies subject to perpetual change and movement. It is this concrete data which analysis must break up into its constitutive elements. In the first place, the very fact that beings become something other than they were supposes the basic distinction of two points of view toward being: what being is; what it can still become. This is the distinction between *act* and *potency,* to which we have been constantly referring. That which is capable of being a certain thing, but is not that thing, is that thing in potency. That which that thing already is is so in act.[9] This notion of possibility or passive potency does not express sheer nothingness, absolute lack of actuality. It signifies, rather, the aptitude toward a certain eventual actuality which is realizable even though not yet realized. The block of marble is in potency to the form of the statue; a liquid mass is not. It is not that the outline of the statue is more present in the marble than in the liquid. It is not in the marble, but can be drawn out of it. The marble is *in potency* to it as long as no sculptor makes it a statue in act.

Of all the kinds of potentiality, the first to present itself is the potency to substantial being. What is "that which can become a substance?" This pure "possibility of being a substance" is called *prime matter*. Taken by itself and separately, it cannot be conceived, for the simple reason that it possesses no being of its own. *Nullum esse habet,* Averroes says of it. That it is nothing in itself does not prove that it is incapable of existing. Prime matter exists in the substance from the very moment that the substance itself exists, and by virtue of the act which makes it exist. This act which constitutes the substance is the *form*. From and by the form, substance receives whatever is positive in its being, since, as we have said, it is in and by the form that its act-of-being penetrates it. This also remains true of matter: *forma dat esse materiae*.[10] Prime matter is the very possibility of substance. It is to the form of the substance that matter owes whatever actual being it has.

Form, accordingly, is an act. The form of the substance is the act which constitutes the substance as such. Hence this is called the *substantial form*. Once substance is constituted by the union of form with matter it is in potency to further determining factors. Substance, regarded as in potency to such factors is called a *subject*. The further determining factors are themselves called its *accidents*.[11] The relation of matter to form is the inverse of that of subject to accidents. Matter has no being but what it has from the form, while accidents have no being but what they hold from the subject. Moreover, this whole ontological structure is, in each substance, but the unfolding of an individual act-of-being created and continually kept in existence by God's power. In and by its form, the creative *Esse* penetrates substance to its very matter, and the subject to its very accidents.

These elements permit us to understand the complex act of becoming. Form explains what a substance is, because it is the act and the reality of its being. Form will not explain, by itself, how a being can acquire something which it is not or lose something which it is. In either case there is the actualizing of a potency or possibility. This actualization of any kind of possibility is called movement or change. For there to be movement, there must first be a being which moves. There must be a being and, consequently, an act. On the other hand, if this act were perfect and complete, the being which it constitutes would have no possibility of changing. For there to be change, therefore, there must be an act which is incomplete and which admits of a margin of potency for actualizing. Thus we say that movement is the act of what is in potency, insofar as it is merely in potency. A good example of change is to be found in the act of learning a science not already known. In order to learn a science there must be an understanding, and an understanding which already knows something. Insofar as this understanding exists, and insofar as it knows, it is in act. But this understanding must also be capable of learning if it is to be in potency. Finally, this understanding must not already possess the science in question. This is a privation. The very change which we call learning is, accordingly, the progressive actualization of an already existing act. And because it has act it actualizes, step by step, its possibilities. Because to learn is to transform step by step an aptitude to know into acquired knowledge, to learn is a kind of changing.[12]

Thus conceived in its most general sense, movement is a passage from potency to act under the impulse of an act which is already realized. Or again, it is the introduction of a form into matter suitable to receive it. These terms and expressions must not be allowed to make us forget the concrete reality they express: an imperfect act that is being completed; or more simply, a being on the way to realization. If this is the way it is, the body we have been speaking of cannot be reduced either to its matter or to its form. For a pure form, capable of subsisting apart, as an Intelligence, would not be suitable for a body. And as for pure matter, since it is mere possibility of all becoming without actually being anything, it would truly be nothing and consequently could not subsist. The correct expression for designating God's production of bodies and of their substantial principles is to say that God *created* bodies and *concreated* their form and their matter; that is, the one in the other indivisibly.[13]

We must realize that God governs by Providence beings constituted in this way. He is intimately present in their substance and operations. But the intimacy of the assistance He gives them leaves their efficacy absolutely intact. That the world is governed in the first place is clear to unprejudiced eyes when they examine the universal order of things. But we are forced to the same position by the very idea of God which we obtained from the proofs for His existence. For reason demands such a God as the first principle of the universe. And since the principle of a being is also its end, God must be the end of all things. Hence He relates and directs them to Himself. And this amounts to governing them. The final term in view of which the Creator administers the universe would seem, therefore, to be transcendent and exterior to things. Once again, what is true of the principle is equally so of the end.

The aspect richest in metaphysical consequences which God's government of things presents to the reflecting mind is the notion of their conservation. St. Thomas takes us to the heart of his metaphysics of bodies by a steady progress of thought. He first develops rigorously all the rigid implications of this notion of divine conservation. Then, when he has, so to speak, left to things nothing in their own right, he shows that the divine concursus which seems to take away their powers and their being, in reality actually confers these things upon them.

Every effect is dependent upon its cause. It depends upon its cause in the very measure in which it is produced by it. The word "cause" here designates something very different from that "constant relationship between phenomena" to which empiricism had reduced it. For St. Thomas, an efficient cause is an active force; that is, it is a being which produces being.[14] Now if we look into this closely, we find that acting or causing is still being. It is only the unfolding or procession of being from its cause in the form of an effect. There is no occasion for introducing any new notion in order to pass from being to causality. If we regard the act-of-being as an act, we shall see in this first act, by which each thing is what it is, the root of this second act by which being, which is first posited in itself, is also posited outside of itself, in its effects. Hence it is that just as God's causality extends to the act-of-being of all beings, it extends to all their operations.

To begin with, the divine efficacy extends totally to the being of creatures. Let us consider the case of the artisan who produces a work, or of the architect who constructs a building. This work or this building is indebted to its author for its exterior form and for the outward shape of its distinguishing parts. But it is indebted to him for nothing else. The materials out of which the work is fashioned already existed in nature. The artisan did not have to produce them; he had only to make use of them. The definite nature of the causal relationship is very well expressed by the manner in which the two terms (the artisan and his work) depend upon each other. Once it has been made, the work subsists independently of the artisan. Since it is not indebted to him for its being, it has no need of him in order to preserve its being.

It is precisely the same with natural beings. Each generates other beings by virtue of a form which it has itself received and of which it is not the cause. But it generates them in such a way that it produces their form but not the act-of-being by which their effects subsist. Thus we see that the infant continues to live after the death of its father in the same way as a house remains standing long after its builder has disappeared. In both cases we have to do with causes which make a thing *become* what it is but which do not cause it to exist.[15]

It is quite different with the relationship between things and God. First, because God is not only the cause of the form which clothes things, but of the very *esse* in virtue of which they exist, so that for them to cease for a moment to depend upon their cause would be to cease to exist at all. Secondly, this relationship between things and God is different because, somehow or other, it would be contradictory that God should make creatures capable of doing without Him.[16] It is of the essence of a creature that it have its existence from another, whereas God has His existence from Himself and subsists independently. For a creature to be able to subsist even for an instant without God's assistance, it would have to be existing by itself during this instant. That is, it would be God.[17] Thus the first effect of the Providence of God over things is the immediate and permanent influence by which He assures their conservation. This influence is, in some way, but the continuance of the creative act. Any interruption of this continued creation by which God maintains things in being would send them instantly back into nothingness.[18]

Now let us go further and follow closely God's influence within things and we shall see that it extends from their existence to their causality. Since nothing exists save in virtue of God's being, neither can anything act save by virtue of the divine efficacy. Accordingly, if any being causes the existence of another being, it only does so because God confers on it the power. This truth is immediately evident if we but remember that *esse* is an effect proper to God alone. Creation is His proper action and to produce being is, properly speaking, to create.[19]

We must go still further, however, and say that what is true of the causal efficacy of beings is equally so of their operations. God is the cause of and the reason for the operation of all beings. Why so? Because, in a way, to act is always to produce. What produces nothing does nothing. Now we have just pointed out that every real production of being, insignificant as it may be, belongs properly to God alone. Therefore, every operation presupposes God as its cause. Let us add to this that no being acts save in virtue of the faculties at its disposal. It applies to the effects of these faculties the natural forces which it is able to utilize. Neither these forces nor these faculties come, in the first instance, from the being itself, but from God who is its author in that He is the universal cause. So much is this so that, in the last analysis, it is God who is the principal cause of all actions performed by His creatures.[20] In His hands, creatures are like a tool in the hands of the workman.

Because He is the supreme Act-of-Being, God is everywhere present and acting by His efficacy. He is intimately present in the very *esse* whose operation proceeds from creatures. He supports them. He animates them from within. He leads them into their operation. He applies them to their acts in such a way that they neither are nor do anything except by Him, just as they would not exist without Him. This is the teaching of the Holy Scripture: "Do not I fill heaven and earth sayeth the Lord." [21] Or, again: "If I ascend into heaven, thou art there; if I descend into hell, thou art present." It must also be the necessary conclusion to which we are led by the notion of a God who is the universal cause of all being. Thus envisaged, the entire world is but a unique instrument in the hands of its creator.

At this very point, where St. Thomas seems to be dissolving beings in the divine omnipotence and submerging their activity in His efficacy, he turns brusquely against those irreconcilable enemies of his who would strip natural things of their own operations. This is the most unexpected change of direction for the unsuspecting reader of the *Summa Contra Gentiles*.[22] Nowhere is this characteristic trait of St. Thomas's technique —never to weaken one truth in order the more firmly to establish another —more perceptibly illustrated. Although we do not actually have to take back a single word of what we have just said, we do have to establish now quite a new proposition. Thomistic philosophy, in which the creature is nothing and does nothing without God, is set off against any teaching which would refuse to confer upon second causes the full share of being and efficacy to which they are entitled.

The varieties and shades of error misrepresenting the proper activity of second causes are innumerable. It is not a question here of adopting or rejecting any particular solution but rather of taking a position for or against an entire philosophy. Behind each of the doctrines he is refuting, St. Thomas detects the hidden presence of Platonism. If he rejects them it is because he feels that the philosopher's task is to interpret the real world of Aristotle, not the world of appearances described by Plato. And if he attaches himself firmly to Aristotle's real world it is in order to verify simple good sense, beyond which it is impossible to go. Causes and effects regularly generate one another in the sensible world. A warm body always warms a body that is brought near it. It never chills it. A man never begets anything but a man. Clearly, the nature of the effect produced is inseparably bound to the nature of the cause that produces it. It is this constant relationship between natural effects and their second causes which prevents our supposing that there is a pure and simple substitution of God's power for theirs. For if God's action were not diversified according to the different beings in which it operates, the effects which it produces would not be diversified in the way that the things themselves are, and anything might produce anything.[23] The existence of the laws of nature prevents our supposing that God has created beings deprived of causality.

A more remarkable thing, perhaps, is that those who deny all efficacy to second causes in order to reserve the privilege of causality to God Himself do no less injury to God than to things. The excellence of the work shows forth the glory of the workman, and how poor indeed would be a world entirely bare of efficacy! In the first place, it would be an absurd world. In giving the principal, no one denies the collateral. What sense would there be in creating heavy bodies incapable of moving downwards? If God, in imparting being to things, gave them some likeness to Himself, He ought also to have given them more of this likeness in imparting to them the activity which issues from being, by attributing to them actions of their own. Moreover, a universe of inert beings would point to a less perfect first cause than a universe of active beings capable of communicating their perfections to one another, when they act upon one another, just as God communicated to them something of His own in creating them, bound and ordered by the reciprocal actions which they perform. The urge by which certain philosophers are driven to withdraw everything from nature in order to glorify the Creator is inspired by a good intention, but a blind one. Actually, *detrahere actiones proprias rebus est divinae bonitati derogare:* to deprive things of actions of their own is to belittle God's goodness.[24]

The problem in the final analysis comes to this. We must hold firmly to two apparently contradictory truths. God does whatever creatures do; and yet creatures themselves do whatever they do. It is a question of understanding how one and the same effect can proceed simultaneously from two different causes: God and the natural agent which produces it. At first sight this is incomprehensible. Most philosophers seem to have cringed before it. They could not see how one action could proceed from two causes. If a natural body is doing it, then God cannot be doing it. Nay more! If God is performing the action, then it is much less intelligible that a natural body can be performing it at the same time, because God's causality reaches to the very depths of being and no longer leaves anything to be produced by its effects. Indeed, the dilemma appears unavoidable, unless we are to resign ourselves to placing contradiction within the very heart of things.[25]

Actually the opposition which metaphysics here encounters is not so irreducible as it seems. Perhaps, indeed, it is only superficial. It is contradictory to say that God and bodies are causes of natural effects at the same time and under the same relationship. They are such at the same time but not under the same relation. An example will enable us to see how this is so.

When an artisan produces something, he must of necessity employ tools and instruments of one kind or another. His choice of instruments is justified by their form. He himself does nothing more than move them in order to put them to work and make them produce their effects. When an axe cuts a piece of wood, the axe is certainly the cause of the effect produced. However, we can say with reason that the workman who wields the axe also causes it. We cannot divide the effect produced into two parts, one coming from the axe, the other from the workman. The axe produces the whole effect and so does the workman. The real difference is that the two of them do not produce it in the same manner. The axe only cuts the wood by virtue of the efficacy which the workman imparts to it. He is the first and principal cause, while the axe is the second and instrumental cause of the effect produced.

We must imagine some analogous relationship between God, the first cause, and natural bodies which we see acting before our eyes. We say *analogous relationship* because God's influence upon the second cause penetrates far more deeply into it than does the influence of the workman into his tool. When God imparts existence to things, He confers upon them at the same time their form, their movement and their efficacy. Nevertheless, it is to them that this efficacy belongs from the moment they receive it. Hence it is they who perform their operations. The lowest being acts and produces its effect, even though it does so by virtue of all the causes superior to the action it is subjected to and whose efficacy is transmitted to it by degrees. At the head of this series is God, the total and immediate cause of all the effects produced and of all the activity released therein. At the foot comes the natural body, the immediate cause of the proper action which it performs, even though it only performs it by virtue of the efficacy conferred upon it by God.

When we examine in this way the operations and movements continually performed in the universe, we notice that no part of this double causality can be considered superfluous. God's operation is clearly necessary to produce natural effects, since second causes owe all their efficacy to the first cause, God. But it is not superfluous that God, who can produce all natural effects Himself, should accomplish them by the mediation of certain other causes. These intermediaries which He has willed, are not necessary to Him in that He is unable to do without them. Rather it is for themselves that He willed them. The existence of second causes points to no lack in His power but to the immensity of His goodness.[26] The universe, as represented by St. Thomas, is not a mass of inert bodies passively moved by a force which passes through them, but a collection of active beings each enjoying the efficacy delegated to it by God along with actual being. At the first beginnings of a world like this, we have to place not so much a force being exercised as an infinite goodness being communicated. Love is the unfathomable source of all causality.

This is also, perhaps, the best point from which to view the general economy of the Thomistic philosophy of nature. From here, too, arise the various criticisms which such a philosophy directs against all other existing systems. Looked at from without, such a doctrine appears to its adversaries rather like a defense of the rights of creatures against those of God. This accusation is the more dangerous in that St. Thomas is ostensibly inspired by Aristotle. In this, at least, he appears to be yielding to the influence of pagan naturalism. Those who take their own interpretation to the extreme have never forgiven him for introducing *natures* and *efficacious causes* between natural effects and God.[27]

Looked at from within, St. Thomas's metaphysics seems, on the contrary, to extol a God whose principal attribute is not power, but goodness. Certainly productive fecundity and efficacy are divine things. If God did not communicate them outside of Himself to the multitude of beings which He has created, none of them would be able to provide itself with the least particle of them; and it is in His power that all efficacy originally shares. Or better, divine power is so perfect and eminent in itself that we can readily imagine how a religous soul will be very slow to attribute to itself the slightest share of it.

But we saw, when we studied the nature of the creative act, that the infinite expansiveness of the Good is at its first beginnings. Consequently, the conception of a universe willed by a Good which communicates itself cannot be that of a universe willed by a Power which reserves its efficacy to itself. Whatever this power would have the right to retain, the Goodness will wish to give away. And the higher the gift, the higher will be the brand of love with which it will be able to satisfy itself. The profound metaphysical intuition which welds together these two key pieces of the system is that a universe like Aristotle's demands as its cause a God like the God of Denis the Areopagite. Our highest glory is to be the coadjutors of God through the causality we wield: *Dei sumus adjutores*.[28] Or, as Denis says elsewhere, what is most divine is to be God's co-operator: *omnium divinius est Dei cooperatorem fieri*.[29] Therefore it is into the original effusion, which renders this co-operation possible, that the efficacy of second causes returns as to its source. No other kind of universe would be equally worthy of infinite goodness.

A consequence of this doctrine is to make its meaning true to what is called the "naturalism" or the "physicism" of St. Thomas. If no philosophy was so constantly busy safeguarding the rights of creatures, it is because it saw in this the one means of safeguarding the rights of God. Far from encroaching upon the Creator's privileges, the perfections attributed to second causes can only increase His glory, since He is their first cause and since this is a new occasion for glorifying Him. It is because there is causality in nature that we can go back step by step to the first cause, God. In a universe stripped of second causes the most obvious proofs of the existence of God would be impossible, and His highest metaphysical attributes would remain hidden from us. Inversely, this whole swarm of beings, natures, causes and operations which the universe presents us with, can no longer be regarded as existing or acting for itself. If God has conferred efficacy upon them as the highest mark of their divine origin, then it is their constant effort to assimilate themselves with God which makes them work and moves them toward their operations. Beneath each natural form there lies hidden a desire to imitate by means of action the creative fecundity and pure actuality of God. This desire is quite unconscious in the domain of bodies, which we are examining for the moment. But it is that same straining toward God which, with intelligence and will, will blossom forth into human morality. Thus, if a physics of bodies exists, it is because there exists first a mystical theology of the divine life. The natural laws of motion, and its communication from being to being, imitate the primitive creative effusion from God. The efficacy of second causes is but the counterpart of His fecundity.

As soon as we realize the significance of this principle, all shadow of antinomy between God's perfection and that of created being disappears. On the contrary, a universe which is only willed by God as resembling Him will never be too beautiful nor too powerful. It will never realize itself too completely. It will never tend too vehemently toward its own perfection in order to reproduce, as it should, the image of its divine model. "Anything which tends toward its own perfection, tends toward the divine model." [31] This is a principle of inexhaustible fruitfulness in Thomistic philosophy because it governs both human morality and the metaphysics of nature. Let us be perfect as our heavenly Father is perfect.

Looked at in this way, St. Thomas's real reason for criticizing earlier systems of metaphysics is easily grasped. He sees all systems, save Aristotle's from which he drew his inspiration,[32] falling into two classes according to two ways of denying to second causes the efficacy which is theirs by right.

First, there is Platonism and its derivatives—the systems of Avicenna, Ibn Gabirol, etc. According to this doctrine, anything new appearing in the world of bodies comes from outside. Hence it is a question here of a basic extrinsicism, whether the exterior cause of forms or operations of the sensible world reside in the efficacy of the Ideas as with Plato, in that of a separated Intelligence as with Avicenna, in that of the divine Will with Gabirol. In every case, the problem is amenable to the same solution, whether it is a question of explaining the physical operations of bodies, the cognitive operation of the reason or the moral operations of the will. In the three cases the entire efficacy resides in an extrinsic agent which imparts from without the sensible form to the body, or the intelligible form to the intellect, or virtue to the will.

Secondly, there is what may be called Anaxagorism, with all the modifications under which it may disguise itself. Here we have in intrinsicism no less basic than the extrinsicism which we have just been discussing, and its result is about the same. In this second case, the various effects we have been speaking of come, not from outside, but are already performed and realized virtually from within. There are seminal reasons included in matter and developed under the excitation of an exterior agent. There are innate ideas included in the soul, and which blossom forth of themselves under the gentle shock of sensation. There are natural virtues, residing in a crude way in the will, and which perfect themselves spontaneously as life provides them with an occasion for doing so. In the first case the second cause did nothing at all because it was receiving everything from outside. Here in the second case, it does very little more since the effects which it seems to produce are already virtually realized either in itself or in others. Its action is limited to removing the obstacles standing in the way of its development.[33]

These errors are closely related, in spite of their apparent contradiction, and hence certain philosophers do not hesitate to combine them. For such as these, knowledge comes to the soul from outside by way of divine illumination, while sensible forms develop in matter from within, thanks to seminal reasons enclosed therein. Actually we have here but two different ways of derogating from the order of the universe whose very structure is fashioned from the order and the connection between causes. All causes are indebted to the infinite goodness of the first cause both for the fact that they are and that they are causes. This we are now about to verify in the particularly important case of the human composite.

CHAPTER IV

MAN

AT THE SUMMIT of the world of forms are the Intelligences which are completely separated from matter—angels. At the bottom are those forms, which we have just been discussing, which are entirely embedded in matter. Between the two come human souls which are neither separated forms nor forms whose existence is tied to matter. Let us begin with an accurate statement of their condition.

The notion of soul is much wider than that of a human soul. In its wide sense soul is defined as the first act of an organized body capable of performing the functions of life.[1] Thus, like all form, a soul is an act. Like all act, it is not directly known to us. We simply infer it from its effects[2] and affirm it by judgment. The effect to strike the observer first is the presence within it of centers of spontaneous movement. Bodies are of two kinds. Some are by nature inert; others seem to grow, to change and, in the case of the most perfect among them, to move about in space by virtue of a kind of internal energy. The latter are called "living beings," a name extending to vegetable, animals and man. Since they perform operations proper to themselves, they must have some principle proper to themselves. This principle is called soul.

We must not regard a living being as a machine inert in itself but with a soul as its motor. This is what Descartes wanted to substitute for Aristotle's notion of living being. For St. Thomas, following Aristotle, the soul does not first make a body move, it first makes it a body. A corpse is not a body. The soul makes it exist as a body. It is the soul which assembles and organizes what we call today the bio-chemical elements (organic, or even inorganic, elements, but never *informes*) in order to make a living body from them. In this complete sense, the soul is its *first act;* that is, is what makes it to be. Thanks to this first act, the living thing can exercise all its second acts, the vital functions which are its operations.

The soul, the form of organized matter, is immaterial and incorporeal, as is the very humblest of forms.[3] But there is a vast difference between the conditions of souls in the various grades of the hierarchy of living things. The human soul, which is under discussion here, not only exercises the physiological operations of every living thing but also cognitive operations. Notably, it knows the existence and properties of bodies. In order to know a thing, it is necessary not to be that thing oneself. To be exact, in order to be able to know a given genus of beings, one must not oneself be one of the species of beings in that genus. For example, when a sick man has a bitter tongue he finds that everything he eats is bitter. He can no longer distinguish other tastes. Similarly, if the human soul were a species of body, it would not know other bodies. Therefore human knowledge is the operation of a form which, insofar as it is fitted for knowing bodies, is essentially a stranger to all corporeity. Since the human soul performs operations in which the body has no part, it is a form in which the body has no part. To operate by itself it must subsist by itself, because being is the cause of operation, and everything acts according as it is. What subsists by itself is a substance. The human soul, therefore, is an immaterial substance. And this is what we set out to demonstrate.[4]

To understand that the human soul is an immaterial substance is to see at the same time that it is immortal. Properly speaking, the immortality of the soul need not be demonstrated, at least for one who knows its nature. It is a kind of evidence *per se nota* and follows from the definition of a rational soul, as it follows from the definition of the whole, that the whole is greater than the part. However, there is sometimes much to be said for pointing out something which really needs no demonstration.

To be immortal is to be incorruptible. What is corruptible can only corrupt by itself (*per se*) or by accident (*per accidens*). Now things lose their existence in the same way they acquire it. They lose it *per se* if, being substances, they exist *per se*. They lose it *per accidens* if, being accidents, they only exist *per accidens*. Since the soul is a substance, it exists *per se*. Therefore it cannot corrupt *per accidens*. But this is what would be happening if the death of the body entailed the death of the soul, as happens in the case of plants and of animals deprived of reason. The rational soul, as a substance, is not affected by the corruption of the body. Indeed the body only exists by the soul whereas the soul does not exist by the body. If there is anything that can cause the soul to corrupt, we must look for it in the soul itself.

But it is impossible to find it there either. Every substance, which is a form, is indestructible by definition. What belongs to a being by virtue of its definition cannot be taken away from it. Now just as matter is potency by definition, so form is act by definition. And just as matter is a possibility of existence, so form is an act-of-being. This is easily seen in the case of bodies, because they acquire being when they receive their form, and lose being when they lose their form. But if we can conceive of a body separated from its form and from the act-of-being which the form confers upon it, we cannot conceive of a subsistent form capable of being separated from the act-of-being that it has. Therefore, as long as a rational soul remains itself, it exists. This is what we mean when we say that it is immortal.[5]

Doubtless we will not be surprised that the soul, a subsistent form, is subject to the same imperfection as angelic substance. By definition, the soul is form in the totality of its being and has no mixture of matter. If we claimed to discover some matter in it, this matter would not be the soul itself but merely the body which the soul animates.[6] But it is true that the soul, like the angel, is composed of potency and act. In it, as in all creatures, existence is distinct from essence. Thus the soul is a form very different from God, who is pure act. It only possesses the degree of being that its nature calls for, in conformity with the general law that the quantity of being shared by each creature is in proportion to the capacity of the essence which shares it.[7]

But here is a new determination which will permit us to establish a distinction between the spiritual substances we call souls and separated intelligences which we already know are infinitely removed from God. The human soul, which is neither matter nor body, is, on the other hand, by its own essence, capable of being united with a body. No doubt some will object that the body united to the soul is not of the essence of the soul considered by itself. Consequently, they will say that the human soul, considered precisely as a soul, remains a pure spiritual substance of the same species as angels. Such an objection only reveals a hazy notion of the new grade of imperfection that is here being introduced into the hierarchy of created beings. In saying that the human soul is naturally capable of union with a body, we do not wish to point out merely that the soul is only accidentally united to the body. Association with the body is, on the contrary, essential to the soul and characteristic of its nature. We are no longer dealing with a pure intelligence like the angelic substance but with a simple intellect; that is, with a principle of intellection whose natural light is so weak that it necessarily requires a body in order to carry out its own operation. Hence the human soul marks off a lower degree of intellectuality than the angel.[8] The truth of this conclusion will become more fully evident when we determine in what way the soul is united to the body to make the human composite.

What is this corporeal nature? And what genus of beings are these composites? The body is not to be considered as evil in itself. When the Manichaeans considered matter to be evil and assigned it a creative principle distinct from God, they were not only guilty of a theological error, but of a philosophical one as well. If matter were evil in itself, it would be nothing. If it is something, it is that, in the very measure in which it is, it is not evil. Like everything else belonging to the realm of creatures, matter is good and created by God.[9]

Moreover, not only is matter good in itself, but it is a good and a source of good for all the forms which can be united in it. It would be completely foreign to the Thomistic perspective to regard the material universe as the result of some calamity and the union of soul and body as the consequence of a fall. A radical optimism runs through this doctrine because it presents a universe created out of pure goodness. It interprets all its parts, in the measure in which they subsist, as so many reflections of God's infinite perfection. Origen's teaching that God created bodies in order to imprison sinful souls in them is most repugnant to St.

Thomas's thought. The body is not the prison of the soul, but a servant and instrument placed in its service by Almighty God. The union of soul and body is no chastisement of the soul but a salutary bond through which the human soul will reach its full perfection.

This is not a theory forged expressly for the particular case of the soul. Rather, it is the case which is necessarily governed according to metaphysical principles, and their scope is universal. The less perfect is ordered toward the more perfect as toward its end; it is for it, not against it. Within the individual, each organ exists with a view to its function, as the eye to allow vision. Each lower organ exists in view of a higher organ and a higher function, the senses for the intellect, the lungs for the heart. The array of organs, in its turn, exists only in view of the perfection of the whole, as matter for form, the body for the soul. For the parts are, as it were, the matter of the whole. It is exactly the same if we consider the disposition of individual beings within this whole. Each creature exists for its own act and its own perfection. Less noble creatures exist for the more noble. Individuals exist for the perfection of the universe; and the universe itself exists for God. The reason for the existence of a determined substance or determined mode of existence is never to be found in an evil but in a good. Let us now seek to discover just what good the human body can bring to the reasonable soul which animates it.[10]

Since it is in the good, which defines essence, and consequently in the form that sufficient reasons and final causes reside, we must, accordingly, look into the soul itself for the body's reason for existing. If the soul were an intelligence of the same degree of perfection as an angel, it would be pure form subsisting and operating without the assistance of an exterior instrument, fully realizing its own definition, and concentrating in a single individuality the total perfection of an essence. We might say again that each angel describes and determines in itself in a complete way one of the possible degrees of participation in God's perfection. But the human soul, lower on the ladder of beings, still belongs to that order of forms which do not possess enough actuality to attain their perfection in the separated state. While each angelic intelligence subsists apart in a clearly defined degree, there does not and cannot exist anywhere a form which corresponds to the human soul's degree of perfection and realizes it fully. Now it is a constant principle that an inaccessible unity is imitated by a multiplicity. Individual human souls are renewed in unceasing succession and assure the perpetuation of the species. They permit the degree of perfection corresponding to man to be continually represented in the universe. But if the human representation of God's perfection demanded by the order in creation is safeguarded in this way, each soul, taken individually, is only the incomplete realization of its ideal type. Insofar as it satisfies its own definition, it is an act and has the pleasure of being what it ought to be. But insofar as it only realizes its definition imperfectly, it is in potency; that is, it is not all that it could be. Indeed, it is even in a state of privation, because it feels that it ought to be what it is not.

A human soul, or any corporeal form, is a kind of incomplete perfection. But it is fitted for completion and feels the need and experiences the desire for it. This is why form, tormented by privation, is the principle of the operation of natural things. Each act-of-being, according to the measure in which it is, wishes to be. It only acts in order to preserve itself in existence and to assert itself more completely. Now man's intelligence is the faintest ray in the order of knowledge. The light illuminating it is so weak and feeble that there is no intelligible in it. Left to itself or placed before a pure intelligible, one easily read by angels, it is blind and discerns nothing. It is an incomplete form fundamentally incapable of completing itself by itself. It is in potency to all the perfection which it lacks, but has nothing to draw it from. The operation which might complete it is an impossible one in its case. So there it is, condemned to sterility and inaction, unless some instrument is placed at its service, an instrument like it incomplete, which the soul may organize and animate from within, an instrument which will permit it to enter into relationship with an intelligible assimilable to itself. That it may become conscious of those things which it lacks and that, under the stimulus of the sense of its own privation, it may begin to seek out the intelligible residing in the sensible, human intelligence simply must be a soul and must profit from the advantages which union with a body can bring it. How can such a union be achieved?

First let us state the condition which must be satisfied by any attempted solution of the problem. The proper act of an intelligible soul is obviously intellectual knowledge. We must discover, then, a mode of union between body and soul permitting us to attribute intellectual knowledge not only to the soul, but to the entire man. Such a condition is quite legitimate. Every human being knows from intimate experience that it is its entire self and not just a part of itself which knows. We have only two hypotheses to choose from. Either man is no more than his intellective soul, in which case it is self-evident that intellectual knowledge belongs to the whole man. Or else the soul is only a part of man, and in this case there must be a sufficiently close union between the soul and the body that the activity of the soul may be attributed to the man himself.[11] But it is quite impossible to hold that the soul alone is the whole man. A general definition of anything is: "that which performs the operation proper to it." In this case man is to be defined as "that which performs the operations proper to man." Man does not perform only intellectual operations. He performs sensitive operations too. These clearly cannot be effected without modification in a corporeal organ. Sight, for example, supposes a modification of the pupil by the species of color. The same holds for the other senses.[12] Thus, if sensation is truly an operation of man, even though it is not his proper operation, then it is perfectly obvious that man is not just his soul but some kind of composite of soul and body.[13] What is the nature of this union?

We must at once eliminate the hypothesis that the soul and body make up a mixed being whose powers participate at the same time in both the spiritual and corporeal substances which constitute it. In any real mixture, the component parts no longer subsist, save virtually, after they have once been mixed. If they subsisted actually, we should not have to do with a mixture but with sheer confusion. Thus, in a mixture, we do not encounter the separate elements which compose it. But although they are composed of essence and existence, intellectual substances are not composed of matter and form, they are simple and therefore incorruptible.[14] They are quite incapable of constituting, along with a body, a mixture in which their own nature would no longer exist.[15]

In opposition to this doctrine which confounds the soul with the body to the point of removing its very essence, we encounter another which makes such a radical distinction between the two that nothing remains but an external contact and the relationship of mere contiguity. This is Plato's position. He would have the intellect united to the body only as its motor. This kind of union is inadequate if the action of the intellect is to be attributed to everything which the intellect and the body do. The action of the motor is never attributed to the thing moved, save by instrumentality, as when the carpenter's action is attributed to the saw. If intellectual knowledge is attributable to Socrates himself only because it is the action of an intellect which is moving his body, then it follows that Socrates is only the instrument of such action. Now Socrates is in this case a corporeal instrument, since he is composed of soul and body. And, as intellectual knowledge requires no corporeal instrument, it may legitimately be concluded that, in placing the soul as the motor of the body, we do not acquire the right to attribute the soul's intellectual activity to the entire man.

Moreover, it should be noted that the action of one part can sometimes be attributed to the whole as when we say that it is the man who sees. But the action of one part is never attributed to another part, unless by accident (*per accidens*). We do not say that the hand sees because the eye does. If, therefore, Socrates and his intellect are two parts of the same whole, joined as a thing moved to its motor, it follows that the action of his intellect cannot, properly speaking, be attributed to the whole Socrates. If, on the other hand, Socrates himself is a whole, composed of the union of his intellect with the rest of what goes to make up Socrates, without his intellect being united to the body other than as its motor, it follows that Socrates has only an accidental unity and an accidental being. We cannot legitimately say this about the human composite.[16]

It is not very difficult to see that we have here to do with an error that we have already refuted. Plato only wished to unite the soul to the body as its motor because he did not place man's essence in the composite of soul and body, but in the soul alone using the body as an instrument. Hence we find him saying that the soul is in the body as the pilot in his ship. To suppose that man is composed of a soul and body is, for Plato, to consider Peter to be a composite formed out of his humanity and his clothes. Plato would say that the truth is, on the contrary, that Peter is a man who uses his clothes, as man is a soul who uses his body. But such a doctrine is quite unacceptable. The animal and man himself are sensible and natural beings; that is, physical composites in which a matter and a form meet. Clearly it would not be thus in the hypothesis stating that the body and its parts do not belong to the essence of man and animal, for the soul, taken in itself is in no way sensible nor material. If we remember, moreover, the consideration already proposed, namely, that the soul not only has operations such as pure intellection, in which the body has no share, and that it also has many operations which it does share with the body, as, for example, sensations and passions, we are led perforce to maintain that man is not merely a soul using his body as the motor uses what it moves but that he is the true whole, the composite of soul and body.[17]

There remains, therefore, but one possible mode of union between the soul and the body—that proposed by Aristotle when he makes the intellective principle the form of the body. Besides, if such a hypothesis succeeded in being verified, the soul's intellection might legitimately be attributed to the man, the substantial unity of the soul and body. And we cannot doubt that this is actually the case. That by which a being passes from potency to act is, indeed, the proper form and the act of this being. Now the living body is only alive in potency until the soul has come to inform it. Only while it is vivified and animated by its soul does the human body really deserve its name. The eye or the arm of a corpse is no more a real eye or arm than if painted on canvas or sculptured in stone.[18] It is the soul that places the body into the species of human body. It is the soul that confers upon it in act the being it possesses. The soul, then, is really its form as we have supposed.[19] Not only can we deduce this conclusion from a consideration of the human body which the soul animates and vivifies, but also from the definition of the human species. When we wish to find out the nature of a being, we have only to determine what its operation is. Now the proper operation of man, considered as man, is intellectual knowledge. Through it he surpasses in dignity all the other animals. It is for this reason that Aristotle places man's sovereign happiness in this characteristic operation.[20] Hence it is this principle of intellectual operation which puts man in the species in which he finds himself. But the species of a being is always determined by its proper form. Therefore the intellective principle, that is, the human soul, is the proper form of man.[21]

However, certain philosophers find it difficult to be reconciled to this conclusion, and only accept it reluctantly. They find it hard to admit that an intellectual substance of great dignity like the human soul is united to the matter of a human body. In order to reduce what might be regarded as shocking in such a disproportion, they introduce between the highest substantial form of the human being—that is, the intellectual principle itself, and the prime matter it informs—a large number of intermediary forms. Matter, as subjected to its first form becomes next the subject of the second form, and so on until the last form. In a hypothesis like this the subject next to the rational soul would not be corporeal matter pure and simple, but the body already informed by the sensitive soul.[22]

This opinion is easily explained if we but put ourselves in the place of the Platonist philosophers. They begin from the principle that there is a hierarchy of genera and species and that within this hierarchy the higher degrees are always intelligible in themselves and independently of the lower degrees. Thus man in general is intelligible *per se*. When abstraction is made from a particular man, animal is intelligible independently of man, and so on. These philosophers reason as though there always existed in reality a distinct and separate being corresponding to each of the abstract representations which our intellect can form. Thus, noting that it is possible to consider mathematics after abstraction has been made from the sensible, the Platonists held for the existence of mathematical beings subsisting outside sensible things. Similarly, they placed man in himself above particular human beings and moved on up to being, to the one, and to the good which they placed at the highest degree of things.

In thus considering universals as separated forms in which sensible beings participate, they are led perforce to say that Socrates is animal insofar as he participates in the idea of animal, man insofar as he participates in the idea of man. And this amounts to placing in him a multiplicity of hierarchical forms. If, however, we consider things from the point of view of sensible reality, which is that of Aristotle and of true philosophy, we shall see that this cannot be true. Among all the predicates which can be attributed to things, there is one that belongs to them in a particularly intimate and immediate fashion, *being* itself. And since it is the form that confers on matter its actual being, it is absolutely necessary that the form from which the matter holds its being belong to it immediately and before everything else. Now it is the substantial form that confers substantial being on matter. Accidental forms confer merely a relative and accidental being on the thing in which they reside. They make it a white being or a colored being. But these things do not make it a being. If, therefore, we suppose a form which does not confer on matter its substantial being, but is merely added to matter already existing by reason of a preceding form, this second form cannot be considered as a true substantial form. This really means that it is by definition impossible to insert a number of intermediary substantial forms between the substantial form and its matter.[23]

If this be so, we must posit only one substantial form within each individual. To this single and unique substantial form, which is the human form, man owes not only his being man but also his animal, living, body, substance and being. This can be explained as follows. Any being which acts impresses its own resemblance in the matter on which it acts. This resemblance is called a form. Now it can be observed that the greater the dignity of an active and operative power, the more other powers it synthesizes and includes in itself. It does not contain them as distinct parts which would constitute it in its own perfection. Rather, it gathers them into the unity of its own perfection, and this form is more perfect according to the degree of perfection in the agent. And since the form resembles the agent which produces it, a more perfect form must be able to effect by a single operation as much as, and even more than, forms lower in dignity effect by several operations. If, for example, the form of the inanimate body enables matter to be and to be a body, the form of the plant will confer these things too, and will in addition enable it to live. Now let a rational soul supervene, and it will be able by itself to bestow being, corporeal nature and life; and in addition it will give it reason. So, in man as in all other animals, the coming of a more perfect form always entails the corruption of the form which preceded it. This happens in such a way, however, that the second form possesses everything the first one had.[24]

We observe at the heart of this thesis, as we have already seen several times and as a simple look at the universe shows, that the forms of natural things are only distinguished from one another as the perfect from the more perfect. The species and forms determining them are differentiated by the greater or less degree of the act-of-being which they share. Species are like numbers. Add or substract a unit and the species is changed. Better still, we can say with Aristotle that the vegetative is in the sensitive, the sensitive in the intellect, just as the triangle is in the tetragon, the tetragon in the pentagon. The pentagon contains virtually the tetragon because it has all that the tetragon has, and more. But it does not have it in such a way that what belongs to the tetragon can be distinguished separately from what belongs to the pentagon. Similarly, the intellective soul contains virtually the sensitive soul, since it has everything the sensitive soul has, and more. But it does not have this in such a way that it is possible to distinguish two different souls in it.[25] Thus, one single substantial form, the human intellect, is enough to constitute man in his own being, bestowing upon him at one and the same time being, body, life, sense and intellection.[26]

The immediate consequences of this conclusion must be noted: We see, in the first place, why the word *man* cannot properly mean either human body or human soul, but the composite of soul and body taken in its totality. If the soul is the form of the body, it forms with the body a physical composite of the same nature as all other composites of matter and form. In such a case, it is not the form alone which constitutes the species but the form and matter which are united therein.[27] We are, therefore, justified in considering the human composite as one single being and in attributing intellectual knowledge to it. It is not the body alone, nor even the soul alone, but the man, who knows. The union of soul and body is so close that the soul compenetrates or envelops the body to the point of being wholly present in each of its parts.[28] This is self-evident, if the soul is truly the form of the body. The union of soul and body is a substantial union, not merely an accidental union. In an attempt to be more explicit about the meaning of this statement, we shall proceed to determine the exact position occupied by the human soul in the hierarchy of created beings.

An accidental composition is one which unites the accident to the subject supporting it. A substantial composition is one which results from the union of matter with the form investing it.[29] And the kind of union established between the beings under consideration is very different in the case of these two compositions. Accidental union amounts to grafting one essence upon another one which could have subsisted without it. Substantial union, on the contrary, makes one complete substance of two beings each incapable of subsisting without the other. Matter and form are realities which are incomplete, considered in themselves, but which, by reason of their union, make up one complete substance.

This is the exact relationship of man's intellective soul to the body it animates. St. Thomas expresses this relationship by saying that the human soul is one part of man and the body another part.[30] This is what is meant by those who say that St. Thomas teaches that the human soul and body are two incomplete substances which, when united, form the complete substance, man.

This second formula is not the better one. It tends too much to gratify our natural desire for an oversimplified Thomism—one thing for each concept, one concept for each thing. If there were a rule to this effect, we should here be confronted by an exception. But there is no such rule. The substantial unity being discussed is man himself, taken as one. It would be contradictory to think of this being as one and yet as composed of two other beings, his soul and body. Just let us recall—and we cannot insist too much on this—that the constitutive functions of the body and soul in the human composite are very unequal. If we consider the problem from the basic point of view of the act-of-being, that of the soul in no way depends upon the body's. The reverse is true. The soul is substantial form and possesses in itself its own act-of-being. This act-of-being is so sufficient that it is even enough for the body whose act it is. Indeed there is only one single act-of-being for the soul and the body. And this act-of-being of the composite is furnished by the soul alone.[31] The unity of the man is not some kind of deft adjustment which makes its component parts interdependent, it is the unity proceeding from his very act-of-being.

But why, then, do we still speak of the soul as a part? Because it is a part of man. We have said several times that species differ as do numbers. Just so, the species "soul" does not exist alone. There is no real being which is a "human soul" and neither is nor was anything more than that. The hierarchical chain of real substances is: angel, man, animal, plant, mineral. The human soul is not listed here because it does not constitute by itself a grade of being specifically distinct from the others. To find it, we must look for it where it is—in man in whom it has this body without which it cannot exist, and which it makes exist. The human soul has to have a body in order that its definite operation, human knowledge, may be performed.[32] In order to constitute a complete human species, there must be the means of performing the proper operation belonging to that species. The characteristic operation of the human species is intellectual knowledge. What the rational soul lacks in order to exercise this operation is not intelligence but sensation. Sensation requires a body. Hence the soul must have a body in order, by its union with this body, to constitute the specific degree of being known as man, and to perform its works.

The only concrete and complete reality corresponding to all these concepts is the human composite. Certainly the two concepts of soul and body correspond to realities, and even to substances. But they do not correspond to real subjects each possessed of the wherewithal to subsist without the other. A finger, an arm, a foot, are substances, yet they only exist as parts of the whole, the human body. Similarly, the soul is a substance and the body is a substance. But every substance is not a distinct subject nor a distinct person.[33] The concepts of human soul and human body must not be thought to signify distinct existences in reality.

When we use such concepts correctly, we conceive each of them to signify a part of a whole along with the place it occupies therein. It is not always easy to do this, but St. Thomas certainly asks us to do so. For example, it is insofar as it is an intellect that the human soul is an immaterial substance. However, remembering that the intellectual operation presupposes sensation and demands the collaboration of the body, St. Thomas says without hesitation that the intellect is the form of the human body: "We must assert that the intellect which is the principle of intellectual operation is the form of the human body." [34] Nothing could be more exact, provided that in reading it we remember by what title the intellect is the form of the body. It is so by the single act-of-being whose efficacy places the concrete human being, body and soul, as an individual reality outside of thought. This is why although the human soul is not man, the notion of the soul is meaningless save in relation to the notion of man, which it connotes much as the concept of a cause does that of its effect. While he goes as far as possible in this direction, St. Thomas does not stop with the concept of soul. He goes on to the affirmation of *esse*. To posit a human *esse* is to posit at the same time a human soul and with it the body of which it is the form. In short, it is to posit a concrete and really existing individual. It becomes true to say, then, that every subject has individuation in the same way that it has existence.[35] This is why the individuation of the soul survives the death of the body just as surely as the soul itself does. When the body dies, it is because the soul ceases to make it exist. But why should the soul cease to exist because of this fact? It does not receive its being from its body, but only from God. And if it keeps its being how could it lose its individuation? "The act-of-being and individuation of a thing are always found together." Just as the soul owes its existing in its body to God's power and not to the body, so does it owe its existing without its body to God's power. No doubt, St. Thomas adds, in a significant remark, the individuation of the soul has some relation to its body, but the immortality of the soul is the immortality of its *esse*. The survival of its *esse* involves as a consequence that of its individuation.[36]

Thus conceived, the human soul occupies an important place in the hierarchy of created beings. On the one hand, it is at the bottom of the order of intellects; that is, the farthest removed from the divine intellect. "The human intellect is the lowest in the order of intellects and most remote from the perfection of the divine intellect."[37] On the other hand, if it is important to note emphatically the close dependence of the human soul on matter, it is equally important not to involve it so deeply in matter as to deprive it of its true nature. The soul is not a separate Intelligence, but is still a principle of intellection. Last in the order of intellects, it is first in the order of material forms. So we see it, as form of the human body, exercising operations in which the body cannot participate.

If there is any doubt that such beings, which are at the same time dependent on and independent of matter, can come naturally into the hierarchy of created beings, a rapid induction will suffice to establish it. It is clear that the nobler a form is, and the more it dominates its corporeal matter, the less deeply is it immersed in it and the more does it exceed it in power and operation. So the forms of the elements, which are the least of all forms and the closest to matter, exercise no operation extending beyond such active and passive qualities as rarefaction and condensation and other similar qualities which seem to be capable of being reduced to the simple dispositions of matter. Above these we find the forms of mixed bodies whose operation is not to be reduced to the forms of the four elements. If, for example, the magnet attracts iron, it is not by reason of the heat or cold that is in it, but because it participates in the power of celestial bodies which constitute it in its own species. Above these forms, there are the souls of plants. Their operation is higher than that of mineral forms and produces nourishment and growth. Next come sensitive souls possessed by animals. Their operation extends to a certain degree of knowledge, although their knowledge is limited to matter and is accomplished exclusively by material organs. Thus we arrive at human souls, which surpass in nobility all the preceding forms. We know they are raised above matter because they have a power and operation in which the body does not participate. It is precisely this power in them that is called intellect.[38]

Thus we verify once again the continuity of order which binds the universe to the creative activity which produced it. "If the human soul, inasmuch as it is united to the body as a form, has an act-of-existing which transcends the body and does not depend on it, obviously the soul itself is established on the boundary-line dividing corporeal from separate substances." [39] The transition established by separated substances between God and man is also established in turn by human souls between the pure intelligences and bodies deprived of intelligence. Thus we pass from extreme to extreme by way of some mean. If we are to conform to the principle that has guided this present work from its beginning, we must now examine in some detail the operations of man.

CHAPTER V

THERE EXISTS in man but one substantial form, and consequently, but one soul. From this soul, he has his reason, senses, movement and life. The one soul has many powers and it must therefore occasion no surprise if we proceed to consider again man's place among created beings. The lower beings are naturally incapable of attaining complete perfection. But they do attain a mediocre degree of excellence by means of certain movements. There are higher beings which acquire a complete perfection by means of a large number of movements. Still higher beings attain their complete perfection by a small number of movements; and highest among these are those which possess their perfection without executing any movements in order to acquire it. So it is those men who have the poorest health who are quite unable to achieve perfect health, but who do manage to keep themselves in a rather precarious state of health by having recourse to a number of remedies. More satisfactory is the state of those who achieve perfect health by using many remedies. Still more satisfactory is the state of those who achieve the same thing by means of few remedies. Completely satisfactory is the state of those who have the most excellent health without ever taking any remedies. Thus, things lower than man can lay claim to certain particular perfections. They perform a small number of fixed and determined operations. Man, on the contrary, can acquire a universal and perfect good, since he can attain the Sovereign Good. But he is at the lowest grade of beings capable of attaining beatitude because he is the least of intellectual creatures. Therefore, it is fitting that the human soul should acquire its proper good by means of many operations presupposing some diversity of powers. Above the human soul come the angels who attain beatitude by fewer means. Finally, there is God in whom there are no powers nor any action outside His one simple act-of-being. There is also a fairly evident consideration which brings us to the same conclusion directly. Man is placed on a frontier where the world of spirits and the world of bodies meet. The powers of both must necessarily belong to him.[1] What distinctions can we find in these various powers?

All potency, considered as potency, is ordered to its act. Thus the nature of each power derives from the act to which it is ordered. In other words, powers are distinguished from one another in the same way as their acts are distinguished. From other sources, we know that acts are distinguished according to their various objects. For an act which plays the role of a principle and motive cause, there is a corresponding passive power which is subject to its action. Thus color, insofar as it moves sight, is the principle of vision. For an object which plays the role of terminus and end, there corresponds an active power. Thus the perfection of stature, which is the end of growth, is the terminus of the faculty of growth belonging to living beings.[2] A consideration of the actions of heating and chilling brings us to the same conclusion. These two actions differ in that the principle of one is heat, of the other cold. But they are even more distinguishable from the ends toward which they tend. For the agent only acts in order to induce its similitude in some other being. Heat and cold act in order to produce hot and cold. Thus actions and the powers from which they come are distinguished from one another by their objects.[3]

We can use this conclusion to distinguish the powers of the soul. We shall see that they fall into hierarchical order, because the many always proceed from the one in some kind of order: *ordine quodam ab uno in multitudinem proceditur*.[4] Moreover, this hierarchy of the powers of the soul is based on the degree of universality in their objects. The greater the dignity of a power, the more universal the corresponding object. At the bottom we find a power of the soul whose one object is the body to which it is united. This power is called vegetative, because the vegetative soul only acts on its own body. There is another genus of powers of the soul corresponding to a more universal object, namely, to all sensible bodies, and not merely to the one sensible body with which the soul is united. They belong to what is called the sensitive soul. Above these, there is a power of the soul with a still more universal object; that is, not merely sensible bodies in general, but all being taken in its universality. This is called the intellective soul.[5]

It is clear, moreover, that according to these differences among the objects of the soul there are corresponding differences in the manner of its operations. The soul's action is more transcendent with regard to the operations of corporeal nature according as its object becomes more universal. From this point of view we can discern three distinct degrees. First, the soul's action transcends the action of nature considered as operating in inanimate things. The proper action of the soul is life. Now whatever moves itself to its own operation is said to be alive. Therefore the soul is an intrinsic principle of action, while all inanimate bodies receive their movement from an exterior principle. The vegetative powers of the soul are only exercised on the body to which it is immediately united, but they place it in a grade of being clearly higher than purely corporeal nature. However, it should be recognized that if the mode in which the soul accomplishes its vegetative operations is not reduced to the mode in which bodies act, the actual operations are identical in both cases. Inanimate things receive their act from an external principle. Animate things receive their act from their soul. Hence there is room, above the vegetative actions of the soul, for actions of a higher order. These surpass those performed by natural forms both from the point of view of what they do and how they do it. These operations depend on the soul's natural aptitude for receiving all things into itself by an immaterial mode of being.

It is to be noted, indeed, that insofar as it is endowed with sense and intellect, the soul is, in a way, all being. But although all things can be in the soul under an immaterial mode of being, there are degrees of immateriality in the mode in which they come into it. At the first degree are those things which are in the soul, deprived to be sure of their proper matter, but yet according to their particular being and with conditions of individuality which they have from their matter. It is thus with the senses. Species come into them from individual things. They receive these species, denuded of matter, but into a corporeal organ. The higher and very perfect degree of immateriality is that of the intellect which, without a corporeal organ, receives species totally deprived of matter and of the conditions of individuality belonging to them.[6] Thus the soul performs, from within, operations of a natural order in the body to which it is united. It performs also operations of a sensible order which are indeed immaterial, but accomplishment by means of a corporeal organ. Finally, it performs without a corporeal organ operations of the intelligible order. Thus all its actions fall into a hierarchy and with them their corresponding powers. We have now considered them in their proper order. It remains to consider them in themselves. Here, however, the order of generation is the reverse of the order of perfection.[7] So we shall examine first the least perfect of all, the vegetative power.

The object of the vegetative power is, as has been indicated, the body considered as receiving the life of the soul which informs it. The nature of the body demands that the soul exercise a threefold operation in it. Hence there is a threefold division of the vegetative power. By the first of these operations the body receives actual existence. The soul confers this by means of its generative power. Moreover, we noted elsewhere that inanimate, natural things, receive simultaneously with their being, their due size or quantity. This cannot be the case with living beings. They are brought forth from a seed. At the beginning of their existence they have only an imperfect being as far as quantity is concerned. For them there must be, besides the generative power, an augmentative power, through which they achieve their proper natural stature. But this increase of being would be impossible unless something were changed into the substance of the being to be increased and was thereby added to it.[8] This transformation is the work of the bodily warmth which assimilates and digests all the foods introduced from without. Thus the very conservation of the individual demands a nutritive power to restore continually what it has lost, and to bring to it what it needs if it is to attain its perfection of stature, as well as what it needs to produce the seed necessary for its own reproduction.[9] Thus the vegetative power itself supposes a generative power which confers being, an augmentative power which confers fitting stature, and a nutritive power which preserves it in existence and in its own proper quantity.

We must, once more, introduce hierarchical order among these powers. The nutritive and augmentative produce their effect in the very being in which they reside. It is the body united to the soul which is thus increased and preserved by the soul. But the generative power does not produce its effect in its own body. It produces it in another, for nothing begets itself. This power, then, is closer than the other two to the dignity of the sensitive soul whose operation is about exterior objects, although the operations of the sensitive soul are of a higher excellence and greater universality. Once again we find Dionysius' principle borne out: the highest grade of a lower order is contiguous to the lowest grade of the higher order. The nutritive power is subordinate to the augmentative, the augmentative to the generative.[10] By the generative we almost attain to the sensitive which will definitely deliver the individual from bondage to its particular mode of being.

The sensitive power of the soul is the lowest degree of the knowledge to be encountered in the universe. When we take a complete view of sensitive knowledge, we see that it must have five operations in order to look after the necessities of animal existence. Some of these operations can themselves be broken down into an orderly series of subsidiary operations. The simplest of all depends upon the *particular sense,* which is first in the order of sensitive powers and corresponds to an immediate modification of the soul by sensible realities. But the particular sense is in turn subdivided into distinct powers according to the various kinds of sensible impressions it is equipped to receive. Sensibles act upon the particular sense by the species which they impress upon it.[11] Contrary to what is generally imagined, these species are not taken into the sense in a material form—otherwise the sense would become the sensible itself, the eye would become color and the ear sound. Yet, some types of sensation are accompanied by very definite organic modifications in the animal which experiences them. Let us begin, then, from the principle that the senses receive sensible species denuded of matter; and let us classify them according to the increasing immateriality of the modifications which they undergo.

First of all we find some sensibles whose species, although received immaterially into the sense, modify materially the animal which experiences them. Such are the qualities presiding over the transmutations of material things themselves; namely, heat, cold, dryness, humidity and the like. Since sensibles of this kind produce material impressions in us, and since every material impression is made by contact,[12] such sensibles must touch us in order that we may perceive them. Hence the sensitive power which apprehends them is called touch.

There is a second kind of sensible whose impression does not itself modify us, but yet it is accompanied by an accessory material modification. Sometimes this supplementary modification affects both the sensible and the sense organ. This is the case with taste. Although, indeed, flavor does not modify the organ which perceives it to the extent of making it itself sweet or bitter, still it cannot be perceived without both the flavored object and the tasting organ being modified in some way. Both the tongue and the object seem to require moistening. This is not like the action of heat which warms the part of the body on which it acts. We simply have here a material transmutation which conditions sensible perception but does not constitute it. Sometimes, again, the material transmutation associated with sensation only affects the sensible quality itself. It can consist in a sort of alteration or decomposition of the sensible, such as is produced when bodies give off odors, or are reduced to a simple local movement, as is the case when we perceive sound. Hearing and smell suppose no material modification of the sense organ. They perceive from a distance and across an exterior medium, the material modifications which have affected the sensible object.[13]

Finally, we have a last class of sensibles which act upon the sense without any corporeal modification accompanying their action. These are color and light. The process by which such species emanate from the object to act upon the subject is totally spiritual.[14] Here, with the noblest and most universal of the senses, we achieve an operation very similar to intellectual operations properly so-called. Numerous, indeed, are the comparisons which can be drawn between intellectual knowledge and sight, between the eye of the soul and the eye of the body.[15] These, then, are the five external sensitive powers. Above them we can also place four internal sensitive powers whose role and purpose can easily be ascertained.[16]

Nature neither makes beings in vain nor multiplies them needlessly. Yet she never refuses them anything they need. Therefore the sensitive soul must exercise as many operations as are required for the life of a perfect animal. Those operations of the soul which cannot be reduced to one common principle suppose the existence within the soul of various powers corresponding to themselves. After all a power of the soul is only the proximate principle of an operation of the soul.[17]

Once we have admitted these principles, we have to consider that the particular sense is not self-sufficient. The particular sense judges the particular sensible and discerns it from all other sensibles which fall under its comprehension. It discerns, for example, white from black or from green. Here it is self-sufficient. But it cannot discern a white color from a sweet flavor. Sight can distinguish between one color and all other colors because it knows them all. It cannot distinguish between a color and a flavor because it does not know flavors. And, in order to distinguish between sensible qualities, it is first necessary to know them. Thus we must posit a *common sense,* to which we can refer, as to a common term, all sense apprehensions so that it may judge them and distinguish them from one another.[18] This common sense will not only perceive the sensibles whose operations are transmitted, but also the sensitive operations themselves. Indeed, it is quite obvious that we are aware that we see. Such knowledge cannot belong to the particular sense which only knows the sensible form which affects it. But when the modification which this form has impressed upon the particular sense has determined the vision, then the visual sensation, in its turn, modifies the common sense. Thus the common sense perceives the vision itself.[19]

Again, if we consider the conditions which must be satisfied in order that an animal live a perfect animal life, we must concede that it is not enough only to apprehend sensibles while they are being presented. The living being must be able to represent them to itself even when they are absent. The objects apprehended by an animal determine what its movements and actions will be. Thus it would never make a move toward satisfying its need if it could not represent these same objects to itself even in their absence. Thus the animal's sensitive soul must be capable, not only of receiving sensible species but also of holding and preserving them within itself. Now, it is easy to observe in bodies that it is not the same principles which receive and which preserve. What is moist, for example, receives readily but preserves badly; while what is dry receives badly but preserves quite well what it has received. Since, therefore, the sensitive power of the soul is the act of a corporeal organ, it must have two different powers, one to receive sensible species, the other to preserve them. This power to preserve is called *fancy* or *imagination*.[20]

The sensible knowledge of a living being must, in the third place, be able to discern a number of properties in things which the sense, left to itself, would be unable to apprehend. All sensibles, perceived by the animal, are not equally worth preserving. Some are useful, other harmful. Man can compare his particular knowledge, reason about it and thus come to distinguish the useful from the harmful. This he does by means of what is called his *particular reason* or his *cogitative* reason. But the animal, which has no reason, must apprehend immediately the useful and harmful aspects of objects, even though these are not, strictly speaking, sensible qualities. It must have, therefore, an additional sensitive power. It is by this power that the sheep knows it must flee when it sees the wolf, and by which the bird is advised to pick up the wisp of straw. The sheep does not avoid the wolf, nor the bird glean the straw because the shape and color of these objects are pleasing or displeasing, but because they perceive them directly as either opposed to their nature or in accord with it. This new power is called the *estimative* power.[21] It makes possible the fourth internal sensitive power, *memory*.

The living being needs to be able to recall for actual consideration species that have been previously apprehended by the senses and interiorly preserved by the imagination. Now although it may seem so at first, the imagination is not itself adequate for this purpose. It is, in some way, the treasury in which the forms apprehended by the senses are stored. But we have just noted that the particular sense is unable to apprehend all aspects of the sensible. The useful and harmful as such escape it. Hence a new power is required in order to preserve their species.[22] Moreover, it must be conceded that different movements suppose different motive principles, that is, different powers which determine them. Now, in the imagination movement proceeds from things to the soul. These objects are impressed first in the particular sense, then in the common sense in order that the imagination or fancy may preserve them. But it is not the same with the memory. Here movement begins in the soul and is terminated in the species evoked. With animals, it is the recollection of the useful or harmful that causes the representation of previously perceived objects to arise. Here we have a spontaneous restoration of sensible species which depend upon the memory, properly so-called. With man, on the contrary, there has to be a searching effort in order that the species stored by the imagination may again become the object of actual consideration. Here we have no longer merely memory, but something that is called *reminiscence*. Let us add that, in both cases, the objects are presented again in the character of something past—quite a different quality, indeed, than the particular sense, left to itself, could attain.[23]

It is to be seen in the preceding discussion that the examination of the highest sensitive power of the soul brings us to the very threshold of intellectual activity. In man the power of reminiscence corresponds to that of memory in the animal. Similarly, corresponding to the estimative power by which animals apprehend the harmful and useful, there is in man what we have called *particular reason*, or, as it is sometimes called, *passive intellect*.[24] It is not here a question of an intellect, properly so-called. The passive intellect remains a power of the sensible order because it only receives particular knowledge, while the characteristic mark of the intellect is its power to apprehend the universal. In the same way reminiscence differs from the spontaneous resurrecting of the recollections which specifies animal memory. It supposes a sort of syllogistic dialectic by which we move from one recollection to another, until we reach the one desired. But this search only has to do with particular representations. Here too the universality required for intellectual knowledge is completely wanting.[25] It can be affirmed, then, that the sensitive powers of the soul are of exactly the same nature in animals and in men, if only what is properly sensitive in them is considered. Their higher efficacy in man comes from the intellect with which they are in contact, in relation to which their operations are ordered, and whose high dignity seems to flow down into their operations.[26] We shall now take an important step, and move up to a consideration of the intellectual powers of the soul.

CHAPTER VI

THE INTELLECT AND RATIONAL KNOWLEDGE

THE INTELLECT is the power which constitutes the human soul in its own degree of perfection, and yet, properly speaking, the human soul is not an intellect. The angel, whose virtue can be reduced to intellectual power and to the will which issues from it, is a pure intellect. Thus it is also called an Intelligence. But the human soul exercises vegetative and sensitive operations and cannot rightfully be given this title. We can only say that intellect is one of the powers of the human soul.[1] Let us examine its structure and principal operations.

In its humblest aspect, the human intellect appears to be a passive power. The Latin verb *pati* may be given three different meanings. First, and properly, it signifies that a thing has been deprived of something which belongs to its essence or which is the object of its natural inclination. Thus water losing its cold temperature because it is being heated, or man falling sick or becoming sad are said to suffer. Secondly, and less properly, it signifies that a being is deprived of something which may or may not rightly pertain to it. Thus we may suffer either a recovery or a loss of health, we may suffer joy as well as sorrow. Thirdly, and this is the most general sense of the word, it signifies not loss or deprivation of one quality in order to receive another, but merely the actualizing of a potency. Hence, whatever passes from potency to act can be regarded as passive or suffering. But such passivity is a source of riches and not of impoverishment. It is in this third sense that our intellect is passive. The reason for this passivity can at once be deduced from the relatively low degree man occupies in the hierarchy of being.

An intellect is said to be in potency or in act according to its relationship with universal being. Examining the possibilities of this relationship we find in the highest degree that intellect whose relationship with universal being consists in its being the pure and simple act of existing. This is the divine intellect, the divine essence itself, in which all being exists originally and virtually as in its first cause. Because it is actually the total act-of-being, the divine intellect is nothing in potency, but is pure act.

It is different with created intellects. For one of these intellects to be the act of universal being, taken in its totality, it would have to be an infinite being. But this is contradictory to the very condition of created being. Therefore, no created being is the act of all intelligibles. It is finite and participated being and so is in potency to all the intelligible reality which it is not. Intellectual passivity is, then, a natural correlative of limitation of being.

There are two ways of looking at the relationship uniting potency and act. There is, indeed, a kind of potentiality in which potency is never deprived of its act. This is to be found in the matter of celestial bodies. There is also a kind of potentiality in which potency is sometimes deprived of its act and must pass into act in order to possess it. Such is the matter of corruptible beings. We see at once that the angelic intellect is characterized by the first of these two grades of potency which we have just defined. Its proximity to the First Intellect, Pure Act, makes it always possess its intelligible species in act. The human intellect, however, last in the order of intellects and as far removed as possible from the divine intellect is in potency to intelligibles not only in the sense that it is passive in relation to them when receiving them, but also in the sense that it is naturally deprived of them. This is why Aristotle says that the soul is at first like a blank tablet (*tabula rasa*) on which there is nothing written. We are forced, then, to posit a certain passivity at the source of our intellectual knowledge because of the extreme imperfection of our intellect.[2]

But we must also admit the existence of an active power if we are to explain human knowledge. Since the possible intellect is in potency to intelligibles, it is absolutely necessary that intelligibles move such an intellect if human knowledge is to be possible. But in order to move something, it must be. Now there would be no intelligible, properly so called, in a universe in which there were only completely passive intellects. The intelligible, indeed, is not such that it is to be encountered as a subsistent reality in nature. Aristotle showed, against Plato, that the forms of natural things do not subsist apart from matter. Now forms which are in matter are clearly not intelligible of themselves because it is immateriality which confers intelligibility. It is necessary, then, that natures, that is, the forms which our intellect knows in sensible things, be made intelligible in act. But only a being already in act can reduce what is in potency from potency to act. An active power, therefore, must be attributed to the intellect so as to render intelligible in act the intelligible which sensible reality contains in potency. This power is called the agent or active intellect.[3]

It can easily be seen that this fact dominates the whole structure of human knowledge. Since sensible things are endowed with an actual existence outside our soul, it is unnecessary to posit an agent sense. This is why the sensitive power of our soul is entirely passive.[4] But since we reject the Platonic doctrine of ideas as realities subsisting in the nature of things, we must have an agent intellect so as to disengage the intelligible from sensibles. Since, finally, there do exist immaterial substances intelligible in act, like the angels or God, we shall have to recognize that our intellect is incapable of apprehending such realities in themselves but that it must be resigned to acquiring some knowledge of them by abstracting the intelligible from the material and from the sensible.[5]

Is this agent intellect, which we have just shown to be necessary, a power of the soul, or is it a being superior to the soul, extrinsic to its essence and conferring on it from without the faculty of knowing? Certain philosophers subscribe to this last solution. They say that there is, above the rational soul, a higher intellect from which it holds its faculty of knowing. What is participated, movable and imperfect, always presupposes some being which is essentially being, immutable and perfect. The human soul is an intellective principle only by participation, as can be seen from the fact that it is only partially, not totally, intelligent, and also from the fact that it ascends to truth by discursive movement and not by direct and simple intuition.

Hence the soul has to have an intellect of a higher order which can confer upon it its power of intellection. For this reason some philosophers consider the agent intellect to be an intellect of this kind. They regard the agent intellect as a separated substance which illumines phantasms of sensible origin, impressed in us by things,[6] and makes them intelligible. But even though we granted the existence of this separated agent intellect, we should still have to posit in the soul of man a participated power of this higher intellect capable of making sensible species intelligible in act. Whenever universal principles exercise their action, we find that there are particular principles of activity which are subordinate to them and which preside over the proper operations of each being. Thus the active power of the heavenly bodies which extends to the whole universe does not prevent lower bodies from being endowed with powers of their own governing determined operations. The same is particularly easy to note in perfect animals. There are, indeed, lower animals which are produced by the activity of heavenly bodies; for example, animals engendered by putrefaction. But for the generation of perfect animals there is required, besides the activity of a heavenly body, some particular power which is to be found in its seed. Now, by far the most perfect operation exercised by sublunary beings is intellectual knowledge; that is, the operation of the intellect. Consequently, even after positing a universal active principle for all intellection, such as the illuminative power of God, there must also be posited in each one of us an active principle of our own which confers actual intellection on the individual concerned. It is this that is called the agent intellect.[7]

This conclusion obviously denies the existence of a separated agent intellect. Since the intellectual knowledge of each man and each soul demands an active principle of operation, we must admit the existence of many agent intellects. Indeed, there are as many intellects as their are souls; that is, as there are men, because it would be absurd to attribute a numerically one and the same principle of operation to a multitude of different subjects.[8] This eliminates the errors which follow the position that there is but one agent intellect for all men, as, for example, the denial of personal immortality or of free-will. Let us see now what are the principal functions of this intellect.

In the first place, memory is fittingly attributed to it. All philosophers do not agree on this point, even among those who adhere to Aristotle. Avicenna denies it because he accepts the doctrine of the unity of the agent intellect which we have just refuted. If we believe him on the matter, we can imagine that the passive intellect, bound to a corporeal organ, preserves sensible species while not actually apprehending them. The same, he says, does not hold for the active intellect. In this totally immaterial power, nothing can subsist save under an intelligible and therefore an actual form. As soon as an intellect ceases actually to apprehend an object, the species of this object disappears from this intellect. If it wishes to know it again it must turn to the agent intellect, a separated substance; and it will reflect these intelligible species back into the passive intellect. Repetition and exercise of such movement by which the passive intellect turns toward the agent intellect creates in it a kind of habit or ability to accomplish this operation. This, says Avicenna, is what is meant by the possession of a science. Knowing, for him, does not consist in preserving species which are not being actually apprehended. This means that he eliminates from the intellect what we properly call memory.

Such a conclusion is most unsatisfying in view of the exigencies of human reason. We have a very important principle, that "whatever is received into something else is received according to the mode of the receiver." Now the intellect is naturally more stable and immutable than corporeal matter. If, however, we find that corporeal matter not only retains forms while it is receiving them but also preserves them for a long time afterwards, much more should the intellect preserve immutably and indefectibly the intelligible species which it apprehends. If, by the term *memory*, we designate merely the capacity to retain species, we must acknowledge that there is a memory in the intellect. If, on the contrary, we consider, as characteristic of the memory, the apprehension of what is past with its very character of something past, we must acknowledge that there is no memory save in the sensitive power of the soul. The past as such is reduced to the fact of existing in a determined moment of time. This mode of existence is proper only to particular things. But it is the sensitive power of the soul that perceives what is material and particular. We can conclude, therefore, that if memory of the past is dependent upon the sensitive soul, there also exists a memory properly intellectual, which preserves intelligible species and whose proper object is the universal, abstracted from all conditions which determine it to any particular mode of existence.[9]

Memory as we have just defined it is constitutive of intellectual operation itself. It is not, properly speaking, a power distinct from the intellect.[10] The same conclusion holds equally for reason and intellect, strictly so called. They are not powers differing from each other; and this is easily seen, if we examine their characteristic acts. Intellection is the simple apprehension of intelligible truth. The act of reasoning is the movement of thought from one object of knowledge to another in order to attain intelligible truth. The angels, for example, who possess perfectly the knowledge of intelligible truth proper to their particular degree of perfection, arrive at the knowledge of that truth by a simple act that is in no way discursive. They are Intelligences, in the fullest sense of the word. Men, on the contrary, know intelligible truth by proceeding from one object of knowledge to another. Hence they are not properly called intelligences, nor even intelligent beings, but rather rational beings.

Reason, then, is to intellection what movement is to repose or acquisition to possession. The relationship between these terms is that of imperfect to perfect. Now we know that movement proceeds from an antecedent immobility and terminates in repose. And so it is with human knowledge. Reason proceeds from initial terms apprehended purely and simply by our intellect; that is, from first principles. Its final term is also marked by first principles to which it returns with the conclusions of its searchings. The intellect is in the repose of agreement at the beginning and at the end of its act of reasoning. Now, obviously, repose and movement fall under one single power. This assertion is to be verified even in natural things where we can observe the same nature putting things into motion and maintaining them in repose. Much more, then, do the intellect and the reason depend upon one single power. Therefore, in man, the names intellect and reason refer to one and the same power.[11]

Thus do we find the precise point at which the human soul and the separated intelligence meet in the hierarchy of created beings. The mode of knowledge which is characteristic of man is reason or discursive knowledge. Discursive knowledge, however, must have two fixed terms, an initial term and a final one. Both of these consist in the simple apprehension of truth by the intellect. The intellection of principles opens and closes the steps of reason. Thus, although the knowledge proper to the human soul follows the way of reason, it presupposes, nevertheless, some kind of participation in that simple mode of knowing which we find in higher intellectual substances. Once more the words of Dionysius ring true: divine wisdom always joins the end of what comes first with the beginning of what comes next (*divina sapientia semper fines priorum conjungit principiis secundorum*).[12] But it is only verified if we deny that man has any intellectual power distinct from his reason.

The universal hierarchy is not based on the assumption that the lower possesses whatever the higher possesses, but on the fact that the lower has a feeble participation in what the higher possesses. Thus the animal, whose nature is purely sensitive, is deprived of reason but is endowed with a kind of prudence and natural power to evaluate which is a feeble participation in human reason. Similarly man does not possess a pure intellect permitting him to apprehend truth immediately and without discourse. But he participates in this mode of knowing by a kind of natural disposition— the intellection of principles. In brief, human knowledge, as it appears now at the close of this discussion, is nothing other than the activity of a reason which participates in the simplicity of intellectual knowledge: "Hence, the discursive power and the power that perceives truth are not different, but one and the same . . . reason itself is called understanding because it shares in intellectual simplicity, by reason of which it begins and through which it terminates its proper activity." [13] Let us now examine this operation; that is, the manner in which human reason apprehends its various objects.

The basic problem, the solution of which dominates all subsequent conclusions, is to know how the human intellect knows corporeal substances lower than itself.[14] Plato teaches that the human soul has natural, innate knowledge of all things. No one, he says, can give the right answer about things he does not know. But a man in complete ignorance will always give the right answer to questions put to him, provided they are asked according to a proper method. This we find in the *Meno*.[15] Therefore, everyone possesses knowledge of things even before acquiring science of them. This amounts to asserting that the soul knows all things, including bodies, by innate species that are in it by nature.

This doctrine, however, runs at once into a very grave difficulty. Since form is the principle of all operation, it is necessary that everything maintain the same relationship with form as with the operation produced by this form. Granted, for example, that motion upwards is produced by lightness, we can say that what is in potency to such movement is potentially light; and that which actually is moving upwards is light in act. Now it is clear that both from the point of view of the senses and from the point of view of the intellect, man is often in potency to his knowledge. It is reduced from potency to act by the sensible things which act upon his senses, and by teaching and research which act upon his intellect. Hence it must be acknowledged that the rational soul is as much in potency to sensible species as to intelligible species. But while it is in potency to these species, it obviously does not possess them in act. Therefore, the soul does not know everything by naturally innate species.[16]

It is true, of course, that a form can be possessed in act and yet be incapable of performing the operation of this form because of some exterior impediment. Thus what is light sometimes fails to rise because there is an obstacle in its way. Plato, too, observed that the soul does not always possess its knowledge in act. He claimed, nevertheless, that the human intellect naturally possesses all its intelligible species, but is sometimes prevented from knowing them in act by the body with which it is united.

One observation is quite enough to reveal how wrong this position is. When a sense is lacking, all the knowledge which that sense apprehends vanishes with it. Where a sense is lacking so too is a science. Men born blind know nothing of colors. But they would know them if the intellect possessed naturally innate, intelligible motions of all things. We can go beyond mere observation of this fact, however, and show that such knowledge would not be in accord with the human soul.

If we adopt the Platonic point of view, we thereby regard the body as a sort of veil or screen dropped between our intellect and the object of our knowledge. We must say, in this case, that the soul does not acquire its knowledge with the help of the body to which it is united, but in spite of it. Now we have already observed that it is natural for the human soul to be united with a body. If we accept Plato's position, we must suppose that the soul's natural operation, intellectual knowledge, meets its greatest obstacle in the natural bond uniting it to the body. This is disturbing to contemplate. Nature, which makes the soul for knowing, can surely not have united it to a body which would prevent it from knowing. Nay more, it ought not to have given a body to this soul unless to render intellectual knowledge easier for it.

There is nothing paradoxical in a statement like this when we recall the modest dignity of the soul and its imperfection. In all intellectual substances there is a faculty of knowing which borrows its force from the influence of the divine light. Considered in the First Principle this light is one and simple. But the farther intelligent creatures are removed from the First Principle the more divided and dispersed is this light, like rays diverging from a common center. This is why God knows all things by His one act of existing. Higher intellectual substances know, to be sure, by many forms, yet they only use a limited number of these forms. Moreover, they apprehend very universal forms and, as they are endowed with an extremely efficacious faculty of knowing, they discern within these universal forms the multiplicity of particular objects. In lower intellectual substances, we can make out a very large number of less universal forms. As we get farther away from the first source of all knowledge, these forms no longer permit particular objects to be apprehended with the same distinction. If, therefore, lower substances only possessed universal intelligible forms like those found in angels, they would not succeed in discerning the multiplicity of particular things in these forms because the tiny ray by which they are enlightened is so feeble and dim. Their knowledge would be vague and confused. It would be like that of ignorant men who cannot discern in principles the innumerable consequences which the learned can. Now we know that in the order of nature, the last of all the intellectual substances are human souls. It was necessary either to give them but general and confused knowledge or else to unite them with a body of such a kind that they might be able to receive from sensible things themselves the determined knowledge of what these things are. God has dealt with the human soul as we do with rude minds that can only learn with the help of examples borrowed from the sensible order. Therefore, it is for its own greatest good that the soul is united to the body since it is helped by it to acquire knowledge. "It is clear then that it was for the soul's good that it was united to a body, and that it understands by turning to the phantasms." [17] "It is necessary for them (souls) to seek their intelligible perfection from bodies, and through bodies, otherwise they would be united to bodies in vain." [18] In brief, it is in turning toward the body that the soul is raised to knowledge of its objects, not in turning away from it, as the Platonic doctrine of innate ideas demands.

We must try to be precise as to how this human intellect apprehends objects. According to St. Augustine, whose doctrine can definitively set us on our way toward the truth, the intellectual soul discovers all things in eternal essences; that is, in the immutable truth which is in God. "If we both see that that which thou sayest is true, and if we both see that what I say is true, where, I ask, do we see it? Certainly not I in thee, nor thou in me, but both in the unchangeable truth itself, which is above our minds." [19] (*Writings of St. Augustine,* I, N.Y., 221.) Augustine felt that we should always take over the truths contained in pagan philosophies. As he had himself been steeped in Platonist doctrine, he constantly endeavored to gather in anything good he encountered among the Platonists, and even to ameliorate and utilize things to be found in them contrary to our faith. Now Plato designated under the name of *Ideas* the forms of things considered as subsisting by themselves and apart from matter. Thus the knowledge which our soul acquires of all things is reduced to its participation in such forms. Just as corporeal matter becomes stone insofar as it participates in the idea of stone, so our intellect knows stone insofar as it participates in this same idea. But it was too obviously contrary to faith to posit separated Ideas in this way, subsisting by themselves and endowed with a kind of created activity. Hence St. Augustine substituted for Plato's Ideas the essences of all creatures which he considered as gathered together in God's thought. All things he held to be created in conformity with them, and through them, too, the human soul knew all things.

There is a sense in which such a doctrine is unacceptable. When it is affirmed with St. Augustine that the intellect knows everything in the eternal essences, and consequently in God, the expression *to know in* can signify that the eternal essences constitute the very object which the intellect apprehends. But we cannot admit that in our present state the soul can know all things in the eternal essences, which are God. And we have just discovered the exact reasons for this in our criticism of Plato's innate ideas. Only the blessed who see God, and who see all things in God, know all things in the eternal essences. Here below, however, the human intellect has for its object the sensible, not the intelligible.

But the expression *to know in* can designate the principle of knowledge rather than its object. It can signify *that by which* we know and not *that which* we know.[20] Taken in this sense, it only serves to hand down a great truth; namely, the need for positing at the source of our intellection the divine light and the first principles of intellectual knowledge which we owe it. The soul knows all things in the eternal essences as the eye sees in the sun all that it sees with the aid of the sun. It is important to grasp the exact force of this statement. We note that there is in the human soul a principle of intellection. This intellectual light that is in us is nothing other than a participated resemblance of the uncreated light. And since the uncreated light contains the eternal essences of all things, it can be said, in a certain sense, that we know all in the divine exemplars. Therefore, *to know in the eternal essences* simply means: to know by means of a participation in the divine light in which the essences of all things are created. Hence, in Psalm IV, where we read: "Many say: who showeth us good things?" We find the Psalmist replying: "The light of the countenance, O Lord, is signed upon us;" as though to say: *By the seal of the divine light in us, all things are made known to us.* But this faculty of knowing which God has given us does not suffice by itself. We have seen that by nature it is quite without the intelligible species which Plato attributed to it. Far from possessing innate knowledge, it is at first in potency to all intelligibles.

Thus understood, natural light does not confer upon us knowledge of material things by participation alone in their eternal essences. It still requires the intelligible species which it abstracts from things themselves.[21] The human intellect possesses therefore a light just sufficient in order to acquire the knowledge of the intelligibles to which it can raise itself by means of sensible things.[22] In a certain sense, indeed, we possess in us the germ of all knowledge: *praeexistunt in nobis quaedam scientiarum semina.*[23] These pre-formed seeds, of which we have natural knowledge, are first principles: *prima intelligibilium principia.*[24] What characterizes these principles is that they are the first conceptions which our intellect forms when we enter into contact with the sensible. To say that they pre-exist in the intellect is not to say that the intellect possesses them actually in itself, independently of the action which bodies exercise on our soul. It is simply to say that they are the first intelligibles which our intellect conceives starting immediately from sensible experience. The actual intellection of principles is no more innate in us than are the conclusions of our deductive reasoning.[25] But while we discover the former spontaneously, we have to acquire the latter at the price of our research. Some examples will enable us to grasp this truth.

Principles can be complex, e.g., the whole is greater than the part; or simple, e.g., the notion of being, of unity, and so on. Complex principles, like the one cited, can be said to pre-exist *in some way* in our intellect. From the moment that the rational soul of man knows the definitions of the whole and of the part, it knows that the whole is greater than the part. It was, accordingly, naturally apt for forming this knowledge immediately. But it is no less evident that, taken in itself, it did not possess it, and that, abandoned to its own resources, the intellect would never have acquired it. To know that the whole is greater than the part, we must know the definitions of the part and the whole. These can only be known by abstracting certain intelligible species from matter.[26] If therefore we cannot know what the whole is and what the part is without appealing to the perception of bodies; and if we cannot know that the whole is greater than the part without possessing this preliminary knowledge, it follows that the apprehension of the first intelligible conceptions themselves necessarily supposes the intervention of the sensible.

This conclusion is still more evident if we envisage the simple principles of knowledge. We should not know what being or unity are if we had not previously perceived sensible objects from which we could abstract intelligible species. The exact definition of principles would then be as follows: "the first conceptions of the intellect which are known at once by the light of the agent intellect through species abstracted from sensible objects." [27] These principles are the first source and the guarantee of all our certain knowledge. It is from them that we set out to discover truth; and we have noted that reason is always in the end referred back there in order to verify its conclusions. On the other hand, our aptitude for forming them on contact with the sensible is, among human souls as a whole, like an image of that divine truth in which they participate. Thus we can say in this sense, but only in this sense, that, in the measure in which the soul knows all things by the first principles of knowledge, it sees all things in the divine truth or in the eternal essences of things.[28]

Thus we have posited that there must be an intellectual light coming from God Himself, and that this light, reduced to its own resources, is impotent. Here we have, in fact, determined the necessary and sufficient conditions of human knowledge. The conclusion to which we are continually returning is that intellectual knowledge begins from sensible things: *principium nostrae cognitionis est a sensu*. The one problem which we have still to resolve is, therefore, to determine what is the exact relationship between the intellect and the sensible within knowledge.

Opposed to Plato, who has the intellect directly participating in separated intelligible forms, we find Democritus who assigns no other cause to our knowledge than the presence within the soul of the image of the bodies about which we are thinking. According to Democritus, all action can be reduced to the influx of material atoms passing from one body into another. He imagines that little images are issuing from objects and penetrating into the matter of our soul. But we know that the human soul has one operation in which the body does not share;[29] namely, intellectual operation. It is clearly impossible that corporeal matter should succeed in impressing its mark upon an incorporeal substance like an intellect and modifying it. Merely the impression of sensible bodies could never produce an operation like intellectual knowledge, and is not enough to explain it. We must appeal to some nobler principle of operation without however turning to the separated intelligibles of Plato. This is what we come to if we take the middle trail which Aristotle blazed between Democritus and Plato; that is, we posit an agent intellect capable of extracting the intelligible from the sensible by means of an abstraction whose nature we shall now analyze in some detail.

Let us suppose that subsequent to the operations described above[30] a sensible body impressed its image in the common sense. And let us designate this image by the term phantasm (*phantasma*). We still should not have the total and perfect cause of intellectual knowledge; we should not even have its sufficient cause; but we should at least have the matter on which this cause works.[31] What, indeed, is a phantasm? It is the image of a particular thing: *similitudo rei particularis*.[32] Still more accurately, phantasms are images of particular things, impressed or preserved in corporeal organs: *similitudines individuorum existentes in organis corporeis*.[33] In brief, we are here in the domain of the sensible both from the point of view of the object and the subject. Colors, for example, have the same mode of existence whether in the matter of an individual body or in the visual power of the sensitive soul. In both cases they subsist in a determined material subject. This is why colors are by nature able by themselves to impress their resemblance in the organ of sight. But for this same reason, it is to be seen that, from this stage on, the sensible as such—and this holds for phantasms—will never penetrate into the intellect.

Sensation is the act of a corporeal organ suited for reception of the particular as such; that is, the universal form existing in an individual corporeal matter.[34] The sensible species, or medium through which it passes, and the sense itself are realities of the same order since they fall, all three, into the genus of the particular. The same is true of the imagination, in which phantasms reside. But it is not the same when it comes to the possible intellect. As intellect, it receives universal species. The imagination, on the contrary, contains only particular species. Between the phantasm and the intelligible species, the particular and the universal, there is a difference of genus: *sunt alterius generis*.[35] And this is why phantasms, which are necessary requisites for intellectual knowledge, only constitute its matter and serve it, so to speak, as instruments.[36]

For an exact notion of just what human intellection is, it is well not to forget the role we have just assigned the agent intellect. Man has been placed in a universe in which the intelligible is not encountered in its pure state. Moreover, his intellect is so imperfect that intuitive apprehension of the purely intelligible is beyond him. The proper object of the human intellect is quiddity; that is, nature existing in a particular corporeal matter. Thus it is not ours to know the idea of stone, but the nature of such and such a determined stone. This nature is the result of the union between a form and its proper matter. Similarly, the abstract concept "horse" is not presented to our mind as an object. It is the nature, rather, of a horse that has been realized in a given, determined, concrete horse.[37] In other words, it is easy to discern in the objects of human knowledge a universal and intelligible element which is associated with a particular and material element. The proper operation of the agent intellect is to dissociate these two elements in order to furnish the possible intellect with the intelligible and universal which lay implied in the sensible. This operation is abstraction.

The object of knowledge is always in due proportion to the knowing faculty which grasps it. Three degrees of faculties of knowing are to be distinguished. Sensible knowledge is the act of a corporeal organ; namely, sense. Thus the object of all the senses is form insofar as it exists in corporeal matter. And since corporeal matter is the principle of individuation, all the powers of the sensitive soul are incapable of knowing anything but particular objects. At the opposite extreme, we find knowledge which is neither the act of a corporeal organ nor so much as bound in any way to a corporeal organ. Such is angelic knowledge. The proper object of this knowledge is form subsisting outside of matter. Even when angels apprehend material objects, they only perceive them through immaterial forms; that is, in themselves or in God. The human intellect occupies an intermediate position between the two preceding. As has been said, it is one of the powers of a soul that is the form of a body. This is why it is proper to this intellect to apprehend forms which, to be sure, exist individually in corporeal matter, but not to apprehend them inasmuch as they exist in this matter. Now, to know what subsists, in individual matter without taking into account the matter within which this object subsists, is to abstract the form from the individual matter which the phantasms represent.[38]

If we take this abstraction under its simplest aspect, it therefore consists first in what the agent intellect considers in each material thing—what constitutes it in its own proper species, leaving aside all the individuating principles belonging to matter. Just as we can consider separately the color of a fruit without taking account of its other properties, so can our intellect consider separately, in the phantasms of the imagination, what constitutes the essence of man, of horse or of stone, without taking into account what distinguishes given, determined individuals within these species.[39]

But the operation of the agent intellect is not limited to separating in this way the universal from the particular. Its activity is not merely separative. It is, in addition, productive of the intelligible. But we must not think that the agent intellect, in abstracting the intelligible species from the phantasms, merely transports as it is into the possible intellect the very form previously existing in the phantasm. In order that the sensible species of the thing may become the intelligible form of the possible intellect, it must undergo a considerable change, and the agent intellect must be turned upon the phantasms in order to illumine them. This illuminating of the sensible species is the very essence of abstraction. It is it which abstracts from phantasms the intelligible they contain[40] and which engenders in the possible intellect the knowledge of what is presented by the phantasms. But it considers in the phantasms only the specific and universal, abstraction having been made from the material and particular.[41]

It is extremely difficult to see what St. Thomas means here because we unconsciously tend to picture this operation and to try to form a concrete image of what takes place. But there is no psycho-physiological mechanism to be included in the description of this act of knowing. We are here in a different order—that of the intelligible. The solution of the problem of knowledge which St. Thomas here describes consists particularly in defining the conditions required for the carrying out of an operation which we know takes place. This cannot be grasped without returning to the very data of the problem posed.

It is a question of knowing, indeed, whether there is in the universe a knowing being whose nature is such that the intelligible cannot reach it unless mixed with the sensible. We know that the hypothesis is probable, *a priori,* because it agrees with the principle of continuity governing the universe. It still remains to be known whether the thing is possible and what order of relations an operation of this kind would establish between the intelligible in act, the higher term in the operation, and matter, its lower term. To solve the problem, we must find some intermediate points to fill in the gaps between them.

A first intermediary is to be seen in the sensible itself. As we have said, the sensible is the union of a form, and hence an intelligible, with determined matter. Therefore, the sensible contains in potency some intelligible, but it is an intelligible determined in act to a given mode of particular being. If we pass on now to man we find something intelligible in act, his intellect—the part of him that is contiguous with the lowest orders of angels. But we know that this intelligible lacks determination. It is a light by which we can still see, but in which we no longer see anything. If it is to enable us to see, this light must fall upon some objects. But for it to fall upon objects, there must exist objects related to it. The intelligible in act, our intellect, will die of inanition unless it finds nourishment in the world in which we are placed. Obviously, it will only find it in the sensible. Thus the solution of the Thomistic problem of knowledge is only possible when the sensible, which is determined in act and intelligible in potency, can communicate its determination to our intellect, which is intelligible in act but only potentially determined.

It is to resolve it that St. Thomas admits the existence in the same individual substance—and not in two distinct subjects as Avicenna and Averroes maintain—of a possible intellect and an agent intellect. If it is not contradictory to hold for the co-existence of these two powers of the soul in a single subject, we can claim to solve the problem, since such a hypothesis satisfies all the data.

Now to hold this is not contradictory. Rather, it is contradictory that one and the same thing should be at the same time and under the same relationship, in potency and in act. It is not contradictory that it be in potency under one relationship and in act under another. Indeed this is the normal condition of every finite and created being. It is also the condition of the rational soul in relation to the sensible and to the phantasms presenting it. The soul has intelligibility in act, but determination is wanting. Phantasms have determination in act, but intelligibility is wanting. The soul confers intelligibility on the phantasms, and in this is an agent intellect; it receives determination from them, and in this is a possible intellect. For the operation to be realizable, one condition is required—a metaphysical condition based upon the exigencies of order—and it is this: the action of the agent intellect which makes phantasms intelligible must precede the reception of this intelligible into the possible intellect: *Actio intellectus agentis in phantasmatibus praecedit receptionem intellectus possibilis.* The sensible as such cannot penetrate the intelligible as such; and so it is our intellect which, aspiring to receive determination from the sensible, begins by rendering its action possible in raising it up to its own dignity. This is the price of knowledge; and this was the only problem to be resolved: "the tiny intelligible light which is connatural to us is enough for our knowing." [42]

Such is the manner in which the human soul knows bodies. This conclusion is true not only for the acquisition of knowledge, but holds equally for the use we make of it after we have acquired it. Serious injury to common sense, imagination or memory removes at the same time phantasms and knowledge of intelligibles corresponding to them.[43] This conclusion also enables us to learn how the human soul knows itself, as well as how it knows objects above itself. The intellect knows itself in exactly the same manner as it knows other things. We now know the conditions of such an act. The human intellect, as it carries on in this present state of life, can only know by turning toward the material and sensible. It only knows itself in the measure in which it passes from potency into act under the influence of species abstracted from sensible things by the light of the agent intellect.[44]

From this result the numerous operations which such knowledge demands as well as the order in which they are presented. Our soul only comes to knowledge of itself because it first apprehends other things: *ex objecto enim cognoscit suam operationem, per quam devenit ad cognitionem sui ipsius.*[45] It knows first its object, then its operation, and finally its own nature. Now it perceives merely that it is an intellectual soul, since it apprehends the operation of its intellect. Then it is raised to universal knowledge of what is the nature of the human soul by a methodical reflection on the conditions required by such an operation.[46] But in both cases, the thought moves forward in the same way. "And there is yet another, namely the human intellect, which is not its own act of understanding, nor is its own essence the first object of its act of understanding, for this object is something extrinsic; it is the nature of a material thing. And therefore that which is first known by the human intellect is an object of this kind, and that which is known secondarily is the act by which that object is known; and through the act the intellect itself is known, whose perfection is the act itself of understanding." [47]

In order to determine the way in which the human soul knows what it perceives above itself, we have only to examine the consequences of the preceding analysis. Whether it be a question of totally immaterial substances like angels or of the infinite and uncreated essence which we call God, direct apprehension of the intelligible as such is completely impossible for man.[48] We can claim no more than to form some very imperfect representation of the intelligible from sensible nature or quiddity. Hence just as the soul does not know itself first, neither is God the first object of its apprehension. It has to begin with the consideration of material bodies; and it will never advance farther in its knowledge of the intelligible than the sensible from which it sets out will allow it to go. Here our method of demonstrating God's existence and analyzing His essence, finds its complete justification. "The knowledge of God that can be gathered from the human mind does not transcend the genus of the knowledge gathered from sensible things; since even the soul knows what it itself is through understanding the natures of sensible things." [49]

It is impossible to insist too much upon this truth because it dominates the whole of philosophy. Failure to grasp it fully makes us assign objects to the human intellect which it is by nature incapable of grasping, and so we mistake the proper value and limits of our knowledge. The most treacherous form this illusion takes is in thinking that the more knowable in itself and more intelligible something is, the better we know it. By now we know that our mind is constructed for extracting the intelligible from the sensible. Because it can disengage from individuating matter the universal form to be found there does not mean, except for a sophist, that it can *a fortiori* apprehend the purely intelligible. The intellect can be compared fairly exactly to an eye capable of receiving colors and at the same time luminous enough to render these same colors actually visible. If we assume that such an eye could see a moderate light, it would be totally helpless before an intense one. There are certain animals whose eyes are said to produce enough light to illuminate the objects they see. Such animals see better by night than by day. Their eyes are weak. A little light makes things clear to them, a great deal of light blinds them. So it is with our intellect. Before the highest intelligibles it is blinded and confused like the eye of an owl unable to see the sun in front of it. Thus we have to be content with the tiny intelligible light which is ours by nature and sufficient for the needs of our knowledge. We must be careful not to ask of it more than it can give. We only know the incorporeal by comparing it with the corporeal. Each time we aspire to some knowledge of intelligibles, we have necessarily to turn to the phantasms which bodies put in us even though there are no phantasms of intelligible realities.[50] Acting in this way, we behave like the very low intellects we are and we accept the limitations imposed upon our knowing faculty by our place in the hierarchy of created beings.[51]

CHAPTER VII

WE HAVE DESCRIBED the cognitive operations of the rational soul and, in doing so, have in some sort brought man to his place in the hierarchy of created beings. It is fitting to pause here in order to disengage, by some detailed reflection, the nature of human knowledge as St. Thomas conceives it and his particular conception of what truth is.

Necessary as such an enterprise is, it is full of risks. More than five centuries separate us from St. Thomas, centuries that have seen so many new systems and new statements of .old problems which tend to offer us Thomism, as it were, through refracted light. The very legitimate preoccupation of finding in Thomism the reply to questions formulated since his day leads us imperceptibly to a modification of the sense of the problem actually confronting him. It tends to make us change the meaning of texts so as to adapt them to new questions, sometimes even to force them in such a way that we compromise the balance of his entire synthesis for the sake of some new interpretation. Neither philosophy nor history profits from such experiments. If we want the Thomistic solution of the problem of knowledge, it must come first from St. Thomas. If it is to come really from him and not from Descartes or Kant, we must not approach it with a Cartesian or Kantian question on our lips, because philosophers' questions are one with their replies. Rather we must approach it by asking St. Thomas what his solution of the problem of knowledge would have been if Thomism, in the course of the internal development of its own principles, had been brought to a position where it might ask such a question.

Such a task is clearly beyond an historian's competence, though he has, indeed, something to say about it. To develop a truly Thomistic noetic presupposes our knowing exactly what the two basic ideas of *knowledge* and *truth* meant for St. Thomas. Only by determining their precise meaning can we understand the role he assigns to the various elements involved in an act of knowing. Any theory of knowledge claiming to be Thomistic can only be valid in the light of such a determination. To treat the question exhaustively would be a very long, perhaps an infinitely long task. But we can at least indicate the principles from which the solution follows.[1]

Preoccupation with knowing what knowledge is is not primitive in man. Most men live and die without worrying about philosophy and use their faculties of knowing all their life without even becoming curious about them. But we cannot examine the nature of the beings given to us in experience without observing that the fact of knowing is not necessarily implied in the simple fact of existing. A quick induction assures us of this. There are, in the first place, artificial beings made by the hand of man, which are inert and incapable of spontaneous movement. If a bed falls, it is as wood not as bed that it does so. If, buried in the earth, it grows, it is not a bed which grows but a tree. Next come natural beings, endowed with an internal principle of movement, such as lightness or heaviness, involved in their form. Such beings move only by an internal principle, without an adaptation to the conditions of the exterior world. Left alone, a stone falls or flame goes up in a straight line; the one is drawn downward, the other upward. There are more complex natural movements too. There is that of the plant animated by a vegetative life which unfolds its roots, branches and leaves into space. Here, too, it is a question of energy, regulated and conditioned from within. The exterior world but permits or prevents its activity. An oak grows, if it can grow, as a stone falls if it is released. When its growth is accomplished, it dies, having never been anything else than an oak, all that it was capable of becoming.

When we come to the animal kingdom, the aspect of beings changes completely. Governed, like the preceding, by internal principles, animal movements are not to be explained by them exclusively. A dog can do more than fall by its own weight or grow by its own life. It moves itself about in space to hunt its prey, springs to seize it, runs to retrieve it. And all these actions presume that the prey in question exists both for itself and for the dog. The goat does not exist for the shrubs it crops but they for it regardless of its way of existing. This existence of one being for another which begins with animality and develops in man is precisely what is meant by knowledge. There is knowledge in the world, and that is the fact of the case. The next question to arise is that of the conditions under which knowledge in general is possible.

Let us put the problem as bluntly as possible. One living being is conscious of another being. What does this mean? If we consider it in itself, the knowing being is, in the first place, its own essence; that is, it falls into a genus, is defined by a species, and is individualized by the various properties which distinguish it from beings of the same nature. As such, it is this, and no more—dog, goat, man. But as a knowing being, it becomes still something other than itself, since the prey which the dog pursues, the shrub which the goat crops, the book which the man reads, exist, from that moment, in some way or other, in the dog, the goat, the man. Since these objects are now in the subjects which know them, it must be that the subjects have in some way become those objects. Thus to know is to be in a new and richer way than before, since it is essentially to cause to enter into a thing which is in the first place for itself alone what another thing is in the first place for itself alone.[2] This fact is expressed by the statement that to know a thing is a kind of becoming that thing.[3]

A preliminary observation is obvious, if we give these remarks their full significance. Whatever their ultimate interpretation, they clearly mean that we are here dealing with two sharply different modes of beings. Between what is never anything but itself, and what is capable of expanding itself so as to possess the being of others, there is considerable distance—the exact distance separating the material from the spiritual. The body or matter in a being contracts and limits it. The spiritual in it, on the other hand, enlarges and amplifies it. At the bottom is the mineral, which is only what it is. At the top, or better, beyond and above all conceivable degree, is God, who is all. Between the two comes man who in a certain way is capable of becoming all things by his senses and his intelligence.[4] Thus, the problem of human knowledge is fundamentally that of the mode of existence of a spiritual being which is not pure spirituality.

A second observation confirming the first also comes to mind: that there are not two conceivable solutions of the problem of knowledge, one for the senses, another for the intelligence. Sensible knowledge and intellectual knowledge can be, and indeed are, two different species or two different steps of the same kind of operation, so they rest inevitably upon a single explanation. If it were necessary to introduce an ideal cleavage in universal order, it would fall between the animal and the plant, not between the animal and man. Restrained as is its field of operation, the animal is still increased by the being of others through the sensation it experiences. It is, therefore, sharply, though still incompletely, disengaged from pure materiality.[5] Hence we have to explain cognitive operations in such a way that we can attach both intelligence and sensation to the same principle and judge them by the same rules.

At this point, the main theses of Thomistic noetic begin to appear. So far we have only considered what is required on the part of the knowing subject for knowledge in general to be possible. But it goes without saying that there are corresponding requirements on the part of the object known. We do not have to describe a universe and then ask ourselves what our knowledge is like for such a universe to become possible. We must do the reverse. Given that there is knowledge, we have to inquire how things must be made in order to explain how we know them.

The first condition for knowledge to be possible is that things too participate in some measure in immateriality. Were we to suppose a purely material universe, one deprived of every intelligible element, it will be, by definition, opaque so far as the mind is concerned. The element in an object assimilable to a thought is its form. To say that the knowing subject becomes the object known is equivalent, therefore, to saying that the form of the knowing subject is increased by the form of the object known.[6] We already know from metaphysics that this intimate relationship between thought and things is possible, since the universe, even to its least parts, is a participation in the highest intelligible, God. Here, however, we can observe that it is also necessarily required if such facts as concepts and sensations are even to be conceivable. It is not enough to provide a meeting point for thought and things; we still have to have the kind of things that can be met there.

When this twofold assimilation is acknowledged to be possible, what becomes of knowledge? A single fact will be offered to us under two aspects, according to whether we look at it from the point of view of what is done by the object known or from the point of view of what is done by the knowing subject. To describe knowledge from one of these two complementary aspects and to speak as though from the other, is to get involved in inextricable difficulties.

Let us first look at the question from the point of view of the object, which is the point of view more easily grasped. If we are to be true to the principles just stated, we must say that the being of the object itself is imposed on the being of the knowing subject. If to know a thing is to become it, it is absolutely necessary that at the moment the act of knowing takes place a new being is constituted, a fuller being than the first, because it envelops into a richer unity the knowing being as it was before the act of knowing and as it has become since enlarged by the accretion of the object known. The synthesis thus produced involves, therefore, the fusion of two beings which fall together at the moment of their union. The sense differs from the sensible, and the intellect differs from the intelligible; but the sense is not different from the object sensed, nor the intellect from the object which it has actually come to know. Thus it is literally true that the sense, taken in its act of sensing, becomes one with the sensible taken in the act by which it is sensed, and that the intellect taken in its act of knowing is one with the intelligible taken in the act by which it is known: "the sensible in act is the sense in act, and the intelligible in act is the intellect in act." [7]

We can regard as an immediate corollary of this fact the Thomistic thesis which states that every act of knowledge supposes that the object known becomes present in the knowing subject. Many texts state this explicitly. We must not minimize their importance merely because, for present purposes, they are only used to put in another way the fundamental thesis of the coincidence of intellect or of sense with its object in the act of knowledge. Nevertheless, a complication does arise, and it will force us to introduce something new into our analysis; namely, sensible species for knowledge by the senses, and intelligible species for knowledge by the intellect.

Let us start with the fact that knowledge of an object is the presence of that object in thought. Now the object must not invade upon thought to the extent that it ceases to be a thought. The sense of sight perceives the form of stone, but does not turn to stone. The intellect conceives the idea of wood, but it does not turn to wood. Rather, it remains what it

was; and it even continues to be capable of becoming still other things.
When we take cognizance of this new factor, the problem of knowledge
takes a new form. Under what condition can the knowing subject become
the object known without ceasing to be itself?

To meet this difficulty we have seen St. Thomas introduce the notion
of *species*. In every order of knowledge there exists a subject, an object
and an intermediary between the object and the subject. This holds for
the most immediate types of sensation, such as touch and taste,[8] and becomes more and more manifest as we go up the ladder of knowledge.
To resolve the difficulty, we have to conceive of an intermediary which,
without ceasing to be the object, would be capable of becoming the subject. Under this condition, the thing known would not encroach upon
thought—as we know it does not do in fact—and it would still be known
through the presence of its *species* in the thought which knows it.

In order to conceive of such an intermediary, which the very fact of
knowledge forces us to posit, we must try not to represent it to ourselves.
It is indeed dangerous to think of sensible species as of sensations being
conveyed off into space. But, when it is a question of an intelligible form,
its extension toward our thought can only be conceived as of an intelligible
nature. We should not even speak here of extension, for we have left the
physical and entered the metaphysical. The operation which we are
analyzing takes place entirely outside of space. The thing is in space
by reason of its matter, but its intelligible aspect has no space to cross
in order to rejoin the intellection of thought, which is dependent upon
space by reason of its body only. The imagination is a deadly obstacle
in the way of understanding such a problem. It is only a matter here of
conceding to thought and to things what they require in order to be
able to do what they do; that is, of assigning them something by which
the object can coincide with our intellect without being itself destroyed,
and without our intellect ceasing to be what it is.

The *species* has to play this role. Hence it is conceived, first, as being
only the intelligible or the sensible aspect of the object itself under
another mode of existence. Practically speaking, it is almost impossible
to speak of it except as if the species were an image, an equivalent or
substitute for the object; and St. Thomas himself so speaks. But it is
important to understand that the species of an object is not one being
and the object another. It is the very object under the mode of species;
that is, it is still the object considered in action and in the efficacy it exerts
over a subject. Under this one condition only can we say that it is not the
species of the object that is present in thought, but the object through
its species. And as it is the form of the object which is its active and
determining principle, so it is the form of the object which the intellect
which knows it, through its species, becomes. The whole objectivity of
human knowledge depends in the last analysis upon the fact that it is

not a superadded intermediary, or a distinct substitute which is introduced into our thought in place of the thing. It is, rather, the sensible species of the thing itself which, rendered intelligible by the agent intellect, becomes the form of our possible intellect.[9]

A last consequence of the same principle brings to light the continuity of the species with the form of the object.

We have said that it was necessary to introduce the notion of *species* into the analysis of knowledge in order to safeguard the individuality of subject and object. Let us now suppose, in order the better to guarantee their individuality and distinction, that we conceded to the species uniting them an existence of its own. The immediate result would be that the object of knowledge would cease to be the intelligible form of the thing known and would become the intelligible species which has just been substituted for it. In other words, if species were beings distinct from their forms, our knowledge would focus upon species, not upon objects.[10] This is unacceptable for two reasons. First, because in this case all our knowledge would cease to deal with exterior realities and would only extend to their representations in our consciousness. Here we should be falling into Plato's error which regards knowledge as a science of ideas instead of a science of things. Secondly, because there would no longer be any criterion of certitude. Each would be sole judge of what is true, seeing that it would now be a matter of what is thought rather than of something independent of thought. Since, however, there actually is demonstrative knowledge dealing with things, and not with mere opinions, the objects of knowledge must be things in themselves and not individual images distinct from things. The species, then, is not *what* thought knows of a thing, but *that by which* it knows it." In the act of knowledge there is no intermediate being between thought and its object.

Let us shift our approach now and look at the same act from the point of view of thought. How will it now appear to us?

What first meets our attention is that the act of knowledge is immanent in its subject. By this we mean that it takes place in the subject and benefits the subject alone. Beginning with this, the unity between the intellect and its object, which we have been emphasizing, will appear under a new and definite aspect. Up to the present, counting on the fact that the act of knowledge was common to the one knowing and the known, we could speak indifferently of thought becoming its object or of the object becoming the knowledge which a thought has of its object. But now we see clearly that when a thing becomes intelligibilized in thought, it does not become anything more nor anything else than what it was. For an object with no consciousness of being, to be known is no event. It is as if nothing were happening to it. Only the being of the knowing subject has gained anything by the operation.

There is something else too. As soon as we see that knowledge is completely immanent in thought, it becomes meaningless to say that it is thought which becomes the object. This must not be unless the object is accommodated to the thought's manner of being in order that the thought may become it. It is no longer any more its own being than that of its object because the object takes in it a being of the same order as its own: *Omne quod recipitur in altero, recipitur secundum modum recipientis*. For iron or wood to be in thought as something known, they must be there without their matter, and only by their form; that is, according to a universal and spiritual mode of being. This manner of existence which things have in the thought assimilating them is called "intentional" *being*.[12] This, if we only think about it, is a profound transformation of concrete datum by the mind receiving it. Experience furnishes a particular man, form and matter; the senses, and after them, the intellect receive a form more and more released from every material mark; that is, they receive its intelligibility.

But this is not all. The act of knowledge is further liberated from the object in a still sharper way when the interior word or concept is produced. The name "concept" is given to what the intellect conceives in itself and expresses by a word.[13] The sensible species and then the intelligible species, by which we know but which we do not know, is still the form itself of the object. The concept is the similitude of the object which the intellect brings forth under the action of the species. This time, therefore, we are in the presence of a substitute for the object. This substitute is no longer either the substance of the knowing intellect nor the thing known itself, but an intentional being incapable of subsisting outside of thought,[14] which the word designates and which later will be fixed by the definition.

We now have some idea of how complex a relation unites our knowledge with its object. Between the thing, considered in its own nature, and the concept which the intellect fashions out of it, there comes a twofold likeness or resemblance which it is important to be able to distinguish. First, there is the likeness of the thing in us; that is, the resemblance of the form which is the species, here a direct likeness, expressed from itself by the object and imprinted by it in us. It is as indistinguishable from it as is the action which the seal exerts on wax from the seal itself. Consequently, this likeness is not distinguished from its principle because it is not a representation of it but its promotion and, as it were, its prolongation. Secondly, there is the likeness of the thing which we conceive in ourselves and which is not the form itself but nothing more than its representation.[15] The next question to arise is how to guarantee the fidelity of the concept to its object.

We cannot doubt that the concept of the thing, the first product of the intellect, is really distinct from the thing itself. Their dissociation is accomplished, as it were, experimentally before our eyes. The concept of man, for example, exists only in the intellect which conceives it, while men themselves continue to exist in reality even when they are no longer known. That the concept is no longer the very species directly introduced into us by the object is no less evident since, as we have just seen, the species is within us the cause of the concept.[16] But, lacking identity between knowledge and the object known, or even between the intelligible species and the concept, we can at least observe the identity between the object and the subject which engenders in itself the likeness of the object. The concept is not the thing; but the intellect, which conceives the concept, is truly the thing of which it forms itself a concept. The intellect which produces the concept of book only does so because it has first become the form of a book, thanks to a species which is but such a form. Hence the concept necessarily resembles its object. Just as at the beginning of the operation the intellect was one with the object because it was one with its species, so also at the end of the operation, the intellect has in itself only one faithful representation of the object, because, before producing it, it had in some way become the object itself. The concept of an object resembles it because the intellect must be fecundated by the species of the object itself in order to be capable of engendering the concept.[17]

The operation by which the intellect engenders in itself the concept is a natural operation. In accomplishing it, it is doing what it is its nature to do. Since the process of the operation is as we have described it, we can conclude that its result is naturally unerring. An intellect which only expresses the intelligible, if the object has first impressed it in it, cannot err in its expression. Let us give the term "quiddity" to the essence of the thing thus known. We shall be able to say that the quiddity is the proper object of the intellect, which never errs in apprehending it. If, to simplify the problem, we abstract from accidental causes of error capable of falsifying an experience, we shall see that this is indeed the case. By rights, and almost always in fact, a human intellect confronted by an oak forms in itself the concept of tree, and confronted with Socrates or Plato forms in itself the concept of man. The intellect conceives essences as infallibly as hearing perceives sounds and sight colors.[18]

Thus the concept is normally in conformity with its object. Nevertheless, its presence in the intellect does not yet constitute the presence of a truth. All that can be said of it thus far is that it is there. The intellect which has made it does not know how it has made it. This concept is not born from the intellect's reflecting upon and considering the intelligible species and being forced then to fashion an image in its likeness. The unity between the intellect and the species, guaranteed by the objectivity of knowledge, prevents our supposing any such duplication.[19] The most evident consequence of this continuity in the operation is that, if the concept is in conformity with the object, the intellect so engendering it knows nothing of it. This simple and direct apprehension of reality by the intellect supposes on its part no conscious and deliberate activity. It is the operation of a being which acts according to its nature and under the action of an exterior reality, rather than the free activity of a mind which dominates and enriches this reality.

In order that this conformity of the concept to the object become something known and take the form of truth in consciousness, the intellect must add something of its own to the exterior reality which it has just assimilated. Such an addition begins when, not content just to apprehend a thing, it makes a judgment upon it and says: this is a man, this is a tree. Here the intellect brings something new—an affirmation which exists in it alone and not in things. Of such an affirmation we can ask whether it corresponds with reality or not. The definition of truth as an adequation between the thing and the intellect, *adaequatio rei et intellectus*, is a simple expression of the fact that the problem of truth can have no meaning unless the intellect is regarded as distinct from its object. Thus far, since it is one with the thing (*species*) or acts only under its immediate pressure (*conceptus*), to be in accord with the object would simply be to be in accord with itself. But here judgment enters, thought's first initiative, and this time there really are two distinct realities; therefore the question of their relation to each other can arise. Truth is only the agreement between reason which judges and reality which the judgment affirms. Error, on the other hand, is but their disagreement.[20]

Adaequatio rei et intellectus is one of philosophy's best known formulas. For some it signifies a profound truth; for others it represents the simplest and most naively sophistic definition of truth. It is not the task of the history of philosophy to refute or to justify this doctrine. Its task is to understand it, which is quite impossible apart from the existential metaphysics of St. Thomas.

Taken in itself, the notion of truth applies not directly to things, but to thought's knowledge of things. As we have said, neither truth nor error is possible except where there is judgment. Now judgment is an operation of reason associating or dissociating concepts. Therefore it is rather in thought that truth is properly said to reside. In other words, it is thoughts, rather than things, which are true. On the other hand, if we look at the relation of thought to things from the point of view of its basis, we have to say that truth is in things, rather than in thought. I say that Peter exists; if this judgment of existence is true, it is because Peter does indeed exist. I say that Peter is a rational animal; if I am speaking truly, it is because indeed Peter is a living being endowed with reason. Let us go further. I say that a thing cannot be both itself and its contrary; if this principle is true, it is indeed because each being is the being that it is and not another. This principle is obviously true because the first basis of everything true which we can say of any being is the primary fact, beyond which thought cannot go, that this being is what it is.

Thus far Thomistic realism is only the heir of everything sound in the Greek realist philosophies with which it rightly claims kinship.[21] Here, as elsewhere, however, it goes beyond them by making them more profound in existential significance. Taken in what we may call its static or essential form, ontological truth merely means that truth is a transcendental: being and truth are convertible (*ens et verum convertuntur*). Indeed, whatever is, is intelligible, that is to say, the object of true knowledge, actual or possible. When we extend this abstract relation of convertibility to the real case of God, we quickly see that not only in right but in fact, all that is is actually known in its truth, adequately and as it is. Nevertheless, this is not the ultimate basis of this thesis, because the priority of being over truth begins where being itself begins, in God. Divine knowledge is true because it is adequate to the divine being. Or better, it is identical with it. If God is truth, it is because His truth is one with His very being. In relation to this identification, the adequation of our true knowledge to its object is but a weak and distant imitation.

Weak and distant though it be, it is no less a faithful imitation, provided it is properly understood for what it is. It is well here to remember that the objects of knowledge are beings only because God creates and conserves them as acts-of-being. Metaphysics dominates noetic as it dominates the rest of philosophy. In such a philosophy, truth will never realize the adequation of understanding with being unless it attains the adequation of understanding with actual existence. The reason why, let us observe with St. Thomas himself, the judgment is the understanding's most perfect operation is that it alone is capable of attaining, beyond the essence of the beings which the concept grasps, that *ipsum esse* which is, as we know, the very source of all reality.[22]

All this shows what a capital role the apprehension of actual existence plays in the noetic of St. Thomas. It is constantly repeated that the first Thomistic principle of knowledge is the notion of being. And rightfully so! Being is first in the order of the simple apprehension of concepts and it is also first in the order of judgment. This must be so, since every judgment is made from concepts. However, it must be added that the word "principle" has two different senses in St. Thomas's, as indeed in any other, philosophy. Descartes reproached Scholasticism for positing as the first principle the universal notion of being and the principle of identity which derives immediately from it. What concrete knowledge, asked Descartes, can anyone hope to derive from such formally abstract notions? Hence his conclusion that it is not the principle of identity or of contradiction, evident as it may be, but rather the first judgment of existence which constitutes the first principle of philosophy. If to know is to progress from existences to existences, the first principle of philosophy can only be the judgment of existence which precedes and conditions all the others: I think, therefore I am.

Descartes was right, at least in the sense that he was here emphasizing, what was never afterwards to be forgotten, the distinction between the principles which govern thought, such as the principle of identity or contradiction, and the principles of acquisition of knowledge, such as the *Cogito* was for him. But his charge that Scholasticism raised the principle of contradiction to a principle of acquisition of knowledge was inaccurate, certainly so far as the teaching of St. Thomas is concerned. The "commencement-principle" of the philosophy of St. Thomas is the sensible perception of actually existing concrete beings. The entire structure of a knowledge of the Thomistic type, from the lowest of sciences right up to metaphysics, rests on this fundamental existential experience. Human knowledge never ceases to make an ever-fuller inventory of its content.

With this central point, we can see how the guiding theses of Thomistic noetic come together and how texts to which his interpreters usually object are in full accord. It is true that the first object known is the thing itself: "that which is primarily understood is the thing," provided that it be present in thought through its species: "the thing of which the intelligible species is the likeness." [23] In saying, with this precise meaning, that the object is the first known, there is no intention of opposing the knowledge of the object to the concept which expresses it, but to the knowledge of the intellectual act which conceives it and of the subject which accomplishes this act. The expression "that which is primarily understood is the thing" signifies therefore that thought first forms the concept of the object, then, reflecting upon this object, it observes the act by which it has just grasped it, and finally, knowing the existence of its acts, it discovers itself as their common source. "And therefore that which is first known by the human intellect is an object of this kind, and that which is known secondarily is the act by which that object is known, and through the act the intellect itself is known, whose perfection is the act itself of understanding" [24]

In the second place, it is equally true to say that the first object of the intellect is not the thing but its concept. This is true, however, on condition that we understand it just as St. Thomas means it when he states it. What is known, absolutely speaking, is not the being considered in its own subjective existence, since this remains what it is whether I know it or whether I do not know it. What is known is only this same being in so far as it has become mine by the coincidence or meeting of my intellect with its species, from which the act of simple apprehension results. To say that the immediate object of thought is the concept is not, therefore, to deny that it is the thing, but rather to affirm that it is the thing, inasmuch as the thing's intelligibility makes all that of the concept.[25]

Once we have grasped these guiding theses of Thomistic doctrine, it becomes possible to conceive of an epistemology faithfully extending and amplifying it. Perhaps we are even in possession of a far fuller epistemology than is customarily imagined.

At our first approach to this doctrine, it is only right to place a criticism of the Critique in order to find out whether the basic Idealist argument does not imply a false position on the problem of knowledge. If we suppose first that things are for themselves and the intellect is for itself, that is, if we suppose that it is impossible for them to meet, then there is no bridge to allow thought to cross over to things, and Idealism is true. It is contradictory to ask whether our ideas conform to things, if things are not known to us save through their ideas. Such an argument is irrefutable, and here again Idealism is true, unless indeed the argument begs the question.

St. Thomas, they say, has not indicated this difficulty. But perhaps it is because he has already resolved another difficulty, which Idealism in its turn has not raised, and whose solution renders impossible the very position from which the Idealist problem emerges. St. Thomas has not asked himself the conditions for a mathematical physics, but he has asked himself what conditions are necessary if we are to have an abstract notion of any physical body whatsoever. The possibility of our knowledge in general is perhaps pre-formed in the conformity of our humblest concept to its object. It becomes possible, contrary to the Idealist thesis, to know whether or not our ideas conform to things, in a doctrine in which the presence of things in us is the very condition of the conception of ideas. The true Thomistic reply to this criticism is to be found in an earlier analysis in which the inquiry into the possibility of knowledge in general precedes the inquiry into science in particular. To demand that St. Thomas refute Kant's Critique is to ask him to solve a problem which from his point of view simply cannot exist.

When the ground is cleared by this preliminary explanation, it would seem that for St. Thomas a complete theory of knowledge does not require what since Kant's time has been called his Critique. There is knowledge, this knowledge is true, at least under certain conditions.[26] It is true each time it is formed under normal conditions, by a normally constituted mind. Whence it arises that agreement among minds may be reached, and that beyond the conflict of opinions, there is a truth. The intellect, in search of this impersonal basis of given truths, reflects upon its act and judges that this basis lies both in the specific identity of nature which connects all human reasons and in the impersonal objectivity of things known by these reasons.

But is it possible to conceive of the act of a thought which extends to a thing? To know it, the regressive analysis, which has brought us to the concept, must mount in the end from the concept back to the intellect. Does there exist in us a principle of such a kind that it can produce a concept whose conformity to the object is assured? Yes, if it is true that we have an intellect; that is, when all is said and done, if it is true that we are not enclosed in our own being, but are capable of becoming the being of others by way of representation.[27]

This is the only possible keystone of a Thomistic theory of knowledge. The adequation of the intellect to the real, which is the definition of truth, is legitimately affirmed in a doctrine in which the intellect reflects upon itself and finds that it is capable of becoming reality: *secundum hoc cognoscit veritatem intellectus, quod supra se reflectitur*. From the moment when the intellect, which judges things, knows that it can only conceive them at the price of its union with them, no scruple can prevent it from affirming as valid the judgments in which the content of its concepts become explicit. The initial factor in knowledge, which this analysis but tries to penetrate, is the direct grasping of intelligible reality by an intellect served by a sensibility.

CHAPTER VIII

APPETITE AND WILL

THUS FAR we have only studied the cognitive powers of the human intellect. But the soul is not only capable of knowing; it is also capable of desiring. This characteristic it shares with all natural forms. In the human soul this characteristic only assumes a particular aspect in that the soul is a form endowed with knowledge. From all forms there emerges some kind of inclination. Fire, for example, is inclined, by reason of its form, to move upwards and to produce fire in the bodies it touches. Now the form of beings endowed with knowledge is superior to the form of bodies without it. In the latter the form determines each thing to the particular being proper to it. In other words, it but confers its natural being upon it. The inclination proceeding from such a form is rightly called a *natural appetite.*

Beings endowed with knowledge are, on the contrary, determined to the proper being natural to them by a form which is, to be sure, their natural form, but which is at the same time capable of receiving species from other beings. It is thus that the sense receives species from all sensibles and the intellect species from all intelligibles. The human soul, therefore, is fitted to become in some way all things, thanks to its senses and intellect. In this it resembles, up to a point, God Himself, in Whom the exemplars of all creatures pre-exist. If, therefore, the forms of knowing beings are of a higher degree than those deprived of knowledge, the inclination proceeding from them must be higher than natural inclination. Here appear the soul's appetitive powers by which the animal tends toward what it knows.[1]

Let us add, moreover, that animals participate more generously in the divine goodness than inanimate things and require a larger number of operations and means of acquiring their own perfection. They are like those men we spoke of above who can acquire perfect health, but only on condition that they utilize a sufficiently large number of means.[2] The natural appetite, determined to one object and to one mediocre perfection, requires but a single operation in order to acquire it. The animal's appetite, however, must be multiform and capable of extending to all the animal's needs. Thus it is that their nature must have an appetite proportionate to their faculty of knowing and which permits them to tend toward all the objects which they apprehend.[3]

We shall observe henceforth that the nature of the appetite is very closely bound to the degree of knowledge from which it proceeds. It will scarcely surprise us to find that as many appetitive powers are attributed to the human soul as it has cognitive powers. Now the soul apprehends objects by means of two powers, one lower which is the sensitive, the other higher which is the intellectual or rational power. Accordingly it tends toward its objects by two appetitive powers, the one lower and called sensuality, which is itself divided into *irascible* and *concupiscible,* the other higher and called *will.*[4]

It cannot be doubted that we here have to do with distinct powers of the human soul. Natural appetite, sensitive appetite and rational appetite are distinguished as three irreducible degrees of perfection. The closer a nature is to the divine perfection, the more clearly is its express resemblance to the Creator to be observed. The characteristic of divine dignity is that He who possesses it moves, inclines and directs everything without Himself being moved, inclined or directed by another. Therefore, the closer a nature is to God, the less does He determine it and the more is it capable of determining itself. Insensible nature, by reason of its materiality, is infinitely removed from God and is therefore inclined toward a definite end. It cannot be said to incline itself toward that end, but it has an inclination which so disposes it. The arrow which the archer aims at the target is like this, and so is the stone which moves downwards.[5] Sensitive nature, on the other hand, is nearer to God and has in itself something that inclines it; namely, the desirable object which it apprehends. However, this inclination is not itself within the animal's power but is determined by the object. In the preceding case the object of the inclination was exterior and the inclination determined. In the present case the object is interior, but the determination remains determined. Animals, in presence of the delectable cannot not desire it, for they are not masters of their inclination. Thus we can say, with John Damascene, that they do not act but rather are acted upon: *non agunt sed magis aguntur.* The reason for this inferiority is that the sensible appetite of the animal is bound, like the sense itself, to a corporeal organ. Its proximity to the dispositions of matter and corporeal things give it the right to a nature less fitted to move than to be moved.

But rational nature, much closer to God than the preceding, cannot not possess an inclination of a higher order distinct from the others. Like animate beings, it has within itself inclinations toward determinate objects, insofar, for example, as it is the form of a natural heavy body which tends downwards. Like the animals, it possesses an inclination capable of being moved by the exterior objects which it comprehends. But it possesses in addition an inclination not necessarily moved by the desirable objects which it apprehends and capable of being moved or not, as it pleases. Its movement, consequently, is not determined by anything other than itself. Now no being can determine its own inclination toward an end if it does not first know the end and the relation of the means to their end. Such knowledge belongs only to rational creatures. An appetite not necessarily determined from without is, therefore, very closely bound to rational knowledge. Hence it is called the rational appetite or will.[6] The distinction, then, between sensuality and will is made first on the grounds that the one is determined in its inclinations while the other determines itself. This supposes two powers of different order. As this very diversity in mode of determination demands a difference in the mode of apprehending objects, we can say that, secondarily, appetites are distinguishable according to the degree of knowledge to which they correspond.[7]

Let us examine each of these powers separately, beginning with the sensitive appetite or sensuality. The natural object, we say, is determined in its natural being. It can only be what it is by nature. It possesses, therefore, but a single inclination toward a determinate object. And this inclination does not require that it be able to distinguish what is desirable from what is not. It is enough that the author of nature has made such provisions in conferring upon each being the inclination proper to it. The sensitive appetite, on the contrary, if it does not tend toward the desirable and the general good which only reason apprehends, tends toward every object useful to it and delectable. As the sense, to which it corresponds, has for its object any particular sensible whatsoever, so the sensible appetite has for its object any particular good whatsoever.[8]

Still we are here dealing with a faculty which, considered according to its proper nature, is solely appetitive and in no way cognitive. Sensuality is so called from sense movement, as sight is so called from seeing, and as, generally speaking, a power receives its name from its act. Indeed, sense movement, if we define it in itself and precisely, is only appetite consequent to the apprehension of the sensible by the senses. Unlike the action of the appetite, this apprehension has nothing of movement in it. The operation by which the senses apprehend their object is completely finished when the object apprehended has passed into the power which apprehends it. The operation of the appetitive power, on the contrary, attains its terminus when the being endowed with appetite tends toward the object it desires. Thus the operation of apprehensive powers is like repose, while that of the appetitive power is more like movement. Sensuality in no way is dependent upon the realm of knowledge but solely on the realm of appetite.[9]

Within the sensitive appetite, which constitutes a sort of generic power under the title of sensuality, two powers, the *irascible* and the *concupiscible*, which form its species, are to be distinguished. The sensitive appetite possesses this in common with the natural appetite, that both always tend toward an object befitting the being which desires it. Now it is easy to observe in the natural appetite a double tendency, corresponding to the double operation performed by the natural being. By the first of these operations, the natural thing strives to acquire what it needs to conserve its nature. Thus the heavy body moves downwards, that is, to the place where it is naturally conserved. By the second operation, each natural thing makes use of some active quality against whatever is capable of being contrary to it.

Corruptible beings must have some such operation. If they could not destroy their contraries, they would quickly perish. Thus the appetite tends toward two ends: to acquire what is in accord with its nature, and to win some sort of victory over each of its adversaries. The first operation belongs to a receptive order, the second to an active order. Action and submission depend upon different principles, and so we should find different powers at the origin of these diverse operations. The same holds for the sensitive appetite. By its appetitive power, the animal tends toward what is friendly to its nature and capable of preserving it. This function is performed by the concupiscible which has for its object whatever it is pleasant for the senses to apprehend. On the other hand, the animal desires domination and victory over everything hostile to it. This function is performed by the irascible, which has for its object not the agreeable but the difficult and arduous.[10]

Obviously, therefore, the irascible is a different power from the concupiscible. The nature of the desirable is not the same in what is attractive and what is adverse. Generally speaking, what is arduous or adverse cannot be overcome without the sacrifice of some pleasure and without running the risk of suffering. In order to fight, the animal will tear itself away from the strongest pleasure and will not give up the struggle in spite of the pain that comes from its wounds. On the other hand, the concupiscible tends to receive its object, for it desires only to be united with what pleases it. The irascible, however, is turned toward action, since it tends in the direction of victory over danger. What we said about the natural is true also of the sensitive. Receiving and acting are always related to different powers. This is even verified in what concerns knowledge, since we have had to distinguish between the agent intellect and the possible intellect. Therefore, we must consider the irascible and the concupiscible as two distinct powers.

Such distinction does not prevent their being ordered to each other. The irascible is ordered to the concupiscible, for it is its guardian and defender. The animal had to vanquish its foes, by means of its irascible, so that the concupiscible might enjoy its agreeable objects in peace. Indeed, it is always for the sake of procuring some pleasure that animals fight— the pleasures, for example, of love or food. The movements of the irascible thus have both their beginning and their end in the concupiscible. Anger starts with sadness and terminates in the joy of revenge, and both of these belong to the concupiscible. Hope begins with desire and terminates in pleasure. Thus the movements of sensuality always proceed from the concupiscible to the concupiscible via the irascible.[11]

The question now arises whether we can distinguish any difference in degree of perfection between these two distinct but closely associated powers. Can we speak of the superiority of either the concupiscible or irascible as we have previously noted the superiority of the sensible appetite over the natural? If we consider the sensitive power of the soul by itself, we observe that, both in what concerns knowledge and what concerns appetite, it includes some faculties which belong to it by the very fact of its sensible nature, and others which it possesses in virtue of a sort of participation in that higher power, reason. This does not mean that there are places where the intellectual and sensible faculties turn out to be confused. But it means that the higher degrees of the sensible lie on the frontiers of the lower degrees of reason, according to the principle of Dionysius: "divine wisdom joins the end of one thing to be beginning of the next." [12]

The imagination belongs to the sensitive soul as perfectly conforming to its proper degree of perfection; what perceives sensible forms is naturally equipped to conserve them. It is perhaps not quite the same in the case of the estimative power. Let us recall the functions we have already attributed to this sensible power: it apprehends species which the senses are not able to receive, since it perceives objects as useful or harmful, and beings as friends or enemies. The appreciation which the sensitive soul thus shows for things confers a kind of natural prudence upon the animal with results analogous to those which reason obtains by very different ways. Now it seems that the irascible is superior to the concupiscible as the estimative is to the imagination. When the animal, in virtue of its concupiscible appetite, tends toward the object which pleases it, it does nothing save what is in perfect proportion to the proper nature of the sensitive soul. But when the animal moved by the irascible forgets about its pleasure in order to have a victory which it can only obtain through pain, it is using an appetitive power that is extremely close to the higher order of the sensible. Just as the estimative achieved results analogous to those of the intellect, the irascible obtains results analogous to those of the will. Therefore, we can place the irascible above the concupiscible even though the irascible's end is to protect the act of the concupiscible. We shall see in the irascible the noblest instrument with which nature has endowed the animal to keep itself in existence and to assure its conservation.[13]

This conclusion concerning animals is also valid for men endowed with will and reason. The powers of the sensitive appetite are of exactly the same nature in both animals and reasonable men. The movements accomplished are identical; only their source is different. If we consider the sensitive appetite as encountered in animals, we see that it is moved and determined by the judgment of their estimative power. Thus the sheep fears the wolf because it spontaneously judges it dangerous. Now we have noted above[14] that in man the estimative power is replaced by a cogitative faculty which collates the images from particular objects. It is the cogitative power which determines the movements of our sensitive appetite. And, as this particular reason itself, which is of a sensible nature, is moved and directed in man by universal reason, so our appetites are made dependent upon our reason.

It is easy to be sure of all this. Syllogistic reasoning proceeds from universal premises in order to make particular conclusions. When we perceive that the sensible object is good or bad, useful or harmful, our perception of this particular *harmful* or of this particular *useful* object can be said to be conditioned by our intellectual knowledge of the harmful or useful in general. When it acts upon the imagination by means of appropriate syllogisms, the reason can make a given object appear as pleasant or fearful, agreeable or painful. A man can calm his anger or appease his fear by reasoning about it.[15]

We should add, however, that in man, the sensitive appetite can have no movement of the soul's motive power carried out unless it first obtains the assent of the will. With animals, the irascible or concupiscible appetite immediately determines certain movements. The sheep fears the wolf, and quickly takes to flight. Here there is no higher appetite to prohibit movements of sensible origin. It is not so with man. His movements are not infallibly set in motion by the inclination of his appetite, but they always await the higher order of his will. In all ordered motive powers, the inferior only move in virtue of the superior. The sensitive appetite is of an inferior order and cannot determine any movement without the consent of the superior appetite. Just as, among the celestial spheres, the inferior are moved by the superior, so appetite is moved by the will.[16]

We have now come to the very threshold of voluntary activity and of free-will, properly so called. To attain it fully, we have only to attribute to the appetite an object in keeping, from the point of universality, with that of rational knowledge. What places the will in its proper degree of perfection is that its first and principal object is the desirable and the good as such. Particular beings can only become objects of the will in the measure in which they participate in the universal reason of good.[17] Let us determine the relations which can be established between the appetite and this new object.

Each appetitive power is necessarily determined by its proper object. In the animal deprived of reason, the appetite is infallibly inclined by the desirable which the senses apprehend. The brute seeing the delectable cannot not desire it. It is the same with the will. Its proper object is the general good. For the will, it is a natural absolute necessity to desire the general good. This necessity proceeds immediately from its definition. The necessary is that which cannot not be. When such necessity is imposed upon a being in virtue of one of its essential principles, whether material or formal, it is said to be a natural and absolute necessity. In this sense,

anything composed of contrary elements is said to be necessarily corruptible; and the angles of a triangle are said necessarily to equal two right-
angles. So too the intellect by definition must adhere necessarily to the
first principles of knowledge. So too must the will necessarily adhere to
good in general; that is, to the last end, which is beatitude.

It is an understatement to say that such natural necessity is not repugnant to the will. It is the formal principle constituting its essence. Just as,
at the origin of all our speculative knowledge there is intellection of principles, so there is at the origin of all our voluntary operations the adhesion
of the will to the last end. It cannot be otherwise. What a being possesses
by the very demands of its own nature and in invariable fashion is necessarily the basis and principle of everything else in it, whether properties
or operations. For the nature of a thing and the origin of all movement
always reside in an invariable principle.[18] Our conclusion, accordingly, is
as follows: the will necessarily desires good in general; this necessity signifies that the will cannot not be itself; and this immutable adherence to
the good as such constitutes the first principle of all its operations.

Because the will cannot not will the good in general—*bonum secundum
communem boni rationem*[19]—does it follow that whatever it wills it wills necessarily? Obviously not. Let us return to the parallel between appetite and
knowledge. The will, we said, adheres naturally and necessarily to the last
end, which is the Sovereign Good, as the intellect adheres naturally and
necessarily to first principles. Now there are propositions which are intelligible for human reason, but which are not bound to these principles by
any necessary connection. Such are contingent propositions, that is, all
those which it is possible to deny without contradicting the first principles
of knowledge. The intellect's immutable adherence to principles does not
force it to accept such propositions. But there are necessary propositions,
so called because they proceed necessarily from first principles and can be
deduced by way of demonstration. To deny these propositions amounts to
denying the principles from which they proceed. If, accordingly, the intellect perceives the necessary connection binding these conclusions to
their principles, it must necessarily accept the conclusions as it accepts the
principles from which it deduces them. But its assent is not necessary
when the necessity of the connection has not been demonstrated. And the
same holds for the will. There is a large number of particular goods the
possession of which is quite unnecessary for happiness. These are not
bound to beatitude by any necessary connection. Consequently, the will
is not bound by any natural necessity to will them.

But there are goods bound to beatitude by a necessary connection. Such
are all the goods by which man is attached to God, in which alone true
beatitude consists. The human will cannot not cleave to them. It is a question here of necessity of right, not of fact. Just as conclusions are only
necessarily imposed upon those who see them implied in their principles,

so man only cleaves indefectibly to God and to what is from God, when he sees with sure vision the divine essence and the necessary connection of the particular goods attached thereto. This is the case of the blessed, who are confirmed in grace. Their will adheres necessarily to God because they see His essence. Here below, however, we are not given to see the divine essence. So our will necessarily wishes beatitude, but nothing more. We do not see with immediate clarity that God is the Sovereign Good and the sole beatitude. And we do not discover with the certitude of demonstration the necessary connection between God and what is truly from God. Thus the will does not will necessarily whatever it wills. But as it is so imperfect that it is never placed in the presence of any but particular goods, we can conclude that, save for the Good in general, it is never under necessity to will what it wills.[20] This truth will be still more apparent when we have determined the relations between the understanding and will within the human soul itself.

It is not without interest for the understanding of what free-will is to inquire whether one of these two powers is nobler and more eminent in dignity than the other. Now the intellect and the will can be considered either in their very essence or as particular powers of the soul exercising determinate acts. Through its essence, the intellect's function is to apprehend being and truth taken in its universality. The will is, in its essence, the appetite for Good in general. If we compare them from this point of view, the intellect appears to be more eminent and noble than the will, because the object of the will is comprised and included in that of the intellect. The will tends toward the good as desirable. Now the good supposes being, because there is no desirable good save where there is a being that is good and desirable. But being is the proper object of the intellect. The essence of the good which the will desires is precisely that which the intellect apprehends. Hence, if we compare the objects of these two powers, the object of the intellect appears to be absolute, that of the will relative. And since the order of the soul's powers follows that of their objects, we can conclude that, taken in itself and absolutely, the intellect is more noble than the will.[21]

By comparing the relation between the intellect and its unversal object with the will as a particular and determinate power of the soul, we also arrive at the conclusion that the intellect is nobler than the will. The proper objects of the intellect, being and universal truth, contain in effect the will, its act, and even its object as so many particular beings and truths. The will, its act and its object are matter for intellection by the intellect just as are stone, wood, and all the beings and truths it apprehends. But if we consider the will by examining its universal object, the good, and consider the intellect as a special power of the soul, we shall reverse our findings as to their relative perfection. Each individual intellect, all intellectual knowledge, and each object of knowledge constitute particular goods. As such they fall under universal good which is the proper object of the will. Thus looked at, the will is superior to the intellect and capable of moving it.

The understanding and the will reciprocally include and move each other. One thing can move another because it constitutes its end. In this sense, the end moves what realizes it, since it acts with a view to realize it. Therefore the intellect moves the will, since the good which the intellect apprehends is the object of the will and moves it as its end. But a being can also be said to move another when it acts upon it and modifies its state. In this sense, that which alters a thing moves that which is altered. The motor moves the mobile object. The will moves the intellect in this sense. In all active powers, reciprocally ordered, the one which looks to the universal end moves those powers which look to particular ends. This is easily verified both in the order of nature and in the social order. The end of the movement of the heavens is to conserve bodies which generate and corrupt. And the heavens move all lower bodies which only act to conserve their own species or their own individuality. Similarly, the king, whose actions are for the general welfare of the entire kingdom, through his orders, moves the officials who govern each city. Now the object of the will is the good and end in general. Other powers of the soul are only ordered in view of particular goods. The eyes, for example, have the perception of color for their end; the intellect has for its end the knowledge of truth. The will, accordingly, moves to their acts the intellect and all the other powers of the soul, except the natural functions of vegetative life which do not fall under our free decisions.[22]

It now becomes easy to understand what our free-will is and in what conditions its activity is exercised. Above all, we can take it as evident that man's will is free from constraint. Certain philosophers would limit human liberty to this absence of constraint. Though this is a necessary, it is not a sufficient condition of liberty. It is only too clear that the will can never be forced. To speak of constraint is to speak of violence, and by definition the violent is that which is contrary to natural inclination. The natural and the violent are mutually exclusive; and we cannot conceive of such characteristics being simultaneously possessed. The voluntary, indeed, is merely the will's inclination toward its object. If constraint and violence were introduced into the will, they would destroy it at once. Consequently, just as the natural is that which is done by the inclination of nature, so the voluntary is that which is done by the inclination of the will. And just as it is impossible for a thing to be violent and natural at the same time, so it is impossible for a power of the soul to be simultaneously constrained; that is, violent, and voluntary.[23]

But we have seen that there is something more. The will is not only free from restraint by definition, but also by necessity. To deny this truth, is to remove from human acts anything to give them a blameworthy or meritorious character. We could hardly merit or demerit by performing acts impossible not to have done. Any doctrine which ultimately removes the notion of merit removes also that of morality, and must be considered as a philosophical—*extranea philosophiae*. If there is nothing free in us, if we are necessarily determined in our willing, then deliberations and exhortations, precepts and punishments, praise and blame, in a word, everything which moral philosophy deals with, would quickly disappear and lose all its meaning. Such a doctrine, we say, is aphilosophical as, indeed, are all opinions which destroy the principles of any part whatsoever of philosophy. Such would be the effect of a principle like "nothing moves," because it would rule out the whole philosophy of nature.[24] Now the denial of free will, except where it merely expresses impotence on the part of certain men to master their passions, is based entirely on sophistry. It shows ignorance of the operations performed by the human soul and of the relation of such operations with their object.

The movement of any power of the soul can be considered from two points of view; that of the subject and that of the object. Let us take an example. Sight, considered in itself, can be moved to see more clearly or less clearly by changes in the disposition of the organ of sight. Here the principle of the movement is in the subject. But it can be in the object, as is the case when the eye perceives something white taking the place of something black. The first of these operations has to do with the very exercise of the act. It causes the act either to be performed or not, to be well or badly performed. The second modification deals with the specifying of the act, for the species of the act is determined by the nature of its object. Let us look at voluntary movement under these two aspects, and let us begin by noting that the will never endures necessary determination where the exercise of its act is concerned.

We have already established that the will moves all the soul's powers. Accordingly, it moves itself as it moves the others. It will no doubt be objected that this means that it is in potency and in act at the same time and under the same relation. But the difficulty is only apparent. Let us consider, for example, the intellect of a man who is seeking to discover truth. He moves himself toward science, for he is proceeding from what he knows in act to what he does not yet know, save in potency. So, when a man wills something in act he moves himself to will another thing which he only wills in potency; that is, which he does not yet will. Thus, when a man wills his health, his willing to recover his health moves him to will to take the necessary medicine. As soon as he wills health, he begins to deliberate on the means to acquire it; and the result of this deliberation is that he wills to take the remedy. What actually takes place in such a case? Here the deliberation itself presupposes the will of a man who willed to deliberate. And since this will has not always willed to deliberate, it must have been moved by something. If by itself, we have to suppose an anterior deliberation itself proceeding from an act of the will. Since we cannot keep this up to infinity, we have to admit that the first movement of the human will is explained by the action of an exterior cause, under whose influence the will began to will.

What can this cause be? The first mover of the intellect and of the will is necessarily, it seems, above both the will and the intellect. It is, accordingly, God Himself. And this conclusion introduces no necessity into our voluntary determinations. God, indeed, is the first mover of all movable things. But He moves each thing in conformity with its nature. He who moves light things upward and heavy things downward, also moves the will according to its nature. He does not impress it with a necessitated movement, but rather with a naturally indeterminate movement which can direct itself toward different objects. If we consider the will in itself, as the source of the acts it performs, we find nothing else than a succession of deliberations and decisions, each decision supposing an anterior deliberation and each deliberation supposing in its turn a decision. And if we go right back to the very beginning of this movement, we find God. He confers it upon the will. But He only confers it as indeterminate. From the point of view of the subject and of the exercise of the act, we can find no necessary determination within the will itself.

Let us consider, on the other hand, the point of view of the specification of the act, that of the object. Here again we find no necessity. What object, indeed, is capable of moving the will? It is the good apprehended by the intellect as suitable: *bonum conveniens apprehensum*. If, accordingly, a certain good is proposed to the intellect, and if the intellect regards it as a good without however considering it suitable, such a good will not move the will. On the other hand, deliberations and decisions deal with our acts, and our acts are individual and particular things. It is not enough then that an object be good in itself and suitable for us in a general way for it to move our will. We must also apprehend it as good and suitable in the given case, taking cognizance of all its discoverable particular circumstances.

There is only one object which presents itself to us as good and suitable under all aspects—beatitude. Boethius defines it as *status omnium bonorum congregatione perfectus*.[25] Obviously, this object does move our will necessarily. But let us note well that this necessity itself only concerns the determination of the act. It is limited strictly to this: that the will cannot will the contrary of beatitude. This reservation can be expressed differently. We can say that if the will performs an act while the intellect is thinking of beatitude, then this act is necessarily determined by such an object. The will will not will any other. But the actual exercise of the act remains free. If we cannot not will beatitude while we are thinking about it, we can, nevertheless, not will to think about beatitude. The will remains in control of its act and can use it as it pleases with reference to any object whatsoever: *libertas ad actum inest voluntati in quolibet statu naturae respectu cujuslibet objecti.*[26]

Let us suppose, on the other hand, that the good proposed to the will be not such according to all the particularities which characterize it. In such a case, not only is the will free to accomplish its act or not, but the determination of the act still has nothing necessary about it. In other words, the will can, as always, not will our thinking about this object. But we can also will a different object, even while actually thinking about the other. It is enough if this new object is present to us as good under some aspect.

How is it that the will, from among all the particular goods offered to us, prefers some objects to others? Three principles may be applied here. One object may surpass another in excellence. In choosing it, the will is moving in conformity with reason. Again, it happens that, as a consequence of its interior dispositions or of some exterior circumstance, the intellect stops over some particular characteristic of one good rather than another. The will then patterns itself according to this thought whose source is quite accidental.

Then too account must be taken of the disposition in which the whole man finds himself. The will of an angry man does not proceed like that of a calm man, for the same objects do not suit both. As a man is, so is his end. The healthy man does not take food like the sick man. Now, the disposition leading the will to consider an object as good and suitable can have two sources. If it is a question of a natural disposition and one withdrawn from the reach of the will, the will conforms to it by natural necessity. Thus do all men desire naturally to be, to live and to know. If it is a question, on the other hand, of a disposition which is not by nature a constituent part of man, but one dependent upon his will, the individual is under no necessity to conform to it. If, for example, some passion makes us consider a particular object to be good or bad, our will can react against this passion and so alter our appreciation of the object. We can govern our anger in order not to judge a given object blindly. If the disposition concerned is a habit, it is more difficult to escape it, because it is far more difficult to break off a habit than to check a passion. However, the thing is not impossible, and so, here too, the will's choice is removed from all necessity.[27]

Let us summarize the preceding conclusions. To suppose that the will can be forced is a contradiction of terms and absurd; hence it is completely free from constraint. Is it free from necessity? Here we must distinguish. The will is always free from necessity in the exercise of its act. We are able not to will even the Sovereign Good, because we are able not to will to think about it. In what concerns the determination of the act, we cannot not will the Sovereign Good nor the objects of our natural dispositions while we are thinking about them. We can, however, freely choose among all particular goods, including those which acquired dispositions cause us to consider to be such, without any of them being able to determine the movement of our will. More briefly yet, the will is always free to will or not to will any object whatsoever. It is always free, when it wills, to determine itself to any particular objects. From this moment, accordingly, we see taking form the elements which constitute the human act. It now remains to determine their relations more exactly by examining the operations by which man moves toward beatitude, his supreme good and his last end.

PART THREE

MORALITY

CHAPTER I

THE HUMAN ACT

IT IS COMMON to regard the creative act as having no other effect than to produce all created being from non-being. Such a view of creation is incomplete. The efficacy of the creative act cannot be restricted to that impulse which causes beings to issue forth from God. At the very moment when creatures receive the movement which gives them a being relatively independent of and exterior to the Creator's, they receive a second movement which puts them on their way back to their point of departure and tends to return them as close as possible to their first source. We have examined the order by which intelligent creatures come forth from God and have defined their characteristic operations. It now remains to establish the terminus toward which these operations tend and the end to which they are ordered.[1]

It is only for man that this very complex problem arises. In the case of the angels, their lot has been definitely decided from the first moment after their creation. This does not imply that angels were created in the state of beatitude.[2] But they were very probably created in the state of grace; and those who so willed, turned toward God by a single act of charity and merited at once their eternal happiness.[3] Inversely, the bad angels, by a single act of their free will, turned irrevocably from Him.[4] As for creatures below man, that is, those wanting intellectual knowledge, the solution of the problem is equally simple. Since they are not endowed with intellect and will, they can only attain their last end, God, by participating in some resemblance to their Creator. Endowed with being, with life or with sense knowledge, they are in their own particular way but so many images of God who formed them. In their case, the possession of this similitude is the possession of their last end.[5]

The truth of this conclusion is obvious. It is manifest that the end corresponds to the principle. If, therefore, we know the principle of all things, it is impossible not to know their end. Now we have already demonstrated that the first principle of all things is a Creator who transcends the universe which He has created. The end of all things, then, must be a good, since only the good, and a good exterior to the universe, can play the role of end. This end is God. It still remains to know how creatures not endowed with intellect can have an end outside themselves. In the case of an intelligent being, the end of its operation is established by what it proposes to do or by the goal toward which it tends. But a being wanting intellect can only possess an end outside itself either by possessing it effectively without knowing it or by representing it. Hercules is thus called the *end* of the statue depicting him. In this sense too the Sovereign Good exterior to the universe can be called the end of all things insofar as it is possessed or represented by them. Insofar as they are and insofar as they operate, all creatures tend to participate in and to represent the Sovereign Good, but each within its own limits.[6]

But man's case is different because he has free-will, that is, intelligence and will. The inclination which God implanted in him at the moment of his creation is not natural. It is a voluntary inclination. It follows, therefore, that man is a creature who, though an image of God like all the others and more excellently than many of them, is master over his choice of acts. We have now to inquire what is his last end and by what means he can come to it.

I. THE STRUCTURE OF THE HUMAN ACT

It has been already established that man is a being endowed with free-will, a property inseparable from a rational and free agent. We know also whence this liberty arises. It results from the gap encountered here below between the will and its object. In conjunction with an understanding open to universal being, the will tends toward universal good. Actually, however, it always finds itself in the presence of particular goods. These particular goods are incapable of satisfying its desire and do not constitute, so far as the will is concerned, absolutely necessary ends, and so the will remains entirely free in respect to them. "If the will be offered an object which is good universally and from every point of view, the will tends to it of necessity, if it wills anything at all; since it cannot will the opposite. If on the other hand, the will is offered an object that is not good from every point of view, it will not tend to it of necessity."[7] But though we have now grasped the general principle governing our whole rational activity, we have still to demonstrate its mechanism and to see how this mechanism functions in practice.

Let us start from the conclusion we have just stated. It can only be understood if we set the will on one side and the object toward which it tends on the other. This movement of the will which moves itself and which moves all the other powers of the soul toward its object is called *intention*. It is essential, moreover, that we determine what are, at this point of departure of human activity, the respective roles of the intellect and the will. They act here upon each other, but under different relations. Let us consider their objects. That of the intellect is universal being and truth. But universal being and truth constitute the first formal principle that it is possible to assign. And the formal principle of an act is also that which puts it in a determinate species. For example, the action of warming is only such by reason of its formal principle, heat. Now the intellect moves the will by presenting its object to it. This object is universal being and truth. By presenting this object, the intellect puts the act of the will into its own species, as opposed to the acts performed by sensitive or purely natural powers. Here, then, there is a real and efficacious moving of the will by the intellect. But, inversely, the will in its turn moves the intellect, in the sense that it can in certain cases put it effectively into motion. If we compare all our active faculties with one another, the one which tends to a universal end will necessarily appear to act upon those tending toward particular ends. For whatever acts, acts in view of an end; and the art whose proper object is a given end directs and moves the arts which procure the means of attaining that end. But the object of the will is the good; that is, the end in general. Therefore since every power of the soul tends toward a particular good which is its own good, as sight toward the perception of colors, and intellect toward the knowledge of truth, the will, whose object is good in general, must be able to use all the powers of the soul, and particularly the intellect, since the will embraces intellect.[8]

Thus the will moves all the faculties toward their end. To it belongs properly the first act of "tending toward," *in aliquid tendere*, called *intention* (in-tention). Insofar as it performs this act of intention, the will turns toward its end as toward the terminus of its movement. Since, in wishing the end, it necessarily wills the means, therefore the intention of the end and the willing of the means constitute but one single act. It is not difficult to see why. A means is to the end as the middle to the terminus. Among natural beings, the movement which passes through the middle is the same as that which reaches the terminus. The same is true of movements of the will. *To-will-a-remedy-in-view-of-health* is one single act of willing. The means is only willed because of the end. The willing of the means, therefore, blends with the intending of the end.[9]

The proper object of the intention is the end willed in itself and for itself. It constitutes, therefore, a simple act and, so to speak, an indecomposable movement of our will. But voluntary activity becomes extremely complex when we pass from the intention of the end to the choice of means. It tends by one act to the end and to the means, when it has opted given determinate means. But opting particular means does not belong properly to the voluntary act of intention. This opting is the actual electing or choosing, and is itself preceded by deliberation and judgment.

Human actions always have to do with the particular and the contingent. Now, when we pass from the universal to the particular, we leave behind the immovable and certain to enter the realm of the variable and uncertain. Hence the knowledge of what ought to be done is inevitably filled with uncertainty. Reason does not risk making a judgment in doubtful matters without preliminary deliberation. This deliberation is called *counsel*. We have just noted that the object of this deliberation is not the end itself. It cannot be a question of the intending of the end, because the end is that very principle which is the action's point of departure. If this end does in some way become the object of deliberation, it cannot be as end. It can only be insofar as it can itself be considered as a means ordered to another end. What is an end in one deliberation can be a means in another, and in this role can come within the scope of this discussion.[10] Whatever the case may be, deliberation must end in a judgment. Otherwise it might be prolonged to infinity, and no decision ever be made. Limited by its initial term, which is the simple intention of the end, it is equally limited by its final term, which is the first action we think ought to be done. Thus deliberation concludes with a judgment of the practical reason. All this part of the voluntary process is carried out in the intellect alone, without the will intervening for anything else than to put it into motion and start it on its way.

Let us now suppose that the will finds itself in the presence of the results of deliberation. Since practical reason is exercised in particular and contingent matter, it will usually arrive at two or more judgments, each representing an action as good under some respect or other. When the intellect shows the will that a number of ways of acting are possible, there is a corresponding movement of complacency in the will by which it tends toward what is good in each of the proposed possibilities. In such complacency and attachment, the will has some kind of experience of the object to which it is attaching itself: *quasi experientiam quandam sumens de re cui inhaeret*,[11] and in so doing, gives it its assent. The act by which the will applies and attaches itself to the result of the deliberation is called *consent*.

But deliberation cannot come to an end with this kind of complacent assent. Here we have reached several judgments, each receiving its assent. But we still require a decisive act by which the will may choose one of its consents in preference to the others. Deliberation brings us to a point where we observe that several means are capable of bringing us to the end toward which we are tending. Each of these means pleases us, and to the extent that it does so, we cleave to it. But of all these means which please us, we at last choose one, and such choice belongs properly to an act of *election* (*electio*). It may sometimes happen that reason only proposes a single means. In this case the one means proposed pleases us, and election or choice can be said to be one with assent.[12]

What is this act of election? It is an act depending in part upon the intellect and in part upon the will. Aristotle speaks of it as: *appetitivus intellectus, vel appetitus intellectivus*.[13] In its fullest sense, it is nothing more than the complete act by which the will is determined, and it embraces both the deliberation of reason and the decision of the will. Reason and understanding are required for deliberation as just expounded and for judgment as to which means seem preferable. The will is required for assent to these means and for election; that is, for preferred choice of one of them.

But we have still to determine whether, considered in its own essence, the act by which deliberation comes to an end depends upon the intellect or the will. To decide this, we must observe that the substance of an act depends upon both its matter and its form. Now, among the acts of the soul, one which depends upon some lower power for its matter can at the same time have form and specification from a higher power, because the lower is always ordained to the higher. If, for example, a man performs an act of fortitude for the love of God, it is truly and materially an act of fortitude, but it is formally and therefore substantially an act of love. We can apply similar reasoning to the act of election. The understanding provides to some extent the matter of the act by proposing judgments for the will to accept. But the formal act of election is a movement of the soul toward the good which it chooses. Election, then, is substantially an act of the will.[14]

Such in its general lines is the structure of the human act. We see in it the intellect and will acting and reacting upon each other, but it is quite erroneous to confuse their roles within the act itself. They are continually crossing each other, but they never mix. This can be clearly seen if we distinguish spontaneous acts from commanded ones. An act of the will is either spontaneous, as when the will tends toward its end as such, or commanded, as when reason says: *Do this*. Voluntary acts are clearly in our power. Consequently, we are always able to issue such a command to ourselves.[15] What takes place in such a case? Reason may simply say: *This is what you should do*. Obviously in this case reason alone is at work. But reason may also issue the command: *Do this*. In this case it moves the will to will it. The serving of notice or "intimation" belongs to the intellect, but the motive element pertains to the will.[16]

Again, let us consider the operations of reason involved in a human act. If it is a question of the very exercise of the rational act, it can always be the object of a command; as when someone orders someone else to pay attention or to listen to reason. But if it is a question of the possible object of such an act, we have to distinguish carefully between two cases. On the one hand, the intellect can, on some question, simply apprehend a certain truth. This depends solely upon our natural light, and not at all upon our will. It is not in our free power to perceive or not to perceive the truth when we actually discover it. On the other hand, the intellect can give its assent to what it apprehends.[17] If, then, what it apprehends falls into the category of propositions to which by its very nature it must give its assent, for example, first principles, it is not in our power either to give or to refuse them our assent. If, on the contrary, the propositions apprehended do not so convince our intellect that it can yet affirm or deny them, and can at least suspend its refusal or consent, it is clear that in such cases the assent or the negation remains in our power and falls within the scope of our will.[18] In every case, it is the understanding alone which apprehends truths, which accepts or rejects them, and which gives orders, but the movement which it receives or transmits always comes from the will. All movement, therefore, remains voluntary, even when it seems to come from the intellect. All knowledge remains intellectual, even when it originates in a movement of the will.

2. HABITS

We have just defined human acts in themselves and, as it were, in the abstract, but it is not in the abstract that they occur. Concrete individuals perform them. These individuals, these men, are not pure substances, but have their accidents too. Each acting subject is not just a schematic agent theoretically constituted with reason and will. He is also influenced in his activity by certain ways of being which are proper to him. He is affected also by permanent dispositions, the principles of which are called habits and virtues. Let us first examine the nature of habits.

Man is a discursive being whose life must be of some duration if he is to attain his end. Now this duration is not that of an inorganic body whose being remains invariable throughout its whole course, but the duration of a living being. Man's efforts to attain his end are not reduced to nothingness but are inscribed in his name and leave their mark upon him. Man's soul as well as his body has a history. It conserves its past in order to enjoy and utilize it in a perpetual present. The most general form of this fixing of past experience is called habit. Habit, as St. Thomas thinks of it, is a quality, that is, not the very substance of man but a disposition added to his substance and modifying it. The characteristic which differentiates this disposition or habit from other species of quality is that it is a disposition of the subject in relation to its own nature. In other words, a being's habits determine the manner in which it realizes its own definition.

Hence no habit can be described without the qualification of good or bad figuring in its description. Now it is the form of a thing which defines a thing; and the form is not only the essence of a thing and its *raison d'être;* it is also its end. To say that habits determine how a being realizes its own definition is to say at the same time how it realizes its essence and how far it is from its proper end. If the habits of a being draw it close to the ideal type toward which it is tending, they are good habits. If, on the contrary, they draw it away from this ideal, they are bad habits. Their general definition is as follows: "habits are dispositions according to which a being is well or ill disposed." [19] Habits are not only qualities and accidents, but they are the qualities and accidents which lie closest to the nature of a thing, and which come closest to entering into its essence and integrating themselves into its definition.[20]

What conditions are required for a habit to develop? The first, and the one which basically implies all the rest, is a subject in potency to different determinations and in which several different principles can combine to bring about one of these determinations.[21] This means, for example, that God, who is totally in act, cannot be the subject of habits. Heavenly bodies, whose matter is totally and definitively fixed by their form, have not this indetermination which we regard as necessary for the birth of habits. Nor can the qualities of elementary bodies, which are necessarily and inextricably bound to their elements, provide the occasion for habits. Actually, the true subject of habits is a soul like that of man because it is comprised of an element of receptivity and potency.

It is the principle of a host of operations by the various faculties which it possesses and satisfies all the conditions required for their development.[22] But within the human soul itself we can determine with still more precision the ground in which they develop. They cannot reside in sensitive powers as such. These powers, considered independently of reason, are determined to their act by a kind of natural bent and have not that indetermination necessary for the development of habits. This leaves, then, only the intellect, in which habits can conveniently be placed. Only in it do we encounter that multiplicity of indeterminate powers capable of being combined and organized among themselves according to widely differing arrangements. And as it is, indeed, potency which provides a basis for habits, we must ultimately decide that they reside in that part of the mind called the possible intellect. The will, too, must be judged a subject of habits since it is a faculty of the rational soul with free indetermination based on the universality of reason itself.

We see, moreover, what is their nature and what very special place they hold in St. Thomas's anthropology. When we were examining the faculties of the soul, we necessarily dealt with them as something static and inorganic. But habits introduce a dynamic element of progress and organization into the study of these faculties. Taken in their most profound significance, habits in the Thomistic sense call for either progress or retrogression. They demand life within the human intellect, and, through it, in the entire soul. We say they "demand" life, because where all the conditions for the development of habits are present, their development is not only possible but necessary. Necessary, that is, if we are willing to concede to each nature all the instruments necessary for it to attain its end. Now, if the natural form necessarily attains its end by reason of the very determination which compels it toward a single operation, the intellectual form, by reason of its universality and indetermination, would never attain its end unless there were some complementary disposition to incline it to do so. Habits are just such complements of nature. They are super-added determinations which establish definite relations between the intellect and its objects or possible operations.[23] Thus any given intellect is *de facto* inseparable from all the habits enriching or degrading it. Habits are but so many self-provided instruments among which the intellect may always freely choose and over which it is finally the master. But it has only provided itself with them because it has had to acquire them in order to satisfy the conditions demanded by the proper nature of its operation.

If we set aside those which are but simple dispositions to being, like the aptitude of matter to receive form, we note that all habits are orientated in view of certain operations, either cognitive or voluntary. Some of them are in some sort natural to us, and as it were innate. This is the case with knowledge of first principles. It is as though our intellect was born with a natural disposition to know them from our first sense experience. Moreover, from the point of view of the individual, and not of the species, each of us is born with the beginnings of cognitive habits. Indeed, our sense organs, whose collaboration is so indispensable to the act of knowledge, predispose us to know well or poorly. The same is true for the will, with this difference, that in the case of the will it is no longer the habit itself that is already present in outline, but only principles which can constitute a habit as, for example, the principles of common law, sometimes called the seeds of the virtues. In the body, on the other hand, certain voluntary habits already exist in outline, because some men, by natural constitution and temperament, are at birth predisposed to kindness, chastity and other similar habits.

As a general rule, however, habits come less from natural dispositions than from acts. Sometimes a single act is enough to conquer the passivity of the power in which the habit develops. This is the case with an immediately evident proposition which is adequate to convince the intellect definitively, and to make it accept a certain conclusion permanently. Sometimes, on the contrary, and this is by far the most frequent case, many analogous and repeated acts are required in order to generate a habit in a power of the soul. Probable opinion, for example, does not prevail the first time, but it becomes habitual belief only when the agent intellect has impressed it upon the possible intellect by a great number of acts. And the possible intellect in its turn must go on repeating them for the benefit of the lower faculties, as, for example, when it wishes to fix such a belief in the memory. Thus the active power usually requires time in order completely to dominate the matter concerned. It is like fire which does not consume combustible material at once nor set it ablaze at the first try, but gradually overcomes all contrary dispositions and so assimilates it to itself.[24] Thus repetition of acts which pierces matter more and more completely with its form (or enters deeply into a power of the soul with some new disposition) progressively builds up a habit. So, too, does cessation of these acts or the performing of contrary acts destroy and corrupt it.[25]

3. GOOD AND EVIL. THE VIRTUES

If we know the nature of habits, we know the nature of virtues because virtues are habits which dispose us in a lasting way to perform good actions. We have said above that habits are dispositions either for better or for worse. Since a habit draws an individual either toward or away from his end and brings him into greater or less conformity to a given standard, we must distinguish between habits which dispose him to perform acts consistent with his nature and those which dispose him to perform acts not consistent with his nature. The former are good habits and therefore also virtues; the latter are bad habits and also vices.[26] But for a fuller definition of virtue, we have to be quite sure just what kind of acts are more consistent with human nature. Then we shall also know in what moral good and evil consist, and how to distinguish vice from virtue.

Operations and actions are what the beings are who perform them: *unaquaque res talem actionem producit, qualis est ipsa;* and the essence of things is always measured by their degree of being. Man, a deficient and imperfect being, must therefore perform incomplete and deficient operations. Hence good and evil are combined, in varying proportion, in his operations.[27]

The good in human actions can be looked at from four points of view. In the first place, human action falls into the genus *action;* and as every action is estimated by the perfection of the being who performs it, there is already in the very substance of every action an intrinsic value corresponding to a given degree of excellence and goodness. Secondly, actions derive good from their *species.* As the species of each action is determined by its object, it follows that an action is said to be good from the point of view of its species according as it is or is not applied to a suitable object.[28] Thirdly, actions are good or bad by reason of the *circumstances* which accompany them. A natural being does not receive its full perfection from its substantial form alone. Its form gives it its species. Its full perfection comes from its many accidents. These, in the case of man, are figure, color and so on. So, too, with an action. It not only draws its goodness from its species, but also from its many accidents. These accidents of an action are the circumstances without which the action is vitiated.[29] Fourthly and lastly, human action draws its goodness from its proper *end.* We have already said that the order of the good and of being are proportionate to each other. Now there exist beings which, as such, do not depend on any other being. To evaluate their operations, it is enough to consider in itself the being from which they issue. But there are beings which are dependent upon some other being. It is impossible to evaluate their operations without considering the cause upon which they depend.

Thus we have to consider the relations which human acts have with the first cause of all goodness, God.[30]

Let us be specific on this last point. In every voluntary action two acts are to be distinguished; namely, the interior act of the will and the exterior act. Each of these acts has its corresponding object. The object of the interior voluntary act is the end. The object of the exterior act is that toward which it is referred. Of these two acts, one must command the other. The exterior act receives its specification from the object which is its terminus or to which it is applied. The interior act of the will receives its specification from its end as from its proper object. What the will brings here imposes inevitably its form on what constitutes the exterior act. For the members are instruments the will uses in order to act, and exterior acts have morality only in the measure in which they are voluntary. This is why if we wish to go back to the highest principle which specifies acts as good and bad, we must conclude that human acts are formally specified by the end toward which the interior act of the will tends, and they are materially specified at the most by the object to which the exterior act is referred.[31]

But what must this end be? Dionysius gives the correct answer to this question. Man's good, he says,[32] is to be in accord with reason. And inversely, whatever is contrary to reason is evil. Each thing's good is what is suited to it in view of its form. Each thing's evil is whatever contradicts this form and tends, consequently, to destroy its order. Since man's form is his rational soul itself, every act conforming to reason must be called good, and every act contrary to it called evil.[33] Thus, when a human act includes something contrary to the order of reason, it falls by that very fact into the species of bad actions. In this way, for example, theft is a bad action because it consists in taking possession of another's goods. But it becomes obvious, too, that when the end or object of an act has no relation to the order of reason, as when someone picks up a wisp of straw from the ground, it must be described as morally indifferent.[34] If we consider each individual act which conforms to reason, we shall find that it does so insofar as it is ordered to an end and to a series of means which the reason, after some investigation, declares good. So, the many particular good acts which man does are an ensemble of acts ordered to their end and justifiable by reason.

Of all the conditions required for a human act to be morally good, the first and most important is that it be subordinate to its legitimate end. Now, as we have seen, the movement by which the will tends toward a certain end is called *intention*.[35] Thus it would seem that we are being led to what is essentially a moral doctrine of intention. There is some justification for this conclusion, provided we do not understand it in a narrow and exclusive sense. Taken in itself, the intention by which a will turns toward its end can be considered as the germ of the completed voluntary act. It is because I will the end that I will the means, that I deliberate, that I choose, that I act. As the intention is, so is the act it brings forth. It is good if the intention is good, evil if it is evil.

But act and intention are not good or evil in the same degree nor in the same way. When the intention is evil, the act is irremediably bad, because each one of its constitutent parts has been called into existence in the service of evil. When, however, the intention is good, such initial orientation of the will toward the good cannot fail to impregnate the entire act which follows, but it is not sufficient to define it. We cannot fairly give equal ranking to two acts of equally good intention if in one means or execution were faulty whereas they were not in the other. A moral act always gains by being inspired by a good intention. Even one that fails in execution, at least retains the merit of having meant well, and often merits more than it accomplishes. But a perfectly good moral act is still one which fully satisfies the demands of reason both in its end and in each of its parts; and not content to will good, realizes it.

Such being the nature of moral good, it is easy to see what is the nature of virtue. It consists essentially and primarily in a permanent disposition to act in conformity with reason. But the complexity of the human being necessarily makes our notion of its proper virtue quite involved. It is certain, of course, that the first principle of human acts is the reason. All other principles of human acts obey reason. If man were a pure spirit, or if the body to which his soul is united were completely docile, he would only have to see what he should do in order to do it. Thus Socrates' thesis would be valid, and there would only be intellectual virtues. But we are not pure spirits, and, since original sin, it is not even true that our body is in perfect submission. Hence, for man to act well, not only must his reason be well disposed by the habit of intellectual virtue, but his appetite, too, or his faculty of desiring, must be well disposed by the habit of moral virtue. Thus moral virtue must be distinguished from intellectual virtue and added to it. And just as the appetite is the principle of human acts in the measure in which it participates in reason, so moral virtue is human virtue in the measure in which it is in conformity with reason.[36]

Thus, it is as completely impossible to reduce one of these two orders to the other as it is to isolate them. Moral virtue cannot do without intellectual virtue. Moral virtue must determine a good act. Now an act supposes election; and, as we have seen in our analysis of the structure of the human act, election supposes the deliberation and judgment of reason. So intellectual virtues, which are not directly related to the action can, indeed, dispense with moral virtues. But prudence cannot do so. It must terminate in precise acts. The intellectual virtue of prudence does not merely determine what should be done in general. For this task, the help of moral virtues would not be necessary. But its action goes right down to the detail of particular cases. Here it is no longer a pure spirit that judges; it is a composite of soul and body. The person in whom concupiscence is the master, judges his own desires to be good, even when such a judgment contradicts the universal judgment of reason. It is to neutralize such sophistries of passion that man must be strengthened with moral habits, thanks to which a sane judging of the end will become in some way connatural to him.[37]

Four intellectual virtues stand out as most important: understanding, knowledge, wisdom and prudence. The first three are purely intellectual and are arranged in order under wisdom as the lower powers of the soul are under the rational soul. Truth can be either evident and known *per se* or deduced and known mediately. Truth known *per se* and immediately plays the role of principle. The immediate knowledge of principles at the very moment of sense experience is the first habit of the intellect and its first virtue. It is the first permanent disposition which the intellect contracts and the first perfection with which it is enriched. Accordingly the name understanding or intelligence is given to this virtue which helps the intellect with its knowledge of immediately evident truths or principles.

If, on the other hand, we consider truths not immediately evident, but deduced and concluded, they no longer depend upon the intellect, but on the reason. Now reason can tend toward conclusions which are last in a given genus. It can tend toward them provisionally. It can also tend toward conclusions which are absolutely last—the highest conclusions of all. In the first case we are dealing with knowledge (or science); in the second, with wisdom. Since a science is a virtue which puts reason into a state in which it can judge certain objects of knowledge soundly, there can be and must be many sciences in a human mind. But since wisdom, on the contrary, bears on last causes and on the object which is both the most perfect and most universal, there can be but one object of knowledge in this order, and consequently but one wisdom. Hence these three virtues (understanding, knowledge and wisdom) are not distinguished merely by juxtaposition, but they fall into hierarchical order. Science or knowledge, the habit of conclusions deduced from principles, depends upon understanding, which is the habit of principles. Both science and understanding depend upon wisdom, which contains and rules them, because it judges not only understanding and its principles, but also science and its conclusions: *convenienter judicat et ordinat de omnibus, quia judicium perfectum et universale haberi non potest, nisi per resolutionem ad primas causas.*[38]

Thanks to these three virtues, the possible intellect, which at first was rather like a blank tablet on which nothing was yet written, acquires a series of progressive determinations which make possible for it the operations of knowledge. But thus far it is only capable of performing its operation. In order to bring it nearer to its perfection, there must be a supplementary determination rendering it, not merely capable of knowing, but capable of using virtues which it has just acquired. It is not enough that man should think; he must live, and live rightly. Now to live rightly, is to act rightly. To act rightly, we must take into account not only what we ought to do, but how we ought to do it. It is not enough merely to decide to act well. We must also decide to act according to reason, not merely by blind impulse or passion.

The principle of this kind of deliberation is not provided by the intellect, but by the end which the will seeks. Ends are, in human acts, what principles are in the speculative sciences. To will the fitting end depends once more on a virtue, but this time on a moral virtue not an intellectual one. Once the end is willed, it is an intellectual virtue which will deliberate and choose the means suited to that end. Thus there must be an intellectual virtue which will put reason into a state where it can fittingly determine the means to the end. This virtue is prudence, *recta ratio agibilium,* and it is a virtue necessary for right living.[39]

The moral virtues introduce into the will the same perfections which the intellectual virtues introduce into knowledge. Some moral virtues regulate the content and nature of our operations themselves, independently of our personal dispositions at the moment of acting. This is the particular case of justice, which assures the moral value and rectitude of all operations in which ideas of what is due and not due are implied. Thus, for example, the operation of buying and selling supposes the acknowledgment or rejection of a debt to a neighbor, and depends upon the virtue of justice.

Other moral virtues bear upon the qualities of acts, considered in relation to the one performing them. Thus, they deal with the interior dispositions of the agent at the moment of acting. They deal, in a word, with passions. If the agent is drawn by passion toward an act contrary to reason, he has to call on that virtue whose particular function is to restrain and check passion; namely, the virtue of temperance. If the agent, far from being drawn into action by some passion, is actually prevented from acting by fear of danger or of effort or the like, he needs another moral virtue to strengthen him in the resolutions his reason dictates. This is the virtue of fortitude.[40] These three moral virtues, together with one intellectual virtue—prudence—are commonly known as principal or *cardinal* virtues. They alone imply both the faculty to act aright and the actual accomplishing of the good act. They alone, consequently, perfectly fulfil the definition of virtue.[41]

Thus we arrive gradually at the notion of virtue in its most perfect form. It owes its quality of moral good to the rule of reason, and operations and passion are its matter: "moral virtue derives its goodness from the rule of reason." [42] It is this, too, that makes moral and intellectual virtues consist in a just mean. The act regulated by a moral virtue is in conformity with right reason; and what reason does is to assign a just mean, equally removed from excess and defect in each given case. Sometimes it happens that the mean fixed by reason is the mean of the thing itself, as in the case of justice which regulates operations relating to external acts, and must assign to each his due, neither more nor less. Sometimes, on the contrary, it happens that the mean fixed by reason is not the mean of the thing itself, but one that is a mean in relation to us. It is thus with all the other moral virtues bearing not on operations but on passions. Temperance and fortitude have to take into account internal dispositions which are not the same in all men, nor even in the same individual at different times. They fix a just mean in conformity with reason, in relation to us and to the passions affecting us. It is the same with the intellectual virtues. Every virtue follows the determination of a measure and a good. Now the good of an intellectual virtue is truth, and the measure of truth is the thing. Our reason attains truth when what it says exists does actually exist, and when what it says does not exist does not exist. It errs by excess when it affirms the existence of what does not exist, and by defect when it denies the existence of what does exist. Truth, therefore, is the just mean, determined by the thing itself. And it is this very truth which confers moral excellence upon a virtue.[43]

Voluntary acts dictated by practical reason, habits, and especially virtuous habits: these are the internal principles which regulate our moral activity. We have now to deal with the principles regulating this activity from without, that is, with laws.

4. LAWS

The preceding considerations tend to make us think of moral activity as totally dependent upon itself, or, to use a non-Thomistic expression, as entirely *autonomous*. Now Thomist morality is unquestionably autonomous. But if we are to understand it properly, we must also consider the laws which govern man's will, even though this means that we shall have afterwards to explain how the will can be master of itself when external legislation imperiously prescribes its end.

First of all, what is a law? It is a rule which prescribes or forbids an action. It is the rule of an activity. If this is so, then the notion of law must be universal in extension. Wherever anything is done, there ought to be a rule in conformity to which this thing is done, and, consequently, a law. Yet a definition like this is incomplete and vague, and we must try to make it more precise.

Actually, when we try to get hold of the essential meaning of the word "law," we find, beyond the idea of mere rule, the much more profound notion of obligation. Whenever any activity is subjected to a rule, that rule becomes, so to speak, the measure of its legitimacy. The activity is attached to the rule as to a principle, and is obliged to respect it. Now, with what principle which regulates activities are we at present familiar, other than reason? It is everywhere reason which is the rule and measure of what is done. If law does not in fact go beyond this rule of reason, it at least seems to be bound by it.[44] Law is a determination that is at the very least based on custom and is in accord with universal conscience. The prescriptions of an unreasonable tyrant can usurp the name, but they can never be true laws. Where reason is wanting, there is neither law nor equity but sheer iniquity.[45]

Moreover, a command or order from reason is not enough to constitute law. This order must be directed to a determined end, other than our purely individual ends. Indeed, to say that law is a prescription of reason determining what ought to be done is to link law with practical reason, whose proper duty it is to prescribe what acts should be performed. But this practical reason, in its turn, depends upon a principle which controls it and according to which it rules itself. It only prescribes a given act with a view to leading us to a given end. Consequently, if there exists an end common to all our acts, that end constitutes the first principle on which all the decisions of practical reason depend. It is not hard to discover this principle. A being which acts rationally must pursue its own good; and the good which each of its actions seeks, beyond the particular ends which they realize, is the supreme good. This supreme good would satisfy man fully if only he could take possession of it. Such possession would dispense with everything else.[46] We can assert, then, even before we have fully determined the object it pursues, that the will sees, across and beyond its many particular acts, one single end, which is beatitude. Every law, as a prescription of practical reason, is the rule for some action which is ordered for the attaining of happiness.

Let us add one last condition to these determinations, a condition which seems at first rather external, but which constitutes an important element in the definition of law. Since law aims essentially at the realization of good, without reservation of any kind, it cannot restrict itself to the good of particular individuals. What it prescribes is absolute good, the common good, and consequently, the good of a community. This is why the authority required for the legitimate establishing of law can only be possessed by someone entrusted with the interests of a community, or by this community itself. It is not simply the practical reason decreeing what has to be done with a view to happiness that is at the origin of law. Indeed the individual's own reason is constantly telling him what he must do to be happy, and its orders are scarcely laws. Rather, it is practical reason decreeing what the individual must do with a view to the good of the community of which he is a part. The people, or the people's representative invested with regular powers to lead his community toward its normal end, alone have the qualifications to establish laws and to promulgate them.[47]

What is true of a people is true of every community of beings ruled with a view to their common good by a sovereign whose decisions are dictated by reason. We shall have as many laws as there are communities of this kind. The first, and the most vast of all, is the universe. All beings created by God and maintained in existence by His will, can be regarded as one huge society in which all of us are members, along with animals, and even with things. There is not a single creature, animate or inanimate, which does not act in conformity with certain ends. Animals and things are subject to these rules and tend toward their ends without knowing them. Man, on the contrary, is conscious of them, and his moral justice consists in accepting them voluntarily. All the laws of nature, all the laws of morality or of society ought to be considered as so many particular cases of one single law, divine law. Now, God's rule for the government of the universe is, like God Himself, necessarily eternal. Thus the name *eternal law* is given to this first law, sole source of all others.[48]

Man, as a rational creature, has the strict duty of knowing what eternal law exacts of him and of conforming to it. This might be an insoluble problem, were this law not in some way written in his very substance, so that he has only to observe himself attentively in order to discover it there. In us, as in every thing, the inclination which draws us toward certain ends is the unmistakable mark of what eternal law demands of us. Since it is eternal law that makes us what we are, we have only to yield to the legitimate inclinations of our nature in order to obey it. Eternal law, thus shared by each one of us, and which we find written in our own nature, is called *natural law*.[49] What are the prescriptions of this law?

The first and most universal of all is that which all living beings, in yielding to it declare: *do good and avoid evil*. This almost seems to be a truism, but it records the least contestable and most universal experience. It is a fact that every living being moves under the impulse of its desires or its aversions. What we call good is really only the object of a desire, and what we call evil the object of an aversion. If we suppose an object which all desire, it would be by definition Absolute Good taken in itself. To say that we must do good and avoid evil is not arbitrarily to decree a moral law; it is merely to read a natural law which is written in the very substance of beings and to bring to light the hidden spring of all their operations. We have to do it, because it is our nature to do it. Such a precept is but a verification of fact.

Granted this, it is clear that the precepts of natural law correspond exactly with our natural inclinations and that their order is the same. Man is, to begin with, a being like all others. More particularly, he is a living being, like all other animals. Finally, by the privilege of his nature, he is a rational being. Thus it is that three great natural laws bind him, each in its own way.

First, man is a being. As such, he wishes to conserve his being, that is, he wishes to conserve himself by making sure of the integrity of whatever belongs by right to his nature. What we commonly call "the instinct of self-preservation" is but a statement of the following law: each tends with all his might, and must tend, toward whatever can conserve his life or protect his health. To tend to persevere in his being is, accordingly, the first precept of natural law to which man is subject.

The second precept embraces all those which bind him by the fact that he is an animal and exercises its functions: to reproduce himself, to raise his children, and other similar natural obligations. The third devolves upon him as a rational being and enjoins upon him the task of seeking what is good according to the order of reason. To live in society in order to unite the efforts of all and help one another; to seek truth in the realm of the natural sciences or, what is better, in what concerns the highest intelligible, God; correlatively, not to injure those with whom we are called to live; to avoid ignorance and to do what we can to dissipate it. These are the binding prescriptions of natural law, which is but one aspect of the eternal law willed by God.[50]

Thus understood, natural law is literally and indelibly written on the fleshy tablets of the heart. We may well wonder how it comes about that all men do not live in the same way. It is because there is between natural law and the deeds of men a third order of precepts, those from *human law*. What is their *raison d'être*?

So long as it is a question of formulating the most general and most abstract principles of conduct, men easily agree. That we must do good, avoid evil, acquire learning, avoid ignorance and obey all the dictates of reason, no one doubts. But what good is, or evil, how we are to act so as to satisfy reason, these things present the real difficulties. Between the universal principles of natural law and the infinitely complex detail of the particular acts which should be in conformity with it, an abyss opens up which no individual reflection can cross by itself and which it is the particular mission of human law to close.

From this arise two important consequences touching the nature of this law. First, it is clear that human law has no principle of its own to invoke. It is strictly limited to defining ways of applying natural law. When princes or States legislate, they only deduce from the universal principle of natural law the particular consequences necessary for life in society. Secondly, it is clear, through the preceding, that he who spontaneously follows natural law is more or less predisposed to acknowledge human law and to receive it willingly. When human law is promulgated, it embarrasses the vicious or rebellious man, but the just man conforms to it with so perfect a spontaneity that it is as though, so far as he is concerned, civil law does not exist.[51]

Human laws aim at prescribing particular acts which natural law imposes upon individuals for the common good, and they only bind in the measure in which they are just, that is, to the extent they satisfy their own definition. Even when they are just, they may be hard to bear and demand difficult sacrifices from the people, but there is still a strict duty to obey them. If on the other hand, the State or the prince establishes laws solely to satisfy their own cupidity or their thirst for glory, or if they promulgate such laws without the authority to do so, or if they distribute the burdens of the State among the citizens unfairly, or if the burdens they try to impose are excessive and disproportionate to the good which is sought, then they are unjust laws and no one is bound in conscience to obey them. There can, of course, be a temporary obligation to observe them in order to avoid scandal and disorder, but sooner or later they must be modified. Human laws in any way contrary to God's rights are not to be obeyed under any pretext because, as Scripture says, it is better to obey God than men.[52]

The true nature of laws—natural, human or divine—permits us to understand the exact sense to be attributed to the notion of sanction. For too often rewards and punishments are considered to be accidental spurs to moral progress, like the expedients used by legislators to encourage men to good or to turn them from evil. The spectacle of human law and social order in which sanctions play so important a role, as we have seen, obscures their true nature and the place they occupy in universal order. They lose their legitimate significance and by the same token find themselves justly excluded from the moral order by all consciences which recognize as good only actions performed for the pure love of the good.

The true relation of an act to the sanction attached to it best appears in the realm of purely natural beings; that is, beings which act in virtue of their natural form and not of a will. We have said above that such beings already obey a rule, although they do not know it. It is written, in some way, in their own substance. They do not act, they are acted upon. Now the very fact that they obey the nature God gave them, and act in conformity to it, puts these beings deprived of knowledge in a situation similar to that of rational persons governed by a law. This universal legislation, promulgated by God for nature, is expressed by the Psalmist: "He hath made a decree and it shall not pass away."[53] But it happens that animals and things, by reason of the situation and role which is theirs in the general economy of the universe, are prevented from satisfying the demands of their nature, from acting as nature would have them act, and consequently, from attaining their end. The result is that they suffer in their operations and substance, die and disintegrate. The death of the animal or the destruction of the inanimate object are not accidental complements of the disorder which prevents their acting according to their nature. It is not even a consequence of it. To put it exactly, death or destruction is the state in which the animal or thing is placed by the very fact of this disorder; death and destruction actually give order to the disorder which caused them. Nothing escapes law. When something claims to be escaping law, it is actually destroying itself in the measure that it succeeds in doing so. In this way is attested the infrangible character of the legislation which it claims to violate.

In this permanence of bodies which observe the law, and this destruction of bodies which break it, we see in a concrete and, as it were, material way, all that is essential in moral sanction. Man, like the rest of the universe, is subject to divine law. He is at the same time endowed with a will, thanks to which it is up to him whether he submits to this order or revolts against it. But whether this order exists or does not, whether effects are realized or not in the universe, these things are not up to him. God can leave it to the will of man to ensure respect for the law in certain points, but not to abandon the law itself to his caprice, because law is an expression of divine order. The will that submits to law and the one that sets itself against it may temporarily appear to be removed from the consequences of their acts. But ultimately they must come to a state where they find themselves face to face with eternal law.

It is the role of sanction to place them there. The only difference between the consequences of natural law and sanction is that the first result naturally from observing or transgressing the law, the second (i.e., sanction) is the effect of a will replying to the act of a will. When bodies are in order, good follows necessarily from any activity that is in conformity with natural law. But in the case of the will, this good is freely conferred by God on the man who has freely observed the natural law. The evil which necessarily befalls disordered bodies is, in the case of a bad will, freely inflicted by God on the man who freely rebelled against order. It is this willed character of reward and punishment which makes sanctions properly so called of the good and evil suffered by individuals.[54] But this should not make us forget that, in either case, there is nothing more in a sanction than strict observance of the law, the satisfaction found in order, and the realization of a perfect balance between acts and their consequences. To the extent that a man has not willed to fulfil the divine law, he will have ultimately to submit to it, and herein will lie his punishment.[55]

Understood in this pure and strict sense, sanction does not destroy the autonomy of morality. Reward or punishment do not confer on an act its morality or immorality. The act I do is not good because it will have its recompense, but it will have its recompense because it is good. Similarly, it is not to avoid punishment that I do good. But if I do good, I shall avoid punishment, just as I have only to do good to be recompensed. To be sure, there is no intention of denying that hope of a reward or fear of a penalty are efficacious aids to moral progress. But man stands in relation to divine law as the citizen to civil and human law. In order not to suffer the restraint of law, he has only to embrace it. The good we first willed because of something else, or because of what we thought was something else, we gradually come to love and will for itself, as the universal good and universal order in which our own good is steadfastly assured. It is in this that the liberty of the children of God ultimately consists, for they obey Him as a Father whose loving law only binds them for their own good.

CHAPTER II

LOVE AND THE PASSIONS

AN ANALYSIS of the general principles of a moral philosophy of this kind is not enough to give an accurate idea of what it is like. It is the application of these principles to the concrete details of moral experience which most concerns St. Thomas. This becomes quite evident as we watch him working out his treatise: "General remarks about moral matters," he writes, "are useful because actions are about particular things." [1] A sound comment like this places both the author and his historian face to face with an insoluble problem. Since the details of moral problems are infinite, St. Thomas had himself to choose from among them. We, in our turn, have even to make a further choice from among his selections. Besides this difficulty, there is another concerning the order to be followed in such an analysis. We have only two methods at our disposal: that of his commentary on the *Nichomachaean Ethics* which adopts Aristotle's order entirely directed toward the morality of the city-state, and that of the *Summa Theologiae* in which the moral virtues are integrated with the Gifts of the Holy Ghost. We are inevitably condemned, then, to some kind of compromise in presenting these moral problems. But we can at least try to say nothing that St. Thomas himself has not already said.

When the moralist comes to discuss concrete cases, he comes up against the fundamental fact that man is a being moved by his passions. The study of the passions, therefore, must precede any discussion of moral problems, in which we will continually be encountering the passions as the matter, as it were, on which the virtues are exercised. These are "human" factors, in the highest sense, since passions belong to man as a unified composite of soul and body. A purely spiritual substance like an angel cannot experience passions, but the soul, which is the form of the body, necessarily experiences repercussions to the profound changes which the body undergoes. Inversely, since it is the soul that moves the body, it can be the principle of changes which the body must undergo. We can, then, distinguish the passions according to their source. *Corporeal* passions arise from the action of the body on the soul, which is the form. *Animal* passions arise from the actions of the *anima* on the body which it moves. In either case, the passion ultimately affects the soul. An incision made upon a member causes a sensation of pain in the soul: this is a corporeal passion. The thought of danger causes in the body the disturbances that accompany fear: this is an animal passion. But we all know from experience that disturbances in the body have repercussions in the soul, so that ultimately every passion is a modification of the soul resulting from its union with the body. [2]

In all this, we have as yet but an approximation to passion. Strictly speaking, all we have said applies also to sensations, for they too are modifications of the soul resulting from its union with the body. Nevertheless, we do know that if sensations are, in what concerns their matter, passions of the soul, they make up a class of facts quite distinct from what we call the passions. The latter are not knowledge, but disturbed states which arise within us when we perceive objects which more or less directly concern the life and well-being of the body. Passions, properly so called, affect the soul in its function of animator of the body at the point where it is most actively engaged in this function. Just as will accompanies the intellectual activity of the soul, so a more modest form of desire accompanies its animating activity. It is the sensitive appetite, which is called sensuality, and which is but the desire that is born from the perceiving of an object which is of interest to the life of the body. It is this lowest form of desire which is the seat of the passions. They are its intensest movements; and it is through them that man experiences most strongly, sometimes most tragically, that he is not a pure Intelligence but the union of a soul and a body.

In studying this form of the appetite, we noted the dual nature of its reactions, according as it found itself face to face with useful or harmful objects. Its behavior with reference to the first forms what we called the concupiscible, with reference to the second, the irascible. Passions fall naturally into two groups according to this basic distinction. The first of them all we call love.

The inadequacy of language to express the complexity of the real is nowhere more noticeable than in the analysis of the life of the soul. Love, the root of all the passions, is many-sided. It changes its aspect according to the various activities of the soul with which it can be associated. Fundamentally, it is a modification of the human appetite by some desirable object. This modification consists in the fact that the appetite takes pleasure in this object. Such pleasure or complacency is, so to speak, an immediate experiencing of natural affinity, of the fact that the living being and the object it is meeting are somehow complementary. It is this complacency (*complacentia*) which constitutes love itself as a passion. Scarcely is it produced, when this passion arouses a movement of the appetite toward a real, and not merely intentional, taking possession of the object agreeable to it. Such a movement is the desire that is born of love. If it reaches its ends, the terminus of this movement is repose in the possession of the object loved. Such repose is joy, the satisfying of desire.

It is here in the order of vital and organic desire that the passion of love, in the proper sense of the term, is encountered. It is only by extension that the name is generalized to include a higher order, that of the will.[3] Wherever the appetite moves toward a good there is love, but its nature varies according to the nature of the movement concerned.[4] Let us first look at inanimate things. Even these desire whatever agrees with their nature. At least, it is as though they desired it, because someone does desire it for them. In creating them, God endowed them with active natures, capable of operating for some end which they do not know but which He does. This natural bent of all beings to follow their nature is natural appetite. We can give the name *natural love* to this selective affinity (*connaturalitas*) which inclines a thing toward what suits it. The corporeal world does not know the love that moves it, but Love knows the world which He moves, because He loves it. He loves it with the same love with which He loves His own perfection. We are not, here, in the order of passion, strictly so called.

Above these desires which are lived are desires which are felt and which animals experience because they have powers of perception. Thus the sensitive appetite is the seat of a sort of "sense love." But just as sensation is necessarily determined by the object, this love is necessarily determined by sensation. It is a passion properly so called, but poses no moral problem because it does not offer any matter for choice. Man experiences this passion of love in his capacity of animal, but in a quite different way, because in him it stands in relation to a higher appetite, the *rational* or *intellectual appetite*, which we have called *will*. The complacency of a will in its object is called *intellectual love*. Like the will which experiences it, this love is free. Intellectual love is the soul's complacency in a good decreed by a free judgment of the reason. Here we are in the order of the intellect and immaterial where it is no longer a question of a passion properly so called. Passions, however, remain in man, and in him alone are they matter of morality. As animal, man experiences all the passions of the sensitive appetite; as endowed with reason, he dominates this appetite and these passions by free judgments. Hence human sensuality differs from that of the animal in that it is capable of obeying reason and therefore participates in liberty. Man's love, like all his passions, is free. If it is not actually so, it can and must become free. And so it is that the passion of love poses moral problems.

Because love has dealings with reason it is diversified in man according to several aspects, each with its special name. First, there must be some way of indicating that a rational being can freely choose the object of its love; accordingly we speak of *dilection*. The object which is thus freely chosen can be desired for its very great value, a value which renders it eminently worthy of being loved; the sentiment experienced in this case is called *charity*. Finally, we can try to express the fact that a love has lasted sufficiently long to have become rather like a permanent disposition of the soul, a habit; in this case love is called *friendship*.[5] It continues to be true, however, that all these affections of the soul are but so many variations of love. It can be seen, then, that this single notion of love extends to many situations and many moral problems. This brings us into the inexhaustible order of particular acts.

There is, however, one general distinction which makes it possible to bring some order into all this multiplicity. The distinction arises from the nature of friendship which we have just distinguished as a variety of love. A man can be said to love wine, but he cannot ordinarily be said to have friendship with wine. This difference in linguistic usage indicates a difference in the feelings concerned. I love wine for the pleasure it gives me. But if I love a person only for the advantages I receive, can I truly call myself his friend? We have, accordingly, to distinguish between the love of a person and the love of a thing. The former goes straight to the person; it loves him for himself because his great worthiness entitles him to be loved. It is this kind of love that is called friendship. This, indeed, is love, pure and simple.

Actually, love consists in taking pleasure in the good. Love, pure and simple, takes pleasure in a good because taken in itself it is good. Other love is not addressed to a good as good and in itself, but only as good for another. It is called love of concupiscence (*amor concupiscentiae*) because the other for whom we covet the good is ourself. Since this love is not directed to the good directly and for itself it is subordinate to the former and only in a secondary way deserves to be called love.[6] Hence we see already St. Thomas's lofty notion of friendship. To be sure, anyone may love the pleasures and advantages he draws from the love of his friend. But in this case he is coveting rather than loving. Such covetousness or cupidity may go along with friendship, but is not itself friendship.[7]

What, then, is the cause of love? First, as has just been said, the good, because our appetite for something or our tendency toward something finds in the good the full satisfaction that makes it take pleasure and repose therein. Added to the good, however, is that other object of love, the beautiful. Between the good and the beautiful, both inseparable from being, there is only a distinction of reason. In the good, the will is at rest. In the beautiful, it is the sensible or intellectual apprehension which is at rest. Every one of us has often experienced this in the case of sight and hearing, the two senses which reason uses. The perception of colors or of sounds and harmonies is accompanied by the feeling that the perception is itself its own end. The beautiful is that thing the very seeing and hearing of which is the totally sufficient reason for seeing and hearing it. Moreover, it is also true that what is known by way of the understanding is the complete justification for the act of knowing it: "It pertains to the nature of the beautiful, that our vision of it finds in it its repose."[8]

Two misconceptions appear to have obscured this profound notion of the beautiful in the mind of scholars, and so to have prevented the full development of an aesthetic such as we might rightly look for from them. First, we must avoid confusing the finality of an apprehension with the finality of knowledge. Knowledge need not be last in the order of knowing for its apprehension to be so. When A. N. Whitehead speaks of "the divine beauty of Lagrange's equations" he does not mean that such equations occupy the same place in the structure of knowledge as the notion of God. What he means is that quite apart from what these equations teach us, they do offer the understanding the object of an apprehension so perfect that, *as apprehension,* it leaves nothing to be desired. This is the concrete meaning of the frequently quoted expression: beauty is the splendor of truth. Literally, this is nothing but a brilliant metaphor. But in a broad sense, it means that certain truths present themselves in so bare a form, so free from mixture of any kind, that they offer thought the rare joy of a pure apprehension of truth. Sensible beauty is of such a nature. Fair colors, beautiful forms, beautiful sounds fill to overflowing the expectation and power of sight and hearing in offering them sensibles so pure in their essence that their perception becomes an end in itself and leaves no more to be desired.

From this, we have that other definition of beauty, no less well known than the preceding: "that which on being seen, pleases." [9] As a definition it is true, but it contributes to the second misconception we should try to avoid. Beautiful colors and beautiful forms are those which are pleasing to sight. But it is not enough that the sight of them please for them to be beautiful. There is no aesthetic joy whose cause is not in the beauty of the object. We know now in what this beauty consists. The joy it gives is a joy *sui generis,* the distinctive quality of which we all know from experience. This is the radiance with which certain perfect acts of knowing are surrounded, and which confers on certain acts of sensible knowledge the very character of contemplation. Then too is born the love of beauty, the complacency of a knowing faculty in an object in which the act which apprehends it finds, along with its ultimate contentment, its perfect repose.

Whether it is a question of the beautiful or the good, love presupposes knowledge of the object loved. It is, therefore, the sight of sensible beauty or good that is at the source of sensible love. Similarly, the spiritual contemplation of beauty or good is at the principle of spiritual love.[10] Nevertheless, love is not measured by knowledge. We can love perfectly an object very imperfectly known. It is enough that knowledge offer it to love, just as it is, for love to take possession of it as though it were a whole. Love loves what it does not yet know for the love of what it does know of it. Who is there who has not experienced what it is to love a science when, in the first enthusiasm of discovery, love hurls thought upon a knowledge which it already loves in its entirety and wishes therefore to know in its entirety? And how would perfect love of God be possible if man could only love in proportion to what he knows? [11]

Knowledge is actually the principle or source of love rather than its cause. We might say, perhaps, that it is a necessary condition for it. The cause properly speaking of love lies in the relation between the lover and the loved. This relation itself is of two kinds. When a being lacks something and meets what it lacks, it covets it. Love of concupiscence arises then out of the fact that two beings are complementary, or to speak in technical fashion, out of the fact that one is in potency what the other is in act. But sometimes two beings meet and are both in act and in the same relation. This is so when an artist meets an artist or a scholar a scholar. There is a specific community of form or resemblance between them: *convenientia in forma*. In this case there is usually established a love of friendship. We say, usually, because we must not forget the extreme complexity of situations of this kind. The first love of all, that is, interested love which each has for himself, underlies all other loves. In principle, artists love artists, but a virtuoso does not much love another virtuoso who is to play in the same concert.[12]

Thus defined, love presupposes no other passion; but the other passions all presuppose love. Love underlies each of them. Indeed, every passion requires either a movement toward some object or repose in some object. Hence every passion presupposes this connaturality which begets friendship or this complementariness which begets covetousness or cupidity. In both cases the necessary and sufficient condition of love is present. Hence it can happen and frequently does happen that a passion, admiration for example, contributes to the birth of love. But it is because, just as one good can be the cause of another, one love can be the cause of another love.[13]

The most immediate and most general of the effects of love is the union between the lover and the loved. An effective union too, which extends even to the real possession of the loved by the lover when it is a question of love of concupiscence. It is a union of feeling, and purely affective, if it is a question of love of friendship wherein one wishes the other the good he wishes himself. This second union is no less intimate for being spiritual than is the first. On the contrary, to will for another what we will for ourselves, to love another for himself as we love ourselves for ourselves is to treat the beloved as another self. It is to make an *alter ego* of him. It is no longer just a union like that of the knower with the thing known that is at stake here. That union was effected by means of the species and its resemblance to the object. But love, as it were, makes two things become a single thing. The unitive power of knowledge is less than that of love.[14]

To appreciate the closeness of this union, it is well to observe the curious tranference of personalities which naturally accompanies love. In some way the personalities can be said to pass into each other. The beloved is as it were in the lover, and the lover in the beloved by knowledge and by desire. By knowledge, for the beloved rests in the thought of the one who loves him; and in his turn the latter never grows weary of listing in thought the perfections of the beloved. So the Holy Ghost, who is Divine Love,[15] is said to "search even the deep things of God." (I Cor., II, 10.)

Of human love it can also be said that it seeks to penetrate by thought to the heart of what it loves. And so too is it in the realm of desires. It can be seen in the joy of the lover in presence of what he loves. Let the beloved be absent and the good wishes of his friend accompany him, or the desire of his lover pursues him, depending on whether he loves him in friendship or concupiscence. There is no juster epithet than *intimate* to characterize this invisceration of the beloved in the lover. Indeed do we not speak of the "bowels of charity"? And this is exactly what we mean. But the lover is no less intimately in the beloved. If he covets him, he will not rest satisfied until he has taken perfect possession. If he loves him in friendship, it is no longer in himself that the lover lives but in the one he loves. Whatever good or evil befalls one of two friends, befalls the other as well. The joys and sorrows of one are the other's too. For two to have but one will, *eadem velle*, this is true friendship.

And how could it be otherwise? We have reasoned as though the lover was in the beloved *or* conversely. It is *and* conversely that we should say. In love of friendship, the lover is the beloved and the beloved the lover, so that in rendering love for love, they are doubly the one in the other and the other in the one. Perfect love allows but one life to subsist for two beings. Each can speak of his "self" and his "other self." [16]

Another way to put it is to say that love is ecstatic. For a "me" to be in ecstasy is to be transported out of itself. Ordinarily what is designated by this term is the state of a faculty of knowing elevated by God to the understanding of objects that are beyond its reach. But it can also be applied to the state of an insane man who is also said to be "out of himself" or "out of his mind." The case of love is rather different. Although this passion disposes thought toward a kind of ecstasy, since the lover loses himself in meditation upon the beloved, any ecstatic quality in love pertains rather to the will. We already see it in the love of concupiscence in which the lover, not content with the good he has, transports his will out of himself to attain the good he covets. But it is more apparent in the love of friendship. The affection we have for our friends simply ceases to concern ourselves. It goes out from us. The friend wills nothing but the good of his friend, does nothing but what is good for his friend, takes care of his friend, provides for his friend. In brief, friendship takes us out of ourselves and is ecstatic by definition.[17]

When love is thus tensely directed toward the object loved, it seeks naturally to exclude all that can stand in the way of its attaining it, or if it possesses it already, that might threaten its possession. Thus does jealousy arise, that complex sentiment in which love blends with hatred but of which, when all is said and done, love is the cause. In love of concupiscence there is nothing more common than the jealousy of the husband who wants his wife for himself alone, or of the ambitious man who is jealous of every rival capable of disputing his place. But even friendship knows jealousy. Who is not aroused in indignation against those whose acts or words threaten the reputation of their friend? And when we read in John (II, 17): "The zeal of thy house hath eaten me up," do we not see that this zeal is a holy jealousy ceaselessly occupied in correcting evil committed against God, or failing this, in deploring it? [18]

Taken in itself, love is not necessarily that destructive passion which the poets have so often described. Quite the contrary, it is natural, and therefore beneficial, to desire something we lack in order to attain our perfection. Love of what is good can only improve the lover. The ravages produced by love arise from two causes, neither of which is a necessary consequence of love. Sometimes love is deceived in its object; it mistakes an evil for a good. Again, even when the love is genuine, it is so violent that the organic disturbances accompanying it threaten the body's equilibrium. Normally it is not thus. Love usually begets tenderness in the heart of the lover, delight in the beloved's presence, listlessness and fervent desire in his absence. The nature of the passion of love demands that certain organic modifications accompany these various sentiments but their intensity follows that of the passion. They have, therefore, nothing of the pathological about them unless the passion itself be unregulated.[19]

Such is love, that universal force which we find everywhere in nature by its works, since whatever acts only acts with a view to an end, and since this end is, for each being, the good which it loves and desires. It is therefore manifest that, whatever action a being performs, it is moved by some kind of love in performing it.[20]

The contrary of love is hate. Just as love is the consonance or accord of the appetite and its object, hate is dissonance or discord between them. Hate is a rejection of what is antipathetic and harmful. As love has the good for its object, hate has evil.[21] This is why hate has love as its cause, for we hate the contrary of what we love. Again, although the emotions of hate are often stronger than those of love, love is in the last analysis the stronger of the two.[22] We cannot not love the good, either in general or particular. We cannot even not love being and truth in general. It may happen that a certain being stands in the way of a good which we covet, or that between our desires and their object there stands our knowledge of a particular truth. We might sometimes too be less well informed about morality than we are. But we only hate beings and truths which interfere with us; we never hate being or truth itself.

To the basic linking of love and hate there is immediately joined another, that of desire and aversion. Desire is merely the form which love takes when its object is absent. Aversion is the kind of repulsion with which the mere thought of an evil inspires us. Closely related to fear, it is sometimes confused with it, but it is quite separate. Fear is of slight importance in comparison with desire. The two chief varieties of desire are concupiscence or covetousness and cupidity. Concupiscence is common to men and animals, and is the desire for the goods of animal life such as food, drink and sexual needs. Cupidity, on the contrary, is proper to man. It extends to whatever knowledge, rightly or wrongly, represents to us as good. Although acts of cupidity are reasoned acts, they are not always reasonable. This is because reason in these cases is only serving our appetites. Acts of cupidity belong to the sensitive appetite and are less acts of choice than of passion.[23] What limits are we to assign to them? Concupiscence is infinite. There are no limits to what reason can know and none to what cupidity can desire.[24]

Let us suppose for the moment that desire is satisfied. If it is a question of the satisfaction of a natural concupiscence, it is called pleasure (*delectatio*). If it is a question of the satisfaction of cupidity, it is called joy (*gaudium*). Pleasure is a movement of the sensitive appetite produced when the animal possesses the object capable of satisfying its need. It is therefore truly a passion. In a being endowed with reason, certain pleasures can be joys at the same time, but there are pleasures from which an animal draws no joy nor even takes any pride. Corporeal pleasures are more vehement than spiritual joys but are nevertheless inferior to them in many ways. By themselves, pleasures are passions in the strict sense. They are accompanied therefore by corporeal disturbance to which they owe a violence which joys never have. In compensation, the joy of understanding far surpasses the pleasure of feeling. So true is this that no one would prefer loss of reason to loss of sight. If many prefer the pleasures of the body to the joys of the mind, it is because the latter presuppose the acquisition of those virtues and habits called sciences. For those qualified to choose, hesitation is out of the question. The good man will sacrifice all his pleasures for the sake of honor. The scholar simply cannot limit himself to the superficialities of sense perceptions. He wishes to go to the very essence of things by way of the intellect. Finally, how are we to compare the precarious nature of sense pleasure with the stability of the joys of the mind? Corporeal goods are corruptible, incorporeal goods incorruptible. And as the latter reside in the thought, they are naturally inseparable from sobriety and moderation.[25]

A moral doctrine whose principles are so profoundly rooted in the real, so strictly dependent upon the very structure of the being they rule, experiences no embarrassment in solving the much-debated problem of the basis of morality. The basis of morality is human nature itself. Moral good is every object, every operation enabling man to achieve the virtualities of his nature and to actualize himself according to the norm of his essence, which is that of a being endowed with reason. Thomistic morality is, accordingly, a naturalism. But it is by that very fact a rationalism because reason acts as its rule. Just as nature makes those beings which are not endowed with reason act according to what they are, so it insists that beings endowed with reason find out what they are so that they may act accordingly. Become what you are is their highest law. Actualize to their ultimate limits the virtualities of the rational being that you are!

This kind of naturalism in morals is quite different from that expressed as follows: whatever is, is in nature, and is, therefore, natural. A statement like this appears to be obvious, but only because it is imprecise. Before it can have any real meaning a number of things have to be made definite. Literally, the statement signifies that there must be a point of view from which whatever is seems equally explicable. Understood in this way, it puts the normal and the pathological on the same plane. We can only do this provided we do not thereby abolish the distinction between what is normal and what is not. Whatever is, even sickness and monsters, can be explained by the laws of nature. It is natural for a monster to conduct itself according to its monstrous nature. But it does not therefore follow that it is natural to be a monster. For St. Thomas and the Greeks, nature is not a juxtaposition of chaotic facts without order, structure or hierarchy. Quite the contrary, it is an architecture of natures. Each of them is the concrete realization of some type. And although none is a perfect realization of nature, all represent it in their way. When they achieve themselves through their proper operations, they are striving to represent nature to the best of their power. This type is normal. Any corruption of type is a deviation into the pathological. Whatever is in nature is natural, but not everything in nature is normal. It is natural to the abnormal to be pathological. Such a distinction must be strongly emphasized in any discussion of the value of the passions called pleasures.

Any discussion of this kind should show that the natural principles pertaining to a species can fail or be perverted in individual cases. Pleasures which are contrary to nature so far as the species is concerned become natural to certain individuals. It is natural for an invert to satisfy his sexual cravings with individuals of his own sex. But though it is natural for an invert to conduct himself like an invert, it is not at all normal for a man to be an invert, *cujuslibet membri finis est usus ejus*.[26] "Corydon's sophism" can be plainly seen if we extend its arguments to other cases. Homosexuality is not the only sexual inversion. Bestiality is also one. If it is natural for certain men to seek their pleasure with animals, it is certainly not natural for man to use his power of reproduction in these sterile unions. Thus all pleasures are in nature, but there are in nature pleasures opposed to nature. For the individual whose idiosyncrasy relegates him to the margin of his species, the need for such pleasure is a regrettable misfortune. Moral science alone is not enough either to condemn men or to absolve them, but it does suffice to distinguish good from evil, and it sees to it that vice is not exalted into virtue.[27]

The moral quality of pleasures does not, then, directly depend upon either their intensity or their causes. Every operation which relieves a natural craving is a cause of pleasure. We are changeable creatures and take pleasure in our very mutability, to such an extent that there is hardly any change without its share of pleasure. "Still, it's a change," people say, and we know what they mean. The very memory of a pleasure is still a pleasure, and hope of a pleasure is a still greater one, particularly when the excellence or rarity of the desired good gives rise to admiration. Even memory of pain has its share of pleasure, since the pain exists no longer. When a man "nurses his tears," it is because he finds repeated comfort in them.

What men most delight in is the unity which arises from resemblance. Love tends toward this oneness and attains it in pleasure. Man then experiences a dilation and enlargement of his whole being to the accompaniment of lively pleasures and great joys. Yet, the act is better and more quickly accomplished in intense concentration.[28] Moreover, whatever their causes or effects, the moral value of pleasures depends upon that of the loves from which they result. All sense pleasure is good or evil according to whether or not it is in accord with the demands of reason. In morals, reason is nature. Man remains, therefore, in the norm and in order while he is taking sensible pleasure from an act in agreement with moral law. Good pleasures only become better by being more intense; the bad only become worse.[29]

Thomistic morality is, accordingly, frankly opposed to that systematic destruction of natural tendencies which is often considered characteristic of the medieval mind. Nor does it even include that hatred of sense pleasures in which some would find the specific difference between the Christian spirit and Greek naturalism. It is wrong, according to St. Thomas, to hold, as certain heretics do, that all sexual relations are sinful.[30] If they were so, it would mean that sin lies at the very source of that eminently natural cell, the family. The use of the sexual organs is natural and normal when regulated by its proper end, which is reproduction. Now in man's case, the generation concerned is that of a being endowed with reason and capable of using it well. The function of reproduction, accordingly, includes, in addition to the biological process of generation properly so called, the education of the beings thus begotten. Thus even among animals not endowed with reason, the male remains with the family during the period necessary to raise the young when the female is not able to raise them herself. It is the same, and much more obviously so, in man's case. Sometimes, of course, the woman herself has the necessary resources to raise the children; but the general rule in the human species is that the father should provide for their education. And morality must first of all concern itself with the general rules of action.

Moreover, the very word "education" which is used with reference to human beings, is enough to show that something more than mere rearing is at stake. Education implies instruction; and all instruction takes time. It takes longer to educate men than to teach birds to fly. The father therefore must remain with the mother the whole time required in order to ensure the education of all the children born successively of their union. It is thus that the natural society we call marriage is constituted. It is natural for a man to remain thus with his wife, and all sexual relations outside of marriage are contrary to moral law because contrary to nature.[31]

For the same reason marriage must be indissoluble. It is, indeed, natural that the father's solicitude for his children endure as long as life, and that the mother be able to count on him for help until the task of education is done. Besides, it would hardly be just that a man should marry a woman in the flower of her youth and cast her off when she has lost her fruitfulness and beauty. Finally, marriage is more than a tie; it is a friendship. Indeed, it is the most intimate of all friendships. It adds to carnal union, which alone is enough to render the common life sweet to animals, the union of days and hours which the family life of human beings implies. Now the grander friendship is, the more solid and durable it is too. And the grandest of all friendships ought also to be the strongest and most lasting of all.[32]

All this supposes, certainly, that the society in question be that of one man and one woman, the father tending naturally to provide for the children whom he knows surely to be his own, and the friendship between father and mother being such that any notion of sharing each other becomes revolting.[33] Thus although sexual pleasure pursued as its own end is gravely immoral and unnatural, it is both natural and moral when directed to that higher end of the conservation of the species. This end itself implies another—the setting up of the social cell, called the family. And the family is based on the most perfect of all friendships, the mutual love of father and mother united for the education of their children.[34]

The opposite of pleasure is pain. Taken as a passion in the strict sense, pain is the sensitive appetite's perception of the presence of evil.[35] This evil affects the body, but it is the soul that suffers. Corresponding to joy, a mental apprehension of good, we have here grief, caused by an internal apprehension of some evil. Grief does not imply the complete absence of joy. We can, for example, be sad about one thing and joyful about something else unrelated to it. Grief and joy are also perfectly compatible when their objects are contraries. Thus to rejoice about the good and to grieve over evil are two closely related sentiments. Moreover, there is a joy that has no contrary grief; the joy of contemplation, for example, has no contrary. When contraries are grasped by the intellect, they contribute to the understanding of each other. Even the contrary of truth can contribute to the knowledge of truth. Moreover, since intellectual contemplation is the work of thought, fatigue and weariness have no part in it. Only indirectly, that is, through the exhaustion of the sense faculties which the intellect uses, do weariness and sadness keep man from contemplating.[36]

Pain and grief are caused by the presence of evil and result in a general diminution of activities in the one who experiences them. Corporeal suffering does not prevent our remembering what we already know. A deep love of learning can even help a man to forget about his pain. As a rule, however, violent pain renders learning practically impossible. Even simple sorrows can cause depression, render action impossible, and plunge a person into a dull stupor. Grief can affect physiological as well as psychological activity.

Hence it is important to resist that weakening of vital forces which follows pain and grief. Here all pleasures and all joys can be useful. Even tears are a consolation because they give exterior expression to pain and enable the sufferer to do something related to his state. The compassion of a friend is the surest remedy for grief. Since we regard grief as a burden, we feel that our friend is helping us to bear it. Above all, the grief which a friend experiences for us is a proof of his love for us. Since every joy effectively combats grief, it is helpful to know that we have a friend. Moreover, we have to attack this evil from two sides at once—in thought, by study and contemplation, in body by such appropriate remedies as sleep, baths and other sedatives. Although all grief is an evil in itself, all grief is not bad. Just as joy, itself a good, becomes bad if it is joy in evil, so grief which is itself an evil becomes good when experienced over what is evil. The grief which is a protest against evil is morally praiseworthy. The grief which invites us to fly from evil is morally useful because there are worse evils than pain and sorrow. It is far worse, for example, not to judge evil what is truly evil, or, judging it so, not to avoid it.[37]

Love and hate, desire and aversion, pleasure and pain, are the six basic passions of the concupiscible. We have still to consider the passions of the irascible, the second group of movements of the sensitive appetite distinguished above. Here too, with the exception of one single case, the passions turn up in pairs of contraries.

The first of these pairs is hope and despair. Like all the passions of the irascible, hope presupposes desire. This is why we have already spoken of hope as the desire of a future good. However, hope is more than this, and rather different too. We do not hope for what we are sure to obtain. What characterizes hope is the feeling that difficulties stand between our desire and its fulfilment. We only hope for what is more or less difficult to obtain. Hope is interior; it is maintained in the face of some obstacle, annihilating it so to speak by desire; and thus it belongs with the passions of the irascible.[38] If the difficulty becomes extreme to the point of appearing insurmountable, a sort of hate succeeds the desire. Then, not only is the pursuit abandoned but we no longer wish to hear this impossible good so much as mentioned. This retreat of the appetite from itself, and the accompanying rancor against its former object, is called despair.[39]

Hope is intimately bound up with man's constant effort to live, act and realize himself, and beats in the heart of all. Men of age and wisdom are men of great hope because experience enables them to undertake tasks which seem to others to be impossible. In the course of their long life, how often have they not seen the unhoped-for come to pass! The young are full of hope too, but for the opposite reason. They have little past and a vast future, little memory and large expectations. The ardor of youth which has never encountered a check makes them believe that nothing is impossible. In some respects, they are not unlike drunkards and certain kinds of lunatics. They are unable to figure things out and believe everything possible.[40] They will try almost anything and, sometimes to the surprise of everyone, succeed. Hope is a driving force. A man will often fail simply because he judges a task impossible and takes it up without conviction. It is very difficult to jump a ditch we despair of clearing. To hope to make it is like having a second chance. Even despair can give additional strength, provided it is seconded by a hope. The soldier who despairs of safety through flight can battle away like a hero if he hopes at least to be avenged thereby.[41]

The second pair of passions of the irascible comprises fear and daring. Next to sadness, fear best reveals the characteristics of passion, because it is eminently passive; and the organic disturbances which it produces are most apparent. Fear is a reaction of the sensitive appetite, not before a present evil as sadness is, but before a future evil which is imagined as present. There are many kinds of fear as, for example, shame, anguish, stupor, fright and so on. All of them are related to some evil or to the possible occasion of evil. We fear death; we fear too the company of the wicked. But in the second case it is not so much the actual company that is feared as the enticement to evil. If the evil is sudden and unusual, we fear it more; and fear reaches its peak before a difficult evil that it is impossible to avoid. The feeling that we are without friends, without resources, without power in the face of peril, always contributes to increase fear. Man shrinks back into himself. The strength remaining in him melts away, like the inhabitants from the ramparts of an invaded city. A chill passes through him, his body trembles, his knees buckle, he becomes incapable of speech. And although his mind can still deliberate about what he ought to do still, as he thinks about the dangers confronting him, his fear exaggerates them and all his calculations go awry. A lively fear causes extreme weakness, but a slight fear is often very useful because it may warn its victim to be careful and to take measures against danger.

Daring or boldness is the contrary of fear. It can even be called its extreme opposite since, instead of wilting before threatening peril, it attacks it in order to overcome it. It is a passion commonly found in men of good hope who readily believe that victory is possible. As in all the passions, the body has a part to play. A certain warmth of heart accompanies it, and the use of stimulants contributes to it. Just as drunkenness facilitates hope, so can it make a man more daring.[42] We must not take this passion for a virtue. Boldness is an impulse of the sensitive appetite and is not based on prudent calculation of the chances of success. A daring man instinctively hurls himself into danger. Once he is at grips with it, he often finds more difficulties than he expected. The merely daring man gives up, while the strong man, once he has taken on the danger after reasoned deliberation, often finds the task less arduous than he feared, and carries it through successfully.[43]

There remains only the passion that has no contrary, anger. Anger is a reaction of the sensitive appetite against a present evil whose effects are actually being experienced. It arises from the meeting of several causes, themselves passions: sadness or grief over a present evil, the desire and hope of revenge. The proof of this is that if the cause of the evil is beyond our reach, if it is, for example, a person of exalted rank, we experience sadness but not anger. Anger implies hope of vengeance, and is not without a certain pleasure. It tends toward vengeance as toward a good and sets itself against an adversary as against an evil. It does not will evil against an evil as does hatred, but seeks to be avenged on evil.

The fact that it is made up of contrary passions, one of them being a desire for the good, renders it much less grave than hatred. Basically, anger is a substitute in the passions for a desire for justice. Justice can seek to punish evil too. Hence all that is wrong with anger is that it is a blind passion. It does not proceed from an objective moral judgment of the reason.[44] The angry man always has the impression that he is a victim of injustice. He thinks that he is being opposed, scorned, misunderstood, outraged, belittled, and he is offended at it. The more reason he has to think that the injurious words were deliberate, the more indignant he becomes. The more violent his anger, the surer he is that injustice lies back of his passion. Personal integrity is no protection against anger. Indeed, it is but an occasion for others to hurt him the more and for him to become the more annoyed. The pleasure we seek in revenge is actually found there. We find consolation in the very bodily agitation it creates. But when our anger becomes excessively violent, it is positively dangerous and imperils our use of reason.[45]

Such are the basic passions which are, as it were, the matter on which the virtues are exercised. In themselves passions are neither good nor bad. The Stoic notion of the wise man as one whom no passions ever disturb is a grand ideal but hardly a human one. To be completely free of passion, we should have to be without a body, to be something more than just a man. Cicero was wrong in describing the passions as "maladies of the soul." [46] For the soul to be united to its body and to feel its organic modifications in a sensible way is no malady. It is absolutely normal. Morally speaking, passions are neutral. If they get out of reason's control, they become real maladies. On the contrary, it is normal that in a completely regulated moral life, nothing in man escape reason's rule. To say that man must pursue truth with his whole soul is to say that he must pursue it with his whole body, for the soul does not know without the body. Similarly, man must pursue good with his whole body, if he wishes to pursue it with his whole soul. To act in any other way, is to pretend to the moral code of angels and thereby run the risk of not attaining even the moral life that belongs to man. Practical wisdom does not exclude the passions but busies itself with regulating, or ordering and using them. The passions of the wise man are an integral part of his moral life.

CHAPTER III

THE PERSONAL LIFE

THE MORAL LIFE of man consists in the highest development of the potentialities of his nature by acting at all times and in all circumstances under the direction of his reason. Accordingly, man's perfection and happiness consist now not so much in deducing knowledge from its principles as in regulating and ordering his actions in view of their common end. To the science of the general principles of morality must be added an art of applying them. Now it is the virtue of prudence which permits us to choose means in the order of practical reason. Hence we can regard prudence as a kind of general moral virtue whose duty it is to guide the other virtues themselves in choosing the means leading to their ends.[1]

The great problem is not so much to know what prudence is but to acquire it. It is a life's work. It is a far cry from the practical experience garnered by individual men in the give and take of daily life which we commonly call prudence to the carefully and patiently constructed virtue of prudence of St. Thomas. In order to become prudent it is necessary to set about it early and deliberately. Experience is necessary, and so is memory. The memory must be trained by being made to accumulate useful data and then frequently to recall it so as not to lose it.[2] There are habits of intellect, too, which are indispensable to the prudent man and which must be carefully cultivated. In sum, in deciding every particular case he must know how to begin, in order to arrive at its ends. What he has to acquire in order to become prudent is the ability to discern the particular act that must be done if the desired result in a given case is to be obtained.

This is truly an art. How am I to deal with such and such a man in particular circumstances without humiliating or injuring him? This is the kind of problem which the virtue of prudence places before the understanding. In order to solve these problems it is not enough just to be able to grasp principles and deduce their logical consequences. There must be acquired as well a sort of special sense which is the privilege of a reason long accustomed to move among the details of the concrete case and effectively to resolve practical problems.[3]

Everything has to be put to work in order to acquire this quality. We must know how to listen, how to follow the advice of those whom knowledge and age have equipped to counsel us. Docility is a part of prudence.[4] But it is not enough to learn from others. We must be prepared to discover on our own how to act in a particular case. This is called address (*eustochia, solertia*), and is a part of prudence. It is a practical presence of mind.[5] All these qualities demand a well-trained reason, capable of working out the particulars of a problem, of foreseeing the probable consequences of an act, of using powers of circumspection, of weighing the individual circumstances of a situation, of exercising caution lest good intentions ultimately do more harm than good. Reasoning, foresight, circumspection, precaution are all essential elements of prudence, and there is no real prudence without them.

In general, prudence seems principally to depend upon that freedom of mind by which a man judges accurately the particular data of a practical problem, appreciates the moral quality of acts, and assesses their significance. Whatever disturbs this balance of judgment diminishes prudence. Now there is nothing which more directly disturbs this balance than sense pleasures. Carnal lust is perhaps the worst enemy of prudence. Such lust completely blinds the judging faculty,[6] and is the mother of imprudence in all its forms. First, it prevents a man from acquiring prudence, and makes him scorn her counsel. Then it drives out all the virtues annexed to prudence. The power to deliberate wisely (*eubulia*), for example, is completely expelled by rash haste. Instead of giving evidence of good judgment (*synesis, gnome*), the lustful man is notoriously wanting in powers of deliberation. And when it is a question of making an actual decision, inconstancy and negligence are the very mark of the imprudent man.[7]

Since prudence is everywhere called upon, we must not be surprised that false prudence often insinuates itself into the moral life. Its counterfeits and imitations abound. There is prudence of the flesh, which consists in placing the goods of carnal life as the highest end of life, as though man should not tend beyond material goods to the perfection of reason.[8] Less radical, but only too frequent, is the vice of allowing oneself to be overwhelmed by temporal cares. Some devote such efforts to the pursuit of material goods that they have no time to attend to the things of the spirit, the most important of all. Others fear that if they do what they should they will lack the very necessities of life, forgetting that to those who seek first the goods of the soul, the rest will be added.[9] Others, finally, not content with their daily task, live in a state of perpetual anxiety about tomorrow. These all flow from a false prudence because they seek false ends.[10] There is also a false prudence which uses false means. There is crafty guile which invents means, or there is deceit (*dolus*) which works them, or there is fraud which deceives not by word but, as it were, by actions. All these caricatures of prudence are but so many forms of avarice. Continually willing all things for oneself is the surest way of missing the highest and noblest gifts whose constant characteristic is always to be common to all.

The liberty of mind which prudence demands presupposes complete mastery over all the passions. Above all it presupposes mastery over that passion which most disturbs the judgment of reason, namely, fear. The virtue which makes this possible is fortitude.[11] Fortitude of mind makes the will capable of pursuing the good which reason proposes to it in spite

of difficulties and dangers. It is a genuine virtue since it helps man to follow the law of reason.[12] But it is not to be confused with other things which
sometimes produce similar effects. We sometimes describe men as strong
who accomplish difficult things easily, whether they do so because they
hope to escape danger, as they have so often done, or because they rely
upon their experience to carry them through, as old soldiers do who do
not regard war as so very dangerous because they have learned how to
defend themselves. All these things have the same effects as fortitude but
are not the same thing. Nor is it fortitude to throw oneself into danger in
anger or despair. These two passions can imitate the virtue of fortitude,
but they are not virtues. We can go farther and say that there are those
who face danger courageously and deliberately, without the ardor of
passion, but only to win honors, to assuage the thirst for pleasure or the
desire of money, sometimes merely to avoid shame or blame or an evil
worse than the danger itself.[13] There is no virtue of fortitude in such cases
because there is no deliberate exposing of oneself to danger in order to
obey the dictates of reason.

Thus fortitude is also to be distinguished from the simple firmness of
soul which it presupposes and to which it adds, nevertheless, the power
to endure in the face of grave peril. The object of fortitude is the overcoming of fear and the restraining of rash audacity which is hardly a healthy
attitude in the face of danger.[14] It is before the greatest of all dangers,
that of death, that this virtue is revealed in all its fullness, and especially
death in time of war. Let us not forget, however, that fortitude is a virtue. It is of its essence that it tend toward a good. To be in danger of
death as the result of an illness, or because caught in a storm, or attacked
by criminals is assuredly an occasion for displaying fortitude of soul. Some
conduct themselves better than others in such circumstances, but the only
merit to be derived out of it is in the act of showing a stout heart against
misfortune. A truer fortitude of soul is present where we deliberately ex-
pose ourselves to contagion in order to care for the sick, or in braving the
perils of the sea in order to accomplish some holy work. But it is truly in
war, provided of course that it is a just one, that courage shines forth in
all its purity. There are, indeed, just wars, those for example in which a
man engages in order to defend the common good. A man can fight in a
general conflict as a soldier in the army, or he can fight alone as does the
judge who, at peril of his life, risks a monarch's displeasure in order to
maintain law and justice. To act thus is still to join battle, for is it not,
indeed, braving martyrdom and entering into a combat to serve God? [15]

We have said that the virtue of fortitude consists in overcoming fear
and restraining audacity. The first is more difficult than the second. It
takes more courage to hold one's ground in danger than to attack, and it
is in this that fortitude principally consists. To hold firm is above all to act
in a manner worthy of oneself. It is to confirm oneself in an attitude which

the strong man wishes to adopt because it resembles himself. How often does the person who is overcome by weakness in the face of danger say: "I hardly recognized myself!" But fortitude keeps in view a more distant end, an ultimate end. To be strengthened in this way is to maintain in the gravest peril the intention of attaining the last end in spite of all obstacles. This last end, as we shall see, is happiness or God.[16]

No matter how it manifests itself, the virtue of fortitude has something of the heroic about it, because it normally appears in circumstances of pain and sorrow. There are bodily pains corresponding to the bodily pleasures of touch, and it is up to fortitude of soul to withstand blows and torture. There are griefs of the soul corresponding to the delight the soul takes in some of its perceptions, and fortitude of soul consists properly in facing these griefs with courage. Losing one's life is always a cruel prospect because all men love to live. For the upright man, it is a still harder sacrifice because he knows that to surrender his life is also to renounce the completing of the works he has begun; the devoting of his life to others, and the practising of virtue.

No doubt there is always some satisfaction in acting as virtue demands. Courage includes its own satisfaction, but bodily pain prevents our experiencing it. It takes a special grace from God to feel joy in the midst of suffering, as when St. Tiburtius was able to walk barefooted over burning coals and say that he seemed to be walking on roses. No moral doctrine can promise such consolations. But if fortitude does not give joy, at least it enables the soul not to allow itself to be absorbed in pain. Hence, though the man of fortitude does not actually rejoice in his sufferings, he is not sad about them.[17] Trained to meet danger, he is not taken unawares even when it comes suddenly upon him. Nor is he what is commonly called a Stoic. Fortitude of soul is not sheer impassivity. The man of fortitude does not neglect anything that can help him against danger. If anger helps him to fight it, then he is not above anger; and his anger in this auxiliary capacity to fortitude becomes a means to virtue.[18]

Fortitude is not the highest virtue. Prudence is the highest of them all, and even justice excels fortitude, for reasons shortly to be discussed. But fortitude is none the less a cardinal virtue of the first rank. A cardinal or principal virtue is one that enters into composition with all the other virtues. There is, accordingly, no virtue which does not comprise some element of fortitude.[19] And fortitude itself can be subdivided, but none of the parts displays the perfect purity of the whole.

Fortitude has been defined in relation to the fear of death, because it is in overcoming this fear that fortitude is supremely necessary. But some fortitude of soul is necessary in facing less difficult tasks. Some people have a natural taste for great and noble actions deserving of honor and glory. This taste is possible matter of a virtue—greatness of soul or magnanimity. The acquiring of this virtue does not consist in wasting our taste for honor and greatness on unworthy objects. This would hardly be magnanimity but its opposite, littleness of soul or pusillanimity. Greatness of soul is a virtue because it enables us to distinguish real from apparent greatness, true from false honor, and to choose with proper measure the means which best assures our attaining them.[20]

Great hearts, animated by this noble desire are always simple. They neither flatter nor despise others. We must not mistake for disdain the reticence and reserve which they are bound to keep. How can they confide in those who cannot understand them? But they open their hearts freely and completely to other souls engaged like themselves in some noble enterprise. Although their ends are very different, the great scholar, the great artist, the great statesman are like brothers. They can understand one another. They all have this in common that they live for a great cause. Moreover, noble enterprises are easily recognized by this sign, that they do not pay.[21] To give oneself to them is truly, as has been said, to labor for the sake of honor. Certainly it is not for the honors that are but the counterfeit of true honor. What the magnanimous man receives is the homage paid in his own work to whatever that work was intended to honor. Such homage is honor itself.[22] It is the recompense due to all excellence, and the latter ought to know how to receive it properly.

We are perhaps beginning to have some idea of the vast scope of the moral teaching of St. Thomas. It is an outlook inherited from the Greeks, and in particular from the *Nichomachaean Ethics*. What St. Thomas is trying to describe, classify and recommend is all virtue possible to man, all possible types of human perfection. The world he is thinking about is not a world of monks. Even though he feels that monks have chosen the better part, St. Thomas is mindful that there are princes and subjects, soldiers and business men, philosophers, scholars, artists, all at grips with the problem of doing well whatever they have to do, and above all with the problem of problems, not to ruin the only life it is theirs to live. Little do the extent and wealth of their personal gifts matter; what is essential is that each make the best possible use of them. Some can aspire to but very little, but there is great virtue in their achieving it and finding contentment in it. Others may aspire to great things, and they will sin seriously if they remain deaf to the call of their nature, indifferent to the duty which their gifts lay upon them.

Such a moral doctrine little resembles the conventional Middle Ages which the historians have described. Let us try to realize, too, that the Middle Ages are not Thomas Aquinas, but that Thomas Aquinas does belong to the Middle Ages. We cannot be mindful of him and at the same time write to the effect that the Middle Ages scorned man and all that contributes to his human greatness. If we do, it is because we no longer know the meaning of fortitude and human glory and are only familiar with shallow ambition and vanity. St. Thomas values highly the virtue of fortitude. He knows how much an entire life devoted to the service of honor depends upon it. He rightly judges that the deserving man receives glory from it. And he is right in all this for the simple reason that nothing can dispense us from our duty, our joyful duty indeed, of honoring true excellence wherever it is to be found. Yes, the very greatest man does honor to himself in honoring the greatness he finds in things much less great than he.[23] And the greater he really is, the more readily does he find greatness in them, and the more willingly does he pay his homage. True greatness is mindful of all the greatness which it lacks itself. If we but consider how true greatness evaluates its own work, we will realize that all true greatness, even to the most sublime limits of glory, has no more faithful companion than humility.[24]

It is a far cry from St. Thomas's man to the stunted human plant which some have imagined he would have him. He aimed at the cultivation of the whole man, including his passions. He assigns him virtues whose object is to provide strength for the conquest of happiness. St. Thomas loves the daring, provided their daring be good, for it must be so to undertake great things and to succeed in them. There must also be that confidence (*fiducia*) which authorizes the magnanimous man to rely upon his own strength and on the help of his friends. Confidence in self is a form of hope. It is a kind of fortitude. It is the strength which the magnanimous man draws from the just evaluation of the means at his disposal and from the hopes they inspire in him.[25] And just as he does not despise his own worth, neither does the magnanimous man despise the goods of fortune. The matter of the soul's greatness is honor; its end is the doing of something great. Now wealth attracts the crowd, itself sometimes a useful force, and wealth is a powerful means of action, at least in a certain order and for the attaining of certain ends.[26] This eulogy of self-confidence, of wealth, of love of honor and glory, does not come from the fifteenth-century court of some prince of the Italian Renaissance but from a thirteenth-century monk with vows of poverty and obedience.

It is true that greatness of soul is mighty rare because it supposes a difficult victory—the maintaining of the mean in greatness itself. To presume too much on its strength, to undertake more than can successfully be accomplished, is not real greatness of soul but presumption. The presumptuous man is not necessarily one who aims higher than the magnanimous man. He is one who merely aims too high for himself. The excess that vitiates his attitude lies in the disproportion between the end and the means at his disposal to attain it. Some are mistaken about the amount of means, as are those who think themselves more intelligent than they are. Others are mistaken about their quality, as are those who think themselves great because they are rich. Such men mistake the means to greatness for greatness itself.[27]

Nevertheless, this is not the most common fault nor the most difficult to avoid. The disorder most fatal to greatness of soul is the vain longing for great things merely to make oneself great. It is just here in this greatness of soul free from all pride that history is right in contrasting modern tendencies with the moral ideals of the Middle Ages. As St. Thomas conceives him, the magnanimous man knows his greatness but knows too that he owes it to God. His excellence is something of the divine residing in him. If he deserves any honor because of it, God deserves it even more. The magnanimous man only receives that honor which others pay him on account of his merits as belonging to God. He accepts them, too, for the greater facilities which they provide him for rendering service to others. To seek honor for the pleasure of being honored and as a last end is not greatness of soul; it is ambition.[28]

It is not the actual winning of glory which destroys magnanimity; it is not the knowledge that we merit it; it is not even the desire to obtain it. Nothing is more natural than that a truly great man should be admired by the crowd. But it is also possible to aspire only to the approval of the elite, or of one single person, even of oneself. And if we know that we deserve glory, why pretend that we do not? Why not desire for our work the approval which we know it deserves? The real fault comes in seeking glory in what is unworthy of it, in perishable and passing things. It is wrong, too, to rely upon the uncertain judgment of men to be assured that we deserve it. And it is wrong not to relate to the proper end the desire for glory which we experience. To commit any one of these faults is to fall from true greatness of soul into vainglory. There is only one glory that is not vain, the glory which the truly deserving great man wisely offers as homage to God.[29]

As to the petty cash of vainglory, it superabounds and is met with everywhere. Its best-known form is boasting, that braggadocia that wastes itself in idle words. Again, a man may itch with the desire to be noticed and, as they say, to make himself conspicuous. Hence arises that mania to cause astonishment by acting differently from everyone else (*praesumptio novitatum*). Some are satisfied merely with seeming to do wonderful things which they actually do not do. Such men are called hypocrites. Finally, there is nothing more common than the desire to glorify oneself by proving that one is better than someone else. There are the stubborn, too, who refuse to give up their opinions because to do so would be to admit that someone else is more intelligent than themselves. With others there is a different reason—their will refuses to yield. It is no longer a case of stubbornness (*pertinacia*), but of crass obstinacy, the mother of discord. Then there are others too who pride themselves in surpassing others, not in depth of intelligence nor firmness of will, but in words. They are wranglers or arguers with a contentious outlook. Lastly, come those who prefer to demonstrate their own worth by refusing to listen to the orders of their superiors. This is disobedience. None of these faults is simple. There is arrogance in boasting, as there is anger in the spirit of discord and contention. However, fundamentally they derive from vain-glory, and are a desire for excellence badly regulated by reason.[30]

There is a virtue which is sometimes confused with magnanimity or greatness of soul but yet is distinct from it, though both arise from the same cardinal virtue of fortitude, the virtue of magnificence. For magnificence is, after all, a virtue. And why not? Every human virtue is a participation in the divine virtue, and God makes things magnificently: "His magnificence and his power are in the clouds." (Ps. LXVII, 35.) To be sure of this, we have only to consider creation.

To be magnificent is not simply to tend toward something great but to make something great or, at least, to tend to make it. The notion of the work to be made is essential to this virtue, and it is by this that it is distinguished from magnanimity. In other words, just as a man is magnanimous in the order of doing, he displays magnificence in the order of making, by undertaking to make a truly great work or even merely to make things in a great way. The ideal of magnificence is to make a great thing in a great way.[31]

Thus understood, magnificence consists fundamentally in knowing how to spend money. Not all rich men know how to do this and many of them display meanness, in wishing to build splendid buildings at very little expense or to entertain their friends at little or no cost. Unfortunately this is impossible because it takes money to do a great many things. The magnificent man is one who does not shrink from expense in order to realize truly great projects. The matter upon which this virtue is exercised, is, accordingly, the expense which the magnificent man must lay out for a great work, the actual money which he must spend, and also the love of that money, which he must be able to control in order to bring his work to a good end.[32] There is room for magnificence in the simplest of lives, in proportion to the means at one's disposal, be it only, for example, to celebrate a marriage. But it is a virtue which belongs particularly to the rich and to princes. The moral teaching of Thomas Aquinas stood ready waiting for Lorenzo the Magnificent.

To move spontaneously into difficult situations is good. But it is also good to endure such situations when they are inevitable. To put up with them is not the same thing as letting oneself be crushed by the sadness they cause. To keep a calm soul in the face of adversity, not to allow sadness to deprive one of the energy necessary to escape from the difficulty is a virtue—the virtue of patience.[33] Like magnificence it is a secondary virtue attached to the principal virtue of fortitude. By fortitude, we hold firm against fear. By patience, we support grief,[34] a less difficult thing. Patience is not the same thing as perseverance. The virtue of perseverance consists in being able to persist in a virtuous action as long as necessary to bring it to a successful conclusion. Accordingly, perseverance is attached to fortitude in that it permits the surmounting of the supplementary difficulty implied always by a prolonged effort. Certainly it is far from equalling fortitude itself, for it is easier to persevere in good than to stand firm in the presence of death. Yet it is a very important virtue by the very breadth of the domain in which it is exercised, since there is not a single virtuous pursuit in which it is not necessary to persevere a long time before succeeding in it. It is by this virtue that we efficaciously resist indolence or lack of fortitude, and stubbornness which we have already described as its counterfeit imitation.[35]

It is of the essence of a virtue to be a solidly established habit of acting well. In a man's case, to act well is to act according to reason. Now one of the reason's most important functions is to introduce moderation and balance into all things. It is temperance which introduces this balance into all human acts.[36] Temperance must be exercised on anything which directly threatens these qualities; that is, on covetousness and voluptuousness particularly in what concerns our animal nature. Thus temperance is exercised principally on drinking, eating and the pleasures of sex; in brief, on the pleasures of touch. Pleasures of taste, smell, sight can also depend upon temperance insofar as they prepare for pleasures of touch, accompanying or reinforcing them. The taste and even the odor of food and the beauty or elegance of a woman are of this kind.[37]

The object of temperance is not the elimination of these pleasures. Taken by themselves, sensible and corporeal goods are not irreconcilable with reason. They are instruments in its service, and it must use them to attain its proper ends. If they hinder it, it is in the measure that the tendency of the sensitive appetite toward these goods breaks away from the rules which right reason imposes upon them. Reason itself finds these rules in the nature of things. It is a question here of pleasures bound to acts necessary to conserve life. The general rule which reason imposes upon us is to use these pleasures to preserve our lives. This is in itself a strict rule, but a flexible one in its applications, because the pleasures necessary for life do not just include those without which it is impossible to live, but also those pleasures without which life cannot be passed in a fitting manner. The temperate man will never use what is injurious to health or well-being, but he will put the rest into harmony with measure according to place, time and convenience of his fellow creatures. Even personal resources and duty of state come into consideration. The rule of temperance in eating and drinking is not the same for a monk, for an athlete, and for a dignitary who has continually to offer hospitality, even give banquets, in either his own interests or in those of the State.[38]

We have given the name "cardinal" to those virtues whose principal merit is one of those elements which go to make up the very notion of virtue. Now measure enters into the composition of every virtue, and since it is in sense pleasures that it is hardest to observe measure, be it only because they are to a certain point necessary, temperance is *par excellence* the virtue of measure. It is not the greatest of the virtues; indeed it is the least heroic of all, but it is a cardinal virtue. No other virtue can exist without it.[39]

In order to regulate his desires a man must have desires to regulate. Just as courage does not consist in inaccessibility to fear[40] but in dominating it, temperance does not consist in being insensible to pleasure but in ruling one's own sensibility. Every natural operation necessary for life is accompanied normally by pleasure; and since this pleasure invites us to perform these operations, it serves a useful vital function. To be incapable of experiencing pleasure is a thwarting of being, a lacuna, a vice. But we must not confuse with insensibility the voluntary abstention from certain natural pleasures imposed upon oneself for some higher end. We must be able to give up the pleasures of the table and to refrain from sexual relations for the sake of health; if an athlete, then to keep fit; if in need of doing penance, then in order to recover health of soul; if anxious to contemplate, then in order to keep the mind free.

Some accuse contemplatives of sinning against nature by refusing to contribute toward the propagation of the species. But there is a hierarchy of natural operations, and it can be the vocation of many to give themselves up to that highest of all operations, the contemplation of truth. The contemplative's life is far from sterile. We can very properly speak of "spiritual paternity" and "spiritual filiation" between those who produce the life of the spirit in others and those who owe them their birth therein.[41] Indeed it is not asceticism properly understood and prudently regulated which hurts nature; it is that dishonorable and execrable vice of intemperance which, by degrading man to the level of the beast, extinguishes in him the light of reason which is the very source of his humanity and honor.[42]

Temperance includes many different kinds of temperance. The virtuous man finds as many occasions of practising temperance as there are orders of sense pleasure. The temperate man is the "honnête homme" in the classical sense of the expression, because honesty of manners is a kind of spiritual beauty. Beauty accompanies every virtue, but it is most at home with temperance which saves man from the worst of all indecencies, that of behaving like a brute.

Honesty or uprightness of manners is not a virtue added to temperance but an integrating part of it and, so to speak, the very condition of the temperate man.[43] He is one capable of a frugality, even abstinence, in eating and of sobriety in drinking. He avoids gluttony (*gula*) in all its numerous forms. The frugal man can await the hour of meals. He does not concern himself about choice dishes. He does not stuff himself with food. Such measured use of nourishment protects him from the usual faults arising from intemperance: mental dulness, full-blown foolishness, the manners of a clown, endless chatter, and that perpetual eroticism of people gorged with food.[44] Frugal in his eating, the upright man is equally sober in his drinking. He does not condemn wine as a blameworthy drink. No food or drink is blameworthy in itself; blame only attaches to the use that is made of it. But temperance strictly excludes the inebriety which results from an abuse of the use of wine. Anyone may be taken by surprise by a drink whose strength he has no reason to suspect. This happened once to Noe and could happen again. It is an accident rather than a fault. On the contrary, to know that a drink is intoxicating, and to prefer drunkenness to the effort of abstaining from it is a grave fault. It is all the more degrading in that it deprives man of his essential dignity, his use of reason.[45] Only sins against God are more serious than sins against reason.[46]

Just as it stands guard over the pleasures of eating and drinking, temperance is also in control of sexual pleasures. In this particular form, it is called chastity when it concerns the sex act itself, and modesty when it is a matter of words, gestures and attitudes which prepare for or accompany this act.[47] In its extreme form, temperance in these matters extends to the complete refraining from all sexual pleasures and to the firm resolve to abstain from them. In this case it is called virginity which is not only a licit virtue, since it is quite legitimate to forbid ourselves certain pleasures completely in order to keep the mind wholly free for higher objects, but it is also a very exalted virtue because it seems to realize the very type or model of spiritual beauty. Those who condemn virginity as a sin against the species are needlessly and wrongly disturbed about it. There is little danger of it becoming very widespread. When God commanded man to increase and multiply he was speaking to the human species, taken as a whole. He did not say that each individual man was bound to collaborate. Individuals divide among one another the functions for attending to the needs of the species. Some do their part toward assuring the actual propagation of the species, and rightly so. But the human species has other needs than this. It has, for example, the need for spiritual progress, and it is excellent that there should be men busy about satisfying this need by keeping themselves totally free for contemplation.[48]

At the opposite extreme of the virtue of chastity is luxury; that is, the inability to govern the sexual passions. To say of a luxurious or lustful man that he is "dissolute" is literally true because the direct effect of luxury is a general dissolution of personality. The sexual pleasures, considered in themselves, are as normal and legitimate as those of the table. As the latter naturally accompany acts necessary for the conservation of the individual, the former naturally accompany acts necessary for the conservation of the species. If sexual pleasures become vicious more readily, it is because they are so intense, and because it is so difficult for reason to master them. When they are unregulated, the entire human person slowly disintegrates.[49]

The luxurious man becomes less and less capable of using intelligence and reason. Desire deceives him about beauty, and even beauty blinds him to his inability to keep his promises. He is incapable of seeing things as they are, and he is incapable of deliberating on them. He becomes so rash and headstrong that he ceases to be able either to reflect naturally or to judge correctly. When he has made a decision, no matter what its value, the dissolute man is only rarely capable of keeping to it. We are familiar enough with these quarrels of lovers who only want to believe what they like to be told. The least false tear is enough to make them change their opinion. But luxury dissolves the will no less completely than the intelligence. To pursue pleasure in everything is to take self for an end, without troubling about others, and still less about God, in spite of the fact that God does remain our true end. It is also to be deceived as to means, since the dissolute man seeks happiness in his carnal pleasures and scorns spiritual joys which alone can lead to it. As he speaks from the abundance of his heart, the one whom luxury leads astray is easily recognized by the grossness of his language. He can no longer use his reason; he breaks out into thoughtless speech, into absurd jests and statements. In his foolishness he regards as uniquely wonderful the illusions created by his desire.[50]

But this is not the worst. To abuse nature is to go beyond her limits; and one who transgresses nature's boundaries is in grave danger of turning against her. Our study of the passions has enabled us to see that there are pleasures which are contrary to nature. There are therefore also vices contrary to nature and consisting in the habitual pursuit of these pleasures. To violate nature is to set oneself against God who has ordained nature. Now the worst way of violating nature is to carry corruption into its very principle. Fornication, rape, adultery, incest are certainly grave faults, but they are not as serious as vice against nature. Moral errors, even incest, respect nature's order in the performing of the sexual act. Unnatural vice, however, refuses to respect this order. The worst form of luxury is bestiality, and after it, sodomy, irregularities in the sexual act and onanism.[51] Whatever its form, this vice affects man in what is most intimate to him, his very human nature; and herein lies its exceptional gravity.[52]

Temperance is best expressed in control of sense pleasures, but it is also exercised on the passions of the irascible appetite. We speak often of "mastering" anger, and this is the act of the virtue of meekness. To be capable of moderation in inflicting punishment is the virtue of clemency. Both deserve to be called virtues because they consist in subduing two passions, anger and the desire of vengeance, and putting them under the control of reason. To measure their importance, we have only to consider the character of a man who lacks these virtues.

The quick-tempered man is not merely a man who gives in to anger. Anger is a passion which we examined along with the others and which, like them, is of itself neither good nor bad. Its moral value depends upon the use we make of it. A man absolutely incapable of becoming angry is abnormal. His will is defective. In brief, his nature is vitiated because it is incapable of a reaction quite normal in certain circumstances.[53] The same must be said of the man who is incapable of the effort of will necessary to inflict punishment. We speak with some justice of "weak parents" or "weak judges" when referring to those unable to administer proper punishment where it is deserved. Meekness and patience are not exercised upon the passions as passions but upon the passions as vicious because out of control. Violent and unjust anger on the slightest provocation is always evil. Some people are given to such outbursts and are difficult to live with. Others dwell ceaselessly upon their grievances and are said to be bitter. There are still others who insist at every turn upon getting all the satisfaction to which they think they are entitled. These are hard men who do not calm down until justice has been done.[54] These last are very likely to exaggerate their wrongs and consequently the punishment they demand. Hardness easily degenerates into cruelty,[55] unless the virtue of clemency or mercy is there to temper it.

Fortunately, man has not always to struggle against such intense passions as love and anger. Yet, he needs virtues for all occasions even the most common ones. Magnificence is only required in great enterprises. When it is a question of offering a gratuity, magnificence becomes ridiculous. All that is called for here is generosity or liberality. Similarly, temperance is only required in the case of passions which are only overcome with difficulty. Otherwise, we speak not so much of self-mastery as of restraint, measure, moderation, or, in brief, of modesty.[56]

Modesty is a quiet virtue, but it is the more useful for its quietness because it is the virtue by which we deal with the little difficulties with which life is so full. These difficulties spring from many sources, the most common being pride. Pride has not all the immediate urgency of those movements subject to temperance, but it is deeply rooted in the will. It is praiseworthy to strive to actualize fully the perfection of our own nature. This is the very principle of morality. But it is perverse and unreasonable to wish to be more than we are and to act accordingly. Pride is the movement by which the will is borne toward ends beyond its real limits. There is not pride in all sins, but there is no sin from which pride may not eventually spring.[57] To will as though we were no longer what we are is a deep-seated disorder from which any other may well follow. Pride is more than this; it is primarily the revolt of a being against its own nature; it is the permanent and deliberate refusal to accept its own limitations. Since these limitations sometimes hurt us, we only accept them reluctantly. Hence pride is related to the irascible, although there is also an intellectual pride into which even pure spirits may fall, since men speak of the pride of demons.[58]

The specific or remedy for pride is humility which keeps us from willing beyond the limits of our nature as members of the species, and of our personal capacities as individuals. This virtue is mainly exercised over desires, which it restrains and directs toward fitting ends. It also implies self-knowledge by which each can know his own limitations and forestall any ambition to exceed them. Humility does not consist in considering ourself the least of men but in understanding that we owe all we are to God, and that, in the measure we are good, the merit is to be attributed to Him. The humble man recognizes superiority in others and acts accordingly. But humility does not demand that we feel inferior to others when we are not actually so. We must respect God's gifts in ourselves as in others. In sum, true humility consists in evaluating ourselves accurately, in judging our own abilities, and in conducting ourselves on all occasions as befits the place we justly occupy. To rule human ambition in this way is to respond directly to the movements of the passion of hope. Humility, accordingly, is a form of temperance in so far as it restrains immoderate hopes and holds them within the bounds of reason.[59]

Any desire, even the desire to know, is subject to intemperance. Taken in itself, the taste for study is an excellent thing, but it can become pathological in many ways. It is possible, for example, to choose the wrong object of research. There are many people who study everything but what they really ought to learn. Others pursue the knowledge of creatures for itself rather than in relation to its legitimate end, which is the knowledge of God. Others, too, obstinately seek to know truths which they are not intelligent enough to understand, and they risk all kinds of misconceptions and errors.[60] This is the vice of curiosity. It is a positive threat to the intelligence, and its ravages become more and more widespread as it takes possession of one's sensibility.

Our senses have been given to us for two ends; first, as to other animals, to enable us to find the wherewithal to conserve life; secondly, since we are rational creatures, to make possible both speculative and practical knowledge. It is a natural, and consequently a legitimate thing to use our senses for these different ends. But to use our senses merely for the using of them, to be devoured by the need of seeing everything, understanding everything, touching everything, without any other object than the pleasure found in it, is the lowest form of idle curiosity.[61] Therefore, we need a special virtue to restrain these disorders of knowledge. This virtue is called *studiositas* and consists in knowing how to study. The studious man is no less skillful at collecting sense experience than the curious one, but his curiosity is useful and regulated. He pursues sense knowledge for the sake of his science, but he never gives himself to studies of which he is incapable. And what knowledge he can acquire in his study is but another means of knowing God.[62] His is what is called a "modest" mind; that is, he is able to "moderate" his desires even in the order of the things of the mind.

Temperance regulates more than our animal passions and the desires of our soul. It extends also to the movements of the body and even to the care we take of its appearance. Modesty of bearing and modest dress obviously pertain to the virtue of modesty. But so too does the regulating of physical posture.

Let us consider, for example, the activity of the human body in games. Sport is a necessary diversion which relaxes the mind and enables it to return to its occupation healthier than it was before. A bow that is always stretched ultimately breaks. Thus we rightly speak of sport as a relaxation of the mind. Here again measure is needed, not only in the sense that we should shun base and obscene amusements, but also that games may be adjusted to age, sex, persons, time and place. Enjoyment (*eutrapelia*) is a virtue;[63] the passion for sport is a vice. Inability to amuse oneself is still another vice. No doubt this latter is the less vicious of the two. We only amuse ourselves in order to be able to work better. Therefore, it is better to work without ever amusing oneself than to amuse oneself without ever working. Nevertheless, the man who works always would work the better if he consented to some distraction. Again, one who does not amuse himself amuses others still less. Such folk are said to be *duri et agrestes*. They are boorish and tiresome.[64]

Problems of the same kind arise with regard to clothes and dress. Some women, and some men too, affect a studied elegance either to attract attention or for the personal pleasure they take in it. There is nothing evil in dressing well. Clothes are a necessity of human life and there is nothing more natural than to use them as a protection against cold, heat and the inclemencies of the weather. But they should be used with decency and simplicity, taking into account accepted customs and the duties of one's state in life. Neither ostentation nor neglect is to be displayed in dress;[65] and each particular case must be judged from this double point of view.

There is, for example, the case of feminine elegance, where some would be inclined to see a mortal sin. To this St. Thomas replies in the most astonishing *sed contra* in the entire *Summa Theologiae* that if feminine elegance were a mortal sin, then all dressmakers and milliners would be in the state of mortal sin. Actually, the problem is a little more complicated. If a married woman neglects her dress, what happens? Her husband pays less attention to her. And when a husband is not occupied with his wife, he begins to be interested in other women. It is, accordingly, perfectly legitimate for a woman to try to please her husband, if for no other reason than to prevent his being tempted to adultery. But the problem is different when it is a question of women who are not married and neither can marry nor wish to marry. The latter have no reason for seeking to please men unless it is either to seduce them or to tempt them. To seek to be elegant in order to provoke to evil is a mortal sin. However, many elegant women are merely light-headed or vain. They dress up well just to show off and nothing more. Their case is not so grave as the preceding, and their sin but venial. Many other considerations must be taken into account. Thus the apostle Paul does not want women to go out with head uncovered. Neither do St. Augustine nor St. Thomas. But what are women to do in a country where it is not customary to cover their head? It is a bad custom, St. Thomas firmly maintains; but, if it is not in style to wear hats, then it is not even a venial sin not to do so.[66] For a man who has been reproached as not knowing women except through his books,[67] all this has not been badly worked out.

As we can see, there are no universals in morals except principles. When it is a question of deciding upon any voluntary action whatsoever, a whole set of principles becomes necessary plus detailed discussion of all the circumstances which meet in it. Every moral act is a particular act. Even when he seems to be discussing particular cases, St. Thomas can do no more than select certain typical cases by way of example, knowing very well that the diversity of the concrete is infinite and that the moralist must be content with first stating the principles and then putting some order into the complex facts and classifying them.

On St. Thomas's aptitude for defining and classifying, there is nothing left to be said that has not already been said a hundred times. His genius for order is incontestable and nowhere is this more evident than in his moral teaching where he systematically exploits the whole treasure of Christian and pagan wisdom. The study of the moral teaching of St. Thomas could go on indefinitely. Bernard, Bede, Isadore, Gregory, Augustine, Jerome, St. Paul, Seneca, Macrobius, Cicero and always, of course, the *Nichomachaean Ethics* and twenty other titles that we could cite, keep turning up at one point or another, furnishing definitions, proposing classifications, specifying shades of meaning, as though so many original works had only been conceived to prepare for the synthesis of St. Thomas Aquinas.

Nevertheless, this synthesis and this order do not result from mere skill and intellectual know-how. If the elements which St. Thomas uses lend themselves so readily to the order he imposes on them, it is because his moral doctrine is primarily a creation. To speak of personal morality is to use an expression which does not belong to the language of St. Thomas. But the term person is part of it, and it is certainly no betrayal of his thought to emphasize at least, by means of this expression, the intensely personal character of his moral doctrine.

A person is an individual endowed with reason. This notion, which enjoys so considerable a rôle in Christian theology, and hence in Christian philosophy, seems to have been foreign to Aristotle's thought. It was probably borrowed from a quite different source, that is, from Roman Law.[68] As St. Thomas understands it, it signifies that definite class of individual substances which are distinguished from one another in that they have mastery over their acts: *dominium sui actus*. Masters of what they do, these substances are not merely "acted upon" by others, they act; that is, each of them is directly and ultimately the cause of each single act it performs. There is, then, in all nature nothing superior to the person: *persona significat id quod est perfectissimum in tota natura*.[70] Now every man is a person. As a substance he forms a distinct ontological cell which owes its being only to its own act-of-being. As a rational substance, it is an autonomous center of activity and the source of its own determinations. What is more, it is his act-of-being which gives man that combination of gifts which he alone possesses, the double privilege of being a reason and a person. All he knows, all he wills, all he does issues from that very act by which he *is* what he is.

If we apply this notion of man to morality, we quickly see what consequences it has. However we look at them, it becomes necessary to relate all our moral acts to that which makes us a person in order to determine whether they are good or evil. Personal morality will thus signify primarily the morality of the person taken as a person; that is, the morality in which the person is at once legislator, judge and judicable of the law of good and evil which it promulgates, applies and sanctions itself in the name of the demands of reason alone. But one of the principal acts of this reason is to recognize itself, on the one hand as dependent upon its proper source, on the other as determined by the concrete conditions under which it is exercised.

Personal morality demands, therefore, in the name of this same reason which constitutes the person, that the moral agent feel bound by a law of which its conscience is but the mouthpiece. This is a limitation of its independence, no doubt, but it doubly respects the inalienable and coessential part of its being. It is metaphysical knowledge alone which imposes this limitation. Now to posit the person as a divine effect is to make it an image of God. And as the person is the very peak of nature, it is the most perfect image of God which we can contemplate in nature. Man accordingly is not rational and free in spite of the fact that God created him in His own image but for that very reason. The person is not autonomous save insofar as it depends upon God. It is so in virtue of the creative act which constitutes it as a participation in an infinitely wise and free power and generously creates each person as an act-of-being endowed with the light of knowledge and the initiatives of the will.

What an enlarging of the perspectives which so limited Aristotle's moral

teaching! We should see this much better if St. Thomas had himself believed it necessary to take the trouble to expound his own moral doctrine
in purely philosophical terms. This is what we are making him do today,
but he never actually did it himself. Why construct a completely self-
sustaining moral philosophy as if there were no Christian revelation or
as if it were not true? Christian revelation does exist, and it is true. This
at least is St. Thomas's point of view. As a Christian Doctor it was his
duty of state to live only with God in order to speak only with Him: *aut
de Deo aut cum Deo*. Above all, he could not speak of morality in any
other way because, if God exists, there are no personal duties prior to
those toward Him.

In this, as St. Thomas clearly saw, his moral doctrine profoundly differed from Aristotle's. The *Nichomachaean Ethics* is and remains a work
of worldwide importance which must ever inspire those whose ideal it is
to mold moral subjects completely adapted to the social and political
life of the city. But we must know that there are virtues which Aristotle
overlooked because they played no rôle in the collective life the exigencies
of which for him were the norm of good and evil. For a man to accept his
own limitations, to limit his ambition to what his worth and resources
permit is assuredly a virtue. We may say that this submission to the
established order which, to the extent that this order is just, is a part of
the virtue of justice. It is a long way from here to that respect which we
experience for the excellence of others to that very joy which we experience in recognizing true greatness wherever we meet it, and in bowing
before it even when it goes against our vanity. Here, of course, it is a
question of humility, and society does not like the humble. It sees in them
only weaklings who are but justly conscious of their weakness, and it
regards their very seriousness as an admission of such weakness. Deliberately to incur such social disfavor, the humble man has to place before
everything his duty of being sincere and clear-sighted in what concerns
himself. Just as the superiority he sees in others is from God, the humble
man knows that he is great in bowing before others because all virtue
is great and particularly humility before God. These are thoughts quite
foreign to Aristotle who never mentions the virtue of humility.[71]

This is only the omission of a virtue to which we would attach no
importance did it not reveal a general and serious difference between the
two moral doctrines. The systems of Aristotle and St. Thomas move in
different directions because they are founded upon different natural theologies. However we interpret Aristotle's, we cannot go so far as to pretend that Pure Thought is much concerned with the details of our acts,
has a right to demand that we render it an account of them, and that
we should relate each one of them to it. Aristotle's God lives his eternal
beatitude; each man aims to the best of his ability to imitate this beatitude; but even though it is given to the occasional wise man during rare

moments to participate in the joys of a quasi-divine contemplation, it is not on the life of their God that these privileged persons order their moral life. So extravagant a measure would be folly in their eyes. The ideal they never lose sight of in their pursuit of a strictly human wisdom is that of a human good under its most perfect form, the good of the city.

But it is rather different in St. Thomas's morality. Created by a God who remains intimately present in his being, in his faculties, in their operations, and in every act proceeding from them, man can do nothing save through Him. And since man is aware of this, then he must do nothing save for Him. The question here is not to know whether man can or cannot aspire to life in God as his supreme beatitude. Whether or not God has decided to grant him this grace, man's moral duty remains exactly the same. Just as Aristotle's moral doctrine follows his own metaphysics, so does St. Thomas's moral doctrine follow St. Thomas's theology. This is why not only humility but also fortitude and temperance, with all the particular virtues related to them, appear here as so many means which man acquires by patient exercise to achieve ever more perfectly within himself that image of God which it is his end to become.

CHAPTER IV

THE SOCIAL LIFE

THE NOTION of social morality immediately calls to mind that of social justice, and justice in its turn evokes the notion of right. Right (*jus*) demands what is just (*justum*). And to do what is just under all circumstances in the life of society is the object at which the virtue of justice (*justitia*) aims.[1] In order to analyze the various forms of justice, we have first to examine the various forms of right.

Justice is distinguished among the virtues by the fact that it governs relations among men. The simplest form under which we can first conceive what such relations ought to be is that of equality. When two things must be made equal, they are commonly said to require "adjusting." The virtues thus far discussed can be defined completely from the point of view of the agent. Here, however, it is absolutely necessary to take into account something besides the agent; and in a certain sense we can speak of justice without even considering the agent. Certainly we speak properly of a just man, but only with reference to someone else. Similarly we can speak correctly of "something just" meaning by the expression to point out that justice demands that someone do it, even though no one actually does so. It is this "what is just" which is designated by the word "right." [2]

This notion is by no means a simple one. Right appears under two aspects, according to the two aspects of the just and of equality. There is first the natural equality of things themselves. This equality is adequate for establishing a relationship of right and therefore of justice. For example, I can give so much in order to receive so much, be it only coin for coin. This is called "natural right," an expression signifying primarily what is naturally just, and, consequently, of right. A rather different case is that in which there is equality or equivalence in virtue of a convention whether private or public. Two men can agree that the tenure of a property is worth a certain sum of money; a whole people can agree upon a fixed scale of prices; the people's representative or head of the State can validly do it in their place. These decisions create more flexible relations of equivalence than those of strict natural equality. All this is in accord with right as a convention, and is called "positive law." [3] Finally, certain notions of equity proceed obviously from the exigencies of reason as they are found in almost every human society. As reason is common to all men, the conventions deriving from it are so too. There is, thus, a positive law common to all men and called the "law of nations." The law of nations is dictated by natural reason and is not the object of a special institution. It arises spontaneously wherever reason prevails.[4]

Still other distinctions appear if we examine, besides the different kinds of right, the different relationships which rights establish among persons. To keep to fundamental cases, we shall put first the relation established by rights between two persons who are not united to each other by any bond; for example, a contract made between two citizens. It is here a question of legal relations, pure and simple. Such a right is the same for all and in all cases. The fact that certain citizens are soldiers, others magistrates, and so on, does not change the fact. Certainly there is a military law or right, a law for magistrates, a sacerdotal law and many others. But, whatever their functions, citizens have no *personal* authority over one another. All are bound immediately to the national community and its chief. The relations which unite them, therefore, are relations of right and justice, properly so called.

It is the same within a family between the father and the son, inasmuch at least as the child is a person distinct from the father. The proof that relations of strict right exist between them is that certain rights of the child are sanctioned by law. Here however all the relations no longer depend upon strict right. The child is not completely distinct from the father who is prolonged in and will survive in him. As St. Thomas puts it, *filius est aliquid patris*, the son is something of the father. Now we have no rights in relation to ourselves. Hence the father can do certain things in virtue of a right which is something quite different from what we call "the law." It is his paternal right. On the other hand, strict relations of law and justice must be established in the very interior of the family between husband and wife. No doubt the woman belongs to her husband, for St. Paul says: "Husbands must love their wives as their own body" (Ephes., V. 28). The wife is not thereby less but more distinct from her husband than the child from the father. Her husband has freely taken her as a partner in order to found a kind of society. Their relations accordingly are more completely matter of strict right and justice than those of the father and son. To distinguish this case from the others, we might call it "domestic justice," because the relations of right are here governed by the common good of the family as their end.[5]

Now that we have determined what right is, in what does justice consist? It is a permanent disposition of the will to render to each his right.[6] We are, therefore, always just or unjust in regard to another. But as the effect of this disposition is to assure that we act rightfully toward another according as reason would have us, it renders its possessor better. In short, it is a virtue.[7] In a certain sense, we can even say that it is virtue itself, or that every virtue is justice and justice is all the virtues. Aristotle affirms this in the *Nichomachean Ethics*.[8] And he is right, at least from his point of view. The virtue he is thinking of, as we have had occasion to observe, is the citizen's. The justice of which he is speaking in this passage is legal justice; that which law specifies in prescribing how each person should conduct himself in view of the common good of the city. From this point of view, each individual is no longer considered except as a part of that whole known as the social body; and as the quality of the part is of some consequence to the quality of the whole, even the personal virtues which each of us can acquire contribute to that common good toward which the justice of law ordains all citizens. If, therefore, we only consider men as members of the social body all their virtues refer to justice. This makes of justice a kind of general virtue which includes all other virtues.[9]

Let us observe, nevertheless, that even from Aristotle's point of view we cannot consider the essence of justice as identical with the essence of any other virtue. Legal justice only includes the others because it governs them and orders them all to its own end, the good of the city. Aristotle himself recognizes this. A good man and a good citizen are not exactly the same thing.[10] St. Thomas hastens to profit by this admission to make a distinction between Greek justice, which is entirely directed to the good of the city, and a particular justice, enriching the soul which acquires and exercises it as one of its most precious perfections. This time it is no longer in Aristotle that St. Thomas finds the text which authorizes him to proclaim that this justice exists, it is in St. Matthew's Gospel: "Blessed are they who hunger and thirst after justice" (V, 6). Here we see how striking a metamorphosis through which Greek morality must pass in order to be able to endure in a Christian climate. Like the other virtues, justice must be interiorized if it is to become Christian. Before being just in the City, we must be just in our own eyes in order to be just in the eyes of God.[11]

Thus we distinguish between legal justice, the virtue of acting justly toward a group, and particular justice, a virtue quite as characterized as either temperance or fortitude, and by which each man in particular conducts himself justly in regard to each man in particular.[12] The matter on which it is directly exercised is no longer the passions of the soul, as was the case with the personal virtues which we have studied, but the actions of men in their relations with other men, their comportment, their dealings with one another. But what is its bearing upon the passions?

Acts governed by justice are voluntary acts: and the will does not belong to the order of the sensitive appetite, the seat of the passions, but to the order of rational desires. No doubt it frequently happens that the passions lead to injustice, for example, vengeance or perhaps the unrestrained coveting of riches, lead a man to steal. It is not up to justice but to fortitude or temperance to redress these passions. Justice only intervenes to redress the unjust act as such. Whatever a man's reason for stealing, justice demands that the ill-gotten goods be restored to their legitimate possessor. It therefore focuses upon the very acts which this virtue produces,[13] and not upon what these acts should be interiorly, in relation to those performing them, as in the case of fortitude and temperance. It focuses upon what our exterior acts ought to be, given the person or persons they affect. In other words, the virtues which govern the passions permit the virtuous man to keep them in a just mean in relation to himself. They allow him to be angry or to experience fear when he should, as he should, and just as often as he should. But justice seeks this just mean in the relationship between two things that are outside the virtuous man himself: his act, and the person whom his act concerns. It is no longer a question, therefore, of *someone who keeps himself in the just mean* but of *keeping the just mean of some thing*. What justice has in common with other virtues is that the just mean it seeks is the mean of reason. This makes it a moral virtue in the full sense of the term.[14]

This just mean is the right of the person concerned through the act which determines it. We can see its nature very well from the vices which destroy this type of relationship. Legal justice is thwarted by illegality— a contempt for the common good which disposes the vicious to pursue only their own immediate individual interest without any thought to the possible effects of their acts upon the general interest of the community. Illegality is a vice that is as general as the virtue it destroys. It can lead the vicious man into all kinds of faults because it disposes him to violate all laws which interfere with him in any way. But injustice, properly so called, consists in falsifying the equality in our relations with other persons, that is, in not respecting the equality which it is fitting to establish between each of our acts and each of their rights. An unjust act is an "iniquitous" act, an "iniquity," or "in-equity" committed upon someone. Thus to wish to take more money from a buyer than the thing being sold is worth, or to wish to get an object away from a seller for less than it is worth, or to wish to obtain more money than the labor supplied warrants or more work than the money paid warrants is to break this fundamental equality between the act and the right which justice demands. Under given conditions of existence, an hour's work or a stated amount of the product of a specified piece of work is worth in a material way a definite sum of money with a determined purchasing power. It is up to a reason that is well-informed to establish this relation honestly.[15]

We must not, however, blandly identify the doing of something just with justice or the doing of something unjust with injustice. The just and the unjust are, as it were, the matter of justice or injustice, but they are not enough to constitute it. A just man may, through ignorance or error commit an injustice and be no less just because of it. We can go even further and say that we can be fundamentally just and yet be led by anger or covetousness to commit injustice. We are then just, but wrongly neglecting to appeal to our justice when we should be doing so. For all this, we do not lose our virtue of justice but show that it is incomplete and still lacks the stability of a true virtue. Injustice, properly so called, is the habit of performing unjust acts, which we know to be unjust and yet deliberately perform. The *habitual intention* to do what is unjust is, therefore, essential to the vice of injustice, as the contrary intention is co-essential to justice taken as a virtue.[16] To do things that are just or unjust in ignorance or in an outburst of passion is to fall into justice or injustice *per accidens*.

Since the just man's will is regulated by reason we can regard him as a judge continually meting out justice and pronouncing judgments. But this is only a metaphor or at least a wide extension of meaning. Strictly speaking, the judgment which defines justice is the privilege of the head of the State, for it is he who establishes positive rights by promulgating laws. The judge merely applies laws thus established. When he passes judgment he merely carries out the ruler's judgment. As for personal judgments based on the reason of individuals, they are only called judgments by analogy. The original meaning of the term "judgment" was "the correct determination of what is just." From this the term was extended to signify the correct determination in any matter whatsoever, whether speculative or practical.[17] In any case, when we take the term "judgment" in the strict sense, it is the reason that judges. We designate this act by the name judgment (*judicium*) because it is governed by that stable disposition for judging accurately which is called justice (*justitia*). A judgment in the order of rights is, therefore, an act of justice, *actus justitiae;* that is, an act whose origin and cause are the very virtue of justice of the one pronouncing the judgment.[18] As an act of justice, judgment is a legitimate act, provided always that it satisfies two other conditions.

The first condition is that the one who exercises justice should have authority from the ruler to do so and should only pass judgment in matters over which he has effective authority. Judgments handed down, without this condition are "usurped" judgments. The second condition is that the judge only pass judgment where there is rational certitude. We do not of course, mean that here, where we are speaking of contingent matters, there must be a conclusive certitude of a scientific kind. But the judge's reason must at least be as certain as it can be in such matters. A judgment handed down in a doubtful or obscure case on the strength of more or less flimsy conjectures must be qualified as a "rash" judgment.[19] Indeed, such a judgment is only based on suspicion. And as Cicero says, to be suspicious is to presume evil on slight evidence.

The wicked are quick to be suspicious because they judge others by themselves. But it is enough to despise someone, to hate him, to be irritated with him in order readily to think evil of him. And old men have seen so much that they generally display much suspicion. Indeed, we are all suspicious. To doubt someone's goodness on flimsy evidence is a human temptation which no one escapes and to succumb to it is not a grave fault. But it is a grave fault to judge a man to be decidedly bad on mere conjecture, because although we are not masters of our suspicions, we are of our judgments.

The judge who in justice condemns on mere suspicion commits the most serious of sins against justice, since instead of judging according to rights, he is violating them. His act is a direct offense against the very virtue it is his duty to exercise.[20] Where there is no certitude, the benefit of the doubt should be given to the accused. The judge's duty, to be sure, is to chastise the guilty, and all of us must condemn the wicked in our inner forum. But it is better to err many times by acquitting the guilty than even rarely to condemn the innocent. The first of these errors harms no one; but the second is an injustice and must be avoided.[21]

Let us leave judgment for the present and return to justice in order to distinguish its various species. In Book V of the *Nichomachaean Ethics*,[22] Aristotle distinguishes between the justice which governs exchange and that which governs distribution. They are called commutative justice and distributive justice. Both depend upon particular justice (as distinct from legal justice) because they both deal with some particular person taken as part of the social body which is its whole. If it is a question of judging the relations between two of these parts, that is, between two private persons, it is a matter of commutative justice. If, on the contrary, it is a question of regulating a relationship between the whole and one of its parts; that is, of assigning to some particular person his part of the goods collectively owned by the group, it is a matter of distributive justice. Between two private persons, indeed, everything boils down to some kind of exchange. Between the social body and its members everything can be reduced to a problem of distribution.[23]

These two sorts of relationships justify the distinction between two species of justice because they proceed from two different principles. When the State wishes to distribute among its members the part of the community's goods which reverts to them, it takes into account the place occupied by each of these parts in the whole. Now these places are not equal, for each society has a hierarchical structure and it is of the very essence of the organized body politic that all of its members be not of the same rank. It is like this under all regimes. In an aristocratic state classes are distinguished by worth and virtue; in an oligarchy wealth replaces nobility; in a democracy it is liberty or the liberties enjoyed which arrange the members of the nation into a hierarchical order. In all cases, and we could cite others, each person's advantages are in proportion to the rank arising from his nobility, wealth, or the rights he has been able to win. These relationships are not based upon an arithmetic equality but rather, according to Aristotle, on a geometric proportion. Hence it is natural that some should receive more than others, since the distribution of advantages is carried out according to rank. When each, according to his place, receives in proportion to the rest, justice is done and rights respected.

In exchanges between persons, these problems are rather different. It is here a question of rendering something to someone in return for what he has received from him. This is pre-eminently the case in buying and selling, the very type of all exchange. Here it is a matter of so adjusting transactions that each gives or receives in proportion as he receives or gives. And so we have to reach an arithmetic equality where both parties end up with as much as they started with. Whether the end which justice seeks to establish be proportional or arithmetic relationship, it is always a relationship of equality.[24]

Like all virtues, these two kinds of justice are threatened by corresponding vices. What most frequently destroys justice is respect of persons. Here the term "person" signifies any condition not related to the cause which justifies a gift. We have said that distributive justice consists in giving to each according to his merits. To show respect of person is to find something other than merit on which to proportion the gift. It is not a case of retribution for a right, but favor to the person of Peter or Martin under the guise of acknowledging a right. Understood in this sense, "person" varies according to case. Taking ties of blood into account in order to regulate an inheritance is not to show respect of persons but is a notable case of taking them into consideration. But it is showing respect of person to appoint a man professor because he happens to be our relative or the son of a friend. In this case only the candidate's knowledge should enter the question. Everything attaches to his person save his competence as a professor, which alone should affect this situation.[25]

All this is perfectly simple and clear-cut in theory. In practice, it is a different matter. So long as it is only a question of distributing public posts or of meting out justice in the courts, respect of persons is always reprehensible. But it is very rare that the distinction between what attaches to the person and what does not is perfectly clear-cut. Knowledge alone does not make the professor, nor does even sanctity make the good bishop. A substantial personal fortune, close personal friendship with rulers can increase a man's diplomatic ability and strengthen his title to an ambassadorial post.

We must particularly distinguish between the granting of posts and the granting of honors. In the second case, it is a well-known fact that honors attach to the post, and rightly so. No doubt only virtue deserves to be honored. But the man who holds public office always represents something more than himself, namely, the authority he holds. A bad bishop represents God; and we must respect God in the bishop. An instructor ought to be a scholar; parents ought to be good; old men ought to have found time to become wise. Therefore we honor instructors, parents, old men even though all are not scholars or good or wise. As for rich men, whether we like it or not, they have a larger place in society than the poor. Their resources give rise to duties. And if it is only for what it is able to do, their wealth is honorable. Let us therefore honor the rich since we have to. But let us honor in them that power to do good which they represent. To honor *their wealth*, the very sight of which draws respect from so many persons is to show respect of persons. It is no longer a virtue but a vice.[26] Very decidedly, we can always count on St. Thomas's good sense.

The vices opposed to commutative justice are more numerous, because of the diversity of the goods that can be exchanged. The gravest are those which consist in taking without giving anything in return. The gravest of all breaches of justice is to take someone's life, because loss of life involves the loss of everything else as well. To sacrifice plants for animals and animals for men is to remain within the scope of order. Homicide is the unjustified slaying of one who is, through reason, our associate and brother. There are justifiable killings, as when a judge inflicts the death penalty. In any given society individuals are only parts of the whole. And just as a surgeon has to cut off a gangrenous member in order to save a man's life, it can become necessary to cut off a member of society if its corruption is a menace to the social body. In such a case the death penalty is justified.[27] Still this penalty can only be inflicted by regularly constituted justice. No private person has the right to set himself up as a judge. The courts alone have the right to condemn malefactors to death.[28]

Suicide is homicide against oneself. We have no right to kill either others or ourself without authority. Suicide is against nature because everyone loves himself and naturally works to conserve himself. If the natural law has in the eyes of reason the value of moral law, then it is a grave fault to violate it. Moreover, each part as such belongs to the whole. Now every man forms a part of the social group. In killing himself a man injures the community which has a right to his services; and to do so is an act of injustice, as Aristotle observes.[29] What Aristotle does not say, and what is much more important, is that suicide is injustice toward God. For it is God who gave us life and conserves us. To deprive ourselves of life is to commit against God the sin we commit against a man in killing his servant. Moreover, it is to commit the sin of usurping to ourself a right to judge which we do not possess. God alone is judge of the limits of our life. "I will kill and I will make to live," (*Deuteronomy* XXXII, 39). Both natural and divine law are one in condemning suicide as a fault against the person, against society and against God.[30]

The taking of life, one's own or another's, is in St. Thomas's eyes so serious an act that it can be said, in spite of apparent exceptions, there is *no case* in which this act is morally justified. We mean by this that in no case is it licit to kill with the intention of killing. It can happen that the pursuit of a quite different and legitimate end may necessarily involve us in killing. Even here the killing must not be willed for itself and as an end. We have several times had occasion to observe that moral acts are specified by the intention which directs them. To kill with the final intention of killing is always a crime. For killing to be excusable, it must remain, as it were, outside one's line of intention and be considered as accidental to the end sought. Such is the case of killing in legitimate self-defense. It is legitimate in a case like this to wish to save one's own life, but it is not legitimate even to have the intention of killing an assailant in order to defend oneself. We ought only to have the intention of defending ourselves against him, and we may only kill him in defense of our own body.[31]

It is possible to injure another in his goods as well as in his person. From this arise many breaches of justice, all of them violations of the right to property. This right has given rise to many controversies. Some, indeed, have denied this right, but they are certainly mistaken. Man is endowed with reason and will, and is naturally capable of using things; as he cannot subsist without using them, he naturally possesses the right to do so. Power to use a thing according to one's needs is to have proprietorship or ownership over it. We cannot conceive human life to be possible without, as a minimum, the right to own the goods necessary in order to live. To this extent, the right to ownership is a natural right.

In addition to this, it is a sacred right. Man is only capable of exercising his dominion over the things he uses because he is endowed with reason. Reason is the image of God in him. The supreme and absolute proprietor of nature is God, who created it. But He made man to His own image and likeness, and consequently capable, not of changing nature to his liking, but at least of exploiting its resources to his own profit. Thus man holds by divine delegation the power to use things put at his disposal in this way and he has the right to do so in the just measure of his needs.[32]

It is true that the right to ownership as ordinarily understood seems to extend beyond the simple right to the use of property. To possess something is to have it not only for oneself but as one's own. So much so, that it seems that the goods possessed constitute, as it were, a very part of the person. If we take the point of view of natural law, no such appropriation of goods is called for. We do not say that natural law prescribes community of goods nor, consequently, that their individual appropriation is contrary to natural law, but simply that it ignores it. It is reason which has added private appropriation of goods to natural law, because it is necessary for human life that each man possess certain goods as his own. In the first place, when a thing belongs to everyone, nobody takes care of it, whereas everyone is willingly busy with what belongs to him alone. Then too things are carried out with far more order than when each is charged with a particular task than when everyone is put in charge of everything. This division of labor, as it is called today, seems to imply in St. Thomas's thought a certain individualization of property. Finally, more peaceful relations among men are thus established. The satisfaction which all experience from the ownership of something makes each man content with his lot. It is enough to see how often the joint possession of goods is a source of disputes in order to be convinced of this. As lawyers say: joint possession must always be broken.

When this has been said, we must not forget that by natural law the use of all things is at the disposal of everyone. This fundamental fact cannot be removed by the progressive establishment of private ownership. That each should possess as his own what is necessary for his own use is quite sound as a safeguard against want and neglect. But it is a very different matter when some accumulate more goods than they can use under the title of private property. To assume ownership of what we do not need is to make fundamentally common goods our own. The use of such goods should remain common. The remedy for this abuse is never to consider even the goods possessed in our own name as reserved for our own use. Let us have them, since they are ours, but let us always keep them at the disposal of those who may need them. The rich man who does not distribute his superfluous wealth is robbing the needy of the goods whose use is theirs by right. He is defrauding them by violence. Wealth, let us recall, is not bad in itself. But we must know how to use it reasonably.[33]

Since it is licit to possess certain goods as our own, anything that impairs this right is a sin. Larceny, which consists in stealthily taking possession of another's goods, is a sin. So too is rapine, or the taking of another's goods by violence.[34] If such acts became general, human society would disintegrate. Moreover, they not only go counter to the love we ought to have toward our neighbor but also that we should have toward God.[35]

On the other hand, there is no larceny or theft involved in taking what we need in case of necessity. As we have already said, by natural law, things have been placed by God at the disposal of all men to provide for their needs. The fact that human rights have divided and appropriated the possession of goods cannot abolish natural right to which it is an addition. What the wealthy possess over and above their needs is intended *by natural law* to provide for the needs of the poor. No doubt those who possess these goods are free to dispose of them according to their best judgment in order to feed the hungry and clothe the naked. But in the case of urgent and manifest necessity, a man in need can take possession of the goods of another either by ruse or by violence without any sin on his part.[36]

So much for injustice in acts. There is also an injustice in words.[37] The most important words in this regard are those of the judge whose proper function is to render justice. A judge's sentence is a kind of particular law made to cover a particular case. So it is that a judge's sentence, like general law itself, has constraining force. It binds both parties, and its power of constraining private persons is the sure token that the judge who pronounces it is speaking for the moment in the name of the State.

No one, then, has the right to judge without a regular mandate.[38] The character of public person is so inseparable from the judge that he has not even the right to take into account in his judgments what he knows about the case as a private person. He can only base his judgments on what he knows *as a judge*. In the exercise of his public function, the judge only knows, on the one hand, divine and human law, on the other the evidence of the witnesses and other pertinent matter placed in the official dossier of the case. To be sure, what he knows of the case from private sources can help him bring about a more coherent and contracted discussion of what are alleged to be proofs and thus show the weakness of the case. However, if he cannot juridically challenge such evidence, he has to base his judgment upon it.[39]

For the same reason, a judge cannot pronounce on a case in which he is in any way an accuser or plaintiff nor must he act like an accuser in a case of which he is the judge. As judge he is only the interpreter of justice. As Aristotle says, he is a living justice.[40] Just as a judge must forget what he may happen to know as a witness, he must abstract completely from what he might have to say as an accuser. In brief, one cannot be judge and party to an action at the same time. It would be to exercise justice toward oneself which cannot be said save by way of metaphor because, as we have said, the virtue of justice directly concerns another.[41]

Finally, the judge has no authority to shield a guilty person from punishment. If the complaint is upheld, the plaintiff has the right to have the guilty person punished and it is up to the judge to recognize this right. Moreover, the judge is charged by the State to apply the law. If the law exacts the punishment of the guilty, the judge is bound to abstract from his feelings as a private person and to apply the law strictly. Of course the head of the State who is the highest judge is not in the same position as other judges. Having full power, he can save a guilty person from punishment if he feels he can do so without prejudice to the interest of the community.[42]

Constrained to restrict himself to what is pertinent to the trial in order to pass sentence, the judge would be at the mercy of plaintiff, defendant and witnesses unless they too were bound to observe justice. It is our duty to accuse when it is a question of a fault which threatens the public good and we are in a position to prove our charge. On the contrary, if it is only question of a fault which appears not to prejudice public interests there is no obligation to make accusations. Moreover, we are not bound to become involved in this way if we do not feel that we are in a position to back up our accusation with proofs, for we are never bound to do what we cannot do as it should be done.[43]

If we should and can accuse, we should do so in writing so that the judge may know exactly what to believe. Above all, we must be careful never to make an accusation which is not well-founded. To fall into this fault is calumny. Some commit calumny because they are shallow and put faith in mere heresay. Others do so deliberately and maliciously, and this is a great deal more serious. There is no justifying a calumnious accusation, not even the intention of serving the common good, because we have no right to serve the common good by injuring someone unjustly.[44] On the other hand, if the accusation is well-founded and it has been decided to lay a charge, then it is our duty to push it as far as possible. To dissimulate in a fraudulent manner facts relating to the accusation being made, to refrain from bringing forward proofs, is to enter into collusion with the guilty party and become his accomplice. This fault is prevarication.[45]

Like the plaintiff, the accused has his obligation in justice. The first of these is to acknowledge the judge's authority and to submit to it. The accused must then, first of all, tell the judge the truth when he asks it, within the limits set forth by the law. To refuse to speak the truth that he is bound to speak, or to lie about it, is a grave fault. But if the judge pushes his enquiry beyond the legal limits, the accused can refuse to reply, denounce it as an abuse or have recourse to any other subterfuge which procedure allows. But he must never lie. He who lies in order to excuse himself sins against the love of God to whom judgment belongs, and he sins doubly against love of neighbor, by refusing the judge the truth to which he has a right, and by exposing his accuser to the punishment usually inflicted upon false accusers.[46]

The question now arises whether the accused who knows himself to be guilty must admit it. He is bound to admit an accusation when it is true. But he is not at all bound to admit something of which he is not accused; and nothing forbids his using the necessary reticence to prevent faults which are not yet known from being brought out into the open. We sometimes hear of criminals who not only acknowledge the crime with which they are charged, as they should do, but who spontaneously confess other crimes of which no one ever dreamed of accusing them. They are not bound to do so. They may even legitimately conceal by suitable means the truth they are not obliged to admit.

To consider the accused as morally bound to acknowledge the fault of which he is justly accused is to go beyond what the justice of the courts demands. St. Thomas knows this. As an objection to his own position he brings up the article in the civil law which declares that in cases involving capital punishment a person is permitted to bribe his adversary. Moreover he notes that if the law punishes collusion between accuser and accused, it does not provide any sanction against collusion between the accused and his accuser. Why should our moral teaching forbid what the laws allow? Because, St. Thomas replies, human laws allow many acts to go unpunished which God's judgment condemns as wrong. There is no law against fornication, yet it is a very grave moral fault. So too here. An accused tries to corrupt his accuser so that he will withdraw his charge. This is manifest deception, but what can the judge do about it if there is no longer any charge? Obviously nothing. What St. Thomas is expecting from the guilty man is, as he says himself in so many words, an act of perfect virtue (*perfectae virtutis*)—the refusal to bribe his accuser even though by refusing to do so he is exposing himself to capital punishment. The law does not demand this kind of heroism from anyone. The proper function of human law is to keep people in order. Such scrupulous respect for all the virtues can hardly be looked for in a very large number of men but only in a few. Law then permits bribing an adversary, but God forbids it.[47] The man who knows himself to be guilty will refuse to have recourse to such subterfuges and, once condemned, he will not even appeal a sentence which he knows has been justly handed down.[48]

After plaintiff and defendant come the witnesses. Their moral code is complicated enough and their problems begin with the question of knowing whether they are actually bound to give testimony. They are, of course, if an injunction has been issued by the judiciary and the facts are common knowledge or plainly evident. But when we are asked to reveal hidden faults knowledge of which is not current, we are not bound to give testimony. It can happen, moreover, that the one who is asking for our testimony is merely a private person without authority over us. Two cases are to be distinguished here. If it is a question of saving an accused from an unjust conviction, we are morally bound to appear as a witness for the defense and even, if we can do so, to inform someone who can vouch for the truth. On the other hand, if it is a question of having someone convicted, there is no obligation to intervene, not even in order to save the accuser from the penalty he will have to pay for making an accusation which, though morally justified, is juridically unsound. There is after all nothing to oblige him to take such a risk. Before he is under obligation to lay a charge, he has to be able to prove it. He ought to have seen ahead of time that he would be unable to prove his accusation.[49]

The next problem is how to proceed after one has become a witness. Certainly a witness has to tell the truth. First of all, to take the witness stand, he has to bind himself under oath, and he cannot make false statements without committing perjury. Moreover, he sins against justice if he unjustly makes or denies charges against the accused. Finally, the giving of false testimony is forbidden because it is a lie.[50] But the real difficulties only start at this point. To bear witness according to justice demands that we only affirm what we are really sure of, and that we only question what we have reason to question. This is not all. Feeling sure of something is no proof that what we affirm is certain. Memory is treacherous, and although errors in memory committed in good faith excuse from perjury,[51] it is necessary to take every precaution possible in order to avoid them.

The judge is also bound to take into account the possibility of such faults. It is to guard against this that witnesses are asked to testify under oath. When a witness has sworn to tell the truth and fails to do so he is guilty of perjury, one of the gravest of faults anyone can commit since it directly affects God himself.[52] But a witness's good faith is no safeguard against error. This is why, as a rule, one single piece of testimony is not considered to be a proof, and two or more concordant testimonies are demanded. Even agreement by three witnesses is still not strictly speaking a proof, nor indeed is agreement by twenty always one. Legal evidence concerns that very particular, contingent and variable matter—human acts. In most cases, there is no hope of reaching more than probable certitude. We expect a certain percentage of error and never expect conclusive certitude. Therefore it is reasonable to admit the validity of the plaintiff's evidence when confirmed by two witnesses.[53]

Again, witnesses must be in agreement on what is essential. If several witnesses agree on the fact but not on certain essential circumstances capable of affecting the nature of this fact; for example, time, place or persons, it is just as though they disagreed on the fact itself. Indeed, they are not speaking about the same thing and each of them is no longer any more than an isolated witness. However, if one of them merely declares that he no longer remembers one of these principal circumstances, their general agreement stands, though somewhat weakened. Finally, if the disagreement is only on details of secondary importance, for example, whether it was fair weather or foul, or on the color of a house, the fundamental agreement of the witnesses does not lose its value. After all, these are things to which we do not generally attach much importance and they easily slip our mind. These petty disagreements tend to increase the trustworthiness of testimony because when several witnesses agree on the least details there is room to suspect that there has been collusion and that their testimony is false. But even this is not sure, and it is up to the prudence of the judge to decide. Finally, it is always up to him to weigh the evidence submitted. If he finds the witnesses contradicting one another, some favoring the plaintiff, some the defendant, it is his delicate duty to estimate the credibility of the witnesses who appear before him and then to pass sentence in favor of the party whom the evidence supports. If the value of the testimony appears to be equal, the accused is to be given the benefit of the doubt.[54]

We are not yet through with the actors in this little court-room drama. After the judge, the plaintiff, the accused, the witnesses comes the figure who willingly assumes the leading role, the advocate or lawyer. Pleading is a profession. Hence it is only just that he who pleads should receive an honorarium or retainer for doing so. When a pauper requires a lawyer's services, it is hardly fair to say that the lawyer is personally bound to take his case. If he does so, it is as a work of mercy. He has only to take it under this title if it is an urgent case and no one is a more obvious choice than himself. To devote oneself to the legal defense of the poor is a splendid work, but demands as a rule the sacrifice of other duties. As St. Thomas says, "We are not bound to go about looking for indigents; it is enough if we show mercy towards those we meet."

The case of doctors is a very similar one. Like the lawyer, the doctor is bound to give free assistance to the poor in urgent need of it, provided no other doctor is more obviously bound to undertake it than himself. Certainly, he does a good work when he looks after those who ought to be the charge of a colleague richer than himself or who is closer to the particular patients. It is a good work on his part to do so, but he is not strictly bound to do it. A lawyer or doctor who spent their time looking for indigents would find their clientele growing too rapidly for their income. If merchants followed this principle they would not sell their goods but distribute them to the needy.[55]

In order to carry on his profession properly, a lawyer must be capable of proving the justice of the causes he is to defend. He must have special professional competence plus the natural gifts required for public speaking. It is difficult to imagine a deaf-and-dumb lawyer. But a lawyer lacking morality ought to be even more unthinkable, because no lawyer is allowed to plead an unjust cause. If he does so in error and good faith, he commits no fault. But if he knows that the cause he is defending is unjust, he gravely offends against justice. He should even regard himself bound to repair any injury unjustly caused to the opposite party.[56]

The lawyer is in a different situation here than is the physician who undertakes to look after a desperate case. To cure a desperate case, and to win an evil cause no doubt demand exceptional talent. But if the doctor fails he does not injure anyone, while the lawyer does cause injury to someone in the event that he is successful. His professional triumph is a moral lapse.[57] Let the lawyer, then, only take on cases which he has every reason to believe just, and let him defend them as skillfully as he can, never resorting to falsehoods but allowing himself those ruses and reservations necessary for the triumph of justice. If in the course of the trial he becomes convinced that his cause is not just, he is hardly to be expected to betray it, go over to the other side and reveal the secrets he has learned. But he can and even should give up his defense and try to make his client acknowledge his guilt, or at least try to obtain from his adversary a friendly arrangement recognizing his rights.[58]

Let us here leave the courtroom and return to common life. Breach of justice by speech is not rare. It can come about through verbal assaults upon a neighbor's honor. In this sense, contumely (*contumelia*) becomes

more and more harmful as it is spoken in the presence of more people.[59]
What makes contumely and insult serious faults is the very thing that
constitutes them what they are; that is, that they are words uttered with
the intention of depriving someone of his honor.[60] This is no less serious
an offense than larceny or rapine because a man is as attached to his reputation and honor as to his goods. Therefore extreme discretion and prudence must be shown in administering public rebukes. We can be within
our right in inflicting them, it can even be our duty to do so, but in no
case nor under any pretext have we the right to disgrace another. This is
not merely saying that we must never *have the intention* of disgracing
anyone, but that we must never rob a man of his honor. To do so by a
blundering choice of words can be a mortal sin even when there is no intention of causing dishonor.

Contumely must not be confused with teasing, a favorite pastime of
playful people. We do not tease in order to wound but to entertain and
create laughter. Within limits, there is no evil in it. But we should only
tease in order to make the one we are teasing laugh. If we go a little too
far, we hurt him and this is no more legitimate than wounding another
physically by hitting him too hard in playing. Above all, teasing is for the
entertaining of the one being teased, not for the amusement of others. The
latter is a real affront.[61]

In general, contumely arises from an angry impulse. We may remember
that this passion of anger implies a desire for vengeance. Now the first
form of vengeance to which anyone is disposed, and which stands ready
for every occasion, is an insulting remark directed toward the person who
has offended us. Feeling that he has slighted us or attacked our honor, we
seek to attack his. It is not, then, pride which directly inspires insulting
words, but it disposes us to make them because it is those who think they
are superior to others who are quick to speak scornfully to others. The
proud regard any resistance to their will as an injury and are quick to
anger and have a ready insult on their lips.[62] When we find that we are
the victims of such anger, we should bear it patiently. Patience concerns
what is said against us as well as what is done against us. True patience
under these circumstances resides in the ability to accept an affront without saying a word. In other words, there is no affront which a patient man
is unable to put up with.

However, this does not mean that it is always necessary to endure such
things without protest. The virtue consists in being able to put up with
them if we have to, but we do not always have to. It is good for those who
insult others to have their boldness checked and to be put in their place. To
treat them like this is to render a service to many others too. We are not
only responsible for what we are ourselves, but for what we represent as
well. A preacher of the Gospel, for example, who would allow himself to
be publicly insulted without a word of protest would be allowing dishonor

to fall upon the Gospel. Those whose morals he ought to correct would only be too happy to believe that his are bad too. They could hardly ask for a better pretext for not correcting their own.[63]

What calumny does openly, sometimes publicly, detraction continues secretly.[64] Some detract in order to attack the good name of another; others take a guilty pleasure in whispering embittered words in the ears of mutual friends so as to destroy their friendship.[65] Others have recourse to derision in order to cover another with confusion. Ridicule is a fearful weapon; and although mere mockery can be but a game or at most a light fault, derision properly so called is a grave fault, graver than detraction and even than calumny. The calumniator at least takes seriously the evil of which he is accusing others, but the one who ridicules pretends that they are so despicable that he is only amused at them.[66]

We have thus far been speaking of the vices opposed to commutative justice. We have been describing those vices which consist in simply seizing possession of some good or other without in any way compensating its possessor. Such, for example, are the vices of larceny and rapine. We must now examine those vices which crop up in voluntary exchange, and particularly fraud, which introduces injustice into buying and selling and into commercial exchange in general.

Fraud is the selling of an object at a higher price than it is worth. The price it is worth is called its just price. The great problem is to determine just what this notion really is. It is bound up in the two actions of buying and selling. It is a question here of practices introduced for the convenience of both buyer and seller. Each needs what the other has and so they must proceed to an exchange of goods. But as the object of this exchange is to render service to both of them, it must not become a burden for either. The contract established between buyer and seller ought to show an equality. In other words, there ought to be equality between what is delivered by the seller and the price paid by the buyer. The price is the measure of the extent to which things are useful for life. Each amount of these things is measured by a given price. Money was invented to represent this price.[67] If the price is higher than the value of the thing or if, inversely, the value is greater than the price, the equality required by justice is abolished. Therefore, it is obviously unjust and illicit to sell a thing dearer or cheaper than it is worth.

So much for the principle. In practice things are not quite so simple. The mean and normal value of an object is not always identical with the real value it has for a particular buyer or seller. The seller may need it very much, be strongly attached to it and consequently experience great repugnance at parting with it, while the buyer may need it badly enough to pay more than it is worth. In such a case the just price should take into account the seller's sacrifice. The seller can licitly sell the object

above what it is worth in itself and at the price it is worth to him. On the
other hand, the buyer's need does not justify the seller increasing his price
if he is not himself making an exceptional sacrifice in consenting to sell.
We can only sell what we have. If selling involves some loss or detriment,
it is *our* detriment; if it is ours, we can demand payment for it. But the
buyer's urgent need is *his* need; since it is his, we cannot sell it to him. In
such a case a buyer may spontaneously add something to the price asked
of him in order to show his gratitude for the exceptional service rendered
him.[68]

These conditions may appear very strict, perhaps even excessive, and
certainly civil law does not go so far. The law wisely leaves a margin to
permit both buyer and seller to deceive each other a little. It is only in a
grave and unmistakable case of fraud that a court binds either party to
restitution. But we should recall once more that the object of law and of
morality is not the same. Human laws are made for the people, that is, for
more than merely the virtuous. Accordingly the civil code cannot prohibit
everything contrary to virtue. It is enough if it prohibits whatever renders
life in society impossible. It is of little consequence to it that sellers over-
charge slightly provided that the very regularity of commercial exchange
be not affected. But for the present we are concerned with morality whose
rule is not civil law but reason, that is, when all is said and done, the law
of God. Now Divine Law does not allow anything contrary to justice to
go unpunished; and as it demands just balance between merchandise and
its price, the seller who receives more than his merchandise is worth is
bound to restitution. Let us hasten to add, however, that measure is necessary even in the evaluation of measure. The just price is not rigidly
fixed. It is a matter for appraisal, and neither a little more nor a little less
prevents a transaction from being just. What matters in morality is that
the seller have the firm intention of always adhering as closely as possible
to the just price and that he succeed in doing so.[69]

As we can see, this is not very easy. If the seller knows that what he is
selling is something other than he pretends to be selling, or if he wittingly
deceives the purchaser about the quantity he claims to be delivering, the
case is clearly one of fraud and the defrauder is bound to restitution. The
real difficulties concern the appraisal of the quality of the products sold. In
certain cases the object for sale is obviously inferior and the seller takes
this into account when he fixes its price. Let us suppose, for example, that
I sell a blind horse and that for this reason sell it very cheaply. I am not
at all bound to announce at the time of the deal that my horse is blind;[70]
it is up to the buyer to see this inasmuch as the exceptionally low price I
am asking is sufficient warning that something is wrong. If the purchaser is
dishonest enough to pay so little for a sound horse, he deserves what he
is getting. But the seller must reduce his price proportionally and, if the

defect is not apparent, is in every way bound to declare it. We should sell a house much more cheaply if its foundations are dangerously weak,[71] so that it will bring its proper price.

Indeed, a merchant who wishes to be honest will find himself faced by many a trying case of conscience. If I take my wheat into an area where there is a shortage, I can get a good price for it. Even without exploiting the situation, I shall only have to sell it at what I am offered in order to do very well. But if I know that many other sellers are following me, attracted by the hope of gain, am I bound to warn buyers of this fact? If I do so, they will pay me less for my wheat or they will await the arrival of the others to put me into competition with them. St. Thomas does not feel that the seller offends justice in not announcing the coming of competitors and in selling his wheat at the price offered him. But, he adds, it would be more virtuous either to announce this fact or to reduce his price.[72]

All questions of this kind turn upon one problem: "Is it just to sell at a profit?" Many hardly see any problem here. But if for this present discussion we think of "the useless retailer" we shall see that there is a very real problem. Like all problems closely bound to the nature of things, there is always the question of the *status quo*. The society of which St. Thomas is thinking is very different in structure from free-trade societies where everything is a matter of trade and commerce and of a trade regulated by the law of supply and demand. As St. Thomas sees it, commerce is reduced to exchange in general, whether of money for money or money for goods or goods for money, which has for its object gain. Commerce, in his eyes, is an essentially private affair, pursuing a private end, which is to enrich the tradesman. St. Thomas would never admit that trade could legitimately control, as happens in capitalistic society, the exchange and distribution of goods necessary for life. All problems of this kind depend directly or indirectly on the State, whose proper function is to assure the common good of its subjects. In a society as St. Thomas would have it and as justice demands, the providing of families and of the citizens in general with goods necessary for life, pertains to the economists (*oeconomicos*) and to those endowed with public office (*politicos*). These things are not part of commerce, which is always a private enterprise, but rather of public service.

Let us understand well St. Thomas's position. There is no system here; there are only principles. The principle which he holds above all is that public service is not trade and that, consequently, members of the body politic should receive the goods necessary for life at cost. How the State is to be organized to obtain this result is the business of politicians and economists. Such enterprises might be socialized provided that this does not turn out to be more expensive than leaving them in private hands. Merchants could be entrusted to supply the public and they might legitimately do this, even finding profit in it, provided that this profit represents the just salary for the work they accomplish for the public, and not that superfluous profit which is gain as such. What governs the question is the fact that every man has the right by natural law to the means necessary for existence. To make a profit on a right is an injustice. No exchange therefore of this kind ought to be an occasion for the enrichment of those who take part in it.[73]

We have still to discuss trade, properly so-called. We have already seen that the end which the merchant proposes is gain (*lucrum*). Of itself, there is nothing wrong with the gain of money. In the present state of our society it is almost necessary, since otherwise life would be impossible. We can even have a noble end in the pursuit of gain. This is the case of the merchant who expects his trade to enable him to support his house, raise his children properly and leave him enough to help the poor. Certain businesses under given circumstances can render a service to the State. If they do so there should be profit for those who conduct them. The important thing in all these cases is that the gain have a measure and limits. It is limited to needs and is measured by the service rendered. But when gain itself becomes its own end, measure no longer remains and limits disappear. This is why St. Thomas seems to think, in spite of what has just been said, that there is something essentially base in commerce *as such*. Indeed, its proper end is gain which is in itself (*in se*) boundless. In order to make it honorable, we have to make of this end a simple means in view of an honorable and necessary end: "Trading, considered in itself, has a certain debasement attaching thereto, insofar as, by its very nature, it does not imply a virtuous or necessary end." If it has an honest or necessary end, let the merchant give himself to his business without scruple and realize a just and moderate profit. Like gain itself, trade is not a vice unless it is its own end.[74]

The problem of interest is still more complicated. It is remarkable that St. Thomas uses the term, *usura,* for both interest and usury. Usury in its most general sense is the price paid for the use of certain goods: *pretium usus, quod usura dicitur*. In a strict sense it attaches to the notions of borrowing and lending. I need a sum of money; I borrow it from someone; someone lends it to me. If I am asked for recompense for the possession of the money thus temporarily conceded me the sum which is exacted is *usura,* interest. Now according to St. Thomas it is illicit to accept interest on a loan. It is illicit because it is unjust; it is unjust because it amounts to selling something which does not exist: *quia venditur id quod non est.*[75]

There are things whose use entails their destruction. To use wine is to drink it. To use bread is to eat it. In such cases it is impossible to reckon the use of the thing as separate from the thing itself. To possess the one is to possess the other: *cuicumque conceditur usus, ex hoc ipso conceditur res*. This is obvious when it comes to selling it. To sell separately wine and the right to drink the wine is to sell the same thing twice or to sell what does not exist. In either case an injustice is done. It is the same when it is a question of a loan. When a thing is loaned to someone it is so that he can use it. If it happens to be wine that is lent to him, it is for drinking. All anyone has a right to expect is the return of the equivalent of what was loaned. It is unreasonable to claim in addition indemnity because the wine has been drunk.

Money happens to be one of those things the use of which entails its destruction. Wine is made to be drunk, money to be spent. This is literally true because money is a human invention designed expressly to make exchange possible. If money is loaned to someone it is that he may make use of it; that is, spend it. When he returns the money later on, to demand that he add to the sum borrowed an indemnity for having used it, is to ask to be reimbursed twice for the same sum.[76]

St. Thomas certainly did not foresee the complexities of modern banking. This led him into a rather uncompromising position on the principle at stake. He is clearly thinking of the simple case in which a solvent man asks for a loan from a wealthier neighbor whose money is lying unused in his coffers. Thus St. Thomas is not swayed by the classic objection that to lend money is to forego the gain which might otherwise be had from it. True enough, he replies, but the money which you might have made, you do not actually possess. What you might have been able to make you might very well never have seen. To sell money which you might have made is to sell something you don't yet possess and perhaps never would have possessed.[77]

If this objection does not stop St. Thomas, there is at least one other whose value he certainly recognizes. Let us suppose the case where a lender suffers real loss in lending his money. Has he not then some right to compensation? Yes, replies St. Thomas, for the loss suffered but not for the use of the money. This is particularly so where the borrower, thanks to the loan he has received, avoids a more serious loss than the lender has incurred in making the loan. The borrower can easily deduct from the loss he has avoided enough to compensate the lender for any loss on his part.[78]

But the Master goes even further than this. St. Thomas remains faithful to his principle and stoutly maintains that the use of money which is loaned cannot be sold, but he recognizes other ways of using money than merely spending it. For example, a sum of money can be laid out in wages, and this is not spending it. In such a case the use made of the money remains distinct from the money itself; hence it can be sold separately and consequently the lender has the right to receive more than he has loaned.[79] Many loans drawing interest in our days might very well call upon this distinction for justification. But lenders are not of great concern to St. Thomas. It is, rather, borrowers who find his indulgence. He is pitiless with usurers and lenient with those who use them. If there is injustice in usury, he says, it is the usurer who commits it. The borrower is but its victim. The poor man needs money; if he can only obtain it from a usurer, he has no choice but to accept the conditions imposed on him. None more thoroughly hate usury than those who have to resort to it. It is not usury they want but a loan.[80]

If the obligations of justice between private citizens are many and complex, they are simple in comparison with those which fall upon the head of the State in relation to his subjects. Political problems are inevitable because it is of man's nature to live in society. When we define man as a "social animal" we are often simply thinking of him as driven to seek the company of his fellows by a kind of instinct or sociability. Actually it is quite another matter. Man's nature is such that it is practically impossible for him to subsist unless he lives in a group. Most other animals can go off and live alone. They have teeth, claws and physical strength for attack, speed for safety, fur for vesture. Man has none of these. But he has his reason by which to invent tools and he has hands to use them. It is difficult for an isolated individual to prepare alone all those things he requires for himself and his family. Common life facilitates the solution of this problem through the division of labor which is therein established.

This collaboration which calls for the existence of social groups is a collaboration of minds before it is one of hands and arms. Men put their reason together by means of language. Terms and propositions enable each to express his thought to others and to be instructed by theirs. The word "society" designates, then, groups of very different nature depending upon whether it is applied to human societies or to what are sometimes called "animal societies." There is no comparison between the eminently practical collaboration of ants or bees among themselves with the commerce established among men by articulate language. The ultimate bond of human societies is reason.

To speak of *a* social group is to imply that it is *one*. It is so, indeed, in about the same way as those organisms called living bodies are one. In other words, the social group is not an organism in the physiological sense of the term, but it can neither exist nor endure unless it is organized. This necessity derives from the distinction between the good of the individual and the good of the group, or common good.[81] The first of these is that which is offered as immediately desirable to the individual as such; the second is that which is presented as finally desirable for the good of the group as such.

Between these two points of view conflict is inevitable. Each naturally prefers to do only what pleases him, as though he existed in an isolated state. But he lives in a group and he has to collaborate in the good of others as others do in its good. He must be a specialist in his own work and submit to common rules set up with an eye to the common good. The social body cannot reach its end unless conducted thereto. Just as the head governs the members of the body and as the soul governs the body itself, so must the social body have its head (*caput*), its *chief*, to organize and lead it. By whatever title he is designated, king, prince or president, the chief's first and principal duty is to govern his subjects by the rules of right and justice in view of the common good of the whole. To the extent that he has regard for right and justice, he governs men with respect for their nature which is that of free beings. A chief among men in very truth! But if he loses sight of the end for which he exercises his power and uses it in his own service rather than for the welfare of the group, he but rules a band of slaves. He is no longer the head of a state but a tyrant.

Tyranny is not necessarily confined to one man. It can happen among a people that a tiny group of men succeed in dominating all the rest and in exploiting them for their own ends. The fact that such a group is careful to identify the common good of the people with its own private ends does not alter the situation. Such tyranny can be exercised by a group of financiers, or by a political party, or by the military. Those who exercise such power are said to form an *oligarchy*. If the dominant group reaches the dimensions of a social class determined to exercise power to its own profit, or to impose on the rest of the people its own way of life, such tyranny is given the name *democracy*. The term "democracy" is given quite a different sense here from that commonly assigned to it today. It signifies the kind of tyranny which the people themselves exercise over certain classes of citizens. Each one of these tyrannies is the corruption of a corresponding form of just government. When the people assume power and exercise it justly in the interest of all, we have a *republic*. When a small group governs righteously, the country is said to be in the hands of an aristocracy. If the government is in the hands of a single person, and if he rules justly, the head of the State is called a prince or king and his regime is described as a *monarchy*. The term "king" also designates in a generic way anyone who is sole head of any political group of any size whatsoever—city, province, kingdom—and who governs it with a view to the common good of the group concerned, and not to his own profit.[82] In this sense, a President of the Republic is a king.

Which of these forms of government is best? St. Thomas is aware, in posing this question, that it is a theoretical problem whose solution, to be sure, has practical conclusions but no practical consequences applying *hic et nunc* regardless of political scene. He knew that there was an actual diversity of political regime; both Roman and Jewish history were there to show that countries are not governed according to what is wanted but according to what is possible. The Romans were first governed by kings. Their monarchy degenerated into a tyranny and kings were replaced by consuls. Thus Rome became an aristocracy. When the aristocracy became tyrannical, it degenerated into an oligarchy which, after several attempts to set up a democracy, reverted by reaction to monarchy in the form of the empire. Jewish history indicates an analogous situation,[83] and several modern instances would seem to confirm such observations. It is not here a question of some necessary law, but merely of facts depending upon what is called today collective psychology. That people often react in this way is no proof that they are right. Rather than ask themselves which is the sounder form of government and adhering to it, they waver between the desire for a monarchy at the risk of getting a tyrant and the fear of tyranny which makes them hesitate to take a king. People are made this way. Their bitterness against the corruption of a regime lasts far longer than their gratitude for the benefactions they have received from it.

The moralist must, accordingly, avoid two contrary fallacies. The first of these is to conclude that the better form of government is intrinsically inferior because it has no chance of succeeding for the moment. The other is to conclude, on the pretext that a given regime is intrinsically better, that every citizen ought to direct his political action *hic et nunc* toward the establishing or re-establishing of this form of government. As with all other action, political action is exercised *in particularibus*. It can only have two things in view: the avoiding of tyranny in all forms, for it is always evil; and, with all due consideration given for circumstances, making the form of government as like as possible to what moral science recommends as absolutely best.

This form of government is monarchy, provided it be completed by all that is good in other forms of government, as we shall show.[84] If monarchy is in itself the best form of government it is because, in the first place, the existence of the social body is in proportion to its unity. Whatever assures it of unity assures it of existence; and nothing can assure unity more completely nor in a more simple manner than the government of one single person. In the second place, it is fear of tyranny that turns some people away from monarchy; and it is important to note that all forms of government can degenerate into tyranny and that, of all tyrannies, that of a single ruler is the least intolerable. The tyranny that arises from a collective government leads as a rule to discord; while the tyranny of one ruler generally preserves order and peace. Moreover, it is rare that the tyranny of one man reaches down to all members of the social body. It usually falls heaviest on a few individuals. Finally, history shows that collective governments more often and more quickly lead to this so-dreaded tyranny than does the government of one man.[85] Essentially, therefore, monarchy is the best form of government.

We are to understand by this that the best form of government is that which places the social body under the direction of one man, but not that the best form of government is one in which the direction of the state is in the hands of one man. The prince or king can only ensure the common good of the people when he is dependent upon them. He must, therefore, appeal for the collaboration of all social forces useful to the common good if he is to direct and unite them. Hence we find St. Thomas speaking of a "properly-proportioned" form of government and regarding it as best.[86]

This kind of government is hardly the same thing as those absolute monarchies based on blood-ties whose supporters have sometimes appealed to the authority of St. Thomas. In order to describe it, St. Thomas simply turns to the Old Testament. He derives his politics from Scripture[87] and Aristotle and presents them in a text which we must quote in its entirety as a typical example of those doctrines which he would lead us to believe he has borrowed and which, nevertheless, are to be found nowhere save in his works.

"For a good disposition of power in a city or among any people whatsoever, two precautions must be taken. First, all citizens should have some share in authority. This is the way to preserve peace among people, because everyone likes an arrangement such as this and strives to maintain it, as Aristotle says in *Politics*, II, 14. The second concerns the various forms of government or the distribution of authority. Aristotle speaks of several forms of government in *Politics*, III, 6, of which the following two are most important: government by a king (*regnum*) in which one man exercises power because of his virtue; government by an aristocracy, that is, the rule of the elite (*potestas optimatum*) in which a small number of men hold sway because of their virtue. Consequently the best distribution of power in a city or kingdom should be as follows: first, a single head, chosen for his virtue, who is above all others, and secondly, under him, several heads, chosen for their virtue. Although authority attaches to certain persons, it still belongs to everyone because those persons can be chosen from among all the people or because they are actually so chosen. Here then is the best form of polity (*politia*). It is properly proportioned (*bene commixta*), consisting of kingship to the extent that one person is in charge, or aristocracy to the extent that several persons exercise power because of their virtue, of democracy, that is, of the people's power (*ex democratia, id est, potestate populi*), to the extent that the heads can be chosen from the ranks of the people and that the choosing of the heads belongs to the people." [88]

It is clear, then, that St. Thomas's monarchy is different from what has since his time been designated by that word. It is not an absolute monarchy; and St. Thomas has even expressly refuted the thesis of the Divine Right of Kings. God did not originally set up kings, absolute or otherwise, but Judges because He was afraid that the kingdom might disintegrate into a tyranny. It was only later, in what can almost be called a new burst of anger, that God conceded kings to His people. And with what precautions He did so! Far from establishing the divine right of absolute monarchy, God "announced rather that the kings were usurpers who were arrogating to themselves an iniquitous right because they were becoming tyrants and robbing their subjects." [89] St. Thomas regarded the Judges as the rulers of the only people who had God for their king. They alone were leaders by divine right. If the Jews wanted kings it was only because God was no longer their ruler. Thus, although St. Thomas firmly holds the principle that monarchy is the best form of government, he is far from thinking that people stand a good chance of being well-governed from the mere fact that they have a king. Unless his virtue is perfect (*nisi sit perfecta virtus ejus*), the man who holds such power may easily degenerate into a tyrant. But perfect virtue is rare: *perfecta autem virtus in paucis invenitur.*[90] We can see, then, what a slight chance there is of people being well-governed.

It is not likely that St. Thomas did any more in this matter than set forth a number of principles. He was not providing a political reform nor a political constitution for future ages. Rather his thought seems to have been moving in an ideal world where everything unfolds according to the demands of justice under a perfectly virtuous king. We are, we know not where, in some city or kingdom, some kingdom of, say, three or four cities. Popular elections have returned a number of leaders, all of them chosen for their wisdom and virtue: *"And I took out of your tribes men wise and honorable, and appointed them rulers."* (Deut. I, 15) An aristocracy, someone will say! To be sure, says St. Thomas, "this was aristocratic; but it was democratic in that these rulers were chosen from among all the people. We read in *Exodus*, XVIII, 21: *Provide out of all the people wise men."* [91] From among these wise men who have come from the ranks of the people, the wisest and most virtuous was elected king.[92] Here he is, then, charged with the frightening task of leading an entire people to its last end, which is to live according to virtue so that its life may be good in this world and blessed in the next.

It is for this reason that it is of the essence of monarchy that the king be virtuous. If man's end were health, kings would have to be physicians or surgeons. Were his end wealth, they would have to be bankers. If knowledge, professors. But the end of the social life is right living. To live right is to live according to virtue and hence we need virtuous kings. When this virtuous king ascends the throne, what is he going to do? He has to know what are the ways leading from earth to eternal happiness. Priests know these ways (*Malachy*, II, 17). The king, therefore, should learn from them what he has to do, and this can be reduced to three points: to establish a life of virtue and honor among those he governs; to maintain this state of affairs after establishing it; not only to maintain it but to improve it. The whole art of governing is herein contained. Without clean, well-managed and adequately provided cities, there is no moral virtue;[93] without just laws, no peace; without peace, no order nor tranquillity to live truly human lives in the practice of justice and charity. The good king is concerned with this alone, and it is in this that he finds his recompense here below.

As the soul in the body, as God in the world, so is the king in his kingdom. He is loved by his people and finds in this love a support altogether different from the fear protecting the thrones of tyrants. Riches flow to him without extortion, glory surrounds him, his renown spreads afar. But even if he is denied these terrestrial rewards, he can look forward to the recompense which God is reserving for him with the certitude of obtaining it. The ruler of the people is the servant of God, and it is from God that this faithful servant will receive his reward. Those truly royal recompenses—honor and glory—will be his in fuller measure in the degree that his kingly office is higher and more divine. The pagans were confused in thinking that their kings became gods after their death. This is not the king's motive for governing justly. But he has been God's vicar among his people and can justly expect, having led his people toward Him, to be closer to Him in the next world and, so to speak, more intimately united with Him.[94]

With the virtuous sovereign we attain the noblest form of that virtue of justice which Aristotle describes as virtue itself. Let us say at least that it is the rule of our relations with other men and the guardian of the social life. We might close our study of it right here in a system of morality directed to no other end than adapting man to the common good of the city. But the moral doctrine of St. Thomas has higher aims imposed upon it by the very metaphysics from which its principles are derived. Aristotle's man was not a creature, but St. Thomas's is. Is it surprising then that the intimate bonds uniting Creator and creature should establish some kind of society between them? If such a society exists, is it not also subject to the supreme rule of the virtue of justice? This is an almost infinite broadening of perspective which moral doctrine cannot reject since metaphysics demands it.

CHAPTER V

THE RELIGIOUS LIFE

TO PERFORM AN ACT of justice is to render someone his due in such a manner that what is rendered is equal to what is owed. Thus two notions are inseparable from that of justice, the notion of debt and the notion of equality. But there are virtues in whose definition only one of these notions, that of debt, is contained. Through the notion of debt, they are linked with justice and so are annexed thereto, but they are to be distinguished from it in this, that they do not bind the one practising them to pay all that he owes.

The most striking example of this sort of relation is the one binding man to God. What does man owe to God? He owes everything. It is hardly to be expected that man will completely pay off his indebtedness to God. It is precisely because he owes everything to God that man cannot return him measure for measure. If my neighbor gives me some of his wheat and I give him some of my wine, there is justice. But what sense would there be in my giving him some of my wine if, in order to be able to do so, he should first have to give it to me? This is exactly man's case. We cannot give God anything which He has not first given us. We have been created rational, and we are the object of a special arrangement of His Providence which governs man for man's own good and all the other creatures of this world for this same good.

This is why Divine Providence aims not only at the common good of the human species, but the good of each particular human being. Divine law is addressed personally to each human being in order to make him subject to God, to attach him to God and to unite him finally to God by means of love. For such is the end of this Law which thus prepares the supreme good of man, making him enter, by charity, a society of union with God.[1] Assuredly, such benefactions cannot be repaid. But not being able to repay a debt is no authorization to deny it. On the contrary, we are thereby the more strictly bound to acknowledge it and to declare ourselves under obligation to him to whom we know we are indebted. For this a special virtue is required, a substitute for justice which cannot in this case be exercised. The virtue by which we acknowledge a debt toward God which we are unable to acquit is the virtue of religion.[2]

Man can practise the virtue of religion toward God alone. As Cicero says, it is religion which gives worship to that higher nature called the divine nature.[3] It establishes a bond (*religio—religare*) which attaches us before all else to God as to the unceasing source of our existence and as to our last end, the object of all our voluntary decisions.[4] Since the stable disposition to act in this way can only make us better, religion is a virtue.

333

And since there is only one true God, there can only be one virtue of religion worthy of the name.[5] This is sometimes put more succinctly by saying that there is only one true religion. Moreover, it is a distinct virtue since it alone ensures the definite good of rendering to God the honor that is His due. Anything which is superior has a right to homage. God is superior in a unique way since He infinitely transcends all existing things and surpasses them in every way. To unique excellence, unique honor is due. We honor a king differently than a father, and we ought to pay a different honor to Him whose perfection infinitely exceeds all other things than we do to all those things.

Religion is not to be confused with any other virtue. And this has to be taken in the strongest sense. It does not merely mean that the virtue of religion consists in honoring God more than anything else. The goodness of the infinite being is not only *very much greater* than that of the best of finite beings, it is *essentially something else.* To honor God as He should be honored, an *essentially different* honor must be paid Him. This is the full sense of the expression. Its force is only too easily lost by repetition. The virtue of religion consists in rendering God the homage due *to Him alone.*[6]

It might very well seem that in speaking of religion we are definitely quitting the order of ethics for that of theology. But the very fact that St. Thomas borrows his definition from Cicero is enough to show that for him the virtue of religion does not exclusively nor necessarily depend on Christian revelation. Cicero was a religious man. His religion was that of a pagan who, although he did not suspect the existence of grace, was persuaded that there is a "divine nature" and that since it exists it has the right to man's worship. The virtue which enables the accomplishing of this duty is, therefore, a moral virtue related to justice. Consequently moral science is perfectly in order in dealing with it.[7]

This conclusion may be surprising to those whose notion of religion is vague and who confuse it in practice with the supernatural or Christian life. St. Thomas does not understand it in this way. The act by which man renders to God the worship due to Him is, to be sure, directed toward God, but it does not reach Him. What gives such an act its value is the intention of rendering homage to God which inspires it. A sacrifice, for example, is the concrete manifestation of one's desire to acknowledge the infinite excellence of the divine nature. Nevertheless, the object of this desire is not God but the rendering of homage to God. St. Thomas formulates this important distinction when he says that by the virtue of religion God is not object but end. If religion were a theological virtue, God would not be its end but its object.[8] It is thus with the virtue of faith. The act by which we believe not only that what God says is true but by which we believe in God, the act by which we entrust ourselves to Him and attach ourselves to Him as to the first truth justifying our faith in His word, is indeed an act of virtue with God as its direct object. It is for this reason that faith is a theological virtue and that religion is not.

Let us hasten to add that religion, simple moral virtue that it is, is the highest of them all because the function of the virtues is to direct us toward God as toward our end and that no virtue brings us as near to Him as that which honors Him through worship. To be sure, man can do little enough to honor God and we are here very far from that perfect equality achieved through the virtue of justice. But it is the intention of the will that gives virtue its merit; and although religion fails to repay man's debt with all the exactness called for by the excellence of the virtue of justice, still it exceeds justice in the nobleness of the intention from which it springs.[9] If such a thing were possible, religion would be justice toward God.

Insofar as possible religious worship consists primarily in interior acts by which we recognize that we are subject to God and by which we affirm His glory. These acts constitute the main part of religion. There are those who would like to think they constitute it in its entirety. They take themselves, as it were, for angels or at least (because a superstition like this horrifies the idealist) they argue as though the professor of philosophy were what, in less enlightened ages, theologians would have called an angel. Anything pertaining to cult and ceremony strikes them as a corruption of true religion which consists only in serving God in spirit and in truth.

We all know how profound has been the influence of the *Tractatus theologico-politicus* in this regard. Spinoza was raised in Judaism and could never understand religious rite save in terms of Jewish ritualism. Hence we can say of him, and of many another too, that they remain most Jewish in their very opposition to Judaism. The worship about which St. Thomas is thinking is very different from the kind of worship they are criticizing. It is a worship rendered to God by man considered in the concrete and substantial oneness of his body and soul. If his body is a sharer in it, it is because, in the first place, man is his body and God suffers no indignity in the homage paid by a body which was not beneath His dignity to create. It is also because man does not think without his body, nor even without those bodies which are the occasion of dispatching him by way of contemplation toward knowledge of the Divine Nature. The body has full right to a place in religion. Indeed, it actually holds a place therein because knowledge of God is dependent upon it. Rites and ceremonies are but the means by which it takes advantage of this fact. There must be signs which make it possible for human thought to ascend to those interior acts by which its union with God is accomplished.[10]

Thus religion is established as a moral virtue. But after this rather surprising step, St. Thomas takes a second and perhaps even more surprising one. He identifies religion and sanctity. He has to do this, however, if the meaning of ceremony and rite lies in honoring and striving to render homage to God. Sanctity or holiness is not a virtue distinct from religion. It does not differ from it at all, save with regard to reason which considers in religion not so much ceremonies, offerings, sacrifices taken in themselves, as the intention which confers upon them their religious sense. Doing something for God demands that thought first turn aside from everything else in order to dwell completely upon Him. This movement of conversion is a purification. As silver is purified from the lead which debases it, so thought (*mens*) is disengaged from the inferior things which are ever drawing it downwards. It strives not to become involved in them and separates itself from them as much as possible. When it does use them it is as props or pulleys to raise itself toward God. From the fact that it directly seeks the highest things, the virtue of religion implies a purification of thought. The resulting purity (*munditia*) is one of the first elements of sanctity.

Religion fastens this purified thought upon God in a twofold fashion: it worships Him as a principle and approaches Him as its end. The *sanctum* for the Latins was both what had been *purified* and *sanctioned* (*sancitum*). The Ancients called *sanctum* anything whose violation the law forbade. A pure thought, one guided and steadied by its two unshakable poles, its First Principle and its Last End, is accordingly a holy thought. Thus sanctity and religion are in reality identical.[11]

But religion demands still more. When thought renders to God the worship that is His due, it cannot dwell upon its own principle without recognizing its indebtedness to this principle for everything it has and is. This holds not only for thought itself, but for the man as well. To be aware of this dependence is to accept it spontaneously. The man who knows he is entirely God's wants to be entirely God's. When the will is dedicated to God from within, and yields itself to Him, and devotes itself to His service, it is in possession of the virtue of devotion. The Ancients were well aware of this. Let us but remember those heroes who were "devoted" to their false gods and who sacrificed their very lives for the safety of an army, men like Decius of whom Livy speaks. Here is to be found devotion; that is, the virtue consisting in a will ever ready to serve God.[12]

Starting from this point, this highest of the moral virtues discloses some of its hidden riches. The carrying out of a ceremony that is not vitalized by holiness of mind is neither worship nor religion. Such rites are signs signifying nothing. If the mind is to be fixed upon God so firmly that it is oblivious to anything else, if from holiness there is to spring the will to offer one's entire self to God, the soul must first consider God's goodness and generosity and its own deficiency and need of help. It matters little that such considerations be called meditation or contemplation but they are the indispensable sources of devotion.[13]

Religion, holiness, devotion and contemplation are inseparable. The contemplation referred to is not necessarily something scientific. Indeed, it is quite possible for science completely to absorb the mind, to make a man over-confident, and to prevent him from yielding himself entirely to God. A simple and holy woman, unhindered by science, may possess deep and abiding devotion. But we must not conclude from this that devotion increases with ignorance. The more science a man has, or the more he has of any perfection, the more homage he is able to render God. The more he can place in God's service, the greater is his devotion.

In this way does the society between God and man which is the essence of religion become firmly established. Man speaks with God, and this is prayer, in which human reason contemplates its Principle and dares turn confidently to Him to make known its wants. God the Creator is no Necessity, but a Father. And although man cannot expect God to alter the order of His providence to answer his prayers, he can and should pray that God's Will be done. Thus through prayer will man become deserving of what God has decided from eternity to grant him.[14]

St. Thomas is clearly thinking here of Christian prayer; but he does not exclude other kinds of prayer nor other forms of worship nor other manifestations of the virtue of religion. How could he, after all, ignore the fact that false religions, even paganism itself, were still religions? Nevertheless the problem of knowing what morality and what virtues we are dealing with in following St. Thomas arises with some urgency, and the answer is not simple. Assuredly, since we are following the *Summa Theologiae,* it is a question of Christian and supernatural morality. But everything points to the fact that St. Thomas is not unmindful of natural morality. He does not claim that Christianity discovered the four cardinal virtues; indeed it would take a long time to point out his borrowings from Aristotle, Cicero, and other pagan moralists in dealing with them. Once more does the revealed take hold of the revealable in order to perfect and rectify it.

St. Thomas often affirms that the pagans knew and practised virtue. This very human nature demanded it. The germ and seed of the acquired moral virtues are innate in every man. And these seeds are themselves of a higher nature than the very virtues they are capable of bringing forth.[15] These are the natural virtues. They are formed by the exercise of morally good acts through which man acquires the stable habit of performing them. Pagan virtues are of this kind. Christian virtues are of quite another nature. All virtues are defined in relation to the good toward which they are directed. The end of natural moral virtues is the welfare of the city or state which is the highest human good because it embraces and rules all the others. It concerns, indeed, the terrestrial city, that is, political bodies whose history we are acquainted with: Athens, Rome or the place we happen to be living in, no matter where it is.

Now the Incarnation, which is at the very center of Christianity, has completely transformed man's condition. By making human nature divine in the person of Christ, God has made us sharers in the divine nature: *consortes divinae naturae* (II Peter 2, 4). Here we have a profound mystery. The Incarnation is the miracle of miracles, the absolute miracle, the norm and measure of all others. For the Christian at least, it is the source of a new life, the pledge of a new society, a society founded on friendship between man and God, and among all those who love one another in God. This friendship is charity itself. So when Christianity substitutes God for the human city as the end of the moral life, it is obliged to add to the natural moral virtues an entirely new order of virtues as supernatural as the end whose attainment they make possible. In other words, as the terrestrial city has its own virtues, so too has the City of God—virtues by which we become no longer merely fellow-citizens of the Athenians or Romans but "fellow citizens with the saints and the domestics of God" (Ephesians 2.19).[16] Supernatural in their end, these moral virtues must also be supernatural in their source. The natural man is quite unable to transcend his own nature. The germs of the virtues necessary to do this are not in him. They come to him from without, infused into him by God like gifts or graces, for no man can be expected to acquire by himself something he is by nature incapable of acquiring.[17]

There is therefore a twofold distinction to be made among virtues: first, between theological and moral virtues; secondly between natural moral and supernatural moral virtues. Theological virtues and supernatural moral virtues have this in common, that they are neither acquired nor acquirable by the practice of what is good. As we have said, the good of which it is a question here cannot be naturally practised by man. How then can he form a habit of doing something of which he is quite incapable? On the other hand, the theological virtues are distinguished from the supernatural moral virtues in that the former have God for their immediate object while the latter bear directly upon certain definite kinds of human acts. Since they pertain to supernatural moral virtues, these acts are directed toward God as to their end. But they are only directed toward Him; they do not reach Him. The virtue of religion furnishes us with a striking example of this difference. It is in every way a virtue directed toward God. A man who possesses this virtue of religion must render to God the worship which is His due when, where and as it should be rendered. The supernatural moral virtues allow him to act *for God;* the theological virtues allow him to act *with God* and *in God.* By faith we believe God and in God. By hope we entrust ourselves to God and hope in Him because He is the very substance of our faith and hope. By charity the act of human love attains to God Himself. We cherish Him as a friend whom we love and by Whom we are loved, and Who through friendship is transported into us and we into Him. For my friend I am a friend; hence for God I am what He is for me.[18]

As to what moral virtues St. Thomas is actually speaking about in the

Summa, the answer in principle is simple. He is speaking of the infused supernatural moral virtues and not the acquired natural moral virtues. However, we must not forget that philosophy is never absent from this synthesis of the revealed and the revealable. It is present in the moral parts as well as elsewhere. Perhaps it is especially present in the moral parts because here it represents that nature which is presupposed by grace in order to perfect it and bring it to its end. Thus we are brought back by circumstances to that problem with which we were faced at the start of our inquiry, save that now it is in the realm of morals whereas then it was in metaphysics.

Is there a "natural morality," founded on natural moral virtues, which can lay claim to the authority of Thomas Aquinas? The only way of approaching this problem historically is to raise it as St. Thomas himself raised it. Are there moral virtues worthy of the name without the theological virtue of charity? Put this way, the problem is clear-cut, because every moral virtue residing in man through charity is a supernatural infused moral virtue. Thus we have first to know whether St. Thomas recognizes a moral order anterior to charity, then whether he recognizes a natural moral order subsisting side by side with charity.

Certainly natural moral virtues are possible apart from charity. The virtues of the pagans were and still are of this order. Now what good were they? Only the theologian can explain the relationship between nature and grace. To reject theology is to sidestep the issue. Theology's first comment on the natural state of man without grace is this. His will has been wounded by Original Sin with a consequent disordering of his concupiscence which no longer allows him to act always as his reason prescribes. Now the philosopher may not admit this essentially religious teaching. But he should at least understand it as a religious sentiment very much alive in St. Thomas and the basis of Kant's entire moral teaching. For both St. Thomas and Kant, man is capable of being better than he actually is. The divorce between reason and sensibility, however we regard it, is the underlying problem of many of our moral difficulties. The Christian solution of this problem is the doctrine of Original Sin. To accept it as Genesis explains it is to be a theologian. To prefer the *Critique of Practical Reason's* conceptual representation of this account is to be a philosopher, and the deeper the mystery we pretend to understand, the deeper metaphysician we seem to be. St. Thomas proceeds as a theologian, saying simply that without Original Sin our will would be naturally capable of complying with the orders issued by our reason. But this is no longer the case. Here, then, we have one reason for the weakness of any natural moral virtue not informed by charity.[19]

With relation to their end, however, the virtues have a far more serious limitation. Indeed, the whole value of a virtue, what actually makes it a virtue, consists in the fact that it makes the one possessing it better. But the only way of making him better is to direct him toward the good. The role of the good in morality is the same as that of undemonstrable principles in science. Sciences are derived from such principles. Now if we are mistaken about these principles, can we acquire a true science? Assuredly not. If, then, we are mistaken about the end, can we acquire virtues deserving of the name? No, and for the same reason.[20] The Gospel alone has revealed to men that their true end is union with God. Hence it is essential to purely natural moral virtues that they have ends that fall short of man's supernatural end. Since all natural moral virtues suffer this limitation, none of them is fully capable of satisfying the definition of virtue.[21]

If it is objected that the pagans could establish sciences and techniques fully satisfying the demands of learning and art, we have to reply that the argument does not hold. Every science or technique is referred by definition to some particular good. The mathematician seeks to know the relations of quantity, the physicist to inquire into the nature of bodies, the metaphysician to analyze being as being. Even in this last case where the object is more general than the others, it is still a particular object, since it is the object of metaphysics only and not of physics or mathematics. These sciences have always been and still are accessible to men without grace. When they attain the definite objects which specify them, they attain their ends.

It is different, however, with the virtues. A virtue makes both the one who possesses it and the work which he does good. The proper function of the moral virtues is, pure and simple, to make a man good: *virtutes morales . . . simpliciter faciunt hominem bonum.* To do this they have to refer a man not to a given particular good but to the highest and absolute good which is the last end of human life. It is only the virtue of charity which can do this. Hence no natural moral virtue satisfies perfectly the definition of virtue. Since it does not possess perfectly the essence of a virtue, it is not perfectly a virtue.[22]

Having gone this far, the question inevitably arises whether they are true virtues. St. Thomas develops this point with his customary brevity and precision in an article in the *Summa Theologiae* in which he asks whether there can be a true virtue where there is no supernatural charity. We can see at once what is at stake. Had he replied that without supernatural charity there is no true virtue, it would immediately follow that natural morality and moral philosophy were impossible. If he decides that true virtues can exist even without charity then both are possible. His reply is definite: true virtues can exist where there is no charity. Then he adds that although these are true virtues, they are not perfect without charity.

To be a true virtue is to be really a virtue, that is, to satisfy the definition of a virtue. For a virtue to be real it must first dispose its possessor toward the good. In this sense any stable disposition toward acting which has the effect of rendering its possessor better is a true virtue. On the other hand, there is a hierarchy of goods. In the case of any given being, there can always be assigned a principal and absolute good which is the rule and measure of all others. The closer its virtues approach this limit, the more will they merit the name of virtue. Every one of them is, indeed, a true virtue, but the only one that will satisfy the definition perfectly is the one that disposes it to the highest good. For man this highest good is the sight of God, and the virtue which helps him to this is charity. Only charity, and virtues directed and informed by charity, fully deserve this name. In this absolute sense there can be no unqualifiedly true virtue without charity: *simpliciter vera virtus sine caritate esse non potest.*

It does not follow from this that, even where charity is wanting, the other habits of doing good are not truly virtues. Let us for a moment consider one of them, that pagan "devotion" of the Roman heroes who "devoted" or dedicated themselves as a sacrifice to the gods for the safety of the army. The object of this virtue was a real good—the common good of both army and city. Every act dictated by the will for a good is a virtuous act. This sacrifice, therefore, took its origin from a true virtue because it was willingly undertaken for a true good. However, the good at stake was a particular good, not the highest good. What was wanting in this sacrifice was that it was not dictated by, in addition to the love of country, the love of God, the highest good in which all goods are included. We have to say of every act performed under these conditions that the virtue accomplishing it is a true but imperfect virtue: *erit quidem vera virtus, sed imperfecta.*[23] To quote a more recent example, the sacrifice of Decius was one thing, that of Joan of Arc another.

We see at once the consequences of all this for morality. Charity is a theological and supernatural virtue. Without it, there is no perfect virtue. Hence there can be no perfectly virtuous moral life where this supernatural virtue is wanting and where there is no grace.

At the same time, since every firm disposition to do good is a true virtue, a virtuous moral life is still possible without charity and without grace. The *Nicomachean Ethics,* the treatises of Cicero, the works of Livy still bear witness that such virtues really existed. The moral lives which such virtues directed were not perfectly virtuous, but the men possessing them were truly virtuous men.

This remark does not solve the problem raised by the Thomistic notion of morality or, better, by the notion of a Thomistic natural morality. When St. Thomas looks into the past, he sees the race of men before the coming of grace submerged, as it were, in darkness or struggling along in a sort of twilight. The best of them possessed imperfect moral virtues, temperance or fortitude for example, but in them there were only natural or acquired inclinations to do good. Not only were these good habits inconstant, but they were somewhat wanting in integration. They were not firmly rooted in the final end which, once charity has made it a reality, so arranges things that the presence of one virtue implies that of all the others. As St. Thomas puts it, only perfect virtues are "connected," the imperfect virtues are not.[24]

Only the infused virtues are perfect. They alone merit unreservedly to be called virtues because they alone ordain man absolutely to his ultimate end. Other virtues, acquired virtues which only ordain man to a relatively ultimate end, that is, ultimate within a defined order only, are only virtues in a relative sense. In the light of the Gospel, the moral splendor of antiquity is but darkness. "All that is not of faith is sin" says St. Paul (Rom. 14:23), and the Gloss cites this phrase of St. Augustine which St. Thomas makes his own: "Where the knowledge of truth is wanting, even when *mores* are excellent, the virtue is false." [25]

We can hardly imagine that St. Thomas foresaw the return of such times, save perhaps just before the final catastrophe. Whatever the case, he wrote his *Summa Theologiae* for his own age and was setting forth a moral code for Christians. To ask ourselves what kind of purely natural morality St. Thomas would propose for our century and to attempt an answer is to seek to go further than history can properly take us. But it seems rather likely, judging from what he has to say about it, that this moral teaching would rely upon theology to lead natural virtues to their point of perfection.

A purely natural code of ethics would probably assign the common good of the City, as man's final end. It would have to exact of everyone all that the common good demands, and nothing more. A primary order of moral law would then become strictly necessary. This means that there would be civil laws, promulgated by the head of the State, and that they would ensure the submission of individuals to their common end. Thus the moral regime would be a kind of social eudaemonism with rules which fall into line with civil law. The State would only concern itself with acts. Occasionally, perhaps, some determination of intention would be necessary in order to establish the nature of the act. It would be necessary, for example, to distinguish between homicide, manslaughter and accident in given cases. But outside of such cases as these, the order of intention would not fall under a civil moral code. Even the order of acts would be largely outside of the State's control. There are all kinds of morally good acts which it would not prescribe, and many bad acts which it would not forbid. St. Thomas remarks several times that laws are made for men; to ask all to do what can only be expected of a few is to be constantly placing people in the wrong. The common good demands that civil law should exact neither all the virtues nor all virtue from everyone.

Is there such a thing as a natural virtue beyond what the law demands? There is indeed. And even Aristotle said that to be good is a different thing than to be a good citizen. This modification, however, does not affect the nature of the last end, which is the rule of moral action. Good and evil can still be determined from the point of view of the common good. A man is virtuous when he obeys reason spontaneously and simply, behaving as the common good demands, and as his moral conscience prescribes. Friendship will ease the rigors of justice, and the long list of personal virtues will bring bare respect for law to its fullest perfection. The common good will also be served because nothing is of greater advantage to the State than to be able to count among its citizens only virtuous men. We are all of us so aware of this that, in the conduct of our lives, we do all we can to regulate our acts by the prescriptions of morality. We live under the law better than the letter of the law demands because our will accepts beyond the law the very principle of law.

The root of the whole confusion on this problem is once more to be found in the same misconception of the relationship of grace to nature. Grace does not suppress nature (*gratia non tollit naturam*); so also theology does not suppress philosophy, not even ethics; nor do the supernatural infused virtues do away with the natural virtues; on the contrary, they add to them and they bring them to perfection. Hence this conclusion: *There is no sense in pretending to arrive at natural virtues by separating them from grace, in a doctrine in which grace, by healing nature, actually makes nature capable of having virtues.* Once again, in dealing with the concrete, we must cast out the phantoms of pure essences. Thomism does not ask us to choose between nature and grace, but to perfect nature through grace. We do not have to choose between natural virtues and theological virtues; we have only to ask the theological virtues to help the natural virtues to realize fully their proper perfection as virtues.[26]

Some concrete examples will help us to understand this problem. Let us take again the virtue of humility. We have already noted with St. Thomas that Aristotle says nothing, nor needed to say anything, about it because his morality was essentially a morality of the City. But there is another side to the problem. Whether Aristotle knew about humility or not, it is none the less a moral and not a theological virtue. If Christians live in the City, and if they can modify their ambition by showing constant respect for the grandeur of God, there will be humble men residing in that city. We might have suspected this since St. Thomas classifies humility among the moral virtues, even while recognizing that a good citizen doesn't have to be humble, and that he doesn't owe the city any more than to keep his proper place and obey its laws.[27]

But there is no need for conjecture on this point because this very objection is raised in the *Summa Theologiae* and St. Thomas's reply is as formal as it can be: "Humility, it seems, is not a part of moderation or temperance. Indeed, it deals primarily with man's submissiveness to God. And to have God for their object is characteristic of theological virtues.

Humility, accordingly, should be placed among the theological virtues rather than made a part of temperance or moderation. The answer to this is that the theological virtues deal with the last end, that is, with the first principle in the appetitive order, and accordingly they are the causes of all the other virtues (*sunt causae omnium aliarum virtutum*). The fact that humility is caused by reverence for God does not, therefore, prevent its being a part of moderation or temperance." [28] This is a definite instance where a moral virtue owes its existence to a theological virtue.

An analogous though not identical case is that of the virtue of patience. We are apt to think this virtue very common since the occasions on which we are forced to exercise it are far from rare. But if we have any such notion, then we hardly realize what patience is, because (unless I am mistaken) it is the only moral virtue of which St. Thomas asked, in an article especially devoted to the question, whether it was possible to possess it without grace. Once again, we have to do with a moral virtue properly so called. St. Thomas showed less hesitation over it since he had already attached it to the cardinal virtue of fortitude, citing Cicero's *De Inventione Rhetorica*, c. 54: "Tully takes it as a part of fortitude." [29] Cicero knew nothing about the Incarnation nor the theological virtues. When he spoke about patience, he certainly had in mind a natural virtue. St. Thomas was so conscious of this that he brought up the same objection: "Among those not in the state of grace, there are some who have greater horror of the evils of vice than of corporeal evils. Hence we read that there were pagans who put up with many evils so as not to betray their country nor be guilty of any other shameful deed. Now this is truly to be patient. It would seem, therefore that there can be patience without the help of grace."

It can be seen that St. Thomas knew the story of Horatius Cocles. However, if fortitude of soul such as this is what is meant by patience, it is necessary to start much lower. A man can submit to a surgical operation in order to save his life. In a more rugged age, when amputations were carried out without anesthetic, it took considerable fortitude of will to undergo such an operation. But was this patience? To put up with pain in order to get well is but loving one's body well enough to submit to suffering in order to save it. We might better call this endurance (*tolerantia malorum*). It is a good thing to have, but it is a specifically distinct virtue from that of the hero who accepts torture in order to save, not his body, but his country. To undergo death for one's country is quite different from undergoing suffering in order to avoid death. The ancients called this "patience," and not without reason, for, humanly speaking, to die for one's country is the highest and grandest sacrifice a man can make. However, even here it is not a question of superhuman virtue. When God created man to live in society, He made him capable of the natural virtues necessary for the maintenance of that society: "The good of a political virtue is commensurate with human nature." There must, then, be men naturally capable of such sacrifices. Their will can make such an endeavor though not (for St. Thomas does not confuse the heroic with the ordinary) "without the help of God." But this divine assistance which takes human nature to its very limit is still not the same thing as grace, which takes nature beyond its limits. This supernatural grace, however, must be present if one is to endure all evils and sufferings rather than lose grace itself. To prefer this supernatural good to all natural goods is to love God above all things. In this does charity consist. Therefore it is no longer the same thing at all: "it is impossible to have patience without the help of grace." [30]

There is therefore no point in trying to isolate supernatural charity from the virtues of the personal and social life. Natural religion, which is only one natural moral virtue among many, is unable itself to perfect them as virtues. Accordingly, the supernatural religious life is the practical, necessary condition of any personal or social life built around virtues fully deserving of the name. This religious life within us is the work of grace. This participation in the divine life is in man's case the germ of a new life. From the moment man, a natural being, receives this free gift, he has something supernatural about him, something that comes from God. This something is very much his. He truly possesses it so that henceforth he will be able to attain of himself that supernatural good which is his ultimate end. Here he is, then, by reason of the presence and life of this principle within him, leading a life of participation in the divine life. This is what is meant by supernatural life. Grace, which is the germ of this life, affects man deeply, regenerating and, as it were, re-creating it.

The soul thus affected is still a soul endowed with reason and intelligence. It is because it is capable of intellectual knowledge and therefore of friendship with God, that the human soul is able to receive this divine, supernatural gift. Thus it can be seen that grace, in spreading from the essence of the human soul into its various faculties, first affects the highest of all the soul's faculties, its intellect or knowing faculty, along with reason which is actually only its movement. What makes the nature of man an intelligent nature, or, better perhaps, the nature of man insofar as it is intelligent, is designated by "mind" or *mens*, the term associated with his thinking. It is this which permits man, unlike creatures lacking reason, to be called the created image of God.

This quality of being the image of God is co-essential to man because it is one with the rationality of his nature. To be a mind is to be naturally capable of knowing and loving God. To be able to do this is one with the very nature of thinking. It is as natural for man to be the image of God as to be a rational animal, that is, as to be man. The first effect of grace is, therefore, to perfect this resemblance of man to God by divinizing his soul, his mind and consequently his whole nature.[31] From the moment he has grace, man can love God with a love worthy of God since this love is divine in its origin. God can accordingly accept it. By the grace of God man has become holy and just in the eyes of God. The life of grace consists therefore in the knowledge and love of God by a rational soul that has been made a sharer in the divine nature and capable of living in society with Him.[32]

Socrates' precept, taken over and provided with a deeper significance by Christian thought, comes at last fully into its own. It is man's duty to know himself and to discern what in his nature confers eminent dignity upon him.[33] Not everyone does this. Man is a substantial union of intellect and body; he is the meeting-place of two worlds: the intelligible which he attains through intelligence and the material which he perceives through his senses. So man has only one natural life but two ways of using it, depending upon whether he chooses to turn toward the intelligible or the corporeal. In fact, nature demands that he move in both worlds. We have already seen that human knowledge can only approach the intelligible by way of the senses. Thus the natural movement of reason necessarily begins by directing man toward the world of bodies whose existence and qualities he perceives by his senses. Gradually he can construct a science of material bodies determining with increasing accuracy their nature and laws. Thus step by step there is acquired a habitus, an intellectual virtue already designated in its proper place as a science. No matter how high or perfect they are, all sciences have this in common that they deal with the intelligible enclosed in something sensible. Even mathematics is tied to the sensible by its object, quantity. But matter endures in time. Hence all sciences of nature deal with temporal things.

To the extent that human reason, which always remains one and the same, is applied in the acquiring of science, it is called "inferior reason," a term designating reason itself in the use (officium) which has just been defined.[34] On the other hand, reason is capable of being directed toward the world of such supra-sensible realities as "being as being," the good, the true, the beautiful. Here we have the incorporeal, the non-temporal, the eternal. Since its object is specifically distinct from that of the sciences, we must regard the knowledge we can acquire in this way as specifically distinct from scientific learning. It is called wisdom. The use man makes of his reason in struggling to acquire wisdom, whether the wisdom of metaphysics, or still more, that of theology, is called "superior reason." If it is by his intellect that man is specifically constituted in his proper dignity, in the image of God and above the beast, it can be seen that he ought to move, as though by natural inclination, toward the noblest objects which his intellect can know. By rights he should be like this. That he is in actual fact otherwise is only a further indication of a lack of balance in human nature which puts to philosophy a question which only the theologian can answer.

But this is not the most serious problem. Man is not satisfied to prefer science to wisdom in such a way that he thinks he can better understand the higher when he can reduce it to the lower. But he usually finds that even science is far too deep for him. Held down by the fearful weight of an uncontrolled sensibility, only too many are no longer aware of the call of the intellect and reason. Their soul has sunk into their belly. It is in its sense of truth that Platonism is so profoundly right. When man has buried his mind in the tomb of his body, he can no longer be said to know himself. He knows, to be sure, that he is made up of soul and body, but he has so completely forsaken his kingdom that he seems to have lost even its memory. Forgetting it, he forgets himself. Because when a man does anything, it is his "head" that does it, his *mens rationalis*, his rational mind. He cannot ignore the very existence of his rational mind and still know what he is.[35]

When grace divinizes the human soul it not only re-establishes the balance which had once been destroyed, but causes a new life to spring up, a life freely given to nature. This life participates in the divine and so, by reason of its source, will move spontaneously into the order of the eternal. It is called the "spiritual life," a term which implies that absolute transcendence of body and time which is characteristic of divine things. And since it is by charity that man's participation in the divine is accomplished, the spiritual life is the supernatural life of a soul divinized by charity.[36]

It is from here that we should set out to discover how the natural moral virtues dovetail into the infused moral virtues and the theological virtues according to the mind of St. Thomas. To attempt to disentangle the virtues in this theological organism so as to arrive at purely natural virtues is dangerous indeed, particularly if the objective is to discover a moral doctrine that can be called Thomistic. To dissociate the virtues from grace is not to take them back to the state of nature, but to the state of fallen nature. It is to transfer them from one theological state to another. It is to bring them to that state in which of all its possible states nature is least itself, because in its fallen state nature is wounded in its power to move toward the good and to fortify itself with genuine virtues, that is, with such virtues as alone make it capable of fulfilling its own end. Hence the natural morality which St. Thomas describes pertains to a nature healed by grace, a nature which has at last achieved a kind of fulness by reason of the divine life that has been introduced into its very depths.

It is impossible, then, from a truly Thomistic point of view, to imagine a natural morality without binding it to that spiritual life the perfection of which is the perfection of that morality. Those who would attempt such a study should be on their guard against the fundamental error of considering each moral virtue to be crowned with a theological double whose function is to do the same thing in a better way. The natural virtues remain what they were; it is the one who possesses them who has changed.

Natural superior reason acquires, after a long and patient effort, the virtue of wisdom, the summit of the intellectual and the moral life. The man who possesses it is called a wise man. Thanks to this intellectual virtue he has become capable of knowing divine and eternal things as correctly judged by a well-informed reason. But the supernatural gift of Wisdom acts in a very different way. It relates the wise man's soul to divine things, at the same time making it divine. The Gift of Wisdom, then, does not add a superior reason to the natural superior reason, but it causes reason, in its investigation of the divine, to feel as it were at home therein, instinctively sensing what is true long before grasping its demonstration. The Gift of Wisdom makes reason capable of guiding the soul toward truth if man is seeking it and, in many cases, sufficient to excuse him from doing so. Natural theology for a Christian is the work of a superior reason essentially identical with that of any other metaphysician, but of a reason penetrated with a deep spiritual life which gives it a connaturality with the realities it is dealing with. It is, accordingly, better able to deal with them.[37]

All wisdom is a knowledge of divine things making possible a sane judgment about them. The Gift of Wisdom dwells in the understanding and makes it connatural with divine things and causes it to share in the light and stability of God's ideas. The wise man not only contemplates in the light of what St. Augustine loved to call the "eternal" rules in order to know, but he also consults them in order to act. His spiritual life connects his soul to the divine and so the Gift of Wisdom has not only a speculative but a practical efficacy. It not only directs contemplation but action as well.[38]

Nothing better illustrates the "vital" character of spirituality than this claim of supernatural Wisdom's to a practical function. Considered as an acquired natural virtue, wisdom is one of those purely speculative intellectual habits of which St. Thomas states that "they do not perfect the appetitive part, nor affect it in any way, but only the intellective part." [39] They are made by knowledge, and their function is to regulate all other knowledge as such, that is, to permit us to see what is true, not to do what is good. Natural wisdom is, accordingly, a virtue for which the intellect is not only the seat but the cause. This is not the case of infused Wisdom, the Gift of the Holy Ghost. Its proper function is not to make us see in God the first principles of knowledge, but to make us share in them insofar as they are divine truth itself. This supernatural virtue does not disclose for us the Ideas, those divine rules by which human reason judges all things. Nor does it constitute in any way an intellectual view of the highest cause, God. But it is a participation in God which is lived, and it enables us to peer into Him, as it were, and handle the first principles of knowledge with an understanding that has been made divine.

The root of this Wisdom is, then, less a cognitive intuition than a com-

munion between nature as knowing and the divine. Its effect, "rectitude of
a judgment made according to divine reasons," is not in this case produced
by the metaphysician's habit of using his reason correctly in such matters.
Its rectitude of judgment comes from elsewhere, from its supernatural relationship in the family of divine things. Now it is only charity that can give
man kinship with God. To be "in sympathy with" the divine, as Dionysius
says, that is, to see it from within rather than from without, to be impregnated with it, to absorb it into one's very substance, it must be loved
with a love of friendship: "Sympathy with or connaturality with divine
things is brought about by charity which unites us with God." This is
why supernatural Wisdom, whose essence has its seat in the understanding,
has its cause in the will. This cause is Charity.[40]

Supernatural charity firmly establishes man in his last end. Wisdom,
which is born of supernatural charity, has a particular practical function,
legitimate only in certain definite cases. It is by Wisdom that Charity
reaches, penetrates and directs all our acts, orientating them toward the
supreme Good which they have to attain if they are not to be wasted acts.
This is not simply a transference of general intention. Natural morality
cannot be taken as such and included in Christian morality. Charity never
leaves a moral virtue as it finds it. There is not a single moral act which
does not through it *become another act*, as can be seen by a simple glance
at the metamorphosis to which Charity subjects it.[41]

In the last analysis this virtue depends upon the humanly unforeseeable
and impossible fact that man is one day to share eternal beatitude with
God. We have friendship with our parents because we live with them. We
can have friendship with our fellow citizens because we share the same
natural life. By the grace of the Incarnation which made human nature
divine, we can have friendship with God because we can live with Him.
To have a part in God's life, to be of value in His eyes, to count for
something in His life, and to know Him, this is the principle of our friendship with Him.[42] No other virtue, even among those freely given, can be
compared with this one because no other touches God so intimately. By
faith and hope we attain to God as cause of the truth which He reveals
and of the good He promises. Through them we approach Him as the
cause of His gifts to us. But charity brings us to God Himself. We believe
in God's truth; we hope for His beatitude; we believe and hope *in God*
as the cause and substance of revealed truth and promised beatitude. But
we love God for God because He is God.[43] Charity attains God and comes
to rest in Him. It has nothing further to attain since in Him it has all
things.

A soul living by supernatural Charity is no longer able to will anything
but God Himself, or if it wants anything else it can only be in union with
His will. To love what God loves as He loves it is indeed that "to will the
same things, not to will the same things" (*eadem velle, eadem nolle*)

in which friendship consists. As we have just said, this friendship depends upon the fact that God shares with man a very definite good, His beatitude, which is Himself. This is why man must love God above everything, as the cause and substance of his friendship with Him.

Thus supernatural Charity brings to its conclusion the profoundest and most universal yearning of nature. Every natural movement is the operation of a body which, whether it knows it or not, is moving in view of some end. Each natural operation is accordingly the actualization of a desire. Whatever moves itself or is moved, loves. The stone which falls, the flame which arises, the tree that grows, the animal in search of its prey, living or not, each being is moved by a love—natural love in the case of a being lacking knowledge, animal in a knowing being.

Endowed with intelligence and reason, man is capable of knowing that God exists, that He has created us and invited us to share these goods in communion with Him. Hence there is a natural love of man for God, a sort of first natural friendship by which man naturally loves God above all things. Perhaps we should say, *should* love Him, because man's nature is no longer sound.[44] The first effect of grace is to restore this natural love of God above all things. It will not destroy it but integrate it with the supernatural love of man for God. Supernatural friendship, based on the sharing of divine beatitude, restores to man the natural friendship which he originally had with God. Then the whole natural morality returns with its order and hierarchy of virtues. But it will not last if deprived of the conditions which brought about its rebirth. For man in his fallen state, grace alone makes possible that firm willing of the good which, even in nature, seeks only the will of God.

CHAPTER VI

THE LAST END

ALL CREATURES COME from one cause and move toward one end. We can expect, therefore, that the same principle will regulate both moral action and physical laws. It is the same deep cause which makes the stone fall, the flame rise, the heavens turn and men to will. Each of these beings is seeking by its operation to achieve its own perfection and, at the same time, to realize its end which is to represent God: "Everything tending to its own perfection, tends to a divine likeness." [1]

However, each being is clearly defined by its own essence and it will have its own way of realizing the end common to all. Since all creatures, even those devoid of intellect, are ordered to God as toward their last end, and since all things attain their last end in the measure in which they share in its likeness, intelligent creatures must attain their end in a manner peculiar to them, that is, by the operation proper to them as intelligent creatures. They must *know* it. It is immediately evident, then, that the last end of an intelligent creature is to know God.[2] This conclusion is inevitable, and other arguments equally direct could be found to convince us of its necessity. To be completely convinced, however, we shall have to see how this last end gathers together all intermediate ends and orders them to itself, and how each particular happiness is but a premise of this beatitude.

Man is a voluntary and free being. He always acts in view of an end, and his acts are specified by this end, that is, his acts are arranged into various species according to the ends which are both their principle and end.[3] Now it cannot be doubted that there exists, over and above the host of particular ends, a last end of human life looked at as a whole. One end is ordained and willed because of another, and, if there were no last end, the series of ends would have to be taken to infinity. It would be the same as if the series of movers and of things moved were infinite, and nothing would ever be desired and no action would ever be brought to an end. Every act starts from an end and comes to rest in it. Therefore we have to conclude that there is a last end.[4]

At the same time it can be seen that whatever man wills, he wills in view of this last end. The last end moves the appetite in the same way as the first mover moves all other moveable things. Now it is clear that while the second cause transmits movement, it can only do so in so much as it is itself moved by the first mover. In the same way, second ends are only desirable and only move the appetite inasmuch as they are ordered toward the last end, which is the first of all desirable objects.[5] Let us see in what this last end consists.

Various and strange are the aspects under which men place this end before their eyes. Riches, health, power, all imaginable corporeal goods, and so on, have been taken for the highest good and the last end. But all of these are erroneous. Man is not the last end of the universe. He is a particular being ordered, like all the rest, in view of a higher end. Neither the satisfying of his body nor its conservation can be constituted his Sovereign Good or his last end. And even if we concede that the end of the human reason and will is to conserve the human body, it still does not follow that man's last end consists in a corporeal good. The human being is, indeed, composed of soul and body. But if it is true that the being of the body depends upon the soul, it is not true that the being of the soul depends upon the body. On the contrary, the body is ordered to the soul as matter to form. In no case can the last end of man, which is beatitude, be considered as seated in a corporeal good.[6]

Does it rest, then, in pleasure or in some other good of the soul? If by "beatitude" we mean not the acquiring of beatitude nor its possession, for these, of course, do depend upon the soul, but that very thing in which beatitude consists, then beatitude is not a good belonging to the soul but subsists outside the soul and infinitely above it. "Beatitude pertains to the soul, but consists in something outside the soul."[7]

It is actually impossible that man's last end be the human soul or anything belonging to it. If we consider the soul in itself, it is only in potency. Its knowledge, its virtue have to be reduced from potency to act. What is in potency is related to its act as the incomplete to the complete. Potency only exists in view of act. It is manifest, therefore, that the human soul exists in view of something else and that as a consequence it is not its own last end. And it is even more manifest that no good of the soul constitutes its Sovereign Good. The Good which constitutes the last end can only be the perfect good, the good which fully satisfies the appetite. Now the human appetite, the will, tends toward universal good, as we have shown. But, as we know from elsewhere, every good inhering in a finite human soul like ours is by that very fact a finite and participated good. Hence no such good can be man's Sovereign Good nor become his last end.

Let us say then, as a general thesis, that man's beatitude cannot consist in any created good. It can only reside in a perfect good, one fully satisfying the appetite, for indeed it could not be the last end if, once acquired, it still left something further to be desired. Now, since nothing can fully satisfy the human will save universal good, which is its proper object, no created and participated good can constitute the Sovereign Good and last end. Therefore man's beatitude is in God alone,[8] who is the first and universal good, the source of all other goods.

We know, then, where beatitude resides. But what is its essence? Let us consider the precise meaning of this question. The term "end" can have two meanings. It can refer first of all to the very thing we wish to obtain. In this sense money is the "end" which the miser seeks. But it can also refer to the acquisition, possession, use and enjoyment of what is desired. In this sense, it is the possession of money which the miser is seeking. These two senses of "end" must be distinguished in a discussion of beatitude. We know well enough what beatitude is in the first sense: it is the uncreated good which we call God, who alone by His infinite goodness can perfectly fill up the will of man. But what does beatitude consist in? It is this second sense of beatitude which we must now examine.

From this point of view, beatitude appears to be a created good. The cause or object of beatitude, as we have shown, is certainly uncreated. But the essence of beatitude, its acquisition by man, the enjoyment of the last end is necessarily something human and consequently something created.[9] We can add that this something is an operation and act, since beatitude constitutes man's highest perfection, and perfection implies act just as potency implies imperfection.[10] Finally, this operation is the operation of the human intellect, excluding all other powers of the soul. We cannot claim that beatitude is reducible to an operation of the sensitive soul. We have established that the very object of beatitude does not reside in corporeal goods; and these goods are the only ones which the sensitive operations of the soul can attain; hence they are radically powerless to confer beatitude upon us.[11]

We already know, however, that of the intellect and will which together form the rational part of the soul, only the intellect is able to grasp immediately the object of beatitude and our last end. Now we should distinguish between the very essence of beatitude and that delectation which always accompanies it, but which, compared with beatitude considered essentially, is in the last analysis but an accident.[12] Once this is posited, it becomes clear that beatitude cannot consist essentially in a voluntary act. All men desire their last end. Its possession represents for them the highest degree of perfection and, consequently, of beatitude. But it is not the will that apprehends ends. The will moves toward absent ends when it desires them, and toward present ends when it rests complacently and pleasurably in them. But desiring an end is not to comprehend it, it is merely to move toward it. As for pleasure involved, it only surges in the will because the very object sought is present. The will takes pleasure in the object because it is present, and it is wrong to reason as though the object were present in it. The very essence of beatitude, therefore, consists in an act of the intellect; and it is only the delight which accompanies it that can be considered as an act of the will.[13]

All the preceding arguments presuppose the principle that if beatitude can be acquired by an operation of man, it can only be by the most perfect and highest of his operations. Using the same principle, we can hold further that beatitude must consist in an operation of the speculative rather than of the practical intellect. The most perfect power of the intellect is the one whose object is the most perfect, that is whose object is the essence of God. This essence is the object of the speculative not of the practical intellect. The act constituting beatitude must therefore be of a speculative nature, and this amounts to saying that it must be an act of contemplation,[14] although we still have to be more precise about this object.

Does the contemplation which is the source of beatitude consist, for example, in the consideration of speculative science? To answer this question, we have to make a distinction between the two kinds of beatitude accessible to man—perfect beatitude and imperfect. Perfect beatitude is that which attains the true essence of beatitude; imperfect beatitude does not attain it but shares, on some particular points, in some of the characteristics pertaining to true beatitude. Now it is certain that that true beatitude cannot be reduced, insofar as its very essence is concerned, to knowledge of the speculative sciences. In considering the speculative sciences, our vision cannot extend further than the first principles of these sciences, for the whole of any science is contained virtually in the principles from which it is deduced. Now the first principles of the speculative sciences are only known with the help of sense knowledge. Therefore our consideration of speculative sciences as a whole cannot take our intellect beyond the point to which the knowledge of sensible things can bring it. It is enough then that we know whether knowledge of sensible things can constitute man's higher beatitude or highest perfection.

It immediately appears that it cannot. The perfection of the superior is not found in the inferior as such. The inferior can only contribute to the perfection of its superior in the measure in which it participates, however wretchedly, in a reality which is beyond itself and beyond the superior as well. The form of a stone, or of any sensible thing, is inferior to man. If in sense knowledge the form of the stone confers some perfection on the human intellect, it is not inasmuch as it is merely the form of the stone, but inasmuch as this form participates in a reality of an order higher than the human intellect; e.g., intelligible light or something of this kind. All knowledge capable of conferring some perfection on the human intellect presupposes an object above this intellect. This would be especially true of the absolutely perfect human knowledge which confers beatific contemplation upon it.

Here we reap the fruits of the conclusion we reached about the value and import of human knowledge. Its proper object is the sensible. It is not, therefore, in the consideration of the sensible, to which speculative sciences are confined, that the human intellect can find its beatitude and its highest perfection.[15] But it can find imperfect beatitude therein, the only beatitude we can achieve here below. Just as sensible forms participate in some resemblance of higher substances, so the consideration of speculative sciences is a sort of participation in true and perfect beatitude.[16] Through them our intellect is brought from potency into act, but they do not bring it to its complete and ultimate actuality.

This means that true and essential beatitude is not of this world. It can only be found in the clear sight of God's being. To grasp the truth of this conclusion, two principles must be known: First, that man is not perfectly happy as long as he has something to wish for and to seek; secondly, that the perfection of the powers of the soul is measured by the nature of their objects. Now the proper object of the intellect is *quod quid est,* that is, the quiddity or essence of the thing. Thus the perfection of the intellect is measured by the depth of its knowledge of the essence of its object. If, for example, an intellect knows the essence of some effect without this knowledge enabling it to know the essence of its cause, then it can be said to know that the cause exists but it cannot be said to know the nature of that cause. It knows the *an sit,* but not the *quid est.* In a word, it does not know this cause, purely and simply. There subsists, then, in the man who recognizes and knows that this effect has a cause, a natural desire to know what this cause is. This is the source of the curiosity and surprise which lie, according to the Philosopher, at the origin of all research.

When a man sees an eclipse of the sun, he immediately judges that this fact has a cause. But he does not know what the cause is. He is surprised and, because surprised, seeks to find it out. His research will not end until he does find out the cause of the phenomenon in its very essence. Let us recall for a moment what the human intellect knows about its creator. Properly speaking, it knows no other essences than those of sensible, created objects. From these it comes to know that God exists, but it never attains the essence of the first cause. Therefore man experiences the natural desire to know fully and to see directly the essence of this cause. But if he naturally desires beatitude, he does not know as man and without the light of revelation, what beatitude is. At least, he only knows it in the measure that God can be known from sensibles. He will only, then, attain his last end and highest perfection through union with God, the only object of contemplation which can entirely satisfy the highest powers of his soul and raise him to his total perfection.[17]

This beatitude, which transcends man and nature, is no adventitious term trumped up to put morality and religion into accord. There is an intimate accord, indeed almost a continuity of order between the earthly beatitude accessible here below and the heavenly beatitude to which we are called. The last end is not the negation of our human ends, rather it gathers them together sublimates and refines them, because human ends are but partial imitations of our last end and imperfect substitutes for it.

Of all the desires which man experiences there is not one which when properly governed and interpreted by reason cannot be given a legitimate significance. Here below we desire health and corporeal goods; and these, indeed, are favorable conditions for cognitive operations through which the most perfect human happiness is attained. We desire, in this life, exterior goods such as the goods of fortune; we desire them because they enable us to live and to perform the works of contemplative and active virtue. They may not be essential for beatitude, but they are at least instruments of it. Here below we desire the society of our friends, and rightly so because the man who is happy in this world must have friends. But he does not need them because they are useful to him—the wise man, indeed is sufficient to himself—nor because they are a source of pleasures —the wise man finds perfect pleasure in the exercise of virtue—but because he has to have matter on which to practice virtue. His friends are there to receive his good deeds; they provide him with opportunities, to acquire virtue or to perfect it.

Inversely, all goods come together again, sublimated and put in order, in heavenly beatitude. Even when he sees God face to face in the beatific vision, even when the soul has come to resemble some separated Intelligence, man's beatitude is not that of a soul separated from its body. The composite will turn up once more within the very glory of heaven: "For since it is natural for the soul to be united to a body, the natural perfection of the soul cannot exclude the perfection of the body." Before beatitude, the body is the soul's minister; it is the instrument of those lesser operations which facilitate its approach thereto. But during beatitude, the soul rewards its servant, confers incorruptibility upon it and lets it share in its own immortal perfection. "The soul's beatitude redounds to the body so that it too may taste of its perfection." [18]

The soul, which is united to that body which was once animal but is now spiritualized in glory, has no longer to pursue the material goods which are ordained on earth to the animal life. She no longer needs any other friend than her God who comforts her with His eternity, truth and love. We can believe, however, that the joy of heaven is not solitary, and that heavenly beatitude is accompanied by the vision which the blessed have of one another's joy, and that is embellished with eternal friendships. [19]

Thus Thomism continues nature into supernature. When it has described the total man, and not merely the human soul, as the immediate object of philosophy, it goes on to deal with the destiny not merely of the human soul but of the total man. For St. Thomas, the Christian's beatitude is the beatitude of the whole man.

CHAPTER VII

THE SPIRIT OF THOMISM

THUS FAR we have been examining the more important philosophical problems dealt with by Thomas Aquinas. In discussing these problems we have attempted to show the bond which ties them together and gives continuity to their solutions. Perhaps it will be useful, here at the end of this study, to take a comprehensive look over our course and to pick out, as precisely as possible, what is constant in St. Thomas's philosophical outlook.

One has no doubt perceived the unified character of a doctrine which provides an explanation of the universe and of man from the point of view of human reason. This character is due to the fact that the texture of Thomism is made from a very small number of principles which are finely interwoven. Perhaps, when all is said and done, all these principles are various aspects of one central notion, the notion of being. Human thought is only satisfied when it grasps an existence; but our intellection of a being never limits itself to the sterile apprehension of a given reality. The apprehended being invites our intellect to explore it; it invites intellectual activity by the very multiplicity of aspects which it reveals. Inasmuch as a being is not distinguished from itself, it is one. In this sense we can say that being and oneness are the same. No essence divides itself without losing at the same time its being and its unity. But since a being is by definition inseparable from itself, it lays the basis of the truth which can be affirmed about it. To say what is true is to say what is, and is to attribute to each thing the very being which it is. Thus it is the being of a thing which founds its truth; and it is the truth of a thing which underlies the truth of thought.

We think the truth of a thing when we attribute to it the being that it has. It is thus that accord is established between our thought and its object; and it is this accord which provides the basis for what is true in our knowledge just as the intimate accord which subsists between its object and the eternal thought which God has of it establishes the truth of the thing outside our thought. The line of the relationships of truth is therefore only one aspect of the line of the relationships of being.

We find exactly the same thing in the case of the good. Every being insofar as it is knowable is the basis of truth. But insofar as it is defined by a certain quantity of perfection, and consequently insofar as it is, it is desirable and presents itself to us as a good; and hence the movement to take possession of it which arises in us when we find ourselves in its presence. Thus the same being, without the addition of anything from outside, displays before us its unity, its truth and its goodness. Whatever the relationship of identity which our thought can affirm in any one of the moments of the doctrinal synthesis, whatever the truth we set forth or good we desire, our thought always refers to being in order to establish its accord with itself, in order to assimilate its nature by way of knowledge or to enjoy its perfection through the will.

But Thomism is not a system if by this is meant a global explanation of the world deduced or constructed, in an idealistic manner, from *a priori* principles. The content of the notion of being is not such that it can be defined once and for all and set forth in an *a priori* way. There are many ways of being, and these ways must be ascertained. The one most immediately given to us is our own and that of corporeal things among which we pass our life. Each one of us "is," but in an incomplete and deficient manner. In the field of experience directly accessible to us we only meet substantial composites analogous to ourselves, forms engaged in matters by so indissoluble a bond that their very "engagement" defines these beings and that God's creative action, when it puts them into existence, directly produces the compounds of matter and form that constitute their beings. However imperfect such a being may be, it does possess perfection to the extent that it possesses being. We already find in it transcendental relations of unity, truth, goodness and beauty which are inseparable from it and which we have defined. But we note at the same time that, for some deep reason which we have still to determine, these relations are not fixed, closed, definite. Everything takes place—and experience verifies this—as though we had to struggle in order to establish these relationships instead of enjoying them peacefully. We are, and we are identical with ourselves, but not completely so. A sort of margin keeps us a little short of our quiddity. We do not fully realize human essence nor even the complete notion of our individuality. Hence, it is not simply a matter of being, but of a permanent effort to maintain ourselves in being, to conserve ourselves, realize ourselves. It is just the same with all the other sensible beings which we find around us. There are always forces at work. The world is perpetually agitated by movements. It is in a continual state of becoming, like man himself ceaselessly passing from one state to another.

This universal becoming is normally expressed in terms of the distinction of potency and act, which extends to all given beings within our experience. These notions add nothing to the notion of being. Act always is being; potency always is possible being. Just as Aristotle had stated the universal extension of this principle without attempting to define it, St. Thomas readily uses it without explanation. It is a sort of postulate, a formula stating as a fact the definite modes of being given to us in experience. Any essence which does not completely realize its definition is act in the measure in which it does realize it, potency in the measure in which it does not, and privation in the measure in which it does not realize it. Insofar as it is in act, it is the active principle which will release the motion of realization. It is from the actuality of form that all endeavors of this kind proceed; it is the source of motion, the reason of becoming; it is cause. Once more, it is the being in things which is the ultimate reason of all the natural processes we have been stating. It is being as such which communicates its form as efficient cause, which produces change as motive cause, and assigns to it a reason for being produced as final cause. We are dealing, then, with beings which are ceaselessly moved by a fundamental need to save and complete themselves.

Now we cannot reflect upon an experience like this without becoming aware that it does not contain the explanation of the facts it places before us. This world of becoming which grows active in order to find itself, these heavenly spheres continually seeking themselves in the successive points of their orbits, these human souls which capture and assimilate being by their intellect, these substantial forms forever searching out new matters in which to realize themselves, do not contain in themselves the explanation of what they are. If such beings were self-explaining, they would be lacking nothing. Or, inversely, they would have to be lacking nothing before they could be self-explaining. But then they would no longer move in search of themselves. They would repose in the integrity of their own essence realized at last. They would cease to be becoming and enjoy the fulness of being.

It is, therefore, outside the world of potency and act, above becoming, and in a being which is what it is totally, that we must look for the cause of the universe. But this being which thought can reach is obviously of a different nature than the being we have been talking about, for if it were not different from the being which experience gives, there would be no point in positing it. Thus the world of becoming postulates a principle removed from becoming and placed entirely outside it.

But then a new problem arises. If the being we postulate from experience is radically different from the one given to us in experience, how can we know it through this experience and how shall we even explain it in terms of this experience? Nothing can be deduced or inferred about a being from some other being which does not exist in the same sense as the first one does. Our thought would be quite inadequate to proceed to such a conclusion unless the reality in which we moved formed, by its hierarchical and analogical structure, a sort of ladder leading toward God.

It is precisely because every operation is the realization of an essence, and because every essence is a certain quantity of being and perfection, that the universe reveals itself to us as a society made up of superiors and inferiors. The very definition of each essence ranks it immediately in its proper place in this hierarchy. To explain the operation of an individual thing, not only must we have the notion of this individual, but we must also have the definition of the essence which it embodies in a deficient manner. And the species itself is not enough because the individuals which go to make up the species are ceaselessly striving to realize themselves. Thus it becomes necessary either to renounce trying to account for this operation or else to seek for its explanation at a higher level, in a superior grade of perfection.

From here on, the universe appears essentially a hierarchy and the philosophical problem is to indicate its exact arrangement and to place each class of beings in its proper grade. To do this, one principle of universal value must always be kept in mind: that the greater or less can only be appraised and classified in relation to the maximum, the relative in relation to the absolute. Between God who is Being, pure and simple, and complete nothingness, there come near God pure intelligences known as angels and near nothingness material forms. Between angels and material nature come human creatures on the borderline between spirits and bodies. Thus the angels reduce the infinite gap separating man from God and man fills in the gap between angels and matter.

Each of these degrees has its own mode of operation since each being operates according as it is in act and as its degree of actuality merges with its degree of perfection. The orderly and arranged hierarchy of beings is thus made complete by the orderly and arranged hierarchy of their operations, and in such a way that the bottom of the higher degree invariably comes into close contact with the top of the lower. Thus the principle of continuity gives precision and determination to the principle of perfection. Actually, both of these principles but express the higher law governing the communication of being. There is no being save the divine being in which all creatures participate; and creatures only differ from one another by reason of their greater or lesser degree of participation in the divine being.[1] Their perfection must, accordingly, be measured by the distance separating them from God. It is in thus differentiating themselves from one another that they arrange themselves into a hierarchy.

If this is true, it is analogy alone which enables our intelligence to arrive at a transcendent God from sensible things. It is analogy, too, which alone permits us to say that the universe has its existence from a transcendental principle and yet is neither confused with it nor added to it. The similarity of the analogue has, of course, to be explained, and it can only be explained by means of what the analogue imitates: "For (being) is not said of many equivocally, but analogically, and thus must be reduced to unity." [2] But at the same time that it possesses enough of its model's being to require it as its cause, it possesses it in such a manner that the being of this cause does not become involved in that of the thing caused. And because the word "being" signifies two different modes of existence when applied to God and to creatures, no problem of addition or subtraction can arise. The being of creatures is only an image, an imitation of the divine being. Even as reflections appear about a flame, increasing, decreasing and disappearing, without the substance of the flame being affected, so the likenesses freely created by the divine substance owe all their being to this substance. They subsist only through it, yet borrow nothing from its *per se* mode of being, a mode very different from their own. They neither add to it nor subtract from it even in the least degree.

These two principles, analogy and hierarchy, enable us to explain the creature through a transcendent Creator. They also permit us to maintain relations between them and to extend bonds between them which become the constitutive principles of created essences and the laws which serve to explain them. Whatever physics or natural philosophy ultimately shows to be the nature of things, it has necessarily to remain subordinate to a metaphysics of being. If creatures are similitudes in what concerns their basic origin, then it is to be expected that analogy will serve to explain the universe just as it explains creation. To account for the operation of a being, we shall always have to show that its operation is based, beyond its essence in its act-of-being. And to give account of this essence will always be to show that a definite degree of participation in being, cor-responding exactly to what this essence is, ought to have a place in our universe. But why was such a determined similitude required by a universe like ours? It is because the similitudes of any model can only be es-sentially different if they are more or less perfect. A finite system of images of an infinite being must have all the real degrees of likeness which can appear within the bounds assigned to the system by the free will of the Creator. The metaphysical explanation of a physical phenomenon must always be concerned with putting an essence in its place in a hierarchy.

This sense of hierarchy shows the profound influence of the Pseudo-Dionysius on the thought of St. Thomas. There is no denying this influ-ence; and it explains why some have wished to rank the author of the *Summa Theologiae* among the disciples of Plotinus. Only when we strictly limit its range does such a thesis become acceptable. The Areopagite furnishes the framework of the hierarchy. He firmly implants in thought the need for a hierarchy. He makes it impossible not to consider the universe as a hierarchy. But he left for St. Thomas the task of completing it; and even though Dionysius assigns the various grades in the hierarchy, he does not know the law which governs their arrangement and distribu-tion.

But is it true to say that St. Thomas thought of the content of this universal hierarchy in a neo-Platonic spirit? If we except with numerous reservations the case of pure spirits, it is quite apparent that the answer is no. The God of St. Thomas the Christian is the same as St. Augustine's. That St. Augustine was under neo-Platonic influence does not mean that his God could be confused with the God of Plotinus. Between Plotinian speculation and the theology of the Fathers of the Church there stands Jehovah, the personal God who acts by intelligence and will, and who freely places outside Himself that real universe which His Wisdom chose from an infinity of possible universes. Between this freely created universe and God the Creator there is an impassable abyss and no other continuity than the continuity of order. Properly speaking, the world is an ordered discontinuity. Must we not see that we are here far removed from neo-Platonic philosophy? To make of St. Thomas a Plotinian, or even a neo-Platonizer, is to confuse him with the adversaries he resisted so energetically.

The distance between the two philosophers is no less noticeable when we move from God to man. We said that St. Thomas's God was not the God of Plotinus but the Christian God of Augustine. Neither is St. Thomas's man the man of Plotinus. The opposition is particularly sharp right at the heart of the problem: in the relation between soul and body, and in the doctrine of knowledge which results from this. In Platonism there is the affirming of the extreme independence and almost complete aseity of the soul; this allows for Platonic reminiscence and even for the momentary return to the One through the ecstatic union. But in Thomism there is a most energetic affirming of the physical nature of the soul and vigilant care to close all paths which might lead to a doctrine of direct intuition of the intelligible in order to leave open no other road than that of sense knowledge. Platonism locates mystical knowledge in the natural prolongation of human knowledge; in Thomism, mystical knowledge is added to and co-ordinated with natural knowledge, but is not a continuation of it. All we know about God is what our reason teaches us about Him after reflecting upon the evidence of the senses. If we want to find a neo-Platonic doctrine of knowledge in the Middle Ages, we will have to look elsewhere than in St. Thomas.

This becomes clearer when we put aside the consideration of this particular problem and examine directly the Thomistic hierarchy of the universe. We have had a great deal to say about God and His creative power, about the angels and their functions, about man and his operations. We have considered, one after the other, all creatures endowed with intellect, and the First Intelligence itself. What we have seen is that the nature and compass of the many kinds of knowledge it has been given to us to acquire have varied very considerably according to the greater or less perfection of the reality which was its object. One who wishes to extract a clear notion of the spirit of Thomistic philosophy must first examine the ladder of being, and then inspect the values which locate each order of knowledge in its proper degree.

What is knowing? It is apprehending what is. There is no other perfect knowledge. Now it is immediately apparent that all knowledge, properly so-called, of the higher degrees in the universal hierarchy is relentlessly refused us. We know that God and pure intelligences exist, but we do not know what they are. There is no doubting, however, that the awareness of a deficiency in our knowledge of God leaves us with a burning desire for higher and more complete knowledge. Nor can it be doubted that, if knowing consists in grasping the essence of the object known, God, angels and, generally speaking, anything of the purely intelligible order, is by definition beyond the grasp of our intellect. This is why, instead of having an intuition of the Divine Essence, we have but a vast number of concepts which, taken together, are a confused sort of imitation of what would have been a true notion of the Divine Essence. When all that we have been able to say about such a subject is put together, the result is a collection of negations or analogies, nothing more.

Where, then, does human knowledge find itself at home? When is it in the presence of its own object? Only at that point where it comes into contact with the sensible. And although it does not here totally penetrate the real, because the individual as such implies or presupposes matter and is therefore beyond expression, still reason is in control of the field in which it is working. In order to describe man, that is, the human composite, to describe the animal and its operations, the heavenly bodies and their powers, mixed bodies or the elements, rational knowledge remains proportioned to the order or rank of the objects it is exploring. Although its content is incomplete, it is nevertheless positive. What is original and truly profound in Thomism is not an attempt either to establish science more solidly or to extend it. St. Thomas places the proper object of the human intellect in the sensible order, but he does not consider the study of this order to be the highest function of the knowing faculty. The proper object of the intellect is the quiddity of the sensible, but its proper function is to make the sensible intelligible.[3] From the particular object on which its light falls it draws something universal. It can do this because this particular object carries the divine image naturally impressed upon it as the mark of its origin. The intellect is, in the proper sense of the term, born and made for the universal. Hence its straining toward that object which is by definition vigorously inaccessible, the Divine Being. Here reason knows very little, but what little it knows surpasses in dignity and value any other kind of certitude.[4]

All great philosophies, and St. Thomas's is no exception, present a different front according to the particular needs of the age which turns to them. It is hardly surprising, then, that in a time like ours when so many minds are seeking to re-establish between philosophy and concrete reality bonds which idealism has broken, Thomists of different varieties should be insisting upon the notion of the act-of-being in his philosophy. The fact that they have reached analogous conclusions quite independently of one another makes their convergence still more significant. Restricting ourselves to recent statements, we can find any number of remarks like the following: The proper object of the intelligence is being, "not only *essential* or quidditative but existential." Or again: The entire thought of St. Thomas "seeks existence itself, though not, as in the case with practical philosophy, to produce it, but to know it." [5] Or again: "Thomistic philosophy is an existential philosophy." Mr. Maritain, the author of these statements, explains them at length in a special section of his *A Digression on Existence and Philosophy.*

When Maritain speaks in this way about St. Thomas, he is trying to make us understand that all human knowledge, including the metaphysician's, begins from sense knowledge and ultimately returns to it "not in order to know their essence. It (i.e., metaphysics) does so to know how they exist, for this too metaphysics should know, to attain their mode of existence, and then to conceive by analogy the existence of that which exists immaterially, which is purely spiritual." [6]

This is a lesson of the greatest importance. The only trouble is that the various statements of it are so compact that they tend to obscure its full significance. To insist on the existential character of Thomism in the above sense is to resist the very natural tendency of the human mind to remain on the level of abstraction. The very art of teaching fosters this tendency. How is anyone to teach without explaining, simplifying, abstracting? We tend to keep both ourselves and others on this level of conceptual abstraction which is so satisfying to the mind. First we disentangle essences from concrete reality; then we hold back the moment when we must again blend these essences into the unity of the concrete. We are afraid that we may fall back into the confusion from which we set out and which it is the very object of analysis to remove. Some hold back this moment so long that they never allow it to arrive. In this case, philosophy is reduced to making cuts into the real, following the cleavage-plane of essences, as if knowing from what essences the real is composed were the same as knowing existing reality. This reality is only directly apprehended by us in and through sensible knowledge and this is why our judgments only attain their object when, directly or indirectly, they are resolved into it: "In other words the *res sensibilis visibilis,* the visible object of sense, is the touchstone of every judgment, *ex qua debemus de aliis judicare,* by which we must judge of everything else, because it is the touchstone of existence." [7]

Lest the metaphysician forget this principle, or rather, lest he be unaware of the point of view which it imposes on him, he should immerse himself in existence, enter ever more deeply into it "by means of as keen a sensitive (or aesthetic) perception as possible, and also by his experience of suffering and of existential conflicts, in order that, away up in the third heaven of the natural intelligence, he may devour the intelligible substance of things." After this comes the almost inevitable remark: "Need we add that the professor who is only a professor, who is withdrawn from existence, who has become insensible to this third degree of abstraction, is the direct opposite of the true metaphysician? Thomistic metaphysic is called *scholastic,* from the name of its most bitter trial. Scholarly pedagogy is its particular enemy. It must ceaselessly combat and subdue the professorial adversary attacking from within." [8]

It could hardly be put better. But just let us see what happens when we neglect to push judgments beyond abstract essences to the actually existing concrete. St. Thomas has noted that the properties of the essence are not the same when it is taken abstractly in itself as when taken in the state of concrete actualization in a really existing being. In fact he explains himself so explicitly on this point that we might as well let him speak for himself.

"Whatever be the object considered in the abstract, we can truly say that it contains no foreign element, that is, nothing outside and beyond its essence. It is in this way that we speak of *humanity* and *whiteness* and everything else of this kind. The reason for this is that *humanity* is then designated as that by which something is a man, and *whiteness* as that by which something is white. Now, formally speaking, a thing is only a man by something pertaining to the formal reason of man. Similarly, a thing is only formally white by what pertains to the formal reason of whiteness. This is why abstractions like these can include nothing foreign to themselves. It is quite different in the case of something signified concretely. Indeed, *man* signifies something possessing humanity, and white, something that has whiteness. Now the fact that man has humanity or whiteness does not prevent him from having something else which does not depend on the formal reason of humanity or whiteness. It is enough that it be not opposed to it. This is why *man* and *white* can have something more than humanity and whiteness. Moreover, it is for this reason that *whiteness* and *humanity* may be called parts of something, but are not predicated of concrete beings themselves, because a part is never predicated of the whole of which it is a part." [9]

If we apply these observations to philosophy, we shall see how, in the approach to problems, perspectives vary according to whether we avoid or face them. The philosopher begins with the experience common to everyone. And he ought in the end to return to this same common experience in so far as it is this which he set out to explain. The only way to succeed is to begin with an analysis, pushed as far as possible, of the various elements included in the factual data which go to make up this experience. Here we have as first task the breaking up of the concrete into its intelligible elements. Whatever we find out has to be separated into its parts and each part isolated from the others. This can only be done by means of a distinct concept for each element. A necessary condition in thus distinguishing any concept is that it contain everything its definition includes, and nothing else. This is why every abstract essence is distinguished from the others as its concept is from theirs, and is only distinguished from them in that it excludes them. *Humanity* is that by which a man is a man, and it is that exclusively. So far is *humanity* from including *whiteness,* that there are men who are not white. Inversely, *whiteness* is that by which what is white is white. This does not include *humanity.* There can be an incredible number of white beings none of them men. Thus our inquiry into the real leads us to break down the confusion of the concrete into an enormous number of intelligible essences each quite distinct insofar as it cannot be reduced to the others.

Does philosophy consist in these abstract essences taken in the state of abstraction in which we are right now considering them? To say Yes is to become involved in a philosophy of the quiddity. We mean by this not simply a philosophy that calls upon quiddities, for this necessity is co-essential to all human knowledge, but a philosophy whose notion of the real reduces it to the essence, or quiddity. History shows us many such philosophies. Indeed their very classifications are innumerable, but there is no need to go into them here. This attitude concerns us primarily in that it expresses a natural tendency of the reason to think by "clear and distinct ideas," and consequently to reject as obscure and confused whatever does not allow itself to be included within the limits of purely quidditative notions. From this point of view, the "simple natures" on which Descartes worked are no different from the essences of the tree of Porphyry which he denounced as sterile.

Let us go further. Whatever method we invoke, and even if we begin by admitting that the concept cannot be the ultimate object of philosophy, we end up in actual fact with a philosophy of the quiddities whenever we fail to carry research beyond the level of abstract notions. A simple glance at the history of the various philosophies leads to this same conclusion. Restricting ourselves to Thomistic philosophy, we have to choose between locating its ultimate object in the grasping of the essences out of which the concrete real is made up, in which case our highest mode of knowing is a sort of intellectual intuition of pure essences, or assigning to Thomistic philosophy as its ultimate term, rational knowledge of the concrete real through the essences engaged in the metaphysical texture of that concrete real.

Whatever we may think, there can be no doubting that the thought of St. Thomas, in first intention, turned toward knowledge of the existing concrete given in sensible experience and of the first causes of this existing concrete whether they be sensible or not. The whole philosophy we have been studying, from metaphysics to moral philosophy, bears testimony of this. This is why it is and remains philosophy in the proper sense and not, in the widely spread pejorative sense of the term, a "scholasticism." Every philosophy engenders its own scholastic presentation, its own school-doctrine, its own scholasticism. But the terms "philosophy" and "scholasticism" designate specifically distinct facts. Every philosophy worthy of the name starts out from the real and returns thereto. Every scholasticism starts from a philosophy and returns thereto. Philosophy degenerates into scholasticism the moment when, instead of taking the existing concrete as object of its reflections in order to study it deeply, penetrate it, throw more and more light upon it, it applies itself rather to the statements which it is supposed to explain, as if these statements themselves and not what they shed light on, were the reality itself.

To fall into this error is to become quite incapable of understanding even the history of philosophy. Because understanding a philosophy is not merely reading what it says in one place in terms of what it says in another; it is reading it at each moment in terms of what it is actually speaking about. An error like this is far more harmful to philosophy itself than to the history of philosophy. St. Thomas's teaching has degenerated into scholasticism whenever and wherever it has been cut off from the real, the only object on which its illuminating rays can properly be focused. This is not a reason for believing that Thomism is a scholasticism, for its object is not Thomism but the world, man, and God, attained as existing beings in their very existence. It is therefore true that in this first sense the philosophy of St. Thomas is existential in the fullest sense of the word.

Beyond this first sense, there is another far more radical one which commands our attention even more imperatively. In this case, however, the very expression "existential philosophy," which is so inviting in itself, lends itself to so many misunderstandings that we stand in dread of the birth and spread of new "scholastic" controversies if, that is, certain necessary precautions are not taken. It is a rather modern expression; and although it has arisen out of problems as old as Western thought, it can hardly be applied to the doctrine of St. Thomas without giving the impression of striving to rejuvenate it from without by fitting it up in modern dress. To attempt something like this is hardly wise. It even has the effect of aligning Thomism with philosophies which in certain fundamental points are its direct contrary. To speak of "existential philosophy" today brings immediately to mind such names as Kierkegaard, Heidegger, Jaspers and so on. In these we find divergent tendencies. No Thomism conscious of what it really is itself could under any circumstances fully align itself with any of them. To do so would only lay it open to the charge of seeking artificial rejuvenation, of postponing its threatening dissolution by laying claim to a title generally conceded to recent philosophies still full of vitality. The whole undertaking would be undignified and profitless to all parties concerned and could only lead to misunderstandings which it would take generations to remove.

The first and most serious of these misunderstandings would be to give the impression that Thomism was *one more* existential philosophy; whereas what really ought to be the issue at stake is whether or not these philosophies to which Thomism is being likened have really any right to be called existential philosophies at all. Assuredly these are philosophies very much concerned with existence. But they really only deal with it as an object of a possible phenomenology of human existence, as though the primacy of existence signified chiefly that primacy of ethics which Kierkegaard so strongly insisted upon. If we look here for a philosophy that passes beyond the phenomenological and establishes the act-of-being as the keystone of metaphysics, we shall look in vain. But this is just what St. Thomas has done. As philosophy of the act-of-being, Thomism is not *another* existential philosophy, it is the only one. All those phenomenologies which are on the hunt for an ontology seem unconsciously to be moving in its direction as though driven on by the natural desire of their own justification.

What characterizes Thomism is the decision to locate actual existence in the heart of the real as an act of transcending any kind of quidditative concept and, at the same time, avoiding the double error of remaining dumb before its transcendence or of denaturing it in objectifying it. The only means of speaking about the act-of-being is to grasp it in a concept, and the concept which directly expresses it is the concept of being. Being is *that which is,* that is, *that which has the act-of-being.* It is quite impossible to come to the act-of-being by an intellectual intuition which grasps it directly, and grasps nothing more. To think is to conceive. But the proper object of a concept is always an essence, or something presenting itself to thought as an essence; in brief, an object. The act-of-being, however, is an act. It can only be grasped by or in the essence whose act it is. A pure *est* is unthinkable; but an *id quod est* can be thought. But every *id quod est* is first a being. And because there is no concept anterior to this, being is the first principle of knowledge. It is so in itself; it is so in the philosophy of St. Thomas. Such a philosophy has every claim to be called a "philosophy of being."

If it is true that even the possibility of philosophy is tied up with the use of the quidditative concept, it is also true that the name which correctly designates a philosophy is drawn from the concept its first principle is based on. This cannot be the act-of-being because, taken in itself, the act-of-being is not the object of a quidditative concept. It must, then, inevitably be being. To call Thomism an existential philosophy does not call into question the legitimacy of its traditional title, but only confirms it. Since existence can only be conceived in the concept of being, Thomism is always a philosophy of being, even though called existential.

It seems proper to make this point because the abstract notion of being is, by its very definition, ambivalent. In a "that which is" (*id quod est*), or a "having being" (*esse habens*), we can spontaneously emphasize either the *id quod* and the *habens* or the *esse* and the *est*. Not only can we do this, but we actually do so and usually it is the "that which" (*id quod*) and the "having" (*habens*) which we emphasize because they place before us the "thing" which exists, that is, being as the object of the quidditative concept.

This natural tendency to abstract and to confine ourselves to the abstract concept is so strong that it has been responsible for the appearance of several forms of Thomism in which *esse,* that is, the very act-of-being, seems to have no effective rôle to play. By yielding to this natural tendency, we abstract from *esse* and make Thomism a philosophy of the *id quod.* In order to rectify this situation, it is just as well to qualify Thomism as an "existential philosophy." To recall in this way the full meaning of *ens* in St. Thomas's language is to guard against impoverishing both *ens* itself and the philosophy whose first principle it is. It is to forget that the concept signified by *ens* implies direct reference to existence: *nam ens dicitur quasi esse habens.*[10]

It might be argued that a new expression like this is superfluous, because everyone is quite aware of what it is meant to express. This may be so. But it is not enough that everyone know it. Everyone must think it as well, and it is perhaps harder to do this than might be suspected. The history of the distinction between essence and existence and the endless controversies to which the same distinction is giving rise in our own day show that there is a very real difficulty. The very controversy itself is revealing. It shows how easy it is to substitute the abstract concept of existence for the concrete notion of the act-of-being, to "essentialize," the act-of-being, to make an act into the object of a simple concept. The temptation to do this is so strong that scholars began to do it in the first generation after St. Thomas. So far as we can tell from research done up to the present, Giles of Rome is the starting point of the controversies over essence and existence. Now it has often been noted that this resolute defender of the distinction spontaneously expressed himself as though essence were one thing, existence another. Whether he consciously went so far as to reify the act-of-being has not been adequately demonstrated. But for our purposes it is quite enough merely to observe that his language betrays a marked tendency to conceive of *esse* as though it were a thing, and consequently to conceive the distinction between essence and existence as between two things. Indeed, he actually writes: "Existence and essence are two things." [11] Many other professed Thomists since his time have expressed themselves in identical terms. But little is to be gained by making this distinction if existence itself is taken as an essence. To call Thomism an "existential philosophy" serves to focus attention on this very important point.

But we have still to come to the chief justification of the expression "existential" as applied to Thomistic philosophy. It is not enough to say of all being that its concept connotes its *esse,* and that this *esse* must be taken as an act. It must also be said that this *esse* is the act of the same being whose concept connotes it. In every *esse habens* the *esse* is the act of the *habens* which possesses it, and the effect of this act upon what receives it is precisely this—to make a being of it.

If we accept this thesis in all its force and with all its ontological implications we come immediately to that well-known Thomistic position: *nomen ens imponitur ab ipso esse.*[12] So we might as well say that the act-of-being is the very core of being since being draws everything, even its name, from the act-of-being. What characterizes Thomistic ontology thus understood is not so much the distinction between essence and existence as the primacy of the act-of-being, not over and above being, but within it. To say that Thomistic philosophy is "existential" is to stress more forcibly than usual that a philosophy of being thus conceived is first of all a philosophy of the act-of-being.

There would be no advantage in making a great to-do about the act-of-being to the point of forgetting about the reality of the essence or even in allowing oneself to belittle its importance. Essences are the intelligible stuff of the world. Hence ever since Socrates, Plato and Aristotle, philosophy has been one long hunt for essences. But the great question is to know whether we will bring home the game dead or alive. An essence is dead when it is deposited in the understanding as a quiddity, without preserving its contact with the act-of-being. It is certainly a lot easier to handle dead essences. Reason surrounds them from all sides through the definitions she can give them. The mind knows what each of them contains, is assured that none of them either is or can be anything other than it is, and is secure against surprise from any quarter. One can, without fear, deduce *a priori* the properties of essences, and even calculate beforehand all their possible combinations.

But a philosophy of the act-of-being cannot be satisfied by such methods. It wants to know which, among all the possible combinations of these essences, has actually been realized. This will very probably lead it to assert that many real combinations of essences are the very ones which would have been regarded as rather unlikely or perhaps even judged *a priori* to be impossible. No doubt living essences find in their own acts of existing a fertility and invention quite beyond the powers of the bare definitions of their concepts. Neither essence nor existence has any meaning apart from the other. Taken separately they are but two abstractions. The only finite reality which the understanding can fruitfully explore is concrete being itself, the original, unique, and, in the case of man, unpredictable and free actualization of an inexhaustible essence by its own act-of-being.

It is rather difficult to find in St. Thomas a single concrete problem whose solution is not ultimately based on this principle. He is primarily a theologian; and it is in constructing his theology with such striking technical originality that he best proves his fertility of mind. Wherever his philosophy touches his theology there is to be seen that new light with which the act-of-being illumines all it touches. Sometimes, when St. Thomas brings up problems and notions not central to his real interests, he allows them to stand like hardened essences in the margin, as it were, of his work. He neither takes the time to rejuvenate them by bringing them into contact with the act-of-being, nor appears to feel the need for doing so. But had he undertaken to do something like this, his philosophy would still remain with its face turned to the future. It will always be thus because the principle to which he makes his appeal is the fertile energy of an act rather than the fixed expression of a concept. A universe like this will never stop surrendering its secret unless, some day, it ceases to be.

This is because it is an ordered plurality of real essences perfected by their acts-of-being. Such must perforce be the case, since this universe is made up of beings, and since a being is "something having an act-of-being." Each being has its own proper act-of-being, distinct from that of every other: *Habet enim res unaquaeque in seipsa esse proprium ab omnibus aliis distinctum.*[13] Let us go further: it is by this act-of-being which it has that it is a being, because it is by it that it is—*unumquodque est per suum esse.*[14] And if we can say, as it is often said, that a being's acting proceeds from its act-of-being—*operatio sequitur esse*—it is not merely in the sense of "like being like operation," but also, and especially because the acting of a being is only the unfolding in time of the first act-of-being which makes it to be. It is this way that we get a notion of the efficient cause which is in agreement with the immediate certitudes of common sense and confers on them that metaphysical profundity which they lack by nature. There are many who feel that the efficient cause extends right to the very existence of its effect. And it is here precisely that they find complete justification: *causa importat influxum quemdam in esse causati.*[15]

God is the only being to which this formula, which is valid for others, cannot as such be applied. Of Him it cannot be said that He is *by* His act-of-being, He is His act-of-being. Since we can only think in terms of being, and since we can only grasp a being as an essence, we have to say that God has an essence. But we must hasten to add that what in Him serves as an essence is His act-of-being: *In Deo non est aliud essentia vel quidditas quam suum esse.*[16] The act-of-being is the act of acts; it is the primary energy of a being and from it all operations proceed (*operatio sequitur esse*). Since God is very *Esse,* the operation belonging to Him and only to Him is the producing of acts-of-being. To produce an act-of-being is what we call creating. Creating is, therefore, action proper to God: *Ergo creatio est propria Dei actio.* And as it is as Act-of-Being that He alone has the power to create; the act-of-being is His proper effect: *esse est ejus proprius effectus.*[18]

The linking of these fundamental notions is rigidly necessary. As God is by essence the Act-of-Being itself, the created act-of-being must be His proper effect: *Cum Deus sit ipsum esse per suam essentiam, oportet quod esse creatum sit proprius effectus ejus.*[19] Once this conclusion has

been reached, it becomes in its turn the principle of a long line of consequences, for every effect resembles its cause, and that by which the effect
is most profoundly indebted to its cause is that by which it resembles it
most. If therefore being is created, its primary resemblance to God lies
in its own act-of-being: *omne ens, in quantum habet esse, est Ei simile*.[20]

From this we see right away that it is the act-of-being in each being
that is most intimate, most profound and metaphysically primary. Hence
the necessity, in an ontology which does not stop at the level of abstract
essence, of pushing right to the existential root of every being in order
to arrive at the very principle of its unity: *unumquodque secundum idem
habet esse et individuationem*.[21]

Such is, in a particular way, the solution of the problem of the metaphysical structure of the human being. Where the essence of the body and
the essence of the soul are taken separately, there can be no return to
that concrete unity which a man is. The unity of a man is first of all the
unity of his soul, which is really only the unity of his own *esse*. It is the
same act-of-being which has issued forth from the divine *Esse*, which
passes through the soul, which animates the body, and which penetrates
even the tiniest cells of that body. When all is said and done, this is why,
although the soul is a substance, its union with the body is not accidental:
"It does not follow that the body is united with it accidentally because the
self-same act-of-being that belongs to the soul is conferred on the body." [22]

Thus that knowing being, man, is bound to God by its deepest ontological root, and has to look no further for the entrance to the paths which
will lead it to the knowledge of its cause. If it pursues its metaphysical
analysis far enough, any being whatsoever will place it in the presence of
God. God is in everything as its cause. His action affects it in its very
act-of-being. Hence it is at the heart of what it is that God is actually
present: *Oportet quod Deus sit in omnibus rebus, et intime*.[23] To prove
God is to re-climb by reason from any finite act-of-being whatsoever, to
the pure Act-of-Being which causes it. Here the knowledge of man reaches
its ultimate terminus. When God has been established as the supreme Act-
of-Being, philosophy ends and mystical theology begins. More simply
put, reason asserts that what it knows depends in its very root upon the
God it does not know: *cum Deo quasi ignoto conjungimur*.[24] To understand St. Thomas in this way is not at all to de-essentialize his philosophy.
It is rather to restore real essence to it, to re-establish it in its full right.
Essence is far more than the quiddity which satisfies reason; it is that
by which, and in which, being has existence: *quidditatis nomen sumitur
ex hoc quod diffinitionem significat; sed essentia dicitur secundum quod
per eam et in ea ens habet esse*.[25] There is nothing further to be said. But
it is worth repeating, because the human mind is so constituted that anyone is quite capable of forgetting it.

It has been rightly insisted that we must distinguish whatever separates the *problem* from the *mystery,* and upon the need for the metaphysician to pass beyond the first plane into the second. But neither is to be sacrificed for the sake of the other. When philosophy abandons the problem in order to immerse itself in the mystery, it ceases to be philosophy and becomes mysticism. Whether we like it or not, the problem is the very stuff out of which philosophy is fashioned. To think is to know by concepts. Yet as soon as we begin to interpret the real in terms of quidditative concepts we are right into the problem. We are here face to face with the inescapable, and even those who tend most strongly to escape from it must perforce recognize it. "What cannot be problematized, cannot be examined nor objectified, and this by definition." [26] If philosophizing is a kind of examining of the real, philosophy can only deal with the real to the extent that the real can be problematized. The philosopher can only get to God by way of the problem of His existence, which the problem of His nature follows hard upon. He is then confronted with the problem of God's action and of God's government in the world. There are as many problems as there are mysteries, and they are not only met when philosophy talks about God. Man's science is alive with mysteries, as knowledge and liberty so eloquently testify.

Nor does mystery dwell only in the world of matter. Reason has for centuries been challenged by such obscure facts as efficient causality and the presence of quality. To renounce the problematizing of mysteries would be to renounce philosophizing. This is not the way to seek the solution of the crisis confronting philosophy today. But if we must not leave the problem alone, neither ought we to leave the mystery alone either. The real danger begins where the problem is confronted by the mystery and pretends to be sufficient to itself and to lay claim to an autonomy which it does not actually possess. The moment a philosophy makes this mistake it is victimized by its own combinations of abstract concepts and enters a game which will never finish. It moves into the realm of the antinomies of pure reason. Kant was not wrong when he said that escape was impossible. We need only add that everything invites philosophic reason not to enter, because such reason ought not to be discussion of pure problems or flight from mystery. It ought to be a perpetually renewed effort to treat every problem as though it were bound up in a mystery. It ought to problematize the mystery by examining it with the help of the concept.

There is a mystery which can be called the object *par excellence* of philosophy, since metaphysics presupposes it, namely, the act-of-being. The philosophy of St. Thomas locates this mystery in the heart of the real and so insures itself against the risk, so fatal to metaphysical thought, of growing sterile in the very purity of abstraction. To a certain point, Aristotle had already walked in this way. His reformation had been to give philosophy an object which was not the ideal essence conceived by thought but was real being as it is and as it behaves. With Aristotle, the οὐσία reality, is no longer the Idea, it is the substance properly so designated. In order to measure the scope of this revolution we have only to compare the solutions to the problem of the first principle of all things proposed by Aristotle and Plato. When Plato takes up the problem, he sets out from an analysis of the real which disengages the intelligible element from it and then proceeds back from one intelligible condition to another until he comes to the first condition. It is the Good in itself; an Idea, that is, an hypostasized abstraction. Aristotle sets out from the concrete substance given in sensible experience, that is, he sets out from the existant. Then, contrary to Plato, he begins by bringing into evidence the active principle of its being and of its operations. Then he proceeds back from one ontological condition to another until he comes to the first condition. Thus pure Act becomes the highest reality because it alone fully deserves the name of being. On it everything else depends because everything else imitates it in an eternally recommenced effort to imitate in time its immovable actuality.

The peculiar work of St. Thomas has been to carry on into the interior of being itself. He has pushed back as far as the secret principle which establishes, not the actuality of being as substance, but the actuality of being as being. To the age-old question (even Aristotle referred to it as old) What is being? St. Thomas replied: it is that which has actual existence. An ontology like this sacrifices nothing of the intelligible reality accessible to man under the form of concepts. Like Aristotle's, it never grows tired of analyzing, classifying, defining. But it always remembers that in what is most intimate to itself, the real object it is struggling to define is incapable of definition. It is not an abstraction; it is not even a thing. It is not even merely the formal act which makes it to be such and such a thing. It is the act which locates it as a real being in existence, which actualizes the very form that makes it intelligible.

A philosophy like this is at grips with the secret energy which causes its object. It finds in the direction of its limitations the principles of its very fertility. It will never believe that it has come to the end of its inquiry because its end is beyond what it can enclose within the bounds of a definition.

We are not dealing now with a philosophy which *leans against* existence and consequently cannot *see* it. Rather we have to do with a philosophy which stands in front of existence and never stops staring it in the face. Of course we cannot see existence, but we know it is there and we can at least locate it, by an act of judgment, as the hidden root of what we can see and of what we can attempt to define. This is also why Thomistic ontology refuses to be limited to what the human mind knew about being in the thirteenth century. It even refuses to allow itself to be checked by what we know about it in the twentieth. It invites us to look beyond

present-day science toward that primitive energy from which both knowing subject and object known arise.

If all beings "are" in virtue of their own act-of-being, each one of
them breaks through the enclosing frame of its own definition. Better,
perhaps, it has no proper definition: *individuum est ineffabile*. Yes, the
individual is ineffable, but because it is too big rather than because it is
too little. St. Thomas's universe is peopled with living essences sprung
from a source as secret and rich as their very life. His world, by a filiation
more profound than so many superficial dissimilarities might indicate,
projects into Pascal's world rather than into Descartes'. In Pascal's world,
the imagination is more likely to grow weary of producing concepts than
nature to tire of providing them. There "all things hide a mystery; all
things are veils hiding God." [27] Is not this what St. Thomas had already
said with a simplicity no less striking than Pascal's: God is in all things,
and that intimately—*Deus est in omnibus rebus, et intime*? For of such
a universe two things can be said at the same time. Everything in it possesses its own act-of-being, distinct from that of all others. Yet, deep within
each of them there lies hidden the same Act-of-Being, which is God.

If we want to recapture the true meaning of Thomism we have to go
beyond the tightly-woven fabric of its philosophical doctrines into its
soul or spirit. What lies back of the ideas is a deep religious life, the interior
warmth of a soul in search of God. There have in the recent past been
prolonged and subtle disputes as to whether, according to St. Thomas,
men experience a natural desire for their supernatural end. Theologians
must ultimately decide such questions. They have to reach some kind of
agreement about expressions and formulas which concern God's transcendence and still do not allow man to be separated from Him. The
historian can at least say that St. Thomas leaves questions only partially
settled, like the projecting stones of an unfinished wall awaiting the hand
of a second builder. The very gaps in St. Thomas's work suggest that
nature awaits the finishing touches of grace.

At the basis of this philosophy, as at the basis of all Christian philosophy, there is a deep awareness of wretchedness and need for a comforter
who can only be God: "Natural reason tells man that he is subject to a
higher being because of the defects he discerns in himself, defects for
which he requires help and direction from some higher being. Whatever
this being may be, it is commonly spoken of as God." [28] This is the natural
feeling which grace excites in the Christian soul and which the perfection
of charity brings to fulfillment when this soul is the soul of a saint. The
burning desire of God which in a John of the Cross overflows into lyric
poems is here transcribed into the language of pure ideas. Their impersonal formulation must not make us forget that they are nourished
on the desire for God and that their end is the satisfaction of this desire.

There is no point in seeking, as some appear to do, an interior life underlying Thomism which is specifically and essentially different from Thomism itself. We ought not to think that the learned arrangement of the *Summa Theologiae* and the unbroken advance of reason constructing stone by stone this mighty edifice was for St. Thomas but the fruit of a superficial activity beneath which there moved deeper, richer and more religious thinking. The interior life of St. Thomas, insofar as the hidden stirrings of so powerful a personality can be revealed, seems to have been just what it should have been to be expressed in such a doctrine. Nothing could be more desirable, nothing more indicative of an ardent will than his demonstrations fashioned from clearly defined ideas, presented in perfectly precise statements, and placed in a carefully balanced arrangement. Only a complete giving of himself can explain his mastery of expression and organization of philosophic ideas. Thus his *Summa Theologiae* with its abstract clarity, its impersonal transparency, crystallizes before our very eyes and for all eternity his interior life. If we would recapture the deep and intense spirit of this interior life, there is nothing more useful than to re-assemble for ourselves, but in terms of the order he gave them, the various elements that go to make up his remarkable *Summa*. We should study its internal structure and strive to arouse in ourselves the conviction of its necessity. Only that will to understand, shared between ourselves and St. Thomas the philosopher, will serve to make us see that this tremendous work is but the outward glow of an invisible fire, and that there is to be found behind the order of its ideas that powerful impulse which gathered them together.

Only thus does Thomism appear in all its beauty. It is a philosophy which creates excitement by means of pure ideas, and does so by sheer faith in the value of proofs and denials based on reason. This will become more evident to those who are disturbed by the very real difficulties encountered in the beginning, if they consider what St. Thomas's spirituality really was. If it were true that his philosophy were inspired by one spirit, his spirituality by another, the difference would become apparent by comparing his manner of thinking with his manner of praying. But a study of the prayers of St. Thomas which have been preserved and which are so satisfying that the Church has placed them in the Roman breviary, shows that they are not characterized by the note of rapture or emotion or spiritual relish common enough in many forms of prayer. St. Thomas's fervor is completely expressed in the loving petitioning of God for what He should be asked for, and in becoming manner. His phrases tend to be rather rigid because the rhythms are so balanced and regular. But his fervor is genuine, deep and readily recognizable and reflects the careful rhythms of his thought: "I pray Thee, that this holy Communion may be to me, not guilt for punishment, but a saving intercession for pardon. Let it be to me an armor of faith and a shield of good-will. Let it be to me a casting out of vices; a driving away of all evil desires and fleshly lusts;

an increase of charity, patience, humility, obedience, and all virtues; a firm defense against the plots of all my enemies, both seen and unseen; a perfect quieting of all motions of sin, both in my flesh and in my spirit; a firm cleaving unto Thee, the only and true God, and a happy ending of my life." [29] Spirituality like this is more eager for light than for taste. The rhythm of his phrases, the pleasing sonority of his Latin words never modifies the perfect order of his ideas. But the discriminating taste can always perceive, beneath the balanced cadence of his expression, a religious emotion that is almost poetic.

Indeed, because he serves reason so lovingly, St. Thomas actually becomes a poet, and, if we believe a disinterested judge, the greatest Latin poet of the Middle Ages. Now it is remarkable that the lofty beauty of the works attributed to this poet of the Eucharist depend almost entirely on the aptness and concentration of his expressions. Poems like the *Oro te devote* and *Ecce panis angelorum* can almost be called little theological treatises and they have supplied generations of faithful Christians with inspiration and devotion. Perhaps the most distinctive of all his poems is the *Pange lingua* which inspired Remy de Gourmont to say, in words matching, almost, the flawless beauty of the style he was attempting to describe: "The inspiration of St. Thomas is fired by an unwavering genius, a genius at once strong, sure, confident and exact. What he wants to say, he speaks out boldly, and in words so lovely that even doubt grows fearful and takes to flight." [30]

> *Pange lingua gloriosi corporis mysterium*
> *Sanguinisque pretiosi quem in mundi pretium*
> *Fructus ventris generosi Rex effudit gentium.*
>
> *Nobis datus, nobis natus ex intacta Virgine*
> *Et in mundo conversatus, sparso verbi semine*
> *Sui moras incolatus miro clausit ordine.*

We pass from St. Thomas's philosophy to his prayer, and from his prayer to his poetry without becoming aware of any change of level. And indeed there is no change! His philosophy is as rich in beauty as his poetry is laden with thought. Of both *Summa Theologiae* and *Pange lingua* we can say that his is an unwavering genius, strong, sure, confident and exact. What he wants to say, he speaks out boldly and with a firmness of thought that doubt itself grows fearful and takes to flight.

Nowhere else, perhaps, does so demanding a reason respond to the call of so religious a heart. St. Thomas regards man as marvelously equipped for the knowledge of phenomena; but he does not think that the most adequate human knowledge is the most useful and most beautiful to which man can aspire. He sets up man's reason in its own kingdom, the sensible.

But to equip it for exploring and conquering this kingdom, he invites it to prefer another which is not merely the kingdom of man but of the children of God. Such is the thinking of St. Thomas. If we grant that a philosophy is not to be defined from the elements it borrows but from the spirit which quickens it, we shall see here neither Platonism nor Aristotelianism but, above all, Christianity. It is a philosophy that sets out to express in rational language the total destiny of the Christian man. But it has constantly to remind him that here below he travels the paths of exile where there is no light and no horizon. Yet it never ceases to guide his steps toward that distant height from which can be seen, far off in the mists, the borders of the Promised Land.

APPENDIX

A CATALOGUE OF ST. THOMAS'S WORKS

BIBLIOGRAPHICAL NOTES

BY I. T. ESCHMANN, O.P.

THE following Catalogue of St. Thomas's works consists of ninety-eight items. This counting should not be considered as definitive; indeed it is debatable. With regard to not a few titles (cf. nos. 4, 5-16, 26-27, and others) it is as yet impossible to know whether they comprise one or several works. The beginnings of the Thomistic editions, made by either the author himself or his posthumous editors, are still too obscure to allow a firm judgment in this matter.

By far the greater part of these works are undoubtedly authentic. However the authenticity of nos. 90-98 is especially debated and debatable, and at the present moment can be neither definitely accepted nor rejected.

To each number a note is attached informing the reader, as fully and precisely as possible, about the nature of the work, the condition of its known text, the chronology, the available editions and English translations.

The classification adopted in the present Catalogue departs from the usual methods. A special case is the so-called *Opuscula*. This traditional category has been abandoned and several others have been substituted. The notion of *Opusculum,* i.e., minor or smaller work, in itself devoid of precise meaning, has in fact disserved the cause of Thomistic bibliography, if not even that of Thomistic studies. A spacious and commodious receptacle was, with the help of this very notion, opened up in the Thomistic museum, a catch-all, as it were, into which everything was thrown after the "main" halls had been duly furnished. The numerically greater part of St. Thomas's writings need not be left to the insignificant qualification of miscellaneous matter. From the point of view of their literary *genre* they bear, for the most part, quite distinct and easily recognizable characteristics. Only in certain cases is some hesitation possible. Thus the distinction between "Treatises on special subjects" and "Letters" may sometimes be of doubtful application. The first editors of

St. Thomas's works, dry and solid schoolmen as they were, had little use for letters. They wanted "tractates." They are known to have cut away from not a few letters the conventional formulae of salutation. In the whole early tradition there is but one Ms which preserved (or, better perhaps, dared to set forth) the appellation *Epistola* for the letter to the Duchess of Brabant (Oxford, *Bodleiana, Cod. Canonici, Script. Eccles.* 76, fol. 63ʳ).

The "List of Books Used," p. 431, is not an exhaustive bibliography but a complement of the notes. In the text of these notes, only the names of the authors referred to are given; the titles will be found in the List. Each author's books or studies are numbered. Thus, for example, the reference Keeler (2, 435) signifies: L. Keeler, *The Vulgate text of St. Thomas' Commentary on the Ethics,* in *Gregorianum* 17 (1936), p. 435.

Concerning the editions of Aquinas's works the following sigla are used:

Leon. (*Editio Leonina*) i.e., *S. Thomae Aquinatis Opera Omnia, iussu Leonis XIII edita,* 16 vols. (to date), Rome 1882-1948.

Parm. i.e., *S. Thomae Opera Omnia,* 25 vols., Parma (Fiaccadori) 1852-1873. Photographic reproduction by Musurgia Publishers, New York 1948/9.

Vivès i.e., *D. Thomae Aquinatis Opera Omnia* (ed. S. E. Fretté and P. Maré), 32 vols., Paris, L. Vivès, 1871-1880.

Taurin. (*Editio Taurinensis*) i.e., the various editions published by the Casa Marietti, Torino-Rome.

Taurin. Phil. i.e., *D. Thomae Aquinatis Opuscula Philosophica* (ed. R. M. Spiazzi), Torino-Rome 1954.

Taurin. Theol. i.e., *D. Thomae Aquinatis Opuscula Theologica* (ed. R. A. Verardo, R. M. Spiazzi etc.), 2 vols. Torino-Rome 1954.

Mand. i.e., *S. Thomae Aquinatis Opuscula Omnia* (ed. P. Mandonnet), 5 vols. Paris 1927.

Perrier i.e., *S. Thomae Aquinatis Opuscula Omnia necnon Opera Minora,* tom. I (ed. J. Perrier), Paris 1949.

The designation "Vulgate text," used in the notes, refers to the text found in most current editions, such as *Parm., Vivès, Taurin.* etc. Its essential characteristic is that its relation to the earlier Ms tradition is not specified by the editors and, for the most part, still unknown. In some way or other, all these editions go back to the *Editio Princeps,* i.e., the Roman or *Piana* edition of 1570/1 (Pope St. Pius V). If, sporadically, they are found to differ from the *Piana,* such differences are not based on textual criticism. *Vivès* presents sometimes, but very rarely and intermittently, some variants taken from Parisian Mss. The *Piana* itself was not drawn from Mss but from earlier printings.

The following dates of St. Thomas's scholastic career are important for the chronology of his works:

1252-1256	"Graduate studies" at the University of Paris.
1256 (Sept.)-1259 (July)	First teaching period as a Master of Theology in the University of Paris.
1259-1268 (Dec.)	Sojourn in Italy. Regent Master in the Dominican *Studium* in Rome (1265-?).
1269 (Jan.)-1272 (April, May)	Master of Theology in Paris for the second time.
1272-1273 (Dec.)	Professor in the Dominican *Studium* in Naples.

THEOLOGICAL SYNTHESES

1. Scripta super libros Sententiarum. Around the middle of the thirteenth century it was customary for the scholastic theologian to prove his skill and to secure his professional standing by elaborating a theological synthesis on the basis of the theological handbook of the times, the *Sententiae* of Peter the Lombard. These elaborations were, antonomastically, called "Writings" (*Scripta*), and were not commentaries. Their expository part occupies but a limited space, their main part consisting of discussions of the theological positions which were held in the schools. According to Tocco (p. 8) Aquinas composed his *Scripta* while he was a Bachelor (*baccalaureus sententiarius*) and in the beginning of his career as a Master. Hence the best dating of this work is to say that it was composed around 1256, for in March of that year Aquinas was granted his teaching licence and in September, with the beginning of the term, he started exercising his scholastic functions. Scholars have attempted to fix this date more precisely. Mandonnet (4, xv) set the *terminus a quo* at 1254, Pelster (4, 108) at 1253. Mandonnet's hypothesis, however (cf. 8, 495, n. 6), viz., that this work on the Sentences resulted from the very discussions between the Bachelor and his students and should be regarded as the day-by-day account of St. Thomas's scholastic activity, is unverified and unverifiable. The exact distribution, moreover, of young Thomas's premagisterial studies and teaching assignments is impossible to obtain from contemporary documents. The other end of our chronology, viz., the *terminus ad quem*, was investigated by Motte (1, 49) who through a comparison between 4 *Sent.*, 49, 2 and De verit. 8 attempted to prove that the composition of 4 *Sent.* was achieved when, in May/June 1257, *De verit.* 8 was written. But this date for *De verit.*, fundamental in Motte's reasoning, is far from having the absolute certainty attributed to it (no. 4). The Vulgate text of Book 3 differs to a certain extent from the autograph preserved in Vat. *lat.* 9851 and seems to be due to a later revision by the author (Rossi 1, 538; A. Dondaine 5, 101). It was suggested by Hayen that the current text of Book 1 also is a revised text and may not be comprised in the general chronology of the work. But this theory was on good reasons rejected by A. Dondaine (5, 100). The article on the Divine Attributes (1 *Sent.*, 2, 3) is an authentic *Quaestio Disputata*, probably from the years 1265-1267, which was inserted in the place where we find it now, perhaps on the authority of Aquinas himself (A. Dondaine 3, 253). 1 *Sent.*, prol. 3, 2 (*Vel dicendum* . . .) also seems to be a later though authentic interpolation (Chenu 2, 153).

EDITIONS: *Parm.* vols. 6-8; *Vivès*, vols. 7-11; Mandonnet (Books 1-2), 2 vols., Paris 1929; Moos (Books 3-4, dist. 22), 2 vols., Paris 1933, 1947 (the text is to a certain extent corrected by Mss). A small part of 4 *Sent.*, 15 was edited by Käppeli (2, 395) from a Spanish autograph folio.

2. **Summa contra Gentiles.** This title brings to light the true nature of the work. It is a *Summa*, i.e. a synthesis comprising the whole range of Catholic truth (*Tractatus de fide catholica*), but this *Summa* is not written for the purpose of academic teaching or discussion; rather it is aimed at defending the faith against "the errors of the unbelievers" (*contra errores infidelium, contra Gentiles*). Who are these Gentiles? The evidence of the work itself is that mainly the "philosophers" are envisaged, i.e., authoritative non-Christian thinkers whose rationalism may furnish reasons to oppose revelation. The testimony of a certain Peter Marsilio in 1313 (*Leon.* 13, vi) serves to identify these thinkers. They were those philosophers who had shaped the Mohammedan intellectual atmosphere with which the Dominican missionaries in the kingdom of Aragon had to cope. According to Marsilio it was upon the invitation of St. Raymond of Penyafort, O.P., the famous Jurist-Theologian and third Master General of the Dominican Order (1238/40), that Aquinas wrote the work as a guide for the Dominican missionaries in Spain. This traditional explanation of the origin and historical context of the *S. c. G.* was questioned by Gorce. Following certain trends in recent Thomistic bibliography, which tend to explain, as far as possible, St. Thomas's literary activity with the facts and data of the University of Paris, this author suggested viewing the *S. c. G.* in the same light. The defense of orthodoxy against some sort of Latin Averroism *ante litteram* which had invaded the teaching of Parisian professors would then be the object of Aquinas's work. This theory was rejected, on solid reasons, by Salman. The tradition linking the work with the Dominican missionary cause much cherished by every Dominican in the thirteenth century is still sound. And if it is felt that such an exacting treatise as the *S. c. G.* could not have been written for missionaries, the objection surely is not a strong one. "St. Thomas himself may well have thought that the *S. c. G.* was precisely the sort of work needed by Christian missionaries in Spain face to face with the high intellectual culture of the Moslem world" (Pegis 21). The works infra nos. 55 and 64 also attest Aquinas's interest in the missionary activity of his confrères.—Tolomeo of Lucca (Mandonnet 1, 60) affirms that this work was

written during the pontificate of Urban IV (1261/4). Not infrequently Tolomeo's chronologies are defective but in this case he seems to be right (cf. *infra* no. 55). Book 4 would appear to have been terminated before the *Contra errores Graecorum* (no. 56). On the other hand, the criterion of the *De animalibus*, chronologically of great interest, applies to Book 2. The criterion consists in the following facts: The Aristotelian work on the animals existed at first in an Arabic-Latin translation comprising only 19 books and bearing one general title, viz., *De animalibus*. William of Moerbeka (nos. 28-39) made a new complete Greek-Latin translation distinguishing the five sections of the original work and heading them with their original titles, viz., *De historiis animalium, De partibus animalium, De generatione animalium, De causa motus animalium, De progressu animalium*. The new translation of *De partibus animalium* was finished in Thebes on Dec. 23, 1260. When, therefore, St. Thomas quotes *De generatione animalium* in chs. 21, 88, 89, and *De causa motus animalium* in ch. 72 of Book 2, these quotations uncontrovertibly point to the years 1261/2 as the earliest date of composition (Grabmann 2, 189; Pelster 6, 75; Gauthier 2, 72). It is possible that this work was begun in Paris, as one witness in the canonization proceedings seems to imply (*Leon.* 13, vi). But no stringent confirmation of this has been found (see however Synave 5, 362; Motte 2, 806). Large parts of the autograph of the *S. c. G.* are preserved in Vat. *lat.* 9850.

EDITIONS: *Leon.* vols. 13 (1918), 14 (1926), 15 (1930). *Leon. Manualis*, Rome 1934.

Engl. trans. London-New York 1928/9 (5 vols.); A. C. Pegis, *Basic Writings of St. Th. A.* (Book 3, 1-113, vol. 2), New York 1945; Id., *On the Truth of Catholic Faith* (Book 1), New York 1955; J. F. Anderson, *On the Truth of Catholic Faith* (Book 2), New York 1956.

3. **Summa theologiae.** St. Thomas's main work was written for students of theology (*"incipientes," "novitii"*). It was to replace, by a new and didactically more adequate synthesis (*"ordo disciplinae"*), the conventional theological syntheses of the time, Aquinas's own former *Scripta* (no. 1) not excluded, which were built around the *Sententiae* of Peter the Lombard. These *Scripta*, often also called *Summae*, St. Thomas judged to be both pedagogically deficient and systematically incompetent, dependent as they were on the plan and organization of the *Sententiae* (cf. Prologue to *Summa* I). The main and most properly Thomistic feature of the *Summa* is its plan by which for the first time in history theology obtained the status of a science (Chenu 5, 255).—Chronological investigations must needs begin with the available documentary evidence. Tolomeo of Lucca (Mandonnet 1, 60) places Parts I, I-II and II-II between the years 1265 and 1271/2, i.e., in his own words, in the pontificate of Clement IV (1265 to Nov. 1268) and the subsequent vacancy which lasted for almost three

years. The successor of Clement IV, Teobaldo Visconti, was elected on Sept. 1, 1271 and arrived in Italy from the Holy Land on Feb. 12, 1272. In Viterbo he accepted the papal dignity and was then ordained a priest and consecrated under the name of Gregory X. The composition of Part III, Tolomeo affirms, took place during the pontificate of this pope. Tocco (1, 108) relates that the Saint was writing the qq. 46 ff. of Part III in Naples, 1272/3.—This chronology may be confirmed and supplemented on the basis of textual evidence. Part I, q. 79, a. 4 was written after Nov. 22, 1267, since it makes use of the Greek-Latin translation of Themistius's paraphrase of Aristotle's *De anima*, a translation whose date of edition is certain (Verbeke 1, 337). When Tolomeo positively states that Part I was begun in the autumn of 1265 when St. Thomas took over the rectorship of the Dominican Study House of *Santa Sabina* in Rome, his testimony is very probably true, at least in the sense that the project to write the *Summa* was known among the Master's friends and confrères as early as 1265. It seems that St. Thomas's first idea was to re-work his *Scripta* (Tolomeo: Mandonnet 1, 63). It may reasonably be assumed that Part I was terminated during the sojourn in Italy.—The main chronological problem of the *Summa* is the precise dating of Parts I-II and II-II. Two criteria are helpful for obtaining at least an approximate solution. The first is the criterion of Metaphysics *Lambda*, which is founded on the following facts. Up to the day when William of Moerbeka (infra nos. 28-39) translated the first twelve Books of the Metaphysics (according to mediaeval counting), the existence of Book *Kappa*, preceding *Lambda*, was unknown to the Latins. Bk. *Lambda*, therefore, bore the number XI, and only after the *Moerbekana* was known did it count as Bk. XII. In the *Summa* the last text to refer to *Lambda* as XI is I-II, q. 111, a. 5 (Gauthier 2, 88; verification in Mss). On the other hand, the first evidence of *Lambda* as Bk. XII is found in II-II, q. 1, a. 8, ob. 1. Scholars are agreed in fixing the earliest date of St. Thomas's knowledge of Bk. *Kappa* at the end of 1270 or the beginning of 1271. This chronology is arrived at with the help of Aquinas's polemical writing against the Averroists (*De unitate intellectus;* infra no. 47). In this way the approximate latest date of the termination of I-II as well as the approximate earliest date of the beginning of II-II, may be set at the turn of the year 1270. It is probable that the composition of the I-II took place in Paris where St. Thomas arrived in Jan/Febr. 1269; but more definite chronological determinations are difficult to obtain (cf. Lottin 1, 373). According to Synave (6, 9) the II-II might have been ready for publication in Paris, during the first months of 1272, since it seems that the work on Part III was begun while St. Thomas was still Professor at the University.—The criterion of doctrinal comparisons was applied to the II-II by Glorieux (9, 59). In this Part the discussions of controversial matters of topical interest discussed especially in Quodlibets I-VI (nos. 5-10) are frequently resumed and their arguments reconsidered. These Quodlibets are very close to the actual controversies and, since according to Glorieux their dating is secure, they lend themselves especially well to being the starting point of chronological investigations. Whatever may be said about this method (cf. infra nos. 5-16), the results, on the whole, confirm the conclusions arrived at in other ways.—Part III breaks off with q. 90, a. 4, when in Naples, 1273, St. Thomas was no longer able to continue this work of which an important part remains unwritten. The so-called *Supplementum*, put together with scissors and paste from pieces cut out of Aquinas's writings on the Sentences (especially Bk. 4), is of no direct interest to the cataloguist of St. Thomas's works. If, as Grabmann (1, 296) is not disinclined to believe, Reginald of Piperno, the Master's most capable secretary, should be its author or inspirer, it will not be amiss to take note of one contemporary of Aquinas, perhaps an important editor of his posthumous works, who did not fully realize the unique grandeur of the *Summa*. Between this Supplement and the *Concordantiae in seipsum*, a certainly apocryphal work, the spiritual affinity is close and worthy of note.

EDITIONS: *Leon.* Part I (vols. 4-5), 1888/9; Part I-II (vols. 6-7), 1891/2; Part II-II (vols. 8-10), 1895/7/9; Part III and *"Supplementum"* (vols. 11-12), 1903/6. The last five vols. are a definitive critical edition, specifically different from the Vulgate text. The former vols. are substantially a reproduction of the *Piana* (1570) with which the editors interfered only when it seemed to be "intrinsically erroneous." The notations, however, of the readings found in a limited number of Mss are more and more frequent. Their purpose is, according to the editors (*Leon.* vol. 8, p. xxx), "to present to the attentive reader the material out of which he may himself form a judgment about the correct text to be followed."—*Taurin.*, 4 vols., 1948; this edition contains the *Leon.* text, without however any apparatus.—*Ed. Biblioteca de Autores cristianos*, 5 vols. Madrid 1952 (*Leon.* text, no apparatus).—Ed. Ottawa, 5 vols., 1941 (*Piana* text with a number of Leonine corrections; outstanding for its notes comprising matters of editorial interest).

Engl. trans. English Dominicans (22 vols.), 2nd ed., London (New York) 1912-1936. Re-print, revised and annotated, of I, I-II, 6-21, 49-114, II-II, 1-7: A. C. Pegis, *Basic Writings of St. Th. A.*, New York 1945.

ACADEMIC DISPUTATIONS

THE Disputation is the most characteristic scholastic exercise in the University of the thirteenth century. There were what we might call regular and solemn disputations. The former were held in the Master's school. A question or problem was presented by the Master. It was formulated, in accordance with the Aristotelian rules, in such a way that it left room for alternative answers and these alternatives were disputed by two students or two groups of students, the "formal Bachelors," who were immediately preparing for their Master's degree, after they had passed through their ordinary studies and, for several years, given "cursory" lectures on the Bible and the Sentences. Two moments are to be distinguished in the procedure of such a disputation: first, the disputation proper, an affair of the students who thoroughly explored those alternatives; second, the "determination" which was given by the Master. —The solemn disputations were called Quodlibets. Everybody was admitted to them and allowed to argue whichever subject he wanted to be discussed. These disputations were held twice a year, viz., during Advent ("Quodlibet of Christmas") and during Lent ("Quodlibet of Easter"). The Masters were under no obligation to hold such disputations (Glorieux 6, 9)—The *Quaestiones disputatae* and the *Quaestiones de Quolibet* of St. Thomas are not recordings of the actual disputations in school but elaborate and stylized compositions which the Master wrote on the basis of these scholastic performances. The difference between the written works and the school disputation may best be studied with the help of an as yet unedited transcript of an actual scholastic exercise of this sort, viz., the *Quaestio disputata: utrum anima coniuncta cognoscat seipsam per essentiam* (cf. Pelster 9, 624).

4. **Quaestiones disputatae. De potentia Dei, De malo, De spiritualibus creaturis, De anima, De unione Verbi incarnati, De virtutibus, De veritate.** These titles are here enumerated in the order in which they are given in the *Ed. Princeps*, 1570/1. Each of these comprises a series of disputations set up at a certain date, either during Aquinas's life or perhaps even posthumously, and presented to the reading public. "Extra-serial" disputations, i.e., such as did not find their place in these collections but were inserted in other works of Aquinas, are the following: [**De pueris in religionem admittendis**] in *Quodl.* 4, 23/4; [**De sensibus s. Scripturae**] in *Quodl.* VII, 14/16; [**De opere manuali religiosorum**] in *Quodl.* 7, 17/18; [**De attributis divinis**] in 1 *Sent.*, 2, 3. Another *Quaestio disputata*, viz., **De immortalitate animae** was recently discovered and is probably to be admitted among the authentic works (A. Dondaine 6, 112; Fries 18). The unedited *Quaestio disputata:* **Utrum anima coniuncta cognoscat seipsam per essentiam** (Oxford, *Bodl., Cod. Laud. Misc.* 480) probably also belongs to Aquinas (Dondaine 6, 112; Pelster 8, 618).—It seems that at certain intervals in his literary career St. Thomas, or some secretary on his instruction, gathered together a number of Questions and edited them in one volume. Such a volume does not necessarily take its unity and shape from the fact that therein one subject is systematically treated. In certain cases at least, a

collection of disputations may be a merely editorial composite taking its name from the first question. The group *De unione Verbi incarnati*, for instance, seems to have been edited together with, and comprised under the title of, the group *De virtutibus in communi*. An editorial device, if not an editorial accident, might have caused Q. 6 of *De malo* (*De libero arbitrio*) to be at the spot where we find it now and where, surely, it is out of place if the organic structure of the collection *De malo* is considered. In the same collection, Q. 16 (*De daemonibus*), which certain Mss separate from its actual context (Axters 1, 157; Gauthier 2, 90), may owe its location to an intervention of the editor of the collection. The group *De veritate*, although from olden times held to be a compact *Summa* On Truth (*Summa de veritate:* Ms St.-Omer 289, Axters 1, 138), appears in other ancient documents also with the designation *Quaestiones de veritate et ultra* (Nicolas Trivet: Mandonnet 1, 48). It is impossible however, at least at the present moment, to reconstruct these collections in their original shape and, consequently, to say how many editions or volumes there were in the beginning, and by whom they were made.— The outstanding chronological essay is that of Mandonnet 3 (cf. also Mandonnet 6). It rests on the testimony of Bartholomew of Capua. Dividing these works into three groups, Bartholomew says that Aquinas "disputed" (*disputavit*) the first, viz., *De veritate* in Paris (1256/9); the second, viz., *De potentia et ultra* in Italy (1259/68); the third, viz., *De virtutibus et ultra* in Paris (1269/72). Mandonnet assumed two facts to be implied in this testimony; first, that each article of our editions presents the very text of one disputation read by the Master to his students as his final word or "determination"; second, that Aquinas indifferently held disputations with whatever students happened to be around, year in, year out, at various but, within each scholastic term, regular intervals, from 1256 (Sept.) to 1272 (April, May). The chronological problem, then, of these Questions turns out to be the problem of how Aquinas may have arranged his teaching routine. He held disputations, according to Mandonnet, either once or twice a week, or one a fortnight, a routine to be determined by the length or the actual text and its relation to the forty or forty-one weeks of the school year. Following out Mandonnet's method, Synave (5, 355) went so far as to compute for each article of the *De veritate* the very day on which it was written.—To be sure, some of the *Quaest. disp.* contain in their text certain traces of the classroom, e.g., the words *sed dicebatur* (*De anima* 10, 11, 18, 21) or in their stead *sed diceretur* (*ibid.* 2). But critics, such as Birkenmajer, Glorieux (4, 29) and others, have long since felt it difficult to follow Mandonnet in his strict literal interpretation of the traditional word *disputavit*. The tendency in more recent bibliography is rather to dissociate the composition, and especially the edition, of these works from the school disputation and to restore to the author the liberty to write what he pleases, when he pleases (cf. Keeler, 1, x).—The chronological indications of Bartholomew, as far as they go, are to-day accepted against those of Tolomeo of Lucca. As to some particular groups of Questions note the following: The Questions *De potentia* were "disputed" in Rome (1265-?) if the evidence of one Ms, viz., Subiaco 211, is to be trusted (Grabmann 1, 306). The Italian origin of the Questions constituting the collection *De spiritualibus creaturis* is affirmed in two Mss, viz., Munich *Clm* 3287 and Lisbon, *Bibl. nac.* 262 (Grabmann 1, 304). The citations of Simplicius, found in its art. 3, and of Themistius *In de anima* (art. 10) furnish definite earliest dates, viz., March 1266 and Nov. 1267 respectively. But this Italian origin of the disputations would not, of course, exclude a Parisian edition. The group *De anima* is qualified as a Parisian "disputation" in Ms Klosterneuburg 274 (Glorieux 4, 21) and Ms Angers 418 (Axters 1, 147). However Q. 2 of this group is known in Italy before 1270 (Pelster 3, 410) and this fact should warn us against too hastily identifying the actual disputation, the composition, and the edition of these works. These acts are different, indeed, and they may, in some cases at least, have proceeded under entirely different conditions. The same distinction seems to have a peculiar importance in the *Quaestiones disputatae de malo.* Certain Catalogues and Mss list or transcribe these Questions after the group *De virtutibus* (Glorieux 4, 16) but it would be unsafe to interpret this fact chronologically. Various tests applied to certain passages strongly suggest these to have been composed before *Summa* II-II (test of Metaph. *Lambda:* Gauthier 2, 89) and even before *Summa* I-II (test of doctrinal criticism: Lottin 1, 373). An Italian origin of Qq. 1-5 and again Qq. 7-15 is not to be excluded, while Q. 6 seems to belong to Paris (1270) on account of doctrinal affinities with the controversies of the time. In short, then, it would seem that, except for a few certainties (*De veritate,* Paris 1256/9; *De potentia,* Italy 1259/68; *De virtutibus,* Paris 1269/72) the chronological problem of these works remains open to research and discussion. For the extra-serial Questions, their chronology etc., see Synave (2, 38), Glorieux (10, 286), Dondaine (3, 253).

EDITIONS: Critical *Leon.* text of *De veritate* in preparation. Vulgate text in *Parm.,* vols. 8, 9; *Vivès,* vols. 13, 14; Mandonnet, 3 vols., Paris 1925; *Taurin.,* 2 vols., 1953. For *De spiritualibus creaturis* the critical, though not definitive, text established by Keeler, Rome 1946, should be used. E. Gomez, *De immortalitate animae. Cuestio inédita de s. Tomás. Biblioteca de Tomistas Espagnoles* 3, Madrid 1935.

Engl. trans. On the Power of God, 3 vols., London, New York, 1932/4; A. C. Pegis, *On Free Choice (De Malo 6),* New York n.d.; Fitzpatrik-Wellmuth, *On Spiritual Creatures,* Milwaukee 1949; J. P. Rowan, *The Soul,* Saint-Louis 1949; J. P. Reid, *On Virtues (in generali),* Providence R. I. 1951; Mulligan-McGlynn-Schmidt, *On Truth* (trans. from the definitive Leonine text [?]), Chicago 1952/4.

5-16. Quaestiones de quolibet I-XII.   Twelve such Questions are traditionally attributed to St. Thomas. Quodl. XII, which is a Reportatum or perhaps better a rough sketch of a Quodlibet, is a relatively late addition, made around 1300, to a pre-existing group of eleven Quodlibets. These eleven again fall into two groups, distinct both in the history of their performance and of their composition and edition. I-VI apparently was the earliest group to be constituted as a compact, never varying series. To these the other five (VII-XI) were added later but their sequence shows a great variety in the early editions (Glorieux 10, 282). I-VI are now commonly held to be Parisian productions (1269/72), after Denifle (1, 320) discovered the dates of several of them given in Mss. According to this evidence, III would be from Easter 1270, II from Christmas 1270, V from Christmas 1271. Adhering strictly to this Ms evidence, Pelster (6, 69) conjectured the following chronology of the entire group I-VI (E = Easter, C = Christmas): I (C 1269); III (E 1270); II (C 1270); IV (E 1271); V (C 1271); VI (E 1272). Others consider the traditional sequence of these pieces in the text (II before III!) to be an indication of their chronological order. They moreover suggest XII to be a Parisian Quodlibet, fitting the doctrinal controversies of 1270 (infra nos. 45-47) especially well. Hence Glorieux (cf. 9, 94) proposes the following chronology: I (E 1269); II (C 1269); III (E 1270); XII (C 1270); IV (E 1271); V (C 1271); VI (E 1272). It will be noted, however, that in VI there are two quotations of Metaph. *Lambda* (art. 19) and that both refer to Book XI (Ms evidence in Gauthier 2, 87, n. 52). It would seem therefore that the chronology of these works, which some scholars are wont to consider a closed question, is still open to further inquiry. St. Thomas himself never edited a volume of, let us say, six Quodlibets, not to speak of eleven or twelve.—As to Quodlibets VII to XI, they were definitely recognized as Parisian disputations (1256/9) by Mandonnet (8, 487). Documentary evidence however for a more detailed chronology is lacking. Therefore scholars are dependent on the rather precarious criterion of doctrinal evaluations and comparisons and, as may be expected, there are *tot sensus, quot capita*. It will be of no avail to describe all these widely divergent conjectures. Even the authenticity of at least some of these Quodlibets, especially of IX and XI, has come up for discussion (cf. Glorieux 11, 235, whose views were contradicted by Pelster 5, 88, and Isaac 1, 145). These Quodlibets were attributed to St. Thomas in their very first editions and they will always be a legitimate part of our literary heritage from him. But they doubtlessly have their share in the obscurities, not uncommon in Thomistic bibliography, which surround certain works edited posthumously by unknown editors according to unknown editorial rules. In Thomistic bibliography authenticity might, and indeed most often does, refer to St. Thomas's direct authorship. Sometimes however it might also, immediately, refer to a posthumous, "authentic" collection of Aquinas's works (Glorieux 10, 297) in such a way that it is impossible for us to turn this relative authenticity into an absolute one (cf. infra no. 55; Eschmann 2, xxii).

EDITIONS: Vulgate text in *Parm.* 9; *Vivès,* 15; Mandonnet, Paris 1926; *Taurin.* 1949.

EXPOSITIONS OF HOLY SCRIPTURE

THESE expositions are here enumerated according to the canonical order of the books of Holy Scripture with which they deal. This merely pragmatic arrangement, adopted by the *Ed. Princeps* (1570/1) and Grabmann (1, 251), seems preferable to the chronological order, elaborated by Mandonnet in a series of remarkable studies (Chronologie des écrits scripturaires, *Revue thomiste* 1928/9). Mandonnet's method and results were widely accepted in recent bibliography but also submitted to serious criticism (Glorieux 12, 243). Of this method we retain only the rule that lecture transcripts (*Reportata*), of which there are not a few in this class of works, may not be crowded into one short period, e.g., the few years in Paris, 1269/72, when it appears physically impossible for the Master to have given these lectures. As to the expositions written or dictated by Aquinas, it seems unprofitable to establish their chronology with reference to his teaching obligations. The notion of "academic work," however useful it be in Thomistic bibliography, should not be developed into a system of "scholastic" determinism depriving St. Thomas of the liberty to write what he pleases, when he pleases.

17. Expositio in Job ad litteram. This is a typically Thomistic exposition of Holy Scripture, a "scientific" work (*expositio secundum sensum litteralem,* as opposed to the *sensus moralis* of the *Moralia* of Gregory the Great). It exploits to the full the philosophical and scientific sources of the time for the explanation of Holy Writ. Aristotle, Plato, Cicero, Pliny, Porphyry, Avicenna, Averroes and others are quoted abundantly in the elucidation of this scriptural work to which another Dominican, Roland of Cremona, had already applied a vast amount of scientific knowledge (A. Dondaine, 7, 128). The central theme is God's Providence. The discussion between Job and his friends is considered as a regular University disputation; Job speaks *more disputatoris* (13, 2) and the Lord appears as the *quaestionis determinator* (38, 1). Mandonnet (10, 147) and Glorieux (12, 260) are of the opinion that this work was composed in Paris, 1269/72. It is, they say, "a ripe fruit of Aquinas' exegetical skill"; "it fits best into those years with their specific doctrinal preoccupations concerning the Averroïstic negation of Divine Providence." Tolomeo however definitely places this commentary in the times of Urban IV, i.e., 1261/4 (Mandonnet 1, 60). He is very probably right. In 27, 1 a tacit but clearly recognizable use is made of the Politics (*divitiae artificiales . . . divitiae naturales:* Pol. 1, 8/9, 1256b 27, 29; 1257a 5). All St. Thomas's writings composed in Paris, 1256/9, are free of any reference to the Politics and it may be concluded with security that this Aristotelian work was unknown to him during those years. On the other hand, it is worthy of note that we find only one reference to the Politics in the commentary on Job, which at several points would lend itself to such quotations (cf. nos. 24, 39). All this suggests a date close to 1260. Moreover, in 40, 2, and 41, 2, there are several citations of *De animalibus* which is the title of the older Arabic-Latin translation of Aristotle's *Historia animalium* (no. 2). Hence Tolomeo's chronology seems to be confirmed by the circumstantial evidence of the work itself.

EDITIONS: *Parm.* 14, 1-147; *Vivès* 18, 1-227. Critical *Leon.* edition in preparation.

18.   **In Psalmos Davidis expositio.**   According to mediaeval usage this work often is described, in our sources, as an exposition of the first four nocturns of the (ancient) Office, i.e., the nocturns of Sunday to Wednesday. It is incomplete, terminating with Ps. 54, which is the third psalm of the Office of Wednesday. Its literary character is obviously that of a lecture transcript. The Master speaks to the students: *Legamus primo litteram secundum historiam* (7, 3); in the characteristic manner of the lecturer, verifiable in all lecture transcripts, he introduces his problems by direct questions: *Sed numquid spirituales delectationes sunt delectabiliores?* (18, 7 and often elsewhere); he quotes from memory and is informal in these quotations (e.g., 44, 5: *Eth.* 10, 10: 1180a 18); the reporter (Reginald of Piperno) uses his well-known abbreviated style (26, 1: *Sed contra de Absalone* . . . or again 17, 11: *Philosophus: subversio est* . . .) As a lecture transcript the work is also listed by that group of the ancient Catalogues which is most explicit about the *Reportata*, viz., the Catalogue of Bartholomew of Capua and its related documents (Mandonnet 1, 31 ff.) No objection against their statements should be raised on the strength of one Ms (Synave 4, 33) which affirms this exposition to have been in the possession of Reginald "who had all the Master's writings" (!) (*habuit omnia scripta sua*); the word *scripta* does not need to be understood in the narrowest possible sense. Concerning chronology, certain facts, especially the unfinished condition, seem to lend probability to the common opinion that these lectures were given in Naples, 1272/3 (cf. Glorieux 12, 250).

EDITIONS: The Vulgate text containing 51 Psalms is printed in *Parm.*

14, 148-353; *Vivès* 18, 228-556. Three more expositions (Ps. 52-54) were edited by Uccelli 243.

19.   Expositio in Canticum Canticorum.   The fact that Aquinas wrote an exposition of the Song of Solomon is too well attested to be controvertible. Three ancient Catalogues, independent one on the other, affirm it, viz., Bartholomew of Capua, Bernard Guidonis (Mandonnet 1, 31, 69) and the *Tabula* of Stams (Meersseman 59). However the text is unknown. The two works printed in the Vulgate editions of *Opera Omnia* (*Parm.* 14, 354; *Vivès* 18, 557: *Incipit: Salomon inspiratus; Parm.* 14, 387; *Vivès* 18, 608: *Incipit: Sonet vox tua*) are not authentic. The first is a much older work (Haymo of Auxerre; Spicq 303), the second belongs to Egidius of Rome and seems to have nothing whatever to do with Aquinas (Bruni).

20.   Expositio in Isaiam prophetam.   An autograph fragment of this exposition, comprising chs. 34-50 (last words: . . . *a meo dominio quod paratus sum benefacere quantum ex me est*), is preserved in Vat. *lat.* 9850. St. Thomas's hand was not easily legible (*littera inintelligibilis*). Shortly after his death, the *Exp. in Is.* was copied, for the purpose of publication, by Jacobinus of Asti. Throughout the whole work there are found so-called *Collationes*, i.e., sermons not elaborated fully but compendiously presented in diagram form (facsimile in Destrez 2, 172, 184). They comprise about one eleventh of the entire text. On the problem of their authenticity see Destrez (2, 183), who declares them to be interpolations due to Jacobinus, and Axters (2, 513), who holds them to be the work of Aquinas himself. These *Collationes* are a peculiar feature of this exposition which it shares only with the work on the Prophet Jeremias (no. 21).—Two parts, heterogeneous in style and method, are distinguishable. Chapters 1-11 are written in the usual form of a scholastic University commentary composed by the Master of Theology; the theological developments are frequent and abundant. From ch. 12 to the end, these developments are lacking and the exposition confines itself to a merely literal gloss.—The chronology of the work is quite uncertain. Some scholars would assign to it an early, others a later date. The years 1256/9 are proposed by De Guibert (1, 107) and Mandonnet (10, 132), the years 1269/72 by Roy (1, 179) and Glorieux (12, 253). This diversity of chronological opinion rests on diverse interpretations of the same texts, taken from chs. 1-11. Considering the autograph fragment, it may be profitable to point to the improbability of a Parisian composition in the years 1269/72. Indeed it seems unlikely that during those years, when his literary production attained almost incredible proportions, St. Thomas would have found the time to write down by hand any of his works himself. Rather he dictated them, having not only one secretary but a staff of several at his disposition.—The following text taken from 3, 3, might prove to be of chronological interest: *sindones, i.e. subtilia velamina quibus operiuntur humeri, sicut fit in Campania in* (read *a*) *mulieribus.*

EDITIONS: Vulgate text in *Parm.* 14, 427-576; *Vivès* 18, 688-821; 19, 1-65. Uccelli's text (144 ff.) is established with the help of the autograph.

21. Expositio in Jeremiam prophetam.   The colophon in the Vulgate editions qualifies this work as *expositio litteralis*. Its literalism should not of course be mistaken for that of the *Exp. in Job ad litteram*. In the 16th cent. Sixtus of Siena (Echard 324) judged its *doctrinae sterilitas* so severely that he denied its authenticity. There can however be no doubt about the authenticity. Yet it is true that theological developments are rare and extremely succinct (chs. 1, 18, 20, 23, 28, 29), so much so that one is tempted to think of the lectures given by the *Baccalaureus Biblicus,* whose task it was to read the Bible "cursorily," i.e., merely insisting on the text and its articulations. The *Collationes*, regular and abundant up to ch. 23, are not found in the remainder of the text. The work is unfinished, breaking off at the end of ch. 42. The usual chronology (Glorieux 12, 259:1267/8) is based on the supposition that the work was written in connection with the lectures of the Master.

EDITIONS: *Parm.* 14, 577-667; *Vivès* 19, 66-198.

22. Expositio in Threnos Jeremiae prophetae.   This exposition of the Lamentations of Jeremias is, like the preceding, significant for its literalism. Doctrinal investigations are completely absent. The author restricts himself to a few summary discussions of discordances found in the Bible or the Glosses. There are no *Collationes*. This may be due to an accident of the text tradition. While the exposition of the prophecy of Jeremias is extant in at least four Mss (Stegmüller, n. 8040), no Ms of this work ascribing it to St. Thomas seems to survive. Recently a Ms of the text was discovered in Salzburg (*Oeffentl. Studienbibliothek* V.4. G. 153: Kürzinger), in which however the exposition is attributed to Augustinus Triumphus (scholastic author of the beginning of the 14th cent.) The chronological problem presents the same aspects as no. 21.

EDITIONS: *Parm.* 14, 668-685; *Vivès* 19, 199-225.

23. Glossa (expositio) continua in Matthaeum, Marcum, Lucam, Joannem.   This is a Gloss in the technical mediaeval sense of the word, a string or series of passages selected from the works of various Fathers or Ecclesiastical writers, and arranged for the elucidation of some portion of Scripture, in this case, the four Gospels. Its publication, in the sixties of the thirteenth century, was an immediate success. It counts among the most widely diffused works of Aquinas both in the manuscript and in early printed editions. Biographers and cataloguists are loud in its praise. From the fourteenth century on, it was called *Catena aurea*, the Golden Chain. In the nineteenth century, M. Pattison, fellow of Lincoln College, Oxford, wrote the following note, worthy of quotation: All former Glosses had been "partial and capricious, dilating on one passage, and passing unnoticed another of equal or greater difficulty. But it is impossible to read the Catena of St. Thomas, without being struck with the masterly and architectonic skill with which it is put together. A learning of the highest kind, not a mere literary book-knowledge, . . . a thorough acquaintance with the whole range of ecclesiastical antiquity, . . . a familiarity with the style of each writer, so as to compress into few words the pith of a whole page, and a power of clear and orderly arrangement in this mass of knowledge, are qualities which make this Catena perhaps nearly perfect as a conspectus of Patristic interpretation. Other compilations exhibit research, industry, learning; but this, though a mere compilation, evinces a masterly command over the whole subject of Theology." A remarkable statement, and a distant echo of Tocco's words: (*opus*) *sanctorum auctoritatibus miro ordine contextum, ex quibus sic evangelio-rum continuavit historiam, quasi unius doctoris videatur esse postilla* (Mandonnet 1, 79). This Gloss was commissioned by Urban IV to whom the *Glossa in Matthaeum* is dedicated. The Ms Parma, Bibl. palat. 1, written in 1263 and containing the *Glossa in Matth.*, definitely fixes the date of this part of the Catena (Masnovo 202). The other Glosses are dedicated to Cardinal Annibaldo degli Annibaldeschi, O.P., Aquinas's disciple and friend; their composition thus was completed after the death of Urban IV (1264). Beginning with the *Glossa in Marcum*, St. Thomas's research in Greek Patristic sources becomes more and more intense. For the purpose of broadening the range of his information, he procured new translations of certain Greek Fathers (on Nicetas of Heraclea see Tonneau 179). Because of this research into Greek theological sources, the Catena marks a turning point in the development of Aquinas's theology as well as in the history of Catholic dogma (Backes; Simonin 2, 941).

EDITIONS: Vulgate text in *Parm.*, 11-12; *Vivès* 16-17; *Taurin.* 2 vols. 1953.

Engl. trans. Catena Aurea, Oxford 1841/5.

24. Expositio in evangelium s. Matthaei. This exposition is a lecture transcript. According to certain documents (Nicolas of Trivet: Mandonnet 1, 50; the two lists of Prague: Grabmann 1, 92, 98), there were two reporters, viz., *frater Petrus de Andia, O.P.,* and *quidam scolaris (secularis) Parisiensis.* The latter is identified in two Mss as *Magister Leodegarius Bissuntinus* (Besançon), whom Synave (4, 37) holds to be the one and only reporter. The almost common opinion of recent bibliographers is that Aquinas pronounced the lectures on St. Matthew during his first sojourn as a Master in Paris, 1256/9. This chronology needs however to be re-examined. There are four quotations from the Politics (Eschmann 2, xxix). Two of these are explicit, viz., 10, 1 (*Taurin.* no. 822: *Hoc est quod dicitur quod quaedam divitiae sunt artificiales: Pol.* I, 9: 1257a 5) and 11, 2 (*ed. cit.* 931: *Unde philosophus: omnis homo* . . . : *Pol.* I, 2: 1253a 27). The two other quotations are tacit but un-controvertible, viz., 8, 2 (701: *Prima est dominativa potestas* . . . : *Pol.* I, 5: 1254b 4) and 12, 2 (1011: *Domus est communitas* . . . : *Pol.* I, 2: 1252b 12-30). If account is taken of the fact, established long ago by Hertling, that all the writings of the first Parisian period are free of references to the Politics, the impact of these four passages appears in its proper perspective. It should however be noted that the text contains several indications unmistakably pointing to Paris and France (26, 7 . . . *sicut patet in Francia et Picardia et Burgundia;* 9, 1 . . . *sicut si aliquis esset de aliqua villa iuxta Parisios*). If these passages are not due to the Parisian reporter, they would, taken together with the quotations from the Politics (nos. 17, 39), suggest a composition of the work during the years 1269/72. Yet it should be noted that very soon the *Lectura in Matth.* was recognized to be a "defective" lecture-transcript (Bartholo-mew of Capua: Mandonnet 1, 31). Its defect, possibly, consists in the reporters interferences with the text. The general condition of the Vulgate text also seems to be subject to caution (Echard 325).

EDITIONS: *Parm.* 10, 1-278; *Vivès* 19, 226-668; *Taurin.* 1951.

25. Expositio in evangelium Joannis. This exposition has been much admired from the earliest days to our own age. "None better may be found," says Bartholomew of Capua who qualifies the *Lect. in Matth.* as *"defectiva."* "None of St. Thomas's other works on Holy Scripture at-tains the sublimity of thought, the breadth of vision, the perfection of the commentary on St. John" (Synave 1, 460). Tolomeo of Lucca emphatically states that the first five chapters are written by Aquinas (*scripsit* . . . *super quinque capitula stilo proprio*) while the rest is a lecture transcript (made by Reginald of Piperno and) corrected, i.e., prepared for publica-tion by the Master himself (Mandonnet 1, 63, 68). A colophon however, written by Reginald, fails to mention these details. Together with the *Glossa continua* (no. 23) this exposition appears in the first University Stationer's list known to us (Chartularium U. P. 646); it was thus, a few years after St. Thomas's death, an acknowledged University text. The above mentioned colophon has Reginald undertake his report at the re-quest of Adenulf of Anagni who was the Provost of the Chapter of St.-Omer in Paris while St. Thomas was at the University, 1269/72 (Glorieux 12, 246). This detail makes the chronology of the work evident.

EDITIONS: *Parm.* 10, 279-645; *Vivès* 19, 669 ff., 20, 1-376; *Taurin.* 1952.

26-27.   Expositio in s. Pauli Epistolas.   The text of our editions is composed of three, if not four, heterogeneous pieces: (a) a text written (or dictated) by St. Thomas (*"Ordinatio"*), covering Rom. 1, 1—I Cor. 7, 9; (b) an exposition cut out of the *Postilla* of Peter of Tarentasia (2nd redaction traditionally attributed to Nicolas of Gorran O. P.; Simonin 1, 226, 228); this exposition extends from I Cor. 7, 10 to the end of ch. 10; its first words are: *dicens Mtth. XIX, 6: Quos Deus coniunxit* . . . ; (c) lectures on the rest of the Epistles transcribed, according to Bartholomew of Capua, by Reginald of Piperno (*"Lectura"*). Since the commentary on *Hebr.* is apparently elaborated with greater care than the foregoing lecture transcript, it would seem reasonable to regard this part, as well, as a direct composition of the Master (cf. Bernard Guidonis, Mandonnet 1, 68, n. 14). When and by whom this work was patched together is unknown; certain indications would suggest an early date, not long after the death of Aquinas (Simonin 1, 228). If this is correct, the reader will not miss the interesting lesson on the editorial rules which guided some early editors of St. Thomas's works. Mandonnet (11, 222) established the chronological priority of the *Lectura* over the *Ordinatio*. St. Thomas, according to Mandonnet, lectured twice on the Epistles, first, in Italy, 1259/65; second, in Naples, 1272/3. The first course, comprising the entire Pauline *Corpus* was taken down by Reginald, the second was written by the Master himself but left unfinished; according to Bartholomew of Capua it ended at I Cor. 10. Hence the history of the original edition of this commentary would have to be reconstructed thus: From the complete lecture course the part dealing with Rom. 1, 1—I Cor. 10 was cut away, destroyed (!) and replaced by the *Ordinatio*. The last pages of this *Ordinatio* were lost in some way and the lacuna was filled by the text of Tarentasia. Although this theory leaves many questions unanswered, it is generally approved as a reasonable solution of the difficulties surrounding this work, *salvo meliore iudicio*. Some authors prefer a vaguer dating of the *Lectura*, viz., 1259/68. For the *Ordinatio* the years 1269/72 were proposed by Bouillard (1, 225). Cf. also Lottin (2, 306; *ibid.* 310; Eschmann (1, 23); Glorieux (12, 258). The *Ordinatio* may reasonably be taken as a mere revision of the former lecture transcript. It is therefore by no means sure that Aquinas really did lecture twice on the Epistles.

EDITIONS: *Parm.*, vol. 13; *Vivès*, vols. 20-21; *Taurin.*, 2 vols., 1953.

EXPOSITIONS OF ARISTOTELIAN WORKS

UP TO 1259, when St. Thomas came to Italy, his knowledge of Aristotle, vast and impressive as it was, nevertheless depended to a considerable extent on rather second hand information and sources. At the court of the great and inspiring Urban IV (1261/4) he realized the necessity of introducing Greek Patristic thought into theology (no. 23). It might have been during those same years that he also conceived the plan of a vast investigation into the letter and the original teaching of Aristotle in order exactly to define Aristotelianism and its place in Christian thought. Certain chapters of the *Contra Gentiles*, e.g., 2, 61, show a significant preoccupation with the *littera* and the *intentio* of the Stagirite, which is to characterize St. Thomas's whole expository work. The first and preliminary task to be accomplished was a literal translation of Aristotle's works of which a considerable part was available only in either Arabic-Latin or in fragmentary Greek-Latin versions. Tradition credits Aquinas with the initiative in regard to new, more accurate translations not only of the Aristotelian writings but also of the Greek commentators. His expert in this field was William of Moerbeka, a Flemish Dominican who had been in Frankish Greece and whom Aquinas met personally in the times of Clement IV (1265/8) if not earlier at the court of Urban IV. Tolomeo of Lucca states that St. Thomas, while Regent of the Dominican Studium in Rome (from 1265 on), explained almost the whole moral and natural philosophy and also put these expositions in writing (Mandonnet 1, 60). If this witness is not devoid of all significance, we may assume Aquinas to have started executing his plan in Italy, in the form of oral lectures of which there are still certain traces in our actual text (no. 34; see also Pelster 1, 384). But none of the written expositions can be proved to have been terminated during those years. Three main chronological criteria were elaborated by recent scholars and, at least with partial success, applied to these expositions. First, the criterion of *Metaph. Lambda* (see no. 3); second, that of the sources used by Aquinas, especially the Greek commentaries, several of which furnish a definite earliest date since the time of their translation is known by direct evidence; third, the criterion of the Latin versions of the Aristotelian text. These investigations, which are in progress, cast an interesting light on the Aristotelian writings of Aquinas. The Master's main intention was not to elaborate a system of philosophy but simply to make the pure and unadulterated Aristotle known to the Occident which was passing through a crisis of heterodox Aristotelianism. All these expositions are preoccupied with the quality of their textual basis. Some of them give us to understand that Aquinas was eagerly waiting for Brother William to deliver his translations on which a secure *Sententia* could be pronounced. In listing these expositions we follow the Aristotelian canon. The many continuations of Aquinas's commentaries are of no interest to the Thomistic bibliographer. Since, however, some of them at least were tacked on to the unfinished works at an early date, they illustrate the editorial rules guiding the editors of Aquinas's works.

28. In libros Peri Hermeneias expositio. This exposition is unfinished, terminating probably, in the middle of a phrase, with the words (2, 2, 14: 19b 26): *Dicit enim quod id, quod in supradictis dictum est, intelligi potest.* The Commentary of Ammonius is certainly used in its Greek-Latin version completed by William of Moerbeka on Sept. 12, 1268. On the other hand, Metaph. *Lambda* is quoted as XI in 1, 3, 5. The extreme dates thus are 1268 and 1270/1. Certain indications definitely point to Paris (1269/72) as the place of composition, e.g., the discussion, in 1, 13-15, of contingency in propositions and events. See Isaac (2, 126).

EDITIONS: *Leon.* I (1882): Vulgate text with only "necessary" corrections (supra no. 3) based on a restricted number of Mss; for some corrections of this text see Isaac (2, 107). Isaac (2, 160) also published the Moerbekana together with certain excerpts from Moerbeka's translation of Ammonius. *Taurin.* 1955 (Ed. Leon. manualis).

29. In libros posteriorum Analyticorum expositio. St. Thomas wrote this exposition on the basis of the translation of Jacobus Venetus but had also at his disposition a version revised and corrected most probably by William of Moerbeka (Minio-Paluello 2, 397). He seems to have been the only *Expositor* of his time to avail himself of the opportunity offered by the *Moerbekana* to throw light on a notoriously obscure text (cf. 1, 6, 5). The date of this new translation, however, is unknown. The *Lambda* test also is here inoperative since there are no pertinent quotations. The sources moreover of this exposition have not been analyzed so far. Hence the chronological problem remains open. Mandonnet, manifestly inspired by the much debatable testimony of Tolomeo, suggested: "around 1268 or thereafter." Grabmann, considering this work to be one of the two commentaries on treatises in the Organon, tentatively advanced a date close to the composition of *Expos in Periermeneias.*

EDITIONS: *Leon.* I (1882); *Taurin.* 1955 (*Leon. Manualis*).

30. In octo libros Physicorum expositio. Ms evidence shows that throughout the exposition Metaphysics *Lambda* is quoted as XI. A summary investigation of the translations used by Aquinas revealed to Pelster (2, 393) that the author changed from the *Physica veteris trans-*

lationis to the Moerbekana (whose date is unknown) during the composition of the work. Grabmann (1, 275) and Mansion (4, 304) agree on the priority of this commentary with regard to *Summa* I. This priority is affirmed on the ground of doctrinal comparisons. Grabmann considers St. Thomas's teaching on the problem of the eternity of the world (cf. Castagnoli 1, 270), Mansion his interpretation of the Aristotelian theory of time. The work would accordingly have been written between 1268 and 1271.

EDITIONS: *Leon.* 2 (1884). On the unreliability of the Latin Aristotelian text presented in this edition see Mansion (3, 68). *Taurin.* 1954 (*Leon. Manualis*).

Engl. transl. of Bk. 1, R. A. Kocourek, St. Paul Minn. 1947.

31. In libros De caelo et mundo expositio. According to Tolomeo (Mandonnet 1, 60) the composition of this work fell in the time of Gregory X (1271/6). The year 1271 as the earliest date is also confirmed by the fact that this commentary not only is based on the Moerbekan translation but also uses Simplicius' commentary, whose translation by the Flemish Dominican is dated June 15, 1271. Mansion (6, 277) observed that in this exposition (cf. 1, 3, 7; 1, 10, 1; 2, 11, 6 and elsewhere) Aquinas seems to be more familiar with Simplicius than in *Exp. in Metaph.* 12, 7: 2567. Moreover, the commentary of Simplicius appears to have been unknown in Paris even as late as 1274 (Pelster 2, 387). All this strongly suggests that our work was composed in Naples 1272/3. It represents the high water-mark of St. Thomas's expository skill. Whether it is an unfinished work, as is commonly asserted, seems doubtful. The beginning of Aquinas's exposition of *De generatione et corruptione* gives us to understand that he knew no more Aristotelian text of *De caelo* than which he explained.

EDITIONS: *Leon.* 3 (1886); *Taurin.* 1952 (*Leon. Manual.*)

32. In libros De generatione et corruptione expositio. This unfinished exposition comprises not quite 5 chs. of Bk. 1 of the Aristotelian text (up to 321b 34.) Its textual basis is an anonymous older version revised perhaps by Moerbeka (Arist. Lat. 55, 788; Minio-Paluello 1, 259.) This fragment was composed in Naples, 1272/3, where Tocco, in the Canonization Proceedings 345, attests having seen the Master writing on it. The witness believed it was "his last work in philosophy." The evidence of 7, 2 (*Met. Lambda*-XII) confirms this chronology. The work was composed after the exposition of the Physics as well as that of *De caelo;* cf. 7, 1: . . . *manifestavimus in VIII Phys. et in I De caelo.*

EDITIONS: *Leon.* 3 (1886); *Taurin.* 1952 (*Leon. Manual.*)

33. In libros Meteorologicorum expositio. This is again a fragment, whose authentic length was fixed by the *Leon.* at 2, 10, i.e., in Aristotle's text, 2, 5: 363a 20. Metaphysics *Lambda* is not quoted nor is there any explicit reference to Greek or other sources. The version used is the Moerbekana, which probably was done in 1260 and certainly was known by the Latins in 1267 (Roger Bacon: Aristoteles Lat. 57; ibid. 788). Thus the chronology of St. Thomas's work may only be conjectured. Mandonnet (4, xiii) proposed 1269/71; Grabmann (1, 278) 1269/72; Pelster (2, 391) 1272/3.

EDITIONS: *Leon.* 3 (1886); *Taurin.* 1952 (*Leon. Manual.*)

Engl. trans. of I, 8-10 by Thorndike (1, 77).

34. In libros De anima expositio. Bartholomew of Capua and the related Catalogues (Mandonnet 1, 31) state that Book 1 is a lecture course transcribed by Reginald of Piperno, while Bks. 2 and 3 are directly composed by Aquinas. From the beginning to the end, the textual basis seems to be a translation of Moerbeka, whose chronology is however unknown (Pelster 2, 396). Metaphysics *Lambda* is always XI (Gauthier 2, 86). Throughout the work Themistius' commentary on *De anima* is used in its Greek-Latin translation (Verbeke 320). This translation was terminated by Moerbeka in Viterbo, Nov. 22, 1267 (Millas Vallicrosa 1, 54). The end of 1267 may thus securely be set as the *terminus post quem* of the whole work. In 3, 7, 695, the author most probably refers to his own writing *De unitate intellectus* which is from 1270 (no. 47). If then it may reasonably be held that Bks. 2 and 3 were composed after *De unitate intellectus* and before the *Summa,* II-II (no. 3), therefore in 1270/1, it is not easy to determine the exact date of Book 1, i.e., of the *Lectura.* Mansion (6, 282) held for a Parisian origin of the entire work; but the question how it was feasible for a Master of Theology in Paris to lecture on Aristotle is neither stated nor answered. Verbeke (1, 334) suggests that the lectures were given in Italy, fall 1268, and that our actual text of Bk. 1 is the exact reproduction of these lectures.

EDITIONS: *Parm.* 20, 1-144; *Vivès* 24, 1-195; *Taurin.* 1949.

Engl. trans. K. Foster, London 1951 (basic Latin text revised by D. Callus).

35-36. In librum De sensu et sensato expositio. In librum De memoria et reminiscentia expositio. These two expositions are worked out on the basis of a translation made by Moerbeka (Pelster 2, 396). In the former, the author is familiar with the Moerbekan translation (Arist. Lat. 97) of Alexander of Aphrodisias' commentary (Mansion 2, 96). No direct evidence for dating either one of these small works is available. They are usually held to have been composed close to the *Exp. in De anima,* on account of their place in the Aristotelian Corpus.

EDITIONS: *Parm.* 20, 145-214; *Vivès* 24, 197-292; *Taurin.* 1949.

37. In duodecim libros Metaphysicorum expositio. The text of this exposition, as we know it to-day, does not seem to have been composed straight through, according to the succession of the Aristotelian books. In the important Ms Naples, *Bibl. Naz.* VIII, F. 16 (Käppeli 3, 116; Duin 511) two parts, viz., Books 2/3 and Books 5, lect. 7, to 7, lect. 16, are the very text dictated by Aquinas to two different secretaries. In the former part Metaph. *Lambda* is constantly referred to as XII, while in the latter we find XI in Book 6, lect. 2 (ed. Taurin. 1188), and XII in Book 7, lect. 1 (ibid. 1269). It thus looks as though the actual text of Books 2 and 3 was posterior to Book 5, lect. 7-Book 7, lect. 16. On the strength of the same *Lambda* test Books 1 and 4 would also belong to a time when *Lambda* still was XI. After Book 7, lect. 17, up to the end of Book 12, *Lambda* is always designated as XII, but there are certain indications suggesting that nevertheless the composition of Book 11 is posterior to that of Book 12. The Latin version used by Aquinas is not always the same. Only beginning with Book 5, lect. 20-22, is the Moerbekana definitely preferred. Yet in Books 2 and 3, supposedly of later origin than the above indicated part of Books 5 to 7, an older translation is preponderantly used. It is as yet too early to interpret all these facts correctly and, especially, to translate them into chronological terms. A piecemeal setting up of the final text may reasonably be assumed, and it seems clear that this unusual way of composition was necessitated by the Latin history of Book *Kappa* (*supra*, no. 3). An at least partial revision of an already existing text seems probable, all the more so since, at least in one spot, such a revision can be demonstrated by the Neapolitan Ms. But, apparently, the author neglected to extend this revision to each and every detail. Certain parts of the exposition, especially those which in the Neapolitan Ms appear to be written under the author's dictation, may have been composed in Paris, between 1270 and possibly 1272, i.e., largely counting, during the years within which Book *Kappa* arrived. It is possible that St. Thomas began working on the whole commentary before 1270 (lectures given already in Rome?, of Tolomeo, Mandonnet 1, 60), just as it is possible that the completion of the work should be advanced into 1272, when the Master was already in Naples. At any rate, this exposition of the Metaphysics is prior to that of the *De caelo et mundo* (no. 31). See especially A. Dondaine (1, 199); Käppeli (3, 116); Pelster (1, 325 and 2, 377); Mansion (6, 283); Duin (1, 511).

EDITIONS: Only the Vulgate text is available in *Parm.* 20, 245-654; *Vivès* 24, 333-649; 25, 1-229; *Taurin.* 1950.

38. In decem libros Ethicorum expositio. The textual basis here is the version of Grosseteste as revised by William of Moerbeka (Franceschini 150, Mansion 5, 401, A. Dondaine 4, 90). There are two quotations of Metaph. *Lambda,* separated by only a few pages. According to Ms evidence, the first (1, 1, 1) refers to XI, the second (1, 6, 79) to XII. Hence the composition of this work seems to coincide with the moment when the complete *Moerbekana* of the Metaphysics became known to the author. Other circumstantial evidence taken from a comparison of texts, also strongly suggests that the composition of this work was synchronous with that of *Summa.* II-II (1271/2). See Gauthier (2, 66). Note the existence of a transcript, written by young Aquinas, of *lectures* on the Ethics given by Albert the Great (Pelzer).

EDITIONS: Vulgate text in *Parm.* 20, 1-363; *Vivès* 25, 231-614; 26, 1-88; *Taurin.* 1949 (on the unreliability of this text see Keeler 2, 413; Gauthier, 137).

Engl. trans. of Bks. 8, 9: P. Conway, Providence 1951.

39. In libros Politicorum expositio.   The authentic work, according to Ms evidence, terminates at 3, 6 (1280a 6). The text of our current editions, barring slight differences, goes back to the edition Rome 1492, set up by *Ludovicus de Valentia.* The original of Aquinas was here systematically and ruthlessly altered so as to conform with the tastes and standards of a humanist (O'Rahilly 2, 618; C. Martin 1, 35). The Vulgate editions therefore, including the latest *Taurin.* 1951, are scientifically worthless; a serious student must needs have recourse to Mss (*Vat. lat.* 777; Paris, *Nat. lat.* 6457; Cambridge, Peterhouse 82, etc.) St. Thomas explains the version of Moerbeka with which he got acquainted around 1260 (nos. 17, 24). But in all his works up to *Summa,* I-II, 90 ff., his knowledge of the Politics appears to result from a rather perfunctory reading. A proper study of this book seems to have been part of that special preparation to which Aquinas devoted himself in view of the elaboration of certain questions of the *Summa,* I-II and II-II. It is probable, therefore, that the composition of this commentary was connected with these studies. More precise chronological determinations are mere conjectures. The Latin version of Moerbeka is edited by Susemihl, Leipzig 1872.

OTHER EXPOSITIONS

40. Expositio super librum Boethii De Trinitate.   This work is not an exposition in the usual sense of a commentary in which the letter of an "authentic" text is the all-important factor; rather, in its main part, it is a discussion, in due scholastic form, of questions arising out of the basic text. This text is the first of the *Theological Tractates* of Boethius, called *De Trinitate,* a text which in the Middle Ages enjoyed an almost sacred authority and was often made the subject of commentaries and explanations. Aquinas however is, among the great scholastics of the thirteenth century, the only author to have written on this *Tractate*. His work is unfinished; it comprises but a small initial part of Boethius' work. With a fulness and precision unknown in any of his other writings he develops in these discussions some truly fundamental questions: the problem of the nature and division of sciences and of the proper scientific methods in philosophy and theology. With regard to these problems the *Expos. super De Trin.* is St. Thomas's principal text.—The Ms Vat. *lat. 9850* has preserved, in the author's own hand, a section of the work beginning with q. 3, a. 2 (*vers. fin.*) and extending to the end.—The chronological problem was definitively solved, when Chenu (4, 81) discovered that Annibaldo de Annibaldeschi (no. 23) had used this work in his commentary on the Sentences, which was written in 1260/1. Thus a secure approximate dating is possible; Aquinas composed these Questions before 1260/1. The probable *terminus a quo* may be indicated, through doctrinal comparison, with the help of *Script. in Sent.* I (no. 1); the present exposition seems to be posterior to this part of the *Scripta*. On the (improbable) supposition that it is a reproduction of questions disputed in school, see Synave (5, 327).

EDITION: a critical and definitive text has been established by B. Decker, Leiden 1955.

Engl. trans. R. E. Brennan, St. Louis 1946; V. White, *On Searching into God* (Q. 2), Oxford 1947; A. Maurer (Qq. 5-6), Toronto 1953. Engl. trans. of Boethius' Tractate, Stewart-Rand, Boethius, *The Theological Tractates*, London (New York) 1926.

41. Expositio in librum Boethii De hebdomadibus. In this work the basic text is the third of Boethius' Tractates whose correct title reads as follows: *Quomodo substantiae in eo quod sint bona sint, cum non sint substantialia bona.* St. Thomas's work is an exposition in the proper sense of the word. Is is of no slight importance for the knowledge of Thomistic metaphysics and is indeed the starting-point for any study of the Thomistic notion of *participation* and the distinction between "quod est" and "esse." Its date is usually given as identical with that of no. 40. Other and stronger chronological criteria have not been found.

EDITIONS: *Parm.* 17, 359; *Vivès* 28, 468; *Mand.* 1, 165; *Taurin. Theol.* 2, 391.

42. Expositio in Dionysium De divinis nominibus. The Platonic influence in Thomistic doctrine has become a matter of renewed interest in recent years. This exposition is Aquinas's first attempt at a direct exposition of a completely Platonizing work, with a critical assessment of its value, elaborated according to the mediaeval methods of dealing with an "authority" (Chenu 5, 117, 192). The *Piana* editors (1570/1) printed the work as an appendix to *Summa* I (vol. 10), thereby giving to understand that the expositio and the *Prima Pars* are in many respects explanatory one of the other. The chronology is unknown except for the *terminus ante quem* which doubtless is 1268, since the work of Proclus (see no. 43) was translated in that year, yet is unknown to the author of this exposition. Note that some scholars credit Aquinas with a transcription, written in his own hand, of St. Albert's lectures on the Dionysian works (Naples, *Bibl. Naz.*). The Thomistic authenticity of this handwriting is however disputable (see Grabmann 1, 439).

EDITIONS: *Parm.* 15, 258; *Vivès* 29, 373; *Mand.* 2, 320; *Taurin.* 1950.

43. Super librum De causis expositio. This exposition was written after 1270. It is, together with *De substantiis separatis* (no. 54), the last of St. Thomas's dialogues with Platonism conducted in the form of a "reverent" explanation of an authoritative Platonizing text. The thirteenth century schools, and perhaps Aquinas himself in his earlier years, held the *Liber De causis* to be an Aristotelian writing (cf. *In Boeth. De Trin.* 6, 1). In the Faculty of Arts it was read after, and in connection with, the Metaphysics (*Chart. U. P.* 1, 278). When, in 1268, Moerbeka translated the Στοιχείωσις Θεολογική of Proclus, St. Thomas was able to discover its true origin and its nature, viz., that it was a compendium of this neoplatonic treatise of Proclus. With this discovery based, as it was, on literary criticism, the age of humanism begins to dawn upon European civilization (Saffrey xxiv). An approximate date of Aquinas's exposition is easily found. The *termius post quem* certainly is 1268 or, better still, certainly 1270, since Metaphysics *Lambda* (no. 3) is quoted as XII. It may even be set, though with less certainty, at Christmas 1271. Such a chronology would result from a doctrinal comparison with *Quodl.* 5, 7 (no. 9; cf. Saffrey xxxv). A more definite chronology (the first months of 1272, Saffrey xxxiv) seems to venture into the realm of conjectures.

EDITION: Saffrey, Fribourg 1954 (critical text with remarkable introduction).

POLEMICAL WRITINGS

44. Contra impugnantes Dei cultum et religionem. In Mss and in the old Catalogues this work is recognized to be a refutation of William of St.-Amour. William was a secular Master in Paris who, in a bitter harangue (*De periculis novissimorum temporum*), took issue with the Mendicant Friars's right to teach and enlarged his criticism into a diatribe against the religious status as such. St. Thomas's reply comprises, in its apologetic scope, all the elements of the situation of the Friars as it had developed in Paris during the years 1254-6; in chs. 2 and 3 their activity in the University is especially envisaged. This work may not be read fruitfully unless it be referred to the almost incredible history of those years in the University and City of Paris; see Glorieux (1, 75); Rashdall (1, 344). Its date is 1256 (around October), a date (Glorieux 1, 74) which seems preferable to the year 1257 indicated in Ms Rome, *Casanat.* 1533-C. IV. 20 (Käppeli 1, 376). William of St.-Amour was condemned in Rome, Oct. 5, 1256. If the treatise had been composed even at the beginning of 1257, the author would hardly have failed to mention this condemnation.

EDITIONS: Vulgate text in *Parm.* 15, 1-75; *Vivès* 29, 1-116; *Mand.* 4; *Taurin. Theol.* 2.

Engl. trans. Procter, *An Apology for the Religious Orders,* London 1902, Westminster Md. 1950.

45.   De perfectione vitae spiritualis.   After, and in spite of, his condemnation and exile from Paris (no. 44), William of St.-Amour continued his fight. In 1266/7 a voluminous sort of encyclopedia (*Collationes catholicae et canonicae scripturae*) appeared which is nothing but a slightly retouched and considerably enlarged revision of the *De periculis*. When St. Thomas returned to Paris at the beginning of 1269, he found the atmosphere thoroughly poisoned. In the summer of 1269 an anonymous pamphlet was edited with the title: *Contra adversarium perfectionis christianae, maxime praelatorum facultatumque ecclesiasticarum inimicum*. This adversary was the Franciscan Thomas of York and the author of the pamphlet was later revealed to be Gerald of Abbeville, Master of Theology in Paris. Against the *Contra adversarium . . .* St. Bonaventure wrote the *Apologia pauperum contra calumniatorem*. This is the situation and the moment when Aquinas decided again to enter the arena. In its very plan, the *De perfectione vitae spiritualis* proves that the author did his best to take the issue out of the heat of controversy and place it on the level of the serene and systematic theological treatise. Yet in the last chapters (21-26) controversy returns. This change of style finds its explanation in the fact that in Dec. 1269 Gerald, already knowing chs. 1-20 of St. Thomas's work, took the occasion of his *Quodl.* 14 to attack ch. 20. Promptly the Dominican added his rejoinder. Hence the edition of the complete work *De perfectione . . .* is from the beginning of 1270. This work soon became an official University publication, a fact attesting its actuality as well as its popularity. Not long after St. Thomas's death, it appears on the first Stationer's list known to us (*Chart. U. P.* 1, 646). The point of this controversy, to which its protagonist was to lend his name (*Contra Geraldinos*), is hard for us to understand. In the foreground there are the problems raised by the foundation and the rapid development of the Mendicant Orders. Their specific spirituality entailed not only a specific conception of Christian life and the values of contemplation and action, but also a re-examination of the nature and structure of the Church. Certain pages of these discussions read as though a sort of Gallicanism *ante litteram* was animating those "Geraldines." It should also be noted that their contentions and arguments had long since left the not too tightly closed precincts of the University and gone out on the streets, as may be seen in popular French didactic literature of the time, for instance in the *Roman de la Rose* (Paré 1, 169).—Cf. Glorieux 5, 5; 7, 129; 2, 97.

EDITIONS: Vulgate text in *Parm.* 15, 76-102; *Vivès* 29, 117-156; *Mand.* 4; *Taurin. Theol.* 2, 111.

46. Contra pestiferam doctrinam retrahentium pueros a religionis ingressu. "Tormented by their quarrelsome temper" (no. 45, ch. 21), the Geraldines (no. 45) relentlessly kept alive the virus of their "pestiferous doctrine." The present work again belongs to the controversy *Contra Geraldinos*. It is probably to be dated at the end of the summer 1270. Its structure and argumentation reflects a number of pamphlets and academic discussions that came to the fore after Aquinas' *De perfectione* . . . (*Quodl.* 14 and a *Qu. disp.* of Gerald of Abbeville; *De perfectione status clericorum* of Nicolas of Lisieux; Glorieux 7, 143). The necessity for Aquinas's intervention may best be inferred from the two sermons he preached at the same time (no. 89).

EDITIONS: Vulgate text in *Parm.* 15, 103-125; *Vivès* 29, 157-190; *Mand.* 4; *Taurin. Theol.* 2, 159.

Engl. trans. Procter (see no. 44).

47. De unitate intellectus, contra Averroistas. This treatise, of a rare philosophical compactness and vigour, was written against the Parisian Averroists and especially against Siger of Brabant, as is affirmed in two Mss of the beginning 14th cent. (Oxford, *Corpus Christi* 225; *Clm* 8001). "From (its) conclusion . . . it seems probable that St. Thomas was answering an Averroistic writing which so far has not been discovered" (Gilson 396). Its chronology is revealed in the Oxford Ms, viz. 1270 (O'Rahilly 1, 482). The work was most probably written before (but not long before) the condemnation, on Dec. 10, 1270, of a number of Averroistic doctrines (van Steenberghen 547).

EDITION: Keeler, Rome 1936 (this edition, based on 20 Mss, which strictly speaking is not perhaps a critical edition, is however thoroughly reliable); re-print, without the apparatus, in *Taurin. Phil.* 63.

Engl. trans. R. E. Brennan, see no. 40 (the textual basis is the *Parm!*).

48. De aeternitate mundi, contra murmurantes. These "murmurers" are some overorthodox, overzealous theologians muttering complaints about their colleague, who, on the basis of Aristotelian doctrine, holds that an eternally created world is not inconceivable. Aquinas discusses the arguments of these integralists objectively and serenely but cannot refrain from making what is the most biting criticism found in all his works: they speak as though they alone were rational beings and wisdom had originated in their own brains. This treatise is part of a collection of writings of current interest which Godefroy of Fontaines gathered during the years 1270/2 (Glorieux 3, 37). The chronology may, with sufficient probability, be determined accordingly. Glorieux (3, 38, 46) conjectured: the beginning of 1271. Van Steenberghen raised the interesting question whether this short treatise might not be the integral *Corpus* of *Quodl.* 12, 7.

EDITIONS: *Parm.* 16, 318; *Vivès* 27, 450; *Mand.* 1, 22; *Perrier* 53 (text established mainly with Paris, Nat. *lat.* 14546); *Taurin. Phil.* 105. On an addition to the traditional text see Morin (1, 175) and A. Dondaine (2, 49).

TREATISES ON SPECIAL SUBJECTS

49. De fallaciis ad quosdam nobiles artistas. Tocco writes in his Vita (74): *In tali autem carcere* . . . (i.e., when young Thomas was detained by his family who objected to his Dominican vocation) *tractatum fallaciarum Aristotelis, ut dicitur* (*!*), *compilavit*. This remark is repeated by Calò (1, 23) without the restriction. The Catalogue of Bartholomew of Capua (Mandonnet 1, 29) ignores the work but several other Catalogues list it, sometimes adding a dedication: *quibusdam nobilibus* (Tolomeo: Mandonnet 1, 63) or *ad quosdam nobiles artistas* (Guidonis: Mandonnet 1, 70). No identification of these Noblemen, members of the Faculty of Arts, is possible. The authenticity of the treatise was first denied by Mandonnet (1, 108), on the basis of his thesis of the "Official Catalogue" (no. 90), but was later (7, 406; 9, xl) admitted as "very probable." Mandonnet's dating is 1244/5 (7, 405).

EDITIONS: *Parm.* 16, 377; *Vivès* 27, 533; *Mand.* 4, 508; *Perrier* 428; *Taurin. Phil.* 225.

50. De propositionibus modalibus. With regard to this logical treatise Mandonnet again (no. 49) revised a former unfavourable judgment (loc. cit.) Bochenski, its recent editor, holds St. Thomas's authorship to be beyond any doubt (1, 686). The harsh words which this author uses (1, 686) in judging the quality of the work, are restrained considerably in 2, 196. In the face of a passage which it is difficult to harmonize with Aquinas's otherwise known doctrine, the author's more considerate opinion is that the treatise was written by young Thomas earlier than 1252 and that Aquinas possibly followed closely an unknown handbook of Logic (2, 196). Mandonnet, ingeniously combining the various data of our bibliographical documents, proposed for this treatise the same date as for no. 49.

EDITION: Bochenski 1940 (see Bochenski 2; text established with 4 Mss).

51. De ente et essentia. One of the most admired and popular works of Aquinas which the *Piana* (1570/1) printed as an appendix to the *Exp. in Metaphysicam*. The bibliographic documents give its title variously: *De ente et essentia, ad fratres (et) socios; De quidditate et esse; De quidditate entium, etc.* The address *Ad fratres socios* surely refers to the author's Dominican confrères, possibly his fellow-students. To Tolomeo of Lucca we owe the indication that this work was written before the author was made a Master of Theology (Mandonnet 1, 59). The latest date is therefore March 1256. Every attempt to determine its chronology more closely, e.g., to fix its earliest date at 1252, seems bound to be a conjecture.

EDITIONS: Roland-Gosselin (Le Saulchoir 1926, Paris 1948) established a text from 8 Parisian Mss. L. Baur (Münster 1926, 1933) chose a more cautious editorial principle by reprinting the Vulgate and presenting, in notes, the variants of 11 Italian and German Mss and, partly also, of the Parisian tradition. Boyer (Rome 1933) corrected the Piana with the variants of both former editions when they coincided. *Taurin. Phil.* (1954) reprinted the edition of Boyer. Perrier (1949) insisted again on the Parisian tradition, especially on *Bibl. nat. lat.* 14546.

Engl. trans. C. C. Reidl, Toronto 1934 (textual foundation not specified; G. G. Leckie, New York, London 1937 (ed. Roland-Gosselin unduly qualified as "critical"); A. Maurer, Toronto 1949 (ed. Baur).

52. De principiis naturae ad fratrem Sylvestrum. Treatise on the principles of natural things, i.e., matter and form, and the principles of their generation, i.e., the four causes. The addressee is unknown. Tolomeo of Lucca mentions this treatise in the same chronological context as no. 51.

EDITION: Pauson, Fribourg 1950 (good provisional text, established with an exacting critical method).

Engl. trans. Henle-Bourke, St. Louis 1947; Kocourek, St. Paul 1948.

53. Compendium theologiae ad fratrem Reginaldum socium suum carissimum. Although often, and already in the age of the Mss, held to be *quaedam brevis Summa,* or *brevis compilatio totius theologiae* (Grabmann 1, 191, 205), this work is in truth a treatise on faith, hope and charity and stresses the spiritual values of these theological virtues rather than their scholastic elaboration. It was written by Aquinas for his friend and secretary, Reginald of Piperno, and is unfinished, breaking off shortly after

the beginning of the treatise On Hope. In 1310 Jean de Pouilly, Master of
Theology in Paris, stated that Aquinas wrote this work "towards the end
of his days" (Grabmann 1, 315). The same dating is suggested in the colophon of the traditional text, which corresponds to a note in Cod. A 209
(end of 13th cent.) of the *Bibl. commun. dell' Archiginnasio* of Bologna:
*huc usque fecit fr. thomas de aquino, sed proh dolor morte preventus sic
incompletum reliquit* (Grabmann 1, 315). Modern critics are sometimes
of a different opinion. Lottin, on the basis of a doctrinal comparison between *Quaest. disp. De malo* 4, 1 and *Comp.* 202 suggests the work to be
prior to the *Quaestio* as well as to the Summa I-II, 81 (2, 310; see however Eschmann 1, 29). Chenu (5, 283) insists on the doctrinal affinity of
the *Compendium* with the *Contra Gentiles* and also prefers an earlier date.

EDITIONS: *Parm.* 16, 1; *Vivès* 27, 1; *Mand.* 2, 1; *Taurin. Theol.* 1, 13.
Engl. trans. L. Lynch, New York 1947; C. Vollert, St. Louis 1947.

**54. De substantiis separatis, seu de angelorum natura, ad fr. Reginal-
dum, socium suum carissimum.**   One of the most important metaphysical writings of Aquinas, whose critical edition is a major desideratum in
Thomistic studies. It belongs to the small group of works in which St.
Thomas directly confronted the powerful stream of mediaeval Platonizing
doctrines. Its chronology is as yet uncertain and an absolute date is, it
seems, impossible to obtain. The fact that it remained unfinished seems to
have prompted Mandonnet (9, lii) to place it in the Neapolitan years
1272/3. Since however this criterion is to be used with caution, Grabmann (1, 324) preferred to take his clue from the two quotations of
Proclus's *Elements of Theology* found in §§ 111, 114 (ed. Perrier); these
surely indicate a *terminus a quo*, viz., May 18, 1268, which is the date of
Moerbeka's translation. Vansteenkiste (1, 29) took issue with this chronology but failed to establish a convincing case. Saffrey (1, xxxiv) pointed
to the close affinity between the treatise and the *Exp. in Libr. De causis.*
This consideration which seems to be well founded would furnish a new
terminus a quo, viz., the year 1270 (no. 43). Further research may be
directed toward such chronologically important indications as the *alia
littera* (§ 75) and the many literal quotations from the Metaphysics. Once
the textual basis of the *Expos. in Metaph.* (no. 37) is fully known, light
will be thrown upon the present chronological problem. *Metaph. Lambda*
is quoted throughout as XII. Yet, since this work is unfinished and therefore not edited by Aquinas himself, its posthumous editor may perhaps be
supposed to have interfered with details of this kind.

EDITIONS: *Perrier* 123 (text based on Paris, Nat. lat. 14546). Vulgate
text in *Parm.* 16, 183; *Vivès*, 27, 273; *Mand.* 1, 70; *Taurin. Phil.* 21.

55. De regno (De regimine principum), ad regem Cypri.   Three
texts, different at least in length, are transmitted in the Mss tradition:

(*A*) a text consisting of a dedication and 18½ chapters (according to the Vulgate counting). This text ends variously, either . . . *ut animi hominum recreentur*, or with an addition to the word *recreentur* which is either *quia*, or *quia vero*, or *quia vero etcetera*. A second text (*B*) consists of the same dedication and 17½ chapters; its *Explicit* is: *corpora aestate infirma redduntur* (*reducuntur*). The Mss of this text constitute a definite family which is found with surprising regularity in Mss originating in the area of the ancient German Empire (Basel, *Univ.* B VII, 9; Cracow, *Jagell.* 2321; *Vat. lat.* 773; *Vat. Barb. lat.* 499; Madrid *Bibl. reál* 19; Vienna, Dominic. 24/26-26526, and others to which the *Incun.* Utrecht, ca. 1475, may be added). The third text (*C*) consists again of the dedication followed by 81 chs. The whole work is here divided into 4 Bks. In its first portion the text of this tradition is identical with (*A*) and (*B*).—The older and doubtlessly more authoritative *Opuscula* collections always contain the texts (*A*) or (*B*), never (*C*), which in Mss of the thirteenth and early fourteenth cent. is found exclusively in separate editions, e.g., in the outstanding *Vat. lat.* 810. (*C*) was first introduced into these collections at a later date, especially in the age of the Incunabula, whence it passed over into the printed editions, there to stay up to our own day. The title most often used in the Mss of (*A*) and (*B*) is *De regno ad regem Cypri*, or *De rege et regno ad* . . . , while the tradition of (*C*) manifestly prefers *De regimine principum*. A combination however and even a confusion of these two titles is noticeable at an early date; the famous *Vat. lat.* 807 solves this problem of titles in Solomonic fashion by presenting the two titles side by side.—The problem of these various traditions obviously is their relation one to another. The difference between (*A*) and (*B*) was ingeniously explained by O'Rahilly (4, 406): "The words which (in *A*) follow the word *redduntur* are these: *Quia vero ad corporum sanitatem ciborum usus requiritur* . . . Now, after *recreentur* certain Mss (of the tradition *A*) add *quia vero*, i.e., the first words of the section which follows *redduntur*. This is, fortunately, made quite clear by Ms Brussels, *Bibl. Royale* 1573 (15th cent.) in which the scribe after *recreentur* wrote the words: *quia vero etcetera ut supra de ciborum salubritate et cetera*, and then crossed them out. It seems clear then that in the original from which some of these Mss were copied there was, immediately following *recreentur*, a section beginning *quia vero ad corporum sanitatem ciborum usus requiritur* . . . down to *recreentur*, thus duplicating the passage. This extra bit, having become detached from another copy, and thus leaving it to end at *redduntur*, got tacked on to the end of an already complete copy, thus providing a duplication of the passage which began *Quia vero* . . ."—However this be, the crux of the whole matter is the relation between (*A*) (*B*) on the one, and (*C*) on the other hand. A solution of this problem was first suggested by Echard (1, 336) and the discussion is still to-day at essentially the same point where it was left by this great

eighteenth century bibliographer. He knew of the existence of the tradition
(*A*). Second-hand information also made him acquainted with the Ms of an
Italian translation of (*C*), which in the margin opposite the word *recrei*
(*recreentur*) marks the end of St. Thomas's work and in its colophon
reveals the name of Tolomeo of Lucca as the author of the "complement"
of this writing. Echard's Italian Ms was identified by Uccelli as the 15th
cent. Ms *Chigi* M VIII 158: its Latin source was discovered by O'Rahilly
(4, 408) in Padua, *Bibl. Cathedr., Coll.* X 2 A (14th cent.)—Echard's
solution, to be sure, is very probable indeed and widely accepted to-day,
but it stands in need of a further, more direct, proof which may be expected to come forth from a closer research into the whole tradition of
these texts. It is worth noting however that even should scholars succeed
in definitively proving the independent origin of (*A*) (*B*), its priority
with regard to (*C*) and the latter's true nature as a "continuation" of
(*A*), this would not eliminate all the difficulties of the work. The intrinsic
difficulties of the text itself of (*A*) (*B*) are, it seems, more serious than
is generally admitted. They have not infrequently been misrepresented,
e.g., by Flori, but were competently described by Browne (1,300); see
also Eschmann (2, xv). The treatise is, very manifestly, a composite of
several fragments woven together by a clumsy hand which it is difficult
to recognize as that of the great intellectual architect who was Thomas
Aquinas. It would seem that in view of a solution of this problem the
technique of the posthumous editions of Aquinas's works should be studied
more attentively. The text (*A*) (*B*) is to be pronounced authentic without any doubt. But in Thomistic bibliography authenticity is not a univocal notion. In the case of a posthumous edition an interference with the
text or the fragments which the editor found in Aquinas's literary *corpus*
is not to be rejected from the start. We have on several occasions pointed
to the possibility of such interferences and to the curious rules which
seem to have guided the one or the other of these editors (nos. 5-16, 26-
27, 67-68, 73, 98).—The chronology (of whatever St. Thomas did write
to the King of Cyprus) may be conjectured by identifying this king. He
was probably Hugh II of Lusignan, the only Cypriote King of the
Lusignan dynasty to be buried in St. Dominic's of Nicosia, the main
convent of the Preachers' Province of the Holy Land. This fact seems
to denote an especially close friendship between the Dominicans and the
Lusignan dynasty at the time of Hugh II. It throws perhaps light on the
initial words of the treatise: "As I was turning over in my mind what I
might offer to Your Majesty as a gift . . ." The composition of these
notes *De Regno* might have been interrupted by the death of Hugh II
in Dec. 1267. On account of the many quotations from the Aristotelian
Politics, their earliest date may be fixed accordingly (nos. 17, 24, 39).—
Note that Schmeidler (1, xi) suggests Thomas and Tolomeo to have met
not only in 1272/4 but also in 1261/2 and 1265/7. The "continuation"

is dated by the same author (1, xxxi) after May 1301, before September 1303, when Tolomeo was in Florence and Lucca.

EDITIONS: *Perrier* 221 (text (*B*); to be used with caution; see Eschmann 3, 450; Rossi 2, 182); Vulgate text (i.e., *C*) in *Parm.* 16, 225; *Vivès* 27, 336; *Mand.* 1, 312; *Taurin. Phil.* 257.

Engl. trans. (of *A*) Phelan-Eschmann, Toronto 1949.

EXPERT OPINIONS

56. Contra errores Graecorum, ad Urbanum IV Pontificem Maximum. Urban IV asked St. Thomas's expert opinion on the *Liber de processione Spiritus Sancti et fide Trinitatis contra errores Graecorum.* The author of this *"Libellus"* is to be identified as Nicolas of Durazzo, Bishop of Cotrone (South Italy), a Greek and an intermediary between Rome and Constantinople (see A. Dondaine 8). His intention, with the *Liber de processione* . . . , was to show to the Greeks that their own Fathers always taught the main points of Latin orthodoxy. For the most part, the Greek authorities quoted by Nicolas and reproduced by St. Thomas, are falsifications. St. Thomas in this work does not question their authenticity, although he gives us to understand that he feels ill at ease with some words and expressions. Texts taken from the *Libellus* are quoted also in the *Glossa continua in Matth.* (no. 23) and the *Q. D. De potentia* (no. 4). However they are no longer found in the *Summa* or in any of the later works. This fact may be interpreted as indicative of a doubt, conceived by Aquinas at some later time, concerning the nature of Nicolas's documentation (Glorieux 13, 503). The work was written very probably in the summer of 1263, a date established by Glorieux (13, 498), in function of the negotiations between Rome and Constantinople under Urban IV. The chronological relations between the *Contra errores* and the 4th Bk. of *C. Gentiles* are controverted; see H. Dondaine (1, 156) and Glorieux (13, 504).

EDITIONS: *Parm.* 15, 239; *Vivès* 29, 344; *Mand.* 3, 279; *Taurin. Theol.* 1, 315 (*Libellus de processione* . . . *ibid.* 347).

57. Responsio ad fr. Joannem Vercellensem, Generalem Magistrum Ordinis Praedicatorum, de articulis CVIII ex opere Petri de Tarentasia. This work is not mentioned in any of the old Catalogues; it is known to us in only three Mss (Paris, *Nat. lat.* 14546; Bordeaux 131; Innsbruck. *Univ.* 197). It was believed spurious by the older editors and bibliographers and restored to its true dignity only by Mandonnet (1, 123). A more definite proof for its authenticity was furnished by R.

Martin (1, 303). In the Mss of Paris and Bordeaux (13th-14th cent.) the title is: *Explanatio* (*declaratio*) *dubiorum de dictis cuiusdam edita a fratre* (*sancto*) *Thoma*. In the fifteenth century Ms of Innsbruck this veil of anonymity is lifted and the man whose dicta were "explained" bears a name. He is Peter of Tarentasia, one time Master of Theology in Paris (1259-1264 (?), and again 1267/9); later Archbishop of Lyons, 1272, Cardinal of Ostia, 1273, and Pope Innocent V, 1276. The printed editions of the sixteenth century transmitted another information; St. Thomas's work is a memorandum addressed to John of Vercelli, Master General of the Dominicans (1264-1283). Thus the *Responsio,* in itself of a rather mysterious appearance, takes on a definite physiognomy: it is Aquinas's expert judgment, presented to the Master General, on 108 suspected propositions taken from Peter's commentary on the Sentences. All these propositions have been identified in Books 1-2, 3 of Peter's commentary (Smeralda 1, 19). Peter's denouncer who, as Thomas himself shows, not infrequently turned into his detractor, is unknown. Mandonnet dates the letter "after 1264" (beginning of John of Vercelli's generalate); A. Dondaine (3, 259) specified the *terminus ad quem* which a comparison with the *Q. D. De attributis divinis* (nos. 1, 4) would show to be 1266.

EDITIONS: *Parm.* 16, 152; *Vivès* 27, 213; *Mand.* 3, 211; *Taurin. Theol.* 1, 223. Text corrections proposed by R. Martin (1, 319) should be taken into account.

58. Responsio ad fr. Joannem Vercellensem, Generalem Magistrum Ordinis Praedicatorum, de articulis XLII.

These are in truth 43 brief articles representing the expert judgment of Aquinas on as many theological questions submitted to him by John of Vercelli, the Master General. In part, these questions are similar to those raised by Brother Baxianus da Lodi (nos. 67/8). The date of this work is April 2nd, 1271, as results from the text itself and the two Mss of Paris and Bordeaux mentioned in note 57; see Destrez (1, 117). The opinion of the Dominican Robert Kilwardby was also solicited in the same affair (Chenu 1, 191; 5, 283).

EDITIONS: *Parm.* 16, 163; *Vivès* 27, 248; *Mand.* 2, 196; *Taurin. Theol.* 1, 211.

59. De forma absolutionis, ad Generalem Magistrum Ordinis.

St. Thomas's expert opinion on a book or treatise presented to him by the Master General. An unknown author, possibly a Dominican, attempted in this *Libellus* to prove that a certain theory on sacramental absolution, widely held in those times, was right: absolution should be given not by an indicative but a deprecatory formula. St. Thomas vigourously stands for the indicative: *Ego te absolvo,* thereby exercising a decisive influence on later theory and practice. This work was written "on the feast of St. Peter's Chair," i.e., either Jan. 18th, or Febr. 22nd of either one of the years 1269 to 1272 (Castagnoli 2, 414). Mandonnet: 1269 (15, 18).

EDITION: Castagnoli, Piacenza 1933; also *Div. Thom. Pl.* 1933/4 (text based on 31 Mss with rich critical apparatus). Re-print of this edition without apparatus in *Taurin. Theol.* 1, 173.

60. De secreto. In the Dominican Chapter General of Paris, 1269, the following case presented itself. A certain *fr. Ioannes Iuristae de Colonia s. Faustini* (near Viterbo) had written a commentary on the Sentences which circulated under the name of *Ioannina de Colonia*. This title gave rise to the misunderstanding that the work was written by one *fr. Ioannes de Colonia*, thus a "Theutonic" Dominican who existed and had even been a fellow-student of the Italian. He seems to have had little use for the inviolability of a copyright. The case was complicated by the fact that only through indiscretion, through breaking the seal of confession and of a confidential communication was it possible to make the true authorship notorious before the Chapter. A special Commission of Masters and Lectors, among them Thomas and Peter of Tarentasia, was instituted to deliberate about whether the Chapter had authority to take action against the thief. In qu. 5 it appears that St. Thomas responded in the affirmative but was contradicted and overruled. No action was taken and the *Ioannina de Colonia* continued to be so called. The *De secreto* is nothing but the minutes of the above-mentioned Commission. The text is already found among the *Opuscula* in the collection of Paris, *Nat. lat.* 14546 (13/14th cent.) It was re-integrated into this collection by certain editions of the seventeenth century. See Mandonnet (1, 139); Planzer (1, 35, 97). Certain traces of these discussions are found in St. Thomas's works, e.g., *Quodl.* 1, 15/6; *Quodl.* 4, 12; *Summa*, II-II, 70, 1, esp. ad 2. (The chronology of *Quodl.* 1 has not been studied in its relation with the *De secreto*).

EDITION: Mandonnet 4, 497 (from Ms Paris l.c.). Re-print in *Taurin. Theol.* 1, 447.

LETTERS

61. To the Archbishop of Palermo: **De articulis fidei et Ecclesiae sacramentis, ad archiepiscopum Panormitanum.** This letter is clearly marked out as such by the initial words: *Postulat a me vestra dilectio* . . . The identity of the addressee is unknown; it cannot, at any rate, be established on the basis of a chronological judgment for which there is no documentary evidence. The use of doctrinal criticism, in order to arrive at a chronological conclusion, was attempted by Sladeczek (1, 413) but to no avail (cf. Grabmann 1, 321). Since Mandonnet affirmed this letter to have been written in 1261/2 (9, lii), if his dating is correct, the Archbishop would be Leonard de Comitibus (Walz 1, 97, n. 58).

EDITIONS: *Parm.* 16, 115; *Vivès* 27, 171; *Mand.* 3, 1; *Taurin. Theol.* 1, 141.

Engl. trans. (2nd Part), J. B. Collins, *Catechetical Instructions of St. Th.*, New York 1953.

62. To Bernard Ayglier, Abbot of Monte Cassino: **Ad Bernardum, abbatem Cassinensem.** The last of Aquinas's letters written shortly before his death (1274), when the Master on his way to the Council of Lyons stopped at Aquino and, unable to go to the monastery (cf. however Tocco 130), answered the Abbot's question by letter. The monks were disturbed by a text of St. Gregory's *Moralia* concerning predestination. The letter's doctrine is genuinely Thomistic. However the writer's repeated protestations of religious obedience to the Benedictine Abbot are somewhat surprising, all the more so, since Aquinas in his letters to the Master General is much less emphatic in this regard. The letter is written on the margin of Gregory's text (Ms Cassin. 82). It was made known for the first time in 1875 by Dom Luigi Tosti. Not a few scholars consider the Cassinese marginal text to be an autograph of Aquinas, an opinion not accepted by Grabmann (1, 441, 377).

EDITIONS: *Vivès* 32, 834; *Mand.* 3, 249 (one sentence and a considerable passage at the end lacking); *Taurin. Theol.* 1, 249 (re-print of *Mand.*, mistakes included).

63. To the Archdeacon of . . . (?): **Expositio super primam decretalem "De fide catholica et sancta Trinitate" et super secundam "Damnamus autem."** It is difficult to decide whether this is a letter or a work dedicated to the archdeacon. The characteristic salutations at the beginning and the end might have been cut away, as was sometimes done (nos. 67/8). Aquinas explains canons 1 and 2 of the 12th Oecumenical Council (*Lateran.* IV, 1215) which have been integrated into the Decretals of Gregory IX (cc. 1, 2, X, 1, 1). This exposition is concerned with showing in detail the heresies condemned by the Council. It is a theological work not to be classified as a contribution of Aquinas to juristic literature; its style and method are not those of a canonist. Often, as in all our current editions, this piece is counted as two works. A glance at the text suffices to disprove this counting, which however is found already in Guidonis (Mandonnet 1, 71). Other documents (Catalogues, Mandonnet 1, 30 ff, and Mss, Grabmann 1, 92, 135) present the work more correctly as one item. The dedication is impossible to determine with certitude; it varies mainly between *ad Archidiaconum Tudertinum* (Todi in Umbria) and . . . *Tridentinum* (Trent). The Italian sojourn, 1259-1268, is usually given as the time of composition, but no proper chronological investigation seems to have been made. The points of comparison with other works of Aquinas are abundant and interesting. Compare, for instance, *Taurin.* 1163 (*error Aristotelis* . . .) with *De articulis fidei* (no. 61), *Taurin.* 601.

EDITIONS: *Parm.* 16, 300; *Vivès* 27, 424; *Mand.* 4, 324; *Taurin. Theol.* I, 417.

64. To the Cantor of Antioch: De rationibus fidei contra Saracenos, Graecos et Armenos, ad Cantorem Antiochiae. A letter explaining "the moral and philosophical reasons" which may be helpful in the defence of the faith against Mohammedans, Greeks and Armenians. St. Thomas refers the addressee to a work, probably the *Contra Gentiles,* "which treats the same subject more abundantly." The relative chronology is thus ascertained. Walz (1, 96) gives the dating 1261-1264, i.e., the dating of the *Contra Gentiles,* and notes that the Cantor of Antioch might have been recommended to address his questions to Aquinas by his own bishop, the Dominican Christian Elias. The identity of the Cantor is unknown.

EDITIONS: *Parm.* 16, 86; *Vivès* 27, 128; *Mand.* 3, 252; *Taurin. Theol.* I, 253. A text corrected on the basis of three Mss (*Ottob. lat.* 198; *Urbin. lat.* 127; *Vat. lat.* 807) is found in Uccelli (1, 487).

Engl. trans. of ch. 5 by Nash, *Why Did God the Son Become Man? Life of the Spirit* 7 (Oxford 1952) 245.

65. To Master Philippus: De motu cordis, ad Magistrum Philippum. No epistolary formalities are preserved in our traditional text. In the Catalogues and Mss the address is sometimes omitted, sometimes variously given, viz., *ad magistrum de Castroceli; ad magistrum Philippum de Castroceli; ad magistrum Iacobum de Castroceli* (see Mandonnet 1, 30 ff., 62 ff., 92; Grabmann 1, 92 ff. 150 ff.) This treatise is part of a collection of writings assembled by Godefroy of Fontaines (Glorieux 3, 37), probably in 1270/2, with a view to discussions of topical interest. In this collection Aquinas's treatise has its place right next to the *De aeternitate mundi* (no. 48); one scribe wrote both these works. Its date may thus, with a respectable degree of probability, be set at 1270/1. See no. 66. Mandonnet (9, xxv) identifies Master Philippus as a physician, professor first in Bologna and later in Naples. No evidence is shown l. c.

EDITIONS: *Perrier* 63 (basic Ms Paris *lat.* 14546). *Parm.* 16, 358; *Vivès* 27, 507; *Mand.* 1, 28; *Taurin. Phil.* 165. On an additional piece of text found in only one Ms, see Morin and Dondaine (2, 50).

66. To Master Philippus: **De mixtione elementorum.** This small work deals with the much debated problem of the structure of physical being. It takes its starting point in a doctrinal difference between Avicenna and Averroes. While St. Thomas argues this point in earlier writings, the present discussion seems to belong to a later period in his career. The text is closely related to *Quodl.* 1, 6 ad 3 (see also *Q. D. De anima* 9, ad 10) of which it almost would seem to be an elaboration. It is therefore perhaps justifiable to see in Master Philippus a member of the Faculty of Arts in Paris to whom Aquinas obligingly explains in more detail one point of this quodlibetal discussion. This view would also imply a chronological criterion. The chronology of the above letter (no. 65) may perhaps also be applied to the present communication since the addressee is the same. In the documents his name is found with almost the same variations as in the other letter.

EDITIONS: *Perrier* 19 (Paris, lat. 14546); *Parm.* 16, 353; *Vivès* 27, 505; *Mand.* 1, 21; *Taurin. Phil.* 155.

67-68. To Brother Baxianus da Lodi: **Responsio ad lectorem Venetum de articulis XXXVI.** Fr. Baxianus O. P. (Käppeli 5, 181) was professor in the school of the Dominican convent in Venice. By letter he submitted a number of questions of scholastic significance to be examined by Aquinas. The Master wrote two communications in this matter, labelled (*A*) and (*B*) by Destrez (1, 103) who discovered the letter (*A*). (*B*) is longer than (*A*). Sometimes contracting two questions of (*A*) into one, sometimes expanding one of these into two, and adding five entirely new questions, (*B*) arrives at the number of 36 instead of the 28 of (*A*). (*B*) is also at times more eloquent and more polished, it arranges the casual sequence of the questions in (*A*) in a logical order. A third document to be taken into account in this connection is a piece entitled: . . . *articuli . . . iterum remissi sibi a quibusdam scolaribus* . . . which is found in two French Mss, viz. Paris *lat.* 14546 and Bordeaux 131. These articles are eight in number; three of them are in both (*A*) and (*B*), and five only in (*B*). The discussions in these letters are in part very similar to those in St. Thomas's letter to John of Vercelli (no. 58).—How these facts might be made to fit into a coherent story is told by Destrez (see also Mandonnet (3, 134). (*A*) and (*B*) are two different letters both written by Aquinas. The letter (*B*) was prompted by a new inquiry coming, this time, from Brother Baxianus's students (*articuli remissi . . . a quibusdam scolaribus!*) Aquinas however decided to send his answer not to these students but to their professor. In so doing he replied not only to the new questions but also profited by the occasion to re-shape his former letter (which however he largely repeated word for word). All this happened in 1271, in close connection with the letter to the Master General. The conjectural elements of this story are obvious. Note

Destrez' remarks (1, 105) about the interference of some early editors with the epistolary formalities of this letter.

EDITION: Destrez 1, 156-161 (Letter *A*); ibid. 162-172 (Letter *B*); re-print in *Taurin. Theol.* 1, 193. The *Articuli iterum remissi* which are extracted from (*B*) are published in *Vivès* 32, 832 (after Uccelli).

69. To Brother Gerald of Besançon: **Responsio ad lectorem Bisuntinum de articulis VI.** Again an obliging gesture of Aquinas answering a request of this Lector of a Dominican convent (see the initial words). Brother Gerald was troubled by some curious problems of a thirteenth century Friar Preacher: whether it may be said in the pulpit that the star of the Magi had the figure of a cross, that the small hands of the Divine Infant created the stars, that seven times every day, in the fashion of a mediaeval devotion, the Holy Virgin remembered Simeon's words: A sword shall pierce . . . etc. Date unknown.

EDITIONS: *Parm.* 16, 175; *Vivès* 27, 264; *Mand.* 3, 246; *Taurin. Theol.* 1, 243.

70. To Brother Johannes of Viterbo: **De emptione et venditione ad tempus.** A letter on credit in which St. Thomas applies canon law and the Aristotelian doctrine on usury to the rapidly developing commercial life of thirteenth century Florence. Its addressee was in Viterbo in 1233, became Procurator General of the Dominican Order in 1265, was made Archbishop of Taranto in 1270 and died in 1273. This letter is doubtlessly authentic; all the concrete data given in it are verifiable and fit perfectly into Aquinas's life and activity. It is however unknown to all our usual bibliographical sources, i.e., the old Catalogues and Mss; it begins to be known around 1400. The text is fully transmitted to us, including the conventional *Vale* at the end. Its date is very probably 1262 (see Mandonnet 1, 116; O'Rahilly 3, 159).

EDITION: O'Rahilly, *loc. cit.* (Mss foundation); re-print *Taurin. Theol.* 1, 185.

Engl. trans. O'Rahilly, *loc. cit.*

71. To Brother Johannes: **De modo studendi.** This short but admirable letter is believed to be authentic because of the rather late testimony of Bl. Venturino of Bergamo, O.P. (d. 1346) who, around 1330, reveals its existence and text. Echard 341 does not seem to be opposed to admitting its authenticity. Grabmann (1, 372), declares that, unwilling to go any further than Echard, he would more readily consent, if the historical proof could be set on firmer ground.

EDITIONS: *Parm.* 17, 338; *Vivès* 28, 467; *Mand.* 4, 535 ("slightly doubtful work"); *Taurin. Theol.* I, 451.

Engl. trans. White, *Blackfriars,* Dec. 1944, Suppl.

72. To the Duchess of Brabant: **De regimine Judaeorum, ad Ducissam Brabantiae.** In this letter St. Thomas answers eight questions about which his advice was requested by the addressee. Seven of these concern the moral aspect of certain measures of financial policy to be adopted towards Jews as well as Christian officials; the eighth deals with the legality of a distinctive habit to be worn by the Jews in Christendom. The letter is part of the collection of Godefroy of Fontaines, who was a native of Liége (nos. 48, 65). Its date therefore may reasonably be presumed to be 1270/2. The "Duchess of Brabant" was formerly believed to be Aleyde (Alix) of Brabant who was regent of the duchy after the death of her husband Henry III (d. 1261) till her son, John I, took over in 1267. Glorieux (8, 153), who discovered Godefroy's collection, made a plausible bid for Marguerite of France being Aquinas's illustrious correspondent. Marguerite was the daughter of St. Louis IX whom we know to have consulted the famous Master of Paris (Tocco 1, 109, 116). She was married to John I in Febr. 1270 and died in 1271. The chronology of this letter may well be set at 1270/71.

EDITIONS: *Perrier*, 213 (fundamental text Paris lat. 14546; title: *De regimine subditorum*); *Parm.* 16, 292; *Vivès* 27, 414; *Mand.* 1, 488; *Taurin. Phil.* 249.

73. To Sir John of . . . (?): **De sortibus ad Dominum Jacobum de . . .** (?). This letter is clearly identified as such by the initial passage recording the correspondent's request and the writer's willingness to sacrifice some time of his "great summer vacation" on the answer. The conventional salutation at the end seems to have been cut away; the letter terminates in the fashion of a doctrinal treatise as many other works do (nos. 49, 65, 74, 90-92, 94, 96), viz., *Intantum igitur nunc de sortibus dictum est.* About the addressee's status and Christian name there is unanimity in those documents which go into such details. He is *Dominus Jacobus.* As to his surname taken from the place of birth, a confusing medley of names is offered to us in the documents: Turoneio, Togone, Tonongo, Tonago, Bonego, Bonoso, Burgo, Borego . . . The reader may take due account of paleographical rules and chose the name which sounds most French. This gentleman probably was a Frenchman. St. Thomas hardly would have selected *"Gallia"* as an example to make a certain point of his discourse clear to an Italian (*Nullus enim in Gallia existens sorte aliquid inquirendum curat de his quae ad Indos pertinent, cum quibus nullatenus in vita communicat;* ch. 1).—In ch. 4 the *Liber de bona fortuna* is quoted which Aquinas used for the first time in *Contra Gentiles* 3, 89 (Deman 1, 41). All this suggests the second sojourn in Paris, 1269/72, as the place and date of composition. The doctrinal parallelism of our letter and *Summa*, II-II, 95, 3-8 (see moreover *Quodl.* 12, 35) will also be fruitful for a chronological study. Both these texts make almost identical use of the same sources, and the special preparation needed for gathering this material would seem to militate against separating them too far in time. Certain indications would lead us to believe that the letter is posterior to the *Summa, loc. cit.*—This letter is one of the most interesting examples of Aquinas's epistolary style, since it allows a minute comparison with a parallel text in which the same matter is treated in academic style. The most striking feature here is that, writing to a layman, Aquinas does not spare him the thoroughness and even the subtleties of the *Summa*.

EDITIONS: *Parm.* 16, 310; *Vivès* 27, 439; *Mand.* 3, 144; *Taurin. Theol.* 1, 159.

74. To a Gentleman from beyond the Alps: **De occultis operationibus naturae, ad quendam militem ultramontanum.** The epistolary nature of this work treating a matter similar to that of no. 73 is evident at the beginning. The address *ad quendam militem . . .* appears almost exclusively in the ancient Catalogues. We do not know who this gentleman was nor whether he was Italian or French nor, consequently, whether the letter was written in Paris or in Italy. Mandonnet (9, liii) dated it 1269/72, for unspecified reasons. McAllister (1, 53) believed this date to be susceptible of confirmation since the doctrine of this letter seems to have an implicit reference to the controversies of 1270, an argument which, it seems to us, is anything but convincing. Thus the date remains unknown.

EDITIONS: *Perrier* 204 (Paris *lat.* 14546). *Parm.* 16, 355; *Vivès* 27, 504; *Taurin. Phil.* 159.

Engl. trans. McAllister (1, 20-30).

75. To a Gentleman from beyond the Alps: **De iudiciis astrorum, ad quendam militem ultramontanum.** On the strength of Tolomeo and Guidonis (Mandonnet 1, 61, 70) the Vulgate holds Reginald of Piperno to be the addressee, an improbable affirmation since Reginald was not only St. Thomas's secretary and companion but a capable theologian in his own right. It is difficult to imagine a letter addressed to this man, which adds nothing to what the Master had dictated to his secretary on several occasions. Other Catalogues, especially that of Bartholomew of Capua (Mandonnet 1, 29) and part of the Mss tradition (Grabmann 1, 135 ff.) consider this letter to have been communicated to that gentleman from beyond the Alps who is the addressee of no. 74. It seems that there was a special need for the laymen of St. Thomas's times (nos. 73-75) to be instructed about the morality of astrology and divinatory practices. Chronology unknown (no. 74).

EDITIONS: *Parm.* 16, 317; *Vivès* 27, 449; *Mand.* 3, 142; *Taurin. Theol.* 1, 155.

LITURGICAL PIECES AND SERMONS

76. Officium de festo Corporis Christi, ad mandatum Urbani Papae IV. In his *Historia ecclesiastica*, published between 1312 and 1317, Tolomeo of Lucca attests the fact that Aquinas, on the mandate of Urban IV, thus undoubtedly in 1264, composed the *Officium de Corpore Christi* (Mandonnet 1, 60). This testimony, being that of an eye witness (no. 55), is incontrovertible, although there is no earlier or contemporary independent witness to this fact. This lack of notoriety, however, with regard to a work of Aquinas which we are inclined to consider as highly significant, is not hard to explain. A liturgical text naturally did not circulate with the author's name. If, then, the fact that Aquinas composed such a liturgy seems to be beyond discussion, the question what text is his is a matter of much controversy. The text of our current editions is that of the fifteenth century Roman liturgy, which was introduced for the first time in the collection of St. Thomas's *Opuscula* by Antonio Pizzamano in 1497 (Kruitwagen 74). It contains, especially in the Mass *Cibavit eos,* a great number of interpolations and is therefore scientifically useless. The title *Sermo Sancti Thomae,* written at the head of the second nocturn in our breviaries, was introduced in 1568 by St. Pius V. Delaissé (1, 228) established the fact that toward the end of the thirteenth century there existed a Roman liturgy of the feast of *Corpus Christi* which, such as we know it, is not, nor can be, the work of Aquinas. An attempt to reconstruct, at least partially, the original Thomistic text of the Office *Sacerdos in aeternum* was undertaken by Lamont (1, 66). In the years 1318 to 1322 three Dominican Chapters General insisted on introducing the Roman liturgy of the feast of *Corpus Christi* into the Order but, surprisingly, say nothing about St. Thomas's authorship. Then, in the Chapter General of Barcelona, 1323, the provision was made that the liturgy "supposedly written by the Venerable fr. Thomas Aquinas" (*officium de Corpore Christi per venerabilem fr. Th. de A. editum, ut asseritur*) be chosen. These documents were interpreted by Delaissé (1, 236) as weakening, if not destroying, the value of Tolomeo's witness. Their curious hesitation may perhaps be explained by the obscurities which already in those times surrounded the original text. See for documents and details the studies of Lamont, Delaissé and Grabmann (1, 365).

77. St. Thomas's Prayers (**Adoro** [te] and others). These prayers are ranged by Mandonnet, in his edition of the *Opuscula,* among the "all but authentic works." Among them the most celebrated is that which, according to the traditional but relatively recent text, begins with the words *Adoro te*. No Mss from the first fifty years (to say the least) after Aquinas's death is known to us to affirm this authorship, nor does anyone else, during those years, refer to St. Thomas as the author. Tocco's silence seems to be especially significant, since he wrote the *Vita* for the purpose of Aquinas's canonization. After a thorough study of every document available in this matter Wilmart (1, 404) declines to draw a definitive conclusion but gives us to understand that his documentary premises are somehow insufficient for affirming Aquinas's authorship. Raby (1, 236) in a valuable contribution to these discussions, points out that a certain poem of Jacopone da Todi, which may possibly be dated between 1280 and 1294, would be unexplainable if the existence of the *Adoro te* were not supposed. But this, naturally, would not prove the Thomistic origin. The other prayers published in the current editions are, critically speaking, in about the same condition as the *Adoro*. The *Concede mihi misericors Deus* may be traced back to a fourteenth century Ms written perhaps not long after the canonization (Grabmann 1, 371).

EDITIONS: The older form of the hymn (*Adoro devote* . . .) is edited by Wilmart (1, 393). Of the prayer *Concede mihi* . . . Doyle (1, 229) published a text and an early Engl. trans. (ca. 1400). Cf. *Parm.* 24, 241; *Vivès* 32, 819; *Mand.* 4, 538; *Taurin. Theol.* 2, 285.

78.   The Lenten-cycle of sermons, Naples 1273: **De duobus praeceptis caritatis et decem legis praeceptis. Devotissima expositio super symbolum apostolorum. Expositio devotissima orationis dominicae.**   The ancient collectors of *Opuscula* all but neglected one well defined group of minor works, viz., the sermons. The cataloguists were satisfied with a general and vague allusion. In the *Piana*, 1570/1 (vol. 16), a large number of sermons were published under the name of Aquinas, all drawn from Vat. *lat.* 3804 and all spurious (*Parm.* 15, 126; *Vivès* 29, 126). In a Parisian edition of 1660 the collection of spurious sermons was brought up to the imposing number of 210. Such incompetent editorial work practically extinguished the scholars's interest in this category of Thomistic productions, and it was only in the nineteenth century that a new interest began to be shown after the discoveries of Uccelli and others. Uccelli found five sermons and edited them in *Parm.* 24, 220 (*Vivès* 32, 665). In our time the studies of scholars like Grabmann (1, 378), Käppeli and others greatly advanced the knowledge of this long neglected field of Thomistic bibliography. The exact value of former collections is now better established and the number of genuine works of this kind considerably increased. The main part however of the work of sifting and editing authentic sermons from the numerous mediaeval Mss remains to be done. St. Thomas preached assiduously, as may be expected from a Friar Preacher and, more especially still, a mediaeval Master of Theology

whose statutory obligations included preaching just as attendance at University sermons was obligatory for the students.—In the following numbers we list first those sermons which are part of the ancient *Opuscula* collections (nos. 78/9), thereafter, under nos. 80-89, those sermons which were more recently discovered and published. They will be counted according to the Mss in which they are found.

The Lenten-cycle of Naples is part of the earliest *Opuscula* collections. It consists of 57 or even 59 sermons, the number depending on whether the *Collationes* on the *Ave Maria* (no. 79) should be comprised in this cycle (see Mandonnet 14, 161). St. Thomas preached these sermons in the vernacular before students and people. In their actual shape they are therefore Latin *Reportata*. We may assume that they were made part of the *Opuscula* collections by the Neapolitan Dominicans with whom Aquinas lived the last years of his life. It is important to note that these Dominicans had a hand in setting up *Opuscula* collections.

EDITIONS: *Parm.* 16, 97; *Vivès* 27, 144; *Mand.* 4, 349; *Taurin. Theol.* 2, 193, 221, 243. After the first petition in the *Exp. orat. dominicae* Vat. *lat.* 807 adds a piece which was first published by Uccelli, *La scienza e la fede* 117 (1880) 106.

Engl. trans. L. Shapcote, *The Commandments of God*, London 1937; W. K. Firminger (*Lord's Prayer*) London 1927; J. B. Collins, New York 1953 (see no. 61).

79. Devotissima expositio super salutatione angelica. This is a collection of two, if not three, sermons, the authenticity of the third (Incip. *Ave Maria . . . Beatus Hieronymus*) being controverted. Whether these sermons belong to the Lenten-cycle of Naples or are a *Reportatum* from Paris, 1269/72, is also a matter of controversy. The famous variant [*Beata Virgo*] *nec originale nec mortale nec veniale peccatum incurrit,* rejected by the Thomists of the Renaissance, resists the most thorough-going paleographical examination and, it seems, is to be admitted (Rossi 4, 442).

EDITION: Rossi, Piacenza 1931 (*Div. Thom. Pl.* 34, 1931, 445).

Engl. trans. L. Shapcote (no. 78); J. B. Collins (ibid.); L. Every, *Dominicana* 39 (1954) 31.

80. Three Sermons from Ms Venice, *Bibl. marcian. Class* VI, Cod. 36. *Sermo in festo Omnium Sanctorum fr. Thomae de Aquino. Beata gens . . . Multis modis sancta Mater Ecclesia . . .* Ed. *Vivès* 32, 797.—*Sermo in nona dominica post trinitatem fr. Thomae de Aquino. Homo quidam erat dives . . . Omnis affluentia gratiarum . . .* Ed. *Vivès* 32, 791 (cf. Käppeli 4, 61).—*Sermo in festo beati Martini fr. Thomae de Aquino. Beatus vir cuius est . . . Satis expresse verba proposita.* Ed. *Vivès* 32, 803.

81. Three Sermons from Ms Milan, *Bibl. ambros.* A 11. *Sermo fratris Thomae de Aquino editus eadem dominica* (i.e., the first Sunday of Advent) *in domo Praedicatorum Parisius coram Universitate Parisiensi. Caelum et terra transibunt . . . Fratres carissimi, quanta . . . Ed. Vivès* 32, 692.—*Sermo fratris Thomae de Aquino editus eadem dominica in domo Praedicatorum Bononiae coram Universitate. Abiciamus opera tenebrarum . . . Apostolus Christianorum doctor . . .* Ed. *Vivès* 32, 693. —*Sermo fratris Thomae de Aquino editus Mediolani coram clero et populo civitatis. Ecce ego mitto angelum . . . Sumptum est . . .* Ed. *Vivès* 32, 815.

82. Two sermons from Ms. Paris, *Bibl. nat. lat.* 15034. *Sermo in prima dominica post Epiphaniam. Puer Jesus . . . Cuncta quae Dominus.* Ed. *Parm.* 24, 220; *Vivès* 32, 663. *Sermo in tertia dominica post festum Apostolorum Petri et Pauli. Attendite a falsis prophetis . . . Duo esse in verbis istis . . .* Ed. *Parm.* 24, 226; *Vivès* 32, 673. The part of this sermon which refers to the Averroistic controversy (1270) was also published by Mandonnet (2, 109).

83. Sermon on the Holy Eucharist preached in Consistory before Pope Urban IV and the Cardinals. Preserved in Munich, *Clm* 675 (beginning 14th cent.) as *Sermo venerabilis doctoris fr. Thomae de Aquino de Corpore Christi,* and in Troyes 1551 (15th cent.) as *Sermo de eucharistia in Coena Domini, in consistorio coram papa Urbano et Cardinalibus.* Date 1264. Ed. *Parm.* 24, 230; *Vivès* 32, 680.

84. Sermon from Ms Paris, *Nat. lat.* 15956. *Sermo in Nativitate b. Mariae Virginis. Lux orta est iusto . . . Omne datum optimum.* Cf. Lecoy de la Marche (1, 122). Ed. *Parm.* 24, 231; *Vivès,* 32, 682.

85. Two Sermons from Ms Paris, *Bibl. nat. lat.* 14952 (14899, 14923). *Sermo magistri Thomae de Haquino Jacobitae, dominica quinta* (i.e., the fifth Sunday after Easter) *Petite et accipietis . . . Dicit b. Hieronymus . . . ; Sermo magistri Thomae de Haquino Jacobitae* (20th Sunday after Trinity). *Omnia parata sunt . . . In evangelio hodierno . . .* Edited by Hauréau 81-93. In the first sermon the preacher makes use of a popular dictum in French: *A bon demandeeur, bon escondisseeur.* This sermon is also printed, in a slightly different text, in *Vivès* 32, 688.

86. Three *Exordia* (*Prothemata*) of Sermons from Mss Angers, *Ville* 250 (241) and Vat. *Ottob. lat.* 505. These *Prothemata* were brief prolusions by which the preacher invited the hearer's attention and prayed for God's blessing: (a) *Sapientia confortabit sapientem. Verbum istud . . . ;* (b) *Adaperiat Dominus . . . Verba ista . . . ;* (c) *Quae autem in caelis sunt*

... *Verba ista* ... Ed. Gardeil (1, 380). A fourth prolusion found in Ottob. *cit.* is unedited. These *Prothemata* probably belong to the second Parisian sojourn. See Käppeli (6, 414).

87. Two Sermons from Ms Florence, *Conv. soppr.* G. 4. 36. These come from a collection, made by Remigio Girolami O.P. of Florence, a disciple of Aquinas, of *Prologi super totam bibliam seu sacram scripturam.* In the Ms they are presented as: *Sermo I fr. Thomae. Rigans montes* ... *Rex caelorum* ... *Sermo II fr. Thomae. Hic est liber mandatorum* ... *Secundum Augustinum* ... Tocco relates in his *Vita* (1, 85) that St. Thomas inaugurated his lectures as a Master with a development of the Scriptural theme: *Rigans montes* ... Hence, it is held, the first of these sermons is the *Principium* of 1256. The second, by association as it were, becomes the *Principium* of the Biblical Bachelor in Paris, 1252. This latter identification seems to be less secure than the former. The fact that Aquinas ever was *Baccalaureus biblicus* in Paris is not quite sure. The discovery of these sermons was made by F. Salvatore, in 1912, who also identified both of them as *Principia*. He was followed in this by Mandonnet and Grabmann (1, 393).

Editions: *Mand.* 4, 481; *Taurin. Theol.* 1, 435.

88. Sermon on Christ the King from Ms Soissons, *Bibliothèque départementale* 125 and other Mss. *Sermo in prima dominica adventus Domini fr. Thomae de Aquino. Ecce rex tuus* ... *Multa sunt mirabilia* ... Ed. Leclercq (1, 158). Date 1270. See also Käppeli (4, 60).

89. Sermons from Mss Madrid, *Bibl. real* 493 and Sevilla, *Bibl. Colomb.* Y 131-24. From this rich collection part of the fifth, and the entire sixth and eleventh sermons were edited by Käppeli (4, 72); the third is identical with no. 88, the ninth with no. 80, *Omnis affluentia.—V. Sermo de adventu. Osanna filio David* ... *Verba ista sunt* ... VI. *Sermo fr. Thomae in Sexagesima. Exiit qui seminat* ... *Quia de spirituali seminatione* ... XI. *Sermo de Omnibus Sanctis. Beati qui habitant* ... *Unam esse societatem.* The first two are clearly related to the topic of nos. 45, 46. Their date is probably Dec. 1270.

WORKS OF UNCERTAIN AUTHENTICITY

90-96. De instantibus; De natura verbi intellectus; De principio individuationis; De natura generis; De natura accidentium; De natura materiae; De quatuor oppositis. These seven philosophical *Opuscula* are here enumerated according to the order in which they appear in their main source, viz., Cod. Avignon 251 (13th/14th cent.) This Ms originally belonged to the Dominican Convent of Avignon. They are also found, although in different order (Rossi 3, 385) in other authoritative Mss, especially in Vat. *lat.* 807, a magnificent collection of the *Opuscula* offered to John XXII who canonized Thomas Aquinas. In regard to the problem of authenticity, these seven works form a compact group and will therefore have to be treated alike. This problem is an age-old controversial matter, a *solemnis quaestio,* in Thomistic bibliography. Certain items of the group were thought to be spurious as early as the fifteenth cent. (Capreolus; see Grabmann 1, 19), and Cajetan in the sixteenth cent. positively rejected the *De natura materiae* "because its doctrine is incompatible with St. Thomas's general teaching on matter." It was Mandonnet's outstanding accomplishment in his study *Des écrits authentiques de St. Thomas* (1910) to have taken these discussions out of the somewhat hazy sphere of doctrinal appreciation and placed them on the firm ground of historical facts. Mandonnet centered his research around the ancient Catalogues. One group of them, viz., the Catalogue of Bartholomew of Capua and its related documents, does not mention these *Opuscula,* while in others, e.g., those of Tolomeo of Lucca, Bernard Guidonis, the *Tabula* of Stams, they are listed as St. Thomas's works. The Catalogue of Bartholomew was presented in the canonization proceedings of 1319 as part of this witness's formal testimony. Mandonnet therefore declared it to be an "official" list for which, in the last instance, the Dominican authorities were responsible. Hence its silence about the seven Opuscula should be interpreted not as an accidental omission but as an intentional exclusion.—Although recent scholars often continue designating the list of Bartholomew as the "Official Catalogue," the conclusion Mandonnet drew from this qualification is generally abandoned (see especially Synave 4, 102).—The problem, as it stands to-day, may be presented thus: There are two traditions incorporated in the Mss as well as the ancient Catalogues. The one takes no notice of these works, the other affirms their Thomistic authenticity. Are these two traditions contradictory, or are they complementary? As long as the whole history of the *Opuscula* collections is not brought to light in all its details and phases, this question is not susceptible of a definitive solution. The complete story of these collections may be told only by the editors of a truly critical text established not for one or the other *Opusculum,* but for all of them together, and we are still far away from such a text. It would seem, then, that two conclusions may be drawn at the present time: (a) the non-authenticity of these seven works is not as yet sufficiently proved; (b) their authenticity, warranted as it is by important documents, is at the same time (juridically, as it were) in possession and for intrinsic reasons (coherence of doctrine etc.) subject to serious doubt. Latest studies of this problem: Rossi (3, 211: cf. H. Dondaine 3, 92); Pelster (8, 21)..

EDITIONS: *Parm.* 16, 179; *ibid.* 328-352; 17, 1-26; *Vivès* 27, 268; *ibid.* 487, 512-530; 28, 1-30; *Mand.* 5, 177-269; *ibid.* 284-294, 368; *Perrier* 468-586; 591-605; *Taurin. Phil.* 111-118; 131-151; 177-217. *De natura materiae,* ed. Wyss, Fribourg-Louvain, 1953 (reliable edition, founded on Mss).

97. De demonstratione. This work, rejected by Mandonnet (1, 108, 149), was accepted by Grabmann principally on the authority of Vat. *lat.* 807 (*"ein hochbedeutsamer Opusculakodex"*: 1, 173). See Grabmann (1, 246); Rossi (3, 389).

EDITIONS: *Parm.* 16, 375; *Vivès* 27, 531; *Mand.* 5, 171; *Perrier* 465; *Taurin. Phil.* 221.

98. De differentia verbi divini et humani. The Thomistic origin of this work is attested to by Vat. *lat.* 807 and other Mss, but the treatise is not mentioned by Bartholomew of Capua. It is nothing but a piece cut out of the *Exp. in Ioan., lect.* 1 (no. 25). The two texts are substantially identical, differing only in some variants of merely paleographical interest. As the Leonine editors observe on another occasion (vol. 13, p. xxiii), "St. Thomas never composed any of his works with the help of scissors, whatever some scholars may say." For an example of how Aquinas elaborated one of his texts in a letter, see no. 73. The presence of this extract, however, in an ancient and important sector of the tradition throws some light on the editorial principles by which some of the first editors were guided.

EDITIONS: *Parm.* 16, 177; *Vivès* 27, 266; *Mand.* 5, 365; *Perrier* 587; *Taurin. Phil.* 101.

In a fourteenth century Ms (Madrid, *Bibl. nacion.* 8979: Beltrán 1, 110) we find a catalogue of the works of Aquinas consisting of a hundred and thirty items. At the end, the author writes a remark which may fittingly bring to a close the present catalogue: *Summa omnium CXXX. Semper secum habebat quatuor scriptores, et in dubiis semper orabat.* St. Thomas wrote an amazingly large number of imposing works in the short span of twenty-one years. He kept a staff of secretaries busy, "and when in doubt, he turned to God in prayer."

I. T. ESCHMANN, O.P.

Toronto, March 7, 1956

LIST OF BOOKS USED

ARISTOTELES LATINUS. Corpus Philosophorum Medii Aevi. Pars prior, Rome 1952; Pars posterior, Cambridge, Eng., 1945.

AXTERS, E., O.P.
1. Pour l'état des manuscrits des Questions disputées de s. Th. d'A. *Divus Thomas Plac.* 12 (1935) 129-159.
2. Frère Jacobin d'Asti, a-t-il été un faussaire? Ou l'heur et le malheur d'un autographe. *Angelicum* 12 (1935) 502-577.

BACKES, I. Die Christologie des hl. Th. v. A. u. die griechischen Kirchenväter. *Forschungen z. christl. Lit. und Dogmengeschichte* VII, 3-4. Paderborn 1931.

BELTRAN DE HEREDIA, V., O.P. Los manuscritos de s. T. de la Biblioteca Nacional de Madrid. *Ciencia tomista* 34 (1926) 88-111.

BIRKENMAJER, A. Kleinere Thomasfragen. I. Über die Reihenfolge u. die Entstehungszeit der Quaestiones disputatae des hl. Th. v. A. *Philosoph. Jahrbuch* 34 (1921) 31-49.

BOCHENSKI, I. M., O.P.
1. Notes historiques sur les propositions modales. *Revue des sciences philos. et théol.* 26 (1939) 673-692.
2. S. Th. A. De modalibus, opusculum et doctrina. *Angelicum* 17 (1940) 180-221.

BOUILLARD, H., S.J. Conversion et grâce chez s. Th. d'A. Paris 1944.

BROWNE, M., O.P. An sit authenticum opusc. s. Th. "De regimine principum" *Angelicum* 3 (1926) 300-303.

BRUNI, G. Le opere di Egidio Romano. Florence 1936.

CALO, P., O.P. Vita s. Th. *Fontes vitae s. Th.* Ed. Prümmer, Toulouse n.d., 17-55.

CANONIZATION PROCEEDINGS. Processus canonizationis s. Th., Neapoli. *Fontes vitae s. Th.* IV. Ed. M.-H. Laurent, O.P. Saint-Maximin n. d.

CASTAGNOLI, P.
1. I commenti di s. T. ai "Libri naturales" di Aristotile. *Divus Thom. Plac.* 34 (1931) 261-283.
2. L'opuscolo "De forma absolutionis" di s. T. d'A. Piacenza 1933. *Divus Thomas Plac.* 36 (1933) 360-416; 37 (1934) 3-45).

CHARTULARIUM UNIVERSITATIS PARISIENSIS. Ed. Denifle-Chatelain. Vol. I, Paris 1889.

CHENU, M.-D., O.P.
1. Les réponses de s. Th. et de Kilwardby à la consultation de Jean de Verceil. *Mélanges Mandonnet I,* Paris 1930, 191-222.
2. [Book review in] *Bulletin Thomiste* 5 (1937-1939) 153-155.
3. La date du commentaire de s. Th. sur le De Trinitate de Boèce. *Les sciences phil. et théol.* 2 (1941/2) 432-434.
4. La théologie comme science au XIIIe

siècle. 2nd ed. Pro manuscripto. Le Saulchoir 1943.
5. Introduction à l'étude de s. Th. d'A. Montréal-Paris 1950.

DELAISSE, L. M. J. A la recherche des origines de l'Office du Corpus Christi dans les manuscrits liturgiques. *Scriptorium* 4 (1950) 220-239.

DEMAN, Th., O.P. Le "Liber de bona fortuna" dans la théologie de s. Th. d'A. *Revue des sciences phil. et théol.* 17 (1928) 38-58.

DENIFLE, H., O.P. Die Statuten der Juristen-Universität Bologna, I. *Archiv f. Lit. u. Kirchengesch. d. Mittelalt.* 3 (1997) 196-347.

DESTREZ, J.
1. La lettre de s. Th. dite lettre au lecteur de Venise d'après la tradition manuscrite. *Mélanges Mandonnet* I, Paris 1930, 103-189.
2. Etudes critiques sur les oeuvres de s. Th. d'A. d'après la tradition manuscrite. *Bibl. thom.* 18, Paris 1933.

DONDAINE, A., O.P.
1. S. Th. et les traductions des Métaphysiques d'Aristote. *Bulletin thom. Notes et communications* 1 (1931/3) 199-213.
2. [Book review in] *Bulletin thom.* 4 (1934) 49-50.
3. S. Th. et la dispute des attributs divins. Authenticité et origine. *Archiv. FF. Praedic.* 8 (1938) 253-262.
4. [Book review in] *Bulletin thom.* 6 (1940/2) 90-94.
5. [Book review in] *Bulletin thom.* 6 (1940/2) 100-108.
6. [Book review in] *Bulletin thom.* 6 (1940/2) 111-112.
7. Un commentaire scripturaire de Roland de Crémone sur le livre de Job. *Archiv. FF. Praedic.* 11 (1941) 107-137.
8. Nicolas de Cotone et les sources du Contra errores Graecorum de s. Th. d'A. *Divus Thom. Frib.* 28 (1950) 313-340.

DONDAINE, H. F., O.P.
1. Le Contra errores Graecorum de s. Th. et le IVe livre du Contra Gentiles.

Les sciences phil. et théol. 1 (1941/2) 156-162.
2. [Book review in] *Bulletin thom.* 9 (1954-1956) 41-44.
3. [Book review in] *Bulletin thom.* 9 (1954-1956) 92-94.

DOYLE, A. I. A Prayer Attributed to St. Th. A. *Dominican Studies* 1 (1948) 229-238.

DUIN, J. J. Nouvelles précisions sur la chronologie du "Commentum in Metaphysicam" de s. Th. *Revue philos. de Louvain* 53 (1955) 511-524.

ECHARD, J., O.P. S. Thomas de Aquino, in Quétif-Echard, Scriptores Ordinis Praedicatorum I, Paris 1719, 271-347.

ESCHMANN, I. T., O.P.
1. Studies on the Notion of Society in St. Th. A. II. Thomistic Social Philosophy and the Theology of Original Sin. *Mediaeval Studies* 9 (1947) 19-55.
2. St. Thomas. On Kingship. Engl. trans. Toronto 1949. Introduction ix-xxxix.
3. [Book review in] *Div. Thom. Frib.* 27 (1949) 450-460.

FLORI, E. Il Trattato "De regimine principum" e le dottrine politiche di s. T. Bologna 1927.

FRANCESCHINI, E. La revisione moerbekiana della "Translatio Lincolniensis" dell'Etica Nicomachea. *Riv. di filos. neoscol.* 30 (1938) 150-162.

FRIES, A, C.Ss.R. Thomas und die Quaestio de immortalitate animae. *Div. Thom. Frib.* 31 (1953) 18-52.

GARDEIL, A., O.P. Trois exordes inédits de sermons de s. Th. *Rev. thom.* 1 (1893) 379-386.

GAUTHIER, R.-A., O.P.
1. [Book review in] *Bulletin thom.* 6 (1947-1953) 136-140.
2. La date du commentaire de s. Th. sur l'Ethique à Nicomaque. *Rech. de théol. anc. et méd.* 18 (1951) 66-105.

GILSON, E. History of Christian Philosophy in the Middle Ages, New York 1955.

GLORIEUX, P.

1. Le "Contra impugnantes" de s. Th. Ses sources, son plan. *Mélanges Mandonnet* I, Paris 1930, 51-81.

2. Pour qu'on lise le "De perfectione" de s. Th. d'A. *Vie spirituelle* 23 (1930) Suppl. 97-126.

3. Un recueil scolaire de Godefroid de Fontaines. *Recherches de thèol. anc. et méd.* 3 (1931) 37-53.

4. Les questions disputées de s. Th. et leur suite chronologique. *Rech. de théol. anc. et méd.* 4 (1932) 5-33.

5. Les polémiques "Contra Geraldinos." Les pièces du dossier. *Rech. de théol. anc. et méd.* 6 (1934) 5-41.

6. La littérature quodlibétique II. *Bibl. thom.* 21. Paris 1935.

7. "Contra Geraldinos." L'enchaînement des polémiques. *Rech. de théol. anc. et médiév.* 7 (1935) 129-155.

8. Le "De Regimine Judaeorum." Hypothèses et précisions. *Div. Thom. Plac.* 39 (1936) 153-160.

9. Pour la chronologie de la Somme. *Mélanges de science religieuse* 2 (1945) 59-98.

10. Les Quodlibets VII à XI de s. Th. d'A. *Rech. de théol. anc. et méd.* 13 (1946) 282-303.

11. Le plus beau Quodlibet de s. Th. est-il de lui? *Mél. de sc. rel.* 3 (1946) 235-268.

12. Essai sur les Commentaires scripturaires de s. Th. et leur chronologie. *Rech. de théol. anc. et méd.* 17 (1950) 237-266.

13. Autour du "Contra errores Graecorum." *Autour d'Aristote: Recueil d'études offert à Mgr. A. Mansion.* Louvain 1955, 497-512.

GORCE, M.-M. La lutte "Contra Gentiles" à Paris au XIIIe siècle. *Mélanges Mandonnet* I, Paris 1930, 223-243.

GRABMANN, M.

1. Die Werke des hl. Th. v. A. *Beitr. z. Gesch. d. Phil. u. Theol. des Mittelalt.* 22, 1/2. Third ed., Münster 1949.

2. Forschungen über die lateinischen Aristotelesübersetzungen des XIII Jahrh. *Beitr. z. Gesch. d. Phil. u. Theol. d. Mittelalt.* 17, 5-6. Münster 1916.

3. Guglielmo di Moerbeke, O.P., il traduttore delle opere di Aristotile. *Miscell. Hist. Pontif.* 11, 20. Rome 1946.

GUIBERT, J. de, S.J. Les doublets de s. Th. d'A. Leur étude méthodique. Paris 1926.

HAUREAU, B. Notices et extraits de quelques manuscrits latins de la Bibl. Nationale IV, Paris 1892.

HAYEN, A., S. Th. a-t-il édité deux fois son Commentaire sur le livre des Sentences. *Rech. de théol. anc. et méd.* 9 (1937) 219-236.

HERTLING, G. von. Zur Geschichte der aristotelischen Politik im Mittelalter. *Historische Beiträge zur Philosophie.* Munich 1914.

ISAAC, J., O.P.

1. Le Quodlibet IX est bien de s. Th. *Arch. d'hist. doctrin. et litt. du Moyen-Age* 22/23 (1948) 145-185.

2. Le Peri Hermeneias en Occident de Boèce à s. Th. *Bibl. thom.* 29, Paris 1953.

KAEPPELI, Th., O.P.

1. Die Thomashandschriften der Biblioteca Casanatense in Rom. *Arch. FF. Praed.* 2 (1932) 351-381.

2. Zerstreute Autographblätter des hl. Th. v. A. *Arch. FF. Praed.* 2 (1932) 382-402.

3. Mitteilungen über Thomashandschriften in der Biblioteca Nazionale in Neapel. *Angelicum* 10 (1933) 111-125.

4. Una raccolta di prediche attribuite a s. T. d'A. *Arch. FF. Praed.* 13 (1943) 59-94.

5. Fr. Baxianus von Lodi, Adressat der Responsio ad lectorem Venetum des hl. Thomas. *Arch. FF. Praed.* 13 (1943) 181-182.

6. Eine Prothemata-Sammlung aus Pariser Predigten des 13. Jahrh. in Cod. Ottob. lat. 505. *Miscellanea Giovanni Mercati II,* Città del Vaticano 1946, 414-430.

KEELER, L., S.J.

1. S. Th. A. Tractatus de spiritualibus

creaturis. *Text. et docum. Series philos.* Rome. 1946.

2. The Vulgate Text of St. Thomas' Commentary on the Ethics. *Gregorianum* 17 (1936) 413-436.

KRUITWAGEN, B., O.F.M. S. Th. de A. Summa Opusculorum. Anno ca. 1485 typis edita. Vulgati Opusculorum text. princeps. *Bibl. thom.* IV, Le Saulchoir 1924.

KUERZINGER, J. Eine Handschrift zum Klagelieder-Kommentar des hl. Th. v. A. *Biblica* 23 (1942) 306-317.

LAMBOT, C., O.S.B. L'Office de la Fête-Dieu. Aperçus nouveaux sur ses origines. *Revue Bénédictine* 54 (1942) 61-123.

LECLERQ, J., O.S.B. Un sermon inédit de s. Th. sur la royauté du Christ. *Revue thom.* 54 (1946) 158-160.

LECOY de la Marche, A. La chaire française au moyen-âge. Second ed., Paris 1886.

LOTTIN, O., O.S.B.
1. La date de la Question disputée De malo de s. Th. d'A. *Revue d'Hist. Eccl.* 24 (1928) 373-388.
2. Le péché originel chez Albert le Grand, Bonaventure et Th. d'A. *Rech. de théol. anc. et méd.* 12 (1940) 275-328.

MANDONNET, P., O.P.
1. Des écrits authentiques de s. Th. d'A. Second ed., Fribourg 1910.
2. Siger de Brabant et l'averroïsme latin au XIIIe s. Second ed., Louvain 1911.
3. Chronologie des Questions disputées de s. Th. d'A. *Revue thom.* 23 (1918) 266-287; 341-371.
4. Destrez, J. (co-editor): Bibliographie thomiste. *Bibliothèque thomiste* I, Le Saulchoir 1921.
5. Le carême de s. Th. d'Aquin à Naples (1273). *San Tommaso d'Aquino. Miscell. storico-artistica,* Rome 1924.
6. [Editor] S. Th. A. Doctoris angelici Quaestiones disputatae I, Paris 1925. Introduction.

7. S. Th. d'A., novice Prêcheur IV. *Revue thom.* 30 (1925) 393-416.
8. S. Th. d'A., créateur de la dispute quodlibétique I. *Rev. des sciences phil. et théol.* 15 (1926) 477-506.
9. [Editor] S. Th. A. Opuscula omnia I, Paris 1927. Introduction, i-liii.
10. Chronologie des écrits scripturaires de s. Th. d'Aquin. II. Premier enseignement Parisien. *Revue thom.* 33 (1928) 116-155.
11. Chronologie des écrits scripturaires de s. Th. d'A. VI. La lecture et l'exposition sur s. Paul. *Revue thom.* 33 (1928) 222-245.
12. A propos des autographes de s. Th. *Bulletin thom.* 2 (1929) 515-523.
13. [Book review in] *Bulletin thom.* 3 (1930-1933) 129-139.
14. Les "Collationes" sur le "Ave Maria" et la critique récente. *Bulletin thom. Notes et communications* I (1931/2) 155-167.
15. [Book review in] *Bulletin thom.* 4 (1934-1936) 13-20.

MANSION, A.
1. Pour l'histoire du commentaire de s. Th. sur la Métaphysique d'Aristote. *Revue néoscolastique* 27 (1925) 274-295.
2. Le commentaire de s. Th. sur le De sensu et sensato d'Aristote. Utilization d'Alexandre d'Aphrodise. *Mélanges Mandonnet* I, Paris 1930, 83-102.
3. Sur le texte de la version latine médiévale de la Métaphysique et de la Physique d'Aristote dans les éditions des Commentaires de s. Th. d'A. *Revue néoscolastique* 34 (1932) 65-69.
4. La théorie aristotélicienne du temps chez les péripatéciens médiévaux. *Revue néoscol.* 36 (1934) 275-307.
5. La version médiévale de l'Ethique à Nicomaque. *Revue néoscol.* 41 (1936) 401-427.
6. Date de quelques commentaires de s. Th. sur Aristote. *Studia mediaevalia in honorem R. J. Martin.* Bruges n. d., 271-287.

MARTIN, C. The Vulgate Text of Aquinas' Commentary on Aristotle's

Politics. *Dominican Studies* 5 (1952) 35-64.

MARTIN, R., O.P. Notes critiques au sujet de l'Opuscule IX de s. Th. d'Aquin, ses manuscrits, ses éditions. *Mélanges Auguste Pelzer*, Louvain 1947, 303-323.

MASNOVO A. La Catena aurea de s. Th. d'A et un nouveau codex de 1263. *Revue néoscol.* 13 (1906) 200-205.

McALLISTER, J. B. The Letter of St. Thomas Aquinas De Occultis Operibus Naturae. Washington, D. C. 1939.

MEERSSEMAN, G., O.P. [Ed.] Laurentii Pignon Catalogi et Chronica. Accedunt Catalogi Stamsensis et Upsalensis Scriptorum O.P. Rome 1936.

MILLAS VALLICROSA, J. M. Las traducciones orientales en los manuscritos de la Biblioteca Catedral de Toledo. Madrid 1942.

MINIO-PALUELLO, L.
1. Les "trois rédactions" de la traduction médiévale gréco-latine du De generation et corruptione d'Aristote. *Rev. phil. de Louvain* 48 (1950) 247-259.
2. L'ignota versione Moerbekana dei Secondi Analitici usata da s. T. *Riv. di filos. neoscol.* 44 (1952) 389-397.

MORIN, G. A travers les manuscrits de Bâle. *Basler Zeitschr. f. Gesch. u. Altertumskunde* 26 (1927) 175-249.

MOTTE, A., O.P.
1. La date extrême du commentaire de s. Th. sur les Sentences. *Bulletin thom. Notes et communications* 1 (1931/2) 49-61.
2. Note sur la date du Contra Gentiles. *Rev. thom.* 44 (1938) 806-809.

O'RAHILLY, A.
1. Notes on St. Th. Some Manuscripts of the Opuscula. *Irish Eccl. Rev.* 63 (1927) 376-392; 481-490.
2. Notes on St. Th. The Commentary on the Politics. *Irish Eccl. Rev.* 63 (1927) 614-622.
3. Notes on St. Th. St. Thomas on

Credit. *Irish Eccl. Revue* 64 (1928) 159-168.
4. Notes on St. Th. De regimine principium. *Irish Eccl. Rev.* 64 (1928) 396-410.

PARE, G., O.P. Le Roman de la Rose et la scholastique courtoise. Paris-Ottawa 1941.

PATTISON, M. [Preface and Engl. trans. of Catena aurea in Matth.] Catena Aurea. Commentary on the Four Gospels Collected out of the Works of the Fathers by St. Thomas Aquinas I, Oxford 1841.

PEGIS, A. C. St. Thomas A. On the Truth of the Catholic Faith. Summa Contra Gentiles I. Engl. trans. and introduction. New York 1955.

PELSTER, F., S.J.
1. Die Übersetzungen der aristotelischen Metaphysik in den Werken des hl. Th. v. A. *Gregorianum* 16 (1935) 325-348.
2. Die Übersetzungen der aristotelischen Metaphysik in den Werken des hl. Th. v. A. IV. Weitere Ergebnisse und Fragen. *Gregorianum* 17 (1936) 377-406.
3. Les manuscrits de Bombolognus de Bologna, O.P. *Rech. de théol. anc. et méd.* 9 (1937) 404-412.
4. [Book review in] *Scholastik* 15 (1940) 108-111.
5. Literarhistorische Probleme der Quodlibeta des hl. Th. I. *Gregorianum* 28 (1947) 78-100.
6. Literarhistorische Probleme der Quodlibeta des hl. Th. II. *Gregorianum* 29 (1948) 62-87.
7. Neuere Forschungen über die Aristotelesübersetzungen des 12. und 13. Jahrhunderts. *Gregorianum* 30 (1949) 46-77.
8. Die Th. v. A. zugeschriebenen Opuscula De instantibus etc. (the seven philosophical Opuscula) und ihr Verfasser. *Gregorianum* 36 (1955) 21-49.
9. Eine ungedruckte Quaestio des hl. Th. v. A. über die Erkenntnis der Wesenheit der Seele. *Gregorianum* 36 (1955) 618-625.

PELZER, A. Le cours inédit d'Albert le Grand sur la Morale à Nicomaque, recueilli et rédigé par s. Th. d'A. *Rev. néoscol.* 24 (1922) 333-361; 479-520.

PLANZER, D., O.P. De Codice Ruthenensi miscellaneo in Tabula Ord. Praed. asservata. *Arch. FF. Praed.* 5 (1935) 1-123.

RABY, F. J. E. The Date and Authorship of the Poem *Adoro te devote. Speculum* 20 (1945) 236-238.

RASHDALL, POWICKE, EMDEN. The Universities of Europe in the Middle Ages I, Oxford 1926.

ROSSI, G. F.
1. L'autografo di s. T. del commento al terzo libro delle Sentenze. *Div. Thom. Pl.* 35 (1932) 582-585. (Separate edition, Piacenza 1932.)
2. Il Codice latino 14546 della Bibl. Naz. di Parigi con gli Opuscoli di S. T. (I). *Div. Th. Pl.* 54 (1951) 149-188.
3. Gli Opuscoli di s. T. d'A. *Div. Thom. Pl.* 30 (1953) 211-236; 362-390.
4. L'autenticità dei testi di s. T. d'A: "Beata Virgo a peccato originali et actuali immunis fuit," "B. V. nec originale peccatum incurrit." *Div. Thom. Pl.* 57 (1954) 442-466.

ROY, L., S.J. Lumière et sagesse. La grâce mystique dans la théologie de s. Th. d'A. Montreal 1948.

SAFFREY, H. D., O.P. S. Th. de A. super librum De causis expositio. Fribourg-Louvain 1954.

SALMAN, D., O.P. Sur la lutte "Contra Gentiles" de s. Th. d'A. *Div. Thom. Pl.* 40 (1937) 488-509.

SALVATORE, F. Due sermoni inediti di s. T. d'A. Rome 1912.

SCHMEIDLER, B. Die Annalen des Tholomeus von Lucca. *Monum. German. hist., Scriptores,* nova ser. 8, Berlin 1930.

SIMONIN, H.-D.
1. Les écrits de Pierre de Tarentaise.

Beatus Innocentius V, studia et documenta. Rome 1943, 163-335.
2. [Book review in] *Bulletin thom.* 3 (1930-1933) 941-947.

SLADECZEK, F., S.J. Wann ist der Traktat des hl. Th. "De articulis fidei et Ecclesiae sacramentis" entstanden? *Scholastik* 2 (1927) 413-415.

SMERALDO, B., O.P. Intorno all'opusculo IX di s. T. d'A. Pietro da Tarentasia ha errato in teologia? Rome 1945.

SPICQ, C., O.P. Esquisse d'une histoire de l'exégèse latine au moyen âge. *Bibliothèque thomiste* 26, Paris 1944.

STEENBERGHEN, F. van. Siger de Brabant d'après ses oeuvres inédites. II. Siger dans l'histoire de l'aristotélisme. Louvain 1942.

STEGMUELLER, F. Repertorium biblicum medii aevi. aevi. V. Commentaria. Madrid 1955.

SYNAVE, P.
1. Les commentaires scripturaires de s. Th. d'A. *Vie spirituelle* 8 (1923) 455-469.
2. [Book review in] *Bulletin thom.* 1 (1924) 33-50.
3. La doctrine de s. Th. sur le sens littéral des Ecritures. La question disputée De sensibus sacrae Scripturae, Quodl. 7. *Rev. biblique* 35 (1926) 40-65.
4. Le Catalogue Officiel des oeuvres de s. Th. d'A. Critique-Origine-Valeur. *Arch. d'hist. doctr. et litt. du M.-A.* 3 (1928) 25-103.
5. La révélation des vérités divines naturelles d'après s. Th. d'A. *Mélanges Mandonnet* I, Paris 1930, 327-365.
6. [Book review in] *Bulletin thom.* I (Jan. 1926) 1-21.

THORNDIKE, L. Latin Treatises on Comets, between 1238 and 1368. Chicago 1950.

TOCCO, Guil. de. Vita s. Th. Fontes vitae s. Th., ed. Prümmer. Toulouse, n. d.

TONNEAU, R.-M., O.P. [Book review] *Bulletin thom.* 9 (1954-1956) 179.

UCCELLI, P. A. S. Th. A. Doctoris Angelici in Isaiam prophetam, in tres Psalmos David, in Boëthium de hebdomadibus et de Trinitate expositiones. Rome 1880.

VANSTEENKISTE, C., O.P. [Book review] *Bulletin thom.* 8 (1947-1953) 17-30.

VERBEKE, G. Les sources et la chronologie du commentaire de s. Th. d'A. au De anima d'Aristote. *Rev. phil. de Louvain* 45 (1947) 314-338.

WALZ, A., O.P. St. Th. Aquinas. A Biographical Study. Engl. trans. S. Bullough. Westminster, Md. 1951.

WILMART, A., O.S.B. Auteurs spirituels et textes dévots du Moyen-Age latin. Paris 1932.

INDEX OF TITLES FOR

A CATALOGUE OF ST. THOMAS'S WORKS

NOTES TO THE INTRODUCTION

[1] St. Thomas once said that the principal function of his life was to speak about God: Ut enim verbis Hilarii (*De Trin.* I, 37) utar, ego hoc vel praecipuum vitae meae officium debere me Deo conscius sum, ut eum omnis sermo meus et sensus loquatur. *Contra Gentiles* I, 2.

[2] A. Touron, *La Vie de S. Thomas d'Aquin . . . avec un exposé de sa doctrine et ses ouvrages,* Paris, 1737, esp. IV, ch. 2 and 3: "Portrait d'un parfait Docteur selon saint Thomas." On the mystical side of his personality, see *Saint Thomas d'Aquin, Sa sainteté, sa doctrine spirituelle* (Les Grands Mystiques). Editions de la Vie spirituelle, Saint-Maximin. Joret, O.P., *La Contemplation mystique d'après saint Thomas d'Aquin,* Lille-Bruges, Desclée, 1924.—For general bibliographical information: P. Mandonnet and J. Destrez, *Bibliographie thomiste,* Paris, Vrin, 1921, pp. 70-72. V. J. Bourke, *Thomistic Bibliography,* St. Louis University Press, 1945 (for the years 1920/40).

[3] "Ergo quod aliquis veritatem meditatam in alterius notitiam per doctrinam deducat," *S T* II-II, 181, 3, ad 3. For what follows see *ibid.* ad Resp.

[4] "Sic ergo dicendum est, quod opus vitae activae est duplex: unum quidem, quod ex plenitudine contemplationis derivatur, sicut doctrina et praedicatio . . . ; et hoc praefertur simplici contemplationi: sicut enim majus est illuminare quam lucere solum, ita majus est contemplata aliis tradere, quam solum contemplari." *S T,* II-II, 188, 6.

[5] *S T,* II-II, 182, 1, ad Resp. and ad 3. See especially the conclusion of the article: "Et sic patet quod cum aliquis a contemplativa vita ad activam vocatur, non hoc fit per modum substractionis, sed per modum additionis."

[6] On diversity of aptitude for active and contemplative life see *S T,* II-II, 182, 4, ad 3.

[7] *S T,* II-II, 186, 6. Here it is shown that contemplative and teaching orders surpass in dignity the purely contemplative orders. In the ecclesiastical hierarchy they come just below bishops, because *fines primorum conjunguntur principiis secundorum.*

[8] *S T,* II-II, 186, 3, ad 3.

[9] *Contra impugnantes Dei cultum et religionem,* c. II: "Item hoc falsum est, quod magisterium sit honor; est enim officium, cui debetur honor."

[10] *Ibid.,* c. II, ad *Ita, cum nomina* et *Restat ergo dicendum.*

[11] *S T,* II-II, 187, 3, ad 3. *Quaest. Quodlib.,* VII, a. 17 and 18. *Contra impugnantes Dei cultum et religionem,* c. II, ad *Item, sicut probatum est,* where teaching is taken as spiritual alms and a work of mercy. Cf. *op. cit.,* c. V.

[12] St. Thomas was asked the curious question whether a master who had always taught out of vainglory could regain the right to his aureola by doing penance. His reply was that penance restores the right to rewards that have been merited, but that one who has taught out of vainglory has never had a right to an aureola and consequently cannot regain it. *Quodlib.,* XII, a. 24.

[13] *Quodlib.,* III, q. 4, a. 9: *Utrum liceat alicui petere licentiam pro se docendi in theologia.*

[14] "Nam scientia, per quam aliquis est idoneus ad docendum, potest aliquis scire per certitudinem se habere; caritatem autem, per quam aliquis est idoneus ad officium pastorale, non potest aliquis per certitudinem scire se habere." *Quodlib.,* III, a. 9, ad Resp. Cf. ad 3: "sed pericula magisterii cathedrae pastoralis devitat scientia cum caritate, quam homo nescit se per certitudinem habere; pericula autem magisterii cathedrae magistralis vitat

homo per scientiam, quam potest homo
scire se habere."

[15] *S T*, I-II, III, 4. Cf. *In evangel.*
Matth. c. V.

[16] On this point see *S T*, II-II, 177, 1.

[17] To determine the object of theology
properly so called does not directly fall
under the scope of this work. For a study
of the pertinent problems see M. D.
Chenu, "La Théologie comme science au
XIIIᵉ siècle," *Archives d'histoire doctrinale et littéraire du Moyen Age,* Paris,
Vrin (Librairie philosophique), 1927, pp.
31-37; J. F. Bonnefoy, O.F.M., *La Nature de la théologie selon saint Thomas
d'Aquin,* Paris, Vrin (Librairie philosophique), 1939; R. Gagnebet, O.P., "La
Nature de la theologie speculative," *Revue Thomiste,* XLIV (1938), 1-39, 213-
225, 645-674. See also the invaluable discussion of these works by M. J. Congar,
O.P., in *Bulletin Thomiste,* V. n. 8, 490-
505. M. D. Chenu, O.P., *Introduction à
l'étude de saint Thomas d'Aquin,* Paris,
J. Vrin, 1950. G. F. Van Ackezen, S.J.
Sacra doctrina, with an Introduction by
M. J. Congar, O.P., Romae, Catholic
Book Agency, 1952.

[18] Located in its proper place in the
life of the Christian Doctor, the knowledge of nature has the appearance of a
contemplation of the divine effects which,
in turn, is a preparation for the contemplation of divine truth. *S T*, II-II, 180, 4.

[19] The expression *philosophie chrétienne*
is used by Father Touron who had such
a fine feeling for Thomistic thought. See
his *La Vie de Saint Thomas d'Aquin,* p.
450. It was a current expression in the
early nineteenth century, and is tucked
away in the full title of the encyclical
Aeternae Patris which runs: *De Philosophia Christiana ad mentem sancti Thomae
Aquinatis doctoris Angelici in scholis
catholicis instauranda* in the text printed
in *S. Thomae Aquinatis Summa Theologica,* Romae, Forzani, 1894, VI, 425-443.
E. Gilson, *The Church Speaks to the
Modern World,* A Doubleday Image Book,
1954, 23-54.

[20] On the meaning of the phrase, see my
Christianisme et philosophie, Paris, Vrin,
1936. The basic idea in this book is that
the phrase "Christian philosophy" ex-

presses a theological notion of a reality
observable in history; see pp. 117-119.
On the history of this controversy, see
the general work of Bernard Baudoux,
O.F.M., "Quaestio de Philosophia Chris-
tiana" in *Antonianum* XI (1936), 486-
552; and the critical note of A. R. Motte,
O.P., "Le Problème de la philosophie
Chrétienne," in *Bulletin Thomiste,* V (no.
3-4), 230-255; and the remarks of O. N.
Derisi in *Concepto de la filosfia cristiana,*
Buenos Aires, 1935.

[21] Cf. M. D. Chenu, O.P., "Ratio superior et inferior. Un cas de philosophie
chretienne," in *Revue des sciences philosophiques et théologiques,* XXIX (1940),
84-89.

[22] Particularly in the *Contra Gentiles*
where books I to III (which take us as
far as the doctrine of grace) lay claim
to a purely philosophical method ("secundum quod ad cognitionem divinorum
naturalis ratio per creaturas pervenire
potest." *C G* 4, 1) but follows a theological order: *C G* 2, 4, 5.

[23] The term "theology" meaning science
of revelation seems to go back to Abe-
lard; see Jacques Rivière, "Theologia,"
Revue des sciences religieuses, XVI
(1936), 47-57. St. Thomas uses it from
time to time, but he prefers *sacra doctrina,* which means "holy teaching." *Sacra scriptura* (Holy scripture) comes to
be the equivalent of *sacra doctrina* because "holy teaching" is that which deals
with sacred scripture. For the distinctions between and definitions of these
terms, see the remarks of Father M. J.
Congar in *Bulletin Thomiste,* XLV
(1939), 495-503. On the origin of the
expression "natural theology," see St.
Augustine, *De Civitate Dei,* VI, 5. 1; P L
41, col. 180-181.

[24] Cf. J. F. Bonnefoy, *op. cit.,* pp. 19-
20. The author warns us that Scholastic
terms in *-abilis, -ibilis,* "are not always
rendered exactly by our -able, -ible," p.
19. This may well be. But the question
which concerns us here is whether *Fr.*
"revelable," Eng. "revealable" correctly
translate the *revelabile* of St. Thomas.
The only important parallel text cited
which seems to point to the opposite
meaning is *S T* II-II, 2, 6: "Explicatio
credendorum fit per revelationem divinam: credibilia enim naturalem rationem

excedunt." On this Bonnefoy remarks: "The proof would be equivocal unless *credibilia* were here a synonym of *credenda*." This is quite true. But the fact that *credibilia* is a synonym of *credenda* here does not prove that it is so elsewhere, that is in another context. Moreover, this text is somewhat richer than we have been given to understand. The question has been raised whether all the faithful are equally bound to have explicit faith. St. Thomas replies that "the exposition of what is to be believed is made through divine revelation. *Credibilia* are beyond natural reason. However, divine revelation comes in orderly fashion through superiors to inferiors." This is the case with the angels, *ut patet per Dionysium.* "Thus, and for a similar reason, the exposition of faith comes to inferior men from their superiors. . . . Superior men, on whom it falls to instruct others, are thus bound to have a more complete knowledge of what must be believed, and must believe it more explicitly." From this we see that St. Thomas integrates theological *explicatio* with divine *revelatio* which is still active all the while the theologian is struggling to set it forth. Next, we see that St. Thomas is clearly speaking about the theological exposition of *credibilia,* the proper object of *fides explicita.* The *credibilia* in question are therefore the very statements in which Christian dogma is set forth. The question is thus reduced to asking whether all Christians have to be as well informed about dogma as the theologians. Father Bonnefoy adds that St. Thomas "has used, it must be admitted, *revelabile* rather than *revelatum* to indicate a slight difference of meaning." p. 19. This is all we really need. The slight difference of meaning is exactly the same as that which distinguishes the "revealable" from the "revealed."

[25] See below, ch. 4, p. 93.

[26] From the abstract point of view, concepts are mutually exclusive as are the essences they represent. From the concrete point of view, diverse essences can enter into the composition of one and the same object without destroying its unity. See the very important text of St. Thomas, *In Boet. de Hebdomadibus,* c. II, in *Opuscula omnia,* P. Mandonnet, ed., I, 173-174.

[27] Let us remember that the question of how we are to distinguish Scripture from theology taken as the science of faith belongs to the theologian's province. The question whether St. Thomas himself distinguished between the *revelatum* as the proper object of divine faith and the *revelabile* as proper object of theology belongs to the province of the historian of theology. (Cf. J. F. Bonnefoy, *op. cit.,* pp. 19-20.) The only question we have to deal with for the moment is whether St. Thomas's *personal* contribution to philosophy is or is not included in what he himself calls the "revealable." What we are really trying to establish is that it is.

[28] What St. Thomas requires for man's justification is belief in all the articles of faith (*In Epist. ad Rom,* c. 1, 1. 5; Parma, Fiaccadori, 1872, XIII, 14 b), but not belief in the theological science of these articles. As for this science, he thinks of it less as being added to Scripture than as contained in it. Even Scripture is perhaps too wide a term, for St. Thomas finds almost everything in the Epistles of St. Paul and the Book of Psalms. "Quia in utraque scriptura fere tota theologiae continetur doctrina." (*Op. cit.,* Prol. p. 2 b). Sacred teaching, including theology, has no valid existence save as contained in Sacred Scripture. It is when it is cut off from its scriptural source, that the problem of their relations becomes hopelessly complicated.

[29] *S T,* I, 1, 3. The thesis of St. Augustine which has just been under discussion is cited in *S T,* I, 1, 2, *Sed contra.*

[30] *S T,* I, 1, 3, ad 2.

[31] *S T,* I, 1, 2.

[32] On the order followed by the Ancients in their philosophical studies: *Sup. lib. de Causis,* 1. 1, in *Opuscula Omnia,* Mandonnet, ed., I, 195. On this point see E. Gilson, *Thomas Aquinas and Our Colleagues,* The Aquinas Foundation Lecture, Princeton University, Princeton Un. Press, 1953.

[33] Some profess to reconstruct St. Thomas's teaching in the philosophical order proceeding from things to God rather than in the theological order proceeding from God to things fail to take

into consideration the difficulties of such an undertaking. In point of fact, not one of them does so. Those of them who honestly try, either substitute the philosophy of Aristotle for that of St. Thomas, or else, as is happening in our own days, flatly contradict the philosophy which they pretend to teach. To summarize what could not be proved without long and tedious developments, let us say that: *one does miraculously find the theology of Thomas Aquinas at the end of the philosophy of Aristotle.* To isolate his philosophy from his theology is to present the philosophical thought of St. Thomas in an arrangement demanded by a philosophy in which everything is "considered by natural reason without the light of faith." (Descartes, *Principes,* Preface, ed. Adam-Tannery, IX, 4, 1. 19-21 and 5, 1. 13-18). In brief, it is to present a *philosophia ad mentem sancti Thomae* as though it were a *philosophia ad mentem Cartesii.* To discuss the consequences would carry us into the field of dogmatic philosophy which does not concern us here.

³⁴ *C G,* 1, 1. *S T* I, 1. 6.

³⁵ *C G,* 1, 1.

³⁶ *John,* 18:37.

³⁷ *C G,* 1, 1 and 3, 25, ad *Quod est tantum.* Cf. *In II Sent.,* Prol., ed. Mandonnet, II, 1-3.

³⁸ *In IV Met.,* 1. 1, ed. Cathala, n. 533; Turin, Marietti, p. 181. Cf. "ipsaque prima philosophia tota ordinatur ad Dei cognitionem sicut ad ultimum finem, unde et scientia divina nominatur." *C G,* 3, 25, ad *Item, quod est tantum;* A. C. Pegis, *Basic Writings of St. Thomas Aquinas,* II, 45.

³⁹ *C G,* 1, 3.

⁴⁰ *Quaest. disp. de Veritate,* 14, 9, ad Resp and ad 6.

⁴¹ What is more, since every human science receives its principles from a higher science, it accepts these principles on its "faith" in this higher science. Thus the physicist, as physicist, relies on the mathematician, or, if one prefers, music believes arithmetic. Theology itself believes in a higher science, that possessed by God and the saints. It is, therefore, subordinate to a knowledge which transcends all human knowledge—the knowledge of God. In the natural order of knowledge each science is subordinate to that one whose principles it receives, although these principles are rationally knowable by the higher science concerned. Finally, among individuals, the science of one person often has to rely upon the science of another. We usually say that he *knows* something which we don't understand but which we *believe* to be true; *S T,* I, 1, 2. *C G,* 1, 3, Adhuc ex intellectuum gradibus.

⁴² *C G,* 1, 4. St. Thomas's source here is Maimonides as is to be seen from the *De Veritate,* XIV, 10, Cf. P. Synave, "La Révélation des vérités divinies—naturelles d'après saint Thomas d'Aquin," *Mélanges Mandonnet,* Paris, Vrin, 1930, I, 327-370. Note particularly the remark that the same reasons lead the two theologians to two different conclusions. Maimonides proves that conclusions which are beyond the grasp of the common people ought not to be presented them. St. Thomas argues differently, that the common people have a right to metaphysical truths necessary for salvation; since they cannot understand them, they ought to receive them by revelation (p. 348). Cf. Leo Strauss, *Philosophie und Gesetz. Beiträge zum Verstandnis Maimunis und seimer Vorläufer,* Berlin, Schocken, 1935, pp. 87-122.

⁴³ *S T,* I, 1, 1. *De Virtutibus,* art. X.

⁴⁴ *C G,* 1, 5.

⁴⁵ *C G,* 1, 6. *De Veritate,* XIV, 10, ad 11.

⁴⁶ *C G,* 1, 7.

⁴⁷ *De Veritate,* 14, 10, ad 7.

⁴⁹ On this general characteristic of Thomistic thought, see the basic work of Jacques Maritain, *Distinguer pour unir, ou les degrés du savoir,* Paris, Desclée, 1932.

⁵⁰ Even the existence of God, a truth eminently demonstrable in metaphysics, can and ought to be accepted by an act of faith if its demonstrations are not understood. See *S T,* I, 2, 2, and 1.

[51] *C G*, 1, 7. *De Veritate*, 14, 9, ad 2.

[52] See the applications of this principle in *S T*, I, 46, 2 and *C G*, 1, 8 and 2, 38.

[53] *C G*, 1, 1; 1, 2; 1, 9. All this aid which theology seeks in various kinds of human knowledge is embraced in one phrase of St. Thomas: "the other sciences are called her servants." *S T*, I, 1, 5, *Sed Contra*. Hence the well-known expression: *philosophia ancilla theologiae*. St. Thomas does not use the phrase, but its sense is quite old. For its history and significance, see Bernard Baudoux, O.F.M., "Philosophia 'ancilla theologiae,' " *Antonianum*, XII (1937), 293-326.

[54] *C G*, 2, 2, and above all *S T*, 1, 5, ad 2.

[55] *C G*, 2, 4.

[56] "Fidelis autem ex causa prima, ut puta quia sic divinitus est traditum, vel quia hoc in gloriam Dei cedit, vel quia Dei potestas est infinita." *C G*, 2, 4.

[57] *C G*, 2, 4.

[58] On the other hand, see J. LeRohellec

in *Revue thomiste*, XXI, 449; Father Mandonnet in *Bulletin thomiste*, I (1924), 135-136; J. De Tonquédec, *La Critique de la connaissance*, 1929, pp. x-xi. These last objections show clearly where the misunderstanding lies: "To be in a servile manner (sic) attached to this order (*sc.* that of the *Summas*) is certainly not to set forth *philosophy* as St. Thomas conceived it." Granted! But it is certainly to set forth *his philosophy* in the only way he set it forth himself. As for saying that "the order followed in the *Summas* for philosophical developments is external to them: *it does not hold to them*," this is to beg the question.

[59] *S T*, I, 1, ad 2.

[60] *Études de philosophie médiévale*, Strasbourg, 1921, pp. 95-124.

[61] *C G*, 1, 2.

[62] *S T*, I, 1, 5, ad 1; *S T*, I, II, 66, 5, ad 3; *Sup. lib. de Causis*, I in *Opuscula omnia*, ed, Mandonnet, I, 195. Cf. Aristotle, *De Partibus Animalium*, I, 5, translated and commented upon by A. Bremond, S.J., *Le Dilemme aristotélicien*, Paris, Beauchesne, 1933, pp. 14-15.

NOTES TO PART I

CHAPTER 1

[1] On the notion of being as the keystone of the philosophy of St. Thomas, see D. Bañes, O.P., *Scholastica commentaria in primam partem S. Thomae Aquinatis*, ed. Luis Urbano, Madrid-Valencia, 1934; commentary to *S T*, I, 3, 4, pp. 139-160. A practically indispensable starting point. N. Del Prado, O.P., *De Veritate fundamentali philosophiae Christianae*, Fribourg (Switzerland), Societe Saint-Paul, 1911, especially "Introduction," pp. XXVI-XIX and c. I, 1, pp. 7-11. For a general introduction to the problem, see Francesco Olgiati, *L'Anima di san Tommasa, saggio filosofico intorno alla concezione tomista*, Milan, Vita e Pensiero, n.d. Aimé Forest, *La Structure métaphysique du concret selon saint Thomas d'Aquin*, Paris, Vrin, 1931 reprinted 1956. J. Maritain, *A Preface to Metaphysics. Seven Lectures on Being*, New York, 1940, especially pp. 20-24, and 37, n. 13. B. Pruche, *Existentialisme et*

acta d'être, Grenoble, Arthand, 1947. E. Gilson, *Being and Some Philosophers*, Toronto, Pontifical Institute of Mediaeval Studies, 2nd ed., 1952.

[2] St. Thomas must have experienced some misgivings about the expressive strength of the verb *esse* when he had to take it in its full existential sense. In the many texts to be cited in what follows, notice the constant use of the expression *ipsum esse* to emphasize actual existence and not simply being. Cajetan notes this distinction clearly in his *De Ente et Essentia*, ed. M. H. Laurent, Turin, Marietti, 1934, p. 68: "Ad probationem dicitur quod cum esse sit duplex, *quidditativum et existentiae actualis*." St. Thomas seems to have had two reasons for refraining from the technical use of *existere* to designate the act of existing: First, *esse* ought to be especially able to designate this act of existing in that it

is the root from which *ens* and *essentia* are derived. St. Thomas insists on keeping intact the unity of this group of words and the filiation of meanings which it implies. Secondly, *existere* had not in his time the meaning of actual existence which we give it. Nor is it always necessary to translate *ens* with the same rigidity. St. Thomas himself often used *ens* as including the sense of *esse*. But we need almost never translate *esse*, and still less *ipsum esse*, by *ens*, because the use of this infinitive almost always corresponds to the existential meaning in the thought of St. Thomas. The only important exception to this rule of terminology is the case in which St. Thomas preserves the language of Aristotle where it is very clearly outside his own thought, and employs *esse* to designate substance. He is careful moreover to state precisely that in this case the term does not designate *esse* taken absolutely but only *per accidens*. See *S T*, I, 104, 1, and *C G*, II, 21, ad *Adhuc, cum omne quot fit*.

[3] Cf. Cajetan, *De Ente et Essentia*, c. II, 23, p. 42; 24, p. 43; 28, p. 41.—We are maintaining this reference to Cajetan as a monument to a now lost illusion; see our article on "Cajetan et l'existence," *Tijdschrift voor Philosophie*, 15 (1953) 267-286 (note of 1956).

[4] *S T*, I, 3, 5, ad 1. The Thomistic distinction of essence and existence is thus implied in the Thomistic conception and definition of the notion of substance. Strictly speaking, only God is an *ens per se*, that is, as we shall see, a being whose essence is its act-of-being. Also, God is not a substance. The term "substance" always designates an essence, or quiddity, which exists in virtue of act-of-being (*esse*) really distinct from his essence. Thus the definition of a man is to be a substance whose essence is defined as "a rational animal." A man is a substance because he is this essence, just now defined, endowed with an act of being (*esse*), and not existence purely and simply.

[5] "Nam accidentis esse est inesse." *In Metaph.* V, 9, 894; p. 286. It has therefore only a relative and borrowed existence. "Esse enim album non est simpliciter esse, sed secundum quid," *op. cit.*, VII, 1, 1256, p. 377. Accidents are not beings, but the beings of being; "non

dicuntur simpliciter entia, sed entis entia, sicut qualitas et motus." *Op. cit.*, XII, 1, 419, p. 683.

[6] *In Met.* II, 4, 320, p. 109.

[7] "Relinquitur ergo quod nomen essentiae in substantiis compositis significat id quod ex materia et forma componitur." St. Thomas, *De Ente et Essentia*, c. II, ed. M. D. Roland-Gosselin, Paris, Vrin, 1926, p. 8. II. 13-14. Cf. "Essentia in substantiis compositis significat compositum ex materia et forma." Cajetan, *De Ente et Essentia*, 2, 26, p. 45.

[8] *C G*, 2, 54.

[9] *Loc. cit.*, ad *Deinde quia*.

[10] For the history of this distinction, see M. D. Roland-Gosselin, O.P., ed. *Le De Ente et Essentia de St. Thomas d'Aquin*, Paris, Vrin, 1926. The real distinction between essence and being, pp. 137-205.

[11] *C G*, 2, 54.

[12] It is not the same with the pure intellectual substances called angels. Since they are Intelligences, and not souls united to a body, they are simple substances. Therefore in them the composition of act and potency is equally simple. Angels are forms which are by themselves substances. Their only *quo est* is their act-of-existing: "In substantiis autem intellectualbus, quae non sunt ex materia et forma compositae, ut ostensum est (Cf. c. 50 and 51), sed in eis, ipsa forma est substantia subsistens, forma est *quod est*, ipsum autem esse est actus et quo est. Et propter hoc in eis est unica tantum compositio actus et potentiae, quae scilicet est ex substantia et esse, quae a quibusdam dicitur ex *quod est* et *esse;* vel ex *quod est* et *quo est*. In substantiis autem compositis ex materia et forma est duplex compositio actus et potentiae: prima quidem ipsius substantiae, quae componitur ex materia et forma; secunda vero ex ipsa substantia jam composita et esse; quae etiam potest dici ex *quod est* et *esse;* vel ex *quod est* et *quo est*." C G, 2, 54.

[13] "Tertio, quia nec forma est ipsum esse, sed se habent secundum ordinem: comparatur enim forma ad ipsum esse sicut *lux* ad *lucere*, vel *albedo* ad *album*

esse." *C G*, 2, 54. Cf. St. Anselm, *Mono-logium*, 5, P L, 158, 153A, where the comparison is made in almost the same terms but in a diametrically opposite sense. For St. Anselm existence is only a property of essence. On this doctrine and its consequence see below, ch. 2.

[14] "Omne ens, inquantum est ens, est bonum." *S T*, I, 5, 3. "Esse est actualitas omnis formae, vel naturae; non enim bonitas, *vel humanitas* significatur in actu, nisi prout significamus eam esse; oportet igitur, quod *ipsum esse* compare-tur ad essentiam, quae est aliud ab ipso, sicut actus ad potentiam." *S T*, I, 3, 4. "Intantum est autem perfectum unum-quodque, inquantum est in actu: unde manifestum est, quod intantum est ali-quid bonum, inquantum est ens; *esse* enim est actualitas omnis rei." *S T*, I, 5, 1.

[15] "Esse actum quemdam nominat." *C G*, I, 22.

[16] "Nam cum ens dicat proprie esse in actu." *S T*, I, 5, 1, ad 1. It is only in this sense that it is true to say with the Platonists, that God is above *ens*. He is not so as *bonum* or *unum* but only as *esse:* "Causa autem prima secundum Platonicos quidem est supra ens, in quan-tum essentia bonitatis et unitatis, quae est causa prima, excedit etiam ipsum ens separatum . . . sed secundum rei verita-tem causa prima est supra *ens* inquantum est ipsum esse infinitum: ens autem dici-tur id quod finite particysat *esse* et hoc est proportionatum intellectui nostro." *In lib. de Causis,* 7; in Mandonnet, ed. *Opuscula omnia,* I, 230.

[17] *S T*, I, 4, 1, ad 3. Cf. "Hoc quod dico *esse* est inter omnia perfectissimum . . . Unde patet quod hoc quod dico *esse* est actualitas omnium actuum, et propter hoc est perfectio omnium per-fectionum. Nec intelligendum est quod ei quod dico *esse,* aliquid addatur quod sit eo formalius, ipsum determinans sicut ac-tus potentiam; *esse* enim quod hujus-modi est that is, the act-of-existing, of which it is a question here est aliud secundum essentiam ab eo cui additur determinandum." *Quaestio Disputata de Potentia,* 7, 2, ad 9. Note here the vigor of the expression: "The act-of-existing in question is *essentially* other than that

to which it is added for determination."

[18] *In II Sent.,* 1, 1, 4. Mandonnet ed., II, 25.

[19] See what follows in the text just cited, p. 51, n 4: "Nec intelligendum est, quod ei quod dico *esse,* aliquid addatur quod sit eo formalius, ipsum determinans sicut actus potentiam; *esse* enim quod hujusmodi est, est aliud secundum essen-tiam ab eo cui additur determinandum. Nihil autem potest addi ad *esse* quod sit extraneum ab ipso, cum ab eo nihil sit extraneum nisi non ens, quod non potest esse nec forma nec materia. Unde non sic determinatur esse per aliud sicut po-tentia per actum, sed magis sicut actus per potentiam. Nam in definitione for-marum ponuntur propriae materiae loco differentiae, sicut cum dicitur quod anima est actus corporis physici organici. Et per hunc modum *hoc esse ab illo esse* dis-tinguitur, in quantum est talis vel talis naturae." *Quaest. Disp. de Potentia,* 7, 2, ad. 9. Since the act-of-being includes all the real, it necessarily includes its own determination. This is why, while includ-ing it, it is distinguished from it, since inversely, taken in itself, the essence does not include the act-of-being. It does not suffice, then, to say that the possible essence is distinct from the actual es-sence. It is in the actually existing thing itself that the essence remains distinct from the act-of-being. To deny that it is distinct from it, is to affirm that this eminently positive act-of-being (for it truly is so, no matter how modest its degree) is of the same order as that which limits it. In brief, it is to say that act and potency are of the same nature. This St. Thomas refuses to accept.

[20] This text is taken from Djémil Saliba, *Étude sur la métaphysique d'Avicenne,* Paris, Presses Universitaires, 84. Cf., in the same sense, the text from Maimoni-des (*Guide des égarés,* S. Munk, transl., Paris, 1856, I, 230) cited in the same book, 86-87.

[21] Djémil Saliba, *op. cit.,* 82-83 and 85-87. Note nevertheless that, if it is correct to attribute to Avicenna the thesis that existence is an accident of essence, he did not hold it in the naive sense suggested by Averroes' summary of his teaching. What is to be found in Avicenna is the thesis that the essence of composite be-

ings does not include their existence. Moreover, in him as in St. Thomas, the distinction between essence and existence shows the basic absence of necessity in composite substances; the passage of the essence of a possible being to actual existence can only come about through creation. Finally, Avicenna clearly saw that existence was not just one more accident, comparable to the other nine, but that it proceeded in some way from the essence, from the moment that the latter was affected by it. What separates Avicenna from St. Thomas is that, in Avicenna, existence is the ultimate act of essence, whereas it is its prime act (*actus primus*) in the doctrine of St. Thomas Aquinas.—See A. M. Goichon in *La Distinction de l'essence et de l'existence d'après Ibn Sina (Avicenne)*, Paris, Desclée, 1937, esp. 120-121 and 136-145. The most readily accessible texts of Avicenna are in *Avicennae metaphysices compendium,* translated by Nematallah Carame, Rome, Pontifical Institute of Oriental Studies, 1926. See particularly I, 1, 3, 2, pp. 28-29 (where the *one* is posited, with *existence*, as an accident of essence). See also the very curious text, I, 4, 2, 1, pp. 37-38, where there is an excellent statement of the indifferent or neutral character of essence in regard to existence in Avicenna as opposed to the positive ordering of essence to existence in St. Thomas.

[22] J. T. Muckle, C.S.B., *Algazel's Metaphysics, A Medieval Translation*, St. Michael's College, Toronto, 1933, 26, lines 10-11. On the distinction between essence and existence (*anitas* and *quiditas*) see *op. cit.*, 25, ll. 12-25. The text concludes as follows: "Existence (*esse*) is therefore an accident which happens to all quiddities from without, and this is why the first cause is being (*ens*), without a superadded quiddity, as we will show. Being, therefore, is not a genus for any quiddities. This same accident (namely, existence) belongs to the nine [other] predicaments in the same manner. Indeed, each of them has *in se* its own essence by which it is what it is. But accidentality belongs to them in regard to the subjects in which they exist, that is, the name accident belongs to them in regard to their subjects, not according to what they are." For the Latin text, see *op. cit.*, 26. Algazel next extends this same character of accidentality from being to the one. *Ibid.* 26, lines 27-30. On the parallel nature of the two problems of the accidentality of existence and the accidentality of the one, see A. Forest, *La Structure métaphysique du concret,* 39-45.

[23] *De Ente et Essentia,* c. 4; ed. M. D. Roland-Gosselin, 34. The expression *hoc est adveniens extra* here does not signify that the act-of-existing is added to the essence from outside, as in the case of an accident, but that it comes from an efficient cause which transcends essence, and which is therefore exterior to it. This cause is God. Cf. *op. cit.*, 35, lines 6-19. The *esse* caused by God in the essence is as intimate to it as anything can be, since, although it comes from outside, it constitutes it from within.

[24] "Esse enim rei quamvis sit aliud ab ejus essentia, non tamen est intelligendum quod sit aliquod superadditum ad modum accidentis, sed quasi constituitur per principia essentiae. Et ideo hoc nomen *ens,* quod imponitur ab *ipso esse,* significat idem cum nomine quod imponitur ab ipsa essentia." *In IV Metaphys.*, 2, n. 558. The expression *quasi constituitur* clearly indicates that, properly speaking, *esse* is not constituted by the principles of the essence. It is only so constituted in that the *esse* is always that of an *ens,* hence of an essence. What really is constituted by its own principles is, being.

[25] "Esse autem est illud quod est magis intimum cuilibet, et quod profundis omnibus inest, cum sit formale respectu omnium quae in re sunt." *S T,* I, 8, 1.

[26] *Die Epitome der Metaphysik des Averroes,* translated into German by S. Van den Bergh, E. J. Brill, Leiden, 1924, 8-9. Cf. Maimonides' commentary (*Guide des égarés,* transl. S. Munk, I, 231, n. 1), cited by A. Forest in *La Structure métaphysique du concret,* 142-143. On the accidental nature of existence in Maimonides, see L. G. Lévy, *Maimonides,* 2 ed., Paris, Alcan, 1932, 133.

[27] See the text of Averroes' *Metaphysics* as reproduced by A. Forest, *op. cit.*, 143, 2.

[28] The earliest texts of St. Thomas invite us to think that he immediately passed beyond Avicenna's point of view. But his terminology shows that he used him in order to pass beyond him. The number and importance of the quotations

from Avicenna in the *De Ente et Essentia* is remarkable. The *Commentary on the Sentences* calls upon him on this crucial point in I, 8, 1, 1, Solutio.

[29] Whenever St. Thomas proposes this thesis, he usually calls upon Avicenna for support. Besides, Avicenna's "essential" ontology seems to be particularly happy at this point: ". . . primo in intellectu cadit ens, ut Avicenna dicit." (*In I Metaph.*, 2, 46, p. 16.) ". . . est aliquot primum, quod cadit in conceptione intellectus, scilicet hoc quod dico ens . . ." (*op. cit.*, IV, 6, 605, p. 202). "Sic ergo primo in intellectu nostro cadit ens . . ." (*op. cit.*, X, 4, 1998, p. 571). "Ens et non ens, qui primo in consideratione intellectus cadunt . . ." (*op. cit.*, XI, 5, 2211, p. 632).

[30] ". . . hoc nomen *ens* . . . imponitur ab ipso esse." *In Metaph.*, IV, 2, 558, p. 187. Note that in this text the *ipso esse* is referred to the *ipsum esse* and thus to the act-of-existing. "Ens dicitur quasi *esse habens.*" *In Metaph.*, XII, 1, 2419, p. 683. The term *essentia* is similarly connected with the verb *esse:* "quidditatis vero nomen sumitur ex hoc quod diffinitionem significat; sed essentia dicitur secundum quod per eam et in ea ens habet esse." *De Ente et Essentia*, I, Roland-Gosselin ed., p. 4. In order to remove all uncertainty from the mind of the reader, let us get at the exact meaning of this last phrase. It does not mean that *essentia* confers *esse* on substance. It means that in and by the mediation of the *essentia*, the substance receives *esse*. We can be sure of this by comparing what St. Thomas says here of essence with what he said in another place about form: "Invenitur igitur in substantia composita ex materia et forma duplex ordo: unus quidem arius materiae ad formam, alius autem ipsius rei jam compositae ad *esse* participatum. Non enim est *esse* rei neque forma ejus neque materia ipsius, sed aliquid ad eniens rei per formam." *De Substantiis Separatis*, VI, in *Opuscula Omnia*, Mandonnet ed., I, 97.

[31] *In I Sent.*, 1, 19, 5, 1 ad 7, p. 489. On this point, cf. André Marc, S.J., *L'Idée de l'être chez Saint Thomas et dans la scolastique postérieure*, Paris, Beauschesne, 1933, 91-101.

[32] *In I Peri Hermeneias*, 3, 5, 8, Leonine edition, I, p. 35.

[33] "Ideo autem dicit sc. Aristoteles quod hoc verbum Est consignificat compositionem, quia non eam principaliter significat, sed ex consequenti. Significat enim primo illus quod cadit in intellectu per modum actualitatis absolute: nam Est, simpliciter dictum, significat *in actu esse;* et ideo significat per modum verbi. Quia vero actualitas, quam principaliter significat hoc verbum Est, est communiter actualitas omnis formae, vel actus substantialis vel accidentalis, inde est quod cum volumus significare quamcumque formam vel actum actualiter inesse alicui subjecto, significamus illud per hoc verbum Est." *Loc. cit.*, 22, p. 28. Cf. Jacques Maritain, *An Introduction to Logic*, New York, Sheed and Ward, 1937, pp. 51-54.

[34] *In I Peri Hermeneias*, 3, 5, 20, Leonine ed., I, 28.

[35] O. Hamelin, *Le Système d'Aristote*, Paris, Alcan, 1920, 159-160. Consult also the analogous remarks of Waitz and Zeller, p. 150, 1. Aristotle's inability to disengage the very act-of-existing from being probably accounts for the existence of the objection and quandary so judiciously noted and analyzed in A. Bremond, S.J., *Le Dilemme aristotélicien*, IV, 36-40.

[36] *In I Peri Hermeneias*, 3, 5, 20, Leonine ed., I, 28.

[37] J. Maritain, *A Preface to Metaphysics*, p. 44.

[38] J. Maritain, *Les Degrés du Savoir*, p. 551.

[39] See André Marc, S.J., *op. cit.*, 88-89.

[40] Etienne Gilson, *Réalisme thomiste et critique de la connaissance*, Paris, Vrin, 1939, 215-216.

[41] *In Metaph.*, Prooem. p. 2 and IV, 5, 593, p. 199.

[42] Alberto Lepidi, O.P., *De Ente generalissimo prout est aliquid psychologicum, logicum, ontologicum*, Placentiae, Tedeschi, 1881. A perfect example of an entirely "essentialized" Thomist ontology.

[43] For this thesis, see my *The Unity of Philosophical Experience*, N. Y., Scribners, 1937.

CHAPTER 2

[1] *De Verit.*, XIV, 10.

[2] *C G*, I, 11.

[3] For the history of the proofs for the existence of God before St. Thomas, see George Grunwald, *Geschichte der Gottesbeweise im Mittelalter bis zum Ausgang der Hochscholastik*, Münster, 1907. Cl. Baeumker, *Witelo, ein Philosoph und Naturforscher des XIII Jahrhunderts*, Münster, 1908, 286-338. A. Daniels, *Quellenbeiträge und Untersuchungen zur Geschichte der Gottesbeweise im dreizehnten Jahrhundert, mit besonderer Berucksichtigung des Argumentes im Proslogion des hl. Anselm*, Münster i Westf., 1908. R. Arnou, S.J., *De quinque viis sancti Thomae ad demonstrandam Dei existentiam apud antiquos Graecos et Arabes et Judaeos praeformatis vel adumbratis*, Romae, Gregoriana, 1932.

[4] *S T*, I, 2, 1 and *C G*, I, 10.

[5] John Damascene, *De Fide Orthodoxa*, 2 and 3, *P G*, 94, 789 C and 793 C.

[6] *S T*, I, 2, 1, obj. 2 and *C G*, I, 10.

[7] *S T*, I, 2, 1, obj. 3 and *C G*, I, 10.

[8] Alexander of Hales, *Summa Theologica*, I, Quaracchi, 1924: Argument taken from John Damascene, 26, p. 43; from St. Anselm, 26, p. 42; from truth, 25, p. 41, III.

[9] St. Bonaventure, *Opera theologica selecta*, I, *Liber I Sententiarum*, Quaracchi, 1934, dist. 8, p. 1; art 1, 2, pp. 118-121.

[10] Plato, *Sophist*, 244 a.

[11] The provisory definition of being proposed further on in the *Sophist* (247 b): "that which can act or suffer," only indicates how we can recognize the presence of something, of a τι.

[12] Plato, *Sophist*, éd. A. Diès, p. 352, note 1; cf. 242 a, p. 365.

[13] Plato, *Sophist*, 254 a.

[14] Plato, *Sophist*, 257 b.

[15] "Res enim quaelibet, prorsus qualicumque excellentia, si mutabilis est, non vere est: non enim est ibi verum esse, ubi est et non esse." St. Augustine, *In Joannis Evangelium*, 28, 8, 10; *P L* 35, 1680.

[16] "Ecce quod est esse: Principium mutari non potest." *Op. cit.*, 28, 8, 11; *P L* 35, 1682.

[17] St. Augustine, *Epist.* 118, 15; *P L* 33, 439.

[18] Seneca, *Ad Lucilium*, Epist. 59; and St. Augustine, *De Civitate Dei*, 54, 12, 2; *P L* 41, 350.

[19] St. Augustine, *De Trinitate*, 5, 2, 3; *P L* 42, 912. Cf. "cum enim Deus summa essentia sit, hoc est sumne sit, et ideo incommutabilis sit . . ." *De Civitate Dei*, 12, 2; *P L* 41, 350.

[20] St. Anselm, *Proslogion*, 22, *P L* 158, 238. "Quidquid aliquo modo essentialiter est, hoc est totum quod ipsa (*sc.* summa essentia) est." *Monologium*, 17, *P L* 158, 166 C.

[21] For *substantia* see *Proslogion*, 4, *P L* 158, 152 C and 15, *P L* 158, 162 B; 24, *P L* 158, 178. For *natura*, *op. cit.*, 4, *P L* 158, 149 B-C; 5, *P L* 158, 150 B; 15, *P L* 158, 162 B-C; 18, *P L* 158, 167 B.

[22] *Monologium*, 26, *P L* 158, 179.

[23] *Monologium*, 6, *P L* 158, 153 A.

[24] St. Anselm, *Monologium*, 1-4, *P L* 158, 144-150. Cf. *De Veritate*, 1, col. 145 C and 4, col. 148-150.

[25] St. Anselm, *De Veritate*, 13, col. 484-486. Cf. chapter 7: "Est igitur veritas in omnium quae sunt essentia, quia hoc sunt quod in summa veritate sunt." 475 B.

[26] St. Anselm, *Proslogion*, 4, *P L* 158, 229 B.

[27] Richard of St. Victor, *De Trinitate* IV, 11 and 12; *P L* 196, 936-938. Alexander of Hales, *Summa Theologica* I, 349, ed. Quaracchi, 1924, I, 517-518.

[28] From here on, we are usually dealing with texts borrowed from commentaries on the *Sentences* of Peter Lombard. The *Sentences*, Bk. I, distinction 8 contains a precious collection of texts from St. Augustine and St. Jerome in which *Ego sum* of Exodus is interpreted in terms of *essentia* and essential immutability. This no doubt is the proximate source of Alexander, Bonaventure and the disciples of Bonaventure on this important point.

[29] "Si vero intelligatur cum praecisione vel privatione ejus quod est *ab alio,* vel ens mutabile, efficitur *sc.* nomen *essentia* proprium nomen divinae essentialitatis: essentia enim nominat essentialitatem nullo addito." Alexander of Hales, *Summa Theologica,* I, 346, Quaracchi, I, 514.

[30] *Op. cit.,* I, 25, II, Quaracchi, I, 41.

[31] *Op. cit.,* I, 25, III, Quaracchi, I, 41-42. Cf. St. Anselm, *De Veritate* I, *P L* 158, 468-469; and St. Augustine, *Soliloquiorum,* II, 15, 28, *P L* 32, 898. Alexander's editors rightly observe that the *Summa* here only cites St. Augustine *ad sensum,* and refer in addition to *Soliloq.* II, 2, 2, *P L* 32, 886 and II, 17, 31, col. 900.

[32] Alexander of Hales, *Summa Theologica,* I, 25, IV, Quaracchi, I, 42

[33] *Op. cit.,* 26, p. 42.

[34] Etienne Gilson, *The Philosophy of St. Bonaventure,* trans. by Dom. Illtyd Trethowan and F. J. Sheed, New York, 1938; see ch. 3: "The Evidence for God's Existence."

[35] St. Bonaventure, De Mysterio Trinitatis, I, 1, 29; in *Opera Omnia,* ed. Quaracchi, V, 48.

[36] St. Bonaventure, *In I Sent.,* 8, 1, 1, 2; ed. minor, I, 120. The substitution of *melius* for *majus* is hardly a transposition. St. Anselm himself suggested it to St. Bonaventure: "Si enim aliqua mens posset cogitare aliquid *melius* te, ascenderet creature super Creatorem." *Prologion,* III, *P L* 158, 147-148.

[37] St. Thomas observes that what is known to us *per se* becomes immediately known to us through sense. Thus, when we see the whole and the part, we know at once without further search that the whole is greater than the part. *In I Sent.,* 3, 1, 2. It would be difficult to indicate more forcefully the empirical origin of all evidence, however abstract it may be.

[38] St. Thomas Aquinas, *In Sent., ibid;* and *In I Metaph.,* 7, 112, Cathala ed., p. 39.

[39] *In I Sent.,* 3, 1, 2. He is dealing here with Avicenna's *Metaphysics,* chapter 1, Cf. *De Veritate,* X, 12.

[40] *S T,* I, 2, 1 ad 1. *C G,* I, 11 ad 4. *Quaestio Disp. de Veritate,* X, 12 ad 1 and ad 5.

[41] *S T,* I, 2, 1, ad 3.

[42] *S T,* I, 2, 1, ad 2. *C G,* I, 11.

[43] *De Veritate,* X, 12.

[44] *Loc. cit.,* at the beginning of the reply. There is no indication that St. Thomas knew the supporters of this thesis. But see my "Les seize premiers theoremata et la pensée de Duns Scot," in *Archives d'hist. et litt. du Moyen Age,* 1938, p. 55, note 1 and p. 59, note 1.

CHAPTER 3

[1] E. Krebs, *Scholastische Texte,* I, Thomas von Aquin. *Texte zum Gottesbeweis, ausgewahlt und chronlogisch geordnet,* Bonn, 1912, is a handy work. It gathers together in chronological order the texts of the various Thomistic proofs. See J. A. Baisnée S.S., *St. Thomas Aquinas' Proofs of the Existence of God Presented in Their Chronological Order,* Philosophical Studies in Honor of . . . Ignatius Smith O.P., Newman Press, Westminster (Maryland), 1952, pp. 29-64. Gerard Smith S.J., *Natural Theology,* New York, Macmillan, 1951.

[2] *S T,* I, 2, 3.

[3] *Phys.,* VIII, 5, 311, a, 4 and foll. *Metaphysics,* XII, 6, 1071, b, 2 and foll. See on this point E. Rolfes, *Die Gottes-*

beweise bei Thomas von Aquin und Aristoteles, 2 ed., Limburg, 1926, and the texts of Aristotle gathered together and translated into Latin, in R. Arnou, S.J., *De quinque viis sancti Thomae ad demonstrandam Dei existentiam*, pp. 21-46.

⁴ See Baeumker, *Witelo*, p. 322 and foll.

⁵ *Guide*, tr. Munk, II, 29-36. L. G. Lévy, *Maimonide*, p. 126-127. The texts of Maimonides can be found conveniently in Arnou, *op. cit.*, 73-79.

⁶ *S T*, I, 2, 3.

⁷ To be moved is simply to change, whatever kind of change is involved: "Quod autem se aliter habet nunc quam prius, movetur." *C G*, II, 33.

⁸ S. Weber, *Der Gottesbeweis aus der Bewegung bei Thomas von Aquin auf seinem Worthaut untersucht*, Freiburg-i-B, 1902.

⁹ Cf. Aristotle, *Phys.*, VII, 1, 241, b 24-243, 2. See Arnou, pp. 21-25.

¹⁰ We accept the reading *sequitur*, since *non sequitur* seems absolutely unacceptable. On this textual controversy see Grunwald, *op. cit.*, p. 136 and notes, where all the necessary references are to be found. The Leonine edition, XIII, 31, adopts this reading.

¹¹ Cf. Aristotle, *Phys.*, VII, 1, 242, a 14-15.

¹² Cf. Aristotle, *Phys.*, VIII, 4, 255 b 29-256 a.

¹³ Aristotle, *Phys.*, VIII, 5, 257 b 7-12.

¹⁴ Aristotle, *Phys.*, VII, 2, 242 b 5-15.

¹⁵ Aristotle, *Phys.*, VII, 1, 242 a 16-31.

¹⁶ Aristotle, *Phys.*, VI, 7, 237 b 23-238 a 18.

¹⁷ Aristotle, *Phys.*, VIII, 5, 256 a 4-256 b 3.

¹⁸ Aristotle, *Phys.*, VIII, 5, 256 b 3-13.

¹⁹ Maimonides had already used this argument, *Guide*, tr. Munk, II, 36. It

had also been used by Albert the Great, *De caus. et proc. universit.*, I, tr. 1, 7; ed. Jammy, V, 534 b, 535 a. See also Baeumker, *Witelo*, p. 326.

²⁰ Cf. Aristotle, *Phys.*, VIII, 5, 256 b 28-257 a 28.

²¹ Aristotle, *Phys.*, VIII, 5, 258 a b-258 b 9. Cf. *C G*, I, 13, *Quia vero hoc habito*.

²² *C G*, I, 13, *Sed quia Deus*. Cf. Aristotle, *Metaph.*, XI, 7, 1072 a 19-1072 b 13.

²³ *S T*, I, 2, 3.

²⁴ *Compendium Theologiae*, I, 5-41. In the *Contra Gentiles* (I, 13, *Quod autem necesse sit*), St. Thomas only posits the eternity of the first mover which is itself moved, and this from Aristotle's point of view (*secundum suam positionem*). It goes without saying that the first immovable and separate mover is still more necessarily eternal.

²⁵ *C G*, 2, 38.

²⁶ *C G*, 1, 13.

²⁷ St. Thomas is only following Maimonides here. See Levy, *op. cit.*, pp. 125-126.

²⁸ *C G*, 3, 65.

²⁹ *C G*, 2, 21. "Instrument" is the correct technical term to designate an intermediary mover which is both mover and moved: "Est enim ratio instrumenti quod sit movens motum." See also the Commentary on the *Physics*, VIII, 5, 9, where this point is insisted upon: "Et hoc (*scil.* the impossibility of regression to infinity) magis manifestum est in instrumentis quam in mobilibus ordinatis, licet habeat eamdem veritatem, *quia non quilibet consideraret secundum movens esse instrumentum primi*." And the profound remark of St. Thomas which shows the logical basis of the doctrine, *S T*, I II, 1, 4 ad 2.

³⁰ *Compend. Theol.*, 1, 3.

³¹ On this proof consult A. Albrecht, "Das Ursachgesetz und die erste Ursache bei Thomas von Aquin," in *Philosoph. Jahrb.*, 33, 2, 173-182.

[32] *Met.*, II, 2, 994, 1. St. Thomas's II, 2, ed. Cathala, a. 299-300. For the history of this proof, see Baeumker, *Witelo*, 326-335. Cp. S. Van den Bergh, *Die Epitome der Metaphysik des Averroes*, Leiden, 1924, pp. 150-152.

[33] See texts in Baeumker, 328-330.

[34] *Ars fidei*, Prol., *P L* 210, c. 598-600.

[35] *De Causis et Processu Universitatis*, I, 1, 7; ed. Jammy, 5, 534.

[36] Cf. Grunwald, *op. cit.*, 151.

[37] *S T*, I, 2, 3.

[38] A. Audin, "A proposito della dimostrazione tomistica dell'esistenza di Dio, *Rivist. di filosfia neo-scolast.*, IV, 1912, 758-769. See analysis of this article by H. Kirfel, "Gottesbeweis oder Gottesbeweise beim hl. Th. v. Aquin?" *Jahrb. f. Phil. u. spek. Theol.*, 27, 1913, 451-460. J. Owens, "The Conclusion of the *prima via*," *The Modern Schoolman*, 30 (1952/53) 33-53, 109-121, 203-215.

[39] It has even been emphasized, and rightly so, that there is an empirical (in the sense of not being metaphysically necessary) quality in the choice and order of the proofs proposed by St. Thomas. See A. R. Motte, O.P., "a propos des *cinq voies*," *Revue des sciences philosophiques et théologiques*, 37 (1938), 577-582. A. Boehm, "Autour du mystère des *quinquae viae* de Saint Thomas d'Aquin," *Revue des sciences religieuses*, 24 (1950) 217-234. W. Bryar, *St. Thomas and the Existence of God, Three Interpretations*, Chicago, 1951.

[40] *S T*, I, 46, 2, ad 7; and I, 104, 1. Cf. "Quod est secundum aliquam naturam tantum non potest esse simpliciter illius naturae causa. Esset enim sui ipsius causa. Potest autem esse causa illius naturae in hoc, sicut Plato est causa humanae naturae in Socrate, non autem simpliciter, eo quod ipse est creatus in humana natura." *C G*, II, 21.

[41] On this proof see P. Gény, "A propos des preuves thomistes de l'existence de Dieu," *Revue de philosophie*, 31 (1924), 575-601; A. D. Sertillanges, "A propos des preuves de Dieu. La troisième voie thomiste," *Revue de philosophie*, 32 (1925), 319-330; A. D. Sertillanges, "Le

P. Descoqs et la *"tertia via,"* *Revue thomiste*, 9 (1926), 490-502 (cf. P. Descoqs, S.J., in *Archives de Philosophie*, 1926, 490-503. L. Chambat, O.S.B., "La *tertia via* dans saint Thomas et Aristote," *Revue Thomiste*, 10 (1927), 334-338, and the remarks of Ch. V. Héris in *Bulletin Thomiste*, 1928, 317-320. M. Bouyges, S.J., Exégèse de la *tertia via* de Saint Thomas, *Revue de philosophie*, 32 (1932) 113-146. H. Holstein, S.J., "L'origine aristotélicienne de la *tertia via* de Saint Thomas," *Revue philosophique de Louvain*, 48 (1950) 354-370 cf. *Bulletin Thomiste*, 8 (1951) 237-241.

[42] The elements of the proof appear to come from Aristotle, *Met.* IX, 8, 1050 b, 2-20. For Avicenna's demonstration see Nem. Carame, *Avicennae Metaphysices Compendium*, Roma, 1926, 91-111; or J. T. Muckle, *Algazel's Metaphysics*, St. Michael's College, Toronto, 1933, 46-51. On these questions see Carra de Vaux, *Avicenne*, Paris, 1900, 266 and foll., and Djémil Saliba, *Étude sur la métaphysique d'Avicenne*, Paris, 1926, 96-113. What is essential in these texts can be found in R. Arnou, De Quinque viis . . . , 59-68.

[43] See R. Arnou, *op. cit.*, 79-82.

[44] Cf. Baeumker, *Witelo*, 338.

[45] Cf. R. Arnou, *loc. cit.*, or Maimonides, *Guide*, tr. Munk, II, 1, 39 and foll. L. G. Lévy, *Maimonide*, 127-128. E. S. Koplowitz, *Die Abhangigkeit Thomas von Aquins von R. Mose Ben Maimon*, author's home, Mir (prov. Stolpce), Poland, 1935, 36-40.

[46] An Aristotelian conception, according to Baeumker, *Witelo*, 128. See, in L. G. Lévy, *op. cit.*, 128, 1, the explanation given by Maimonides himself when consulted by the translator Ibn Tibbon: "If we concede that writing is possible for the human species, he said, it is necessary that at a given moment there be men who write. To maintain that no man ever wrote nor will write would be to say that writing is an impossibility for the human species."

[47] *S T*, I, 2, 3.

[48] Maimonides, *Guide*, I, 71, tr. Munk, 350.

⁴⁹ On this proof see the studies of R. Joly, *La Preuve de l'existence de Dieu par les degrés de l'être: "Quarta via"* de la Somme théologique. *Sources et exposés*, Gand, 1920. L. Chambat, "La *quarta via* de Saint Thomas," *Revue Thomiste*, 33 (1928), 412-422. Ch. Lemaitre, S.J., "La preuve de l'existence de Dieu par les degrés des êtres," *Nouvelle Revue théologique*, 1927, 331-339 and 436-468, and C. V. Héri's remarks in *Bulletin Thomiste*, 1928, 320-324. O. Bonamartini, "La 'quarta via' di S. Tommaso d'Aquino," *Scuola Cattolica*, 60 (1932) 17-24. P. Muniz, O.P., 'La 'quarta via' di Santo Tomas . . . , *Revista de Philosophia*, 3 (1944) 385-433; 4 (1945) 49-101.

⁵⁰ *Met.*, II, 1, 993 b, 19-31.

⁵¹ *Met.*, IV, 4, *sub fin.* St. Thomas does not appear to have known the fragment of the *De Philosophia* preserved by Simplicius in his commentary on the *De Coelo*, and which contains exactly the same proof which he had himself reconstructed with the help of the Metaphysics (fr. 1476 b, 22-24): "In a general manner, wherever we find the better, we find also the best. Since, among beings, some are better than others, there must be a best, and this is the Divine Being." Simplicius adds that Aristotle borrowed this proof from Plato. This shows that what the first Aristotelianism had kept from Platonism permitted St. Thomas to feel himself to be in agreement with both of these philosophies on this fundamental issue.

⁵² *C G*, I, 13.

⁵³ *Met., loc. cit.*

⁵⁴ *S T*, I, 2, 3.

⁵⁵ *Die Gottesbeweise in der katolischen deutschen Literatur von 1850-1900*, Paderborn, 1910, 77.

⁵⁶ *Geschichte der Gottesbeweise . . . ,* 155.

⁵⁷ T. Pègues, *Commentaire litt. de la Somme théol.*, Toulouse, 1907, I, 105.

⁵⁸ See "Der Gottesbeweis aus den Seinsstufen," *Jahb. f. Phil. und spek. Theol.*, 26 (1912), 454-487.

⁵⁹ E. Rolfes, *Der Gottesbeweis bei Thomas von Aquin und Aristoteles erklart und verteidigt*, Köln, 207 and 222. See his reply to Kirfel's article in *Phil. Jahrb.*, 26 (1913), 146-159.

⁶⁰ *Commentaire*, I, 106.

⁶¹ Kirfel, *op. cit.*, 469.

⁶² Rolfes, *Phil. Jahrb.*, 26 (1913), 147-148.

⁶³ See above, notes 50 and 51. The capital text, *De Potentia*, III, 5, expressly attributes this conception to Aristotle and even makes it the specifically Aristotelian reason for creation: "Secunda ratio est quia, cum aliquid invenitur a pluribus diversimode participatum oportet quod ab eo in quo perfectissime invenitur, attribuatur omnibus illis in quibus imperfectius invenitur . . . Et haec est probatio Philosophi in II *Metaph.*," for the text quoted above. St. Thomas always had the feeling that he was here closely adhering to Plato as closely as his own system and Aristotle's permitted him. Cf. the following note.

⁶⁴ *De Civitate Dei*, VIII, 6; *P L* 41, 231-232. Cf. Plato, *Banquet*, 210 e-211 d.

⁶⁵ Grunwald, *op. cit.*, 157.

⁶⁶ *C G*, I, 28, ad *In unoquoque*, and II, 15 ad *Quod alicui*. Cf. "Quidam autem venerunt in cognitionem Dei, ex dignitate ipsius Dei; et isti fuerunt Platonici. Consideraverunt enim, quod omne illud quod est secundum participationem, reducitur ad aliquid quod sit illud per suam essentiam sicut ad primum et ad summum; sicut omnia ignita per participationem reducuntur ad ignem, qui est per essentiam suam talis. Cum ergo omnia quae sunt, participent esse, et sunt per participationem entia, necesse est esse aliquid in cacumine omnium rerum, quod sit ipsum esse per suam essentiam, idest quod sua essentia sit suum esse; et hoc est Deus, qui est sufficientissima et dignissima et perfectissima causa totius esse, a quo omnia quae sunt, participant esse." *In Joannem evangelistam expositio*, Prologus.

⁶⁷ *De Veritate*, 22, 2, ad 1. This is what permits St. Thomas to give some recognition to the Augustinian proof from the

notion of truth. Cf. *In Joannem evangelistam,* Prologus: "Quidam autem venerunt in cognitionem Dei ex incomprehensibilitate veritatis . . ." But St. Augustine considers this to be the most manifest proof of all because it argues solely from the intrinsic qualities of truth. St. Thomas can only argue from sensible truth, empirically given, because of the care he takes to begin from existences. He necessarily, therefore, considers truth less manifest to the senses than movement. Hence the less prominent rôle of this proof as he uses it. For arguments for and against this form of proof, see M. Cuervo, O.P., "El argumento de *las verdades eternas* segun s. Tomás," Ciencia Tomista, 37 (1928), 18-34; also C. V. Héris, O.P., "La preuve de l'existence de Dieu par les vérités éternelles," *Revue Thomiste,* 10 (1926), 330-341.

[68] *De fide orthodoxa,* I, 3; P G, 94, 795.

[69] *C G,* I, 13; II, 16, ad *Amplius, quorumcumque,* Cf. *In II Phys.,* 4, 7, 8. This for St. Thomas is the classic proof from common sense. It is a kind of "popular" proof. *C G,* III, 38.

[70] *S T,* I, 2, 3. *De Ver.,* V, 1.

[71] St. Thomas himself used this proof, giving it its simplest form, in his *Expositio super Symbolo Apostolorum;* Opusc. 33 in *Opuscula omnia,* ed. Mandonnet, IV, 351-352. The authenticity of this opusculum is generally admitted.

[72] *De Verit.,* V, 2.

[73] On this point see Garrigou-Lagrange, *Dieu, son existence et sa nature,* 3 ed., Paris, 1920, Appendix 1, 760-773. E. Rolfes, "Die Gottesbeweise bei Thomas von Aquin," *Philos. Jahrb.,* 37, 329-338.

[74] A. R. Motte, "A propos des cinq voies," *Revue des sciences phil. et théol.,* 27 (1938) 578-579.

[75] See above, chapter 2, section 2, theologies of Essence.

[76] See above, *ibid.* See also the conclusions of R. Mugnier, *La Théorie du premier moteur et l'évolution de la pensée aristotélicienne,* Paris, Vrin, 1939, 111-122. For the opposite view see R. Jolivet, *Essai sur les rapports entre la pensée grecque et la pensée Chrétienne,* Paris, Vrin, 1931, 34-39. The argument of this book does not in the least weaken the Mugnier's conclusions.

[77] *S T,* I, 2, 3.

[78] *In VI Metaph.,* 1, 1164; ed. Cathala, 354-355.

[79] *In XII Metaph.,* 7, 2534; ed. Cathala, 714-715.

[80] Aristotle, *Metaph.,* XII, 7, 1072 b, 14-30.

[81] *In XII Metaph.,* 7, 2535; ed. Cathala, 715.

[82] The actual commentary on the text on which St. Thomas relies to attribute will to the First Mover does not employ this term (*In XII Metaph.,* 3; Cathala, 717-719). Thus it is in a gloss in the course of his interpretation that St. Thomas uses it (*op. cit.,* 2535, p. 715).

[83] *C G,* II, 6.

[84] We also note that this proof by a first efficient cause, which St. Thomas attributes to Aristotle, is not to be found in the *Metaphysics.* See above, towards the end of section 2.

[85] See above, chap. 1, p.

[86] *Ibid.*

[87] *De ente et essentia,* IV; ed. Roland-Gosselin, p. 35.

[88] *Op. cit.,* V, 37. References to Avicenna, *loc. sit.,* note 1. It is to be observed, however, that in this text St. Thomas does not say that he is making this expression his own.

[89] *De Ente et essentia,* V, p. 38.

[90] *S T,* I, 4, 3.

CHAPTER 4

[1] On the meaning of the expressions from *Exodus* see E. Gilson, *The Spirit of Mediaeval Philosophy*, London, Sheed and Ward, 1936, p. 433, note 9; also the interesting remarks in A. Vincent, *La Religion des judéo-araméens d'Éléphantine*, Paris, Geuthner, 1937, 47-48.

[2] On the agreement of Christian thinkers on this point see *The Spirit of Mediaeval Philosophy*, pp. 51-52, Ch. 3; "Being and the Necessity," pp. 42-63.

[3] St. Augustine, *De civitate Dei*, 8, 11; *PL*, 41, 236.

[4] St. Augustine, *De doctrina christiana*, I, 32, 5; *PL*, 34, 32.

[5] Cf. E. Gilson, *Introduction à l'étude de saint Augustine*, Paris, Vrin, 2 ed., 1943, 88-103.

[6] St. Augustine, *In Joannem Evangelium*; 28, 8, 8-10; *PL*, 35, 1678-1679.

[7] St. Augustine, *De Trinitate*, VII, 5, 10, *PL*, 42, 942. Other texts may be found in M. Schmaus, *Die psychologische Trinitatslehre des hl. Augustinus*, Münster i. W., 1927, 84, 1. In St. Thomas the immutable presence of the divine essence is no longer the first and direct sense of the *Qui est* of *Exodus*. As it concerns time, and as time is "cosignified" by the verb, this meaning is only a "cosignification" of the *Qui est*. Its "signification" is given as *ipsum esse. S T*, I, 13, 11.

[8] *S T*, 1, 3, 1.

[9] *C G*, I, 18, ad *Adhuc, omne compositum*.

[10] *S T*, I, 3, 2. Cf. *C G*, I, 18, ad *Nam in omni composito*.

[11] See above, chapter 1.

[12] *S T*, I, 3, 3. *C G*, I, 21.

[13] *S T*, I, 3, 3, 2 obj.

[14] See A. Forest, "Le Réalisme de Gilbert de Porrée dans le commentaire du *De Hebdomadibus*" *Revue néo-scolastique*

de Philosophie, 36 (1934), 101-110. M. H. Vicaire, "Les Porrétains et l'Avicennisme avant 1215," *Revue des Sciences phil. et théol.*, 26 (1937), 449-482, and especially 460-462.

[15] Boethius, *Quomodo substantiae in eo quod sint, bonae sint* (usually cited as *De Hebdomadibus*); *PL*, 64, 1311 B. Cf. "Omni composito aliud est esse, aliud quod ipsum est," *ibid*. C. On these Platonist sources of Boethius, let me refer to two articles that may well escape most historians of medieval philosophy: P. Courcelle, "Boèce et l'école d'Alexandrie," *Mélanges d'Archéologie et d'Histoire de l'école Française de Rome*, 52 (1935), 185-223; and J. Bidez, "Boèce et Porphyre," *Revue belge de philologie et d'histoire*, 2 (1923), 189-201.

[16] M. H. Vicaire, *op. cit.*, 461.

[17] Boethius, *Quomodo substantiae*, 1311 C.

[18] Boethius, *op. cit.*, 1331 B.

[19] Vicaire, *op. cit.*, 461. Cf. Gilbert de la Porrée, *In librum Boetii de Trinitate*, *PL*, 64, 1268 D; 1269 A.

[20] For this problem, see the article by A. Hayen, "Le Concile de Reims et l'erreur théologique de Gilbert de la Porrée," *Archives d'histoire doctrinale et littéraire du moyen âge*, 1935-1936, 29-102. Note the "Conclusion," 85-90.

[21] Since we cannot here discuss this thorny problem, we are minimizing Hayen's conclusions which themselves seek to avoid all excess. See Hayen, *op. cit.*, 56-60, and particularly, 58, notes 4 and 5.

[22] *C G*, I, 21.

[23] "Unumquodque est per suum esse. Quod igitur non est suum esse non est per se necess est. Deus autem est per se necesse esse; ergo Deus est suum esse." *C G*, I, 22.

[24] See above, p. 88.

[25] "Est igitur Deus suum esse, et non solum sua essentia." *S T*, I, 3, 4. We can reach the same conclusion, beginning from creatures. They *have* the act-of-existing but *are* not it. The cause of their *esse* can only be the *Esse*. Therefore the act-of-existing is God's very essence: *De potentia*, 7, 2.

[26] According to Sertillanges, "St. Thomas formally concedes in the *De ente et essentia* (chapter 6) that God has no essence." (*Le Christianisme et les philosophies*, I, 268.) But actually St. Thomas only says: "inveniuntur aliqui philosophi dicentes quod Deus non habet quidditatem vel essentiam, quia essentia sua non est aliud quam esse suum." St. Thomas explains here in what sense this expression would be true, but he does not seem himself to have used it. But in Avicenna we read: "primus igitur non habet quidditatem." *Met.*, VII, 4, ed. Venice, 1508, 8 99 rl.

[27] It is to be noted that it is the *esse* which absorbs the essence and not *vice versa:* "In Deo autem ipsum esse suum est sua quidditas: et ideo nomen quod sumitur ab esse, proprie nominat ipsum, et est proprium nomen ejus: sicut proprium nomen hominis quod sumitur a quidditate sua." *In I Sent.*, 8, 1, 1, *Solutio*. God is, therefore, more properly called *Qui est* than essentia.

[28] "Quandoque enim significat [sc. ens et esse] essentiam rei, sive actum essendi: quandoque vero significat veritatem propositionis . . . Primo enim modo est idem esse Dei quod est substantia et sicut ejus substantia est ignota, ita et esse. Secundo autem modo scimus quoniam Deus est, quoniam hanc propositionem in intellectu nostro concipimus ex effectibus ipsius." *De Potentia*, 7, 2, ad 1.

[29] *C G*, I, 22.

[30] *C G*, II, 52. The phrase is not absolutely perfect because it seems to indicate that God is composed of *Qui* and *est*. But it is by far the best because it is the simplest which a human understanding can conceive to designate God. The others, *Qui est unus, qui est bonus*, etc. add to composition with *qui*, composition with a third term as well. Cf. *In I Sent.*, 8, 1, 2, ad 3 and ad 4. To say that it is the least imperfect does not mean that it is not proper to God. This name, *qui est*, is His *maxime proprium;* in this absolute sense it belongs to God alone (*S T*, I, 13, 11, *Sed contra*); but it is still not a perfectly simple designation of the *Ipsum esse*. The terms composing it can still be attributed to creatures since it is from them that our intellect has fashioned them.

[31] *S T*, I, 3, 4, ad 2. Cf. *De Potentia*, 7, 2, ad 1.

CHAPTER 5

[1] *Compendium theologiae*, I, 2.—A. Hozwath, O.P., "Der thomistische Gottesbegriff," *Divus Thomas*, Freiburg i. Br., 18 (1940), 141-210. Cf. 18 (1940) 443-496. Ch. Journet, *Connaissance et inconnaissance de Dieu*, Lyons, 1943.

[2] *Ibid.*, I, 36.

[3] *S T*, I, 3, 5. This conclusion proceeds directly from the perfect simplicity of God already established (*S T*, I, 3, 7). It makes it impossible to find in Him the composition of genus and specific difference required for the definition.

[4] *C G*, I, 14.

[5] See chapter 4.

[6] *C G*, I, 28. *S T*, I, 4, 1 and I, 4, 2, ad 2. It goes without saying that even the word "perfect" is inadequate to qualify God. To be perfect is to have been achieved or completely made. Now God is not made, and therefore has not been completely made. Here we are extending the range of the word from what completes itself by a process of becoming to what possesses completeness by full right without ever having gone through a process of becoming. Cf. *C G*, I, 28.

[7] *C G*, I, 28. Cf. *De ente et essentia*, 5, ed. Roland-Gosselin, 37-38.

[8] *S T*, I, 5, 1. The text to which St. Thomas is referring here is *S T*, I, 3, 4. Cf. *C G*, III, 20 ad *Divina enim bonitas*.

[9] *S T*, I, 5, 2, *Sed contra.*

[10] *S T*, I, 5, 2.

[11] *C G*, I, 28.

[12] *Ibid.*, III, 20; *S T*, I, 6, 3.

[13] *Ibid.*, towards the end of the chapter: "Deo vero simpliciter idem est esse et esse bonum simpliciter."

[14] *S T*, I, 7, 1.

[15] *In I Sent.*, 8, 1, 2. Cf. St. Bernard of Clairvaux, *In Cant. Cant.*, IV, 4, *PL*, 183, 798 B.

[16] See above, chapter 1.

[17] *S T*, I, 8, 1. Cf. *In I Sent.*, 37, 1, 1.

[18] *S T*, I, 8, 2.

[19] *S T*, I, 8, 3 and also ad 1.

[20] *S T*, I, 9, 1.

[21] Thus God's immutability is immediately posited, *per viam remotionis* in *C G*, I, 14 end.

[22] *S T*, I, 10, 1.

[23] *S T*, I, 10, 2.

[24] *S T*, I, 11, 1. Note the important ad 1, following this response. St. Thomas distinguishes two kinds of unity: one, quantitative, which is the principle of number, the other metaphysical, which is convertible with *being*. With an historically profound insight, St. Thomas sees in the confusion of these two kinds of unity the origin of two notions which he rejects. Pythagoras and Plato saw that transcendental unity was equivalent to being, but they confused it with numerical unity and concluded that all substances were composed of numbers, themselves composed of units. Avicenna, on the contrary, saw very well that unity of number differed from that of being because substances could be added together, and then the number thus obtained could be subtracted, multiplied or divided. But he confused unity of being with that of number and concluded that the unity of a being was added to it, like an accident. There is a strange parallel between the two notions, the accidentality of number and the accidentality of existence, in relation to substance in the teaching of Avicenna. St. Thomas remarked upon it several times. He, himself, but developed his own principle by reducing the metaphysical and transcendental unity of each being to the undivided character of its act-of-existing.

[25] *S T*, I, 11, 1, ad 3.

[26] *S T*, I, 11, 4. Let us understand here at the same time and for the same reason, one in Himself and unique. For there to be severals gods, God's being taken in itself would have to be divisible, and therefore He would not be one. St. Thomas shows the inconsistency of the hypothesis of a plurality of gods by establishing (*S T*, I, 11, 3) that none of the beings in question would be sufficiently in act in order to be God.

[27] *S T*, I, 12, 12.

[28] *C G*, I, 30. St. Thomas here agrees with the opinion of Dionysius that all names of this kind can be applied to God with regard to what they signify but not with regard to their manner of signifying it.

[29] *C G*, I, 29.

[30] *C G*, I, 31.

[31] *C G*, I, 32; *S T*, I, 13, 5.

[32] *C G*, I, 33, ad *Ex praemissis.*

[33] *C G*, I, 33.

[34] See F. A. Blanche, "Sur le sens de quelques locutions concernant l'analogie dans la langue de saint Thomas d'Aquin," *Revue des sciences philosophiques et théologiques*, 1921, 52-59. B. Desbuts, "La Notion d'analogie d'après saint Thomas d'Aquin," *Annales de Philosophie chrétienne*, 1906, 377-385. B. Landry, *La notion d'analogie chez saint Bonaventure et saint Thomas d'Aquin*, Louvain, 1922. M. T. L. Penido, *Le Rôle de l'analogie en théologie dogmatique*, Paris, Vrin, 1931, 11-78. J. Maritain, *Les Degrés du savoir*, Paris, Desclée de Brouwer, 1932, Annexe II: "De l'analogie," 821-826. L.-B. Geiger, O.P., *La participation dans la philosophie de saint Thomas*,

Paris, 1942. Cornelio Fabro, *La nozione metafisica di partecipazione*, Roma, 1950.

[35] *S T*, I, 13, 5. St. Thomas, as a philosopher, is comforted by Aristotle's example, as a theologian by St. Paul's words, Rom. 1, 20: "Invisibilia Dei per ea quae facta sunt, intellecta conspiciuntur."

[36] *S T*, I, 13, 5.

[37] See A. D. Sertillanges, "Renseignements techniques" after his translation of the *Somme théologique*, Paris, Desclée, 1926, 2, 379-388; and the same author's *Le Christianisme et les Philosophies*, Paris, Aubier, 1939, 268-273, where St. Thomas's position is defined as "an agnosticism of definition." A contrary view is to be found in Jacques Maritain, *Les Degrés du savoir*, Annexe III, "Ce que Dieu est," pp. 827-843.

[38] *S T*, I, 12, 11.

[39] *In Epistolam ad Romanos*, 1, 6; Parma edition, 13, 15.

[40] *Const. Gent.*, I, 30, end of the chapter.

[41] *In Epistolam ad Romanos*, 1, 6; Parma ed., 13, 16. According to St. Thomas, St. Paul might even have said "et divinitas" rather than "et deitas" because "divinitas" signifies participation in God while "deitas" signifies His essence. Moreover, that the expression *bonitas est in Deo* can only be taken as a manner of speaking, can be seen from *C G*, 1, 36, end.

[42] *C G*, 1, 29.

[43] *C G*, 1, 35. *De Potentia*, 7, 6.

[44] *C G*, 1, 36.

[45] *S T*, 1, 13, 12.

[46] *De Potentia*, 7, 5, ad 2.

[47] *De Potentia*, 7, 5. In using this text, on which Jacques Maritain bases his own interpretation (*Les Degrés du savoir*, 832-834), we must keep in mind the exact thesis which St. Thomas is developing, namely, that the divine names signify the substance of God, that is, they designate it as actually being what the names signify. It does not follow from this that these designations give us a positive conception of what the divine substance is.

[48] *S T*, I, 13, 2.

[49] *De Potentia*, 7, 2, ad 1.

[50] *De Potentia, loc. cit.*, ad 11.

[51] *S T*, I, 13, 2, ad *Sed Contra*. Sertillanges says that "He who is . . . is but a name for a creature." Maritain calls this statement "altogether equivocal" (*Les Degrés du savoir*, p. 841). Let us say, rather, provocative, for it is only wrong in that it takes for granted that St. Thomas's teaching is understood. The three words "he who is" are borrowed from common speech. They were fashioned in order to designate everything else except God. Therefore, *quantum ad modum significandi*, the phrase is applicable first of all to creatures. On the other hand, *what* the phrase signifies—existence itself—belongs first of all to God, who is the pure act-of-existing. Maritain himself points out this distinction in his answer to Sertillanges (*S T*, I, 13, 3, and I, 13, 6), when in fact the latter's formula was based upon it. Maritain seems to forget that if, from the time they are first given, the names we attribute to God are creature's names, the concepts corresponding to them in thought remain to the end concepts of creatures. To say that the *id quod*, which in the creature we only know as participation, belongs *per prius*, or by right of priority, to God, is equivalent to saying that what it is in God eludes us. To escape the "agnosticism of quidditative concept" to which some are ill resigned where God is concerned, it is not necessary to seek refuge in a more or less imperfect concept of the divine essence, but in the positive character of affirmative judgments. These start from multiple effects of God and locate, so to speak, the metaphysical position of an essence which we absolutely cannot conceptualize.

[52] *C G*, 1, 44.

[53] *Ibid.*, ad *Ex hoc*.

[54] *S T*, I, 14, 1. *De Veritate*, 2, 1.

[55] *C G*, 1, 45.

[56] *De Veritate*, 2, 2. *C G*, I, 47. *S T*, I, 14, 3.

[57] *C G*, I, 48.

[58] *S T*, I, 14, 5.

[59] *S T*, I, 14, 5 ad 2 and ad 3.

[60] *C G*, I, 50. *S T*, I, 14, 6.

[61] *De Veritate*, 2, 4.

[62] *C G*, I, 63, obj. 1.

[63] *C G*, I, 65, *S T*, I, 14, 11. *De Veritate*, 2, 5.

[64] See Mandonnet, *Siger de Brabant et l'Averroisme latin au XIII siècle*, I, 168; II, 76.

[65] *S T*, I, 14, 9.

[66] *S T*, I, 14, 13. *C G*, I, 67. *De Verit.*, 2, 12.

[67] *S T*, I, 14, 13 ad 1.

[68] Mandonnet, *op. cit.*, I, 164-167; II, 122-124.

[69] *C G*, I, 72.

[70] *S T*, I, 19, 1; cf. *De Verit.*, 23, 1.

[71] *S T*, I, 19, 1. *C G*, I, 73.

[72] *C G*, I, 74. This conclusion also issues directly from the principle that in God *suum esse est suum velle; loc. cit.*, ad Praeterea, principale volitum.

[73] *C G*, I, 75.

[74] *S T*, I, 19, 2.

[75] *C G*, I, 79.

[76] *Ibid.*

[77] *C G*, I, 84.

[78] *C G*, I, 80.

[79] *S T*, I, 19, 3. *C G*, I, 81 and 82.

[80] *C G*, I, 83.

[81] *S T*, I, 19, 5.

[82] *S T*, I, 20, 1.

[83] *Ibid.*, 2.

[84] *Ibid.*, 3.

[85] *Ibid.*, 4.

[86] *C G*, I, 97, ad *Adhuc, vivere*.

[87] *C G*, I, 98. Cf. *S T*, I, 18, 4.

[88] "Cujuslibet enim intellectualis naturae proprium bonum est beatitudo." *C G*, I, 100.

[89] These are what St. Thomas calls *immanent* operations: seeing, knowing, etc., as opposed to *transitive* operations, the effects of which are exterior to the being which is the cause of the operation: building, healing, etc.

[90] *C G*, I, 100 ad *Amplius, illud*.

[91] "Quod per essentiam est, potus est eo quod per participationem dicitur; . . . Deus autem per essentiam suam beatus est, quod mulli alii competere potest. Nihil enim aliud praeter ipsum potest esse summum bonum. . . . ; et sic oportet ut quicumque alius ab ipso beatus est, participative beatus dicatur. Divina igitur beatitudo omnem aliam beatitudinem excedit." *C G*, I, 102.

[92] *De mystica theologia*, I, 1.

[93] *De Veritate*, 2, 1, ad 9.

[94] On this question: J. Durantel, "La notion de la creation dans saint Thomas," *Ann. de philosophie chrétienne*, Feb., Mar., Apr., May, June, 1912; Rohner, "Das Schopfungsproblem bei Moses Maimonides, Albertus Magnus, und Thomas von Aquin," *Beitr. z. Gesch. de Phil. des Mittelalters*, XI, 5 (1913). On the question of the eternity of the world see: Th. Esser, *Die Lehre des heil. Thomas von Aquin über die Moglichkeit einer anfangslosen Schopfung*, Münster, 1895; Jellouschek, "Verteidigung der Moglichkeit einer Anfangslosen Weltschopfung durch Herveus Natalis, Joannes a Neapoli, Gregorius Ariminensis, und Joannes Capreolus," *Jahrb. f. Phil. und spek. Theol.*, XXVI (1911), 155-157 and 325-367; Fr. M. Sladeszek, "Die Auffassung des hl. Thomas von Aquin in seiner Summa

Theologica von der Lehre des Aristoteles uber die Ewigkeit der Welt," *Philos. Jahrbuch,* XXXV, 38-56; A. D. Sertillanges, "L'Idée de création dans saint Thomas d'Aquin," *Rev. de théologie et de philosophie,* Apr. 1907. J. F. Anderson, *The Cause of Being,* St. Louis, 1953.

[95] *De Potentia,* 3, 3. Cf. *S T,* I, 44, 1.

[96] *S T,* I, 45, 1, ad 3.

[97] *De Potentia,* 3, 1, ad 7.

[98] Like the divine *Esse* with which it is identical, the creative act eludes quidditative concepts. It is we who think of it as a sort of causal relation binding God to the creature: "Creatio potest sumi active et passive. Si sumatur active, sic designat Dei actionem, quae est ejus essentia, cum relatione ad creaturam; quae non est realis relatio, sed secundum rationem tantum." *De Potentia,* 3, 3. We shall see, on the contrary, that taken passively, as effect or terminus of the creative act, creation is a real relation or, to be more exact, is the creature itself in its dependence upon God from whom it has being.

[99] "Creatio non est factio quae sit mutatio proprie loquendo, sed est quaedam acceptio esse." *In II Sent.,* 1, 1, 2, ad *Resp.* and ad 2. Cf. *C G,* 2, 17; *De Pot.,* 3, 12; *S T,* I, 45, 2, ad 2 and ad 3.

[100] *S T,* I, 45, 2. It is a question here of *creatio* as a divine act. But the term can be taken as signifying the effects of this act. Thus understood, creation must be defined as an *aliquid,* which brings us back to the ontological dependence of creature upon Creator. To put it in another way, it is the real relation by which the created act-of-existing depends upon the creative act. (Cf. *S T,* I, 45, 3; *De Pot.,* 3, 3.) It is this which St. Thomas calls "creatio passive accepta" (*De Pot.,* 3, 3, ad 2), and which is sometimes called *creatio passiva.* The creature is the terminus of creation as such, and is, as it were, the subject of this real relation to God, *creatio passiva.* It is "Prius ea in esse, sicut subjectum accidente." *S T,* I, 45, 3, ad 3.

[101] *S T,* I, 45, 5. Cf. "Quod aliquid dicatur creatum, hoc magis respicit esse ipsius, quam rationem." *S T,* III, 2, 7, ad 3.

[102] *S T,* I, 45, 6. For Duns Scotus, on the contrary, in whom the ontology of *esse* is overshadowed by that of *ens,* to attach creation to the divine essence would be to think of it as the operation of a *nature,* not as a free act. This is a necessary consequence in a philosophy in which the essence of God is not his pure act of *Esse.* In order to assure the free character of the act of creating, Duns Scotus must locate its root, not in God's essence but in His will. See the criticism of St. Thomas's position in Duns Scotus, *Quaest. quodlib.,* 8, 7, where he clearly has in mind the *Summa Theologiae* (I, 45, 6) of St. Thomas.

[103] *S T,* I, 8, 1.

[104] Cf. Mandonnet, *Siger de Brabant et l'Averroisme latin au XII siècle,* I, 161 and II, 111-112.

[105] Peter Lombard, *Sent.,* IV, 5, 3, Quaracchi ed., 1916, II, 776.

[106] *S T,* I, 45, 5. Cf. *C G,* 2, 21.

[107] *De Pot.,* 3, 4.

[108] *De Pot.,* 3, 4.

[109] *S T,* I, 7, 2.

[110] *S T,* I, 19, 4. *De Pot.,* 3, 10.

[111] *S T,* I, 15, 1.

[112] *S T,* I, 15, 2.

[113] *S T,* I, 15, 2. Cf. *De Verit.,* 3, 1.

[114] *De Verit.,* 3, 5, ad *Sed Contra,* 2. "Sicut sol radios suos emittit ad corporum illuminationem, ita divina bonitas radios suos, id est, participationes sui, diffundit ad rerum creationem." *In II Sent.,* Prol.; *S T,* I, 6, 4. For the phrase cited in the text, see *C G,* 2, 15, ad *Deus secundum hoc.* The term *virtualiter,* to be sure, implies no passivity of the divine substance. It indicates that the divine being contains, by its perfect actuality, the sufficient reason of the analogous being of things. It contains them as the artist's thought contains his works. "Emanatio effluunt formae artificiales in materia, ita etiam ab ideis in mente divina existentibus fluunt omnes formae et virtutes naturales." *II Sent.,* 18, 1, 2.

[115] Let us remember, so as to avoid all equivocation: first, that creatures are "deduced" from God in that they have in Him their exemplar: *omne esse ab eo exempliariter deducitur* (*In de Div. Nom.*, 1, 4), and secondly, that to participate, in Thomistic language, does not mean to be a thing, but rather means not to be it. To participate in God, is not to be God (*S T*, I, 75, 5, ad 1 and ad 5). Here as in all Thomistic ontology, the notion of being is fundamental.

[116] *De Pot.*, 3, 16, ad 24.

[117] *S T*, I, 19, 2.

[118] *De Pot.*, 3, 10, ad 1.

[119] *Ibid.*, ad 6.

[120] *Ibid.*, ad 12.

[121] *De Pot.*, 1, 5. *S T*, I, 25, 5.

[122] *De Pot.*, 3, 16, ad 17.

[123] *S T*, I, 25, 6, ad 3.

[124] *S T*, I, 45, 3, and ad 1. *De Pot.*, 3, 3.

[125] *S T*, I, 19, 5, ad 3. *De Pot.*, 3, 17. This is why the Neo-platonic axiom "bonum est diffusivum sui" ought not to be understood in St. Thomas in the Platonic sense of the efficient causality of the Good, but only in the sense of the final cause: "Bonum dicitur diffusivum sui per modum finis." *I Sent.*, 34, 2 the ad 4 of the only article; *C G*, I, 37, ad *Amplius*. On this point, see the excellent work by J. Peghaire, "L'Axiome *Bonum est diffusivum sui* dans le néoplatonisme et le Thomisme," *Revue de l'Université d'Ottawa*, Jan. 1932, special section, 5-32.

CHAPTER 6

[1] Aristotle, *De generatione et corruptione*, II, 9, 335 b. We are completing the analysis of *S T*, I, 44, 2, with the help of Aristotle's *De generatione*, II, 6 etc. which St. Thomas used in his own work.

[2] Aristotle, *De gen. et corrupt.*, II, 10, 336 a-b; transl. J. Tricot, Paris, Vrin, 1934, p. 141.

[3] *S T*, I, 44, 2. Cf. *De Pot.*, 3, 5, and remarks in *The Spirit of Mediaeval Philosophy*, pp. 68-70.

[4] "Secundus est error Platonis, et Anaxagorae, qui posuerunt mundum factum a Deo, sed ex materia praejacenti, contra quos dictur in Ps. 148: *Mandavit, et creata sunt*, id est ex nihilo facta. Tertius est error Aristotelis, quia posuit numdum a Deo factum non esse, sed ab aeterno fuisse, contra quod dicitur, Gen. 1: *In principio creavit Deus coelum et terram.*" *De articulis fidei* in *Opuscula* ed. Mandonnet, I, 3.

[5] St. Augustine, *De civitate Dei*, 8, 4; *P L*, 41, 228. St. Thomas refers to this text in *De Pot.*, 3, 5. He makes St. Augustine's testimony appear more positive than it actually is. Augustine says: "Fortassis enim . . ." St. Thomas seems to have no doubt that these philosophers are in agreement with Christian teaching on creation: "Cui quidem sententiae etiam catholica fides consentit."

[6] St. Thomas defines creation as an "emanationem totius entis a causa universali." *S T*, I, 45, 1. Elsewhere, in *In VIII Phys.*, 1, 2, 5 (Leonine ed., 1, 368), he asserts that Plato and Aristotle "pervenerunt ad cognoscendum principium totius esse." He even goes so far as to say that, according to Aristotle, even what *esse* prime matter has, derives "a primo essendi principio, quod est maxime ens. Non igitur necesse est praesupponi aliquid ejus actioni, quod non sit ab eo productum" (*loc. cit.*, 1, 2, 4, p. 367). Thirdly, we have just seen (*De articulis fidei, Opuscula*, 1, 3) that Aristotle "posuit mundum a Deo factum non esse." It is difficult to reconcile these texts even granting a development in St. Thomas's thinking on this point, because the respective dates of the *Summa* and the *Commentary on the Physics* are uncertain. They can be brought into agreement, if we remember that *esse* has both a limited meaning and a broad one. Its strict and properly Thomistic meaning is "to exist." Its broader, and Aristotelian meaning, is to indicate substantial being. Now St. Thomas always gave Aristotle (and Plato) credit for recognizing a cause *totius esse*, understood in the sense of total substantial being, that is,

of complete composite including matter and form (Cf. *S T*, I, 45, 1). In this sense the celestial bodies are *causae essendi* for the lower substances which they produce, each according to its species (*S T*, I, 104, 1: "Sed aliquando effectus . . ."). But St. Thomas never admitted that the cause in virtue of which a substance exists as substance was *ipso facto* a *causa essendi simpliciter* (*C G*, 2, 21). Thus he could say, without contradicting himself, both that Aristotle came to acknowledge a first *causa totius esse*, in the sense of substantial being, and also that he never came to accept the notion of a God who was a creator, that is, cause of existential being.

⁷ See Chapter 2, section 2, pp. 48-54, and Chapter 4, pp. 84-88.

⁸ See E. Gilson, *Introduction à l'étude de saint Augustin*, 2 ed., 287-288.

⁹ St. Augustine, *Confessions*, 11, 5, 7. The French text used was that of de Labriolle. See this translation II, 301 and II, 300.

¹⁰ A. Gardeil, O.P., *La Structure de l'âme et l'expérience mystique*, Paris, Gabalda, 1927, II, 313-325.

¹¹ St. Augustine, *De Genesi ad litteram*, 5, 5, 14; *P L* 34, 326.

¹² St. Augustine, *Confessions*, 9, 3, 5.

¹³ St. Augustine, *Sermo VII*, 7; *P L* 38, 66. Cf. *De Civitate Dei*, 12, 2; *P L* 41, 350. *De Trinitate*, 5, 2, 3; *P L* 42, 912.

¹⁴ St. Augustine, *Confessions*, 1, 6, 10, Labriolle ed., 1, 9. Cf. 7, 15, 21, p. 165. On St. Augustine's difficulty in thinking of history as a function of Platonism, see Guitton, *Le temps et l'éternité chez Plotin et saint Augustin*, Paris, Bowin, 1933, 322, at 3.

¹⁵ *Confessions*, 3, 6, 11, Labriolle, 1, 54.

¹⁶ *Op. cit.*, 1, 2, 2, Labriolle, 1, 4. The last words refer to Romans, 11, 36.

¹⁷ St. Augustine certainly was deeply aware of the intimate presence of God. The problem here is rather different. Had St. Augustine, as a philosopher, the tools to think about a presence of which he was so profoundly aware? It might be shown, perhaps, that the intense pathos of the *Confessions* comes, in part at least, from the anxiety experienced by a soul which felt the divine presence within it and yet was quite unable to know that it could actually be there. Such is indicated by that celebrated reaching for God in Book 10 which concludes as follows: "Ubi ergo te inveni, ut discerem te, nisi in te supra me" (10, 26, 37); and in the no less celebrated "ecstasy at Ostia" (9, 10, 25), that veritable fore-taste of the beatific vision. Despite appearances, the Thomistic immanence of the *Esse* in beings is more penetrating than that of the interior Master in the disciple, which St. Augustine so magnificently describes. Once again let us recall that we are here dealing exclusively with the technical comparison of two solutions of the same philosophical problem. What Thomas and Augustine knew as philosophers could never match what they knew as saints.

¹⁸ St. Augustine, *Enarratio in Ps.*, 101, 10; *P L* 37, 1331. In St. Augustine's Trinity, eternity is appropriated to the Father: "O aeterna veritas et vera caritas et cara aeternitas !" *Confessions*, 7, 10, 16. Cf. St. Bernard, *De Consideratione*, 5, 6. When St. Bernard in his turn invokes the text of *Exodus*, he adds: "Nil competentius aeternitati, quae Deus est."

¹⁹ *S T*, I, 13, 11, end.

²⁰ For a study of this problem, see J. Durantel, *Saint Thomas et le Pseudo-Denis*, Paris, Alcan, 1919. He makes a useful collection of the texts of Dionysius used by St. Thomas and of the interpretation he proposes for them.

²¹ The *Corpus Dionysiacum* is made up of a number of works of uncertain date. Sometimes they have been placed in the 3rd Century, sometimes ascribed to a writer of the 5th or early 6th Century. See my *History of Christian Philosophy . . .*, p. 597, note 45.

²² Dionysius the Areopagite, *De divinis nominibus*, 1; transl. by John Scotus Erigena, *P L* 122, 1113 C and 5, *P L* 122, 1148 A-B. Cf. Hilduin's translation of Dionysius in G. Thery, *Études Dionysiennes, II, Hilduin traducteur de Denys*, Paris, Vrin, 1937, 168, 18-20.

[23] Dionysius, *De divinis nominibus,* 5; *P L* 122, 1148 B and 1149 A-B.

[24] *Op. cit.,* 4; *P L* 122, 1128 D-1129 A. Cf. 12, *P L* 122, 1169 B-D.

[25] *Op. cit.,* 4; *P L* 122, 1130 A.

[26] *Op. cit.,* 1; *P L* 122, 1117 B. Cf. 1119-1120.

[27] *Op. cit.,* 5; *P L* 122, 1147 A.

[28] *Op. cit.,* 5; *P L* 122, 1148 A-B. Cf. 1150 A and 1151 A.

[29] *Op. cit.,* 5; *P L* 122, 1148 C-A.

[30] *Op. cit.,* 1147 A.

[31] *Op. cit.,* 5; *P L* 122, 1148 D-1149 A. This text follows from others, in which God is posited, with a remarkable vigor as a *nondum,* (1148 A), which because it does not exist itself is the being of all that exists; in brief, a God who, as principle and cause of being, transcends it (1148 B).

[32] St. Thomas Aquinas, *In II Sent.,* 3, Divisio primae partus textus; Mandonnet ed., 1, 88.

[33] J. Durantel, *S. Thomas et le Pseudo-Denis,* 188. Here the very text of the quotation made in the *In Boetium de Trinitate,* 1, 2, has been corrected in the Thomistic sense. Thus it reads: "cognoscitur (Deus) ut omnium causa, ex excessu et ablatione." The same correction is in *Opuscula omnia,* Mandonnet ed., 2, 532.

[34] Dionysius, *De divinis nominibus,* 7. Erigena's translation reads: "redeundum, omnium ablatione et eminentia, in omnium causa." *P L* 122, 1155 B.

[35] *Op. cit.,* 7; in St. Thomas's Commentary, *Opuscula omnia,* Mandonnet ed., 2, 532.

[36] St. Thomas is generally quite careful to handle Dionysius tactfully, e.g., *S T,* I, 13, 3, ad 2. But he does stand up to him when the Christian notion of God is at stake. Here is an interesting case: "Praeterea, intellectus creatus non est cognoscitivus nisi existentium. Primum enim, quod cadit in apprehensione intel-lectus est ens; sed Deus non est existens, sed supra existentia, ut dicit Dionysius; ergo non est intelligibilis, sed est supra omnem intellectum.—Ad tertium dicendum, quod Deus non sic dicitur non existens, quasi nullo modo sit existens, sed quia est supra omne existens, inquantum est ipsum esse. Unde ex hoc non sequitur, quod nullo modo possit cognosci, sed quod omnem cognitionem excedat, quod est ipsum non comprehendi." *S T,* I, 12, 1, ad 3. It is to be noted that the *Respondeo* of this same article is aimed at, or at least replies to the teaching of John Scotus Erigena that it is impossible to see the divine essence, even in the beatific vision.

[37] Anxious to retain some knowledge of the divine essence, one of St. Thomas's most profound interpreters cites him as follows: "Essentiam Dei in hac vita cognoscere non possumus *secundum quod in se est;* sed COGNOSCIMUS EAM *secundum quod repraesentatur in perfectionibus creaturarum*" (*S T,* I, 13, 2, ad 3). (Jacques Maritain, *Les Degrés du savoir,* p. 836.) Italics and capitals belong, of course, to Maritain. A different emphasis is not impossible. But no typographical artifice can alter the meaning of a well-turned phrase. Taking it without emphasis of any kind, we find that St. Thomas says two things: 1. that we do not know God's essence according as it is in itself; 2. that we do know it according as it is represented by the perfections of creatures. Not to know God's essence according as it is in itself, is not to know it in itself. St. Thomas is therefore repeating here what he says elsewhere; that in itself we do not know it at all. To know it as it is represented in the perfections of creatures is still only to use our concepts of creatures to represent God. In what do these concepts represent God's essence? In nothing. We must not transform into any concept whatsoever of God's essence, knowledge made from judgments which affirm that *what things are, God is,* because that *pre-exists* in Him, but *secundum modum altiorem.* We affirm this eminent mode of existing, but it eludes us. And we must know it if we are to know the essence of God at all.

[38] *S T,* I, 22, 13.

[39] *S T,* I, 13, 7, and ad 1. It is a type of unilateral relation that is being dealt

with here. We have to affirm that these exist, but we can't form a concept of them. This is true of creation, and infinitely more true of the Incarnation, that miracle of miracles towards which all others are ordained (*C G*, 4, 27). The Redemption is only cited here as a particularly striking example of the reduction of an event to the divine Act-of-Existing as to its cause.

PART II

CHAPTER 1

[1] *De Pot.*, 3, 17.

[2] *Topic* 1, 9.

[3] *S T*, I, 46, 1.

[4] Horten, *Die Hauptlehren des Averroes*, 112. Mandonnet, *Siger de Brabant* etc., I, 168-172.

[5] *S T*, I, 46, 1, 9. *C G*, 2, 32, ad *Posita causa. De Pot.*, 3, 17, 4.

[6] *C G*, 2, 32, ad *Effectus procedit. De Pot.*, 3, 17, 26.

[7] *S T*, I, 46, 1, 10.

[8] *S T*, I, 46, 1, 2. *De Pot.*, 3, 17, 2.

[9] *S T*, I, 46, 1, 5. *C G*, 2, 33, ad *Quandoque aliquid*.

[10] Aristotle, *Phys.*, 8, 1; Leonine ed. 2, 365.

[11] Aristotle, *De coelo et mundo*, 1, 12, 26; Leonine ed. 3, 103.

[12] *Gen.*, 1, 1.

[13] *De Pot.*, 3, 17. *S T*, I, 46, 1. *C G*, 2, 35-37.

[14] St. Bonaventure, *Sent. II*, 1, 1, 1, 2, ad *Sed ad oppositum*, 5.

[15] *S T*, I, 46, 1, ad 8. *C G*, 2, 38, ad *Quod autem* and *De Aeternitate mundi contra murmurantes*, sub fin. For the doctrinal milieu in which this controversy was born, see M. Gierens, S.J., *Controversia de aeternitate mundi*, Romae, Pont. Univ. Greg., 1933. W. J. Dwyer, C.S.B., *L'Opuscule de Siger de Brabant De aeternitate mundi*. Introduction, critique et texte, Louvain, Inst. Sup. de Philos., 1937. J. de Blic, "A propos de l'éternité du monde," *Bulletin de littérature ecclesiastique*, 47 (1946), 162-170.

[16] St. Bonaventure, *loc. cit.*, propos. 3.

[17] *C G*, 2, 38, ad *Quod etiam tertio. S T*, I, 46, 2, ad 6.

[18] St. Bonaventure, *loc. cit.*, propos. 1.

[19] *C G*, 2, 38, ad *Quod etiam quarto*.

[20] *C G*, 2, 38, ad *Has autem rationes*.

[21] *S T*, I, 46, 2.

[22] *De Pot.*, 3, 14.

[23] L. G. Lévy, *Maimonide*, 71-72.

[24] Lévy, *op. cit.*, 72-74.

[25] *De Pot.*, 3, 16. See Djémil Saliba, *Étude sur la métaphysique d'Avicenne*, Paris, Presses Universitaires, 1926, "La théorie de l'émanation," 125-146.

[26] *De Pot.*, ad loc., *S T*, I, 47, 1.

[27] *C G*, 2, 45, ad *Quum enim, S T*, I, 47, 1.

[28] Let us recall here that essence circumscribes the proper fulness of each act-of-existing. Each variation, increasing or decreasing this act, implies *ipso facto* a correlative variation of the essence. This is expressed by the symbolic expression: Forms vary like numbers. See above, Part 1, ch. 1. pp. 36-37.

[29] *S T*, I, 47, 2.

[30] *Ibid*, ad 1.

[31] *De Pot.*, 3, 16. St. Thomas brings up the much debated question of the plurality of worlds. He settles it by denying that God did produce several worlds. *S T*, I, 47, 3. But the principle upon which he based his reply imposes no definite limit upon creation. All that he says is that the divine work possesses

unity of order. Whatever the size or number of the astronomical systems created, they still form but one world embraced by the unity of divine order.

[32] *S T*, I, 48, 2.

[33] *In Lib. de div. Nom.*, 1, 1, in *Opuscula*, Mandonnet ed., 2, 232.

[34] *C G*, 4, 7, ad *Nulla creatura*. We keep the term "exodus" deliberately, over the objection of some critics who detect in it a distressingly pantheistic flavor. It is authentically Thomistic: "aliter dicendum est de productione unius creaturae, et aliter de *exitu* totius universi a Deo." *De Pot.*, 3, 47. St. Thomas freely used the terms *deductio, existus, emanatio,* to describe the procession of creatures from God. There is no inconvenience in keeping his language, provided, of course, that we keep his meaning.

[35] *De div. Nom.*, 4, in *Opuscula*, Mandonnet ed., 2, 469. Cf. Durantel, *S.*

Thomas et le Pseudo-Denis, 174, where the various forms of this adage are brought together.

[36] *S T*, I, 48, 1.

[37] *C G*, 3, 6, ad *Ut autem.*

[38] *C G*, 3, 7, ad *Mala enim.* Cf. *De Malo*, 1, 1. *De Pot.*, 3, 6.

[39] *C G*, 3, 11. *S T*, I, 48, 3 and ad 2. *De Malo*, 1, 2.

[40] *C G*, 3, 12, ad *Patet autem. S T*, I, 48.

[41] *C G*, 3, 13, ad *Quidquid enim.*

[42] *S T*, I, 49, 1.

[43] *S T*, I, 49, 2.

[44] *Ibid*, ad 2. *C G*, 3, 10, ad *Ex parte quidem.*

CHAPTER 2

[1] See A. Schmid, "Die peripatetisch-scholastische Lehre von den Gestirngeistern," *Athenaeum, Philosophische Zeitschrift,* hersg. von J. von Froschammer, Bd I, Munchen, 1862, 549-589. J. Durantel, "La notion de la création dans saint Thomas," *Ann. de philosophie chrétienne,* Avril, 1912, 1-32. W. Schlossinger, "Die Stellung der Engel in der Schopfung," *Jahrb. f. Phil. u. spek. Theol.,* XXV, 451-485 and XXVII, 81-117. By the same author, "Das Verhaltnis der *Engelwelt zur sichtbaren Schopfung, ibid.,* XXVII, 158-208. The two latter studies consider the problem for itself. They are useful, however, because their conclusions are generally based on the authentic teaching of Thomas Aquinas. The richest source on this question remains the second part of C. Baeumker, *Witelo,* 523-606: "Die Intelligenzen et Die Intelligenzenlehre der Schrift: *De Intelligentiis.*"

[2] Schmid, *op. cit.,* 594 and foll. Baeumker, *op. cit.,* 523 and foll.

[3] This is not certain and scholars differ about it. It is easier to understand Aristotle's world if stars therein are animate. But the texts concerned are all obscure.

Cf. O. Hamelin, *Le Système d'Aristote,* Paris, Alcan, 1920.

[4] Cf. E. Bréhier, *Les Idées philosophiques et religieuses de Philon d'Alexandrie,* Paris, Vrin, 1925, 126-133.

[5] On these different issues, see Baeumker, *Witelo,* 531-532.

[6] For Dionysius' dependence upon the neo-platonists, see H. Koch, *Pseudo-Dionysius Areopagita in seinen Beziehungen zum Neuplatonismus und Mysterienwesen, Eine litterarhistorische Untersuchung,* Mainz, 1900; H. P. Muller, Dionysios, Proklos, Plotinos, Beitrage, XX, 3-4, Münster, 1918. On the later influence of Dionysius, see J. Stiglmayr, *Das Aufkommen der pseudo-dionysischen Schriften und ihr Eindringen in die christliche Litterartur bis zum Laterankonzil,* Feldkirch, 1895.

[7] Cf. J. Turmel, "Histoire de l'angélologie des temps apostoliques à la fin du Ve siècle," *Rev. d'histoire et de littérature religieuses,* III (1898) and IV (1899); esp. III, 407-434.

[8] *De coel. hier.*, 1 and 7-10.

[9] For copious references and texts, see Baeumker, *Witelo*, 537-544.

[10] *Ps.* 103, 4.

[11] *S T*, I, 50, 1.

[12] *C G*, 2, 91, ad *Natura superior.*

[13] *De spiritualibus creaturis*, 1, 5.

[14] *Op. cit.*, 1, 1, 3d. See St. Bonaventure, *In II Sent.*, 3, 1, 1, 1, ad *Utrum angelus.*

[15] *Op. cit.*, 1, 1, 16. Cf. St. Bonaventure, *ibid.*, ad *Item hoc ipsum ostenditur.*

[16] *Op. cit.*, 1, 1, 17; *S T*, I, 50, 2, 4. In St. Bonaventure, *ibid.* Cf. E. Gilson, *The Philosophy of St. Bonaventure*, New York, 1938, pp. 205-209.

[17] *S T*, I, 50, 2. *De spir. creat.*, 1, 1.

[18] *De spir. creat.*, *ibid.*, ad 3.

[19] *Ibid.*, ad 16.

[20] *Ibid.*, ad *Resp. S T*, I, 50, 2, ad 3. *C G*, 2, 50, ad *Formae contrariorum*, 51 and 52. *Quodlibet*, 9, 4, 1.

[21] St. Bonaventure, *Sent.* II, 3, 1, 1, ad *Item hoc videtur.*

[22] On St. Thomas's agreement with Avicenna on this point and his opposition to most of the doctors, see Baeumker, *Witelo*, 543.

[23] *S T*, I, 50, 4.

[24] *C G*, 2, 93, ad *Id quod est*, and *De spiritualibus creaturis*, 8.

[25] On this distinction, see E. Gilson, *The Spirit of Mediaeval Philosophy*, p. 432, note 8.

[26] Aristotle, *Phys.*, II, 1, 192 b 21-23.

[27] *Op. cit.*, 193 b 6-9.

[28] Physics is, in fact, like the other sciences, the science of a genus of determinate being, that is, of the kind of substance which possesses in itself the principle of its movement and of its rest . . ." Aristotle, *Metaphysics*, IV, 1, 1025 a 18-21. Similarly, we shall see that theology itself is the science of a genus of determinate being: "There are three theoretical sciences: Mathematics, Physics, Theology (φιλοσοφία θεολογική). We call it Theology. Indeed there is no doubt that if the divine is present anywhere, it is in this immovable and separated essence. Science *par excellence* must have as object genus *par excellence*. Thus, the theoretical sciences are the highest of sciences, and Theology the highest of the theoretical sciences." Aristotle, *op. cit.*, IV, 1, 1026 a 18-23.

[29] Etienne Gilson, *The Philosophy of St. Bonaventure*, pp. 207-209. On Ibn Gebirol (Avicebron), considered as the source of this hylomorphism, see St. Thomas Aquinas, *De substantiis separatis*, in *Opuscula*, ed. Mandonnet, I, 82-85.

[30] *S T*, I, 50, 2, ad 3. For the sake of simplicity, we pass over St. Thomas's discussion of the Boethius-inspired thesis which places in the angel a composition of *quo est* and *quod est* (*loc. cit.*). To reduce *esse* to *quo est* in this way is to be confined to the order of essence and not to proceed to that of act-of-existing.

[31] *S T*, I, 50, 3. *C G*, I, 92. *De Potentia*, VI, 6.

[32] On the progressive effort at synthesis on this point to be observed in the thought of St. Thomas, see J. Durantel, "La notion de la création dans saint Thomas," in *Ann. de philosophie chrétienne*, April 1912, 19, n. 2.

[33] *De spirit. creat.*, I, 8, ad 2.

[34] *S T*, I, 108, 3.

[35] *S T*, I, 54, 2 and 3.

[36] *C G*, II, 96.

[37] *S T*, I, 55, 2.

[38] *De Veritate*, VIII, 9. *S T*, I, 55, 2 and ad 1.

[39] *De Veritate*, VIII, 10. *S T*, I, 55, 3.

[40] *De cael. hier.*, c. 7.

⁴¹ *S T*, I, 108, 1.

⁴² *S T*, I, 108, 6.

⁴³ Cf. *Sent.*, IV, 48, 1, 4, 3.

⁴⁴ *C G*, III, 80. *S T*, I, 108, 5 ad 4.

⁴⁵ *S T*, I, 108, 6.

⁴⁶ *S T*, I, 106, 1 and 3.

CHAPTER 3

¹ *S T*, I, 65, 1, Proem.

² *S T*, I, 66, 1, ad 2: "Aerem autem, et ignem non nominat, quia non est ita manifestum rudibus, quibus Moyses loquebatur, hujusmodi esse corpora, sicut manifestum est de terra et aqua." Cf. in the same sense: "Quia Moyses loquebatur rudi populo, qui nihil, nisi corporalia poterat capere . . ." *Ibid.*, 67, 4. "Moyses rudi populo loquebatur, quorum imbecillitati condescendens, illa solum eis proposuit quae manifest sensui apparent . . ." *Ibid.*, 63, 3, 2. "Moyses autem rudi populo condescendens . . ." *Ibid.*, 70, 1, ad 3; and also, 70, 2. The guiding principles of the Thomistic exegesis are as follows: "Primo, quidem, ut veritas Scripturae inconcusse tenatur. Secundo, cum scriptura divina multipliciter exponi possit, quod nulli expositioni aliquis ita praecise inhaereat, ut si certa ratione constiterit hoc esse falsum, quod aliquis sensum Scripturae esse credebat, id nihilominus asserere praesumat, ne Scriptura ex hoc ab infidelibus derideatur, et ne eis via credendi praecludatur." *S T*, I, 68, 1. St. Thomas is here in full agreement with St. Augustine, and expressly claims to have taken this double principle from him: 1. to maintain steadfastly the literal truth of Scripture; 2. not to be so exclusively attached to one of the possible interpretations as to cling to it even when its opposite has been scientifically demonstrated. See Father Synave, O.P., "Le Canon scripturaire de saint Thomas d'Aquin," *Revue Biblique*, 1924, pp. 522-533; also, by the same author: "La Doctrine de saint Thomas d'Aquin sur le sens littéral des Écritures," *Revue Biblique*, 1926, pp. 40-65.

³ *In II Sent.*, 12, 1, 2, Solutio.

⁴ Above the sphere of the fixed stars, the invisible world begins. Naturally, its structure is more Aristotelian: the heaven of waters, or the Crystalline sphere; and the heaven of light, or the Empyrean. *S T*, I, 68, 4.

⁵ See above, p. 122.

⁶ St. Thomas is constantly preoccupied with the Manichaean doctrine which he wishes to refute. This is owing to the development of the doctrine in the Albigensian heresy, a heresy which the Order of St. Dominic fought from the very moment of its birth.

⁷ *S T*, I, 65, 2. Cf. my *The Spirit of Mediaeval Philosophy*, ch. 6: "Christian Optimism," pp. 108-127.

⁸ See above, p. 156.

⁹ Quoniam quoddam potest esse, licet non sit, quoddam vero jam est: illud quod potest esse et non est, dicitur esse potentia; illud autem quod jam est, dicitur esse actu." "De principiis naturae" in *Opuscula*, I, 8 (ed. Mandonnet).

¹⁰ *Ibid.* This absence of form in matter is called *privation*. Thus marble is being in potency, or matter. Its absence of artistic form, is a privation. Its shape as statue is a form.

¹¹ Matter is not a *subjectum*, for it only exists through the determination it receives. Of itself, it is not there in order to receive it. On the contrary, because the *subject* is a substance, it does not owe its being to accidents. Rather, it lends them its being. See above, Part I, ch. 5. Cf. *S T*, I, 66, 1. Note that matter, being in potency, cannot exist apart. However, it is not potentially good but absolutely good, because it is ordained to form. This of itself constitutes it as a good. Thus there is a relationship under which good is more extensive than being. See *C G*, III, 20.

¹² For a purely technical analysis of becoming, see *In III Physic*, I, 2: Leonine ed., II, 104-105.

¹³ St. Thomas accepts Aristotle's classification of the four kinds of causes,

material, formal, efficient, final (*De Principibus naturae*, in *Opuscula*, I, 11). In fact, matter and form are only causes in that they are constitutive elements of being. Matter cannot actualize itself, nor can form impose itself upon matter. Marble does not make a statue of itself. Form does not sculpture itself. For actualization of matter by form, there must be an active principle: "Oportet ergo praeter materiam et formam aliquid principium esse, quod agat; et hoc dicitur causa efficiens, vel movens, vel agens, vel unde est principum motus" (*Ibid.*) Whether Aristotle ever truly got beyond the level of motor cause to efficient causes still requires examination. If not (and see A. Bremond, *Le dilemme aristotélicien*, p. 11 and pp. 50-52), then St. Thomas's notion of the efficient cause must grow out of his analysis of *esse*. In this case, St. Thomas's philosophy of nature must be as far beyond Aristotle's as his natural theology is.

¹⁴ "Hoc vero nomen Causa, importat influxum quemdam ad esse causati." *In V Metaph.*, I, Cathala ed., n. 751, p. 251. This is why the operation of a being (second act) is only an extension of the act which this being is: "Actus autem est duplex: primus et secundus. Actus quidem primum est forma, et integritas rei. Actus autem secundus est operatio." *S T*, I, 48, 5. The expression is not perfect because it does not push out beyond the form to the act-of-existing. In this sense, the classical adage "operatio sequitur esse" is better. Note that we actually know the second act first. A being operates, therefore it acts, it performs an act. It is this that we see. Tracing our way back from there by means of thought to the active energy which causes its act or operation, we locate its origin in the first act-of-being. This act-of-being reaches being by its form and confers *esse* upon it. Thus this first act is posited by a judgment proceeding from its observable effect, operation. See *In IX Metaph.*, lectio 8; ed. Cathala, n. 1861, p. 539.—J. Owens, C.SS.R. "The Causal Proposition —Principle or Conclusion?" *The Modern Schoolman*, XXXII (1955), 159-171, 257-270, 323-339.

¹⁵ To this corresponds the technical distinction between the *causa fiendi* and the *causa essendi*: when man engenders a man independent of himself, he is his

causa fiendi; when the sun engenders light and the light ceases just as soon as the sun disappears, it is its *causa essendi.*

¹⁶ *C G*, II, 25.

¹⁷ *S T*, I, 104, 1.

¹⁸ "Nec aliter res (Deus) in esse conservat, nisi inquantum eis continue influit esse; sicut ergo antequam res essent, potuit eis non communicare esse, et sic eas non facere; ita postquam jam factae sunt, potest eis non influere esse, et sic esse desinerent, quod est eas in nihilum redigere." *S T*, I, 104, 3.

¹⁹ *C G*, III, 66.

²⁰ "Causa autem actionis magis est id cujus virtute agitur, quam etiam illud quod agit, sicut principale agens magis agit quam instrumentum. Deus igitur principalius est causa cujuslibet actionis quam etiam secundae causae agentes." *C G*, III, 67.

²¹ Jeremias, 23, 24. For the text following, see Psalm 138, 8. Cf. *C G*, III, 68. *S T*, I, 8, 1.

²² Here is the order of the chapters in the course of which this rectification takes place: cap. 65, "Quod Deus conservat res in esse"; cap. 66, "Quod nihil dat esse nisi inquantum agit in virtute divina"; cap. 67, "Quod Deus est causa operandi omnibus operantibus"; cap. 68, "Quod Deus est ubique et in omnibus rebus"; cap. 69, "Quod opinione eorum qui rebus naturalibus proprias substrahunt actiones."

²³ "Si enim nulla inferior causa, et maxime corporalis, aliquid operatur, sed Deus operatur in omnibus solus, Deus autem non variatur per hoc, quod operatur in rebus diversis, non sequetur diversus effectus ex diversitate rerum in quibus Deus operatur. Hoc autem ad sensum apparet falsum; non enim ex appositione calidi sequitur infrigidatio, sed calefactio tantum, neque ex semine hominis sequitur generatio nisi hominis; non ergo causalitas effectuum inferiorum est ita attribuenda divinae virtuti, quod substrahatur causalitas inferiorum agentium." *C G*, III, 69.

²⁴ On the Arabian and Latin adversaries

whom St. Thomas opposes here, see Etienne Gilson, "Pourquoi saint Thomas a critiqué saint Augustin," *Arch. d'hist. doctr. et litt. du moyen âge,* I (1926-1927), 5-127. Maurice de Wulf has severely criticized the plan of this article in "L'Augustinisme 'avicennisant,'" *Revue néoscolastique de philosophie,* 1931, p. 15. His reproach falls really on the plan of the *Contra Gentiles,* III, 69, on which the article is but a commentary.

²⁵ *C G,* III, 70.

²⁶ "Patet etiam quod, si res naturalis producat proprium effectum, non est superfluum quod Deus illum producat. Quia res naturalis non producit ipsum, nisi in virtute divina. Neque est superfluum, si Deus per seipsum potest omnes effectus naturales producere, quod per quasdam alias causas producantur. Non enim hoc est ex insufficientia divinae virtutis, sed ex immensitate bonitatis ipsius per quam suam similitudinem rebus communicare voluit, non solum quantum ad hoc quod essent, sed etiam quantum ad hoc quod aliorum causae essent." *C G,* III, 70.

²⁷ From this point of view, the philosophy of Malebranche is the absolute antithesis of Thomism. In Malebranche God alone is cause and reserves efficacy exclusively to Himself. Moreover, the preface to *Recherche de la vérité* opens with a protest against the Aristotelian, and therefore pagan, inspiration of Thomist scholasticism. Cf. the two rich and suggestive volumes of Henri Gouhier, *La Vocation de Malebranche,* Paris, Vrin, 1926, and *La Philosophie de Malebranche*

et son expérience religieuse, Paris, Vrin, 1926.

²⁸ I Cor., 3, 9.

²⁹ *De coel. hierarchi.,* c. 3. Texts cited in *C G,* III, 21.

³⁰ Cf. *The Spirit of Mediaeval Philosophy,* ch. 7, "Glory of God," pp. 128-147.

³¹ *C G,* III, 21, at Praeterea, tunc maxime perfectum.

³² We are here speaking of Aristotle as St. Thomas looked at him, or wish to do so. If, as we have suggested, St. Thomas went far beyond the Aristotelian notion of motive cause to a truly efficient cause, it was Aristotle's Platonism he was effectively leaving behind.

³³ "Utraque autem istarum opinionum est absque ratione. Prima enim opinio excludit causas propinquas, dum effectus omnes in inferioribus provenientes, solis causis attribuit: in quo derogatur ordini universi, qui ordine et connexione causarum contexitur, dum prima causa ex eminentia bonitatis suae rebus aliis confert non solum quod sint, sed etiam quod causae sint. Secunda opinio in idem quasi inconveniens redit: cum enim removens prohibens non sit nisi novens per accidens . . . , si inferiora agentia nihil aliud faciunt quam producere de occulto in manifestum, removendo impedimenta quibus formae et habitus virtutum et scientiarum occultabantur, sequitur quod omnia inferiora agentia non agant nisi per accidens." *Quo. disp. de Veritate,* XI, 1.

CHAPTER 4

¹ *In II de Anima,* 1. 2; ed. Pirotta, n. 233, p. 83.

² *Op. cit.,* 1. 3; p. 91.

³ *Op cit.,* 1. 1; pp. 83-84. Cf. *S T,* I, 75, 1. *C G,* II, 65.

⁴ The very nature of this demonstration implies that the conclusion is valid for the human soul alone, not for the soul of animals. Animals are sentient but have no intellect. Now, sensation implies participation of the body. But the sensitive soul of the animal does not operate

separately and does not subsist apart from the body. Accordingly, it is not a substance. See *S T,* I, 74, 4 and I, 75, 4. *C G,* II, 82.

⁵ *S T,* I, 75, 6. This justification of the immortality of the soul is a transposition of a proof from the *Phaedo* seen through St. Augustine's *De immortalite animae,* XII, 19; *P L,* 32, c. 1031. On the natural desire to exist as a sign of immortality, see *S T,* I, 75, 6 and *C G,* II, 55, 79. Cf. J. Martin, *Saint Augustin,* Paris, 1923, pp. 160-161.

[6] On the other hand, see Saint Bonaventure, *Sent.*, II, 17, 1, 11 ad *concl.*

[7] *S T*, I, 75, 5, ad 4. *De spirit. creat.*, art. 1. *De Anima*, art. 6.

[8] *S T*, I, 75, 7, ad 3.

[9] *De Potentia*, III, 5. *S T*, I, 65 1. *C G*, II, 6 and 15.

[10] *S T*, I, 47, 2 and I, 65, 2. We are here close to the ultimate basis of individuation. Without actually discussing them, let us just notice that the various criticisms to the effect that it is impossible to save personality in St. Thomas's system, in which individuation is by matter, misunderstand a basic Thomistic principle, namely, that matter makes possible the multiplicity of certain forms, but is itself there only in view of these forms. Matter is the passive principle of individuation, form the active principle of individuality. Matter only individualizes the soul as form of the body. This body is only a body because the soul gives it organization, life, act-of-existing. In fact, the body only exists by the soul, and both together only exist by the unity of the existential act that causes them, penetrates them, and contains them. See the basic text *Qu. disp. de anima*, I, and the remark: "Unumquodque secundum idem habet esse et individuationen," *ibid.*, ad 2. Here as elsewhere the *esse* of a substance is not its *being* but its *act-of-existing*.

[11] *S T*, I, 76, 1.

[12] *S T*, I, 75, 3.

[13] *S T*, I, 75, 4.

[14] *C G*, II, 55.

[15] *C G*, II, 56.

[16] *S T*, I, 75, 5. Cf. I, 76, 1. *C G*, II, 56.

[17] *C G*, II, 57. *De Anima*, I, 1.

[18] *De Anima*, I, 1.

[19] *C G*, II, 57.

[20] *Nicom. Ethics*, X, 7, 1177 a 12.

[21] *In II de Anima*, 4; Pirotta ed., 271-278, pp. 97-98. *S T*, I, 76, 1. *De spirit. creat.*, art. 2.

[22] See M. de Wulf, *Le Traité des formes de Gilles de Lessines* (Les Philosophes Belges), Louvain, 1901. Insofar as the actual state of the texts permits us to judge, this conception can be attributed to Alexander of Hales, *Summa*, II, 63, 4. St. Bonaventure's position is open to discussion. Cf. Ed. Lutz, *Die Psychologie Bonaventuras nach den Quellen dargestellt*, Münster, 1909, 53-61.

[23] *De Anima*, I, 9. *C G*, II, 58. *S T*, I, 76, 4.

[24] *S T*, I, 118, 2, ad 2.

[25] *De spirit. creat.*, art. 3.

[26] *Qu. disp. de anima*, art. 9.

[27] *S T*, I, 75, 4.

[28] *S T*, I, 76, 8. *C G*, II, 72. *De spirit. creat.*, art. 4. *De Anima*, art. 10.

[29] *S T*, I, 3, 7. I, 40, ad 1. I, 85, 5, ad 3. *C G*, II, 54. *Quodlibet*, VII, 3, 7, ad 1.

[30] *S T*, I, 75, 2, ad 1.

[31] This is so true that St. Thomas's real difficulty is to prevent the union of soul and body from becoming accidental, as it is in Plato: "Licet anima habeat esse completum, non tamen sequitur quod corpus ei accidentaliter uniatur; tum quia illud idem esse, quod est animae, communicat corpori, ut sit unum esse totius compositi; tum etiam quia, etsi possit per se subsistere, non tamen habet speciem completam; sed corpus advenit ei ad completionem speciei." *De Anima*, art. 1, ad 1.

[32] *De Anima*, art. 1.

[33] *S T*, I, 75, 4, ad 2.

[34] *S T*, I, 76, 1.

[35] See above, note 10, end of the note.

[36] "Unumquodque secundum idem habet esse et individuationem . . . Sicut igitur esse animae est a Deo sicut a principio activo, et in corpore sicut in materia, nec

tamen esse animae perit pereunte corpore, ita et individuatio animae, etsi aliquam relationem habeat ad corpus, non tamen perit corpore pereunte." *De Anima,* art. I, ad 2.

[37] *S T,* I, 79. 2. Cf. *De Veritate,* X, 8.

"Anima enim nostra in genere intellectualium tenet ultimum locum, sicut materia prima in genere sensibilium."

[38] *Qu. de anima,* art. I. *S T,* I, 76, I.

[39] *Qu. de anima,* art. I.

CHAPTER 5

[1] *C G,* II, 72. *S T,* I, 77, 2.

[2] *S T,* I, 77, 2.

[3] *De Anima,* art. 13.

[4] *S T,* I, 77, 4.

[5] *S T,* I, 78, I.

[6] *De Anima,* art. 13. *S T,* I, 78, I.

[7] *S T,* I, 77, 4. *De Anima,* art. 13, ad 10.

[8] *De Anima,* art. 13, ad 15.

[9] *Ibid.*

[10] *S T,* I, 78, 2.

[11] The action of bodies on the senses is explained by the radioactivity of forms into the space around them. Each form radiates an emanation resembling itself. This emanation contacts the sense organ and causes sensation. The activity of the form depends on the fact that it is an act and, naturally, a cause: "Omnis forma, inquantum hujusmodi, est principium agendi sibi simile; unde cum color sit quaedam forma, ex se habet, quod causat sui similitudinem in medio." *In II de Anima,* 14; ed. Pirotta, 425, p. 145.

[12] *In II de Anima,* 14; p. 148. For the kind of scientific explanation to which this qualitative physics corresponds, see E. Meyerson, *Identité et réalité,* Paris, Alcan, 4 ed., 1932, ch. 10 and 11.

[13] *In II de Anima,* 16; p. 152.

[14] *De Anima,* art. 13.

[15] *S T,* I, 67, I. *In II Sent.,* 13, 1, 2.

[16] Avicenna distinguishes five. Cf. *S T,* I, 78, 4.

[17] *S T,* I, 78, 4.

[18] *De Anima,* 13. *S T,* I, 78, 4, ad 2. *In II de Anima,* 13, ed. Pirotta, n. 390, p. 137.

[19] *S T,* I, 78, 4, ad 2. The common sense is like a fountain head from which the faculty of feeling is diffused throughout the organs of the five senses. *In III de anima,* 3; ed. Pirotta, n. 602, p. 206 and n. 609, p. 208. Its proper organ is localized at the very root of the sense of touch, that is, of the particular sense which is spread throughout the whole body. Cf. *In III de Anima,* 3; n. 611, p. 208.

[20] *In II de Anima,* 6; n. 302, p. 106. *S T,* I, 78, 4. On the whole array of problems about the *phantasia,* see *In III de Anima,* 5; pp. 216-223.

[21] *S T,* I, 78, 4. St. Thomas's description of the *aestimativa* closely follows Avicenna's, *Lib. VI Naturalium,* I, 5; ed. Venice, 1508; fol. 5, recto a.

[22] *S T,* I, 78, 4.

[23] *S T, ibid. De Anima,* 13. The difference between human and animal memories is not based on the way they are constituted as sensitive faculties. The superiority of human memory comes from its contact with man's reason which has a sort of reflected influence upon it (*loc. cit.,* ad 5).

[24] *C G,* II, 73.

[25] *S T, ibid.,* ad *Considerandum est autem.*

[26] *Ibid.,* ad 5.

CHAPTER 6

[1] *S T*, I, 79, 1, ad 3. *De Veritate*, 17, 1.

[2] *S T*, I, 79, 2. *C G*, II, 59.

[3] *De Anima*, art. 4. *S T*, I, 79, 3.

[4] *S T*, I, 79, 3, ad 1. On the inutility and even the impossibility of an "agent sense" in Thomism, see the excellent remarks of Father Boyer, S.J., in *Archives de Philosophie*, III, 2, p. 107.

[5] *De Anima, ibid.* With St. Thomas we shall reserve the name "passive intellect" for the faculty of the human composite which Aristotle designates by this name, and "possible intellect" for the immaterial and immortal faculty which St. Thomas, as opposed to Averroes, attributes to us. For the origin of this terminology, see Aristotle, *De Anima*, III, 4, 429 a 15-16. Albert the Great, *De Anima*, III, 2, 1; ed. Jammy, III, 132. St. Thomas, *In III de Anima*, 7; ed. Pirotta, n. 676, p. 226.

[6] Cf. Mandonnet, *Siger de Brabant et l'Averroisme latin*, I, 172, and foll.

[7] *De Anima*, art. 5.

[8] *C G*, II, 76, ad *In natura. S T*, I, 79, 4 and 5.

[9] *C G*, II, 74. *De Veritate*, X, 2. *S T*, I, 79. 6.

[10] *S T*, I, 79, 7.

[11] *S T*, I, 79, 8.

[12] *De Divin. Nom.*, c. 7.

[13] *De Veritate*, 15, 1.

[14] On the Thomist doctrine of knowledge, see principally: P. Rousselot, "Métaphysique thomiste et critique de la connaissance," *Revue néo-scolastique*, 1910, 476-509. La Guichaoua, "A propos des rapports entre la métaphysique thomiste et la théorie de la connaissance," *Revue néo-scolastique*, 1913, 88-101. Domenico Lanna, *La Teoria della conoscenza in S. Tomaso d'Aquino*, Firenze, 1913, with a bibliography. M. Baumgartner, "Zur thomistischen Lehre von den ersten Prinzipien der Erkenntnis," *Festgabe f. G. v. Hertling*, Freiburg i. Breisg., 1913, 1-16; and by the same "Zum thomistischen Wahrheitsbergriff," *Festgabe f. Cl. Baeumker*, Münster, 1913, 241-260. A. D. Sertillanges, "L'Être et la connaissance dans la philosophie de saint Thomas d'Aquin," *Mélanges Thomistes* (Bibl. Thomiste, 111), Le Saulchoir, Kain, 1923, 175-197. G. P. Klubertanz, *The Discursive Power-Sources and Doctrine of the Vis Cogitativa According to St. Thomas Aquinas*, St. Louis, 1952 (extensive bibliography, 331-346).

[15] Meno, 82 b, and foll.

[16] *S T*, I, 84, 3.

[17] *S T*, I, 89, 1.

[18] *S T*, I, 55, 2.

[19] *Confessions*, 12, c. 25.

[20] *S T*, I, 84, 5. St. Thomas knew very well that these differences separate Aristotle's theory from St. Augustine's. See especially the remarkable texts: *De spiritualibus creaturis*, 10, ad 8, and *De Veritate*, XI, 1.

[21] *S T*, I, 84, 5.

[22] *S T*, IaIIae, 109, 1. But since the proper object of the intellect is the intelligible, it cannot know the particular, from which it extracts the intelligible, except mediately and through a reflection. This process is analysed in the *De Veritate*, X, 4.

[23] *De Veritate*, XI, 1.

[24] *C G*, IV, 11, ad *Rursus considerandum est.*

[25] *Ibid.*

[26] *S T*, IaIIae, 51, 1.

[27] *De Veritate*, XI, 1. The interpretation of the Thomist doctrine of the principles of knowledge supported by M. J. Durantel, *Le Retour à Dieu*, pp. 46, 156-

157, 159, etc., seems to me to be very difficult to reconcile with the texts *C G*, II, 78, ad *Amplius Aristoteles*, and *De Anima*, art. 5, ad *Quidam vero crediderunt*. The remark, p. 161, note 3, seems to indicate that the author conceives of no middle term between sensualism and Platonism, namely that "innate-ism" of the intellect without an "innate-ism" of principles which describes exactly St. Thomas's position. As "the theory of first principles is the central and characteristic point of the doctrine of knowledge in St. Thomas" (p. 156), the error made here leads to others. Thus the principles have been taken somewhat like Kantian categories originating in God (p. 162 agrees with p. 159, "car il faut . . ."). The reason for this is that the Thomist term *determination* has been understood and interpreted as the intrinsic development of a virtual content, and not taken, in the proper sense of determining, as the elaboration of a content which the intellect has received from outside and intellectualized.

²⁸ *C G*, III, 47. *Compendium Theologiae*, c. 129. *De Veritate*, X, 6.

²⁹ See above, p. 198.

³⁰ See pp. 204-205.

³¹ *S T*, I, 84, 6.

³² *S T*, I, 84, 7, ad 2. Let us remember that sensible species are not scattered sensations in physical surroundings looking for knowing subjects in which to reside. They are physical radiations emanating from objects. Like their causes, species have no existence distinct from that of the object which produces them and of which they are but the continual emanation. Proceeding from the form of the object (not from its matter), species retain its active virtue. It is by them, accordingly, that the object actualizes the sensory organ and assimilates it to itself. The *phantasma* is the *similitudo* of the object resulting from the action of the species on the proper sense, then on the common sense.

³³ *S T*, I, 85, 1, ad 3. *In III De Anima*, 3, ed. Pirotta, n. 794, p. 258.

³⁴ *S T*, I, 85, 1.

²⁵ *De Anima*, 4, ad 5.

²⁶ *De Veritate*, X, 6, ad 7.

³⁷ *S T*, I, 84, 7. "In mente enim accipiente scientiam a rebus, formae existunt per quamdam actionem rerum in animam; omnis autem actio est per formam; unde formae quae sunt in mente nostra, primo et principaliter respiciunt res extra animam existentes quantum ad formas earum." *De Veritate*, X, 4.

³⁸ *S T*, I, 85, 1.

³⁹ *S T*, I, 85, 1, ad 1.

⁴⁰ *Ibid.*, ad 4.

⁴¹ *Ibid.*, ad 3. *De Anima*, 4. Cf. *Comp. Theol.*, c. 81-83.

⁴² *C G*, II, 77.

⁴³ *S T*, I, 84, 7.

⁴⁴ *S T*, I, 87, 1.

⁴⁵ *De Anima*, III, ad 4. Cf. *De Veritate*, X, 8.

⁴⁶ *S T*, I, 87, 1.

⁴⁷ *S T*, I, 87, 3. *De Veritate*, X, 8. See, on this point, B. Romeyer, "Notre Science de l'esprit humain d'après saint Thomas d'Aquin," *Archives de Philosophie*, I, 1, Paris 1923, pp. 51-55. This work rather augustinizes St. Thomas's doctrine on this point. It is not easy to admit that St. Thomas grants a direct knowledge of the essence of the soul, and one that does not come from sense knowledge. What is true is that the soul's presence to itself gives it a corresponding *habitus* (*De Veritate*, X, 8). Thus we have habitual knowledge of the soul's essence, and we have the immediate certitude of its acts (Cf. Aristotle, *Nic. Eth.*, IX, 9, 1170 a. 25 and foll.), but we infer its existence and its nature from its operations. For a more profound study, see A. Gardeil, "La perception de l'âme par elle-même d'après saint Thomas," *Mélanges Thomistes* (Bibl. Thomiste, III), Le Saulchoir, 1923, pp. 219-236.

⁴⁸ *S T*, I, 88, 3.

⁴⁹ *C G*, III, 47.

[50] *S T*, I, 84, 7.

[51] Besides the works we have indicated and which bear directly on the Thomist doctrine of knowledge, there exists a number of classical studies of the relation between St. Thomas's doctrine of knowledge and those of St. Augustine, St. Bonaventure and the Augustinian school in general. It is a dangerous problem to approach before directly studying the Thomist and Augustinian texts, but it must be tackled afterwards. Many rich philosophical and historical works have grown out of it. See J. Kleutgen, *Die Philosophie der Vorzeit*, Münster 1860, 2 vols. (it can be had in French translation: *La Philosophie scolastique*, Paris 1868-1890, 4 vols.). Lepidi, O.P. *Examen philosophico theologicum de Ontologismo*, Louvain, 1874; and by the same, "De Ente generalissimo prout est aliquid psychologicum, logicum, ontologicum," *Divus Thomas*, 1881, no. 11. Zigliara, *Della luce intellettuale e dell' ontologismo secondo le dottrine dei SS Agostino, Bonaventura, et Tommaso*, Rome 1874 (or in *Oeuvres Complètes*, tr. Murgue, Lyon, 1881, XI, 273 and foll.). There is an interesting, though sometimes debatable, general introduction to the problem in *De Humanae cognitionis ratione anecdota quaedam S. D. Sancto Bonaventurae*, Ad Clara Aquas (Quarrachi), 1883; see especially, Dissertatio Praevia, pp. 1-47.

CHAPTER 7

[1] Besides the works cited in Chapter 5, see P. Mandonnet and J. Destrez, *Bibliographie Thomiste* (Bibliothèque Thomiste, I), Le Saulchoir, Kain, and Libr. philos., J. Vrin, Paris, 1921, pp. 36-39. Particularly, A. D. Sertillanges, "L'Idée général de la connaissance d'après saint Thomas d'Aquin," *Rev. des sciences philos. et théol.*, II (1908), 449-465; M. D. Roland-Gosselin, "Sur la théorie thomiste de la vérité," *ibid.*, X (1921), 222-234 (and see also the important remarks, *ibid.*, XIV, 188-189 and 201-203); L. Noël, *Notes d'épistémologie thomiste*, Louvain, 1925. For a general discussion of the interpretations proposed, see our *Réalism thomiste et critique de connaissance*, Paris, J. Vrin, 1938. C. Van Riet, *L'Épistémologie thomiste*, Louvain, 1946.

[2] In Thomistic language, since a being is defined by its form, a knowing being is distinguished from a nonknowing one in that it possesses, besides its own proper form, the form of the thing it knows: "Cognoscentia a non cognoscentibus in hoc distinguuntur, quia non cognoscentia nihil habent, nisi formam suam tantum, sed cognoscens natum est habere formam etiam rei alterius; nam species cogniti est in cognoscente. Unde manifestum est, quod natura rei non cognoscentis est magis coarctata et limita. Natura autem rerum cognoscentium habet majorem amplitudinem et extensionem; propter quod dicit Philosophus, *III De Anima* (text. 37) quod *anima est quodammodo omnia*." *S T*, I, 14, 1.

[3] This is the meaning of the well known statement of John of St. Thomas: "Cognoscentia autem in hoc elevantur super non cognoscentia, quia id quod est alterius, ut alterius, seu prout manet distinctum in altero possunt in se recipere, *ita quod in se sunt, sed etiam possunt fieri alia a se.*" *De Anima*, IV, 1. This statement is not St. Thomas's, but it is consistent with his thinking. For an interpretation, see the controversy between M. N. Balthasar and P. Garrigou-Lagrange in *Revue neo-scolastique de philosophie*, XXV (1923), 294-310 and 420-441.

[4] *In III de Anima*, 13; ed. Pirotta, no. 790. Cf. "Forma autem in his, quae cognitionem participant, altiori modo invenitur tantummodo forma ad unum esse proprium determinans unumquodque, quod etiam naturale uniuscujusque est ... In habentibus autem cognitionem sic determinatur unumquodque ad proprium esse naturale, per formam naturalem, quod tamen est receptivum specierum aliarum rerum: sicut sensus recipit species omnium sensibilium, et intellectus omnium intelligibilium. Et sic anima hominis fit omnia quodammodo secundum sensum et intellectum, in quo, quodammodo, cognitionem habentia ad Dei similitudinem approprinquant, in quo omnia praeexistunt" *S T*, I, 80, 1.

— "Patet igitur, quod immaterialitas alicujus rei est ratio, quod sit cognoscitiva, et secundum modum immaterialitatis est modus cognitionis. Unde in 2 *de Anima* dicitur quod plantae non cognoscunt propter suam materialitatem. Sensus autem cognoscitivus est, quia receptivus est specierum sine materia, et intellectus adhuc magis est cognoscitivus, quia magis separatus est a materia, et immixtus . . . Unde, cum Deus sit in summo immaterialitatis . . . , sequitur quod ipse sit in summo cognotionis." *S T,* I, 14, 1. Cf. *In II de Anima,* 5; ed. Pirotta, n. 283.

[5] "Hujusmodi autem viventia inferiora, quorum actus est anima, de qua nunc agitur, habent duplex esse. Unum quidem materiale, in quo conveniunt cum aliis rebus materialibus. Aliud autem immateriale, in quo communicant cum substantiis superioribus aliqualiter." *In II de Anima,* 5; ed. Pirotta, n. 282.

[6] See above, note 1.

[7] Unde dicitur *In III de Anima,* quod sensibile in actu est sensu in actu, et intelligibile in actu est intellectus in actu. Ex hoc enim aliquid in actu sentimus, vel intelligimus, quod intellectus noster, vel sensus, informatur in actu per speciem sensibilis vel intelligibilis. Et secundum hoc tantum sensus, vel intellectus alius est a sensibili, vel intelligibili, quia utrumque est in potentia." *S T,* I, 14, 2. Cf. *In III de Anima,* 2, ed. Pirotta, n. 591-593 and 724.

[8] *In II de Anima,* 15; n. 437-438. See M. D. Roland-Gosselin, "Ce que saint Thomas pense de la sensation immédiate et de son organe," *Rev. des sciences philos. et théol.,* VIII (1914), 104-105.

[9] See the striking statement of St. Thomas on this operation: "Cum vero praedictas species (scil. intelligibiles) in actu completo habuerit, vocatur intellectus in actu. Sic enim actu intelligit res, cum species rei facta fuerit forma intellectus possibilis." *Comp. Theologiae,* c. 83. The term "similitude" which St. Thomas often gives to the species (e.g., *C G,* II, 98) ought to be taken in a strong sense: it is a participation in the form; it represents the form because it is only a prolongation of the form. The "similitudo formae" is not a picture or carbon copy of it, without which knowl-

edge would but grasp the shadows of objects: "Sciendum est autem quod, cum quaelibet, cognitio perficiatur per hoc quod similitudo rei cognitae est in cognoscente, sicut perfectio rei cognitae consistit in hoc quod habet talem formam per quam est res talis, ita perfectio cognitionis consistet in hoc, quod habet similitudinem formae praedictae." *In VI Metaph.,* 4, ed. Cathala, n. 1234; cf. 1235-1236. It is because having the "similitude" of the form is equivalent to having the form, that we come to St. Thomas's definition of truth.

[10] "Quidam posuerunt, quod vires cognoscitivae, quae sunt in nobis, nihil cognoscunt, nisi proprias passiones: puta, quod sensus non sentit nisi passionem sui organi; et secundum hoc intellectus nihil intelligit, nisi suam passionem, id est speciem intelligiblem in se receptam: et secundum hoc species hujusmodi est ipsum *quod* intelligitur. Sed haec opinio manifeste apparet falsa ex duobus," etc., *S T,* I, 85, 2. — "Intellectum est in intelligente per suam similitudinem. Et per hunc modum dicitur, quod intellectum in actu est intellectus in actu; in quantum similitudo rei intellectae est forma intelligente per suam similitudinem. Et per hunc modum dicitur, quod intellectum in actu est intellectus in actu; in quantum similitudo rei intellectae est forma intellectus, sicut similitudo rei sensibilis est forma sensus in actu; unde non sequitur quod species intelligibilis abstracta sit id quod actu intelligitur, sed quod sit similitudo ejus." *Ibid.,* ad 1.

[11] "Manifestum est etiam, quod species intelligibiles, quibus intellectus possibilis fit in actu, non sunt objectum intellectus. Non enim se habent ad intellectum sicut *quod* intelligitur, sed sicut *quo* intelligit . . . Manifestum est enim quod scientiae sunt de his quae intellectus intelligit. Sunt autem scientiae de rebus, non autem de speciebus, vel intentionibus intelligibilibus, nisi sola scientia rationalis (*scil.,* logic)." *In III de Anima,* 8; ed. Pirotta, n. 718.

[12] *In II de Anima,* 24; 552-553.

[13] "*Dico autem intentionem intellectam* (*sive conceptum*) id quod intellectus in seipso concipit de re intellecta. Quae quidem in nobis neque est ipsa res quae intelligitur neque est ipsa substantia in-

tellectus, sed est quaedam similitudo concepta intellectu de re intellecta, quam voces exteriores significant; unde et ipsa intentio verbum interius nominatur, quod est exteriori verbo significatum." *C G,* IV, 11.

[14] *In II de Anima,* 12; n. 78-380. *S T,* I, 88, 2, ad 2.

[15] "Intellectus, per speciem rei formatus, intelligendo format in seipso quamdam intentionem rei intellectae, quae est ratio ipsius, quam significat diffinitio . . . Haec autem intentio intellecta, cum sit quasi terminus intelligibilis operationis, est aliud a specie intelligibili quae facit intellectum in actu, quod oportet considerari ut intelligibilis operationis principium: licet utrumque sit rei intellectae similitudo. Per hoc enim quod species intelligibilis, quae est forma intellectus, et intelligendi principium, est similitudo rei exterioris, sequitur quod intellectus intentionem formet illius rei similem. Quia quale est unumquodque, talia operatur, et ex hoc quod intentio intellecta est similis alicui rei, sequitur quod intellectus, formando hujusmodi intentionem, rem illam intelligat." *C G,* I, 53.

[16] "Id autem quod est per se intellectum non est res illa cujus notitia per intellectum habetur, cum illa quandoque sit intellecta in potentia tantum, et sit extra intelligentem, sicut cum homo intelligit res materiales, ut lapidem vel animal aut aliud hujusmodi: cum tamen oporteat quod intellectum sit in intelligente, et unum cum ipso. Neque etiam intellectum per se est similitudo rei intellectae, per quam informatur intellectus ad intelligendum. Intellectus enim non potest intelligere nisi secundum quod fit in actu per hanc similitudinem, sicut nihil aliud potest operari secundum quod est in potentia, sed secundum quod fit actu per aliquam formam. Haec ergo similitudo se habet in intelligendo sicut intelligendi principium, ut calor est principium calefactionis, non sicut intelligendi terminus. Hoc ergo est primo et per se intellectum, quod intellectus in se ipso concipit de re intellecta, sive illud sit definitio, sive enuntiatio, secundum quod ponuntur duae operationes intellectus, in III Anima (com. 12). Hoc autem sic ab intellectu conceptum dicitur verbum interius, hoc enim est quod significatur per vocem." *De Potentia,* XI, 5. Cf. *Ibid.,* VIII, 1 and IX, 5. *De Veritate,* III, 2.

[17] See *De natura verbi intellectus* from "Cum ergo intellectus, informatus specie natus sit agere . . ." to "Verbum igitur cordis . . ."; and especially the words: "Idem enim lumen quod intellectus possibilis recipit cum specie ab agente, per actionem intellectus informati tali specie diffunditur, cum objectum (*scil.* conceptum) formatur, et manet cum objecto formata." Not being able to establish identity between the concept and its object, St. Thomas maintains at least the continuity of the intelligibility of things and of that which it permits the intellect to introduce into the concept. This is why the texts in which St. Thomas declares that the immediate object of the intellect is the concept, not the thing, in no way contradict the objectivity of the concept. On the contrary, if our intellect had an immediate intuition of the object (as sight sees color) the concept formed from this intuition would only be an image of our intuition, and consequently a mediate image of the object. When St. Thomas considers the concept, that is, the intellect's immediate object, as the product of the intellect fecundated by the object itself, he feels that he is guaranteeing the strictest continuity between the intelligibility of the object and that of the concept. It is from this point of view that the necessity for taking the species as a principle and not as an object of knowledge fully appears. First of all, there is the object, and this is not itself grasped by an intuition. Next there is the *species,* and this is still only the object, and it also is still not grasped by an intuition. There, there is the intellect informed by the species, which thus becomes the object, and it still has no direct intuition of what it has thereby become. Finally there is the concept, the first conscious representation of the object. *No intermediary representation, therefore, separates the object from the concept which expresses it.* It is this which confers objectivity upon our conceptual knowledge. The full weight of this doctrine, therefore, rests upon the two-fold aptitude of our intellect, first, to become the thing, and secondly, to bring forth the concept while thus being fecundated.

[18] "Quidditas autem rei est proprium objectum intellectus: unde sicut sensus sensibilium propriorum semper est verus, ita et intellectus in cognoscendo quod quid est." *De Veritate,* I, 12. Cf. *S T,* I,

16, 2: "cum autem omnis res sit vera secundum quod intellectus in quantum est cognoscens sit verus, in quantum habet similitudinem rei cognitae, quae est forma ejus in quantum est cognoscens."

[19] "Sed secundum est quod cum reflexio fiat redeundo super idem; hic autem non sit reditio super speciem, nec super intellectum formatum specie, quia non percipiuntur quando verbum formatur, gignitio verbi non est reflexa." *De nat. verbi intellectus.* "Non enim intellectus noster inspieiens hanc speciem (*scil.*, intelligibilem) tamquam exemplar sibi simile, aliquid facit quasi verbum ejus; sic enim non fieret unum ex intellectu et specie, cum intellectus non intelligat nisi factus unum aliquid cum specie, sed in ipsa specie formatus agit tanquam aliquo sui, ipsam tamen non excedens. Species autem sic accepta semper ducit in objectum primum." *Ibid.*

[20] *Qu. disp. de Veritate,* I, 3.

[21] See the expressions of St. Augustine, St. Anselm, St. Hilary of Poitiers, Avicenna and Isaac Israeli which St. Thomas gathered together in *Qu. disp. de Veritate,* I, 1. On the intrinsic character of the being of truth thus understood, see the reasonable remarks of Father Pedro Descoqs, S.J., in his *Institutiones metaphysicae generalis,* Paris, Beauchesne, 1915, I, 350-363.

[22] See above, Part I, Ch. 1, pp. 40-41. For the epistomological consequences of this principle, see my *Réalisme thomiste et critique de la connaissance,* Ch. VIII, pp. 213-239.

[23] *S T,* I, 85, 2.

[24] *S T,* I, 87, 3.

[25] *De potentia,* VIII, 1 and IX, 5. We fail to see where Father Roland-Gosselin differs from Jacques Maritain on this point (*Rev. des sciences philos. et théol.,* XIV (1925), 202. The identity of the species (and therefore the object) and the intellect which Mr. Maritain rightly affirms is in no way contradicted by Father Roland-Gosselin's equally correct affirmation of the non-identity of object and concept. I fail to see how the texts that affirm the one position can be said to

deny the other. The source of the misunderstanding is probably to be found in the double use of the term *similitudo* mentioned earlier. It is not a question of how the similitude expressed by the object can conform to the object, because it actually is this object. The conformity to the object of a similitude of this object expressed by thought is certain, given the conditions in which thought expresses it, but it is no longer identical with the object. Father Roland-Gosselin is therefore right when he says: "It is always, for St. Thomas, the resemblance of the mental word to the thing it differs from (the resemblance and not the identity) that explains its objectivity." (*Op. cit.,* p. 203). Yes, but this resemblance of the word to the thing presupposes in its turn identity of the species and of the intellect conceiving the word. Otherwise it would not be the very thing which the word (or concept) expresses. We may wonder whether most misconceptions do not arise from the fact these identities are taken as individual whereas as they are only specific. The definition of *similitudo* is *convenientia in forma.* From the form of the object to the concept there is perfect continuity of species. The number of intermediaries is therefore without importance. So long as the specific and formal identity remain constant, the concept always remains the object itself as known.

[26] On this point see the important article by Father Roland-Gosselin, "La théorie thomiste de l'erreur," *Mélanges Thomistès* (Bibliothèque Thomiste, III), 1923, 253-274.

[27] "In intellectu enim est (*scil.* veritas), sicut consequens actum intellectus, et sicut cognita per intellectum; consequitur namque intellectus operationem secundum quod judicium intellectus est de re secundum quod est; cognoscitur autem ab intellectu, secundum quod intellectus reflectitur supra actum suum, non solum secundum quod cognoscit actum suum, sed secundum quod cognoscit proportionem ejus ad rem: quod quidem cognosci non potest nisi cognita natura ipsius actus; quae cognosci non potest, nisi cognoscatur natura principii activi, quod est ipse intellectus, in cujus natura est ut rebus conformetur; unde secundum hoc cognoscit veritatem intellectus quod supra seipsum reflectitur." *Qu. disp. de Veritate,* I, 9.

CHAPTER 8

[1] *S T*, I, 80, 1.

[2] See above, p. 200.

[3] *De Veritate*, XXII, 3 and ad 2.

[4] *De Veritate*, XV, 3.

[5] *De Veritate*, XXII, 1.

[6] *De Veritate*, XXII, 4.

[7] *S T*, I, 80, 2. *De Veritate*, XXII, 4, ad 1.

[8] *De Veritate*, XXV, 1.

[9] *S T*, I, 81, 1. *De Veritate*, XXV, 1, ad 1.

[10] *S T*, I, 81, 2. This distinction might seem to be superfluous (cf. A. D. Sertillanges, *Saint Thomas d'Aquin*, Paris, Flammarion, 1931, 215), but it has just been resurrected and studied at length by M. Pradines, *Philosophie de la sensation*, vol. II, *Les Sens du besoin*, Paris, Les Belles Lettres, 1932; vol. III, *Les Sens de la défense*, Paris, Les Belles Lettres, 1934.

[11] *De Veritate*, XXV, 5.

[12] *De Div. Nom.*, VII.

[13] *De Veritate*, XXV, 2.

[14] See Ch. 5, p. 206.

[15] *De Veritate*, XXV, 4.

[16] *S T*, I, 81, 3.

[17] *De Veritate*, XXV, 1. The whole hierarchy of the relationships among the various types of forms and the various types of appetitive inclination are taken up with matchless dexterity in *C G*, II, 47, ad *Amplius*.

[18] *S T*, I, 82, 1.

[19] *S T*, I, 59, 4.

[20] *De Veritate*, XXII, 6. *De Malo*, III, 3. *S T*, I, 82, 2.

[21] *S T*, I, 82, 3.

[22] *S T*, I, 82, 4.

[23] *S T*, I, 82, 1.

[24] *De Malo*, VI.

[25] *De consolatione philosophiae*, III, prosa 2.

[26] *De Veritate*, XXII, 6.

[27] *De Malo*, VI.

PART III

CHAPTER 1

[1] On St. Thomas's moral doctrine in general, see A. D. Sertillanges, *La Philosophie morale de saint Thomas d'Aquin*, Paris, 1916. Etienne Gilson, *Moral Values and the Moral Life*, Saint Louis, 1941. J. Pieper, *Die ontische Grundlage des Sittlichen nach Thomas von Aquin*, Münster i. W., 1929. Michaël Wittmann, *Die Ethik des hl. Thomas von Aquin*, München, Hueber, 1933. G. Ermecke, *Die natürlichen Seinsgrundlagen der christlichen Ethik*, Paderborn, Bonifacius-Druckerei, 1941. Vernon J. Bourke, *Ethics*, New York, Macmillan, 1951.

[2] *In II Sent.*, 4, 1.

[3] *S T*, I, 62, 5. The reason for this lies in the perfection of the angelic nature. The angel's nature is to live under the regime of direct intuition. It has no discursive knowledge. It can, accordingly, attain its end by one single act. Man, however, has to go searching. He needs time and a life of some duration to attain his end. The length of human life is based upon man's mode of knowing: "Homo secundum suam naturam non statim natus est ultimam perfectionem

adipisci, sicut angelus: et ideo homim longior vita data est ad merendum beatitudinem, quam angelo." *Ibid.*, ad 1. Cf. *S T*, I, 58, 3 and 4; and I, 62, 6.

⁴ *Ibid.*, 63, 6.

⁵ *S T*, I-II, I, 8.

⁶ *C G*, III, 17. *S T*, I, 103, 2, and ad 2. *Qu. disp. de Veritate*, 13, 1 and 2.

⁷ *S T*, I-II, 10, 2.

⁸ *S T*, I, 82, 4. I II, 9, 1. *C G*, I, 72; III, 26. *De Veritate*, XXII, 12. *De Malo*, VI, 1.

⁹ *S T*, I-II, 12, 3, and 4. *De Veritate*, XXII, 14.

¹⁰ *S T*, I-II, 14, 1, and 2.

¹¹ *S T*, I-II, 15, 1.

¹² *S T*, I-II, 15, 3, ad 3.

¹³ *In VI Ethic.*, II, 5, 2.

¹⁴ *S T*, I, 83, 8. I-II, 13, 1. *De Veritate*, XXII, 15.

¹⁵ *S T*, I-II, 17, 5.

¹⁶ *S T*, I-II, 17, 1.

¹⁷ On the distinction between "to assent" which is reserved on the whole to the intellect, and "to consent," by reason of the union which it seems to suppose between the power and the object, is reserved in principle to the will, see *S T*, I-II, 15, 1, ad 3.

¹⁸ *S T*, I-II, 17, 6. *De Virtut*, I, 7.

¹⁹ *S T*, I-II, 49, 2. Aristotle, *Met.* IV, 20, 1022 b 10.

²⁰ *S T*, I-II, 49, 2. This also justifies the insistence upon stability before speaking of a habit. All habits are dispositions, but all dispositions are not habits. A disposition is only transitory, a habit is a permanent disposition. Here again we are not in the realm of the definite and immovable. A disposition is more or less a habit according as it is less or more easy to lose it. A habit is an organism in development: "Et sic dispositio fit habitus, sicut puer fit vir." *Ibid.*, ad 3.

²¹ *S T*, I-II, 49, 4. Cf. D. Placide de Roton, *Les Habitus, leur caractère spirituel*, Paris, Labergerie, 1934, Ch. 5, "La Vie des habitus."

²² *S T*, I-II, 50, 2. *In I Sent.*, 26, 3, ad 4 and 5.

²³ *S T*, I-II, 49, 4, ad 1. *In III Sent.*, 23, 1, 1, 1. Cf. Pègues, *Commentaire français littéral de la Somme théologique*, VII, 562-570.

²⁴ *S T*, I-II, 51, 2 and 3.

²⁵ *Ibid.*, 52, 2 and 53, 1.

²⁶ *S T*, I-II, 54, 3 and 55, 1-4.

²⁷ *De Malo*, II, 4. *S T*, I-II, 18, 1.

²⁸ *S T*, I-II, 18, 2 and 19, 1.

²⁹ *S T*, I-II, 18, 3. For the study of these circumstances, see I-II, 7, 1-4.

³⁰ *S T*, I-II, 18, 4.

³¹ *S T*, I-II, 18, 6.

³² *De Div. Nom.*, 4.

³³ *S T*, I-II, 18, 5. *C G*, III, 9. *De Malo*, II, 4. *De Virtut.*, I, 2, ad 3.

³⁴ *S T*, I-II, 18, 8. *De Malo*, II, 5.

³⁵ "Unde hoc nomen *intentio* nominat actum voluntatis, praesupposita ordinatione rationis ordinantis aliquid in finem." *S T*, I-II, 12, 1, ad 3.

³⁶ *S T*, I-II, 58, 2. On the adequacy of this division, *ibid.*, 3. On the fundamental identity of the two notions *virtus* and *honestum*, see *S T*, II-II, 145, 1. The term *honestum* signifies in effect *quod est honore dignum;* now honor rightly pertains to excellence (II-II, 103, 2 and 144, 2, ad 2); and since men are excellent through virtues, *honestum* properly taken is identical with virtue. *Decorum*, however, is the kind of beauty proper to moral excellence. More exactly, it is the "spiritual beauty" which consists in agreement between action or moral life and the spiritual clarity of reason. Cf. II II, 145, 2.

³⁷ *S T*, I-II, 58, 4-5.

[38] *S T*, I-II, 57, 2 and ad 2.

[39] *S T*, I-II, 57, 5.

[40] *S T*, I-II, 60, 2, and 61, 2.

[41] *S T*, I-II, 56, 3, and 61, 1.

[42] *S T*, I-II, 64, 1, ad 1.

[43] *S T*, I-II, 64, 2 and 3. *De virtutibus cardinalibus*, 1. *De virtutibus in communi*, 13.

[44] *S T*, I-II, 90, 1.

[45] *Ibid.*, ad 3.

[46] See below, Chap. 6, "The Last End."

[47] *S T*, I-II, 90, 3.

[48] *C G*, III, 115. *S T*, I II, 91, 1, and 93, 3.

[49] *S T*, I-II, 91, 2.

[50] *S T*, I-II, 94, 2.

[51] *S T*, I-II, 91, 3, and 95, 1.

[52] *Acts*, 4, 19. *S T*, I-II, 96, 4.

[53] *Psalm* 148. Cited in *S T*, I, 93, 5.

[54] "Sicut res naturales ordini divinae providentiae subduntur, ita et actus humani . . . Utrobique autem convenit debitum ordinem servari vel etiam praetermitti; hoc tamen interest quod observatio vel transgressio debiti ordinis est in potestate human ae voluntatis constituta, non autem in potestate naturalium rerum est quod a debito ordine deficiant vel ipsum sequantur. Oportet autem effectus causis per convenientiam respondere. Sicut igitur res naturales, cum in eis debitus ordo naturalium principiorum et actionum servatur, sequitur necessitate naturae conservatio et bonum in ipsis, corruptio autem et malum, quum a debito et naturali ordine receditur, ita etiam in rebus humanis oportet quod, cum homo voluntarie servat ordinem legis divinitus impositae, consequatur bonum, non velut ex necessitate, sed ex dispensatione gubernantis, quod est praemiari, et e converso malum, cum ordo legis fuerit pratermissus, et hoc est puniri." *C G*, III, 140. Cf. *S T*, I-II, 93, 6.

[55] "Quum igitur actus humani divinae providentiae subdantur, sicut et res naturales, oportet malum quod accidit in humanis actibus sub ordine alicujus boni concludi. Hoc autem convenientissime fit per hoc quod peccata puniuntur; sic enim sub ordine justitiae, quae ad aequalitatem, reducit, comprehenduntur eo quae debitam quantitatem excedunt. Excedit autem homo debitum suae quantitatis gradum, dum voluntatem suam divinae voluntati praefert, satisfaciendo ei contra ordinem Dei; quae quidem inaequalitas tollitur, dum contra voluntatem suam homo aliquid pati cogitur secundum ordinationem. Oportet igitur quod peccata humana puniantur divinitus, et eadem ratione bona facta remunerationem accipiant." *C G*, III, 140.

CHAPTER 2

[1] *S T*, II-II, Prologus.

[2] *Qu. disp. de Veritate*, 26, 2. On this problem, see H. D. Noble, O.P., *Les Passions dans la vie morale*, Paris, Lethielleux, 2 vols., 1931 and 1932.

[3] *S T*, I-II, 26, 2.

[4] *S T*, I-II, 26, 1.

[5] *S T*, I-II, 26, 3. Friendship is not a passion but a virtue. St. Thomas's principal source on this point is the *Eth. Nic.*, Books 8 and 9. See *In VIII Eth. Nic.*, ed. Pirotta, pp. 497-566, and *In IX Eth. Nic.*, pp. 563-621.

[6] *S T*, I-II, 26, 4.

[7] *S T*, I-II, 26, 4. The source of friendship is the virtue *benevolentia*. Benevolence is an internal movement of affection for someone. When it is stabilized into a habit, it is friendship. *In IX Eth. Nic.*, 5; ed. Pirotta, n. 1820, pp. 585-586.

[8] *S T*, I-II, 27, 1, ad 3: ad rationem pulchri pertinet quod in ejus aspectu seu cognitione quietur apprehensio. It is from this metaphysical notion of beauty, rather than from the notion of art, that we should have to begin in order to establish an aesthetic based upon authentic Thomist principles. The notion of art is

common to the fine arts and the useful arts. To proceed from art to aesthetic, it is necessary to return to the notion of the beautiful taken in itself.

[9] For the elements of aesthetics in St. Thomas, see Jacques Maritain, *Art et scolastique,* Paris, 3rd ed., 1935. E. Gilson, *Painting and Reality,* Bollingen Series, to be published during the Fall of 1956.

[10] *S T,* I-II, 27, 2.

[11] *S T,* I-II, 27, 2, ad 2.

[12] *S T,* I-II, 27, 3.

[13] *S T,* I-II, 27, 4.

[14] *S T,* I-II, 28, 1 and ad 3.

[15] On the theological extensions of this doctrine of love, see *C G,* IV, 19.

[16] *S T,* I-II, 28, 2.

[17] *S T,* I-II, 28, 3. But this does not also imply forgetfulnes of self. To love a friend is not to love him more than self but as oneself. The love we always have for ourself does not prevent that detachment from self demanded by all true friendship. Cf. *loc. cit.,* ad 3.

[18] *S T,* I-II, 28, 4.

[19] *S T,* I-II, 28, 5 and replies to the objections.

[20] *S T,* I-II, 28, 6.

[21] *S T,* I-II, 29, 1.

[22] *S T,* I-II, 29, 2 and 3.

[23] *S T,* I-II, 30, 3, and ad 3.

[24] *S T,* I-II, 30, 4.

[25] *S T,* I-II, 31, 5 and ad 2.

[26] *C G,* III, 126, ad *Sicut autem.*

[27] *S T,* I-II, 31, 7. *C G,* III, 122, to *Nec tamen oportet.*

[28] It must be remembered that the pleasure under discussion here is the pleasure of a given act. When pleasure absorbs into its act the one performing that act, it thereby makes any other pleasure difficult or even impossible. Thus intense sensible pleasure and the exercise of reason are incompatible. Cf. *S T,* I-II, 33, 3.

[29] *S T,* I-II, 34, 1. The first object of moral philosophy is not the preventing of the manifestations of nature, but ordering them according to reason. *C G,* III, 121. Thus normal pleasure controlled by reason is morally good. This is so true that Thomas holds that the pleasure that accompanies the sexual act was greater in the state of innocence than since original sin: fuisset tanto major delectatio sensibilis, quanto esset purior natura, et corpus magis sensible. *S T,* I, 98, 2, ad 3.

[30] *C G,* III, 126.

[31] *C G,* III, 122.

[32] *C G,* III, 123.

[33] *C G,* III, 124.

[34] These and other arguments used by St. Thomas are not impaired by exceptions to the contrary (a mother who is capable of raising her children alone, or of raising them better alone than with the help of the father, or for whom it is impossible to raise them otherwise than alone since she is a widow, etc.). The moral law sets a general rule to cover normal cases. It cannot regulate exceptions.

[35] *S T,* I-II, 35, 1.

[36] *S T,* I-II, 35, 5.

[37] *S T,* I-II, 39, 4.

[38] *S T,* I-II, 40, 1.

[39] *S T,* I-II, 40, 4.

[40] *S T,* I-II, 40, 6.

[41] *S T,* I-II, 40, 8 and ad 3.

[42] *S T,* I-II, 45, 3.

[43] *S T,* I-II, 45, 4.

[44] *S T,* I-II, 46, 6.

[45] *S T,* I-II, 48, 3.

[46] Cicero, *Tusculan Questions,* III, cited in *S T,* II-II, 123, 10.

CHAPTER 3

[1] *S T*, II-II, 47, 4. The principal source of this doctrine is *In VI Eth. Nic.*, 4, ed. Pirotta, 386-392, and 7, 398-402.

[2] *S T*, II-II, 49, 1.

[3] *S T*, II-II, 49, 2 and ad 3.

[4] *S T*, II-II, 49, 3.

[5] *S T*, II-II, 49, 4. It is not here a question of *eubulia*, or the ability to deliberate soundly. Some people discover the proper way to act, but very slowly and often too late. Address is promptitude in practical judgment; it is pouncing from the first upon the correct solution: On *eubulia*, a virtue annexed to prudence, see *op. cit.*, II-II, 51, 1.

[6] *De Malo*, 15, 4; and *S T*, II-II, 53, 6 and ad 1.

[7] *S T*, II-II, 53, 2. On negligence as a special vice, see II II, 54, 2.

[8] *S T*, II-II, 55, 1.

[9] *S T*, II-II, 55, 6.

[10] *S T*, II-II, 55, 7.

[11] The source of this teaching is *In III Eth. Nic.*, 14-18, ed. Pirotta, 181-202.

[12] *S T*, II-II, 123, 1. Cf. *De virtutibus*, I, 12.

[13] *S T*, II-II, 123, 1, ad 2. Cf. II II, 126, 2.

[14] *S T*, II-II, 123, 2.

[15] *S T*, II-II, 123, 5 and all of 124.

[16] *S T*, II-II, 123, 7.

[17] *S T*, II-II, 123, 8.

[18] *S T*, II-II, 123, 10. On the other hand, the soldier must not allow himself to fight for the sheer pleasure of killing. The justifiable annoyance with any obstacle standing in the way of performance of duty is very different from the thirst to kill for the very sake of killing. A soldier who yields to this passion is an assassin. He is delighted with war because it provides him with an occasion for killing. See *S T*, II-II, 64, 7, end.

[19] *S T*, II-II, 123, 12.

[20] *S T*, II-II, 129, 1.

[21] *S T*, II-II, 129, 3, ad 5.

[22] *S T*, II-II, 103, 1. Honor is the reward paid by others to the virtuous. But the virtuous man does not directly act in view of this reward. He seeks happiness, which is the end of virtue. Honor is not a very great thing in itself. Its greatness lies in the fact that it is the homage due to virtue. See *S T*, II-II, 131, 1, ad 2.

[23] *S T*, II-II, 103, 2.

[24] *S T*, II-II, 129, 3, ad 4. The contrary of magnanimity is not therefore humility, but pusillanimity or smallness of soul, which prevents man from undertaking tasks worthy of his strength and truly worthy of himself. Cf. II-II, 133, 1.

[25] *S T*, II-II, 129, 6.

[26] *S T*, II-II, 129, 8.

[27] *S T*, II-II, 130, 1 and 2.

[28] *S T*, II-II, 131, 1.

[29] *S T*, II-II, 132, 1, and ad 3.

[30] *S T*, II-II, 132, 5. On *pertinacia*, see II-II, 138, 2.

[31] *S T*, II-II, 134, 1, and ad 4.

[32] *S T*, II-II, 134, 3. On meanness (*parvificentia*), see II-II, 135, 1.

[33] *S T*, II-II, 136, 1.

[34] This is why fortitude depends upon the irascible, while patience depends upon the concupiscible. For the reason why it is connected rather with fortitude, see II-II, 136, 4, ad 2. On longanimity, the virtue of those whose hope is far-reaching, see II-II, 136, 5.

[35] *S T*, II-II, 137, 2. Constancy only differs from perseverance in that it is less concerned with enduring effort and more with overcoming increasingly difficult exterior impediments. See II-II, 137, 3. On indolence and stubbornness, see II-II, 138, 1 and 2.

[36] *S T*, II-II, 141, 1. The principal source is *In III Eth. Nic.*, 19-22, ed. Pirotta, 203-220.

[37] *S T*, II-II, 141, 6.

[38] *S T*, II-II, 141, 7, and ad 2 and ad 3.

[39] *Ibid.*

[40] On fearlessness, or imperviousness to fear, taken as the opposite of courage, see II-II, 126, 2. Fear is a useful natural reaction, and therefore normal. It is just as dangerous to be incapable of fear as to be unable to overcome it. Similarly is it with pleasures.

[41] *S T*, II-II, 142, 1. Cf. II-II, 152, 2, ad 1.

[42] *S T*, II-II, 142, 4.

[43] *S T*, II-II, 145, 4.

[44] On impurity (*immunditia*), see II-II, 148, 6, and 154, 11.

[45] *S T*, II-II, 150, 2. For the influence of drunkenness on the culpability of acts, see 151, 1.

[46] *S T*, II-II, 150, 3.

[47] *S T*, II-II, 151, 4. St. Thomas distinguishes between chastity properly so called, and continence. Continence has not all the qualities of a virtue. It is an aptitude of repressing, occasionally, evil desires. A continence which is stable and firmly rooted becomes a kind of chastity. Cf. *S T*, II-II, 155, 1.

[48] *S T*, II-II, 152, 2 and ad 1.

[49] *S T*, II-II, 153, 1 and 3.

[50] *S T*, II-II, 153, 5, and ad 4.

[51] *S T*, II-II, 154, 12, and ad 4.

[52] Thus unnatural vice is even worse than incest, for "unicuique individuo magis est conjuncta natura speciei quam quodcumque individuum. Et ideo peccata quae sunt contra naturam speciei sunt graviora." *S T*, II-II, 154, 12, ad 2.

[53] *S T*, II-II, 158, 8.

[54] *S T*, II-II, 158, 5.

[55] St. Thomas distinguishes between cruelty, that is, intemperance in the desire to chastize, and ferocity (*saevitia, feritas*) or pleasure in causing suffering for the very sake of causing it. Cruelty is a distorted desire for justice, ferocity is only another form of bestiality. Cf. *S T*, II-II, 159, 2.

[56] *S T*, II-II, 160, 1 and 2.

[57] *S T*, II-II, 162, 1 and 2. On the meaning of *Initium omnis peccati est superbia*, see II-II, 162, 7.

[58] *S T*, II-II, 162, 3. As a movement of aversion of the will from God, refusing to submit to being ruled by Him, pride is really contempt of God. Since all sin is part of a general rebellion against God, and since pride is the very essence of this rebellion, pride is the sin of sins and the gravest of all. Cf. *S T*, II-II, 152, 6.

[59] *S T*, II-II, 161, 3 and 4.

[60] *S T*, II-II, 167, 2.

[61] *Ibid.*

[62] *S T*, II-II, 166, 2.

[63] *S T*, II-II, 168, 3.

[64] *S T*, II-II, 168, 4.

[65] *S T*, II-II, 169, 1.

[66] *S T*, II-II, 169, 2.

[67] J. Webert, *Saint Thomas d'Aquin, le génie de l'ordre*. Paris, Denoel et Steele, 1934, pp. 257-258.

[68] On recent controversies over the notion of the person, see the bibliography in *Bulletin thomiste*, 1939, 466-477. It is useful to be familiar with these controversies, but it is possible to consider this notion peacefully as absolutely essential

to grasping the authropology and moral philosophy of St. Thomas.

69 *S T,* I, 29, 1. See, in general, my *The Spirit of Mediaeval Philosophy,* ch. 10, pp. 189-208.

70 *S T,* I, 29, 3.

71 We mitigate, here, rather than accentuate, the rigor of the precept. If we are sure that St. Thomas was applying it to the Christian doctor it is only because he is speaking in a general way of man's forgetfulness of God as the root of the vice of "vain curiosity." Cf. *S T,* II-II, 167, 1: "Tertio quando homo appetit

cognoscere veritatem circa creaturas, non referendo ad debitum finem, scilicet ad cognitionem Dei."

72 *S T,* II-II, 161, 1, ad 4. The analogous text on the virtue of patience (II-II, 136, 3, ad 2) poses a problem that is specifically theological, bringing into question the very possibility of patience as a natural virtue. Since it is difficult to see *a priori* why this is a case peculiar to patience, the real problem seems to be whether there is such a thing as natural morality in St. Thomas. We will come back to this point when dealing with the virtue of charity.

CHAPTER 4

1 The principal source is *In V Eth. Nic.,* ed. Pirotta, 293-368. For these questions in general, see M. Gillet, O.P., *Conscience chrétienne et justice social,* Paris, 1922.

2 *S T,* II-II, 57, 1. Cf. O. Lottin, *Le Droit naturel chez saint Thomas d'Aquin et ses prédécesseurs,* Bruges, Beyaert, 2 ed., 1931. On the transformation of the Roman notion of law by Christianity, see F. Hölscher, *Die ethische Umgestaltung der romischer Individual-Justitia durch die universalistische Naturrechstlehre der mittelalterlichen Scholastik,* Paderborn, Schöning, 1932. L. Lachance, *Le concept de droit selon Aristote et saint Thomas,* Paris, 1933. C. Riedl, *The Social Theory of St. Thomas Aquinas,* Philadelphia, 1934.

3 *S T,* II-II, 57, 2.

4 *S T,* II-II, 57, 3, and ad 3. On the *jus gentium,* see I-II, 95, 4, ad 1. Serfdom and slavery, for example, are not from natural law. They are only to be justified to the extent that they serve the interest of both master and slave: "inquantum utile est huic quod regatur a sapientiori, et illic quod ab hoc juvetur, ut dicitur in *I Polit.,* lect. 4." (*loc. cit.,* ad 2). Thus St. Thomas is far from considering slavery a natural condition. As soon as it ceases to be useful to both parties, it loses all legal character. On the practical value of St. Thomas's notion of law, see A. Piot, *Droit naturel et réalisme. Essai critique sur quelques doctrines françaises contemporaines,* Paris, Librairie générale de Droit et de Jurisprudence, 1930.

5 *S T,* II-II, 57, 4. St. Thomas likens the relationship between lord and serf to that between father and son, because "servus est aliquid domini, quia est instrumentum ejus." (*loc. cit.*) The historical interpretation of this text would presuppose a study of slavery in the Middle Ages. There are the elements of such a study in M. Bloch, *La Société féodale, la formation des liens de dépendance,* Paris, Albin Michel, 1939; and by the same author, *La Société féodale, les classes et la gouvernement des hommes,* Paris, Albin Michel, 1940.

6 According to *Dig.,* I, 1. *De justitia et jure; S T,* II-II, 58, 2 and 4.

7 *S T,* II-II, 58, 3.

8 *Eth. Nic.,* V, 3, 1130 a 9-10.

9 *S T,* II-II, 58, 5.

10 *In II Polit.,* 3.

11 See my *The Spirit of Mediaeval Philosophy,* ch. 7.

12 *S T,* II-II, 58, 7.

13 *S T,* II-II, 58, 9.

14 *S T,* II-II, 58, 10, and ad 1.

15 *S T,* II-II, 59, 1.

16 *S T,* II-II, 59, 2. What is unjust is not necessarily evil. We can fail to be just both by excess and defect. We can, for example, voluntarily give someone more than is due to him (*loc. cit.*, 3). However, the term is habitually used in its pejorative sense even by St. Thomas.

[17] No doubt this is why St. Thomas usually avoids the term *judicium* to designate what we today, in logic for example, call judgment. *Judicium* for him still connotes fundamentally the judgment of the prince who defines justice or of the judge who administers it.

[18] *S T*, II-II, 60, 1.

[19] *S T*, II-II, 60, 2.

[20] *Ibid.*

[21] *S T*, II-II, 60, 4.

[22] *In V Eth.*, 4; ed. Pirotta, 927-937, pp. 308-311.

[23] *S T*, II-II, 61, 1.

[24] *S T*, II-II, 61, 2. On fines and damages, see II-II, 61, 4. On restitution, see II-II, 62.

[25] *S T*, II II, 63, 1. This vice is more serious than ever in the case of the distribution of ecclesiastical posts, since nothing is more sacred than the spiritual welfare of souls. See art. 2.

[26] *S T*, II II, 63, 3; and *Quodlibet.*, X, 6, 1.

[27] *S T*, II II, 64, 2. Cf. II II, 64, 6.

[28] *S T*, II-II, 64, 3 and 65, 1, ad 2. Clerics are even forbidden to take on such tasks because they are called to serve at the altar where there is a renewal of the Passion of Christ crucified, Who *cum percuteretur, non repercutiebat* (I Pet. 2, 23). Cf. II-II, 64, 6. On mutilation, blows, wounds, incarceration, see II-II, 65, throughout.

[29] *In V Eth.*, 17.

[30] *S T*, II-II, 64, 5.

[31] *S T*, II-II, 64, 7. This concerns a relation between private persons. Where killing is a public function (as in the case of soldiers in battle or policemen in pursuit of a criminal) it becomes legitimate to intend to kill, but only by virtue of delegated public authority, and provided that those who carry out such tasks do so as delegated representatives and not through the personal desire to kill.

Involuntary homicides, where there is no suspicion of imprudence on the part of the killer, are really accidents, not sins. II-II, 64, 8.

[32] *S T*, II-II, 66, 1. A Horvath, O.P., *Eigentumsrecht nach dem hl. Thomas von Aquin*, Graz, Moser, 1929; J. Tonneau. "Propriété" in *Dict. de théologie catholique*, XIII, 757-846. For bibliographical data on property rights, see *Bulletin Thomiste*, 1932, 603-613 and 1935, 474-482. On the very complex question of property rights in St. Thomas, see J. Pères-Garcia, O.P., *De principiis functionis socialis proprietatis privatae apud divum Thomam Aquinatem*, Fribourg (Switzerland), 1924. R. Brunet, S.J., "La propriété privée chez saint Thomas," *Nouvelle revue théologique*, 61 (1934), 914-927, 1022-1041.

[33] *C G*, III, 127; *S T*, II-II, 66, 2, and ad 2.

[34] On the ownership of found articles, see *S T*, II-II, 66, 5, ad 2.

[35] *S T*, II-II, 66, 6.

[36] *S T*, II-II, 66, 7.

[37] We are still in the order of vices contrary to commutative justice. This order is based on relationships where equality obtains.

[38] *S T*, II-II, 67, 1.

[39] *S T*, II-II, 67, 2.

[40] *In V Eth. Nic.*, 6; ed. Pirotta, 955, p. 318.

[41] *S T*, II-II, 67, 3. See above, pp. 307-308.

[42] *S T*, II-II, 67, 4.

[43] *S T*, II-II, 68, 1. This article makes the distinction between denunciation and accusation: "Haec est differentia inter denuntiationem et accusationem, quod in denuntiatione attenditur emendatio fretris, in accusatione autem attenditur punitio criminis." The reason that accusation is not obligatory (save when public

interest is at stake) is that its only object is to punish the guilty party in this life, and it is not in this life that faults are finally punished. Aristotle would have been surprised at this argument.

[44] *S T,* II-II, 68, 3, and ad 1.

[45] *Ibid.,* ad 2. It goes without saying that if, on the contrary, one becomes aware during the course of the trial that one's accusation is groundless, one not only may but should withdraw it. *Ibid.,* ad 2.

[46] *S T,* II-II, 69, 1. The idea that we can fail in charity towards God by lying to a judge is quite foreign to the ethics of Aristotle.

[47] *S T,* II-II, 69, 2, ad 1 and ad 2. This discussion poses, in a particularly urgent way, the problem of the true character of the moral philosophy of St. Thomas. We shall return to it later.

[48] *S T,* II-II, 69, 3, and 4.

[49] *S T,* II-II, 70, 1.

[50] *Ibid.,* 4.

[51] *Ibid.,* ad 1.

[52] *Ibid.,* ad 3.

[53] *Ibid.,* 2, and ad 1.

[54] *S T,* II-II, 70, 2, ad 2. Even this last conclusion is not absolute. A judge has to be slow to release a man who is not guilty if to do so is contrary to the public interest in any serious way. Here he has to rely on his own prudence. On the characteristics of a reliable witness, see II-II, 70, 4.

[55] *S T,* II-II, 71, 1. On the right of lawyers and doctors to fees, see *loc. cit.,* 4 and ad 1.

[56] *S T,* II-II, 71, 3.

[57] *Ibid.,* ad 1.

[58] *Ibid.,* ad 2 and ad 3.

[59] *S T,* II-II, 72, 1, ad 1. On the slight differences between contumely (*contumelia*), insult (*convicium,* to reproach someone for a corporal infirmity) and defamation (*improperium,* words belittling a person), see *loc. cit.,* ad 3.

[60] Contumely consists essentially in words. But it is possible to insult someone by a gesture, an outrage or by an action—a box on the ear, for example. In these cases, the act or gesture is taken as a *sign* of the desire to inflict contumely or affront. They are, therefore, a sort of language. Thus the box on the ear is, by extension, a form of contumely. *S T,* II-II, 72, 1.

[61] *S T,* II-II, 72, 2, ad 1.

[62] *S T,* II-II, 72, 4, and ad 1.

[63] *Ibid.,* 3.

[64] Defamation or calumny (*detractio*) differs from contumely in the manner in which language is used and in the end in view. An insulter speaks openly, a calumniator or defamer in secret. An insulter assaults honor, a calumniator destroys a reputation. *S T,* 73, 1. It is sometimes necessary to lessen a person's reputation; but to do this for its own sake is a sin (*loc. cit.,* 2).

[65] *S T,* II-II, 74, 1. This form of calumny or detraction, St. Thomas calls *susurratio,* the insinuation of the sower of discord.

[66] *S T,* II-II, 75, 2.

[67] On suggested reasons for the selecting gold and silver for money-standards, see *S T,* II-II, 77, 2, ad 1. On problems of just prices in general, see S. Hagenauer, *Das justum pretium bei Thomas von Aquino, ein Beitrag zur Geschichte der objecktiven Werttheorie,* Stuttgart, Kolhammer, 1931.

[68] *S T,* II-II, 77, 1.

[69] *Ibid.,* ad 1.

[70] Purchasers would be frightened off, suspecting from this admission that the horse in question had many other faults. Even blind, a horse is still able to work. *S T,* II-II, 77, 3, ad 2.

[71] *Ibid.,* and ad 1.

[72] *Ibid.*, ad 4.

[73] *S T*, II-II, 77, 4. Exchanges, however, are perfectly licit and St. Thomas approves of them even for clerics when it is a matter of buying or selling in order to come by the necessities of life (*loc. cit.*, ad 3). A unit like a Benedictine monastery, for example, could hardly survive without at least a small amount of such business.

[74] *S T*, II-II, 77, 4, and ad 2. See Aristotle, *Politics*, I, 7 and 8.

[75] *S T*, II-II, 78, 1, and ad 5. The discussion which follows is only a summary of this article. See *S T*, II-II, 78, 1, and 3 where Aristotle is praised for having seen, *naturali ratione ductus,* that this way of making money is *maxime praeter naturam.*

[76] The case is different when the objects used have not been destroyed. To use a house, for example, is to live in it, not destroy it. One can be sold without the other. This is what is done in selling a house and reserving the right to use it during one's lifetime, or in selling the use of it (renting it out, that is) yet keeping the ownership. Receiving rent, therefore, is legitimate. *S T*, II-II, 78, 1.

[77] *S T*, II-II, 78, 2, ad 1.

[78] *Ibid.*

[79] *S T*, II-II, 78, 1, ad 6. Putting money in a business is something else again. It is no longer a loan but a commercial partnership in which profits are shared as well as risks. *Ibid.*, 2, ad 5.

[80] *S T*, II-II, 78, 4, ad 1.

[81] See S. Michel, *La Notion thomiste du Bien commun. Quelques-unes de ses applications juridiques,* Paris, Vrin, 1932. Th. Eschmann, O.P., "Bonum commune melius est quam bonum unius," *Mediaeval Studies,* VI (1944), 62-120. Same author, "Studies in the Notion of Society in St. Thomas Aquinas," *Mediaeval Studies,* XVIII (1946), 1-42; IX (1947), 19-55.

[82] *De regimine principum,* I, 1, in *Opuscula Omnia,* ed. Mandonnet, I, 314.

[83] *Ibid.*, I, 4. *S T*, I-II, 97, 1. Note that St. Augustine is cited.

[84] Jacques Zeiller, *L'Idée de l'État dans saint Thomas d'Aquin,* Paris, Alcan, 1910. Marcel Demongeot, *La Théorie du régime mixte chez saint Thomas d'Aquin,* Paris, Alcan (1927); a useful work which seems, unfortunately, to have been published only as a thesis in Law without date or editor. See also Bernard Roland-Gosselin, *La Doctrine politique de saint Thomas d'Aquin,* Paris, Rivière, 1928. O. Schilling, *Die Staats-und Soziallehre des h. Thomas von Aquin,* Paderborn, 2 ed., 1930.

[85] *De regimine principum,* I, 5, in *Opuscula Omnia,* ed. Mandonnet, I, 321-322.

[86] "Est etiam aliquod regimen ex istis commixtum, quod est optimum." *S T*, I-II, 95, 4.

[87] It is certain that the *regimen commixtum* of the preceding text is under discussion in I-II, 105, 1. Here we read: "Talis enim est optima politia, bene commixta." Indeed, "hoc fuit institutum secundum legem divinam." *Ibid.* A political regime established under God's law is certainly the best of all.

[88] *S T*, I-II, 105, 1. The phrase *secundum virtutem* can be translated: "according to the virtue" (i.e., following the pattern of the virtue), or "by reason of their virtue," "because of their virtue." The second sense seemed better in view of the commentary on the texts of the Scriptures which this response recalls (Eligebantur autem . . . etc.), in which are to be seen the Judges of Israel "chosen . . . by reason of their virtue." Moreover, the virtue of the kings is the only protection the people have against tyranny: "Regnum est optimum regimen populi, si non corrumpatur; sed, propter magnam potestatem quae regi conceditur, de facili regnem in tyrrannidem, nisi sit perfecta virtus ejus cui talis potestas conceditur." *Loc. cit.*, ad 2. The meaning is, therefore, certain.

[89] *S T*, I-II, 105, 1, ad 2 and ad 3.

[90] *Ibid.*, ad 2. The intelligent preface of Father Garigou-Lagrange, O.P., to the French translation of *De regimine principum* sounds an optimistic note. The state-

ment, which he makes his own, that *monarchia est regimen imperfectorum . . . , democratia est regimen perfectorum* (*Du Gouvernement royal,* ed. de la Gazette Française, Paris, 1926, p. XVI), only holds from the subjects' point of view. It is quite the reverse from that of the sovereign. If there is any system which, for St. Thomas, demands that the possession of power be perfect, it is monarchy.

⁹¹ *S T,* I-II, 105, 1.

⁹² *Ibid.,* ad 2: "Instituit tamen a principio, circa regem instituendum primo quidem modum eligendi." The question here under discussion is the Old Law, but we must remember that St. Thomas sees in it the very type of an *optima politia.* See the *Sed contra:* "Ergo per legem populus fuit circa principes bene institutus."

⁹³ The detailed account of the measures to be taken was to have come in Book 2 of the *De regimine principum* which, unfortunately was never finished.

⁹⁴ *De regimine principum,* I, 7-14. On the question as to whether this work is a treatise of political theology or of political philosophy, see Jacques Maritain, *An Essay on Christian Philosophy,* Philosophical Library. New York, 1955, pp. 99-100, and *Science and Wisdom,* London, 1940, p. 120, n. 1. See also, Father M. D. Chenu in *Bulletin thomiste,* 1928, 198. We shall return to this problem in the general framework of Thomist moral doctrine. It is very certain that the *De regimine principum* is a theological writing. But if we were to say that it does not contain St. Thomas's politics, we should also, for the same reason, have to say that the *Summa Theologiae* does not contain his moral teaching. Such an assertion would certainly raise some enormous difficulties.

CHAPTER 5

¹ *C G,* III, 116.

² *S T,* II-II, 80, 1. It is the same with the other virtues annexed to justice. A child cannot give its parents all it owes them. Hence we speak of *filial piety* (see II-II, 101). There are merits which have to be acknowledged, but which it is impossible to recompense. Hence we have the virtue of respect (II-II, 102). On the contrary, we can feel morally bound to render another his due where there is no legal indebtedness, properly speaking. In these cases it is not the equality which presents the difficulty as the debt. For example, "everyone has a right to the truth," but such indebtedness is rather metaphorical. Our debt here is really our strict obligation to tell the truth. Hence a further annexed virtue to justice, *veracity* or truthfulness (see II-II, 109), and its contrary vice lying or prevarication (see II-II, 110). Again, we may have received services for which there is no paying back. These we simply acknowledge by practising the virtue of *gratitude* (see II-II, 107). There are still those social virtues involving a kind of luxury. They bind us to embellish living itself by making it more pleasant: *liberality* and *affability* (II-II, 114 and 117) are such virtues; avarice and quarreling (II-II, 18 and 116) are their contrary vices. We can hardly speak of indebtedness here, save in the sense that we have to do our best to increase honest manners. But this is enough to permit us to attach such virtues to justice.

³ Cicero, De inventione rhetorica, II, 53, cited in *S T,* II-II, 81, 1 ad *Sed contra.*

⁴ *S T,* II-II, 81, 1.

⁵ *Ibid.,* 3.

⁶ *Ibid.,* 4. See especially the important ad 3, which shows why, on the contrary, the virtue of charity remains the same whether addressed towards God or neighbor. It is because God, in creating His creatures, communicates His goodness to them. Charity, as we shall see, consists in loving God's goodness in our neighbor. But God does not communicate His unique and infinite goodness to creatures, and hence only in Him can it be honored as it ought to be.

⁷ *S T,* II-II, 81, 5. This is why St. Thomas shows that the virtue of religion is indispensable to man. *C G,* III, 119 and 120. These are those questions "quae

ratione investigantur de Deo." *C G*, IV, 1, ad *Quia vero*. Here, again, all the problems are directly related to philosophy properly so called.

[8] *S T*, II-II, 2, 2. On the distinction between intellectual, moral and theological virtues, see I II, 62, 2. To the extent that God is their object, the theological virtues bear on an object which exceeds the grasp of human reason. This is not the case with the intellectual and moral virtues. By this one sign it can be seen that religion is not a theological virtue.

[9] *S T*, II-II, 81, 6 and ad 1.

[10] *S T*, II-II, 81, 7. *C G*, III, 119. St. Thomas is not ignorant of the text of St. John: *Spiritus est Deus, et eos qui adorant eum, in spiritu et veritate oportet adorare* (IV, 24), but concludes from it "quod Dominus loquitur quantum ad id quod est principale et per se intentum in cultu divino." *Loc. cit.*, ad 1. Some idealists, who assume the role of exegete as well as of theologian, take another meaning from it. Those who reject theology would do well not to meddle with it, for bad theology is bad philosophy. No one gains anything from such confusions.

[11] *S T*, II-II, 81, 1.

[12] *S T*, II-II, 82, 1.

[13] *S T*, II-II, 82, 3, and ad 3. On the psychological effects—joy and sadness—accompanying devotion, see *loc. cit.*, 4. On the acts of worship—prayer, adoration, sacrifice and offering—, see II-II, 83-86.

[14] *S T*, II-II, 83, 2.

[15] *S T*, I-II, 63, 2, ad 3. Cf. *loc. cit.*, 1.

[16] *S T*, I-II, 63, 4.

[17] *Ibid.*, 3 and 4.

[18] *S T*, II-II, 23, 1. The supernatural moral virtues are distinguished from the natural in a very concrete way because the acts they order can be quite different. Temperance for the good of self or for public order is not the same as temperance for God. The just mean is altered by the end which measures it. *S T*, I-II, 63, 4. Thus, by the standards of natural

temperance, monastic fast appears excessive, but by supernatural standards many a sober and moderate person is not nearly temperate enough.

[19] This thesis is set forth in the discussion of the virtue of patience. *S T*, II-II, 136, 3, ad 1.

[20] *S T*, II-II, 23, 7, ad 2.

[21] This argument is presented in considerable detail and developed without reservation in the profound study of Jacques Maritain, *An Essay on Christian Philosophy*, trans. by Edward H. Flannery, New York, 1955, pp. 61-100. Also in his *Science and Wisdom* trans. by Bernard Wall, London, 1940, pp. 137-241. This last work will bring the reader to the criticisms raised by Mr. Maritain's personal position.

[22] *S T*, II-II, 23, 7, ad 3.

[23] *S T*, II-II, 23, 7. St. Thomas does not say anything different, even in those passages in which he declares that "solae virtutes infusae sunt perfectae, et simpliciter dicendae virtutes." *S T*, I-II, 65, 1. Without charity, it cannot be said *simpliciter* of any virtue that it is a virtue. We have to add, or understand, the word "imperfect." Still, however imperfect, a virtue remains a virtue. For a habit to lose this title, its object would have to be a false good, one that only appears to be good. In this case, the habit is not a "vera virtus, sed falsa similitudo virtutis." *S T*, II-II, 23, 7.

[24] *S T*, I-II, 65, 1.

[25] *S T*, I-II, 65, 2. An extreme expression, which departs from St. Thomas's usual terminology. He prefers, as we have seen, to say that these are virtues, albeit imperfect virtues. That they are false in the order of supernatural merit, and that this is what St. Augustine means, St. Thomas readily admits. When St. Thomas speaks of them as relatively true, or true in a certain sense or under a certain relationship (*secundum quid*), he is maintaining, on a plane which does not interest St. Augustine, that they deserve the name of virtue in the exact measure in which they satisfy the definition of a virtue. To the extent that each of them realizes this, it is a virtue.

[26] Those Thomists who hold for a purely natural moral philosophy show a tendency not to cut the bridges linking them with those who hold for a moral philosophy distinct from religion. They wish, and their motive is a very high one, to salvage morality from the shipwreck which religion has suffered among certain social groups. Perhaps there is a failure to see what is at stake. First, there is the danger of making Christian virtues detestable by transferring their name to acts which imitate them exteriorly but lack their Christian vitality. It is impossible to "do charity" without having it. Secondly, to require people to have the Christian virtues in the name of morality alone is to impose obligations for which there is no basis. This will ultimately be discovered with the result that these false natural virtues will break down. Even the authentically Christian virtues will suffer by reason of the severe criticism to which they will be subjected. The more our duty to God is made to deviate from its first objective and exploited for other purpose, the graver the consequences for religion. When Christian morality is maintained for some other end than Christ, it serves the interest of that other end. Under this aspect, the Christian virtues are too open to the hostile charge that they are "the opiate of the people." To be sure, so long as they are Christian, they are no such thing. But when they cease to be Christian, they can hardly be regarded otherwise. From every point of view, even that of apologetics, the teaching of St. Thomas does not seem to countenance such an attitude. There is in it, quite contrary to the intention of those who adopt it, a distortion of good. It is unfortunate that Christianity should be made a victim in any case, but tragic that it should appear as an accomplice. To have the right to challenge this charge, we must continually remind men that if they still want the natural virtues of Christian morality, they must continue to want Christ.

[27] *S T*, II-II, 161, 1, ad 5.

[28] *S T*, II-II, 161, 4, ad 1. It might be objected that St. Thomas is here considering humility as an infused moral virtue. This is possible, but it would imply that humility should be placed among the natural virtues and excluded

from the moral. Either it is a Christian virtue or it ceases to exist.

[29] *S T*, II-II, 136, 4, *Sed contra.*

[30] *S T*, II-II, 136, 3, and ad 2. This article was written under the direct influence of St. Augustine. St. Thomas refers expressly to *De patientia, PL,* 40, 611-626. See particularly cap. 15, n. 12, c. 617-618, and cap. 6, nn. 13-14, c. 618-619.

[31] For all these theological problems, see A. Gardeil, *La structure de l'âme et l'expérience mystique,* 2 vols., 1927.

[32] On St. Thomas's notion of the spiritual life, see A. Gardeil, *La vraie vie chrétienne,* Desclée de Brouwer, Paris, 1935.

[33] See my *The Spirit of Mediaeval Philosophy,* Ch. 11: Self-knowledge and Christian Socratism, pp. 209-228.

[34] On the Augustinian origin of the distinction *ratio inferior et ratio superior,* see my *Introduction à l'étude de saint Augustin,* p. 142. St. Thomas refers to St. Augustine and interprets him very exactly in *S T,* I, 79, 9, and ad 3. The importance of this distinction for St. Thomas has been pointed out recently by Jacques Maritain in *Science and Wisdom,* pp. 155-161, and by M. D. Chenu, "Ratio superior et inferior, un cas de philosophie chrétienne," *Revue des sciences philosophiques et théologiques,* XXIX (1940), 84-89.

[35] *S T*, II-II, 25, 7.

[36] The supernatural life grows in the mind. The fact that it is the will that is the subject of charity (*S T, I-II, 24, 1*) makes no difference. The will is an *appetitus intellectivus* and belongs to the order of thought. The doctrine of the image of the Trinity in the soul of man clearly implies this.

[37] *S T*, II-II, 45, 2. In this text, St. Thomas uses a classic illustration to which he returns again and again. There are two ways of speaking about chastity: that of the professor of ethics who knows and teaches this virtue because he possesses the science of ethics; and there is that of the chaste man who, even though

he knows no science of morals, instinctively judges correctly as between what is chaste and what is unchaste. He judges it "per quamdam connaturalitatem." Thus it is that the gift of Wisdom enriches higher reason by linking it to its own object, the divine. Note that this gift belongs to every man in the state of grace and free from mortal sin. *S T*, II-II, 45, 5.

[38] *S T*, II-II, 45, 3. Cf. I, 64, 1.

[39] *S T*, I-II, 57, 1.

[40] *S T*, I-II, 45, 2. Very interesting, for the light this theological thesis throws on the deep unity of Thomism, is the position of St. Thomas on the key problem running right through the history of Christianity, including the Reformation. Is the charity that is in man God Himself or is it a supernatural gift created by God? The former might seem to exalt charity to the highest degree, but in fact its effect is to prevent the act of charity from being performed by man himself. Charity, then, is no longer the principle, within man himself, of the movements of charity which direct the will. In brief, the will would move not by its own charity but be moved by God's charity. Hence St. Thomas regards charity as "aliquid creatum in anima." *S T*, II-II, 23, 2. For the historical context of these problems, see P. Vignaux, *Luther commentateur des Sentences*, Paris, Vrin, 1935.

[42] *S T*, II-II, 23, 5.

[43] *Ibid.*

[44] *S T*, II-II, 26, 3.

CHAPTER 6

[1] See above, p. 185.

[2] *C G*, III, 25.

[3] *De virtut.*, I, 2, ad 3; and II, 3.

[4] *S T*, I-II, 1, 4.

[5] *In IV Sent.*, 49, 1, 3; *S T*, I-II, 1, 6.

[6] *C G*, III, 32; *Comp. theol.*, II, 9; *S T*, I-II, 2, 5.

[7] *S T*, I-II, 2, 7.

[8] *C G*, IV, 54; *S T*, I-II, 2, 8; *Comp. theol.*, I, 108 and II, 9.

[9] *S T*, I, 26, 3 and I-II, 3, 1.

[10] *S T*, I-II, 3, 2.

[11] *C G*, III, 33; *S T*, I-II, 3, 3; *Comp. theol*, II, 9.

[12] Note, however, that although beatitude does not consist in the delectation which accompanies it, delectation is *necessarily* joined to beatitude. Cf. *S T*, I-II, 4, 1.

[13] *C G*, III, 26; *S T*, I, 26, 2, ad 2, and I-II, 3, 4; *Quodlib.*, VIII, 9, 1.

[14] *S T*, I-II, 3, 5.

[15] *C G*, III, 48; *S T*, I-II, 3, 6.

[16] *S T*, I-II, 3, 5 and 6, 3. "Et ideo quidam philosophi attendentes naturalem perfectionem hominis, dixerunt ultimam felicitatem hominis in hoc consistere quod in anima hominis describatur ordo totius universi." *De Veritate*, 20, 3.

[17] *S T*, I, 12, 1; I-II, 3, 8. Cf. *De Verit.*, 8, 1; *Quodlibet*, 10, 8.

[18] *S T*, I-II, 4, 6.

[19] *S T*, I-II, 4, 8.

CHAPTER 7

[1] "Necesse est igitur omnia quae diversificantur secundum diversam participationem essendi, ut sint perfectius vel minus perfecte, causari ab uno primo ente quod perfectissime est." *S T*, I, 44, 1.

[2] *C G*, II, 15.

[3] "Contemplatio humana secundum statum praesentis vitae non potest esse absque phantasmatibus . . . , sed tamen

intellectualis cognitio non consistit in ipsis phantasmatibus, sed in eis contemplatur puritatem intelligibilis veritatis." *S T*, II-II, 180, 5, ad 1. Cf. *De Veritate*, 13, 3: "intellectus qui summum cognitionis tenet, proprie immaterialium est."

⁴ *C G*, I, 5, ad *Apparet.*

⁵ Jacques Maritain, *A Preface to Metaphysics (Seven Lessons on Being)*, London, Sheed and Ward, 1943, pp. 21, 24. The lectures published in this volume date from 1932 to 1933.

⁶ *Op. cit.*, p. 23.

⁷ *Ibid.*

⁸ *Op. cit.*, p. 24.

⁹ "Tertiam differentiam ponit [sc. Boetius] ibi, 'id quod est habere aliquid, praeterquam quod ipsum est, potest.' Sciuntur ista differentia per admixtionem alicujus extranei. Circa quod considerandum est, quod circa quodcumque abstracte consideratum, hoc habet vertiatem quod non habet in se aliquid extraneum, quod scilicet sit praeter essentiam suam, sicut humanitas, et albedo, et quaecumque hoc modo dicuntur. Cujus ratio est, quia humanitas significatur et quo aliquid est homo, et albedo quo aliquid est album. Non est autem aliquid homo, formaliter loquendo, nisi per id quod ad rationem hominis pertinet; et similiter non est aliquid album formaliter, nisi per id quod pertinet ad rationem albi; et ideo hujusmodi abstracta nihil ailenum in se habere possunt. Aliter autem se habet in his quae significantur in concreto. Nam homo significatur ut qui habet humanitatem, et album ut quod habet albedinem. Ex hoc autem quod homo habet humanitatem vel albedinem, non prohibetur habere aliquid aliud, quod non pertinet ad rationem horum, nisi solum quod est oppositum his: et ideo homo et album possunt aliquid aliud habere quam humanitatem vel albedinem. Et haec est ratio quare albedo vel humanitas significantur per modum partis, et non praedicantur de concretis, sicut nec aliqua pars de suo toto. Quia igitur, sicut dictum est, ipsum esse significatur ut abstractum, id quod est ut concretum, consequens est verum esse quod hic dicitur, quod 'id quod est, potest aliquid habere, praeterquam quod ipsum est,'

scilicet praeter suam essentiam, sed 'ipsum esse nihil habet admixtum praeter suam essentiam,' " *In Boet. de Hebdomadibus*, II, in *Opuscula Omnia*, ed. P. Mandonnet, I, 173-174.

¹⁰ *In XII Met.*, I; ed. Cathala, n. 2419.

¹¹ Aegidius Romanus, *Theoremata de esse et essentia*, ed. Edg. Hocedez, S.J., Louvain, 1930, p. 127, 1, 12. On the interpretation of this expression, see the Introduction to this work, pp. 54-56. As Father Hocedez puts it, the distinction *inter rem et rem*, taken literally, amounts to making the distinction between essence and existence a distinction between essence and essence (p. 55).

¹² *In IV Met.*, 2; ed. Cathala, 558.

¹³ *C G*, I, 14, ad *Est autem.*

¹⁴ *C G*, I, 22, ad *Item, unumquodque.* Cf. "Ipsum autem esse est complementum substantiae existentis: unumquodque enim actu est per hoc quod esse habet." *C G*, II, 53.

¹⁵ The bond tying the operations of substance to its act of *esse* has been well pointed out in a fairly recent work: J. de Finance, *Être et agir dans la philosophie de saint Thomas*, Paris, Beauchesne, n. d. (1943). For the text quoted, see *In V Met.*, 1, 1; ed. Cathala, 751.

¹⁶ *Op. cit.*, 1, 21, ad *Ex his autem.*

¹⁷ 2, 21, ad *Adhuc. effectus.*

¹⁸ 2, 22, ad *Item, omnis virtus.*

¹⁹ *S T*, I, 8, 1.

²⁰ *C G*, II, 22, ad *Nullo autem.* See also, II, 53: "Assimilatio autem cujuslibet substantiae creatae ad deum est per ipsum esse."

²¹ *Qu. disp. de Anima*, 1, ad 2. To avoid possible equivocation, let us make it clear that this thesis does not oppose the thesis that, in corporeal substance, matter is the principle of individuation. For matter to individuate, it has to be; now it only *is* by the act of its form which in its turn only *is* by its act-of-existing. Causes cause one another, though under different relationships.

[22] *Op. cit.*, 1, ad 1. Let us note, for the theologian, that this solves the much-debated question about the point at which grace is inserted in the soul. See also, *S T,* I-II, 110, 2, ad 3.

[23] *S T,* I, 8, 1.

[24] "Et hoc est ultimum et perfectissimum nostrae cognitionis in hac vita, ut Dionysius dicit in libro *De mystica theologia* (cap. 1): *cum Deo quasi ignoto conjungimur:* quod quidem contingit dum de eo quid non sit cognoscimus, quod vero sit penitus manet ignotum." *C G,* III, 149.

[25] *De ente et essentia,* cap. 1; ed. Roland-Gosselin, p. 4.

[26] Gabriel Marcel, *Être et avoir,* Paris, Aubier, 1935, 183.

[27] Pascal, *Pensées et opuscules;* ed. L. Brunschvicg, edit. minor, 4 ed., 215.

[28] *S T,* II-II, 85, 1.

[29] It is interesting to compare this prayer with the prayer of St. Bonaventure which immediately follows it in the Breviary. The contrast is striking.

[30] R. de Gourmont, *Le latin mystique,* Paris, Crès, 1913, 274-275. All texts dealing with the spirituality of St. Thomas are brought together by Father Sertillanges in his *Prières de saint Thomas d'Aquin,* in *Art Catholique,* Paris, 1920.

ANALYTICAL INDEX

Abstraction, 194, 208, 218, 219.

Accident, 30, 37, 39, 188, 196; its definition, 177; its *esse est inesse,* 30; is *entis ens,* 445 n.5.

Accusation, 316-317.

Accused (the), 317-318; rights and obligations of, 317.

Act, *see* Human acts.

Act and Potency, 59-63, 78, 91, 92, 102, 176-177, 189, 193, 200-201, 207-208, 212, 219, 220, 358.

Act-of-being (*esse*), 29, 32-44, 81-83, 91-95, 98, 99, 104, 108, 109, 115, 118, 121, 132, 133, 135, 167, 179, 188, 191, 196, 232, 361, 370-375.

Active life, 3, 4, 6.

Address (*eustochia, solertia*), 287.

Advocate (lawyer), 319-320.

Affability, 488 n.2.

Agent intellect, *see* Intellect.

Ambition, 291.

Analogy, 105, 135, 360-361.

Anaxagorism, 185.

Angels, 189-190, 207-208, 211, 445 n.12; their existence, 160-162; their incorporeity, 161-164; distinction among, 165-169; essence not one with existence, 169; their mode of knowing, 169-170; hierarchies of, 170-173; lot decided from first moment after creation, 251; sources of teaching on, 160-162.

Anitas, 447 n.22.

Anger, 285.

Anthropology, 257.

Appetite, natural, 236, 272; sensitive, 237, 272; rational, 237-241; analogous to movement, 238; tends toward two ends. *See* Will.

Archangels, 171.

Aristocracy, 328, 329.

Arrogance, 294.

Articles, of faith, 442 n.28.

Arts, 15.

Attributes, of God, known by way of negation, 97-103; simplicity, 91, 97, 118, 125; perfection, 97-100, 104, 107; infinity, 100-101; omnipresence, 101; immutability, and eternity, 102, 117; known by way of analogy, 103-110; by way of judgment, 107-108; intelligence, 110; will, 110, 128; life, 110;

intelligibility, 111; knows Self immediately, 111; His knowledge of singulars, 112-113; of possibles, 113-114; His will, 114-118; His liberty, 117; His love, 118; His life, 118-119; His beatitude, 119-120.

Augmentative powers, 202.

Aureola, 440 n.12.

Avarice, 488 n.2.

Aversion, 279.

Beatitude, 399, 350; definition, 352; essence of, 352-353; conditions, 354-355.

Beauty, 275; spiritual beauty, 297.

Being (*ens*), 29, 34, 194, 444 n.2; being "by itself," 30; *habens esse,* 40; signifies existing thing, 43; abstract notion of being, 44; identified with "the same" by Plato, 49; with the immutable by St. Augustine, 49-50, 135-136; being and essence according to St. Anselm, 50-51; according to Alexander of Hales, 51-53; according to St. Bonaventure, 53-54; *maxime ens,* 72; often includes sense of *esse,* 444 n.2.

Being (*esse*), 29, 30-44, 90-92, 99, 175, 179, 444 n.2; designates act-of-being, 29 (*see* Act-of-being); *esse* of essence and *esse* of existence in Cajetan, 444 n.2; *ipsum esse,* 33, 34, 81, 86, 90; *vere esse,* 49, 86; being and God, 370-372; as heart of Thomism, 368; being and mystery, 373-374.

Bestiality, 280, 483 n.55.

Biology, 174.

Bishopric, 5.

Body, 187, 193, 196.

Calumny, 321.

Cardinal virtues, 263, 290, 295-296.

Causality, 66, 67, 75, 124, 179-184; and existence, 68, 76-77; *importat influxum quemdam ad esse causati,* 468 n.14, 371; and its effect, 162-163, 178-179; presupposes divine efficacy, 67, 180; of second causes, 181-186; assimilation to God, 182-184.

Cause, 178; kinds of, 66, 68, 467 n.13.

Chance, 152, 153.

Change, 48, 134, 148, 177; *see* Motion.

Charity, 273, 339, 341, 345, 349.

INDEX OF PROPER NAMES